LATIN AMERICAN EXPERIENCES WITH TRUTH COMMISSION RECOMMENDATIONS

SERIES ON TRANSITIONAL JUSTICE

The Series on *Transitional Justice* offers a platform for high-quality research within the rapidly growing field of transitional justice. The research is, of necessity inter-disciplinary in nature, drawing from disciplines such as law, political science, history, sociology, criminology, anthropology and psychology, as well as from various specialised fields of study such as human rights, victimology and peace studies. Furthermore, the research is international in outlook, drawing on the knowledge and experience of academics and other specialists in many different regions of the world.

The series is aimed at a variety of audiences who are either working or interested in fields such as crime and justice; human rights; humanitarian law and human security; conflict resolution and peace building. These audiences include academics, researchers, students, policy makers, practitioners, non-governmental organisations and the media.

All books published within the series are subject to a double-blind peer review by recognised authorities in the field.

Published titles within this Series:

11. Ilse Derluyn, Cindy Mels, Stephan Parmentier and Wouter Vandenhole (eds.), *Re-Member. Rehabilitation, Reintegration and Reconciliation of War-Affected Children* (2012), 97894-000-0027-4
12. Anne-Marie de Brouwer, Charlotte Ku, Renée Römkens and Larissa van den Herik (eds.), *Sexual Violence as an International Crime: Interdisciplinary Approaches* (2012), 978-1-78068-002-6
13. Estelle Zinsstag and Martha Albertson Fineman (eds.), *Feminist Perspectives on Transitional Justice: From International and Criminal to Alternative Forms of Justice* (2013), 978-1-78068-142-9
14. Josep M. Tamarit Sumalla, *Historical Memory and Criminal Justice in Spain. A Case of Late Transitional Justice* (2013), 978-1-78068-143-6
15. Catherine Jenkins (ed.), Max du Plessis (ed.), *Law, Nation building and Transformation The South African experience in perspective* (2014), 978-1-78068-184-9
16. Susanne Buckley-Zistel and Stefanie Schäfer (eds.), *Memorials in Times of Transition* (2014), 978-1-78068-211-2
17. Nico Wouters (ed.), *Transitional Justice and Memory in Europe (1945–2013)* (2014), 978-1-78068-214-3
18. Agata Fijalkowski and Raluca Grosescu (eds.), *Transitional Criminal Justice in Post-Dictatorial and Post-Conflict Societies* (2015), 978-1-78068-260-0
19. S. Elizabeth Bird and Fraser M. Ottanelli (eds.), *The Performance of Memory as Transitional Justice* (2014), 978-1-78068-262-4
20. Bo Viktor Nylund, *Child Soldiers and Transitional Justice* (2016), 978-1-78068-394-2
21. Peter Malcontent (ed.), *Facing the Past: Amending Historical Injustices through Instruments of Transitional Justice* (2016), 978-1-78068-403-1
22. Francesca Capone, *Reparations for Child Victims of Armed Conflict: State of the Field and Current Challenges* (2017), 978-1-78068-438-3
23. Cheryl S. White, *Bridging Divides in Transitional Justice: The Extraordinary Chambers in the Courts of Cambodia* (2017), 978-1-78068-440-6
24. Jeremy Sarkin (ed.), *The Global Impact and Legacy of Truth Commissions* (2019), 978-1-78068-794-0
25. Camila de Gamboa Tapias and Bert van Roermund (eds.), *Just Memories: Remembrance and Restoration in the Aftermath of Political Violence* (2020), 978-1-78068-908-1
26. Grazyna Baranowska, *Rights of Families of Disappeared Persons* (2021), 978-1-83970-137-5
27. Elin Skaar, Eric Wiebelhaus-Brahm and Jemima García-Godos (eds.), *Exploring Truth Commission Recommendations in a Comparative Perspective: Beyond Words Vol. I* (2022), 978-1-83970-178-8

For previous volumes in the series, please visit http://tj.intersentia.com

Series on Transitional Justice, Volume 28

LATIN AMERICAN EXPERIENCES WITH TRUTH COMMISSION RECOMMENDATIONS

Beyond Words Vol. II

Edited by
Elin Skaar
Eric Wiebelhaus-Brahm
Jemima García-Godos

INTERSENTIA
Cambridge – Antwerp – Chicago

Intersentia Ltd
8 Wellington Mews
Wellington Street | Cambridge
CB1 1HW | United Kingdom
Tel: +44 1223 736 170
Email: mail@intersentia.co.uk
www.intersentia.com | www.intersentia.co.uk

Distribution for the UK and
Rest of the World (incl. Eastern Europe)
NBN International
1 Deltic Avenue, Rooksley
Milton Keynes MK13 8LD
United Kingdom
Tel: +44 1752 202 301 | Fax: +44 1752 202 331
Email: orders@nbninternational.com

Distribution for Europe
Lefebvre Sarrut Belgium NV
Hoogstraat 139/6
1000 Brussels
Belgium
Tel: +32 (0)800 39 067
Email: mail@intersentia.be

Distribution for the USA and Canada
Independent Publishers Group
Order Department
814 North Franklin Street
Chicago, IL 60610
USA
Tel: +1 800 888 4741 (toll free) | Fax: +1 312 337 5985
Email: orders@ipgbook.com

Latin American Experiences with Truth Commission Recommendations:
Beyond Words Vol. II

Artwork on cover: Author Jan Jordaan, title 'Hurt', medium Linocut, 1999. From the Universal Declaration of Human Rights – International Print Portfolio, Article 5, published by Art for Humanity, South Africa, 1999.

ISBN 978-1-83970-179-5
D/2022/7849/9
NUR 828

GPRC Guaranteed Peer Reviewed Content

British Library Cataloguing in Publication Data. A catalogue record for this book is available from the British Library.

PREFACE

Truth commissions have become an indispensable part of the transitional justice and peace-building tool-kit in recent years. The anticipated impact of such commissions usually relates to three things: the actual work of the truth commission (in particular, its interaction with victims, perpetrators, and society at large); the issuance of a report; and the implementation of the recommendations made in that report. This latter dimension has attracted comparatively little attention from scholars and practitioners. In fact, we know very little about whether, how, why, and which recommendations are actually implemented and, when they are, with what effect. Yet, truth commission recommendations may be highly significant in shaping how societies heal and develop after periods of repression and/or violent conflict. As such, the fate of recommendations overlaps with good governance and development concerns, among other things.

This volume takes stock of the implementation records of the recommendations made by 13 truth commissions across 11 Latin American countries (Argentina, Chile, Brazil, Ecuador, El Salvador, Guatemala, Haiti, Panama, Paraguay, Peru, and Uruguay) in the period from 1983 through 2017. It is the first book ever to provide a systematic comparative analysis of the entire universe of recommendations made by all formal (i.e., state-sponsored) truth commissions in a geographical region. It also is the first book to include a large selection of little known, under-researched cases like the truth commissions of Ecuador, Haiti, Panama, and Paraguay. These commissions addressed a variety of human rights violations committed in the context of repression by authoritarian regimes and civil war. Some were created in the immediate aftermath of democratic transition and/or conflict termination; others came years later. This volume, therefore, offers several important innovations for scholars and practitioners concerned with democratization, peace-building, and transitional justice in general and with truth commissions in particular.

The events covered in this volume start with what is arguably the first truth commission in the world, Argentina's *Comisión Nacional sobre la Desaparición de Personas* (CONADEP). Established right after the country's transition to democratic rule in 1983, CONADEP handed over its famous report, *Nunca Más*, to the Alfonsín government the following year. Chronologically, the book ends with the politics surrounding the implementation of the Brazilian *Comissão Nacional da Verdade*'s recommendations after it handed over its final report to then-President, Dilma Rouseff, in December 2014. During this span of over 30 years, truth commissions across Latin America and the Caribbean have made around 1,000 recommendations to their respective governments concerning a wide range of diverse issues – from reparations to victims of gross human rights violations to proposals for legal, judicial, and administrative reform. Our study is animated by two overarching questions: Why did these truth commissions make the specific recommendations they did, and not others? And, were these recommendations ever implemented?

Addressing these two core questions, this volume forms part of the research project *Beyond Words: Implementing Latin American Truth Commission Recommendations*.[1] The research project is based at the Chr. Michelsen Institute (CMI), Bergen, Norway, and was funded by the Latin America Programme at the Research Council of Norway (2015–17). The editors of this volume form the project core team: Elin Skaar (Chr. Michelsen Institute, Bergen, Norway), Eric Wiebelhaus-Brahm (University of Arkansas at Little Rock), and Jemima García-Godos (Department of Sociology and Human Geography, University of Oslo). However, we have not done this job alone. We have worked closely with three institutional partners in Latin America: *Centro de Estudios Legales y Sociales* – CELS (Argentina), *Instituto de Democracia y Derechos Humanos de la Pontificia Universidad Católica del Perú* – IDEHPUCP (Peru), and *Facultad Latinoamericana de Ciencias Sociales* – FLACSO (Guatemala). We also have worked closely with a research team based at *Universidad de Salamanca* in Spain and a number of individual researchers and research assistants in 11 Latin American countries.

Nearly two dozen people from four continents based in a number of different countries have labored over several years to collect and analyze the data that forms the basis of this volume. As far as we know, this is the first attempt to systematically collect information on a critical part of a truth commission's legacy, namely the recommendations outlined in a report to the government once the truth commission has concluded its investigations into human rights violations. We have done this exhaustively rather than selectively: the volume analyzes all recommendations made by all official truth commissions in Latin America that have ever successfully concluded their investigations by producing a final report.

The main foci of each of the 11 country chapters included in this volume are threefold: (i) to provide a brief introduction to the historical context in which the truth commission was established; (ii) to provide an account of the formulation of the truth commission's recommendations; and (iii) to assess the implementation record of those recommendations. All research teams have used the same analytical framework and collected the same types of data. Findings have

1 See also Skaar, Wiebelhaus-Brahm, and García-Godos (2022).

been shared and discussed electronically as well as at three international workshops spread across the project period: two in Bergen, Norway, and one in Pisac, Peru. Various authors also have presented earlier drafts at a variety of academic conferences, including the annual meetings of the Latin American Studies Association (LASA) and the European Consortium for Political Research (ECPR).

The country chapters are structured in roughly the same way. Geographically, we start in the Southern Cone, where truth commissions in Argentina, Chile, Uruguay, Paraguay, and Brazil sought to address abuses during the era of military dictatorships in the region. In the second part, we move to the Andean countries of Ecuador and Peru, where oppression and marginalization of indigenous populations played a prominent role. Finally, we shift to Central America and the Caribbean to examine the legacies of internal armed conflicts in El Salvador and Guatemala as well as the little-known truth commissions of Haiti and Panama.

The construction of this volume would not have been possible without the hard work and assistance of many people. First and foremost, we would like to thank the following researchers and research assistants for contributing to the 11 country chapters in this volume, either by collecting and analyzing data and/or doing the actual writing: Héctor Centeno-Martín, Federico Ghelfi, Hugo Goeury, Tania Gómez, Martha Gutiérrez-Salazar, Sol Hourcade, Eduardo Hurtado, Camila Barreto Maia, Elena Martínez-Barahona, Luz Palmás Zaldua, Marcela Perelman, Félix Reátegui, Sonia Rubio-Padilla, Augusto Rosas, Adriana Rudling, Luis Raúl Salvadó, Elena San José, Salvador Sánchez, Lisa-Marie Måseidvåg Selvik, and Diego Uchuypoma.

We are grateful to Hunjoon Kim for offering valuable suggestions on the formulation of our original grant proposal for this project. Thanks to Andrea Rocha Granados and María Eugenia Ulfe for their participation in the project at its early stages. We also would like to thank the enthusiastic assistance of Osmund Grøholt, who worked on the datasets at various stages of the project. Special thanks to Lisa-Marie Måseidvåg Selvik for invaluable work on the datasets and tables that form the basis for the country chapters. Thanks also to Aslak Orre and Vegard Furustøl Vibe for patient discussions on how to organize and process the data collected for this project.

We also are grateful for a group of scholars and practitioners who gave graciously of their time in helping us think through the complexities of the project. Special thanks to Onur Bakiner for agreeing to write the Conclusion to this volume. He has provided thoughtful feedback on the overall project as well as the individual chapters at different stages of progress. We also want to highlight the very valuable contributions of our excellent project reference group, who have been actively involved since the project idea was first conceived, and many of whom have provided useful feedback on various chapter drafts: Stener Ekern, Joanna Quinn, Catalina Smulovitz, Astri Suhrke, Patricia Tappatá Valdez,

Hugo van der Merwe, and José Zalaquett. In the many rounds of revisions, we are further thankful to the following people for kindly providing comments and input on country chapters at various stages: Cath Collins, Anita Ferrara, Gabriela Fried, Monica Kirya, Francesca Lessa, Mari Norbakk, Rebecca Root, Nina Schneider, Margaret Scranton, Rachel Sieder, Sofía Tiscornia, Verónica Torras, Vibeke Wang, Sebastián Yerovi, and Jørgen Sørlie Yri. We further thank the many individuals present at various LASA and ECPR panels, as well as members of the Rights and Gender cluster at CMI for helpful comments on various drafts.

A big thank you to Mari Norbakk and Lisa-Marie Måseidvåg Selvik for helping to coordinate, respectively, the first and second project workshops at Solstrand, Bergen. We also would like to warmly thank IDEHPUCP for hosting the third workshop in Pisac, Peru, particularly Elizabeth Salmon, Patricia Barrantes Delgado, and their assistants, Aída Ugarte Cáceres and Emilie de Haas. They gave the project team an unforgettable experience in the Andean highlands of Peru.

The project teams have worked with truth commission reports and data in three different languages (Spanish, Portuguese, and French). Chapters for this volume have been drafted in Spanish and English. We warmly thank Diana Valori for translating the chapters originally in Spanish into English, and Gabriela Fried for proofreading the translated versions.

We want to thank the CMI internal administrative support team who provided invaluable input in the first phases of the Beyond Words project. Thank you to Steinar Hegre, Ingvild Hestad, Lars Ivar Høberg, Chris Jakob, Reidunn Ljones, Aksel Mjeldheim, Guri Stegali, Robert Sjursen, and Hong Kim Tran.

There is a long road to be traveled from the moment in which a project is conceptualized until interested readers may pick up a book summarizing years of labor. We want to warmly thank Intersentia and their staff for all their help and support from the inception phase to publication. Jeremy Sarkin and Stephen Parmentier have been enthusiastic and supportive of our project since we discussed the possibility of publishing the two *Beyond Words* volumes with Intersentia during a conference on truth commissions organized in Lisbon in February 2018. The Intersentia editorial team has patiently waited for manuscript drafts and steered the process towards publication with a steady hand. A warm thank you to Mina Rauschenbach, Ahmed Hegazi, and especially Ella Brice-Jeffreys. We are also indebted to the blind reviewers who provided encouraging and useful suggestions for tightening and finalizing the text. Any errors in this volume are, as always, the chief responsibility of the editors.

Elin Skaar, Eric Wiebelhaus-Brahm, and Jemima García-Godos
Bergen. Little Rock. Oslo.
February 2022

CONTENTS

LIST OF ACRONYMS

ARGENTINA

APDH	*Asamblea Permanente por los Derechos Humanos* (Permanent Assembly for Human Rights)
CELS	*Centro de Estudios Legales y Sociales* (Center for Legal and Social Studies)
CONADEP	*Comisión Nacional sobre la Desaparición de Personas* (National Commission on the Disappearance of Persons)
CONSUFA	*Consejo Supremo de las Fuerzas Armadas* (Supreme Council of the Armed Forces)
ESMA	*Escuela de Mecánica de la Armada* (Navy Mechanics School, Argentina)
FADERAP	*Familiares Detenidos Desaparecidos Por Razones Políticas* (Relatives of Persons Disappeared and Detained for Political Reasons)
FEDEFAM	*La Federación Latinoamericana de Asociaciones de Familiares de Detenidos-Desaparecidos* (Family Members of Persons Disappeared and Detained for Political Reasons)
ILID	*Iniciativa Latinoamericana para la Identificación de Personas Desaparecidas* (Latin American Initiative for the Identification of Disappeared Persons)
LADH	*Liga Argentina por los Derechos del Hombre* (Argentine League for Human Rights)
MEDH	*Movimiento Ecuménico por los Derechos Humanos* (Ecumenical Movement for Human Rights)
PJ	*Partido Justicialista* (Judicialist Party)
RUV	*Registro Unificado de Víctimas del Terrorismo de Estado* (Unified Register of Victims of State Terrorism)
SDH	*Secretaría de Derechos Humanos* (Secretariat of Human Rights)
SERPAJ	*Servicio Paz y Justicia* (Peace and Justice Service)
SsDH	*Subsecretario de Derechos Humanos* (Undersecretary of Human Rights)

UCR	*Unión Cívica Radical* (Radical Civic Union)
UPR	*Subsecretario de Derechos Humanos* (Universal Periodic Review)

CHILE

AFDD	*Agrupación de Familiares de Detenidos Desaparecidos* (Family Members of Disappeared Detainees Group)
CCHDH	*Comisión Chilena de Derechos Humanos* (Chilean Commission on Human Rights)
CNI	*Centro Nacional de Información* (National Information Center)
CNPPT	*Comisión Nacional sobre Prisión Política y Tortura National* (Commission on Political Imprisonment and Torture)
CNRR	*Corporación Nacional de Reparación y Reconciliación* (National Corporation for Reparation and Reconciliation)
CNVR	*Comisión Nacional de Verdad y Reconciliación* (National Truth and Reconciliation Commission)
CODEPU	*Corporación de Promoción y Defensa de los Derechos del Pueblo* (Corporation for the Promotion and Defense of the People's Rights)
COSENA	*Consejo de Seguridad Nacional* (National Security Council)
DINA	*Dirección Nacional de Inteligencia* (National Intelligence Agency)
FASIC	*Fundación de Ayuda Social de las Iglesias Cristianas* (Christian Churches Social Assistance Fundation)
ILAS	*Instituto Latinoamericano de Salud Mental y Derechos Humanos* (Latin American Institute of Mental Health and Human Rights)
INDH	*Instituto Nacional de Derechos Humanos* (National Institute of Human Rights)
PPD	*Partido por la Democracia* (Democracy Party)
PRAIS	*Programa de Reparación y Atención Integral de Salud* (Comprehensive Reparation and Health Care Program)
SELADEH	*Secretariado Latinoamericano de Derechos Humanos* (Latin American Secretariat of Human Rights)
UDI	*Unión Demócrata Independiente* (Democratic Independent Union)

URUGUAY

ASCEEP	*Asociación Social y Cultural de Estudiantes de la Enseñanza Pública* (Social and Cultural Association of Public Education Teachers)
CRYSOL	*Asociación de ex presos y presas políticos/as del Uruguay* (Association of Ex Political Prisoners of Uruguay)
FAMIDESA	*Asociación de Madres y Familiares de Uruguayos Detenidos Desaparecidos* (Association of Mothers and Family Members of Detained Disappeared Uruguayans)
INDDHH	*Institución Nacional de Derechos Humanos y Defensoría del Pueblo* (National Institution for Human Rights and the People's Ombudsman)
PIT	*Plenario Intersindical de Trabajadores* (Inter-Union Workers' Plenary Meeting)
SERPAJ	*Servicio de Paz y Justicia* (Peace and Justice Service)

PARAGUAY

CODEHUPY	*Coordinadora de Derechos Humanos del Paraguay* (Paraguay's Human Rights Coordinating Body)
CVJ	*Comisión de Verdad y Justicia* (Truth and Justice Commission)
DGVJR	*Dirección General de Verdad, Justicia y Reparación* (General Directorate for Truth, Justice and Reparations)
EAAF	*Equipo Argentino de Antropología Forense* (Argentine Forensic Anthropology Team)
ENABI	*Equipo Nacional para la investigación, búsqueda e identificación plena de personas detenidas, desaparecidas y ejecutadas extrajudicialmente* (National Team for the Investigation, Search and Identification of Persons Detained, Disappeared and Extrajudicially Executed)
EPP	Ejército del Pueblo Paraguayo (*Paraguayan People's Army*)
FTC	*Fuerza de Tarea Conjunta* (Joint Task Force)
ICRC	International Committee of the Red Cross
INDERT	*Instituto Nacional de Desarrollo Rural y de la Tierra* (National Institute of Rural Development and Land)
INDI	*Instituto Paraguayo del Indígena* (National Institute of Indigenous People)
ISEPOL	*El Instituto Superior de Educación Policial* (Higher Institute of Police Education)

MNVDS	*Movimiento Nacional de Víctimas de la Dictadura Stronista* (National Movement of Victims of the Stronist Dictatorship)
RAADH	*Reunión de Altas Autoridades sobre Derechos Humanos* (High Authorities on Human Rights and Foreign Ministries of MERCOSUR and Associated States)

BRAZIL

CEMDP	*Comissão Especial de Mortos e Desaparecidos Políticos* (Special Commission on the Dead and Disappeared for Political Reasons)
CFMDP	Sao Paulo Commission for the Family Members of the Persons Killed or Disappeared for Political Reasons
CNDH	*Conselho Nacional de Direitos Humanos* (National Council for Human Rights)
CNV	*Comissão Nacional da Verdade* (National Truth Commission)
CVDMM	*Comissão da Verdade da Democracia "Mães de Maio"* ("May Mothers" Democracy Truth Commission)
ISER	*Instituto de Estudos da Religiao* (Religious Studies Institute)
STF	*Supremo Tribunal Federal* (Federal Supreme Court of Brazil)

ECUADOR

CED	Committee on Enforced Disappearances
CONESUP	*Consejo Nacional de Enseñanza Superior Universitaria Privada* (National Council of Higher Education)
CEDHU	*Comisión Ecuménica de Derechos Humanos* (Ecumenical Human Rights Commission)
LGBTI	Lesbian, gay, bisexual, transgender and intersex
MPL	*Montoneras Patria Libre* (Montoneros Free Fatherland)
SIC-10	Criminal Investigation Service

PERU

CERIAJUS	*Comisión Especial para la Reforma Integral de la Administración de Justicia* (Special Commission for Integral Reform of Justice Administration)

CMAN	*Comisión Multisectorial de Alto Nivel Encargada del Seguimiento de las Acciones y Políticas del Estado en los ámbitos de la Paz, la Reparación Colectiva y la Reconciliación Nacional* (High-Level Multisectorial Commission)
CVR	*Comisión de la Verdad y Reconciliación* (Truth and Reconciliation Commission)
DRE	*Dirección Regional de Educación* (Regional Education Directorate)
ICRC	International Red Cross Committee
ICTJ	International Center for Transitional Justice
IDEHPUCP	*Instituto de Democracia y Derechos Humanos de la Pontificia Universidad Católica del Perú* (Institute of Democracy and Human Rights, Pontifical Catholic University of Peru)
INABEC	*Instituto Nacional de Becas y Crédito Educativo* (National Institute of Scholarships and Educational Loans)
LUM	*Lugar de la Memoria, la Tolerancia y la Inclusión Social* (Place of Memory, Tolerance and Social Inclusion)
PIR	*Plan Integral de Reparaciones* (Comprehensive Reparations Plan)

EL SALVADOR

ARENA	*Alianza Republicana Nacionalista* (Nationalist Republican Alliance)
CIHD	*Comisión Investigadora de Hechos Delictivos* (Commission for the Investigation of Criminal Acts)
CNJ	*Consejo Nacional de la Judicatura* (National Council of the Judiciary)
COPAZ	*Comisión Nacional para la Consolidación de la Paz* (National Commission for the Consolidation of Peace)
CSJ	*Corte Suprema de Justicia* (Supreme Court of Justice)
CVES	*Comisión de la Verdad para El Salvador* (Commission on the Truth for El Salvador)
DNI	*Dirección Nacional de Inteligencia* (National Intelligence Office)
FAES	*Fuerza Armada de El Salvador* (Armed Forces of El Salvador)
FISDL	*Fondo de Inversión Social para el Desarrollo Local* (Fund for Social Investment for Local Development)
FMLN	*Frente Farabundo Martí para la Liberación Nacional* (Farabundo Martí Front for National Liberation)

LCJ	*Ley de la Carrera Judicial* (Law for the Judicial Career)
ONUSAL	United Nations Observer Mission in El Salvador
PDDH	*Procuraduría para la Defensa de los Derechos Humanos de El Salvador* (Office of the Attorney for the Defense of Human Rights of El Salvador)
PNC	*Policía Nacional Civil* (National Civil Police)
UNO	*Unión Nacional Opositora* (Oppositional National Union)

GUATEMALA

SEPAZ	*Secretaría de la Paz* (Ministry of Peace)
AIDPI	*Acuerdo sobre Identidad y Derechos de los Pueblos Indígenas* (Agreement on the Identity and Rights of Indigenous Peoples)
CEH	*Comisión para el Esclarecimiento Histórico de Guatemala* (Commission for Historical Clarification)
CICIG	*Comisión Internacional contra la Impunidad en Guatemala* (International Commission Against Impunity in Guatemala)
CNAP	*Consejo Nacional de los Acuerdos de Paz* (National Council for Peace Agreements)
FAFG	*Fundación de Antropología Forense de Guatemala* (Guatemalan Forensic Anthropology Foundation)
FLACSO	*Facultad Latinoamericana de Ciencias Sociales* (Latin American Faculty of Social Sciences)
IDPP	*Instituto de Defensa Pública Penal* (Criminal Public Defender Institute)
PAC	*Patrullas de Autodefensa Civil* (Civil Defense Patrols)
PAN	*Partido de Avanzada Nacional* (National Progress Party)
PNR	*Programa Nacional de Reparación* (National Reparation Program)
REMHI	*Proyecto Interdiocesiano de Recuperación de la Memoria Histórica* (Interdiocesan Project for the Recovery of Historical Memory)
URNG	*Unión Revolucionaria Nacional Guatemalteca* (Guatemalan National Revolutionary Union)

HAITI

CNVJ	*Commission Nationale de Vérité et de Justice* (National Truth and Justice Commission)
CONAP	National Coordinating Body for Women's Rights

CPRDJ	*Commission préparatiore à la réforme du droit et de la justice* (Preparatory Commission for the Reform of Law and Justice)
CRAD	*Centre de Recherche et d'Action pour le Développement* (Centre for Research and Action for Development)
CSPJ	*Conseil Supérieur du Pouvoir Judiciaire* (Supreme Judicial Council)
FAd'H	*Forces Armées d'Haïti* (Haitian Armed Forces)
FRAPH	*Front pour l'Avancement et le Progrès d'Haïti* (Front for the Advancement and Progress of Haiti)
GARR	*Groupe d'Appui aux Rapatriés et Réfugiés* (Support Group for Repatriated Persons and Refugees)
HNP	Haitian National Police
ICHRDD	International Centre for Human Rights and Democratic Development
JILAP	National Commission for Justice and Peace
MICIVIH	*Mission Civile Internationale en Haïti* (International Civilian Mission in Haiti)
MINUJUSTH	UN Mission for Justice Support in Haiti
MINUSTAH	UN Stabilization Mission in Haiti
OPC	*Office de la Protection du Citoyen et de la Citoyenne* (Office of Citizen Protection)
RNDDH	*Réseau national de défense des droits humains* (National network for the defense of human rights)
SGBV	Sexual and gender-based violence
SOFA	*Solidarité des Femmes Haïtiennes/Solidarite fanm ayisyèn* (Solidarity with Haitian Women)
UN CIVPOL	UN Civilian Police
UNPOL	UN Police
URAMEL	*Unité de Recherche et d'Action Médico-légale* (Unit for Medical-Legal Investigation and Operations)

PANAMA

CIVP	*Comisión Institucional de la Verdad* (Institutional Truth Commission)
COFADEPA-HG	*Comité de Familiares de Detenidos y Asesinados de la Dictadura Militar de Panamá Héctor Gallego* (Committee of Relatives of Detained-Disappeared Persons of the Military Dictatorship of Panama Héctor Gallego)
COPODEHUPA	*Coordinadora Popular de Derechos Humanos Panamá* (Popular Coordinating Committee for Human Rights Panama)

CVP	*Comisión de la Verdad de Panamá* (Panama Truth Commission)
MEDUCA	*Ministerio de Educación* (Department of Education)
PRD	*Partido Revolucionario Democratico* (Democratic Revolutionary Party)
PTC	Panama Truth Commission
RDH-P	*Red de Derechos Humanos-Panamá* (Human Rights Network-Panama)

GENERAL (NON-COUNTRY SPECIFIC TERMS IDENTIFIED)

CIDH	*Comisión Inter-Americana de Derechos Humanos* (IAComHR, Inter-American Commission on Human Rights)
EU	European Union
IACtHR	Inter-American Court for Human Rights
LGBTI	Lesbian, gay, bisexual, transgender and intersex
NGO	Non-governmental organization
OP-ICCPR	Optional Protocol to the International Covenant on Civil and Political Rights
TCR	Truth Commission Recommendations
UN	United Nations
UNDP	United Nations Development Programme
UNOHCHR	United Nations Office for the High Commissioner of Human Rights
USAID	United States Agency for International Development

LIST OF TABLES AND FIGURES

TABLES

Introduction

Argentina

Chile

Uruguay

Paraguay

Brazil

Ecuador

Peru

El Salvador

Haiti

Panama

FIGURES

Ecuador

INTRODUCTION

Elin SKAAR, Eric WIEBELHAUS-BRAHM,
and Jemima GARCÍA-GODOS*

During the past four decades, over 50 countries have established truth commissions to investigate patterns of gross human rights violations committed by repressive regimes and/or in the context of internal armed conflict. Depending upon what types of commissions one counts, more than a third of these commissions have been in Latin America, making it a leading region in this search for truth. Constructing shared memories of the past, many believe, is crucial to healing divided societies after violent conflict and repression. Apart from documenting abuses, most truth commissions make recommendations to governments. The assumption is that these recommendations, if implemented well, will prompt further measures to address past abuses – such as compensating surviving victims and their families for past suffering – and promote the types of reforms that may aid societies in the transition from violence to peace, democracy, and reconciliation.

A significant scholarly literature on truth commissions notwithstanding (Bakiner 2016; Chapman 2009; Ferrara 2014; Freeman 2006; Freeman and

* Elin Skaar is Research Professor at the Chr. Michelsen Institute in Bergen, Norway; Eric Wiebelhaus-Brahm is Associate Professor in the School of Public Affairs, University of Arkansas at Little Rock; and Jemima García-Godos is Associate Professor – Department of Sociology and Human Geography, University of Oslo.

Hayner 2003; Hayner 1994, 2001; Mayer-Rieckh and Varney 2019; Wiebelhaus-Brahm 2010b), to date there is no systematic study of the formulation and implementation of truth commission recommendations. Hence, we know little about whether and under what conditions recommendations are implemented. This knowledge gap has been increasingly recognized (United Nations General Assembly, 2013). As the first United Nations Special Rapporteur on the promotion of truth, justice, reparation, and guarantees of non-recurrence, Pablo de Greiff, warned shortly after taking office in 2012, truth commissions around the world "face various challenges which can lead to the non-implementation of recommendations. Among these challenges are overly broad mandates, flawed choices of commissioners, and insufficient and unreliable funding streams" (Office of the UN High Commissioner for Human Rights 2013).

The research project of which this volume forms part analyzes the recommendations of 13 Latin American truth commissions established by 11 countries since 1982 to gather more knowledge about their implementation. The overarching question we had when we embarked on this project was: *How frequently are truth commission recommendations implemented?* This led to two further questions related to variation in recommendations. First, we are interested in *what factors influence the presence of recommendations and the form they take?* Second, we explore *to what extent do the type and complexity of recommendations influence the degree of implementation?*

As the chapters in this volume aptly illustrate, there is enormous variety in the number of recommendations and level of detail presented in the 13 truth commission reports. The amount of space commissioners have devoted to recommendations ranges from a few pages to multiple, thick volumes. Over time, recommendations have become increasingly numerous, ranging from individual victim reparations to complex structural and institutional reform. This diversity creates a laboratory for examining how the type, range, and complexity of truth commission recommendations influence their implementation record. To be sure, implementation also is determined by broader contextual factors such as political will, available resources, and unforeseen events (such as natural disasters and economic crises that divert attention from implementing recommendations). However, this project has focused on the triangular relationship between the processes that shape the formulation of truth commission recommendations, the nature of the recommendations themselves, and the degree of implementation. Each of the country studies included here addresses three main questions: (i) What kinds of recommendations have the truth commission(s) made, and why? (ii) How, when, and by whom have the recommendations been implemented? and, more speculatively, (iii) What are the short- and long-term impacts of these recommendations in the societies in which they are implemented?

The rest of this introductory chapter is structured in four sections. The next section gives a short overview of the scholarly literature on truth commission recommendations. From there, we derive hypotheses on implementation from the international human rights law and norms literature. The third section briefly outlines the research objectives, case selection, and methodology of the wider research project that underpins the case studies. The fourth section outlines the structure of this volume.

1. TAKING STOCK OF WHAT WE KNOW ABOUT TRUTH COMMISSION RECOMMENDATIONS

In recent decades, Latin American countries have been at the forefront of establishing formal "truth and justice" mechanisms after military dictatorships or civil war (Sikkink and Walling 2007; Skaar, García-Godos, and Collins 2016). Transitional justice encompasses a wide range of measures, including prosecution, truth commissions, amnesty, reparations, lustration and vetting, institutional reform, and local justice processes that address past abuse (Gloppen 2002; Huyse 2008; Roht-Arriaza and Mariezcurrena 2006; Shaw and Hazan 2010; Teitel 2000). Since the 1980s truth commissions have become an important transitional justice (TJ) mechanism through which past human rights abuses committed during repressive regimes or periods of armed conflict are confronted. Latin American truth commissions have served as models for truth commissions established in other parts of the world, including the more famous South African Truth and Reconciliation Commission that was modelled on Chile's National Commission on Truth and Reconciliation (more popularly known as the Rettig Commission after its chairperson).

The establishment of truth commissions often generates broad expectations that they will lead to peace and justice – objectives that typically are cited to justify their creation. The most common, explicit goals of truth commissions have included clarifying and acknowledging past abuses, meeting the needs of victims, contributing to justice and accountability, delineating institutional responsibility for past abuses and promoting reform, and promoting reconciliation and a reduction in tensions over the past (Hayner 2011). Tristan Anne Borer (2006) identifies no fewer than 26 different explicitly stated goals or expectations for truth-finding initiatives, including acknowledgment, co-existence, promoting a human rights culture, justice, *nunca más* (never again), reconciliation, and the rule of law. Truth commissions may play a *ceremonial function* in that the investigation and the giving of testimony affect victims, perpetrators, and bystanders. The process of uncovering information creates a form of theatre. Acts and ceremonies frame the introduction of reports and findings to the public. The *reporting function* (Mendeloff 2004), depending on the truth commission's mandate, may vary from the systematic recollection of facts and data, to the historical interpretation of events and processes.

This forms the basis of a *transformative function* that potentially makes similar abuses less likely in the future.

The transformative potential of truth commissions arguably lies most directly in the body of recommendations put forward in the report. Truth commission recommendations usually include reforms in the legal, political and social fields, as well as reparations of various kinds. The list is often extensive. The tendency over time has been towards longer lists of recommendations. This in itself raises questions about expectations and the possibility of implementation. In general, the task of implementing truth commission recommendations faces many obstacles. A little over a decade ago, Priscilla B. Hayner (2011) concluded that, although "[n]o one has yet analysed how many of the thousands of recommendations by truth commissions have been implemented", the implementation record is generally poor. Upon the tenth anniversary of the Peruvian truth commission, a generally highly regarded truth commission, a report from the International Center for Transitional Justice (ICTJ) found that the implementation record had been abysmal (Correa 2013).

The relationship between the nature of recommendations and the prospects for their implementation has largely been neglected in the scholarly literature. Many qualitative studies of truth commissions make little reference to either (Amstutz 2005; Chapman 2009). Even recent qualitative work that focuses explicitly on the impact of truth commissions gives recommendations rather short shrift. Anita Ferrera's (2014) detailed analysis of the Chilean truth commission and its implications for later transitional justice policies is a notable exception.[1] Some large-N studies have in recent years attempted to evaluate the impact of truth commissions and other TJ mechanisms on outcomes such as peace, democracy, and human rights (Kim and Sikkink 2010; Olsen, Payne, and Reiter 2010; Sikkink and Walling 2007; Wiebelhaus-Brahm 2010b). They come to quite contradictory conclusions, however. Moreover, none of them take into account qualitative differences in truth commission recommendations, such as type of recommendation and degree of implementation. Only recently has the Transitional Justice Research Collaborative collected data on the recommendations of truth commissions.[2] However, the database consists only of categories of recommendations derived from truth commission reports and does not contain any information on their implementation.

A few qualitative studies have looked more closely at truth commission recommendations. Already in 1994, in his analysis of the then recently established truth commissions in Chile and El Salvador, Mark Ensalaco wrote that,

> The most important contributions of these most recent truth commissions, given the manner in which they were constituted, derived from their advisory function.

1 See also Quinn (2010) for a comparative analysis of Uganda and Haiti.
2 See https://transitionaljusticedata.com/.

> The commissions' recommendations concerning the adaptation of the political constitutions and legal statutes to reflect international human rights standards, and institutional reforms of the judiciaries and militaries, consisted of the legal and institutional prerequisites *of* societies that are truly protective and promotive of human rights (Ensalaco 1994, 666).

Mike Kaye (1997) provides an overview of recommendations by investigative commissions in Central America, including the Salvadoran truth commission, and some indication of their implementation status. Note, however, that, for both studies, given the short time-span between the issuing of truth commission reports and the publication of the journal article, the positive evaluation must have been based upon the text of the reports rather than on an actual analysis of their implementation record.

Other case studies provide a bit more historical distance. Some look at a subset of recommendations. In their analysis of the Peruvian truth commission, Lisa J. Laplante and Kimberley Theidon (2007) make a convincing argument for why it is important to trace what happens after a truth commission has issued its report, if one wants to understand the commission's potential impact. They analyze the implementation record of the Peruvian truth commission recommendations related to reparations to victims, exemplified by the government's "Plan of Reparations 2005–2006" approved by executive decree in 2005. They find that, at least initially, the government was unwilling to allocate the resources necessary to implement the reparations plan. Other studies provide a more general assessment of implementation for specific cases. For example, Margaret Popkin (2000) provides a more detailed overview of the implementation of the Salvadoran truth commission's recommendations. Shifting the focus to two other Latin American countries, in his analysis of Chile's Rettig Commission and the Salvadoran truth commission, Eric Wiebelhaus-Brahm (2010b) finds that recommendations are more likely to be implemented when party politics are more competitive and when civil society is more robust.

To date, the most comprehensive analysis of the impact of truth commission recommendations' implementation is Onur Bakiner's examination of truth commission impact based upon empirical evidence drawn from 15 truth commissions around the world. He concludes that, "The processes that generate the largest effects are direct political impact and delayed political impact through civil society mobilization" (Bakiner 2014, 29). He further argues that,

> Truth commissions' positive judicial impact (i.e., human rights accountability) tends to appear several years after the end of the process, in great part as a result of broader changes in politicians' and judges' attitudes on human rights trials. Negative judicial impact (i.e., impunity) favors only a small subsection of perpetrators, while the overall climate of impunity is likely caused by factors other than truth commissions' amnesty procedures (Bakiner 2014, 29).

These are all useful building blocks for constructing a comparative framework with broader application, as this project aims to do. Collectively, previous research highlights the importance of examining the nature of recommendations themselves as well as domestic and international contextual factors if we are to adequately explain patterns of (non)implementation. Moreover, existing studies indicate the value of scrutinizing implementation in the long run. Nonetheless, we still lack a comprehensive, systematic examination of which recommendations are implemented, and the circumstances under which implementation is likely to occur.

2. IMPLEMENTATION AS COMPLIANCE

In the project, we examine the factors that shape the likelihood of recommendations being implemented. In the absence of significant scholarly literature on the implementation of truth commission recommendations, we draw upon research on compliance with human rights treaties and norms. Although abiding by treaty provisions and court rulings issued by international or regional courts like the Inter-American Court of Human Rights exhibits important differences from truth commission recommendations, there is significant overlap in the causal mechanisms potentially at play. In particular, a common puzzle in each of these areas is explaining compliance in situations where enforcement mechanisms are quite weak. Broadly speaking, the two main perspectives within compliance theory are: (i) rational choice approaches that focus on material power and self-interest; and (ii) constructivist approaches that emphasize the power of norms, repeated interactions, and rhetorical argumentation in shaping state behavior (Bates 2014, 1170).

There is some variety among rationalist scholars. Realist accounts of compliance emphasize the power and interests of powerful domestic and/or international actors. Some of the earliest transitional justice accounts emphasize the balance of power in shaping transitional justice choices (Elster 1998; Huntington 1991; Kritz 1995; Skaar 1999). Although it may have shifted between the creation of a truth commission and the issuance of its final report, the balance of power among perpetrators, pro-justice factions, and civil society undoubtedly influences the odds of implementation. Shifting to external forces, existing research is pessimistic about powerful states using their leverage to promote human rights, especially in contradiction to strategic and economic interests (Barratt 2004; Blanton 2005; Carleton and Stohl 1985; Schoultz 1981). The chapters in this volume are attuned to the power and interests of an array of domestic and international influences.

Liberal accounts, by contrast, point to reciprocity and reputational reasons for compliance with international law and norms. Thus, governments, especially if they are fragile and new, may implement truth commission recommendations to build their legitimacy and curry favor with other states. However, existing research questions the extent to which a state's reputation in one issue area is correlated with reputations in other areas (Downs and Jones 2002). As a result, compliance may be influenced more by domestic political factors (Hillebrecht 2014; Simmons 2009). In particular, many argue that civil society, free press and public debate, electoral accountability, and transparency make it more difficult for democracies to renege on international human rights commitments they have made (Dai 2005; Lipson 2005; Simmons 2009). We see indications that these same factors influence the implementation of truth commission recommendations.

Finally, constructivist accounts emphasize a logic of appropriateness; that governments are often driven to behave in accordance with prevailing norms and ideas (Keck and Sikkink 1998; Keck and Sikkink 1999). Early research argued that global human rights norms socialized states to behave in certain ways (Risse et al. 1999). More recent studies find that treaty bodies that are run by committees of independent experts fare better in identifying learning opportunities for states, as they provide technical solutions (Carraro 2019, 12). Nonetheless, the mechanisms leading to the adoption of a norm are often rooted in domestic politics (Betts and Orchard 2014; Cortell and Davis Jr. 2000). Scholars have identified conditions under which domestic civil society collaborated with international actors to induce a positive change in the behavior of a recalcitrant authoritarian state (Keck and Sikkink 1998). All of the cases in our study, though, are democratic to varying degrees. In addressing the gap between commitment and compliance with human rights norms, Risse, Ropp, and Sikkink (2013) identify four social mechanisms at work in explaining the adoption of norms: coercion, persuasion, capacity-building and the use of incentives. Furthermore, they suggest five scope conditions that influence the level of compliance: the regime type, the degree of statehood, the degree of centralized or decentralized rule implementation, material vulnerability, and social vulnerability. While there is not a specific international obligation to create a truth commission and commission recommendations are not norms, many of them would satisfy citizens' rights to truth, reparation, and non-repetition, among other things (Hirsch 2014; Wiebelhaus-Brahm 2010a).

In our study, we see some of these dynamics at work. Transitional states may be more vulnerable to international pressure as they seek to build legitimacy. Several chapters reveal instances in which foreign governments and multilateral institutions have exerted pressure to enact truth commission recommendations. However, those recommendations have typically been in alignment with pre-existing policy interests of domestic and/or international actors. Although the international community may have induced some vulnerable transitional governments in our study to act upon recommendations from commissions established right after political transitions, this mechanism may be less effective for post-transitional commissions created in more stable political environments.[3] Moreover, as our country chapters show, governments are often more likely to implement truth commission recommendations if they coincide with rulings issued by the Inter-American Court of Human Rights, particularly those related to the unconstitutionality of amnesty laws, victims' right to reparations, orders for the uncovering of mass graves based upon rights to truth and reparations, and rulings calling for public apologies. Victims' groups and human rights activists also have collaborated across the region to advance their agendas, including the implementation of truth commission recommendations.

Nonetheless, the chapters in this volume reinforce the primacy of domestic politics in driving implementation. As Alexander Mayer-Rieckh and Howard Varney (2019, 51) argue, "ultimate implementation [of recommendations] depends on a number of factors that are beyond the control of a truth commission such as political will and the level of civil society engagement".

There are no enforcement mechanisms tied to the setting up of a truth commission. Commission mandates may require governments to implement recommendations. We find that, although some of the truth commissions were followed by monitoring bodies established by the governments to oversee the implementation of the recommendations, none of these bodies have had detailed instructions from the government regarding how to implement, or measure the implementation of, the recommendations. Regardless of the motivation for establishing a truth commission, the act of creation may have *ex ante* and *ex post* costs (Fearon 1997). First, there are sunk costs associated with creating the commission. States may have created a commission out of a sincere desire to address the past. By contrast, some see states strategically employing truth commissions, and transitional justice more generally, to alleviate domestic and/or international pressure to address a history of human rights abuses (Cronin-Furman 2019; Grodsky 2008; Loyle and Davenport 2016). In contrast to trials or reparations, governments may see commissions as relatively costless commitments. In such scenarios, states may have little intention to follow through. However, establishing a truth commission which is charged with producing recommendations can be a credible signal to domestic and international audiences about of the seriousness of its commitment to addressing past abuses. In such circumstances, states face the *ex post* costs of not complying with recommendations. Overall, the case studies in this volume point to governments' historical connection to past violence, the degree of pressure from victims' and human rights organizations, and the presence or absence of competing issues on the national agenda as being critical for the prospects of implementation.

---

3 On the concept of post-transitional justice, see Collins (2010) and Skaar (2011), Chapter 2. "Explaining Post-Transitional Justice".

A final important insight from the literature on compliance particularly relevant to our project is that the nature of recommendations matters. In her comparison of the recommendations made by the UN Human Rights Council's Universal Periodic Review (UPR) and by treaty monitoring bodies, for example, Valentina Carraro (2019, 12) finds that both types of reviews can be successful in delivering feasible recommendations. However, their effectiveness derives from very different characteristics: "while UPR recommendations are appreciated for being realistic (albeit often vague), Concluding Observations [from the state reporting procedures of the treaty bodies] are praised for being very detailed, yet criticized for aiming at unattainable standards". As our country studies suggest, recommendations that are clearly (as opposed to vaguely) formulated, that are attainable (as opposed to aspirational), and that have identified specific implementing agencies (as opposed to not mentioning what agency should be responsible to the implementation) are more likely to be implemented. The following chapters similarly reveal that both the subject of truth commission recommendations as well as the explicit language used to craft them may influence the likelihood of their implementation.

3. METHODOLOGY

3.1. RESEARCH OBJECTIVES

Given the lack of systematic data and analysis of the relationship between the recommendations and their implementation record, particularly in a comparative framework, the unique collection of country chapters in this volume amends this knowledge gap by doing three things. First, for each of the truth commissions, the authors have collected and systematized information on recommendations. Second, each chapter identifies the factors that influenced how recommendations were formulated in the truth commission's final report. Finally, the authors assess the extent to which these recommendations have actually been implemented. Furthermore, the authors speculate about the extent to which the implemented truth commission recommendations have influenced behavior and attitudes within the country.

Our goal is that the data collected and the theory developed will advance our understanding of truth commission processes and contribute to broader scholarly debates about the multiple roles truth commissions play in the social, political, and economic reconstruction of societies after periods of conflict and repression. The rich data assembled here also has been used to develop theory-based explanations for variation in implementation across country, over time, and by type of recommendation (Centeno-Martín, Wiebelhaus-Brahm, Nieto-Librero, and Wright, Forthcoming; Martínez Barahona and Centeno-Martín 2020; Skaar, Wiebelhaus-Brahm, and García-Godos 2022; Wiebelhaus-Brahm,

Centeno-Martín, Nieto Librero, and Wright, Forthcoming; Wiebelhaus-Brahm and Wright 2021).[4]

3.2. CASE SELECTION

We geographically focus on Latin America for several reasons. First, Latin America was the first region in the world to employ truth commissions in significant numbers in the early 1980s. Second, since some of the oldest truth commissions in the world are found in Latin America, significant time has passed in which to trace the implementation record of their recommendations. For truth commissions established in the 1990s and the 2000s, the length of time during which implementation may have taken place is naturally shorter, but still often significant. Consequently, a third benefit of a regional focus is that this variation enables us to explore the extent to which the global or regional historical time-period may influence patterns of implementation. The post-Cold War world contained different incentives from previously, arguably more conducive to the promotion of human rights. Finally, the inclusion of all official truth commissions enables us to weigh each country's own unique history. Debt crises and neoliberal economic reform, for example, sometimes have created unwanted distractions from other policy issues, including TJ (Olsen, Reiter, and Wiebelhaus-Brahm 2011). Overall, the region presents a natural laboratory in which to explore truth commission recommendation formulation and implementation.

3.3. CORE DEFINITIONS

Definitional issues have plagued the study of truth commissions. Like many other comparative studies, this project adopts Priscilla Hayner's seminal definition of a truth commission. A truth commission is

> (1) focused on past, rather than ongoing, events; (2) investigates a pattern of events that took place over a period of time; (3) engages directly and broadly with the affected population, gathering information on their experiences; (4) is a temporary body, with the aim of concluding with a final report; and (5) is officially authorized or empowered by the state under review (Hayner 2011, 11).

This is a more restrictive definition than Hayner's (1994, 600) earlier definition of truth commissions as "bodies set up to investigate a past history of violations of human rights in a particular country – which can include violations by the

---

[4] Since the theory and methodology used in the *Beyond Words* project is elaborated upon elsewhere, we only highlight a few points here to provide context to the 11 case studies included in this volume.

military or other government forces or by armed opposition forces". It is, however, similar to Mark Freeman's definition of a truth commission as

> an *ad hoc*, autonomous, and victim-centred commission of inquiry set up in and authorized by a state for the primary purposes of (1) investigating and reporting on the principal causes and consequences of broad and relatively recent patterns of severe violence or repression that occurred in the state during determinate periods of abusive rule or conflict, and (2) making recommendations for their redress and future prevention (Freeman 2006, 18).

Both Hayner's (1994, 2011) and Freeman's (2006) definitions are much more restrictive than the more expansive definition used in recent statistical work on truth commissions by Olsen, Payne, and Reiter (2010), in which they identify about 70 truth commissions world-wide.

Although Hayner's (2011) definition has been used variously in the literature, vagaries in the definition still lead to different conclusions about which investigative bodies are or are not truth commissions (Stewart and Wiebelhaus-Brahm 2017; Wiebelhaus-Brahm 2009). With respect to their "official" nature or otherwise, this volume examines only *state*-sponsored truth commissions because, unlike NGO-based investigations, such sponsorship entails an obligation on the part of the state to implement the recommendations. At the same time, we include only those bodies set up for a limited amount of time specifically to address a period of past violations. By contrast, some previous studies have included investigations by existing state organs as truth commissions (Kaye 1997). Moreover, to reduce ambiguity in the meaning of "pattern of events", we restrict ourselves to truth commissions that investigate a certain political era, defined here as a particular regime's time in power or the length of a civil war. This definition gives us the list of Latin American truth commissions presented in Table 1.

Table 1. Official Latin American Truth Commissions (in chronological order)[5]

Country	Name of Commission (English translation)	Commission established by/Years of operation	Year of final report
Bolivia	National Commission for the Investigation of Forced Disappearances	President (1982–84)	No report completed
Argentina	National Commission on the Disappeared (CONADEP)	President (1983–84)	1984

(continued)

[5] This list does not include the following non-state truth commissions that have examined histories of violence and repression in Latin America: Brazil's truth commission established by Archbishop of São Paulo and the World Council of Churches (1979–85) (report issued

Table 1 *continued*

Country	Name of Commission (English translation)	Commission established by/Years of operation	Year of final report
Uruguay	Investigative Commission on the Situation of Disappeared People and its Causes	Parliament (1985)	1985
Chile	National Commission for Truth and Reconciliation (Rettig Commission)	President (1990–91)	1991
El Salvador	Truth Commission of El Salvador (CVES)	UN (1992–93)	1993
Haiti	National Truth and Justice Commission (CNVJ)	President (1994–96)	1996
Ecuador	Truth and Justice Commission	Ministry of Government and Police (1996–97)	No report completed
Guatemala	Commission for Historical Clarification	UN (1997–99)	1999
Uruguay	Commission for Peace (COMIPAZ)	President (2000–02)	2003
Panama	Panama Truth Commission	President (2001–02)	2002
Peru	Truth and Reconciliation Commission (CVR)	President (2001–03)	2003
Chile	National Commission on Political Imprisonment and Torture (Valech)	President (2003–05)	2004, 2005[6]
Paraguay	Truth and Justice Commission (CVJ)	President (2004–08)	2008
Ecuador	Truth Commission to Impede Impunity	President (2008–10)	2010

(continued)

1985); Uruguay's truth commission established by *Servicio Paz y Justicia* (Uruguay) (report issued 1989); and Guatemala's Recovery of Historical Memory project (REMHI) established by the Human Rights Office of the Archbishop of Guatemala (1995–98) (final report 1998). Furthermore, we have not included the self-described truth commissions in Honduras, which included both the early 1990s investigation by the National Commissioner for the Protection of Human Rights because "the Commissioner's work does not conform to the traditional truth commission model" (Kaye 1997, 700) and the 2010–11 commission that investigated the circumstances surrounding the 2009 coup.

6 The report published on November 29, 2004, detailed the results of a six-month investigation. A revised version was released on June 1, 2005. The commission was reopened in February 2010 for 18 months, adding more cases. For more details on the Valech report, see (Collins 2017).

Table 1 *continued*

Country	Name of Commission (English translation)	Commission established by/Years of operation	Year of final report
Brazil	National Truth Commission (CNV)	President (2012–14)	2014
Colombia	Commission for the Clarification of Truth, Coexistence, and Non-Repetition	President (2018–)	--
Bolivia	Truth Commission	Government of Bolivia (2017–)[7]	--

Sources: Hayner (2011); monthly bulletins from ICTJ (at http://ictj.org/); and reports published by United States Institute of Peace digital Truth Commission Digital Collection, at: http://www.usip.org/publications/truth-commission-digital-collection.

Note: See Appendix for full names of all truth commissions and their reports in their original language.[8]

The country cases listed in Table 1 provide an exhaustive list of 13 countries in Latin America that have had one or more official state-sponsored truth commissions.[9] Excluding from our analysis those truth commissions that did not complete their reports (i.e. Bolivia (1982–84) and Ecuador (1996–97), as well as the Colombian (2018–) truth commission and Bolivian (2017–) truth commission, which had not concluded their work as of mid-2019, we are left with 13 commissions in 11 countries (in bold in Table 1). Some of these are well known, like the truth commissions of Argentina, Chile, El Salvador, Guatemala, and Peru. Others have received much less scholarly attention, such as the commissions set up in Ecuador, Paraguay, Panama, and Uruguay. Brazil's 2014 commission also is included in our study.

These truth commissions can be categorized in at least two ways. A first distinction relates to when they were created, with some established around the time of attempted transition to either democracy or peace (transitional truth commissions), whereas others were established several years after the transition (post-transitional commissions) (Skaar, García-Godos, and Collins 2016).

7 The Bolivian truth commission was formally established in August 2017.

8 The 13 commissions from 11 countries featured in this volume are in bold.

9 All these commissions, except for the Uruguay 1985 commission and Chile 2003 commission, are included in US Institute of Peace truth commission digital library. Several TJ scholars do not count the 1985 Uruguay commission established by Parliament to investigate the fate of the detained-disappeared as a "proper" truth commission because it did not have sufficient autonomy from the executive and legislative branches of government (Bakiner 2014, 6). Rather than make such a qualitative judgement, we err on the side of inclusion.

The first group are commissions that were tasked with investigating violations in the immediate past while the second group typically investigated violations that happened decades ago. According to Onur Bakiner, these two types of commissions may be expected not only to be different in character, but also to have different impact. In his words, "The political stakes, self-declared goals and methodologies are radically different from those characterizing transitional truth commissions" (Bakiner 2014, 15). Second, the truth commissions in this volume vary in terms of the types of violations they investigated. Truth commissions in the Southern Cone, for example, examined military juntas' oppression of perceived leftist opponents. In some other countries, by contrast, truth commissions dealt with atrocities committed in the midst of civil war. We bear these differences in mind when we analyze the implementation record of the truth commissions included in our study, which include transitional and post-conflict, as well as post-transitional truth commissions.

3.4. DATA AND METHODOLOGY

It was a challenge to systematize data collection and analysis across such a large number of cases. Teams based in four different institutions in four different countries – CELS (Argentina), IDEHPUCP (Peru), FLACSO (Guatemala), and at the University of Salamanca (Spain) – contributed to the project. In addition, several individual researchers covered countries where none of the four teams had extensive links.

All researchers relied on a combination of primary and secondary sources (also noted in the data sets[10]). For each truth commission, researchers collected three types of data. First, using the original truth commission reports, researchers recorded all recommendations verbatim in the original language (Spanish, Portuguese, or French), while also providing an English translation. Furthermore, each truth commission recommendation has been classified according to a typology developed by the project team to facilitate comparative analysis across truth commission cases.[11]

Second, researchers collected detailed data on the formulation phase of the truth commission recommendations. They examined why particular recommendations were included or excluded in the final report. We sought to understand commissioners' strategic calculations as they navigated complex,

---

10 https://www.cmi.no/data/beyondwords.

11 See Chapter 2 in *Exploring Truth Commission Recommendations in a Comparative Perspective: Beyond Words Vol. I* (Skaar, Wiebelhaus-Brahm, and García-Godos 2022). For the data sets and code book see https://www.cmi.no/data/beyondwords.

often contradictory domestic and international pressures for justice and impunity. To accomplish this goal, on-site fieldwork was carried out in all 11 countries (see Table 1 above). For data on truth commission recommendation formulation, the teams interviewed former commissioners and staff as well as members of civil society to gain insights into the debates that influenced the inclusion or exclusion of particular recommendations in the truth commission report. They used semi-structured interviews, designed to cover some core questions across all cases, but at the same time allowing sufficient flexibility to capture the specificities of each case. Interviews were supplemented with memoirs and other insider accounts.

Third, researchers collected data on the implementation of each recommendation. For data on truth commission implementation, researchers relied on a wide range of written sources (i.e., government documents, newspaper reports, surveys, etc.) together with interviews conducted with a wide variety of people in government ministries, follow-up commissions/institutions and courts, plus legal experts, and members of civil society. On a basic level, we sought to determine whether a particular truth commission recommendation had been implemented or not. If it had, we outlined how it was implemented and when, and identified the actor that was responsible for doing so.

Note that implementation is not an either/or proposition. Implementation can be a lengthy and piecemeal process, depending on the nature of the recommendation and the political will and resources allocated to its implementation. As noted by Rousseau (2018, 323), compliance with global human rights norms too is not a dichotomous variable, and partial compliance (in our case, partial implementation) is difficult for scholars to accommodate. The country chapter authors who collected the data were challenged to assess whether a particular recommendation had been partially implemented, fully implemented or not implemented at all. We coded recommendations as partially implemented if some action had occurred, such as the introduction of legislation that was never passed, or if it in some other way fell short of what was envisioned by the commissioners. A detailed code book was given to all research teams to ensure consistency in coding across all cases.[12] More generally, for each truth commission recommendation, we analyzed which actors (governmental and civil society, domestic and international) were involved in the politics of implementation and what circumstances supported or obstructed the implementation process.

---

[12] See Appendix III: Excerpts from the Truth Commission Recommendations (TCR) Data Code Book in Skaar, Wiebelhaus-Brahm, and García-Godos (2022). See also https://www.cmi.no/data/beyondwords.

4. STRUCTURE OF THE BOOK

This volume consists of 11 country chapters, technically covering 13 truth commissions. However, in effect, it provides analysis of only 12 commissions in detail. The first Uruguayan truth commission that handed over its report to the government in 1985 receives short shrift here for several reasons, including that hardly any information is available, but also because there is not much to analyze. This commission with the rather complicated name, Investigative Commission on the Situation of Disappeared People and its Causes, made only two recommendations in its final report: that the Commission hand over the report to the President and to the Courts for further action. Both recommendations were completed. No further action was taken. Therefore, with good reason, the truth commission is generally perceived inside Uruguay as well as by TJ scholars as fairly inconsequential (Lessa and Skaar 2016, 88). Many scholars do not even count it as a "proper" truth commission. Thus, though technically included in our dataset of 13 commissions, the 11 chapters in this book effectively analyze only 12 truth commissions in depth.

Following this short introduction, we have divided the rest of the book into three parts. Each part covers a geographical region of Latin America. We have organized the chapters geographically rather than by the year in which the commissions issued their reports for three reasons. First, to make the country analyses comparable, it makes sense to group the countries that share characteristics. Although clearly every country is different, the countries in each region tend to share similarities either with respect to type of conflict (military regimes versus internal armed conflict), or with respect to international involvement in the truth commission and its report. Second, the research teams have worked on a regional basis, meaning that they have had the responsibility for between three and five cases each. They possess the sub-regional expertise to draw out the similarities and differences across cases. Third, there are long histories of cross-national interaction that have facilitated the spread of ideas and practices across the region, but within sub-regions in particular. This has been true not only for tactics of oppression and violence, such as Operación Condor in the Southern Cone, but also in the sharing of strategies and evidence by victims' groups and human rights campaigners. Within each part, however, the country cases are presented chronologically according to when truth commissions issued their reports.

Starting in the south of the continent, Part I covers five Southern Cone countries:[13] Argentina (the first country to establish a truth commission

[13] The core Southern Cone countries are Argentina, Chile, and Uruguay. However, Southern Brazil and Paraguay are politically and socially considered to also be part of the Southern Cone. We have included all five here for these reasons as well as because all five had similar military regimes that were all part of the regional Operación Condor right-wing repression network.

that completed its work and handed over its report to the government); Chile (which had two formal truth commissions – the Rettig Commission and the Valech I Commission); Uruguay (which also had two formal truth commissions – only the latter of which is given detailed attention here); Paraguay (which had one commission); and Brazil (the last country in Latin America to issue a truth commission report as of mid-2019). Part II covers the truth commissions operating in proximity to the Andean region: Ecuador and Peru.[14] Part III focuses on truth commissions in Central America and the Caribbean: the well-known UN-sponsored commissions in El Salvador and Guatemala, as well as the much less well-known commissions in Panama and Haiti.

The first chapter on Argentina shows that all the recommendations made by *Informe de la Comisión Nacional Sobre la Desaparición de Personas* (CONADEP) have been implemented since the commission's report was launched in 1985. Thus, it appears to be a highly successful truth commission. However, the chapter raises the question of causality. Were the reforms undertaken because the truth commission recommended so, or did the recommendations become part of a larger human rights agenda? While many of CONADEP's recommendations were already being discussed by civil society, Sol Hourcade, Federico Ghelfi, Luz Palmás Zaldua, and Marcela Perelman conclude that the recommendations have proven to be an important catalyst for change in Argentina.

Moving to neighboring Chile, the second chapter compares and contrasts two of its central, yet distinct, truth commissions. Whereas the recommendations made by *Informe de la Comisión Nacional de Verdad y Reconciliación* (Informe Rettig) mostly concerned state reform, the *Informe de la Comisión Nacional sobre Prisión Politica y Tortura* (Informe Valech) made recommendations focusing heavily on reparations for victims of torture. In the chapter, Sol Hourcade, Federico Ghelfi, Luz Palmás Zaldua and Marcela Perelman show how the implementation of recommendations for institutional and legal reform has been neglected compared to that of reparations for victims. The Chilean experience is one of gradual expansion of the definition of victimhood and, hence, eligibility for reparation.

Uruguay's experience with truth finding and truth telling is manifold. The next chapter narrows the focus to the experience of the Commission for Peace. Of the eight recommendations made by *Informe Final de la Comisión para la Paz* in 2003, Federico Ghelfi, Sol Hourcade, Luz Palmás Zaldua, and Marcela Perelman conclude that those dealing with insitutional and legal reforms to ensure compliance with human rights norms and practice demonstrate a better

[14] Geographically, The Andes extend through the western part of South America in the following countries: Colombia, Venezuela, Ecuador, Peru, Bolivia, Argentina, and Chile, However, neither Argentina nor Chile are considered to be geopolitically an Andean State and are more commonly known as Southern Cone countries.

implementation record than the recommendations dealing with reparations and human rights education.

Paraguay was different from its neighboring countries in that military repression was carried out under a one-man authoritarian regime that stretched over many decades. A truth commission was established a few years after Alfredo Stroessner finally stepped down in 1989, after 35 years in power. As this chapter shows, the *Informe Final. Anive haguâ oiko* (2008) of the Paraguayan truth commission has the longest list of recommendations of all Latin American truth commission reports. Despite the commission having launched a very ambitious reform agenda, though, Félix Reátegui, Tania Gómez, and Eduardo Hurtado find that very few of the truth commissions' 202 recommendations have been implemented in the decade following their release. Some memorialization and educational initiatives have been successful, whereas the search for the disappeared, high-level prosecutions, and restitution as redress for the illegal appropriation of land have been largely neglected.

The last country in the sub-region, Brazil, is the most recent country in Latin America to launch a truth commission report, in 2014 – more than 30 years after the worst human rights violations had taken place. In spite of being a voluminous report, the *Relatório da Comissão Nacional da Verdade* made relatively few recommendations, most of which were aimed at rectifying persisting democratic deficiencies in the army, security sector, and prisons. "Brazil's National Truth Commission" shows that most of these suggested reforms remain unimplemented, though there have been some advances in truth and memory measures. Federico Ghelfi, Sol Hourcade, Luz Palmás Zaldua and Marcela Perelman have little optimism for the future. When the Commission completed its work, Brazil was in the midst of economic recession and a political scandal that brought down many politicians, especially from the Workers' Party. With the 2018 election of right-wing President Jair Bolsonaro, there is little prospect of progress on implementation in the near term.

Moving to the Andes in Part II of the book, "Ecuador's Truth Commission" takes stock of what happened when Ecuador's Truth Commission concluded its work. One of the least-known truth commission reports, *Informe de la Comisión de la Verdad Ecuador 2010: Sin Verdad no hay Justicia*, issued an ambitious reform agenda with 156 recommendations, dealing with reparations, justice, and institutional reform. The Ecuadorian government has undertaken a number of measures to promote and protect human rights. However, Félix Reátegui, Eduardo Hurtado, and Diego Uchuypoma argue that these measures are not directly related to the Commission's recommendations, but to a more comprehensive government plan. In spite of active participation of victims in the truth commission, the construction of a collective memory about the violent past has proven hard to achieve.

Neighboring Peru's Truth and Reconciliation Commission is much more widely known, particularly for its strong emphasis on reparations to victims of state repression. "Peru's Truth and Reconciliation Commission" takes stock of *Informe Final de la Comisión de la Verdad y Reconciliación* (*Hatun Willakuy* 2003), which made a wide-ranging set of recommendations designed to overcome the legacy of violence in Peru. These include measures of reparation for the victims and institutional reform intended to ensure non-repetition and the strengthening of Peruvian democracy. As Félix Reátegui and Diego Uchuypoma show, however, the implementation record is mixed. Most well-known is the extensive national reparations program, while institutional reforms have been less successful.

From the Andes, in Part III the book moves further north to Central America and the Caribbean. The conflicts in these two regions were of a different character than the right-wing military dictatorships that dominated the southern part of Latin America. The next chapter shows how the recommendations made by El Salvador's truth commission in its final report, *De la locura a la esperanca. La guerra de 12 años en El Salvador* (1993), were deeply entangled with the peace process. The recommendations, aimed at reforming the state and addressing human rights violations, were binding, yet most of them have not been fulfilled. Implementation proved very difficult during the right-wing Alianza Republicana Nacionalista (ARENA)'s 20 years in power, as politicians, the military, and the Supreme Court actively resisted institutional and legal reforms. Although a window of opportunity appeared to open with the inauguration of the first Presidency of the left-wing Frente Farabundo Martí para la Liberación Nacional (FLMN) in 2009, Elena Martínez-Barahona, Sonia Rubio-Padilla, Héctor Centeno-Martín, and Martha Gutiérrez-Salazar find that this generated high expectations that have resulted in significant frustration among those who expected great changes regarding the country's endemic impunity.

Like El Salvador, neighboring Guatemala also was plagued by civil war, and had the largest number of victims of human rights violations of the countries analyzed in this volume. "Guatemala's Commission of Historical Clarification" shows that the truth commission's report, *Guatemala: Memoria del Silencio* (1999), largely succeeded in documenting the atrocities that took place during Guatemala's 36-year-long civil war. However, after close on 20 years, most of its recommendations remain unimplemented, particularly those dealing with the disappeared and reparations to victims. Héctor Centeno-Martín provides a thoughtful analysis of why Guatemala has one of the poorest implementation records of all truth commission reports included in this volume. In the more than two decades since the recommendations were issued, successive governments have generally shown little interest in implementation. As the chapter shows, progress has largely been driven by Guatemalan civil society and the international community.

Haiti's little-known truth commission report, *Si m pa rele: 29 September 1991–14 Octobre 1994*, is the focus of the following chapter. This report was the first in Latin America to focus in depth on sexual violence against women.

Lisa-Marie Måseidvåg Selvik shows that the implementation of its recommendations has been heavily dependent on international actors since domestic political will and resources have mainly been absent. Although the final report is largely forgotten, the demands the Commission vocalized through its recommendations are still very much alive in Haitian society.

"Panama's Truth Commission Recommendations" takes us to the under-researched country of Panama. The truth commission's virtually unknown final report, *Panama: Informe Final de la Comisión de la Verdad. "La verdad os hará libres"*, which was handed over to the government in 2002, gave only 12 recommendations. Based on long-term fieldwork, Adriana Rudling's chapter provides a uniquely detailed account of a report that most truth commission experts have never come across. The chapter concludes that the implementation record overall is "abysmal" due to the lack of political commitment. However, Rudling also shows that there has been limited progress in the implementation of reparation measures and recommendations aimed at criminal investigations into human rights abuses.

Finally, Onur Bakiner concludes the volume with a reflection on the study of truth commission recommendations. In particular, he connects recommendations to broader academic and policy discussions about the impact of truth commissions in societies emerging from periods of violence and repression. The chapter nicely lays out the conceptual and methodological challenges confronted by this project. In his critique of the volume, Bakiner offers several suggestions as to how the field can build upon the authors' findings.

BIBLIOGRAPHY

Amstutz, Mark R. (2005). *The Healing of Nations: The Promise and Limits of Political Forgiveness*. Lanham, MD: Rowman & Littlefield Publishers.

Bakiner, Onur (2014). "Truth commission impact: An assessment of how commissions influence politics and society." *International Journal of Transitional Justice* no. 8 (1): pp. 6–30.

—— (2016). *Truth Commissions: Memory, Power, and Legitimacy*. Philadelphia, PA: University of Pennsylvania Press.

Barratt, Bethany (2004). "Aiding or Abetting: British Foreign Aid Decisions and Recipient Country Human Rights." In *Understanding Human Rights Violations: New Systematic Studies*, edited by Sabine C. Carey and Steven C. Poe, pp. 43–62. Aldershot, England: Ashgate.

Bates, Elizabeth Stubbins (2014). "Sophisticated constructivism in human rights compliance theory." *The European Journal of International Law* no. 25 (4), pp. 1169–1182.

Betts, Alexander, and Phil Orchard (eds.) (2014). *Implementation and World Politics: How International Norms Change Practice*. Oxford: Oxford University Press.

Blanton, Shannon Lindsey (2005). "Foreign policy in transition? Human rights, democracy, and US arms exports." *International Studies Quarterly* no. 49 (4): pp. 647–667.

Borer, Tristan Anne (2006). "Truth Telling as a Peace-Building Activity: A Theoretical Overview." In *Telling the Truths: Truth Telling and Peace Building in Post-Conflict Societies*, edited by Tristan Anne Borer. South Bend, IN: University of Notre Dame Press.

Carleton, David, and Michael Stohl (1985). "The foreign policy of human rights: Rhetoric and reality from Jimmy Carter to Ronald Reagan." *Human Rights Quarterly* no. 7: 205–229.

Carraro, Valentina (2019). "Promoting Compliance with Human Rights: The Performance of the United Nations' Universal Periodic Review and Treaty Bodies." *International Studies Quarterly* no. 63 (4):1079–1093.

Centeno-Martín, Héctor, Eric Wiebelhaus-Brahm, Ana Belén Nieto-Librero, and Dylan Wright (Forthcoming). "Explaining the Timeliness of Implementation of Truth Commission Recommendations." *Journal of Peace Research*.

Chapman, Audrey R. (2009). "Truth Finding in the Transitional Justice Process." In *Assessing the Impact of Transitional Justice: Challenges for Empirical Research*, edited by Hugo Van der Merwe, Victoria Baxter and Audrey R. Chapman, 91–114. Washington, DC: USIP Press.

Collins, Cath (2010). *Post-Transitional Justice: Human Rights Trials in Chile and El Salvador*. University Park, PA: Penn State University Press.

—— (2017). "Truth-Justice-Reparations Interaction Effects in Transitional Justice Practice: The Case of the 'Valech Commission' in Chile." *Journal of Latin American Studies*: no. 49 (1) 55–82.

Correa, Cristián (2013). Reparations in Peru: From Recommendations to Implementation. New York: International Center for Transitional Justice, (ICTJ) available at: http://ictj.org/sites/default/files/ICTJ_Report_Peru_Reparations_2013.pdf.

Cortell, Andrew P, and James W Davis Jr. (2000). "Understanding the domestic impact of international norms: A research agenda." *International Studies Review* no. 2 (1): 65–87.

Cronin-Furman, Kate (2020). "Human Rights Half Measures: Avoiding Accountability in Postwar Sri Lanka." *World Politics* no. 72 (1): 121–163.

Dai, Xinyuan (2005). "Why comply? The domestic constituency mechanism." *International Organization* no. 59 (2): 363–398.

Downs, George W, and Michael A Jones (2002). "Reputation, compliance, and international law." *The Journal of Legal Studies* no. 31 (S1): 95–114.

Elster, Jon (1998). "Coming to terms with the past. A framework for the study of justice in the transition to democracy." *European Journal of Sociology* no. 39(1):7–48.

Ensalaco, Mark (1994). "Truth commissions for Chile and El Salvador: A report and assessment." *Human. Rights Quarterly* no. 16 (4): 656–675.

Fearon, James D. (1997). "Signaling foreign policy interests: Tying hands versus sinking costs." *Journal of Conflict Resolution* no. 41 (1): 68–90.

Ferrara, Anita (2014). *Assessing the Long-Term Impact of Truth Commissions: The Chilean Truth and Reconciliation Commission in Historical Perspective* London: Routledge.

Freeman, Mark (2006). *Truth Commissions and Procedural Fairness.* New York: Cambridge University Press.

Freeman, Mark, and Priscilla B. Hayner (2003). "Truth-Telling." In *Reconciliation after Violent Conflict: A Handbook*, edited by David Bloomfield, Teresa Barnes and Luc Huyse. 122–139 Halmstad, Sweden: International Institute for Democracy and Electoral Assistance (IDEA).

Gloppen, Siri (2002). Reconciliation and Democratisation: Outlining the Research Field. Bergen: Chr. Michelsen Institute, R 2002: 51–52.

Grodsky, Brian (2008). "Justice without transition: Truth commissions in the context of repressive rule." *Human Rights Review* no. 9 (3):281–297.

Hayner, Priscilla B. (1994). "Fifteen Truth Commissions - 1974 to 1994: A Comparative Study." *Human Rights Quarterly* no. 16 (4):597–655.

—— (2001). *Unspeakable Truths. Confronting State Terror and Atrocity.* New York and London: Routledge.

—— (2011). *Unspeakable Truths: Transitional Justice and the Challenge of Truth Commissions* New York and London: Routledge (2nd edition).

Hillebrecht, Courtney (2014). *Domestic Politics and International Human Rights Tribunals: The Problem of Compliance.* New York: Cambridge University Press.

Hirsch, Michal Ben-Josef (2014). "Ideational change and the emergence of the international norm of truth and reconciliation commissions." *European Journal of International Relations* no. 20 (3): 810–833.

Huntington, Samuel P. (1991). *The Third Wave: Democratization in the Late Twentieth Century.* New York and London: Cambridge University Press.

Huyse, Luc, and Mark Salter (2008). *Traditional Justice and Reconciliation after Violent Conflict - Learning from African Experiences.* Stockholm, Sweden: IDEA (International Institute for Democracy and Electoral Assistance).

Kaye, Mike (1997). "The role of truth commissions in the search for justice, reconciliation and democratisation: The Salvadorean and Honduran cases." *Journal of Latin American Studies* no. 29 (3): 693–716.

Keck, Margaret E, and Kathryn Sikkink (1999). "Transnational Advocacy Networks in International and Regional Politics." *International Social Science Journal* no. 51 (159): 89–101.

—— (1998). *Activists Beyond Borders: Advocacy Networks in International Politics.* Ithaca NY: Cornell University Press.

Kim, Hunjoon, and Kathryn Sikkink (2010). "Explaining the Deterrence Effect of Human Rights Prosecutions for Transitional Countries." *International Studies Quarterly* no. 54 (4): 939–963.

Kritz, Neil (1995). *Transitional Justice. How Emerging Democracies Reckon With Former Regimes.* Vols. I–III. Washington DC: United States Institute of Peace Press.

Laplante, Lisa J., and Kimberly Susan Theidon (2007). "Truth with Consequences: Justice and Reparations in Post-Truth Commission Peru." *Human Rights Quarterly* no. 29 (1): 228–250.

Lessa, Francesca, and Elin Skaar (2016). "Uruguay: halfway towards accountability." In *Transitional Justice in Latin America: The Uneven Road from Impunity towards Accountability*, edited by Elin Skaar, Jemima García-Godos and Cath Collins, 77–102. London and New York: Routledge.

Lipson, Charles (2005). *Reliable Partners: How Democracies have made a Separate Peace*: Princeton University Press.

Loyle, Cyanne E, and Christian Davenport (2016). "Transitional injustice: Subverting justice in transition and postconflict societies." *Journal of Human Rights* no. 15 (1): 126–149.

Martínez Barahona, Elena, and Héctor Centeno-Martín (2020). "Comisiones de la verdad y reformas del sector seguridad y defensa en América Latina." *América Latina Hoy* 84: 9–30.

Mayer-Rieckh, Alexander, and Howard Varney (2019). *Recommending Change. Truth Commission Recommendations on Institutional Reforms: An Overview.* Geneva: DCAF (Geneva Centre for Security Sector Governance).

Mendeloff, David (2004). "Truth-Seeking, Truth-Telling, and Postconflict Peacebuilding: Curb the Enthusiasm?" *International Studies Review* no. 6 (3): 355–380.

Office of the UN High Commissioner for Human Rights (2013). Truth commissions become victims of their own success, cautions UN expert on transitional justice (available at: http://www.ohchr.org/EN/NewsEvents/Pages/DisplayNews.aspx?NewsID=13722&LangID=E).

Olsen, Tricia D, Andrew G Reiter, and Eric Wiebelhaus-Brahm (2011). "Taking stock: Transitional justice and market effects in Latin America." *Journal of Human Rights* no. 10 (4): 521–543.

Olsen, Tricia D., Leigh A. Payne, and Andrew G. Reiter (2010). *Transitional Justice in Balance: Comparing Processes, Weighing Efficacy.* Washington DC: United States Institute of Peace Press.

Popkin, Margaret (2000). *Peace without Justice: Obstacles to Building the Rule of law in El Salvador.* Original edition, University Park, PA: The Pensylvania State University Press.

Quinn, Joanna R. (2010). *The Politics of Acknowledgement: Truth Commissions in Uganda and Haiti*, Vancouver: UBC Press.

Risse, Thomas, Stephen C Ropp, and Kathryn Sikkink (eds.) (1999). *The Power of Human Rights. International Norms and Domestic Change.* Cambridge: Cambridge University Press.

—— (2013). *The Persistent Power of Human Rights: From Commitment to Compliance.* Cambridge: Cambridge University Press.

Roht-Arriaza, Naomi, and Javier Mariezcurrena (eds.) (2006). *Transitional Justice in the Twenty-First Century. Beyond Truth versus Justice.* Cambridge: Cambridge University Press.

Rousseau, Elise (2018). "Power, Mechanisms, and Denunciations: Understanding Compliance with Human Rights in International Relations." *Political Studies Review* no. 16 (4): 318–330.

Schoultz, Lars (1981). "US foreign policy and human rights violations in Latin America: A comparative analysis of foreign aid distributions." *Comparative Politics* no. 13 (2): 149–170.

Shaw, Rosalind, and Lars Waldorf with Pierre Hazan (eds.) (2010). *Localizing Transitional Justice: Justice Interventions and Priorities after Mass Violence*. Stanford, CA: Stanford University Press.

Sikkink, Kathryn, and Carrie Booth Walling (2007). "The Impact of Human Rights Trials in Latin America." *Journal of Peace Research* no. 44 (4): 427–445.

Simmons, Beth A. (2009). *Mobilizing for Human Rights: International Law in Domestic Politics*: Cambridge University Press.

Skaar, Elin (1999). "Truth commissions, trials – or nothing? Policy options in democratic transitions." *Third World Quarterly* no. 20 (6): 1109–1128.

Skaar, Elin (2011). *Judicial Independence and Human Rights in Latin-America: Violations, Politics and Prosecution*. New York: Palgrave Macmillan.

Skaar, Elin, Jemima García-Godos, and Cath Collins (eds.) (2016). *Transitional Justice in Latin America: The Uneven Road from Impunity towards Accountability*. London: Routledge.

Skaar, Elin, Eric Wiebelhaus-Brahm, and Jemima García-Godos (2022). *Exploring Truth Commission Recommendations in a Comparative Perspective: Beyond Words Vol. I*. Cambridge: Intersentia.

Stewart, Brandon, and Eric Wiebelhaus-Brahm (2017). "The Quantitative Turn in Transitional Justice Research: What Have We Learned About Impact?" *Transitional Justice Review* no. 1 (5): 97–133.

Teitel, Ruti (2000). *Transitional Justice*. New York: Oxford University Press.

United Nations General Assembly (2013). Report of the Special Rapporteur on the Promotion of Truth, Justice, Reparation and Guarantees of Non-Recurrence A/HRC/24/42 edited by Pablo de Greiff: United Nations, Human Rights Council (Twenty-fourth session).

Wiebelhaus-Brahm, Eric (2009). "What is a Truth Commission and Why Does it Matter?" *Peace and Conflict Review no.* 3 (2): 1–14.

—— (2010a). "Truth commissions." In *Handbook of International Criminal Law*, edited by William Schabas and Nadia Bernaz, 367–381. New York: Routledge.

—— (2010b). *Truth Commissions and Transitional Societies: The Impact on Human Rights and Democracy*. New York: Routledge.

Wiebelhaus-Brahm, Eric, and Dylan Wright (2021). "Temporal Patterns in Latin American Truth Commission Recommendation Formulation and Implementation." *International Criminal Law Review* no. 21 (5): 990–1023.

Wiebelhaus-Brahm, Eric, Héctor Centeno-Martín, Ana Belén Nieto Librero, & Dylan Wright, "Examining Compliance with Domestic Human Rights Bodies: the Case of Truth Commission Recommendations", *Journal of Human Rights* (Forthcoming).

PART I

THE SOUTHERN CONE

ARGENTINA'S PIONEERING CONADEP

A Lasting Human Rights Agenda

Sol HOURCADE, Federico GHELFI, Luz PALMÁS ZALDUA, and Marcela PERELMAN*

1. INTRODUCTION

Raúl Alfonsín, Argentina's first democratically elected president after the last dictatorship (1976–83), took office on December 10, 1983. His government

* This chapter was written by Sol Hourcade, Federico Ghelfi, Luz Palmás Zaldua and Marcela Perelman, researchers from the Centro de Estudios Legales y Sociales (Center for Legal and Social Studies, CELS), from Argentina. Fieldwork was conducted by Hourcade and Ghelfi, the analysis and systematization of sources were in charge of Hourcade. The general analysis and writing is a collective work, under the direction of Perelman. Andrea Rocha Granados participated during the project preparation phase, in 2015. The authors wish to thank Sofía Tiscornia, Verónica Torras, Catalina Smulovitz, and Onur Bakiner for detailed and helpful comments on earlier drafts.

pursued a human rights agenda focused on the discovery of the truth regarding past State repression and the prosecution of the high command of the armed forces and the upper echelons of political-military organizations. One of the milestones of this agenda was the setup of the *Comisión Nacional sobre la Desaparición de Personas* (CONADEP, National Commission on the Disappearance of Persons), which operated between 1983 and 1984, and the Trial of the Junta, which took place in 1985.

CONADEP was a "Commission of Notables", dominated by prominent individuals from civil society and the arts with a history of human rights activism. It was created to investigate the fate of disappeared persons, locate children abducted from their parents, to collect testimony, refer cases to the justice system, and draft a report. The Commission drafted the well-known final report "*Nunca Más*" (Never Again), which constitutes a key point of reference in Argentina's engagement with its past. Moreover, it set an important precedent for other truth commissions throughout the world.

Although it did not originally intend to formulate recommendations, CONADEP included a limited list of substantive recommendations in its report regarding matters of justice, reparation, institutional reform, and guarantees for non-recurrence.

Over the past 37 years, the recommendations set forth in *Nunca Más* have largely been implemented. While the Argentine human rights movement led the push for action, implementation proceeded in fits and starts according to historical circumstances. The content of these measures related to memory, truth and justice have strongly shaped the country's subsequent political development. In the decades since the report was released, the truth of what happened during the State Terrorism have prompted nearly constant social mobilization and driven public debates about several highly contentious issues. Specifically, the fight against impunity for the crimes committed by State terrorism has left an indelible mark on the country's recent history. The relatives of victims, as well as the broader human rights movement jointly with other actors, have implemented a variety of strategies to sustain public demand to investigate and punish the perpetrators of these crimes. With regards to justice and memory, some administrations embraced this agenda, while others were more reactive. The matter of reparations has been less controversial. Even during the so-called "years of impunity" during the 1990s, very important results were achieved in terms of truth-seeking, reparation, and memory-building. Measures oriented towards establishing the unconstitutionality of the impunity laws and pardons passed between 1986 -90, as well as arrests in connection with State terrorism, also occurred during this period. Following the inauguration of Néstor Kirchner in 2003 and continuing through the tenure of his successor Cristina Fernández, a multi-agency, joint State-civil society effort led to the massive reopening of trials and the deepening of the memory, truth and justice process, and became an emblematic point of reference for the region and the world. Under the

Cambiemos government (2015-19), the memory, truth and justice process has once again become a controversial issue in the political debate, but despite some controversies and the fact that several public policies in the matter were interrupted or weakened, in general terms the process continued.

In this chapter, we focus on the recommendations in the final report of CONADEP and examine the specific factors and processes that affected their formulation, as well as the actors involved in the process and the challenges presented by their implementation. When compared to other countries in the world, Argentina stands at the vanguard of matters of accountability for human rights violations of the contemporary era. The local repercussions of CONADEP are evident to this day in Argentina and its international impact is reflected in the truth commissions established throughout the world.

The Argentinean case possesses some special features that place it at the extreme end of the cases included in this volume. The first feature is its *long-term time frame*. CONADEP completed its work in 1984, thus placing it as the earliest case addressed by this project. This complicates efforts to establish causal connections over such an extended time period. Secondly, CONADEP is one of the so-called "transitional commissions". The long-term time-frame requires the research to address *changing circumstances*. In other words, we must take into account different political cycles throughout the analyzed implementation period. This also makes incorporating the "world-time" concept of Elin Skaar and Eric Wiebelhaus-Brahm (2013) essential in connection to the dramatic global legal and regulatory changes seen during the subsequent decades in terms of the treatment of serious violations of human rights. Thirdly, practically all the components included in the recommendations have achieved a *high degree of implementation* in Argentina, both if we consider the original intent of the actors involved and if we compare it to other processes. Although one might think this feature simplifies the task of tracing implementation, in fact it requires a review of multiple events, stages and actors. Thus, it presents a different challenge from cases with few implementation events. Fourthly, CONADEP decided on a *limited and precise group of recommendations*, which allows us to reconstruct longitudinally progress on each recommendation. However, the lengthy time-frame and high degree of implementation make determining the specific causal weight of the recommendations in the implementation of their proposals especially complex. Finally, the Commission members were *national-local figures*, a fact that made it weightier and more rooted than commissions constituted by foreign members or less well-known figures.

Keeping these peculiarities in mind, we analyze CONADEP as a complex social, political and historical event that includes the Commission itself, the effects of the *Nunca Más* report as the official truth and also the institutionalization of CONADEP's Archive as a permanent State agency. This understanding led us to the formulation of equally complex questions: How can we isolate the specific causality of the truth commission recommendations in the Argentinean case?

To what degree can we differentiate the specific weight and the causal drivers of the recommendations and its report and Archive? What are the risks of creating an artificial object (the "CONADEP recommendations") if for the most part the truth commission recommendations were not autonomous relative to the "commission / report / recommendations /Archive" complex? How can we work with "implementation events" which implement part of the content of a recommendation but make no reference to the recommendations or even the Commission?

To answer these questions, we decided to consider CONADEP as a system in itself that includes different components affecting the implementation. Moreover, we discriminate between the recommendations as a specific instrument, in general, and the specific content of the recommendation. The recommendation and its content can have different, although convergent trajectories. This division is also useful to explain the pre-existing trajectories of previously articulated demands; that is taking into account circumstances in which CONADEP recommended things that others had previously called for. For this reason, we decided to adopt certain appraisal strategies. First, although finding "implementation events" in which direct reference is made to specific recommendations is a strong indication of causality, failing to find them does not allow us to discard the possibility of such a connection. Second, we must consider that the implementation process contains actions that later operate as conditions allowing for other implementations; namely, actions that modify the circumstances, thus allowing the realization of other measures that advance implementation. These actions operate as layers or bridges towards other implementation events. In our case, as we shall see, the role of the Undersecretary of Human Rights (created directly by a recommendation) and the continuing work on the CONADEP Archive created the institutional structure that allowed implementation of reparations several years later. The conditions resulting from a first period of implementation can later be considered as a contextual element of the following period.

2. ARGENTINA'S TRANSITION TO DEMOCRACY

Under the pretext of an "anti-subversion war" or "fight against subversion", the last civilian-military dictatorship in Argentina implemented a repressive plan characterized by kidnappings of dissidents and their children, illicit imprisonment in clandestine detention centers, torture, sexual violence, assassination and enforced disappearances. At the end of its rule, however, the armed forces were unable to impose the terms for the transition to democracy. Several factors came together to challenge their version of the facts during those years, thus undermining their legitimacy as an actor in Argentinean politics. Although the socio-economic crisis and the defeat in the Malvinas/Falklands

War (1982) are considered decisive factors, other events also brought about the *Junta*'s downfall. In particular, the reports and documentation produced by survivors and exiles, the relatives of the victims, and human rights organizations drew attention to gross human rights violations. Moreover, the *in loco* visit of the Inter-American Commission on Human Rights (CIDH) in 1979 produced a report verifying the existence of a systematic plan for the disappearance of persons.

At the beginning of 1983, the *Junta* announced a call for elections to be held in October. Before ceding power, the armed forces implemented some measures that were intended to justify its violations of human rights, deny the existence of disappeared persons and insure their impunity for the serious crimes they had committed. These goals were accomplished in the "Final Document of the Military Junta regarding the War Against Subversion and Terrorism", published on April 28, 1983. On the same day, the *Junta* also issued a statute declaring that the crimes committed were acts of service and, therefore, not punishable (Acuña and Smulovitz 1995, 47). In response to these moves, human rights organizations demanded the creation of a bicameral commission to investigate, prosecute and punish those responsible for the disappearances[1] (Crenzel 2008, 58).

A few days before the elections, the *Junta* went further. De facto President Reynaldo Bignone issued Decree no. 2726/83 providing for the destruction of documents connected to persons detained by the State, which implied the loss of evidence needed to clarify disappearances. On September 23, 1983, still under the dictatorship, the government enacted Law no. 22.924 for National Pacification. Known as the "self-amnesty", it shielded from criminal liability "terrorist or subversive" actions as well as crimes committed in the fight against such acts that occurred between May 25, 1973, and June 17, 1982. However, the Law excluded civilians who committed terrorist acts, so, in practice, the sole beneficiaries of the Law were members of the armed forces, security and penitentiary staff.

The presidential candidates for the main parties, the *Partido Justicialista* (PJ) and the *Unión Cívica Radical* (UCR), each publicly rejected the Law. While the PJ candidate, Ítalo Luder, held that, even if rescinded, it would maintain its effectiveness under the principle of application of the most benign criminal law, the UCR candidate, Alfonsín, declared that the Law had to be annulled and declared fully void (Nino [1996] 2015, 134). In the end, the UCR decisively won the October 1983 elections. Among other factors, Alfonsín's ability to interpret the values of the different sectors of a society under the grip of the

---

1 See paid announcement, "They took them alive, and we want them back alive. Political Party request to obtain commitment for the creation of a Bicameral Commission to investigate those responsible for the disappearances and the Judicial Branch to prosecute and punish as applicable by law", *Memoria Abierta* (Open Memory) (FAMILIARES B22.23).

dictatorship proved critical (Catterberg 1985, 259; Landi and González Bombal 1995). In this context, Alfonsín announced a policy of criminal prosecution, but limited to the commanders of the armed forces and leaders of political-military organizations. Lower ranking individuals would be prosecuted only if they had overstepped their duty to comply with such orders. On his third day in power, Alfonsín communicated his human rights policy to the nation (Nino [1996] 2015, 138). Further, he signed Decree nos. 157 and 158, which ordered the Attorney General to initiate the criminal prosecution of seven leaders of political-military organizations and members of the first three military *Juntas* before the Supreme Council of the Armed Forces (*Consejo Supremo de las Fuerzas Armadas*, CONSUFA).

To advance the prosecution agenda, Alfonsín promoted the replacement of the ministers of the Supreme Court of Justice and the judges of the Federal Court of Criminal Appeals. In addition, he repealed the "self-amnesty law" via Law no. 23.040. He also reformed the Military Code of Justice to establish, among other things, the recourse to appeal from CONSUFA judgments to the Federal Court of Appeals and the possibility of civilian courts hearing military cases in the event of unjustified delays or negligence (Law no. 23.049).

3. ARGENTINA'S TRUTH COMMISSION: CONADEP

On December 15, 1983 President Alfonsín issued the decree creating the CONADEP, with the specific purpose of "clarifying the facts connected with the disappearance of persons" and receiving reports and evidence for their referral to the judiciary. The Commission was established with 16 members, all Argentine, summarized in Table 1. They included 10 well-known members of society and six legislators (three representatives and three senators). Addendum I of the decree set forth the CONADEP members. Only one woman was commissioned. In the end, the Senate sent no representatives (Crenzel 2008).

Table 1. CONADEP Commissioners

Ricardo Colombres	Ex-minister of the National Supreme Court of Justice.
René Favaloro	Medical surgeon. Resigned in June of 1984, before the CONADEP completed its work.
Hilario Fernández Long	Ex-Chancellor of the University of Buenos Aires (UBA).
Carlos Gattinoni	Protestant Pastor. Founder of the Ecumenical Movement for Human Rights (*Movimiento Ecuménico por los Derechos Humanos*, MEDH) and the Permanent Assembly for Human Rights (*Asamblea Permanente por los Derechos Humanos*, APDH).

(continued)

Table 1 *continued*

Gregorio Klimovsky	Epistemologist. Dean of the School of Social and Natural Sciences of the University of Buenos Aires.
Marshall Meyer	Rabbi. Doctor in Philosophy. Member of the APDH and Co-President of the Jewish Movement for Human Rights. Commissioner until June 1984.
Mons. Jaime De Nevares	Bishop of the Province of Neuquen. Attorney and Co-founder of the APDH.
Eduardo Rabossi	Attorney specializing in Philosophy of Law.
Magdalena Ruiz Guiñazú	Journalist.
Ernesto Sábato	Writer. Appointed President of the Commission.
Santiago López	National Representative for the UCR.
Hugo Piucill	National Representative for the UCR.
Horacio Huarte	National Representative for the UCR.

Source: Compiled by the authors.

The Commission enacted its own regulations and designated an Executive Committee with four acting members (CONADEP 1984). To manage their work, commissioners established five subcommittees. Those in charge of these subcommittees, summarized in Table 2, were awarded a category equivalent to the position of National Judge (National Memory Archive).

Table 2. CONADEP Subcommittees

Subcommittee	Secretary
Reports	Graciela Fernández Meijide
Proceedings	Raúl Aragón
Documentation and Data Processing	Daniel Salvador
Administration	Leopoldo Silgueira
Legal Matters	Alberto Mansur

Source: Compiled by the authors.

The Decree established that CONADEP would operate for six months, until May 27, 1984. Due to the enormous volume of people filing reports before it, the Commission requested a three-month extension. Its work was financed by the Ministry of the Interior, which provided the material resources, including salaries for 99 staff members plus five secretaries (interview with María Julia Bihurret, 2016).

Table 3 summarizes the key features of the Commission. Although it did not satisfy human rights organizations' demand to form a bicameral commission with investigative power in the Congress (interview with Emilio Crenzel, 2016), several groups and organizations cooperated actively with CONADEP. They supplied personnel to receive testimony and reports from victims, armed forces members and security personnel. These organizations also collaborated with the establishment of branches of the Commission in Córdoba, Mar del Plata, Bahía Blanca and Santa Fe (Crenzel 2008, 69).

Commissioners and staff travelled to different provinces domestically, and travelled overseas, to collect information, as well as to visit jails, morgues, and neighborhoods where kidnappings had taken place. In addition, they received testimonies collected during the dictatorship by national and international human rights organizations (Mignone 1991, 159-160; CONADEP 1984, 445; and Crenzel 2008, 68). They also inspected locations that had been clandestine detention centers, such as military units, police stations, and psychiatric hospitals, and requested reports from various government departments. The Commission had the power to request documents from the National Executive Branch, dependent and autonomous agencies, and the armed or security forces. Furthermore, CONADEP had access to any offices it needed to visit. The Commission submitted 1,086 files to the Judicial Branch,[2] although some of its members believed that the appropriate course of action was to remit these to the CONSUFA.[3] During that time, members of the Commission received threats and were under illicit surveillance by the intelligence services, which were still largely beyond civilian control.

Table 3. CONADEP – Summary of Main Characteristics

Context	Five days after his inauguration, Alfonsín signed Decree no. 187/83 dated December 15, 1983, creating the National Commission on the Disappearance of Persons (CONADEP)
Members	The Executive Branch decided to select as commissioners renowned personalities chosen for their defence of human rights and their representation of various sectors of Argentine society. Ten members were appointed by the Executive Branch and three (originally six) were selected by the National Congress. Selected by the Executive Branch: Ricardo Colombres, René Favaloro, Hilario Fernández Long, Carlos T. Gattinoni, Gregorio Klimovsky, Marshall Meyer, Mons. Jaime F. de Nevares, Eduardo Rabossi, Magdalena Ruiz Guiñazú and Ernesto Sábato (President).

(continued)

2 According to the Commission's conclusions, 1,086 reports were remitted; according to the schedule of remitted cases, 1,091.

3 CONADEP was created before the enactment of Law no. 23.049, which confirmed that CONSUFA would act first. Decree no. 187/83 stated that the cases were to be remitted to the legal authorities and that the trials were to be heard by the Judicial Branch. In light of this issue, CONADEP decided to send the files to the federal and the provincial courts (CONADEP 1984, 451-452, 460; Nino [1996] 2015, 153; Crenzel 2008, 90-91).

Table 3 *continued*

	Selected by Congress (only House of Representatives): Santiago Marcelino López, Hugo Diógenes Piucill and Horacio Hugo Huarte. CONADEP issued its own regulations, designated a President and was empowered to create sub-committees (five were created) and hire administrative personnel for its tasks. The Commission would be dissolved once it delivered its Final Report. It was financed by the Ministry of the Interior.
Mandate and Attributions	Presidential Decree no. 187/83 dated December 15, 1983 Its main purpose was to "clarify the facts connected with the disappearance of persons." Specific Duties a) receive reports and evidence regarding the facts and immediately remit them to the justice system if connected with the alleged commission of a crime; b) determine the fate or location of disappeared persons, as well as any other circumstance connected with location of such persons; c) determine the location of children taken from their parents or custodians as a result of the actions enforced for the alleged purpose of fighting terrorism, and allow the intervention of organizations and courts for the protection of minors; d) report to justice any attempt to hide, remove or destroy evidence connected with the facts to be clarified; e) issue a final report, with a detailed explanation of the investigated facts, one hundred and eighty (180) days after the creation of the Commission. CONADEP was not empowered to "issue judgments regarding the facts and circumstances, which were the exclusive jurisdiction of the Judicial Branch."
Period of Operation	December 1983 – September 1984 The decree established an operating time-frame of six months, until June of 1984. Due to the volume of people making reports, the Commission requested a three-month extension.
Final Report	*Nunca Más* (Never Again) exposed the features and scope of the system of disappearances and the responsibility of the State in such activities. CONADEP gathered 50,000 pages of documentation. *Nunca Más* report is 480 pages; recommendations span one-and-a-half pages. The public significance of CONADEP's investigation was enhanced when its results were used as the main piece of evidence presented by the prosecution during the military *Junta* trial. The court legitimized its veracity by accepting its evidentiary quality. CONADEP was a model for several other Latin American truth commissions.

Source: Compiled by the authors.

The Commission made its preliminary conclusions public on a TV program broadcast on July 4, 1984 (Crenzel 2008, 81). That night, there were military movements. Tanks left from the base at Campo de Mayo (Crenzel 2008, 82) and headed towards the City of Buenos Aires. Although they returned to their base, it was an obvious attempt to intimidate the Commission, the government and society. This pattern of intimidation would recur during the rest of the 1980s and early 1990s whenever the threat of prosecution arose.

During an emotionally powerful public event on September 20, 1984, CONADEP presented its final report, *Nunca Más*, to President Alfonsín. It officially acknowledged that a systematic policy of forced disappearances had been deployed across the country. The report described kidnappings perpetrated by task forces, or "gangs"; it uncovered 340 clandestine detention centers, and detailed torture practices, as well as the particular cruelty directed towards victims with certain characteristics, such as women, Jews and disabled persons. The report acknowledged the participation of members of the Church and the judiciary and exposed the responsibility of some businesspeople in the persecution of union leaders and workers. It concluded that abuses were not the result of individual excesses, but rather a systematic policy of State repression.

The report proved to be a critical event in Argentina's political development. It was published as a book two months after the public ceremony; the first edition sold out in two days (Crenzel 2008, 131). It has been re-published and translated multiple times and is recognized as a milestone for truth commissions globally:

> The book presented a new understanding of the crimes of State terrorism that had been consistently denied and/or justified by its perpetrators, thus laying down the State's responsibility for these crimes. This reconstruction of facts was made possible mainly thanks to the testimonies of the survivors and relatives of the disappeared persons (Chillier and Torras 2018).

An initial criticism was that the printed version did not include the list of perpetrators that had been delivered to the President (Paganetti 1984a; Mignone 1991, 161). With the passage of time, the main criticism concentrated on the interpretive spirit of the prologue, which is known in Argentina as the "theory of the two demons". It cast blame on two supposed "sides": the "political responsibilities of guerrillas and members of the armed forces" were considered to be equivalent and thus this theory reproduced "[the] official discourse that proposed the violence perpetrated by members of the guerrilla as the precursor for state terror" (Crenzel 2008, 135).

While the Commission was making its final report known, *Junta* members were being indicted by the military justice system. Although the armed forces did not issue their opinion regarding CONADEP's report, a few days after its release, CONSUFA informed the Federal Court of Appeals that it would not be able to complete the trial in the 90-day term required. In addition, they argued that they only had general statements that lacked evidential authority and would not allow for a legitimate trial. CONSUFA finally concluded their report to the Court of Appeals by arguing that the decrees, directives and operative orders were "unobjectionable" both in their form and content (Nino 1996, 150 and Camacho 2008, 75). In light of this response, the Court of Appeals took over the case and ordered it to be sent to the Public Prosecutor for the purpose of issuing indictments.[4] CONADEP's investigation[5] was used by the prosecutor's office as the foundation for its work (Moreno Ocampo 1987, 132). The fact that *Nunca Más* was the foundation for the historic "trial of the military *Juntas*" is one of the best examples of the ways in which the modalities of construction of truth and justice have mutually strengthened each other during Argentina's long process of memory, truth and justice.

4. THE INCLUSION OF RECOMMENDATIONS IN THE REPORT

Three months before the delivery of the report, CONADEP President Ernesto Sábato announced that it would produce recommendations – something not originally contemplated by its creation decree (Paganetti 1984b). The final report states that, in view of the reported facts, CONADEP decided to formulate recommendations "for the purpose of preventing, repairing and ultimately avoiding recurrence of the human rights violations," and indicated that they "aim to avoid losing sight of the need for a deep judicial investigation of the facts." The latter strengthens the intimate link established by the Commission between its work and the work to be done by the judiciary, which we now understand as foundational milestones of democracy regarding the construction of truth and justice.

The logic behind formulating recommendations is reflected in the minutes of the Commission's meetings during the first months of 1984. According to Minutes no. 6, drafted for the Commission's meeting held on January 10, 1984, the commissioners approved a proposal made by Ricardo Colombres advising the

> Commission to invite internationally renowned human rights personalities to the country, beginning with Dr. [Edmundo] Vargas Carreño,[6] who prominently participated in the preparation of the report on the violations perpetrated in our country which was published by the OEA. [Organization of American States].

---

4 National Criminal and Correctional Federal Court of Appeals of the Federal Capital (CNACCF CF). Certiorati pursuant to Art. 10 of Law no. 23.049 (Agreed 42, October 4, 1984, in LL, November 19, 1984).

5 According to Graciela Fernández Meijide, in practice, the Commission operated as a pre-trial investigation court (Bruno et al. 1985, 68).

6 Edmundo Vargas Carreño, a Chilean national, was executive secretary of the Inter-American Commission on Human Rights (CIDH) from September 1977 to March 1990. During July 1979, he visited Argentina to prepare for the September *in loco* CIDH visit.

This comment by Colombres marks the continuity between the Inter-American Commission on Human Rights' (CIDH) efforts to reconstruct the truth and CONADEP's work. On March 13, Eduardo Rabossi stated the need to recommence the exchange of ideas to decide on the report's basic format (Minutes no. 15). Colombres agreed with the statement and suggested a tentative format for the report's thematic content. For her part, Graciela Fernández Meijide stated that she had talked about this subject with Noemí Labrune[7] and they had developed a proposal for the summary. According to Crenzel (2008), Fernández Meijide and Labrune used the "Banned Report" presented by the CIDH in 1980 as a model for their proposal. Labrune, together with other members of the Center for Legal and Social Studies (CELS), cooperated with the CIDH in the selection of testimonies previously collected by APDH, and presented the cases that confirmed the participation of members of the armed forces in the detention of disappeared persons (Mignone 1991, 112).

Bishop Gattinoni and Representative Huarte also contributed their ideas regarding the subjects they thought should be included. Sábato synthesized the meeting's predominant opinion regarding the fact that the report's drafting

> needed to flow and have vivid content, including testimonies, photographs and descriptions of exemplary cases, including an appendix listing the names of the victims and statistical data (Minutes no. 15, p. 57 of the Book of Minutes).

On March 27, 1984, Vargas Carreño, Executive Secretary of the CIDH,[8] appeared at the Commission's meeting. He offered as much collaboration as possible to CONADEP as well as the documentation held by the Inter-American Commission. He delivered individual cases and information received in 1979 regarding incidents at the time (Minutes no. 17, pp. 60-61 of the Book of Minutes).

As proposed by Mr. Colombres, on May 15, 1984, they distributed some subjects for the purpose of making progress on the report draft (Minutes no. 24, p. 100 of the Book of Minutes). When the work was distributed, Colombres was tasked with drafting the recommendations. The specific issue of the recommendations is also linked to the structure of the CIDH's 1980 report, which contained recommendations addressed to the Argentinean government. Our evaluation is that the decision to formulate recommendations to the three

---

7 Noemí Fiorito de Labrune is a prominent human rights activist, co-founder of the Permanent Assembly for Human Rights for the Province of Neuquén and co-founder andmember of the board of directors of the Center for Legal and Social Studies between 1979 and 1983.

8 On March 26, 1984, Sábato received Mr. Edmundo Vargas Carreño, Executive Secretary of the CIDH of the OEA, and the specialist for Argentina of that institution, Mr. Guillermo Fernández de Soto at the Ezeiza airport (see: http://imagenes.cedinci.org/index.php/edmundo-vargas-carreno-ernesto-sabato-y-guillermo-fernandez-de-soto).

branches of government, as well as the content of such recommendations, was based on the CIDH report, a format regularly used by international organizations.

CONADEP invited human rights organizations to provide suggestions for recommendations, and some of these were incorporated. For example, the report includes the suggestion made by the Ecumenical Movement for Human Rights (MEDH) to recommend the enactment of protective laws for the family members of disappeared persons. They also included a suggestion from the Argentine League for Human Rights (LADH) requesting the inclusion of academic programs with human rights content, as well as the abolishment of repressive laws.

Among those suggestions not included in the report, one was formulated by the Relatives of Persons Disappeared and Detained for Political Reasons (FADERAP) suggesting the inclusion of the names of the parties responsible for the repression. Another recommendation that was overlooked came from MEDH. It suggested that the date of the report's presentation be declared "National Contrition Day". The report also did not include suggestions made by LADH to eliminate the concept of state of siege from the Constitution and clarify the operation of the repressive apparatus (Crenzel 2008, 94-95).

Finally, Augusto Conte, father of a detainee-disappeared person and founding member of CELS, stated his expectation that CONADEP would finally suggest the creation of a bicameral commission, which many still believed was essential to overcome the entrenched resistance to accountability within the judiciary[9] (Bruno et al., 1985: 86).

5. THE CONTENT OF THE CONADEP RECOMMENDATIONS

Chapter 6 of *Nunca Más* includes a section entitled "Recommendations," with an introductory paragraph that explicitly states the institutional and judicial objectives of the Commission's recommendations:

> The more than eloquent facts reported and declared to this Commission require us to recommend some initiatives to the different branches of the National Government for the purpose of preventing, repairing and finally avoiding the recurrence of such human rights violations in our country. On the other hand, these recommendations

9 On September 28, 1984 the UCR block in the house of representatives rejected the creation of a bicameral commission "praising the mission of the National Commission on the Disappearance of Persons." On his side, Augusto Conte "also highlighted the purpose of the CONADEP, stating that the present circumstances require such Commission, thus referring to the recent decision of the Supreme Council of the Armed Forces." *Clarín*, September 29, 1984, p. 7.

are intended to keep us from losing sight of the need for a deeper judicial investigation of the facts reported to us. We therefore recommend the following:

a)	The organism which substitutes this Commission should accelerate the process of remitting the documents collected during the investigation ordered by the Executive Branch to the justice system.
b)	The Judicial Branch should adequately support the prompt processing of the investigation and the verification of the reports received by this Commission.
c)	Necessary regulations should be enacted to allow the children and/or family members of persons disappeared during the repression to receive economic assistance, study scholarships, social assistance and employment. In addition, measures must be implemented as considered appropriate to help palliate the variety of family and social problems resulting from the enforced disappearance of persons.
d)	Enact regulations tending to: 1. Establish the enforced disappearance of persons as a crime against humanity. 2. Support the acknowledgment and membership in national and international Human Rights Organizations. 3. Establish the mandatory teaching of the defense and dissemination of human rights in State educational agencies, either for civilians, military or security forces. 4. Strengthening and full optimization of resources provided to the civil justice system for the court appointed investigation of human rights violations. 5. Repeal any repressive legislation still in effect.

Recommendations a) and b) are grouped by their content, oriented to the investigation and punishment of past crimes. It is here that the Commission makes a key recommendation: the creation of an agency to continue the work of CONADEP and to "accelerate the process of remitting the documentation collected during the investigation to the justice system." According to the report's conclusions, this recommendation was prompted by the existence of cases which had not yet been reported:

> Up to the date of presentation of this report, the CONADEP estimates that 8,960 persons are still experiencing enforced disappearance, based on the reports received by this Commission, which were compared with lists compiled by national and international human rights organizations. This number cannot be considered final, because the CONADEP has confirmed that many cases of disappearance were never reported. In addition, we understand that the list may include some individuals who did not promptly report the termination of their disappearance to the pertinent agencies (p. 371).

The report recommends that the judiciary "adequately support the prompt processing of the investigation and the verification of the reports" received by the Commission. This recommendation implies that the civil justice system, not the military justice system, should investigate the crimes reported to the Commission. It asks the Judicial Branch to abstain from waiving its jurisdiction in favor of the military justice system, even though Law no. 23.049 established that the latter should be used first.

Within CONADEP, Ricardo Colombres originally proposed remitting the reports to the civil justice system instead of military courts (see Minutes no. 30 dated June 26, 1984, p. 117). This opinion reflects the position of most Commission members, and most of the human rights movement. According to Emilio Mignone (1991), human rights organizations believed that the civil justice system should have exclusive jurisdiction without exception. As stated by Raúl Aragón, Colombres was "the soul" of CONADEP:

> Colombres was the thinker. (...) He was a man with political experience and a great vocation for human rights. The CONADEP'S policy line, the essential steps it took, taking the cases away from the CONSUFA in order to remit them to the federal justice system, that type of thing, were his initiatives. He was the only one committed full time to the task. His position was honorary (*Memoria Abierta* oral archive, AO0179B-3).

Recommendation c) is clearly reparative and was included at the suggestion of MEDH.

The last recommendation formulated by the Commission, recommendation d), includes five initiatives for the purpose of preventing and avoiding recurrence of past human rights violations. Point 1, regarding establishing enforced disappearance as a crime against humanity, adopts the opinion of human rights activists during the dictatorship (Mignone 1981), and a growing consensus in the Inter-American System, as expressed by the OEA's General Assembly on November 18, 1983: "The practice of enforced disappearance of persons in America is an insult to the conscience of the Hemisphere and constitutes a crime against humanity." Point 2, regarding support for national and international human rights organizations, recognizes the central role of Argentine human rights organizations in reporting and collecting information, as well as international organizations, due to the impact and dissemination of the reports made by relatives of the victims, and the existence of a systematic plan. This recommendation also continues a recommendation made by CIDH in its report following the Commission's *in loco* visit (CIDH 1980, 225).

As recorded in the CONADEP minutes, Points 3 and 5, regarding the teaching of human rights and the repeal of repressive legislation, were suggested by LADH (Minutes no. 35 dated July 30, 1984, p. 145). However, the latter was a long-standing demand of the human rights movement (see paid announcement of the FADERAP, published in *Edición Cuatro Reconquista* on July 17, 1981). Finally, point 4 reflects the Commission's interest in generating adequate institutional conditions for the transfer of evidence to the civilian justice system.

6. IMPLEMENTATION OF THE RECOMMENDATIONS

6.1. RECOMMENDATION NO. 1: COMMISSION IN CHARGE

> The organism which substitutes this Commission should accelerate the process of remitting the documents collected during the investigation ordered by the Executive Branch to the justice system.

According to CONADEP's minutes, there was some debate about how to continue its work after its mandate ended. While some preferred the creation of a temporary body and a prosecutor's office, others felt the Commission itself should continue (Minutes no. 35 dated July 30, 1984). In the end, the members stated the need for an organization to continue the task, but they did not articulate an institutional design. On the same day that the CONADEP was dissolved, September 20, 1984, President Alfonsín issued Decree no. 3090 for the creation of the Undersecretary of Human Rights (SsDH) within the Ministry of the Interior. Alfonsín named Eduardo Rabossi, ex-member of the Commission,[10] as head of this body. According to Silvia San Martín,[11] the former SsDH (it became a Secretariat in 2002) was the continuation of the CONADEP (interview dated October 20, 2016).

The SsDH was not specifically created to supervise the implementation of CONADEP recommendations. Rather, it has a wide-ranging human rights agenda. The current Secretariat's duties also include other matters including promoting compliance with human rights legislation; receiving reports about human rights violations and remitting them to the competent legal and administrative authorities; performing research and formulating recommendations for the full exercise of human rights; organizing and promoting academic, educational and community activities aimed at awareness and protection of human rights; and creating technical commissions for the identification of bodily remains (Decree no. 3090/1984).

Nonetheless, creation of the SsDH was a key step for the subsequent implementation of other recommendations. It has played a key role in

---

10 Initially, this organism received disparate evaluations. Although, according to the Undersecretary, a total of 700 "cases" were remitted to the justice system between the date of its creation and January 1985 (Clarín, January 9, 1985), the body was criticized for failing to adequately investigate and promptly remit the reports to the justice system (Clarín, January 21, 1985), although, according to María Julia Bihurret, employee of this body, every report they received was remitted to the judiciary (interview October 26, 2016). The creation of this agency with only 19 employees was insufficient to continue the tasks of the CONADEP (interview with Ernesto Sábato, La Voz, December 1, 1985).

11 Coordinator of the Unified Registry of State Terrorism Victims, an office of the Ministry of Justice and Human Rights.

managing reparation programs. It also was tasked with guarding CONADEP's archives and continuing the process of receiving and processing claims. The records in the archives were essential for drafting the recommendations for reparation and criminal justice, since they are considered evidence both in administrative and judicial proceedings. Many years later, the Ministry created the Unified Register of Victims of State Terrorism (RUV). According to San Martín:

> [The RUV] began operating in 2013 and was formalized by Ministerial resolution in 2014. It includes two projects. The first is the registry of victims and the second one is the Latin American Initiative for the Identification of Disappeared Persons (ILID) (...) The Inter-American Convention on Enforced Disappearance, dated June 9, 1994, in its Article XI, sets forth that "Member States shall establish and maintain updated official registries on their detainees and, in accordance with their internal legislation, shall make them available to family members, judges, attorneys and any other person with a legitimate interest, as well as other authorities." In compliance with this Article, work is permanently ongoing to complete the registry, update existing data and input new information coming from the different subject-related fields (interview dated October 20, 2016).

CONADEP possessed the strength and power of an exceptional organism that performed pioneering work during a limited period of time. This distinctive feature gave it strength, intensity and resources, but the creation of a permanent body in the State bureaucracy was decisive for the sustainability of the implementation of recommendations. With some differences depending on the politics of the administration in power, the SsDH and its successor prompted the implementation of other recommendations and linked the Executive Branch and human rights organizations. In effect, it became the foundation for the advancement of other recommendations, as well as promoting human rights in Argentina more broadly.

6.2. RECOMMENDATION NO. 2: JUSTICE

> The Judicial Branch should adequately support the prompt processing of the investigation and the verification of the reports received by this Commission.

Argentina is among the countries with the greatest number of trials for crimes against humanity in the world. The process began in 1983 and continues to this day. The sheer number of investigations, trials and sentences make it one of the most notable criminal justice processes in the world. Up to the end of 2017, more than 201 decisions have been issued, resulting in the conviction of 864 persons and the acquittal of 109 in judicial proceedings. What is more, the proceedings are widely viewed to be in full compliance with the right to defense and due process.[12]

To establish links between this complex and multi-stage process and CONADEP's recommendation on justice, we must separate different phases. Toward the end of the dictatorship, human rights activists and some politicians were already demanding civilian trials and the rejection of the military's self-amnesty.[13] As we have seen, from the beginning, Alfonsín's government debated whether the trials should be civilian or military: although Law no. 23.049 granted the military justice system initial jurisdiction, CONADEP submitted the reports it received to the civil justice system. At the time of his inauguration, Alfonsín issued a decree to CONSUFA ordering the prosecution of the military *Juntas*. However, since it did not investigate adequately, the Federal Court of Appeals, part of the civil justice system, was put in charge of the commanders' trial. When the defense attorneys questioned the proceedings and stated that it was an alleged violation of the principle of "natural judge", the National Supreme Court confirmed that the cases would be tried in civil courts.

Thus, the "Trial of the Juntas" began seven months after the publication of CONADEP's report, in the National Criminal and Correctional Federal Court of Appeals of the Federal Capital.[14] Prosecutor Julio César Strassera and deputy prosecutor Luis Gabriel Moreno Ocampo used *Nunca Más* as the foundation for their accusations. On December 9, 1985, the Court established the existence of a clandestine State system to repress so-called subversives. It convicted five of the accused military members and acquitted the other four.[15] The trial was a major social and political event nationally, and also proved influential regionally and globally.

The judgment also ordered the remittance of the verdict and supporting documentation to CONSUFA to enable the trial of the upper echelon officers who had commanded the zones and sub-zones created by the dictatorship in the country and of individuals with operational responsibility for repressive actions. However, in 1986, several federal appeal courts in different civil jurisdictions took charge of these cases, superseding military jurisdiction.

Undoubtedly, there is a very strong link between the recommendation in *Nunca Más* and the *Juntas* trial. In addition, the prosecution's accusations were based upon the CONADEP report. The trial and the expectation of trying other

---

12 Justice Process Statistics from CELS, available at http://www.cels.org.ar.

13 For more information on the rejection of the self-amnesty, see Landi and González Bombal, 1995.

14 Judges: Jorge Torlasco, Ricardo Gil Lavedra, León Carlos Arslanian, Jorge Valerga Araoz, Guillermo Ledesma and Andrés J. D'Alessio.

15 Videla and Massera were each sentenced to a life sentence with military dismissal. Viola was sentenced to 17 years in prison, Lambruschini to 8 years in prison and Agosti to 4 years and 6 months in prison, all of them with military dismissal. Graffigna, Galtieri, Lamidozo and Anaya were acquitted.

perpetrators left an indelible mark on the political system at the time. As trials threatened to ensnare a growing number of members of the armed forces, the military became increasingly restless. Through a series of provocative actions, the military intimidated civilian authorities into backing down. The trials ultimately were interrupted by the enactment of the laws known as *Punto Final* (Full Stop) in 1986 and *Obediencia Debida* (Due Obedience) in 1987, under the government of Alfonsín.

In a bid to quell the uprising, Law no. 23.492 (Full Stop) provided a 60-day limitation period for trying perpetrators of crimes committed before December 10, 1983, the date when the new democratic government began. However, the Full Stop Law had a paradoxical effect: by establishing a statute of limitations for the filing of new cases, it caused a strong current of judicial activism which accelerated investigation processes in order to be able to file as many cases as possible within the established term. According to Carlos Nino, the courts of the whole country "entered a phase of frenetic activity, even waiving the summer judicial recess period in January" (Nino [1996] 2015, 171-172):

> [S]ince the courts believed that the Full Stop Law had established a short period of time during which they had the historic responsibility of punishing these crimes, they greatly accelerated their activity, receiving copious amounts of evidence from victims and human rights groups.

This caused further concern among the military and security forces and tensions rose further. With the threat of a military coup heightened, the government passed Law no. 23.521 (Due Obedience). It established the *iure et de iure* presumption, in other words, the law did not admit proof to the contrary, that armed forces, security and penitentiary personnel who committed serious crimes during the military dictatorship were deemed to have done so pursuant to the obedience they owed their superiors and, therefore, were not punishable. Although the law was consistent with the "doctrine of levels of responsibility" originally included in Alfonsín's program, it was enacted in the context of strong military pressure. Although some actors disagree, the most accepted interpretation is that Alfonsín's government made the concession to maintain democracy and civilian rule.

The judiciary, including ultimately the Supreme Court, ratified these regulations, even though they were contrary to the National Constitution and the human rights treaties ratified by Argentina. In this way, the Judicial Branch refrained from exercising its jurisdiction over the investigation of such crimes and violated victims' right to judicial protection.

This first cycle of the trial process is bounded by the trial of the *Juntas*, the expectation of prosecutions extending to other responsible parties, and their curtailment with the impunity laws. This back and forth is characterized by different tensions. First was the jurisdictional struggle between the military justice system and the Judicial Branch.[16] In addition, effective military pressure in the provinces increased the civil justice system's reluctance to take charge of the trials in their jurisdiction (Nino 1996). The links and/or complicity of some members of the Judicial Branch with part of the armed forces also were significant.[17] The strategies used by Alfonsín's government and human rights organizations, and the provocations of the armed forces heightened tensions. María José Sarrabayrouse Oliveira describes the contradictory climate in the Judicial Branch at the time:

> The first years of democratic transition were very uncertain for those in the Judicial Branch. It was a time characterized by the rupture of some loyalties in order to develop new ones, a period of obvious adjustment of power relationships, which for many judicial agents implied a "necessary" adaptation to the environment. (...) On one hand (...) the public servants and magistrates continued to operate much as they had operated during the dictatorship. Thus, they continued acknowledging the legitimacy of the *de facto* regulations (the use and appeal to the law of self-amnesty is a clear example of this), or declaring they lacked jurisdiction for the cases that involved deaths and/or disappearances in the hands of the armed forces, remitting them to the military justice system, or, in other more modest cases, they questioned the constitutionality of a law enacted by the dictatorship, but they immediately acknowledged the legitimacy that, in their opinion, the *de facto* governments had to enact laws (...) But, on the other hand, and in parallel fashion, judicial proceedings became extremely speedy, which resulted in the re-opening of cases of victims of State terrorism that had been filed up to that point, in the acknowledgment of the relatives of victims as plaintiffs, and the unsealing of the records (2015, 191-192).

Between 1989 and 1990, trial processes came to a virtual halt due to the pardon decrees enacted by the recently inaugurated President Carlos Menem. These measures benefited hundreds of sentenced members of the armed forces and the police (including the *Junta* members sentenced in 1985) who had already been prosecuted.

The halt in prosecutions resulted in a period of impunity during the 1990s. However, during the period, the human rights movement implemented a variety

---

16 CONADEP and the families of detainees and disappeared persons presented their reports and stood as plaintiffs before the Judicial Branch, in the national courts. However, CONSUFA claimed jurisdiction over many investigations. It was up to each judge to declare his or her jurisdiction or lack thereof and, if applicable, argue against the jurisdiction of the military justice system. The government of Alfonsín tried to convince CONSUFA to speed up the trials it was performing (Nino 1996, 167), but was unsuccessful. However, with the enactment of Law no. 23.049, the Federal Court of Appeals of the Federal District was able to prosecute two cases and enter their sentences: Case 13/84 "Trial of the Juntas" and case 44/85 known as "Camps," which prosecuted the higher echelons of the Buenos Aires Province Police Department.

17 See Nino (1996) and Verbitsky (1987), 159–164.

of strategies to advance the cause of memory, truth and justice. One example is the report made to the Inter-American System of Human Rights, which drove the "Truth Trials",[18] under the notion that the inability to criminally punish the responsible ones does not relieve the State of its responsibility to provide the truth to victims and society. They asserted, therefore, that the justice system was required to perform trials, although it could not issue criminal sentences.

In 2001, for the first time a federal judge declared the Full Stop and Due Obedience Laws unconstitutional. This ruling allowed the prosecution of two individuals accused in a case involving two disappeared persons and the kidnapping of a female child.[19] During the first few years of the twenty-first century, complaints were filed for several cases and additional trial courts and the Federal Court of Appeals for the City of Buenos Aires ruled the impunity laws unconstitutional.

The year 2003 marked the beginning of a new stage of memory, truth and justice driven by the advances implemented under the administration of Néstor Kirchner. Kirchner presented to Congress a legislative project designed to declare the Full Stop and Due Obedience Laws irremediably null, which the Congress enacted by means of Law no. 25.779. Further, Law no. 25.778 was passed to grant constitutional supremacy to the "Convention on the Non-Applicability of Statutory Limitations to War Crimes and Crimes Against Humanity". The enactment of both regulations allowed the re-opening of the trials for crimes against humanity. The day after their enactment, the Court of Appeals for the Federal Capital ordered the reopening of two cases that had been in limbo since the 1980s: Case 450 "First Army Corps" and Case 761 "ESMA", involving illegal arrest and torture by, respectively, the First Army Corp and by the navy at the Escuela de Mecánica de la Armada. The simultaneous commitment of the three branches of government and the attorney general allowed very significant progress in these trials.

In 2005, the Supreme Court confirmed the nullity of the impunity laws and affirmed the constitutionality of the law that annulled them. Further, in 2007, the Court declared the nullity of the presidential pardons, thus fully reopening the path to prosecute parties responsible for serious human rights violations committed during the dictatorship. The Executive Branch supported this effort by providing reports, documentation and support to the victims and their relatives.

---

18 CIDH, Report no. 21/00, Case no. 12.059 Carmen Aguiar de Lapacó, Argentina, February 29, 2000.

19 It deals with the disappearances of José Liborio Poblete Roa and Gertrudis Marta Hlaczic and the kidnapping of their daughter, Claudia Victoria Poblete. The case is known as "Simón" (the surname of one of the accused, who was sentenced in 2006). The lawsuit was filed by Buscarita Imperi Roa, represented by the Grandmothers of Plaza de Mayo and CELS.

Ultimately, the trial process in Argentina is among those examples of recommendations (i.e. "justice") where a high degree of implementation exists. To be sure, the changing scenarios and the lengthy time-frame complicate the task of establishing causal relationships between CONADEP's recommendation and the many trials. While it is possible to establish a clear connection between the recommendation to try the responsible parties, as formulated by the CONADEP, and the *first* cycle of trials, there are multiple mediating factors to take into consideration over the ensuing decades.

6.3. RECOMMENDATION NO. 3: REPARATIONS

> Necessary regulations should be enacted to allow the children and/or family members of disappeared persons during the repression to receive economic assistance, study scholarships, social assistance and employment. In addition, measures must be implemented as considered appropriate to help palliate the variety of family and social problems resulting from the enforced disappearance of persons.

The reparation recommendation also has a long and complex process of implementation in Argentina, which requires us to characterize each individual measure to determine its precise links to the recommendation. Silvia San Martín states that this "was guaranteed by the laws of economic and historic reparation, which is Law 24321" (interview October 20, 2016). However, since the dates of the milestones of this process are so separated in time, with advances occurring in 1987, 1995 and 2004, once again it is necessary to divide the reparations process to establish a connection with the recommendation.

Law no. 23.466, enacted in 1987, created pensions and other benefits for family members of disappeared detainees. Non-contributory pensions were granted to the family members of disappeared persons, specifically to children under the age of 21, spouses, parents and/or siblings disabled from work or minor orphaned siblings who had lived with the disappeared person (regulated by Decree no. 1228/1987). Access to the pension entitled the beneficiary to receive health-care coverage through the National Institute of Social Services for Retirees and Pensioners (*Instituto Nacional de Servicios Sociales para Jubilados y Pensionados*, INSSJP).

Further, Law no. 24.411 of 1994 (regulated by Decree no. 403/1995) established an indemnification for successors-in-title of persons in a situation of enforced disappearance or for the heirs of those who had died as a result of State terrorism before December 10, 1983. In terms of the resolution of certain bureaucratic and administrative problems faced by family members due to the enforced disappearance of their relatives, another law was enacted in connection with the status of persons and public administration (Law no. 24.321 on absence due to enforced disappearance). This law allowed family members of disappeared persons to dispose of their patrimony and complete paperwork and legal processes, without this implying a legal declaration of death of the person who had been detained and had disappeared.

Finally, Law no. 25.914, enacted in 2004, established an indemnification for any persons born during the imprisonment of their mother or who had been in captivity with their parents, as long as their parents had disappeared or been detained for political reasons.

According to María José Guembe (2004),

> Notwithstanding the specific recommendation made by the CONADEP, the interest expressed by human rights organizations and the directly affected parties and the open attitude of the State, economic reparation was not granted for a long time. The priorities in the democratic transition were the search for truth and justice, although, little by little, the demands extended to the subject of economic reparation.

For the purposes of this project, we can state that the pensions and benefits provided following the 1987 law were directly connected to this recommendation. The programs defined during the subsequent 20 years are the product of different social and political stages. Therefore, it is risky to attribute a direct link between all the reparation programs and CONADEP's recommendation. However, one should keep in mind that, once the first economic reparation measure was established in 1987, it was considered necessary at different stages to establish other lines of economic reparation to address different prejudicial consequences facing family members of disappeared persons. Furthermore, as noted above, the current Secretariat of Human Rights (SDH), created on the recommendation of CONADEP, and the Commission's archives have been integral to managing the reparation programs. Thus, it is hard to envision the reparation program in its current form without CONADEP's work.

6.4. RECOMMENDATION NO. 4: HUMAN RIGHTS

> Regarding the enactment of regulations to guarantee the prevention and non-recurrence of human rights violations:

6.4.1. Sub-Recommendation No. 4.1

> Enact regulations tending to:
>
> 1. Establish the enforced disappearance of persons as a crime against humanity.

The recommendation to declare enforced disappearance a crime against humanity has been fully implemented. However, this is another instance in which this measure is only indirectly linked with CONADEP's recommendation.

In this case, the time-frame is lengthier. The demand to declare enforced disappearance a crime existed during the dictatorship, thus pre-dating the Commission. However, no such step was taken until 10 years after the transition, with the 1994 constitutional reform. When the change occurred, no explicit reference to CONADEP was made. A series of regulations regarding enforced disappearance as a crime against humanity were established during the period of 1995-2007.[20] The country even proved to be a global leader in the development of the International Convention for the Protection of All Persons from Enforced Disappearances (later approved domestically by Law no. 26.298). Argentina and France were the driving forces behind the initiative for the adoption of the text of this treaty.[21] The recommendation's precise formulation has undoubtedly contributed to its full implementation status. However, it is not evident that this is the result of the Commission including it among its recommendations. The activism of human rights organizations and well-known persons in the field of human rights, some of them members of CONADEP, was an essential factor.[22]

20 Among others, the approval of the Inter-American Convention on the Enforced Disappearance of Persons (Law no. 24.556), ratified by the Executive Branch in February of 1996 and constitutionally in 1997, and the approval of the Rome Statute by means of Law no. 25.390, ratified in January 2001.

21 See "The UN adopted today an initiative proposed by Argentina and France to establish the enforced disappearance of persons as a crime against humanity", available at: https://www.mrecic.gov.ar/la-onu-adopto-hoy-por-aclamacion-iniciativa-de-la-argentina-y-francia-que-establece-la-desaparicion; "Una iniciativa de Argentina y de Francia con historia accidentada" (An Argentinean and French initiative with a bumpy history), available at: https://www.pagina12.com.ar/diario/elpais/subnotas/68730-22331-2006-06-20.html; and "The International Protection Convention against Enforced Disappearances becomes effective", available at: https://elpais.com/internacional/2010/12/23/actualidad/1293058812_850215.html.

22 The "Conference on the legal treatment of the enforced disappearance of persons", held by the School of Law and Social Sciences of the University of Buenos Aires on March 24 and 25, 1987 was a milestone. The Conference was organized by the Initiative for an International Convention on the Enforced Disappearance of Persons Group. The group was formed by the Grandmothers of Plaza de Mayo, the Permanent Assembly for Human Rights (APDH), the Buenos Aires Attorneys Association, the American Bar Association (Argentinian Branch), the Latin American Association for Human Rights, the Association of Ex-Disappeared Detainees, the Center for Legal and Social Studies, the Family Members of Persons Disappeared and Detained for Political Reasons, FEDEFAM, the Institute of International Relations, the *Liga Argentina por los Derechos del Hombre* (LADH, the Argentine League for Human Rights), the Mothers of *Plaza de Mayo* (founding line), the Ecumenical Movement for Human Rights (MEDH), the Jewish Movement for Human Rights, the Office of Solidarity with Argentine Exiles, and the Peace and Justice Service (SERPAJ). Ex-members and secretaries of CONADEP, such as Ricardo Colombres and Raúl Aragón participated in the conference. The published edition includes sections with the words of Ricardo Colombres, Ernesto Sábato and Mon. Jaime de Nevares. Raúl Aragón's presentation of this collective effort includes the Paris Colloquium of 1981 as well as OEA's 1983 declaration as part of its background. See APDH (1987).

6.4.2. *Sub-Recommendation No. 4.2*

Enact regulations tending to:

2. Support the acknowledgment and membership in national and international human rights organizations.

The lack of specificity in this sub-recommendation makes it difficult to evaluate its degree of implementation. It could be said that the signing and ratification of international treaties on human rights is one of the ways in which the Argentine government "recognizes and adheres" to the human rights organizations. In addition, the State established awards to recognize domestic and foreign human rights defenders.[23]

The acknowledgment of organizations as spokespersons for certain government policies can also be considered a type of implementation. One example is the collaboration between State agencies specializing in the search for persons who were kidnapped as children and whose identities remain unknown and the Association of Grandmothers of Plaza de Mayo.

The link between the State and Argentine human rights organizations has varied over time. Once again, the current Secretariat of Human Rights is the main liaison between the State and such organizations. However, it would be arbitrary to define what the commissioners were thinking when they formulated this recommendation in order to assess whether the objectives have been fulfilled.

6.4.3. *Sub-Recommendation No. 4.3*

Enact regulations tending to:

3. Establish the mandatory teaching of the defense and dissemination of human rights in State educational agencies, either for civilians, military or security forces.

---

[23] Decree no. 1200/2003 set up an annual award known as the "Azucena Villaflor de Devincenti" award for the recognition of citizens or entities who "stood out for their civic activities in defense of human rights." Azucena Villaflor de Devincenti was one of the founders of the Mothers of *Plaza de Mayo* organization who demanded the live reappearance of their disappeared relatives. In December of 1977 she was kidnapped by task force 3.3 together with other campaigners. She was imprisoned at ESMA and murdered by being thrown out of an airplane, a practice known as "death flights". In 2007, the Ministry of Foreign Relations and Cult established the "Emilio F. Mignone International Human Rights Award" for the purpose of recognizing foreign institutions and/or persons residing overseas who stand out or have stood out in the promotion and protection of Human Rights in their respective countries, both in regard to the struggle against impunity in the face of massive and systematic violations of Human Rights as well as areas of discrimination, economic, social and cultural rights, among others (More information at: https://www.mrecic.gov.ar/premio-emilio-mignone).

Human rights are a subject included in almost every professional training program in Argentina. This has been a part of the democratization process, and it has increased especially since 2003, when the number of universities incorporating the subject into curricular or extracurricular programs has increased significantly. Given the level of decentralization of the Argentine educational system and the way training of military and security personnel is conducted, there is variation in the extent to which human rights have been incorporated around the country.

The most immediate link with CONADEP's recommendation can be established with Decree no. 3090/84 which ordered the Undersecretary of Human Rights to "[o]rganize and promote academic, educational and community activities tending to disseminate, protect and reaffirm the value and foundations of human rights within society" (Article 2, paragraph d). María Julia Bihurret acknowledged the efforts of the Ministry in the teaching and promotion of human rights and highlighted a general human rights course offered in 1985 with 1700 registered students as evidence (interview October 26, 2016). Another method of implementation strongly associated with the recommendation is the fact that the CONADEP report continues to have a strong impact on the policies of memory and education. The "*Nunca Más* [report] was incorporated into the educational curriculum of schools in order to transmit a sense of the past to the new generations and it inspired various museums of memory in curating their exhibitions" (Chillier and Torras 2018).

Public policy in connection with education on human rights was formalized during the 1990s. According to Mónica Fernández (2016), the most important milestone for this period was the 1994 constitutional reform, which increased the visibility of human rights, and which favored

> [t]he inclusion of human rights as basic educational content at every academic level. (…), they are incorporated into the formal educational curriculum, nationally, and at every educational level. This incorporation into the curriculum includes the curriculum design for teacher training as well as academic plans for the academies of the security and armed forces, including the curriculum for every police agent training program in the country.

Emilio Crenzel states that the federal education law that allows private entities to produce school texts made it possible for some academics to incorporate recent history events into school textbooks, which, in many cases, had not been previously modified since the dictatorship (interview October 21, 2016). National Education Law no. 26.206, of 2006, incorporates a perspective on human rights and forbids persons sentenced for crimes against humanity to practice teaching (Article 70). In its Article 92 paragraph c) it establishes that must be included in the curricular content of all jurisdictions

> [t]he exercise and construction of a collective memory of the historical and political processes that infringed the constitutional order and ended up implementing the State terrorism, for the purpose of nurturing in students democratic reflection and sensibilities supporting the defence of the rule of law and the full effectiveness of human rights.

Other measures serve a broader educational purpose for society at large. In 2002, National Law no. 25.633 established March 24 as the National Day of Memory for Truth and Justice "to commemorate the victims of the process that began on that date in the year 1976." Since then, the anniversaries of the *coup d'état* are national holidays. Further, the subject is discussed in classrooms around the country in order to allow children and youth, together with the educational and local community, to

> understand the scope of the serious economic, social and political consequences of the last military dictatorship and obtain their active commitment to actively defend the effectiveness of human rights and the guarantees provided by the National Constitution and the democratic system.[24]

Ultimately, these profound educational and training initiatives throughout the country can be linked directly to CONADEP's work.

6.4.4. *Sub-Recommendation No. 4.4*

> Enact regulations tending to:
>
> 4. Strengthen and fully optimize resources provided to the civil justice system for the courts' investigation of human rights violations.

We have not identified any activity related to the implementation of this recommendation. During the 1980s, on the contrary, regulations were enacted to hinder the civil justice system's efforts to investigate human rights violations that occurred during the civilian-military dictatorship, with consent of the Judicial Branch. There is no evidence to suggest that the government's budget allocations to the justice system have been influenced by CONADEP.

6.4.5. *Sub-Recommendation No. 4.5*

> Enact regulations tending to:
>
> 5. Repeal any repressive legislation still in effect.

---

[24] See: https://www.argentina.gob.ar/24-de-marzo-dia-de-la-memoria-por-la-verdad-y-la-justicia.

The intent of this recommendation was largely fulfilled when CONADEP presented its report. Law no. 23.007, enacted on August 9, 1984, on the initiative of the Executive Power "for the defence of democracy", revoked multiple repressive criminal regulations, such as Law no. 20.840 for "National Security. Penalties against subversive activities of every kind." As mentioned, LADH attorneys had suggested the repeal of repressive legislation during a meeting with CONADEP. Specifically, they identified Laws no. 16.964 and 16.970, both enacted in 1966 during the period of dictatorship prior to the one from 1976 to 1983. In its report, CONADEP did not specify which regulations should be repealed.

Since the repeal of repressive regulations was a demand set out by human rights organizations before the democratic transition, and the main activity occurred before the presentation of *Nunca Más*, the Commission's recommendation can be seen as more of a reinforcement of this position than the reason for its implementation.

More generally, although some of the most repressive State terrorism regulations have been repealed, there are still areas of legislation that have not been reformed in a democratic fashion and continue to be the legal basis for many institutions that are essential for the exercise of human rights. The Code of Military Conduct and its Intelligence System, for example, have undergone recent reforms in their framework laws. By contrast, the Argentine Federal Police still operate by laws created during dictatorial times. The democratization of institutions and their governing laws remains an ongoing process in Argentina.[25]

7. CONCLUSIONS

Our analysis of the implementation of CONADEP's recommendations sheds light on the astounding force and validity of this Commission as a most significant socio-political event in the social, institutional and political lives of the Argentine people. The memory of the Commission's work, the dissemination of its report, the multiple consequences of the creation of the Subecretary, then Secretary, of Human Rights, which continues the Commission's work, and the creation of a still-growing official archive created with the documentation collected by the Commission jointly constitute a complex device for the development of memory, truth and justice which undoubtedly continues to significantly affect the present. It is a foundational democratic milestone that

25 The website "Las leyes de la dictadura y cómo afectan la democracia" lists current de facto laws: http://www.leyesdeladictadura.com/.

has contributed profoundly to the true acknowledgment of State terrorism in every sector of Argentine society.

Although the recommendations precisely adapt to the public policies implemented on the subject, they often have not been invoked as a foundational reference. In general, it has been forgotten that *Nunca Más* contains a recommendations section. Without explicit links in most cases, determining the specific impact the recommendations have had on these matters and their implementation is a methodologically challenging task. In each case, we attempted to establish the nature of the link between recommendations and implementation as precisely as possible. Having analyzed them one by one, we found that most of the recommendations formulated by CONADEP have been implemented to a high degree. The creation of an entity to continue the task of the Commission was a direct and immediate consequence of that recommendation, and this entity became a platform for the implementation of other recommendations.

The lengthy implementation time-frame for more than 35 years requires segmentation, both in order to consider the causal links to each recommendation and for the purpose of compiling a truthful international comparison. Several of the recommendations are closely linked to early implementation events in the 1980s and are indirectly linked to implementation during the following decades. It is necessary to conceptualize how to evaluate the existing links between the different implementation milestones extending for decades through fragmented public policy processes and multiple stages.

There are design aspects of CONADEP and its recommendations program that stand out in our international comparison and deserve further mention. One interesting feature worth mentioning to understand its historical transcendence is the fact that CONADEP commissioners were local actors, members of civil society, with a pluralistic composition and a significant connection to the organized human rights movement. Second, the way in which CONADEP was formed and its connections to civil society provided the Commission with deep societal roots that allowed it to achieve historical impact. Emilio Crenzel believes this influenced the Commission's construction of the truth:

> Both in the CONADEP'S investigation and its report, the voice of the State and the voices of the victims and the human rights movement intermix and become a sort of shared truth about this system of disappearance. (Crenzel 2008)

Chillier and Torras (2018) also share this analysis:

> The work of the CONADEP bore results not only due to being of state character or being comprised of distinct eminent personalities, but its performance must also be understood in the light of alliances and joint efforts between the human rights movement and the state.

Regarding the content of the recommendations themselves, it is worth mentioning for international comparison that the matter of using the judicial process was presented as a main objective and identified as the preferred method to corroborate and direct the investigative efforts of the Commission. Recently, it has become popular to contrast transitional models focused on truth with those focused on criminal justice and, in some cases, it is stated that there are trade-offs in pursing one over the other. The Argentine case shows a process of mutual reinforcement between the Commission and the trials for crimes against humanity:

> the CONADEP report gives continuity to the historical process in which truth and justice are considered as mutually reinforcing strategies, set in motion the process of building social memory, and condemned the perpetrated crimes at a political level (Chillier and Torras 2018).

The fact that Commission members were local personalities and that the Commission cooperated with human rights organizations highly versed on the matter is significant in order to understand the precision of the agenda produced from the recommendations. The connections between CONADEP and the human rights movement are reflected in the formulation of the recommendations: most of CONADEP's recommendations had already been articulated by relatives and other activists during the dictatorship, as was reflected in the CIDH's report following its *in loco* visit, and, as we have established, was used as a model by the commissioners.

When compared to other truth commission cases, the CONADEP recommendations stand out due to their scant number, the juridical style of their drafting and their legally feasible nature in the context of Argentina's democratic system. They evidence a precise knowledge of the operation of the State and its bureaucracies: what it can do and how its agencies are organized. Although political circumstances have changed substantially over the nearly four decades that have elapsed since the beginning of this process, the three branches of government have been able to implement the recommendations of CONADEP through public policies of memory, truth and justice and have even gone beyond them. Since CONADEP was only empowered to investigate enforced disappearances, their recommendations center around that issue. However, subsequent policies were designed to provide reparation to victims of other crimes. For example, ex political prisoners and ex disappeared detainees were indemnified under Law no. 24.043.[26] There are also policies for the promotion of memory, such as the creation of Memory Sites and the National Archive for

[26] For other public policies on the issue of memory, truth and justice, see Torras, Palmás Zaldua and Perelman (2016) and Balardini (2016).

Memory, as well as others for the construction of truth, such as the "trials for truth". This variety of public policies centered on memory, truth and justice lead us to the belief that implementation has gone beyond the recommendations formulated by CONADEP.

Within the complex landscape of the Argentine process of memory, truth and justice, CONADEP's recommendations have largely been forgotten as an instrument of historical narrative, while their content has been widely implemented. In many cases, research has shown links deeper than expected in light of the lack of explicit references to the recommendations. As a group, it could be said that CONADEP's recommendations crystallized public consensus between the State and society on a human rights agenda in the new-born democracy.

BIBLIOGRAPHY

Acuña, Carlos and Smulovitz, Catalina (1995). "Militares en la transición Argentina: del gobierno a la subordinación constitucional." In Carlos H. Acuña et al (eds.), *Juicio, castigos y memorias. Derechos humanos y justicia en la política argentina*, 19-99. Buenos Aires: Ediciones Nueva Visión.

APDH (1987). *La desaparición crimen contra la humanidad*. Buenos Aires: Estudio Sigma.

Balardini, Lorena (2017). "Argentina: regional protagonist of transitional justice." In Skaar, Elin, García-Godos, Jemima, Collins, Cath (eds.), *Transitional justice in Latin America: The Uneven Road from Impunity towards Accountability*, 50–76. New York: Routledge.

Brienza, Lucía (2010). "Los usos del pasado dictatorial en los primeros años de democracia: Argentina, 1983–1989." *Revista. Escuela de Historia* [online] no. 9 (2). Available at: http://www.scielo.org.ar/scielo.php?script=sci_arttext&pid=S1669-90412010000200002&lng=es&nrm=iso. ISSN 1669-9041.

Brodsky, Ricardo (2014). *Violencia, Comisiones de la Verdad y Memorias (anotaciones sobre los casos de Argentina, Chile y Perú.)* Museum of Memory and Human Rights.

Bruno, Ángel, Cavarozzi, Marcelo, and Palermo, Vicente (eds.) (1985). *Los derechos humanos en la democracia*. Buenos Aires: Centro Editor de América Latina.

Camacho, Fernando (2008). "Memorias enfrentadas: las reacciones a los informes Nunca Más de Argentina y Chile." *Persona y Sociedad*, no. XXII (2): 67–99.

Catterberg, Edgardo (1985). "Las elecciones del 30 de octubre de 1983. El surgimiento de una nueva convergencia electoral." *Desarrollo Económico*, no. 25 (98), July-September 1985: 259–267, Buenos Aires: Instituto de Desarrollo Económico y Social (IDES).

CONADEP (Comisión Nacional sobre la Desaparición de Personas) (1984) [1986]. *Nunca Más. Informe final de la Comisión Nacional sobre la Desaparición de Personas*. Buenos Aires: Eudeba. Spanish version available at: http://www.desaparecidos.org/arg/conadep/nuncamas/.

Crenzel, Emilio (2008). *La Historia Política del Nunca Más*. Buenos Aires: Siglo Veintiuno editores.

—— (2009). "La Comisión Nacional sobre la Desaparición de Personas en Argentina. ¿Sólo una comisión oficial de personalidades?" *Iberoamericana. Nordic Journal of Latin American and Caribbean Studies* no. XXXIX (1-2): 15–36.

Chillier, G. and Torras, V. (2018). "Strategies Against Impunity in Relation to Crimes of State Terrorism in Argentina." In Guevara Bermúdez, J.A. and Chávez Vargas, L.G. (eds.), *Eradicating Impunity for Atrocities Committed in Dictatorships, Authoritarian Regimes and Armed Conflicts in Latin America: Challenges and good practices in Argentina, Chile, Colombia, Guatemala and Peru.* Mexico: Comisión Mexicana de Defensa y Promoción de los Derechos Humanos, A.C. Available at: http://www.cmdpdh.org/publicaciones-pdf/cmdpdh-erradicating-impunity.pdf.

Fernández Meijide, Graciela (2009). *Historia íntima de los derechos humanos en la Argentina.* Buenos Aires: Sudamericana.

Fernández, Mónica (2016). "Educación en derechos humanos en Argentina. Notas sobre el proceso de incorporación de los derechos humanos en los contextos educativos." *Revista Latinoamericana de Derechos Humanos* no. 27 (1): 143–166.

Guembe, María José (2004). *La Experiencia Argentina de Reparación Económica de Graves Violaciones a los Derechos Humanos.* Buenos Aires: CELS. Available at: http://www.cels.org.ar/common/documentos/experiencia_argentina_reparacion.doc.

González Bombal, Inés and Landi, Oscar (1995). "Los derechos humanos en la cultura política." In Acuña, C. et al. (eds.), *Juicio, castigos y memorias. Derechos humanos y justicia en la política argentina.* Buenos Aires: Ediciones Nueva Visión.

Inter-American Commission on Human Rights (CIDH) (1980) [2006]. *Informe sobre la situación de los Derechos Humanos en Argentina.* Buenos Aires: New edition by the National Ministry of Justice and Human Rights.

Jelin, Elizabeth (1995). "La política de la memoria: el Movimiento de Derechos Humanos y la construcción democrática en la Argentina." In Carlos H. Acuña et al. (eds.), *Juicio, castigos y memorias. Derechos humanos y justicia en la política Argentina*, pp. 101–146. Buenos Aires: Ediciones Nueva Visión.

Mignone, Emilio (1981). "El caso argentino: desapariciones forzadas como instrumento básico y generalizado de una política" La doctrina del paralelismo global. Su concepción y aplicación. Necesidad de su denuncia y condena. Conclusiones y recomendaciones". Presentation made during the debate: *"La política de desapariciones forzadas de personas"*. Paris, January 31-February 1, 1981.

—— (1991). *Derechos Humanos y Sociedad. El caso argentino.* Buenos Aires: Centro de Estudios Legales y Sociales.

Moreno Ocampo (1987). "La importancia de la prueba en el juzgamiento de la desaparición forzada de personas." In APDH, *La desaparición crimen contra la humanidad.* Buenos Aires: Estudio Sigma.

Nino, Carlos (1996) [2015]. *Juicio al mal absoluto.* Buenos Aires: Siglo Veintiuno Editores.

Presidency of Argentina (2008). *Derechos Humanos.* Legislative Summary 2003–2007. Buenos Aires: National Directorate of the Official Registry.

Sarrabayrouse Oliveira, María José (2015). "Rupturas, continuidades y lealtades en el Poder Judicial." In Bohoslavsky (ed.), *¿Usted también, doctor? Complicidad de jueces, fiscales y abogados durante la dictadura.* Buenos Aires: Siglo Veintiuno Editores.

Skaar, Elin, and Eric Wiebelhaus-Brahm (2013). "The drivers of transitional justice: An analytical framework for assessing the role of actors." *Nordic Journal of Human Rights*, no. 31 (2): 127–148.

Torras, Verónica, Palmás Zaldua, Luz and Perelman, Marcela (2016). "Memoria, verdad y justicia como política de Estado. Análisis de políticas públicas implementadas durante los gobiernos kirchneristas (2003–2015) respecto de los delitos de lesa humanidad ocurridos en la última dictadura argentina." *ANÁLISIS*, no. 11–2016. Buenos Aires: Friedrich Ebert Stiftung.

Verbitsky, Horacio (1987). *Civiles y militares*. Buenos Aires: Editorial Contrapunto.

Press Articles

Clarín (September 29, 1984). "Rechazan la creación de la comisión bicameral de derechos humanos". Buenos Aires.

Edition no. 4 (July 17, 1981). "Solicitada de Familiares de detenidos por razones políticas de Reconquista". Reconquista.

El País (December 23, 2010). "Entra en vigor la Convención Internacional de Protección contra las Desapariciones Forzadas". Madrid.

Paganetti, Arnaldo (1984a). "Acto con bemoles". Buenos Aires. *Clarín*, November 27, 1984.

—— (1984b). "Desaparecidos: El último capítulo". Buenos Aires. *Clarín*, June 27, 1984.

Página 12 (June 20, 2006). "Una iniciativa de Argentina y de Francia con historia accidentada". Buenos Aires.

ANNEX: SOURCES OF DOCUMENTATION

Interviewee List

Emilio Crenzel. CONICET researcher and professor in the School of Sociology of the University of Buenos Aires, October 21, 2016.

María Julia Bihurret. Researcher of the Ministry of Human Rights, Buenos Aires October 26, 2016.

Silvia San Martín. Unified Registry of State Terrorism Victims, Buenos Aires, October 20, 2016 (responded via e-mail).

Archival Search

Testimonies of the Oral Archive of Open Memory. Interviews with:

Raúl Aragón
Julio Strassera
Graciela Fernández Meijide
Luis Moreno Ocampo
Jorge Valerga Aráoz
Ricardo Gil Lavedra

Search of Documentary Fund of the CONADEP- National Memory Archive:

Minutes of the National Commission on the Disappearance of Persons

Book of Minutes of the National Commission on the Disappearance of Persons. Decree no. 187/83. Minutes of the Commission member meetings regarding the disappearance of persons.

Book of Minutes of the National Commission on the Disappearance of Persons. Decree no. 187/83. Minutes on CONADEP administrative subjects.

Statistics of the Justice Process of the Center for Legal and Social Studies (CELS). Available at: http://www.cels.org.ar.

Laws and Regulations

Laws (available at www.infoleg.gob.ar):

Law 23040 (December 22, 1983). Law no. 22.924 – Its repeal.

Law 23049 (February 9, 1984). Military Code of Justice. Its modification.

Law 23077 (August 9, 1984). Law of the Defense of Democracy.

Law 23466 (October 12, 1986). Non-taxable pension for disappeared persons.

Law 23492 (December 23, 1986). Expiration of criminal action against the Armed Forces.

Law 23521 (June 8, 1987). Limits the scope of the duty of due obedience.

Law 24321 (May 11, 1994). Enforced disappearance of persons.

Law 24411 (December 7, 1994). Disappearance of persons. Receivable benefits.

Law 24556 (September 13, 1995). Conventions. Enforced disappearance of persons (OEA).

Law 25390 (November 30, 2000). Rome Statute. Its approval.

Law 25633 (August 1, 2002). Commemorations. National Memory for Truth and Justice Day.

Law 25914 (August 4, 2004). Human Rights. Indemnification.

Law 25974 (December 1, 2004). Location and restitution of children. Historical Reparation Fund.

Law 26001 (December 16, 2004). Commemorations. National Right of Identity Day.

Law 26200 (December 13, 2006). International Criminal Court. Implementation of the Rome Statute. Law 25390.

Law 26206 (December 14, 2006). Law of National Education.

Decrees

Decree 157/83 (December 13, 1983) Orders the criminal prosecution of political-military organization leaders. Available at: https://es.wikisource.org/wiki/Decreto_157/83.

Decree 158/83 (December 13, 1983) Presidential order to put military juntas on trial. Available at: http://www.desaparecidos.org/nuncamas/web/document/nacional/decr158.htm.

Decree 187/83 (December 15, 1983) National Commission on the Disappearance of Persons. Available at: http://www.derechos.org/ddhh/arg/ley/conadep.txt.

Decree 3090/84 (September 20, 1984) Created in the Ministry of the Interior, Office of the Undersecretary of Human Rights. Available at www.infoleg.gob.ar.

Decree 1228/87 (July 30, 1987) Regulations of Law no. 23.466, granting non-tax pensions to family members of disappeared persons. Available at www.infoleg.gob.ar.

Regulatory Decree 403/95 (August 29, 1995). Law no. 24.411 - regulation. Available at www.infoleg.gob.ar.

Decree 1200/03 (December 5, 2003). "Azucena Villaflor de Devincenti" Award. Available at www.infoleg.gob.ar.

CHILE'S RETTIG AND VALECH COMMISSIONS

Truth and Reparation under the Sign of Reconciliation

Sol HOURCADE, Federico GHELFI, Luz PALMÁS ZALDUA, and Marcela PERELMAN*

---

* This chapter was written by researchers from the Centro de Estudios Legales y Sociales (Center for Legal and Social Studies, CELS), Buenos Aires. The general analysis and writing is a collective work by Sol Hourcade, Federico Ghelfi, Luz Palmás Zaldua and Marcela Perelman. Fieldwork in Santiago de Chile and the analysis and drafting of the chapter were in charge of Hourcade. Systematization of sources was in charge of Hugo Goeury. Andrea Rocha Granados participated during the project preparation phase, in 2015.
The authors wish to express their gratitude for the valuable input by Elin Skaar, Jemima García-Godos, and Eric Wiebelhaus-Brahm to prior versions of this text. They also wish to thank Boris Hau for his invaluable contributions to the fieldwork design in Chile, as well as Onur Bakiner for his reading and comments.

1. INTRODUCTION

Two separate truth commissions were created in Chile within different contexts for the purpose of establishing the State's responsibility for gross human rights violations committed during the civil-military dictatorship headed by Augusto Pinochet Ugarte (1973–90). The National Truth and Reconciliation Commission (*Comisión Nacional de Verdad y Reconciliación* – CNVR), ran during 1990–91 in the immediate aftermath of the democratic transition. About a decade later, in 2003–2004, the National Commission on Political Imprisonment and Torture (*Comisión Nacional sobre Prisión Política y Tortura* – CNPPT) delved further into Chile's past.

The National Truth and Reconciliation Commission, known as the Rettig Commission after its chairperson, was one of the first measures enacted by President-Elect Patricio Aylwin Azócar in 1990 to address the dictatorship's human rights violations, shed light on the responsibility of the State and contribute to the process of "reconciliation" of the Chilean people. The Amnesty Law Decree of 1978[1] and the features of the so-called "Chilean Transition", also known as the agreed transition and "*política de empate*" (Even Score Policy),[2] in which the military stepped down but still held real power, constrained what form of transitional justice was possible. "The Chilean transition attempted to neutralize clashes between social and political forces connected to the traumatic past by deactivating the memory of historical violence using an initial mechanism: consensus and its reconciliation discourse" (Richard 2010: 31). In this context, public policy on the matter revolved around developing an agenda of truth and reconciliation instead of establishing criminal responsibility for crimes against humanity.

With members broadly representing the various segments of Chilean society, the Rettig Commission established the existence of 2,298 individuals who disappeared or were executed for political reasons. It further described the role of State agents in those crimes and formulated recommendations to establish symbolic and socio-economic reparations for the victims as well as modify institutions to prevent future human rights violations. Based upon the Rettig Commission's recommendation, Law 19123 established reparation measures for

---

1 The decree was issued by the military *Junta* on April 18, 1978. Article 1 states: "We hereby grant amnesty to any individual who, acting as author, accomplice or accessory, have incurred criminal liability during the effectiveness of the State of Siege beginning on September 11, 1973, and ending on March 10, 1978, provided such individual is not under prosecution or has been sentenced." In view of the decree, most courts declared themselves incompetent to investigate the human rights violations and the cases were referred to the military justice system.

2 Personal interview with Alicia Lira, September 15, 2016.

family members of victims "qualified" as such by the Commission. The Chilean government also created other public policies contemplating the circumstances of individuals dismissed from government or private employment or forced into exile for political reasons.

However, the status of political prisoners and torture victims remained unaddressed. The sole reparation for those cases was the medical care provided by the Reparation and Comprehensive Healthcare Program (*Programa de Reparación y Atención Integral en Salud*) to victims of torture. Former political prisoners began to organize and thus increase the visibility of their suffering, to litigate over the events of torture, and worked to recover clandestine prison and torture centers as memory sites (Collins 2013). Ultimately, a second truth commission was created in 2003 when then-President, Ricardo Lagos Escobar, presented the country with his human rights proposal known as "*No hay mañana sin ayer: para seguir avanzando en el delicado proceso de sanar las heridas*"[3] (Centro de Estudios Públicos 2003). Among other measures, President Lagos announced the creation of a commission to establish a list of individuals who were illegally deprived of their freedom and subjected to torture for political reasons. Also known as the Valech Commission after its chairperson, the National Commission on Political Imprisonment and Torture acknowledged the existence of approximately 30,000 victims and formulated recommendations broadly framed within President Lagos' human rights program.

Both commissions were deeply influential in Chilean society with their acknowledgment of the gross and massive human rights violations perpetrated between 1973 and 1990. This chapter focuses on the different contexts surrounding the creation of each commission, the factors influencing the formulation of recommendations, and the status of their implementation.

2. THE CHILEAN TRANSITION: BETWEEN APERTURE AND AMNESTY

Following a long period of democracy, the military overthrew Chilean President Salvador Allende Gossens on September 11, 1973. Allende had been elected in 1970 on a promise to get to socialism through the democratic way. The Cold War is a determining context: in large part, with respect to the growing concern of the United States and its allies about political sectors that they perceived and pointed out as subversives inspired by the Soviet model. Three years later,

[3] This translates as "There is no Tomorrow without a Yesterday: to continue advancing the delicate process of healing the wounds."

tensions came to a head when the military *Junta* headed by Augusto Pinochet Ugarte violently overthrew the government (CNPPT 2004).

The repressive methods implemented by the armed forces and law-enforcement agencies included imprisonment for political reasons, torture and executions, as well as the forced disappearance of thousands of individuals. Many Chileans were sentenced by court-martial and did not have access to a proper defense. Thousands of others were dismissed from jobs in public administration, State-owned companies, and the education system, and thousands requested asylum or went into exile (Lira and Loveman 1998). Over two-thirds of political prisoners were detained during the first three months of the dictatorship.[4] The judiciary continued to function, though it posed no obstacle to Pinochet's regime. In fact, it rejected all *habeas corpus* appeals. Moreover, political repression was accompanied by a radical neoliberal restructuring of the economy (Collins and Hau 2016, 127).

Over the next decade, Pinochet's control was absolute. Decree 2919 (known as the "Amnesty Law") was issued in 1978 under the pretext of achieving a peaceful resolution of past events, although in reality it promoted impunity for State agents responsible for the human rights violations. In 1980, the *Junta* approved a new Constitution that allowed the military to retain significant power once democracy was re-established (CODEPU 2001). Nonetheless, by the mid-1980s, domestic and international pressure to re-democratize was growing. A popular referendum conducted in 1988 to decide if Pinochet would remain President for an additional eight years resulted in "No". This event triggered democratic elections the following year.

This progress also initiated a debate surrounding constitutional reform (CODEPU 2001). Reformers had many successes. Article 8, limiting the activities of political parties, was repealed. Political pluralism was established as a guarantee. Rights guaranteed in international treaties ratified by Chile were acknowledged. Articles regulating states of emergency were modified. However, although some of the so-called "authoritarian enclaves"[5] of the 1980 Constitution were modified, many others that "distort, limit and deny exercise of popular sovereignty" were left intact (CODEPU 2001, 1). The military remained outside of civilian control through the National Security Council (*Consejo de Seguridad Nacional* – COSENA). The commanders in chief of the armed forces and the Carabineers (Chilean National Police Force, known as *Carabineros*) enjoyed permanent tenure. Many Senate seats were designated and lifelong. COSENA had the power to designate two members of the Constitutional Tribunal.

---

4 Interview with María Luisa Sepúlveda, Santiago, Chile, September 12, 2016.

5 Garretón (2001) defines authoritarian enclaves as military-dominated institutions "which live on in the ensuing democratic regime, preventing it from becoming a full political democracy".

Pinochet himself continued to be in charge of the Army as its commander in chief and, after retiring, as ex-President, became a lifelong Senator pursuant to the 1980 Constitution.

The presidential and legislative elections were organized in accordance with the calendar established by the military regime. Patricio Aylwin, a Christian Democrat who headed the center-left *La Concertación*[6] coalition, was elected in December 1989. During his campaign, Aylwin created a commission to formulate recommendations regarding human rights, particularly dealing with human rights violations during the dictatorship (Collins and Hau 2016). According to Lira and Loveman (1998), *La Concertación*'s program was based largely on recommendations of the Chilean Commission on Human Rights (*Comisión Chilena de Derechos Humanos*, CCHDH).[7]

Thus, Aylwin's transitional justice platform centered on knowledge of the truth, reconciliation and justice "insofar as possible". While Aylwin recognized the political sensitivity of the Amnesty Law, he argued it did not preclude uncovering information about serious crimes like disappearances and assassinations.[8] Further, he argued the Law could only be applied once the facts and responsible parties had been established (Garretón 2008). However, the Judicial Branch was generally applying the Amnesty Law automatically without investigation.

The program also supported the Chilean Commission on Human Rights' calls for reparations for victims of political repression and addressing the status of political prisoners, exiles and individuals deprived of their nationality. Nonetheless, the chances of progress seemed bleak as the Senate was under the control of representatives, either designated or elected, who sympathized with the Pinochet regime (Collins and Hau 2016). Therefore, upon his March 1990 inauguration, Aylwin met with human rights activists, victims' family members, religious leaders, and representatives from a wide range of political parties to define his public policy on the matter. The overarching goals were: i) to offer reparations to individual victims and to society at large; and ii) to prevent recurrence of massive human rights violations (Zalaquett 2002, 6). The National Truth and Reconciliation Commission became a primary policy to achieve these ends.

---

6 Abbreviation for The *Concertación de Partidos por la Democracia* (Parties' Agreement for Democracy) party coalition.

7 The Chilean Commission on Human Rights was created on December 10, 1978. The NGO is dedicated to the effective promotion and protection of the economic, social, cultural, civil and political rights set forth in international human rights law. Web page: http://www.cchdh.cl/nosotros.

8 Speech of March 4, 1991, presenting the CNVR's report.

3. THE CHILEAN NATIONAL TRUTH AND RECONCILIATION COMMISSION (RETTIG COMMISSION)

3.1. CREATION AND MANDATE

The National Truth and Reconciliation Commission (or Rettig Commission) was created on April 25, 1990, by Supreme Decree 355. President Aylwin ordered it to clarify cases of grave human rights violations, which were limited to cases of death or disappearance where the facts involved "moral responsibility by the State"[9] for the actions of its agents or persons at its service, as well as kidnappings and attempted murders committed by individuals "under political pretexts". It was entrusted with the task of collecting information about these human rights violations, identifying the victims and establishing their location. It was empowered to receive testimony, collect information from domestic and international human rights organizations, and request documents from State authorities. The Ministry of Justice was ordered to provide technical and administrative support, as well as the necessary funding (CNRR 1996a, 3).[10] The Rettig Commission was empowered for six months, extendable for another three. Upon completion of its investigation, the Commission was to draft a report to be presented to the President. The Rettig Commission was required to recommend reparations and other measures to restore the reputation and dignity of each victim as well as legal and administrative measures to prevent the recurrence of such crimes. The decree specified that the Rettig Commission would not have judicial authority and, in the event of learning of a crime, it was required to make that information available to the relevant court.

President Aylwin appointed eight individuals to serve on the Commission (see Table 1).[11] Commission members represented a range of political viewpoints in Chilean society. All but one were attorneys, and most were academics. The composition, which included prominent figures linked to right-wing political parties, was designed to enhance the credibility of the investigation in order to achieve a "reconciliation" of diverse ideological groups (Camacho Padilla 2014).[12]

---

9 In its final report, the Rettig Commission observed that this concept does not have a precise technical or legal meaning and stated that this reference must be understood as "the responsibility which, according to sound judgement, can be assigned to the State as a result of the actions of its agents (or others in its service) executed in compliance with State policies or orders; or resulting from actions executed without specific policies or orders, if the State agent possessed express or tacit ratification from State agencies or State protection or failure to act, resulting in the impunity of such actions" (CNRR 1996a, 16).

10 According to Hayner (2008, 289), approximately US$1 million were allocated to the Commission.

11 For more information on the Commission's composition, see Camacho Padilla (2004).

12 See also interview with Jorge Correa Sutil on television program "*Secretos del Informe Rettig*" (Secrets of the Rettig Report), *Ahora Noticias*, Mega, broadcast on March 3, 2016.

According to former commissioner Zalaquett, four of the eight members had either been Pinochet supporters or at least favored ousting Allende, while the remainder were human rights advocates and Pinochet opponents. Zalaquett further states that the President had nominated only men, and it was he who pointed out the absence of women, which led to the inclusion of Mónica Jiménez de la Jara and Laura Novoa Vásquez.[13]

Table 1. Members of the National Truth and Reconciliation Commission

Commissioner	Political and/or social background
Raúl Rettig Guissen (President)	**Professor, attorney and politician**. Member of the Radical Party. Presided over the party in 1950. Senator between 1949 and 1957. Undersecretary of the Ministry of the Interior and Ministry of Foreign Relations during the government of Pedro Aguirre Cerda (1938–41)[14]
Jaime Castillo Velasco	**Attorney, professor, politician**. Founder of the Christian Democratic Party. After the coup, founded and directed the *Secretariado Latinoamericano de Derechos Humanos* (Latin American Secretariat of Human Rights) (SELADEH). Founded the National Commission of Human Rights in 1978.[15]
José Luis Cea Egaña	**Attorney**. Professor of Political Law, Constitutional Law and Political Science at the *Pontificia Universidad Católica de Chile* (Pontifical Catholic University of Chile), University of Chile and Diego Portales University. Docent at the Academy of Police Sciences of the Chilean Carabineers (Chilean National Police Force).[16]
Mónica Jiménez de la Jara	**Social worker**. Ex-Director of the School of Social Work of the *Universidad Católica* (Catholic University). Linked to the Christian Democratic party.[17]
Ricardo Martín Díaz	**Attorney**. Ex-Minister of the Supreme Court of Justice (1964–71) and institutional Senator of the Republic (1990–98).[18]
Laura Novoa Vásquez	**Attorney** of the *Universidad de Chile* (University of Chile) and academic.[19]
Gonzalo Vial Correa	**Attorney, journalist and historian.** Conservative and nationalist intellectual, Minister of Education during Pinochet's de facto government (1978).[20]

(continued)

13 Interview with José Zalaquett on the television program "*Secretos del Informe Rettig*" (Secrets of the Rettig Report), *Ahora Noticias*, Mega, broadcast on March 3, 2016.

14 http://historiapolitica.bcn.cl/resenas_parlamentarias/wiki/Mauricio_Ra%C3%BAl_Rettig_Guissen.

15 https://www.camara.cl/prensa/noticias_detalle.aspx?prmid=122285.

16 http://www.institutodechile.cl/instituto/cea.pdf.

17 http://www.archivochile.com/Gobiernos/gob_paylwin/de/GOBdeaylwin0004.pdf.

18 http://historiapolitica.bcn.cl/resenas_parlamentarias/wiki/Ricardo_Martin_D%C3%ADaz.

19 http://www.archivochile.com/Gobiernos/gob_paylwin/de/GOBdeaylwin0004.pdf http://ciperchile.cl/2013/09/11/laura-novoa-perdon-y-reconciliacion/.

20 http://www.memoriachilena.cl/602/w3-article-100642.html.

Table 1 *continued*

Commissioner	Political and/or social background
José Zalaquett Daher	**Attorney**. As of 1973, directed the Legal Department of the *Comité de Cooperación para la Paz* (Cooperation Committee for Peace) in Chile, after directing the *Vicaría de la Solidaridad* (Vicariate for Solidarity). Following expulsion from Chile in 1976, became a member of Amnesty International (acting as Deputy Secretary General and President).[21]
Secretary	**Political and/or social background**
Jorge Correa Sutil	**Attorney**. Christian Democratic attorney. Dean of the School of Law of the Diego Portales University.[22]

Source: Compiled by the authors.

3.2. THE REPORT AND ITS RECEPTION

The Commission presented its report to President Aylwin on February 8, 1991.[23] The report explained the Commission's organization, operation, and tasks. It exposed the operation of the State's repressive apparatus and the most fundamental human rights violations committed by the armed forces, the Carabineers, and other intelligence agencies (*Dirección Nacional de Inteligencia* (DINA), later the *Centro Nacional de Información* (CNI) acting effectively as Pinochet's secret police). The CNVR acknowledged the existence of 2,298 cases where individuals had either disappeared or been executed for political reasons. Of these, 2,130 were victims of human rights violations committed by the State (CNRR 1996a, 1364). Human rights organizations expected that the report would only include victims of State terrorism. However, it also included the names of members of the armed forces and Carabineers who died during kidnapping operations or other armed operations. According to Garretón, some deceased military and police personnel included as victims in the report did not die as a result of civilian-related confrontations or attacks.[24] Rather, it was an attempt by commissioners to maintain their agreement to have some balance to increase the report's credibility.

The report then included the description of actions committed by "individuals under political pretexts." It contained information that would be beneficial for judicial investigations, such as background on illegal interments and names of

21 http://www.uchile.cl/portal/presentacion/consejo-de-evaluacion/presentacion/50053/prof-jose-zalaquett-daher.

22 http://www.archivochile.com/Gobiernos/gob_paylwin/de/GOBdeaylwin0004.pdf.

23 This chapter uses a new edition of the report published in 1996 by the National Corporation for Reconciliation and Reparation (CNRR 1996a) when referencing the Rettig Commission report. The 1996 edition added a series of attachments to the original document.

24 Interview with Roberto Garretón, Santiago de Chile, September 12, 2016.

alleged perpetrators.[25] The actions of the judiciary during the dictatorship were included in a separate chapter, in which the Rettig Commission concludes that the Judicial Branch "did not react to the human rights violations with sufficient energy."

The Rettig Commission's acknowledgment that the State had violated human rights had great impact. In a national address on March 4, 1991, Aylwin announced the Rettig Commission's report and made a brief presentation of its content as well as its recommendations and preventive measures related to reparations.[26] He also apologized to the victims' families. Reactions to the report across Chile varied considerably. Victims' relatives perceived it as progress, although they criticized the moral equivalence of crimes committed by the State and by non-State actors.[27] They also faulted the report for failing to provide a list of perpetrator names, as Argentina's CONADEP did.[28] The armed forces rejected the report and accused the Commission of bias. They denied the historical and legal validity of the report and stated that they had no reason to apologize (CODEPU 2001). Pinochet declared on behalf of the Chilean Army that he would not accept "to be placed before the citizens in the dock of the accused"."[29] Meanwhile, the Chilean Supreme Court alleged that the report jeopardized judicial autonomy. In a letter dated May 13, 1991, the signatories concluded that the Commission went too far in identifying judges as the authors of such crimes,[30] and rejected calls to reopen dismissed cases. The Court also characterized itself as a victim of the dictatorship, saying that the State's Institutional Acts had restricted their freedom of action.

In its report on human rights in Chile in the 1990s, the Corporation for the Promotion and Defense of the People's Rights (*Corporación de Promoción y Defensa de los Derechos del Pueblo* – CODEPU) (2001, 5) highlighted the achievements and limitations of the Rettig Commission. In particular, it concluded that "[e]fforts to clarify violations committed during the dictatorship are extremely important if we consider that the Chilean transition has had to adapt to limitations imposed by the military regime." Among such limitations highlighted, it pointed out that only individuals *killed* were recognized, and not

25 This differentiates it from the later National Commission on Political Imprisonment and Torture.

26 "*Mensaje a la Nación del Presidente Patricio Aylwin al dar a conocer el informe de la Comisión de Verdad y Reconciliación*" (Message to the Nation from President Patricio Aylwin upon presentation of the report drafted by the Truth and Reconciliation Commission), March 4, 1991 (CNRR 1996a, 1310–1316).

27 Interview with Alicia Lira, Santiago de Chile, September 14, 2016.

28 The list was not included in the *Nunca Más* report but became public after it was released by the media.

29 Archival content from the television program "*Secretos del Informe Rettig*" (Secrets of the Rettig Report), *Ahora Noticias*, Mega, broadcast on March 3, 2016.

30 Published by *El Mercurio* on May 16, 1991. Available at: https://www.cepchile.cl/cep/site/artic/20160303/asocfile/20160303183805/rev42_documento.pdf.

victims who survived the likes of illegal detention, torture, and exile. Criticism also centered on the short time-frame provided to the Commission to complete its task, compared with the extensive period it had to investigate. In addition, CODEPU mentioned that the Rettig Commission did not have authority to force people to testify, which led to a lack of cooperation from members of the armed forces and police force. Finally, CODEPU criticized the fact that, at an apparently favorable time to do so, the recommendations did not include overturning the Amnesty Law. These issues drove the creation of the Valech Commission, among other factors. Before progressing to it, though, we first examine the implementation of the Rettig Commission's recommendations.

4. THE RETTIG COMMISSION'S RECOMMENDATIONS AND THEIR IMPLEMENTATION

4.1. GENERAL FEATURES AND FORMULATION

The decree establishing the Rettig Commission charged it with drafting of reparations recommendations and measures to avoid recurrence. According to Zalaquett, Aylwin asked him, together with Minister of Justice Francisco Cumplido,[31] to collaborate on drafting the decree. As director of Amnesty International, Zalaquett possessed ample experience on international law and human rights and was optimistic about truth commissions that were then being set up around the world.[32] The closest experience was CONADEP in Argentina, and its report *Nunca Más* (Never Again). The idea also was based on the recommendations of the United Nations (UN) Special Rapporteur for Chile and the Commission on Human Rights of the UN Economic and Social Council.[33]

In order to draft its recommendations, the Rettig Commission felt it needed to consult victims as well as domestic and international human rights organizations. It surveyed 109 victims' organizations, human rights groups, universities and academic centers, political parties, and religious entities, and received more than 70 responses (Lira and Loveman 2005). Input from the *Vicaría de la Solidaridad* (Vicariate of Solidarity) stands out.[34] In an October 1990 note from Executive Secretary Alejandro González Poblete, the Vicariate

---

31 Interview with José Zalaquett on television program "*Secretos del Informe Rettig*" (Secrets of the Rettig Report), *Ahora Noticias*, Mega, broadcast on March 3, 2016.

32 Interview with Jorge Correa Sutil on television program "*Secretos del Informe Rettig*" (Secrets of the Rettig Report), *Ahora Noticias*, Mega, broadcast on March 3, 2016.

33 For example, reports E/CN.4/1987/55 y E/CN.4/1990/5 available at: http://dag.un.org/bitstream/handle/11176/187719/E_CN.4_1987_55-ES.pdf?sequence=6&isAllowed=y and http://www.archivomuseodelamemoria.cl/uploads/5/7/57669/E_CN.4_1990_5.pdf.

34 For information on the *Vicaría de la Solidaridad*, see: http://www.vicariadelasolidaridad.cl/vicaria_solidaridad.php.

provided ideas regarding reparations and prevention, some of which were already circulating among human rights organizations. It stated that "[t]he first and greatest reparation gesture is the State's acknowledgment of the reality of human rights violations and its responsibility regarding these" (Lira and Loveman 2005, 129). It further suggested establishing a special legal statement of death procedure for the disappeared detainees. As far as financial reparations were concerned, it recommended granting permanent benefits, such as appropriate lifelong pensions, instead of one-time indemnifications.[35] It also suggested a financial allowance to enable victims' children to access higher education and the creation of a special, free health program for victims' families (Lira and Loveman 2005: 130). These proposals were received by the Rettig Commission and appear in their final report. Consultation with human rights organizations and other social organisms and their input undoubtedly contributed to the formulation of other recommendations as well.

4.2. IDENTIFICATION OF THE RECOMMENDATION: METHODOLOGY

The Rettig report presents an extensive body of recommendations. They are not numbered, and the report alternates prescriptive language with examples and grounds for the recommendations. Due to the features of the text corpus, an initial challenge for the present project was to determine where each recommendation began and ended, in addition to separating sub-recommendations from separate recommendations. In total, we identified 48 recommendations, subdivided into a total of 110 sub-recommendations.

In terms of their content, the Rettig Commission's recommendations can be broadly grouped, as entrusted by Decree 355, into two large sections: "reparation recommendations" and "recommendations for the prevention of future human rights violations (non-recurrence)".

With regards to the first group, the Rettig Commission interpreted the term reparation "as a combination of actions expressing the State's recognition and acknowledgment of its responsibility in connection to the facts and circumstances set forth in this report" (CNRR 1996a, 1253). According to García-Godos (2016, 3), in international law, reparations refer to any type of compensation measure implemented for the purpose of addressing the human rights violations suffered by victims. The Rettig Commission's recommendations include individual and collective symbolic reparations as well as individual material reparations

[35] The Vicariate suggested that an appropriate pension would be the average monthly income of a family above the poverty line in the City of Santiago, which was calculated in August 1990 as 530 US dollars (Lira and Loveman 2005, 130).

(compensation and rehabilitation). The second group of recommendations includes measures intended to avoid recurrence, including legal and institutional reforms to strengthen the rule of law and protect human rights; the creation of other transitional justice mechanisms; establishment of the truth; and judicial or administrative penalties. It further held that "reconciliation" was the best way to guarantee non-recurrence.

Given the passage of time, we faced many obstacles in our attempts to interview Commission members (death, scheduling or contact setbacks, governmental duties). This led us to deepen our research into secondary sources, such as previous interviews given by commissioners, both to the news media and for other academic works. We also interviewed other relevant actors. Below, we present the formulated recommendations divided into two thematic groups.

4.3. IMPLEMENTATION OF THE RETTIG RECOMMENDATIONS

4.3.1. Group I: Recommendations for Victim Reparation and Vindication

This first group of recommendations is included in Volume I, Tome II, Part 4, Chapter 1,[36] which is lengthy because recommendations often are accompanied by detailed descriptions.

4.3.1.1. Symbolic Measures

1) Public reparation of the dignity of victims

The Rettig Commission's first recommendation was that "the authorities see fit to provide the measures and resources necessary to implement cultural projects for the purpose of vindicating the memory of the victims both individually and collectively" (CNVR 1996a, 1254). The proposals of human rights organizations and other institutions consulted by the Rettig Commission influenced the formulation of this recommendation (Lira and Loveman 2005). The establishment of the Commission itself can be understood as a first act of reparation. Since then, the Memorial for Disappeared Detainees and Individuals Executed for Political Reasons was built in 1994 at the general cemetery and is a milestone in a series of memorial sites and monuments created for the victims. Two actions were critical in fulfilling this recommendation. First, Decree 1005 of 1997, enacted by President Eduardo Frei, created the Ministry of the Interior's Human Rights Program, the framework of a continuity plan for the law creating the

[36] CNRR 1996a, 1253–1267.

National Corporation for Reparation and Reconciliation (*Corporación Nacional de Reparación y Reconciliación* – CNRR).[37] An area of symbolic reparation dedicated to memorials was included in the Program.[38] Second, Article 8 of Law 19980 of 2004, enacted during the government of Ricardo Lagos, provides that "the Ministry of the Interior's budget shall reflect the resources it must allocate to finance any agreements entered with organizations, entities and companies, all non-profit, for the creation and maintenance of memorials and historical sites remembering the victims."

2) Solemn re-establishment of victims' reputation

Connected to the prior recommendation, the Rettig Commission proposed that "the State (...) solemnly and expressly re-establish the victims' dignity inasmuch as they were accused of crimes that were never proven and against which they never had adequate means to defend themselves" (CNRR 1996a, 1256).

The first identifiable event implementing this recommendation was Aylwin's March 4, 1991 address on the Rettig Report. In it, he stated:

> Embracing the report's suggestions, I hereby publicly and solemnly vindicate the personal dignity of victims denigrated by the accusation of crimes that were never proven and against which they never had an adequate opportunity or means to defend themselves.

In publicly apologizing to victims and their families on national TV, the former president, on behalf of the State, fulfilled this recommendation.

4.3.1.2. Legal and Administrative Recommendations

3) Special death certification for disappeared detainees

As it worked, the Rettig Commission established the existence of legal and administrative issues affecting victims' family members. Specifically, the lack of a death certificate prevented them from obtaining death benefits, remarrying, and the like. Thus, the Rettig Commission proposed a special legal statement of death procedure for cases of proven detainment and disappearance by State agents.[39] Initially, it was not implemented because, during Congressional debate, the

---

37 As noted below, the CNRR was created by Law 19123 to continue the Rettig Commission's work.

38 Source: *Observatorio de Justicia Transicional Diego Portales* (Diego Portales Transitional Justice Observatory) (2016). See the Ministry of the Interior's Human Rights Program website: "La política de construcción de memoriales del Programa de Derechos Humanos encuentra su base en el mandato de la Comisión Nacional de Verdad y Reconciliación, y de la Corporación Nacional de Reparación y Reconciliación, la cual ha ido perfeccionándose a partir de 2001" (available at: http://www.aerchipro.com/paginas/?pag=129). For more information, see: http://pdh.minjusticia.gob.cl/area-proyectos-memoriales-y-gestion-institucional/.

39 This was among the reparations suggested by the Vicariate of Solidarity.

Group of Family Members of Disappeared Detainees (*Agrupación de Familiares de Detenidos Desaparecidos* – AFDD) objected to the proposal. They demanded to know what had happened to their relatives and to find the location of their remains, claiming that simply acknowledging their death was insufficient (Camacho 2008, 73; Lira and Loveman 2005, 134). Many years later, this issue re-emerged. In 2009, Congress enacted Law 20377, which allows for the statement of absence due to forced disappearance of an individual, and authorizes family members of disappeared persons to use this to process personal and family law matters (Observatorio de Justicia Transicional Diego Portales 2016).

4.3.1.3. Recommendations Connected to Social Welfare

4) Individual pensions for family members

The Rettig Commission proposed the creation of

> a sole pension for the reparation of direct family members of the victims and the deceased, which only requires the person's name to be included in this Report; that is, without necessarily requiring his or her family members to accept the statement of presumed death procedure, for cases of disappeared detainees (CNRR 1996a, 1259).

This recommendation was also among those suggested by human rights organizations consulted by the Commission, including the *Comisión Chilena de Derechos Humanos* (Chilean Commission on Human Rights), the legal department of the *Vicaría de la Solidaridad* of the Archdiocese of Santiago, the *Agrupación de Familiares de Detenidos Desaparecidos* (Group of Family Members of Disappeared Detainees), the *Instituto Latinoamericano de Salud Mental y Derechos Humanos* (Latin American Institute of Mental Health and Human Rights) (ILAS), the *Agrupación de Familiares de Ejecutados Políticos* (Group of Family Members of Persons Executed for Political Reasons), and the *Comité de Defensa de los Derechos del Pueblo* (CODEPU) (Lira and Loveman 2005, 132–134).[40] The intervention of these organizations undoubtedly facilitated implementation of this recommendation. In March 1991, Aylwin presented a bill to Congress to create such a pension. Ultimately, Law 19123, establishing a monthly reparation pension for the benefit of victims acknowledged by the Rettig Report was approved in January 1992. The law specified that beneficiaries would be

> the surviving spouse; mother, or father of the victim if the mother is absent, waives the benefit or is deceased; the mother of any out-of-wedlock children of the victim,

40 *Comité de Defensa de los Derechos del Pueblo* (Defense Committee for People's Rights) was the first name of the Corporación de Promoción y Defensa de los Derechos del Pueblo (Corporation for the Promotion and Defense of the People's Rights, CODEPU), in the year 1980. Lira and Loveman used the former name of the organization.

or the father of such children when the victim is the mother, and any children of the victim under 25 years of age or disabled children of any age.

Critics of the plan objected to its exclusion of special cases (for example, cases of large families) and the amount of the pension (Lira and Loveman 2005).

5) Special health care program

The Rettig Commission also recommended providing specialized health care services for persons and families victimized by gross human rights violations. In addition, it recommended "including in these programs persons who have been victims of serious physical and psychological torture, as well as those who suffered severe injuries as a result of terrorist acts committed by individuals under political pretexts" (CNRR 1996a, 1262). That is, in addition to relatives of victims recognized by the Rettig Report, it recommended providing reparation for ex-political prisoners who had been victims of torture, an issue later considered by the CNPPT. This recommendation also had been suggested by the Solidarity Vicariate (Lira and Loveman 2005, 129–130).

Aforementioned Law 19123 included this measure. Article 28 provided free medical services to beneficiaries of the monthly pension and other family members (such as parents or siblings). Another important step was the creation of the Comprehensive Reparation and Health Care Program (*Programa de Reparación y Atención Integral de Salud* – PRAIS) for victims of human rights violations. Created in 1991, the program was based on the mental health work performed by the Coordinator of Mental Health Teams, which participated in consultations on PRAIS (Lira and Loveman 2005, 377). In December 1992, the Ministry of Health approved PRAIS by Resolution 729 (Lira and Loveman 2005, 383). In 2004, following publication of the Valech Commission's final report, Law 19980 extended the program to victims of political imprisonment and torture.

4.3.1.4. Recommendations on Education

6) Educational reparations: scholarships, debt waivers, and free admission into educational institutions

The Rettig Commission recommended implementing measures for the benefit of victims' children as promptly as possible, entrusting the Ministry of Education to formulate a reparation program with participation of the affected parties, human rights organizations, professional associations, and the education sector (CNRR 1996a, 1264). We identified the following sub-recommendations:

- allot a portion of higher education scholarships to victims' children.

- study the possibility of waiving tax or college debts for victims' children, spouses, or other direct family members.
- allow youth and adults who were unable to complete their studies and who do not have an established trade or profession to enroll in technical and work training centers free of charge.
- promote the same in regard to surviving spouses, domestic partners or other direct family members.

Implementation of this recommendation was partially reflected in Law 19123. However, it failed to address all of the sub-recommendations. This law only provides educational benefits to victims' children under 35 years old in the form of scholarships to cover the cost of registration and monthly school fees. It included as beneficiaries any children completing high school studies by granting them the right to receive a monthly subsidy. This reparation measure was among the most mentioned by the key interviewees during our fieldwork.

4.3.1.5. Recommendations on Housing

7) Special consideration for victims' direct family members who applied to social programs or vacancies within special housing programs

The Rettig Commission recommended that the Ministry of Housing and Urban Development grant special consideration to the victims' direct family members who applied to social programs to acquire housing, and to study the possibility of providing vacancies within special housing programs for victims' direct family members who wished to apply and who fulfilled other requirements. We were unable to draw firm conclusions on implementation. A 2004 decree granted housing access benefits to victims of political imprisonment and torture and their family members but did not mention the relatives of victims of execution or disappearance.[41] The target and timing of this measure suggest it was more the result of the Valech Commission than of Rettig.

4.3.1.6. Other Recommendations Connected to Social Welfare

8) Waiver of debts for victims acknowledged by the Commission's Report

The Rettig Commission recommended studying the possibility of waiving unexpired social security, educational, housing, fiscal and other debts with State agencies for deceased and disappeared detainees mentioned in its report. We have not identified any implementation activity for this recommendation.

41 See "Cartilla informativa. Beneficios establecidos por ley a las víctimas y familiares de violaciones ocurridas durante la dictadura", p. 6. Available at: https://www.indh.cl/bb/wp-content/uploads/2017/01/beneficios.pdf.

9) For the children of the victims to be allowed to refuse mandatory military service

The Rettig Commission recommended considering allowing the children of victims of human rights violations to refuse to join the Military Service, without this being used as a discriminatory factor in their work or studies. This recommendation was implemented by Law 19123 of 1992 (Article 32).

10) Priority attention to certain groups due to their vulnerability and social significance: seniors, children and mapuche families

As its last recommendation regarding reparations, the Commission encouraged the State to make a special effort to support vulnerable groups such as seniors, children and Mapuche families (CNRR 1996a, 1266). In terms of the Mapuche community, Lira and Loveman (1998, 19) point out that the

> reparation measures … [applied otherwise in Chile] were designed for non-Mapuche individuals, without considering the Mapuche grieving process nor the types of solidarity characteristic of these communities. In many cases, these measures had a negative impact on the family and community networks and the symbolic purpose of reparation within the culture was overlooked. This dimension has been fairly absent in Chilean society, especially the symbolic purposes expressed through collective acts, justice, and gestures and commemorations.

Beyond the other measures already noted, we have not identified implementation events in connection to the prioritization of specific vulnerable groups.

4.3.2. Group II: Recommendations for Non-Recurrence

This group of recommendations possesses a high degree of technical and legal detail and is included in Volume I, Tome II, Chapter 2 (pp. 1268–1298) of the report, taking up double the space of reparation recommendations. The development of international human rights law was highly influential in the formulation of these recommendations, which indicates the influence of the attorneys who made up a majority of the Commission. In the introduction to this chapter, the Commission states that the human rights violations and the social tolerance towards them demonstrate the absence in Chile of "a national and sufficiently firm awareness regarding the imperative duty to respect human rights." It goes on to say that, without this awareness, a country produces legislation which is ineffective to protect these rights, as the Chilean legal system's past failures suggest. It pointed out three features of the legal system that enabled past human rights violations. First, the Military Justice Code violated due process. Second, the State Security Law imprecisely defined crimes, thereby enabling arbitrary and politicized application. Finally, the 1925 Constitution's provisions on states of emergency gave the Executive Branch expansive authority without adequate checks by the other branches.

Reforms proposed by the Rettig Commission within the institutional and regulatory fields are designed to promote the rule of law and human rights in Chile. According to the Commission (1996a: 1269), "adequate respect for human rights requires the existence of certain legal conditions which our current system does not satisfactorily fulfil" in regard to:

(i) Concordance between the national legal code and international human rights law.
(ii) A judiciary that effectively fulfils its role as protector of the essential rights of persons.
(iii) Armed forces and law enforcement agencies committed to execute their duties in full compliance with their duty to respect human rights.
(iv) Creation of an institution entrusted with the promotion and protection of human rights.
(v) Modification of regulatory codes at the constitutional, penal and procedural matters for the purpose of improving the protection of human rights.

Based on these five categories, they formulated "a series of suggestions tending to achieve total fulfilment of those conditions" (CNRR 1996a, 1270). In regard to implementation, progress was much slower on these measures, which often makes it difficult to disentangle whether the Rettig Report or the later Valech Report was more influential.

4.3.2.1. Institutional and Regulatory Recommendations to Promote Human Rights

1) Synchronization of the national legal code with international human rights laws

These recommendations refer to the ratification of international human rights treaties, the improvement of national regulations to make them compatible with international law, and the establishment of efficient mechanisms for the defense, promotion and dissemination of human rights in Chile. Some progress actually pre-dates the Rettig Report. In August 1990, the Chilean government ratified the American Convention on Human Rights and recognized the jurisdiction of the Inter-American Commission on Human Rights. At this time, Chile withdrew its prior reservations to the Convention with regard to torture, in accordance with one of the sub-recommendations later published in the Rettig report. Furthermore, the ratification of the First Optional Protocol to the International Covenant on Civil and Political Rights, accepting the individual complaint procedure, was accomplished in May 1992. Finally, the position of Human Rights Advisor was created within the Ministry of Foreign Relations to coordinate bringing national legislation into alignment with international treaties (Lira and Loveman 1998, 8).

2) To strengthen the ability of the judiciary to effectively fulfil its role as protector of the essential rights of persons

The recommendations encourage the adoption of measures to insure the independence and impartiality of the judiciary. Several legislative measures were implemented in the 1990s to accomplish this goal (CNRR 1996a, 1316). For example, Law 19390 of May 1995 modified the Organic Code of the Courts in matters related to the designation, hierarchy and qualification of judges, judicial officers, and administrative employees of the justice system. Law 19541 of 1997, enacted during Frei's administration, ordered a constitutional reform regarding the Judicial Branch. The initiative was prompted by a desire to optimize its efficiency and modernize the procedural code, which is in alignment with regional trends (CEJA 2003). It also allowed the gradual removal of judges aligned with Pinochet's policies (Collins 2003, 19).

The recommendation to reform military jurisdiction to ensure the constitutional guarantee of trial by an independent court also was implemented. Law 20477, enacted in November 2010, established that "[u]nder no circumstances shall civilians and minors be subject to the jurisdiction of military courts. Jurisdiction for these individuals shall be held always by the ordinary criminal courts". The fact that this recommendation was implemented two decades after the Rettig Commission makes it difficult to assert a direct link to its report. According to Anita Ferrara (2017, 17), the reform took so long because many politicians did not wish to challenge military prerogatives and the military's allies in the Senate in the years after the transition.

Ferrara also highlights the importance of perfecting writs of *habeas corpus* in order to turn them into truly effective mechanisms for safeguarding human rights. The Rettig Commission suggested constitutional and legal modifications to extend the protected rights and establish other measures to guard such rights. In addition, it recommended the repeal of Article 41, paragraph 3, first and second part, of the Constitution, which impeded filing writs during states of emergency (states of siege – in the case of internal war or grave internal disturbance – and of assembly – in the case of external war). Specifically, the Rettig Commission proposed making it mandatory for participating judges to visit persons deprived of freedom to verify whether legal requirements are fulfilled. Also that officials preventing visits to detainees should be penalized. Such recommendations were implemented through the 2005 constitutional reform and by Law 20050, which modified the title on states of emergency and guaranteed the ability to turn to judicial authorities in connection to specific measures affecting constitutional rights by filing the relevant appeals. Regarding the writ of protection, Law 19696 of 2000 modified criminal procedure, although the reform did not exactly include the recommendation.

Finally, the Rettig Commission recommended reform of judicial proceedings in order to guarantee the enjoyment and respect of human rights. Law 19374 of 1995 modified the Organic Code of Tribunals, the code of civil and criminal procedure, the organization and operation of the Supreme Court, the writ of *certiorari* and writ of *cassation*. Other measures include Law 19519 of 1997, creating the Attorney General's Office, Law 19696 of 2000, which established a new criminal procedural code, and Law 19718 of 2001, which created the Office of the Public Defender. However, none of these laws mentioned Rettig's recommendations in their formulation.

3) Ensuring the armed forces and law enforcement authorities are committed to executing their functions in a way fully compliant with the duty to respect human rights

This recommendation addresses the inclusion of human rights and international humanitarian law-related content in academic curricula of the armed and security forces. According to interviewees, Pinochet and his allies effectively blocked such action in the 1990s. Constitutional reforms in 2005 made some progress by separating National Defense and Internal Security. Following the reform of Article 90 of the Political Constitution, the Carabineers and Investigations Police were transferred from the jurisdiction of the Ministry of National Defense to the Ministry of the Interior and Public Safety. We were unable to identify direct links between the recommendation and this reform or find evidence of the implementation of any other measures with respect to this recommendation.

4) Creation of an institution entrusted with the protection of human rights

The Rettig Commission recommended studying the establishment of an institution, such as a Public Defender or Ombudsman, to protect people from abuses of power. The demand to create the position of Ombudsman actually pre-dates Pinochet's departure from the presidency.[42] Although numerous proposals for the creation of an independent institution to protect human rights have been presented over the years, none has been created.

5) Specific modifications to constitutional, penal, and procedural codes to improve the protection of human rights

The details of the elaboration of recommendations pertaining to constitutional, criminal, and procedural law are similar to the work of a Commission drafting a bill. Regarding the recommendations to create or modify regulations governing the treatment of persons deprived of their freedom within detention centers

42 The "Chilean Chapter of the Ombudsman – People's Defender" (*Capítulo Chileno del Ombudsman – Defensor del Pueblo*), an organization which defines itself as "pluralistic and independent, not for profit and autonomous from authorities" was founded in 1985 to promote the creation of this institution. See https://www.ombudsman.cl/.

or prisons, Law 19567 of 1998 modified criminal procedure and the criminal code concerning detention by regulating the protection of citizens' rights. The grounds for the bill do not specifically mention the Rettig Commission's recommendation.

In addition, the Rettig Commission proposed increasing the criminal penalty in the event that public officials commit acts of coercion or torture. Currently, coercion is defined as an offense and not a crime. Meanwhile, the crime of torture was newly defined in domestic law in 2016, based on international standards, thus increasing the penalty and eliminating any statute of limitations. Although the systematic violation of human rights during the dictatorship was considered in the parliamentary motion, it contains no explicit mention of the Rettig Commission's recommendation.

Other recommendations to modify the judicial system that stand out are the establishment of a law defining forced disappearance as a crime against humanity and assigning liability to the detaining agent when s/he fails to indicate the location of the victim; the suspension of statutes of limitation when factual circumstances prevent pertinent legal actions; and preventing the application of amnesty for any crimes without prior investigation of the facts (CNRR 1996a, 1289). The only evidence of action was Law 20357 of 2009, which provides legal definitions of crimes against humanity, genocide, war crimes, and forced disappearance. The enactment of the law, however, does not mention the Rettig Commission's recommendation.

4.3.2.2. Recommendations to Promote a Culture of Respect for Human Rights

(i) Creation of a cultural environment that is adequate for the respect of human rights.
(ii) Recommendation that the institution whose creation is suggested in the chapter "Other recommendations" of this report assumes the role of formulating proposals to consolidate a solid human rights culture.
(iii) Conceptual suggestions which could serve as a reference framework for the teaching of human rights.
(iv) Specific suggestions to illuminate the field of education regarding human rights.
(v) Recommendations to address the need to provide spaces for discussion and the adoption of symbolic prevention measures.
(vi) Inclusion of terrorist acts as a human rights violation.

This section is the most general, and generally addresses society as a whole (CNRR 1996a, 1291). It recommends that an entity be charged with proposing the adoption of policies contributing to a culture of respect for human rights, as well as teaching a human rights curriculum. The provision of spaces for discussion and the adoption of preventive measures of a symbolic nature are also suggested (CNRR 1996a, 1296). Finally, under the "even score policy" (política de empate), it urges the inclusion of terrorist acts within the concept of human rights violations.

Verifying implementation of these recommendations is complex due to the absence of explicit links to the Rettig Commission. One of the most important measures to fulfil these recommendations is the creation of the National Corporation for Reconciliation and Reparation (*Corporación Nacional de Reconciliación y Reparación* – CNRR). The CNRR was created by Law 19123 in February 1992, and, among its responsibilities detailed below, it was in charge of "formulating proposals for the consolidation of a culture of respect for human rights within the country" (Article 2, paragraph 6). According to the CNRR's 1996 activity report to the President, the Corporation developed an educational and cultural program and a study and legal investigation program, including several publications.[43]

4.3.2.3. Truth, Justice, and Reconciliation as Preventive Measures

(i) A culture that respects human rights can only be developed in an environment of healthy national coexistence.
(ii) Truth
(iii) Justice
(iv) Reconciliation
(v) Inclusion of terrorist acts in the human rights violation concept

The formulation of this point makes it difficult to determine whether it is a recommendation or a statement of opinion. The fact that it is considered a "preventive measure" leads us to assume it is a recommendation.

At this stage of the report the Commission stated that "this drives us to point out as a preventive measure, the need to achieve fulfilment of basic requirements for national reconciliation, that is, the attainment of Truth and Justice" (CNRR 1996a, 1297). In terms of the truth, the Rettig Commission considers that the information collected in the report serves to achieve the purpose of prevention. In terms of justice, it holds that there are two opposed opinions regarding the

---

43 In 1994, the CNRR published "Diálogo y juventud: instrumento para una cultura de derechos humanos" (Dialogue and Youth: an Instrument for a Culture of Human Rights); "Manual de capacitación para educadores: la incorporación de los derechos humanos al aula" (Educator Training Manual: Incorporating Human Rights in the Classroom); "Para recrear la cultura escolar: experiencias y proyecciones desde los derechos humanos" (Recreating School Culture: Human Rights Experiences and Projection) and "Protección penal de los derechos constitucionales" (Penal Protection of Constitutional Rights). See the catalog of the National Library of Chile at: http://descubre.bibliotecanacional.cl/primo_library/libweb/action/search.do?&vid=BNC.

issue: one that considers it a reparative and preventive measure, and the other that considers it inadvisable because it could foment conflict. The Commission decided in favor of the first opinion (CNRR 1996a, 1298), although it recognized the practical difficulties of the decision: cases barred by statutes of limitations, suspects that benefited by amnesty, lack of investigation by the judiciary, the jurisprudence of the Supreme Court, the rulings of military courts, to name but a few obstacles. Finally, it states that truth and justice constitute the pillars required to build a reconciled society, and that they demand the conciliation of different social sectors (CNRR 1996a, 1298).

During President Aylwin's administration, several measures were taken in connection with this recommendation, especially regarding the Amnesty Law.[44] Regardless of the drive of the Executive Branch, the prosecution of accused individuals was hindered by the Amnesty Law. Pinochet remained powerful and continued as Commander in Chief of Armed Forces after the transition, holding the position that his subordinates had done nothing to be ashamed of and that no government institution had information regarding the final destination of disappeared persons (Collins 2013, 90). While reforms to the Judicial Branch only occurred in the mid-1990s, human rights organizations continued to file criminal complaints. These factors, together with other political events, finally resulted in the initial processing of the demands for justice from 1998 onwards.[45]

4.3.2.4. Other Recommendations

Creation of a Public Law Foundation

- *(i) Collaboration in the search for victims.*
- *(ii) Collection of background information and descriptions of the victims.*
- *(iii) Centralization of information compiled by the Commission.*
- *(iv) Assistance to family members.*
- *(v) Drafting of educational proposals.*
- *(vi) Punishment for concealing information regarding illegal interment and jurisdiction over these investigations.*

The Rettig Commission recommended the creation of a public law foundation for the purpose of continuing the Commission's work, which would cooperate in the search for victims; continue the investigation of cases in which the Commission failed to reach a definitive conclusion; centralize the Commission's information; provide assistance to victims' family members in accessing reparations; and draft educational proposals. These measures were achieved

44 Attachment II of (CNRR 1996a, 1315).

45 For further information on the multiple factors driving the justice process, see Collins (2013).

through Law 19123 of 1992, which created the CNRR. It was legally established for two years.

The internal regulations of the CNRR established a term of 90 days for interested parties to present new information, after which the Corporation had one year to respond. Law 19209 of 1993 granted a new term for the Corporation to receive information on new cases. It examined 2,188 cases: 899 qualified as victims. Of these, 644 were assassinated and disappeared victims of human rights violations and 255 were victims of "political violence" (CNRR 1996b). The term was subsequently extended through 1996 (extensions enacted by Decree 1359 of 1993, Law 19274 of 1993, Law 19358 of 1994, and Law 19441 of 1996). Once the CNRR closed, Decree 1005 of 1997 created the "Human Rights Program" within the Ministry of the Interior to serve the functions laid out in Law 19123. The Program assisted victims' family members in accessing reparations, searching for remains and establishing the circumstances of their relatives' disappearance or death.

The last recommendation formulated by the Rettig Commission with respect to the creation of a public law foundation was to penalize the concealment of information regarding illegal interment and to require notification of such facts to ordinary courts of justice. In a point greatly discussed internationally, it held that the law needed to waive liability for persons providing information. We have not identified any action toward implementing this recommendation.

4.4. PROGRESS IN REPARATIONS BUT OBSTACLES TO INSTITUTIONAL REFORMS

On balance, the Rettig Commission's recommendations have experienced a relatively high degree of implementation. This is particularly true for reparations, which were largely implemented under Law 19,123 of 1992. This law, besides creating a public entity that would continue the Commission's work, established the reparation pension, medical and educational benefits, and the possibility for victims' children to request exclusion from compulsory military service.

There were far greater difficulties in achieving progress on institutional reforms aimed at non-recurrence due to the persistence of authoritarian enclaves. It is difficult to verify implementation of this second group of recommendations. Many are general in nature, making it difficult to establish a direct link between implementation and the recommendations formulated by the Rettig Commission. In addition, progress was hampered by the tense relationship between the armed forces and the government in the 1990s. The armed forces had a great degree of political and financial autonomy at the time and, in addition, had left the matter "well tied down" by appointing loyal bureaucrats and judges (Collins 2013; Ferrara 2017). Such tensions occasionally threatened violence, such as when Pinochet ordered his men confined to barracks in 1990 and the "*Boinazo*" of May 1993.[46] Furthermore, in parliament, the armed forces resisted reforms of military institutions through the efforts of their *Unión Demócrata Independiente* (Democratic Independent Union) (UDI) and *Renovación Nacional* (National Renewal) allies. Issues connected to human rights and constitutional reforms remained pending for this reason (Lira and Loveman 1998). The issue of political prisoners remained unaddressed for similar reasons.

Nonetheless, the Rettig Commission's recommendations created the foundation for further action to deal with past abuses. As we have noted, the creation of the CNRR was instrumental in advancing much of the reform agenda contained in the Rettig report. Moreover, during the parliamentary debate over the Rettig Commission's recommendations, Representative Roberto Muñoz Barra of the Democracy Party (*Partido por la Democracia* – PPD) argued for the need to discuss an initiative related to the victims of torture and the social reintegration of political prisoners (Lira and Loveman 2005). This vision was not fully realized until 2003.

5. A NEW TRUTH COMMISSION: THE VALECH COMMISSION

5.1. THE VALECH COMMISSION'S ORIGINS

The National Commission on Political Imprisonment and Torture (*Comisión Nacional sobre Prisión Política y Tortura* – CNPPT), often known as the Valech Commission, was preceded by new attempts to reconstruct what had happened to detained-disappeared victims, as well as assassinated persons whose remains had not been returned to their relatives and who had been excluded from the Rettig Commission's investigation. The purpose of the so-called *Mesa de Diálogo* (roundtable), which operated between August 1999 and June 2000, was to reconcile the armed forces, the Carabineers and government representatives, human rights attorneys, academics and religious leaders in order to address the situation of disappeared detainees and to attempt to locate them. The idea was that, by protecting responsible parties from possible criminal consequences, they would be more forthcoming with data

46 *El Boinazo* took place on May 28, 1993, during Aylwin's administration, When Pinochet was requested to step down due to accusations of corruption, he ordered the Army confined to their barracks. Simultaneously, paratroopers dressed for combat and with blackened faces surrounded the Defense building. See http://www.memoriachilena.cl/602/w3-article-92406.html.

(Collins and Hau 2016). The initiative was rejected by some victim groups, political parties, and human rights attorneys.[47]

Other events created opportunities for the creation of a new truth commission. Pinochet's detention in London on October 16, 1998, in response to an international arrest order issued by Spanish Judge Baltasar Garzón for crimes against humanity, including torture, is seen as a turning point in Chile's transitional justice process. Nevertheless, Collins argues against the view that claims that Pinochet's arrest was the only factor that caused "the reopening of the question of justice in Chile and of the complex scenario of domestic penal prosecution for crimes against humanity existing in current time" (2013: 96–97).[48]

Another milestone in the path to recognition and reparation for ex-political prisoners and victims of torture was the establishment of the Ethical Commission Against Torture (*Comisión Ética contra la Tortura*). The Ethical Commission Against Torture sought the enactment of a Law for Comprehensive Reparation (legal and medical). In addition, it requested the government to create an official commission to investigate truth, justice and reparation for survivors of torture. In parallel, the Coordinating Committee of Organizations of Ex Political Prisoners of Chile and Ex-Prisoners of Dawson and Magallanes (*Coordinadora de Organizaciones de Ex Presos Políticos de Chile y ex Prisioneros de Dawson y Magallanes*) outlined comprehensive reparation proposals (Lira and Loveman 2005). While reparation policy after Rettig benefited family members of disappeared victims and of persons executed for political reasons, as well as exiles and those discharged from the public administration and State companies, ex-political prisoners and victims of torture who had survived their ordeals were not eligible. According to Lucas Sierra Iribarren, who was later a member of the Valech Commission, the feeling among human rights activists was that the achievements up to that date were insufficient.[49]

In August 2003, Ricardo Lagos presented his human rights proposals, including the Valech Commission, in a document entitled "*No hay mañana sin ayer*"

---

47 See interview with Viviana Díaz, Mesa de Diálogo member and AFDD ex-president, who described the initiative as such: "The *Mesa de Diálogo* responded precisely to Pinochet's detention, to the fact that investigations in the courts were progressing at the time and the military had started to express that they were tired of parading through the courts, under circumstances that one does not parade in court; one appears when one is accused of a crime or offense. That's when Frei filed a request and the roundtable was created. And it so happens that the roundtable, now being a year and four months old, has achieved absolutely nothing for us. That is a reality and it's not that we want to reject every proposal." Source: Latin American Information Agency, April 23, 2002 http://www.alainet.org/es/active/2032.

48 Collins points out there were "previous changes in the internal political and legal constellation in Chile", such as the impulse of new criminal investigations based on the criminal complaints presented by victims of human rights violations and the Supreme Court's ruling in regard to the duty to investigate the disappearances despite amnesty law (2013: 96–97).

49 Interview with Lucas Sierra Iribarren, September 14, 2016.

(There is no Tomorrow without a Yesterday).[50] The document outlines four primary objectives:

1. Achieve full knowledge of the fate of disappeared persons and those executed for political reasons.
2. Ensure the independence, agility, and efficiency of the courts to promote justice by driving legislative initiatives to facilitate and hasten investigations.
3. Deepen and improve reparation policies.
4. Improve the protection, promotion and guarantee of human rights by means of legislative initiatives.

Regarding the third objective, Lagos announced the creation of a commission to establish a list of persons who were deprived of their freedom and tortured for political reasons. He stated that the commission would have the same features as the Rettig Commission. In essence, the Lagos proposal sought to develop certain measures, including some of the Rettig Commission recommendations that had not yet been implemented.[51] The proposal also anticipated many of the recommendations later formulated by the Valech Commission.

5.2. MANDATE AND COMPOSITION

The Valech Commission was created on September 26, 2003, by Supreme Decree 1040 as a presidential advisory body for the purpose of determining the identity of victims deprived of their freedom and subjected to torture for political reasons by State agents between September 11, 1973, and March 10, 1990. It was entrusted with proposing to the President reparative measures to be granted to recognized persons. The Valech Commission was forbidden from determining legal responsibility regarding discovered facts. The President selected seven commissioners, most of whom were attorneys (see Table 2). According to Lucas Sierra, those with the most experience on the subject were María Luisa Sepúlveda, Álvaro Varela, Elizabeth Lira, and Luciano Fouilloux. According to Álvaro Varela, the pluralistic composition of the Commission served to generate discussions without hindering consensus.

50 Interview with Lucas Sierra Iribarren, September 14, 2016.

51 The proposed measures that coincided with the Rettig Commission recommendations that had not been implemented were the proposal to grant immunity to those providing information regarding the location of victims or the circumstances leading to their disappearance or death; the filing of a bill to resolve the state of legal limbo of disappeared detainees; the reform of the Military Code of Justice to reduce the jurisdiction of military courts, such as preventing them from prosecuting civilians and prosecuting common crimes committed by members of the armed forces.

Table 2. Members of the National Commission on Political Imprisonment and Torture

Commissioner	Background
Sergio Valech Aldunate (President)	**Monsignor**, human rights advocate, member of the *Vicaría de la Solidaridad*.[52]
Miguel Luis Amunátegui Monckeberg	**Attorney** and academic, constituent member of the National Renewal party (partido Renovación Nacional).[53]
Luciano Fouillioux Fernández	**Attorney**, ex executive secretary of the Ministry of Interior's Human Rights Program. Participated in the *Mesa de Diálogo*.[54]
José Antonio Gómez Urrutia	**Attorney**, militant in the Chilean Social Democratic Radical Party.[55]
Elizabeth Lira Kornfeld	**Psychologist** recognized for work treating victims of repression during the military dictatorship. Member of the Christian Church Social Assistance Foundation (*Fundación de Ayuda Social de las Iglesias Cristianas* – FASIC). Participated in the *Mesa de Diálogo*.[56]
María Luisa Sepúlveda Edwards (Executive Vice President)	**Social worker**, member of the Pro Peace Committee (*Comité de Cooperación para la Paz – Comité Pro Paz*) and *Vicaría de la Solidaridad* (Vicariate of Solidarity). Advised Ricardo Lagos regarding the outcome of the *Mesa de Diálogo*.[57]
Lucas Sierra Iribarren	**Attorney** and academic. Constitutional Law and political institution specialist.[58]
Álvaro Varela Walker	**Attorney**, human rights advocate. Served on the *Comité de Cooperación para la Paz* in Chile and member of the *Vicaría de la Solidaridad*.[59]

Source: Compiled by the authors.

The Valech Commission was granted six months to work, extendable for another three. It was to present a report upon the conclusion of this term. In its investigation, the Commission was empowered to obtain information from human rights organizations. The commissioners received testimony about repression and consulted with victims regarding what reparation measures they deemed appropriate. Further, the Commission could request collaboration from State agencies, which were required to provide requested information and to provide access to any sites the commissioners wished to visit. The military alleged that they did not have any information, even when victims could document that they had been detained.[60]

52 http://defensoresydefensoras.indh.cl/defensores-as-en-la-historia/dictadura/sergio-valech/.

53 https://www.indh.cl/consejo/miguel-luis-amunategui-monckeberg/ and https://archivojaimeguzman.cl/uploads/r/archivo-jaime-guzman-e-3/7/2/5/725ddfbf61578be523ab77d9df239d638279edfbfe5d33fee897a663330b3e73/REN.87.03.18.pdf.

54 https://cl.linkedin.com/in/luciano-fouillioux-21472764.

55 http://www.defensa.cl/biografia-ministro-gomez-urrutia/.

56 http://derecho.uahurtado.cl/academicos/elizabeth-lira-kornfeld/.

57 http://www.indh.cl/resena-institucional/consejo-indh/maria-luisa-sepulveda-edwards.

58 https://www.cepchile.cl/lucas-sierra-i/cep/2016-03-23/122003.html.

59 Personal interview September 12, 2016 (Santiago, Chile) and http://www.freedomcollection.org/interviews/alvaro_varela_walker/.

60 Interview with María Luisa Sepúlveda. Coincidentally, Álvaro Varela thought the armed forces believed they had cooperated because they responded to official notices, but the truth

Although it did not have a set budget, the Valech Commission had the necessary resources to create a news media and television publicity campaign, as well as to hire a large staff through the Ministry of the Interior.[61] As for expectations regarding the Commission's work, Margarita Romero, physician, ex-political prisoner, and human rights advocate, summed up the views of many activists in saying, "[w]hen the Valech Commission was created, there was a certain level of mistrust towards the State so, in the beginning, many victims did not wish to participate in this process."[62] Nonetheless, human rights organizations mobilized their own initiatives to get victims to testify before the Commission to maximize its impact.

5.3. THE VALECH REPORT AND ITS RECEPTION

In its final report, the Valech Commission listed 27,255 victims of political imprisonment and torture, identified 1,132 detention centers, and formulated recommendations with regard to reparations, as had been ordered by the presidential decree. Due to its drafting style, the Valech Report was much more accessible than the Rettig Report. The report described the context of political imprisonment and torture in Chile. For each period, it indicated the number of detentions and the authority in charge. It described torture methods and sexual violence against women. The victims were profiled, and the consequences of imprisonment and torture were detailed. In fulfilment of its mandate, the Commission included its reparation proposals in Chapter 9 of the report.

Public interest was high. Commissioner Varela reported that,

> Our office was one block away from the *Moneda* Palace and, on [November 10, 2004, the day the Report was delivered], we stepped out of the Commission's offices (...) we received an ovation on the street. People were peeking out of apartment and office buildings. It was something that really affected me, and there were a lot of people around the *Moneda* Palace, waiting for our arrival. (...) it was an expression of how what we were doing had been communicated to the people.[63]

The report was delivered to the President, who took two weeks to read it. During that period, none of the commissioners spoke publicly about the subject. In the silence, the media consulted victims to get their opinions.[64]

---

is they did not deliver a concrete and complete response. Varela added, "although I haven't the slightest doubt that they are in fact in possession of the documentation and information."

61 Interview with Álvaro Varela Walker, September 12, 2016.

62 Romero is currently advisor to the National Institute of Human Rights. For more on her background, see: http://www.indh.cl/margarita-romero-mendez and http://www.memoriaabierta.org.ar/materiales/pdf/margarita_romero.pdf.

63 Interview with Álvaro Varela Walker, September 12, 2016.

64 Interview with Elizabeth Lira, September 12, 2016.

Two weeks later, Lagos made the Valech Report's conclusions public and recognized that political imprisonment and torture constituted unacceptable institutional practices. He wondered how it had been possible to live 30 years in silence and attributed it to fear. President Lagos affirmed that, if State agents were involved and responsible, it was the State's responsibility to implement measures to mitigate the effect of so much pain. He stated that such measures needed to heal injuries and that he agreed with the reparations proposals presented by the Valech Commission. The State needed to deliver an "austere" compensation, a moderate pension in an amount that is compatible with other State obligations.[65]

The armed forces and law enforcement reaction to the report were different from their responses to the Rettig Report. The three branches of the armed forces and the country's most important law enforcement institution issued statements or communiqués acknowledging the Valech Commission's work and the results of the report, and recognizing the human rights violations during the dictatorship. The Army accepted the report's "content and conclusions".[66] The Navy went further, publicly declaring that nobody "could deny that human rights were gravely violated in Chile" by agents of the State.[67] The Carabineers' response offers a more elaborate statement of recognition and condemnation.[68] In every case, the institutions sought to distance themselves from the historical and political context of the 1973 coup, which they intended to use to explain their actions. The Army spoke about the need to remember "the rationale of the confrontation prevailing at that moment and the behavior induced in Chileans by such confrontation at the time".[69] As for the judiciary, the Supreme Court did not modify its position regarding the facts set forth in the Rettig Report. It acknowledged the gravity of the facts and expressed its consternation. However, it presented a strong corporate defense justifying the actions of the courts, by affirming that it had been unable to exercise its duty to protect rights and guarantees due to the decreed state of emergency.

---

65 The President decided to send a bill to Congress to establish a pension equivalent to a minimum and moderate pension. See the prologue to the report "Reflexiones y propuestas de S.E. el Presidente de la República, Ricardo Lagos Escobar. Para nunca más vivirlo, nunca más negarlo", published by the Centro de Estudios Públicos and available at https://www.cepchile.cl/cep/site/artic/20160304/asocfile/20160304093533/r97_informe_lagos.pdf, Press archives https://youtube.com/watch?v=I0IMYXHwTD0.

66 November 3, 2004, speech. Available at: https://www.cepchile.cl/cep/site/artic/20160304/asocfile/20160304093533/r97_cheyre_ejercito_chileno.pdf.

67 Public Statement of the Chilean Navy dated November 30, 2004. Available at https://www.cepchile.cl/cep/site/artic/20160304/asocfile/20160304093533/r97_armada.pdf.

68 See: https://www.cepchile.cl/cep/site/artic/20160304/asocfile/20160304093533/r97_carabineros.pdf.

69 Speech dated November 3, 2004. Available at: https://www.cepchile.cl/cep/site/artic/20160304/asocfile/20160304093533/r97_cheyre_ejercito_chileno.pdf. The Carabineers and Navy texts reflect a similar point. See https://www.cepchile.cl/cep/site/artic/20160304/asocfile/20160304093533/r97_carabineros.pdf and Public Statement of the Chilean Navy dated November 30, 2004. Available at: https://www.cepchile.cl/cep/site/artic/20160304/asocfile/20160304093533/r97_armada.pdf.

Recognition of human rights violations did not imply an apology or request for forgiveness to the victims by these State institutions. The Report was also criticized for failing to include the names of those responsible for the crimes described. However, ex-commissioner Luciano Fouillioux pointed out that 98 per cent of testimonies did not identify a perpetrator.

6. THE VALECH COMMISSION'S RECOMMENDATIONS AND THEIR IMPLEMENTATION

The Valech Commission consulted widely on the design of its recommendations. During their interviews, in addition to providing testimony, victims were asked about the type of reparation they would consider adequate.[70] The Valech Commission also met with experts and civil society organizations as it formulated its recommendations. According to the final report, advice was sought from experts on reparations, and the civil and criminal dimensions of reparation measures. Commissioners studied other countries' experiences with reparations,[71] as well as their incorporation of international human rights laws in the domestic legal system.[72] Furthermore, President Lagos' human rights program, the Rettig Commission's work and the reparations precedent set by Law 19123 that enacted the Rettig Commission's recommendations were all influential.

The Valech Commission's recommendations can be divided into three categories:

1. *Individual* reparation measures in the (a) legal, (b) financial, (c) health, (d) education, and (e) housing sectors.
2. *Symbolic and collective* reparation measures on a) non-recurrence guarantees and preventive measures, b) symbolic gestures of recognition and conciliation, c) acknowledgment of memory, and d) dissemination, promotion and education on human rights.
3. *Institutional* measures, specifically a) the creation of the National Institute of Human Rights (*Instituto Nacional de Derechos Humanos* – INDH), and b) protection and confidentiality of the received information.

We take up each of these recommendations below.

[70] Interview with María Luisa Sepúlveda, September 12, 2016.
[71] Interview with Lucas Sierra Iribarren, September 14, 2016.
[72] Final report from the Valech Commission, pp. 48–49.

6.1. INDIVIDUAL REPARATION MEASURES

6.1.1. Individual Reparation Measures in the Legal Sector

The first measure recommended the elimination of criminal records for cases processed by military courts during the dictatorship. This was implemented by means of Law 19962 dated August 2004 (that is, it pre-dated the issuance of the Valech Report). The legislation stipulated the elimination of criminal records for sentences imposed by military courts for events that occurred between September 11, 1973, and March 10, 1990.[73] Law 20200 of 2007 added the elimination of criminal convictions by ordinary courts.

We have not found evidence of the implementation of the sub-recommendation on the restitution of civil and political rights regarding accessory penalties imposed.[74] We also were unable to identify any progress on recommendations to review arrest orders and on supporting initiatives to recognize the nationality of children of Chilean citizens born abroad.

The last recommendation in this category was to grant the children and grandchildren of victims recognized in the Valech report the ability to opt out of mandatory military service, by applying the provisions of Law 19123. Law 19992 of 2004 implemented the recommendation by establishing that

> [t]he children of victims of human rights violations identified in the attachments "Listing of political prisoners and victims of torture" and "Minors born in prison or detained with their parents" included in the List of Persons Recognized as Victims, which is part of the report of the [CNPPT], shall be exempted from mandatory military service.

In 2009, Law 20405 expanded the program by exempting direct relatives up to the second degree and other relatives up to the fourth degree.

6.1.2. Individual Economic Reparation Measures

Like Rettig, the Valech Commission recommended granting victims a compensatory pension matching the financial benefit provided to victims of other human rights violations under Law 19123. In addition, the Valech

---

73 The following requirements were set forth for the elimination of criminal records: that the sentenced crimes be punishable by Law 12927 on Safety of the State, Law 17798 on Weapons Control, Law 18314 on Acts of Terrorism, Decree 77 of 1973 (on the illegal nature of political parties and their dissolution), or Decree 3627 of 1981 (establishing the jurisdiction of military courts during times of war); that the sentence had been served or the criminal liability had been extinguished; and that these crimes had not been committed against the physical integrity of third parties.

74 According to Leda Berardi (2017: 481), up to 2017, no law existed to restore the civil and political rights of victims affected by State terrorism. They had to bring a lawsuit against the State seeking damage indemnification.

Commission proposed making this pension transferable for life to the victim's spouse (or to domestic partners with whom the victim had had children). It also proposed indemnifying children born in captivity and minors detained with their mothers or fathers by providing them with a one-time payment. The Commission concluded that financial reparation for political imprisonment and torture should be the same for every victim "without considering the length of imprisonment or the intensity of torture."

This recommendation was implemented by Law 19992, enacted on December 24, 2004. Law 19992 established an annual compensatory pension benefiting victims directly affected by political imprisonment and torture, and minors born in prison or detained with their parents. Contrary to the Valech Commission's recommendation, the amount of the pension did not match those established by Law 19123 of 1992 for victims qualified by the Rettig Commission, in accordance to Lagos' statement that the compensation would be "austere and symbolic".[75] In 2009, Law 20405 extended the pension benefit to surviving spouses of beneficiaries of the pension established under Law 19992. It reduced the pension amount from 75 per cent to 60 per cent. This law also granted a pension to minors born in prison or detained with their parents. In 2015, during the government of Michelle Bachelet, victims of political imprisonment and torture were granted a one million pesos lump sum.[76] The payment followed a hunger strike organized by victims of political imprisonment and torture in several cities throughout the country. Among the items demanded were the matching of the Valech pension to the Rettig pension, and a solution to differences between the pension schemes and related benefits. In this manner, Bachelet's government completed "one more chapter in the monetary reparation of human beings that were victims of political imprisonment and torture, thus taking one more step forward on this difficult road which, although possibly not definitive, substantially improves this aspect."[77]

---

75 Law 19123 of 1992 granted a monthly pension of $140,000 plus the percentage matching the health contribution (at least $1,680,000 per year), while Law 19992 of 2004 established a pension of $1,353,798 for beneficiaries under 70 years old, $1,480,284 for beneficiaries between 70 and 75 years old and $1,549,422 for beneficiaries over 75 years old (that is, a monthly amount of $112,816, $123,357 and $129,118, respectively). [1 Chilean peso ($) = 0.0013 US$]. The former executive vice president of the Valech Commission, María Luisa Sepúlveda, stated that, notwithstanding the recommendation, in the end they decided on a pension amount which was lower than the pension for victims of forced disappearance.

76 Law 20874 established this lump sum benefit for victims recognized by the Valech Commission and by the Advisory Commission for the Qualification of Disappeared Detainees, Persons Executed for Political Reasons and Victims of Political Imprisonment and Torture (*Comisión Asesora para la Calificación de Detenidos Desaparecidos, Ejecutados Políticos y Víctimas de Prisión Política y Tortura*), which operated during 2011 and was known as Valech II.

77 Message of Her Excellency the President of the Republic used to launch a bill granting a compensatory lump sum payment to victims of political prison and torture recognized by the government of Chile. Santiago, July 9, 2015. No. 600-363. Available at: https://www.bcn.cl/historiadelaley/nc/historia-de-la-ley/4425/.

6.1.3. *Individual Reparation Measures in the Health Sector*

The Valech Commission recommended providing free comprehensive physical and mental health care to victims of political imprisonment and torture recognized by this Commission and their direct family members. This mirrored a recommendation of the Rettig Commission and was one of the initiatives in Law 19123 that was pushed forward by Lagos' *No hay mañana sin ayer* program. In reality, PRAIS (the Reparation and Comprehensive Health Care Program) was already providing medical attention to ex-political prisoners and victims of torture who requested it. This recommendation, enacted in Law 19992, sought to formalize the practice. In 2009, Law 20405 extended the program to family members.

6.1.4. *Individual Reparation Measures in the Education Sector*

The Valech Commission recommended developing a program to facilitate the completion of basic, high school, or university education for victims who could verify that their education was interrupted by their detention. Law 19992 guaranteed access to free basic, high school and university studies. In addition, the recommendation to grant scholarships to victims' offspring was implemented in 2009 under Law 20405. The legislation enables daughters, sons and grandchildren of victims who were unable to avail themselves of the program to request scholarships to access higher education themselves. The significance of this measure is considerable in a country that does not offer free university education. However, its implementation was limited, since the law only provides a scholarship to one descendant.

6.1.5. *Individual Reparations in the Housing Sector*

Like the Rettig Commission, the Valech Commission considered victims' housing issues. It recommended "granting a special bonus to the victims who were unable to access housing using the state subsidy, do not have housing and are in a precarious housing situation" (CNPPT 2004, 626). While we found no evidence that the Rettig Commission's recommendation was acted upon, Decree 176 of 2004 grants additional points of access to housing programs for persons recognized as victims of imprisonment and torture.[78] Furthermore, Decree 48 of 2005 grants subsidies to pay off punitive interest on the mortgage debts of persons recognized as victims by the CNPPT.[79] Although this measure does not secure access to new housing, it, in fact, does protect possession.

---

[78] National Institute of Human Rights (2017). *Cartilla Informativa: Beneficios establecidos por ley a las víctimas y familiares de violaciones ocurridas durante la dictadura.* Available at: https://www.indh.cl/bb/wp-content/uploads/2017/01/beneficios.pdf.

[79] Consulted at: https://www.leychile.cl/Navegar?idNorma=238119.

6.2. SYMBOLIC AND COLLECTIVE REPARATION

6.2.1. Non-Recurrence Guarantees and Preventive Measures

In this category, the Valech Commission proposed ratification of international treaties and inclusion of the international legal descriptions of certain crimes within national legislation. It also proposed legal and/or constitutional reforms in connection with military jurisdiction, the rights and duties of persons deprived of their freedom, the prevention of torture and states of emergency.

During the Bachelet administration, both the Rome Statute for the International Criminal Court and the Inter-American Convention on Forced Disappearance of Persons were ratified (in June 2009 and January 2010 respectively). However, the ratification of the Convention on the Non-Applicability of Statutory Limitations to War Crimes and Crimes Against Humanity has not yet been approved, despite several years of congressional discussion. Law 20357 of 2009 provided legal definitions for crimes against humanity, genocide and war crimes, and adopted the definition of forced disappearance set forth by the Inter-American Convention. Furthermore, at the end of 2016, legislation that defined torture in accordance with international standards, increased the penalty upon criminal convictions, and established the non-applicability of statutory limitations for such crime was approved. Although the systematic violation of human rights during the dictatorship was considered in the parliamentary motion, the Valech Commission's recommendation was not mentioned in the legislative debate over either piece of legislation.

There have been reforms to military jurisdiction and laws on states of emergency, but they were done without explicit reference to the Valech Commission's recommendations. Military justice reform was enacted by Law 20477 of November 2010. The law established that "under no circumstances shall civilians and minors be subject to the jurisdiction of military courts. Jurisdiction for these individuals shall be held always by the ordinary criminal courts".

In connection to the revision of constitutional and legal regulations regarding states of emergency, 2005 reforms substituted Articles 39, 40 and 41 of the Constitution. The constitutional reform of 2005 and Law 20050 modified states of emergency and guaranteed the ability to resort to judicial authorities in connection to specific measures affecting constitutional rights by filing the relevant appeals. As for the recommendation to issue a law establishing the rights and duties of persons deprived of their freedom, defining offenses and crimes, penalties and procedures, and the recommendation to review regulations on police operations and criminal procedure to eliminate torture, we have not identified any action.

According to the INDH, there has been little movement regarding penitentiary procedure. This is despite the fact that several organizations see a system in crisis in which protection of the human rights of female and male prisoners has declined. In particular, INDH highlighted the diagnosis by the 2008 UN Rapporteur's Report on the Rights of Persons Deprived of Liberty in the Americas, which pointed out issues such as excessive and unnecessary use of force and punishments and the systematic practice of physical abuse and isolation in subhuman conditions (INDH 2012, 132–133).

6.2.2. *Symbolic Gestures of Recognition and Reconciliation*

The Valech Commission recommended public acknowledgment of the violations perpetrated by State institutions, as well as State acknowledgment of its commitment to avoid recurrence and to promote respect for the rights of all people. Further, it called for the establishment of a date to commemorate this human rights commitment. Finally, it urged the State to provide a copy of the report to every person recognized by the Commission as a victim of political imprisonment and torture.

Of these measures, we were only able to identify action on the first item. As noted above, following the delivery of the report to President Lagos on November 10, 2004, official statements were issued by the Investigation Police (November 13, 2004) and the Air force (on December 1, 2004). Statements from the Navy and the Carabineers actually came a week earlier on November 3. To be sure, none of the statements was an explicit apology for past human rights violations. However, each expressed appreciation for the Valech Commission's report, recognized the occurrence of violations of the most fundamental rights, extended condolences to victims and their families, stated that these crimes should never occur again, and reaffirmed a commitment to respect human rights.

6.2.3. *Acknowledgment of Memory*

As measures to acknowledge memory, the Valech Commission recommended transforming the main torture centers into national monuments and creating memorials and sites of remembrance for the victims of human rights violations and political violence. During her government, President Bachelet agreed to inaugurate memorials and recover memory sites (Collins 2013). These are civil society initiatives supported by State contributions. There are currently 25 properties declared monuments in the categories of "memory and commemoration sites" and "memory and human rights".[80] However, we have not seen substantial action on the recommendations to create a permanent grant fund for research projects on the subject of respect for human rights and a publishing fund for the publication of testimonies and literary works. Although the Undersecretary of Human Rights organized a 2017 call for bids for a grant

80 Can be further consulted at http://www.monumentos.cl/monumentos.

fund for projects promoting memory and a culture of human rights, no evidence was found that these funds have been disbursed.

6.2.4. *Dissemination, Promotion and Education on Human Rights*

Among its collective and symbolic measures, the Commission further recommended distribution of its report to schools, universities, public libraries, overseas consulates, and other entities as well as its publication online. In addition, it proposed a continuing education on human rights for members of the armed forces and law enforcement agencies. Finally, in this section, it recommended including human rights education at all educational levels. According to María Luisa Sepúlveda:

> Another recommendation that we presented was sending a copy of the report to every library and school in Chile, and that was done. They respected that. We should have further secured our position with the Ministry of Education, since professors did not dare, and those who agreed did not dare to do it because, even if they had one against them (...) the press was willing to hear that politics were being done in school and who knows what else. Changes in that regard came with the inauguration of this museum [Memory and Human Rights Museum], because this legitimized the possibility of opening discussions on the subject in class, and schools and private individuals from all conceivable sectors have come to see the museum, and they can visit it with their students and discuss the subject.[81]

The recommendation to distribute the report has been implemented, notwithstanding resistance from educators to teaching the subject. Some alleged that educating students about human rights violations committed during the dictatorship was like "doing politics in school". Unlike Rettig, the Valech report only addresses human rights violations committed by State agents, so it appears biased to some.

We have not been able to verify the revision and permanent adoption of human rights education by the armed forces and law enforcement agencies, as well as at every level of the education system. A 2011 investigation completed by INDH concluded that there were insufficient explicit references to human rights in regulations regarding the education of the armed forces. Their report pointed out the difficulty of getting a definitive answer due to the autonomy of the three branches of the armed forces to define their own curricula. While INDH was able to ascertain that human rights are included in general law courses, they found no evidence of a course specifically on human rights (INDH 2011b, 3). In conclusion, we have not been able to verify fulfilment of the human rights education-related recommendations suggested by the Valech Commission.

---

81 Interview with María Luisa Sepúlveda, Santiago, September 12, 2016.

6.3. INSTITUTIONAL MEASURES

6.3.1. Creation of the National Institute of Human Rights

Among institutional measures, the Valech Commission considered it fundamental to support President Lagos' initiative to create the National Institute of Human Rights that was announced in *No hay mañana sin ayer*. In the opinion of the Valech Commission, this public entity was required to help

> Chilean society to reflect on and delve into past's lessons, impulse initiatives which help the development of a society that respects the human rights of persons and to be vigilant to detect possible instances of discrimination or violation of these rights. It must also help continue the work to uncover the truth about past violations and achieve justice regarding such violations. In addition, it must promote the study and development of sound practices in connection with the dissemination and promotion of human rights, as well as the peaceful resolution of conflicts. Finally, it must perform follow-up activities for the implementation of the measures proposed by this Commission.[82]

The formal creation of INDH occurred under Law 20405 of 2009, enacted during the Bachelet administration. It was inaugurated by the government of Sebastián Piñera in July 2010. The law granted the INDH almost all the powers given to the Valech Commission, although it was not entrusted with following up on the implementation of the Commission's recommendations. However, the INDH developed an informative booklet on reparations available to victims identified by both truth commissions. It also continued to evaluate applications from individuals who had not previously been found eligible for reparations. With regards to the follow-up on preventive and non-recurrence measures, although we did not find any specific work on the subject, INDH has produced reports outlining specific institutional reforms required to promote and defend human rights.[83]

6.3.2. Protection and Confidentiality of Received Information

The last two recommendations made by the Valech Commission relate to the protection and confidentiality of information it collected. The Commission recommended filing and keeping source documents at the proposed INDH

82 Translated from the original Valech report in Spanish by Diana Valori.

83 For example, INDH drafted reports on the bill defining the crime of torture based on international standards, on the incorporation of the subject of human rights in training curricula for armed forces and law enforcement personnel, and on international standards regarding persons deprived of their freedom.

or, barring that, to turn them over to the country's national archive for their protection against theft and destruction.

This recommendation was implemented by Law 20405 of 2009, which, upon creating the INDH, entrusted it with not only keeping and protecting background information from the Valech Commission, but also from the Rettig Commission, the National Reparation and Reconciliation Corporation, the Human Rights Program from the Ministry of Interior, and the Advisory Commission for the Qualification of Disappeared Detainees, Persons Executed for Political Reasons and Victims of Political Imprisonment an Torture.

However, the Valech Commission's sub-recommendation about applying a special term for publicly communicating personal files generated controversy. This recommendation led to the enactment of Law 19992, which established the secrecy of documents, testimonies and background information contributed by victims to the Valech Commission for 50 years, extending the 30 years recommended in the final report.[84] This provision generated great anxiety in some parts of Chilean society, who feared the purpose of this secrecy was to avoid legal accountability, since the law prohibited the intervention even of the judiciary. Currently, INDH provides access only to the person whom the documentation is about, regardless of whether they have been classified as victims. As of April 30, 2018, 1,626 folders have been delivered.[85] However, demands to declassify this information continue in hopes of providing access for the Judicial Branch and for the entire society.

The last recommendation was to release commissioners and persons rendering services to the Commission from any legal obligation requiring the disclosure of information regarding the testimonies received. This recommendation was also implemented by Law 19992, which provided the obligation to protect the confidentiality of background information and secret data for the same 50-year period.

6.4. EVALUATING IMPLEMENTATION OF THE VALECH RECOMMENDATIONS

Chile stands out due to the variety of reparation measures proposed and adopted by law, though it has not been immune from criticisms. With some limitations,

---

84 Some Valech commissioners stated that their inclusion of this recommendation resulted from requests made by victims themselves who, in many cases, had never disclosed the torments, humiliation, and sexual abuses they suffered during their political imprisonment to family members and/or close friends. They also argued that the information included in each folder reflected the victim's own words and, therefore, they could freely state the same information in court or to any other institution. Finally, as indicated previously, 98% of the victims did not identify perpetrators.

85 Information available at https://www.indh.cl/destacados/comision-valech/.

most of the reparation recommendations made by the Valech Commission were implemented by Laws 19992 of 2004 and 20405 of 2009. The formulation of individual reparations followed those made by the Rettig Commission: pensions, assistance and health care, scholarships for access to education, exemption from mandatory military service and housing access benefits. However, the measures have been criticized for the amounts as well as the discrepancy between them and pensions granted under the Rettig Commission. The fact that widows of beneficiaries receive only 60 per cent of the benefit and widowers of female beneficiaries cannot access this right is another source of criticism. The State argued that it was fair to provide benefits that were comparable to what it provided to the poor and vulnerable within society.

Many limitations were linked to the transient nature of the Valech Commission and the absence of a permanent State institution "entrusted with a proactive follow-up of the rights of qualified male and female survivors" (Transitional Justice Observatory at the University of Diego Portales 2016b, 68).[86] According to the Transitional Justice Observatory, survivors have to take it upon themselves to do the "advising, informing or contacting persons subject to rights to truth, justice and reparation." As for the pensions, recipients are often confused about what agencies to contact about the programs. The Social Welfare Institute (*Instituto de Previsión Social*) lacks specialized personnel to provide advice. Nonetheless, despite criticisms and limitations, interviews completed for this project evidenced a significant appreciation for reparation measures such as pensions and academic scholarships.

Regarding measures to prevent human rights violations and guarantee non-recurrence, unlike the Rettig Commission, these were not within the mandate of the Valech Commission. Regardless, the Commission categorized them as symbolic and collective reparations and made recommendations in this area. We have found scant evidence of further investigations or other follow-up efforts on these recommendations, unlike with reparations. Furthermore, our interviews generally did not record information about these types of recommendations. Although some degree of implementation can be verified, the causal relationship with the recommendations remains unclear. As with Rettig, recommendations on regulatory and institutional reforms were harder to fulfil, as political obstacles often arise. Particularly when it comes to legal and constitutional reform, support and political will from the Executive Branch is insufficient. It requires bigger commitments at the Legislative Branch and in some cases even requires qualified majorities.

To conclude, we should point out that our research highlighted an absence of institutional design to guarantee non-recurrence of these types of human rights violations. Some of the demands for change relating to democratic

[86] Corroborated by ex-commissioner Álvaro Varela Walker (interview September 12, 2016).

institutionalization and human rights are based on the fact that a new Constitution has not yet been drafted, nor has the position of ombudsman been established. We recorded criticisms due to delays in the creation of the Undersecretary of Human Rights and in issuing a legal definition for the crime of torture, though these issues were later resolved with the designation of lawyer Lorena Fries as Undersecretary of Human Rights, and with the enactment of Law 20968.

7. CONCLUSION: TRUTH AND REPARATION MEASURES UNDER THE PARADIGM OF RECONCILIATION

The paradigm of reconciliation affected the process of both truth commissions, Rettig and Valech, and helps explain what was emphasized and omitted. An initial distinctive feature of the Rettig Commission in this sense was that it included both cases regarding persons disappeared and executed for political reasons involving the responsibility of the State and its agents, and also cases of kidnappings and attacks committed by private parties acting under political pretexts. While implementing its recommendations resulted in a highly developed policy of reparation, there was little progress in judicial matters and on the issues of prevention and institutional reform during the years following the Rettig Commission. According to Ferrara (2017), truth and reparations were seen as political and legal concessions required to promote national reconciliation. Although the Rettig Commission itself transferred background information to the Judicial Branch and held that the State should not waive its responsibility to pursue criminal investigations, the Commission did not recommend repealing or annulling the Amnesty Law, and the achievements of its recommendations in the field of justice were almost non-existent.

Recommendations related to prevention and non-recurrence, particularly institutional and legal reforms, were stymied by the authoritarian enclaves created by Pinochet's 1980 Constitution. Several authors point out that the search for stability of the democratic system within the transitional framework caused reforms to be gradual.

By contrast, the Valech Commission, established about a decade later, addressed the cases of survivors of the civilian-military dictatorship who were victims of political imprisonment and torture. It distinguished itself from the Rettig Commission because it collected only facts involving State responsibility, without comparing them to those committed by "private parties under political pretexts." The Valech Commission was characterized by the secrecy of information and, unlike Rettig, did not hand over any records to the Judicial Branch. Notwithstanding this, lawsuits for torture continued to be filed with the support of individuals and human rights organizations.

Unlike the Rettig Commission, Valech was not entrusted with recommending measures to avoid recurrence. However, it included such recommendations under the category of symbolic and collective reparations, which exhibit a poor degree of implementation. Just as was the case with the implementation of the Rettig's recommendations (and although general expectations were more focused on official acknowledgment than on reparations),[87] individual reparation measures recommended by the Valech Commission experienced a high degree of implementation.

The findings of this study are consistent with existing research, which focuses predominantly on reparation measures, as they stand out when making international comparisons. Little has been written on the implementation of public policy addressing non-recurrence, which is consistent with the much lower implementation rate we found. In our fieldwork, nearly every interviewee referred to reparation measures such as pensions, the PRAIS health care program, the study scholarships and the exemption from the mandatory military service for children of the victims as implementation events but overlooked the evolution of the other recommendations.

Regardless of the implementation record, Chile has experienced a long, tumultuous process of pursuing justice for crimes committed by the dictatorship. We agree with Collins (2013) that this progress is the result of political and institutional processes driven by multiple causes, and, therefore, cannot be causally traced back to one commission or the other. All in all, the Rettig and Valech Commissions provided a valuable service by officially constructing the truth and dismissing attempts to deny the facts in Chile, and, considering the variety of measures oriented towards reparation, helped to highlight the Chilean case.

BIBLIOGRAPHY

Berardi, Leda (2017). "Violación de derechos humanos durante la dictadura cívico-militar de Pinochet y los gobiernos post dictadura en Chile". *Discurso & Sociedad* no. 11 (3): 458–484.

Biblioteca del Congreso Nacional de Chile (March 13, 2013). "Beneficios para prisioneros y torturados políticos". Available at: http://www.bcn.cl/leyfacil/recurso/beneficios-para-prisioneros-y-torturados-politicos.

—— (December 24, 2004). *Historia de la Ley N° 19.992*. Establece pensión de reparación y otorga otros beneficios a favor de las personas que indica.

Brett, Sebastián (2009). *El Efecto Pinochet: A diez años de Londres 1998*. International Seminar Report. Santiago: Universidad Diego Portales.

[87] Interview with Margarita Romero, September 15, 2016, Santiago, Chile.

Brodsky, Ricardo (2014). "Violencia, Comisiones de la Verdad y Memorias. Anotaciones sobre los casos de Argentina, Chile y Perú". Museo de la memoria y los Derechos Humanos. Retrieved from: http://www.cedocmuseodelamemoria.cl/wp-content/uploads/2014/03/ViolenciaComisiones-de-Verdad-y-Memorias-final.pdf.

Camacho Padilla, Fernando (2004). "Una Memoria Consensuada: El Informe Rettig". V Congreso Chileno de Antropología. Colegio de Antropólogos de Chile A.G, November 8–12, 2004, San Felipe.

—— (2008). "Memorias enfrentadas: las reacciones a los informes Nunca Más de Argentina y Chile". *Persona y Sociedad* no. XXII (2): 67–99.

—— (2014). "La construcción histórica de la represión de Argentina y Chile: las Comisiones de la Verdad". *Revista de Historia Iberoamericana* no. 7(1): 35–74.

Centro de Estudios de Justicia de las Américas (CEJA) (2003). *Reformas Procesales Penales en América Latina: Resultados del Proyecto de Seguimiento*, Chile, 2003. Available at: http://biblioteca.cejamericas.org/handle/2015/5366.

Centro de Estudios Públicos (2003). "Propuesta de derechos humanos del gobierno del presidente Ricardo Lagos del 12 de Agosto de 2003". *Estudios Públicos* no. 92: 313–333. Available at: https://www.cepchile.cl/propuesta-de-derechos-humanos-del-gobierno-del-presidente-ricardo-lagos/cep/2016-03-04/093152.html.

CNPPT (*Comisión Nacional sobre Prisión Política y Tortura)* (2004). *Informe de la CNPPT*. Santiago: Ministerio del Interior.

CNRR (*Corporación Nacional de Reparación y Reconciliación)* (1996a). *Informe de la Comisión Nacional de Verdad y Reconciliación de 1991* - CNVR. Reedición elaborada por la CNRR. La Corporación: Santiago.

—— (1996b). *Informe sobre calificación de víctimas de violaciones de derechos humanos y de la violencia política*. CNRR.

CNVR (*Comisión Nacional de Verdad y Reconciliación*) ("Rettig Commission") (1991). *Informe de la Comisión Nacional de Verdad y Reconciliación* (Informe Rettig). Vols. 1-3. Spanish version available at: http://www.ddhh.gov.cl/wp-content/uploads/2015/12/tomo1.pdf (Volume 1), http://www.ddhh.gov.cl/wp-content/uploads/2015/12/tomo2.pdf (Volume 2) and http://www.ddhh.gov.cl/wp-content/uploads/2015/12/tomo3.pdf (Volume 3).

CODEPU (*Corporación de Promoción y Defensa de los Derechos del Pueblo*) (2001). *Informe de Derechos Humanos 1990–2000*. CODEPU.

Collins, Cath (2013). "Chile a más de dos décadas de justicia de transición". *Revista de Ciencia Política* no. 51 (2): 79–113. Available at: https://byzantion.uchile.cl/index.php/RP/article/view/30160.

Collins, Cath and Observatorio de Justicia Transicional de la UDP (2013). "Verdad, Justicia y memoria por violaciones a los derechos humanos en tiempos de dictadura, a 40 años del golpe militar." In Vial T. (ed.). *Informe anual sobre derechos humanos en Chile - 2013*. Santiago de Chile: Ediciones Universidad Diego Portales / Centro de Derechos Humanos.

—— (2014). "¿Una nueva medida de lo posible? Verdad, justicia, memoria y reparaciones posdictadura". In Vial T. (ed.), *Informe anual sobre derechos humanos en Chile - 2014*. Santiago de Chile: Ediciones Universidad Diego Portales / Centro de Derechos Humanos.

—— (2015). "Silencios e irrupciones: verdad, justicia y reparaciones en la postdictadura chilena". In Vial T. (ed.), *Informe anual sobre derechos humanos en Chile - 2015*. Santiago de Chile: Ediciones Universidad Diego Portales / Centro de Derechos Humanos.

Collins, Cath and Hau, Boris (2016). "Chile: Incremental truth, late justice". In Skaar, Elin, Jemima García-Godos, and Cath Collins (eds.), *Transitional Justice in Latin America: The Uneven Road from Impunity towards Accountability*. New York: Routledge.

Corte Suprema de Justicia de Chile (2000). "Texto del fallo de la Corte Suprema que desaforó al General Augusto Pinochet." *Estudios Públicos* no. 79: 509–561.

Estudios Públicos (2000). "Acuerdo de la Mesa de Diálogo sobre Derechos Humanos." *Estudios Públicos* no. 79: 481–487.

Ferrara, Anita (2017). "The Implementation Record of Two Chilean Truth Commissions' Recommendations". Paper presented at Congress of the Latin American Studies Association, Lima, Peru, April 29–May 1, 2017.

Fuenzalida, Paula (2007). "Las políticas de reparación en Chile y sus consecuencias en los hijos de los detenidos-desaparecidos 1990–2000". University of Stockholm.

García-Godos, Jemima (2016). "Reparations". In Simic, Olivera (ed.), *An Introduction to Transitional Justice*. Abingdon and New York: Routledge.

Garretón, Manuel (2001). "Memoria, olvido, reconciliación y justicia en el caso chileno". In Instituto Interamericano de Derechos Humanos, *Verdad y Justicia: Homenaje a Emilio F. Mignone*. San José: IIDH.

Garretón, Manuel and Garretón, Roberto (2010). "La democracia incompleta en Chile: la realidad tras los rankings internacionales". *Revista de Ciencia Política* no. 30 (1): 115–148.

Garretón, Roberto (2008). "Los tribunales con jurisdicción penal durante la transición a la democracia en Chile". Presented at the roundtable conference "El Papel de los tribunales en contextos de justicia transicional. Oportunidades y desafíos actuales en la región Iberoamericana. Los tribunales nacionales en Chile y Argentina" Madrid, May 8–10, 2008.

Guzmán Dalbora, José Luis (2009). "Chile". In Ambos, Kai, Malarino, Ezequiel, and Elsner, Gisela (eds.), *Justicia de Transición: Con informes de América Latina. Alemania, Italia y España*. Montevideo: Fundación Konrad-Adenauer Oficina Uruguay. Available at: https://archivos.juridicas.unam.mx/www/bjv/libros/9/4487/23.pdf.

Hayner, Priscilla B. (2001). *Unspeakable Truths: Confronting State terror and Atrocity*. New York: Routledge.

—— (2006). "Comisiones de la verdad: resumen esquemático". *International Review of the Red Cross* no. 88 (862): 295–310.

—— (2008). *Verdades innombrables. El reto de las comisiones de la verdad*. México D.F.: Fondo de Cultura Económica.

Instituto Nacional de Derechos Humanos (INDH) (November 24, 2009). Ley 20405. Available at: http://www.leychile.cl/Navegar/?idNorma=1008867&idVersion=2009-12-10&idParte.

—— (2011a). "Cartilla Informativa: Beneficios establecidos por ley a las víctimas y familiares de violaciones ocurridas durante la dictadura". INDH. Available at: http://bibliotecadigital.indh.cl/handle/123456789/96.

—— (2011b). "Estudio sobre la integración de educación en derechos humanos en la formación de las Fuerzas Armadas". *Boletín informativo INDH*, no. 2, (December 2011).

Available at: http://bibliotecadigital.indh.cl/bitstream/handle/123456789/253/Bolet%C3%ADn%20N%C2%B02%20EDH%20FFAA.pdf?sequence=1.
—— (2012). "Estándares internacionales en materia de personas privadas de libertad y condiciones de los centros penitenciarios: sistematización, análisis y propuestas". Santiago de Chile. Available at: http://bibliotecadigital.indh.cl/bitstream/handle/123456789/311/ESTANDARES.pdf?sequence=4.
Lira, Elizabeth (2013). "Algunas reflexiones a propósito de los 40 años del golpe militar en Chile y las condiciones de la reconciliación política". *Psykhe*, no. 22 (2): 5–18.
Lira, Elizabeth and Loveman, Brian (1998). "Derechos Humanos en la transición 'modelo': Chile 1988–1999". Documento preparado para la reunión "Chile 1990 1999: The model country for democracy and development?". University of California, San Diego, California, December 10–12, 1998.
—— (2005). *Políticas de reparación Chile 1990–2004*. Santiago: LOM Ediciones.
Ministerio del Interior (December 24, 2004). Ley 19992. Establece pensión de reparación y otorga otros beneficios a favor de las personas que indica. Available at: http://www.leychile.cl/Navegar/?idNorma=233930&idVersion=2009-12-10&idParte.
Ministerio del Interior (January 31, 1992). CNRR; Pensión de Reparación, Ley no. 19.123. Available at: http://www.leychile.cl/Navegar?idNorma=30490.
Novoa Vásquez, Laura (September 11, 2013). "Laura Novoa: Perdón y Reconciliación". Centro de Investigación Periodistica (CIPER). Available at: http://ciperchile.cl/2013/09/11/laura-novoa-perdon-y-reconciliacion/.
Observatorio de Justicia Transicional (2012). "Medidas de reparación en Chile desde 1990. Políticas públicas por violaciones a los ddhh cometidas durante la dictadura militar de 1973 a 1990". Centro de Derechos Humanos – Universidad Diego Portales.
—— (2012). "Tabla leyes y medidas de reparación en Chile. 1991–2011". Centro de derechos humanos – Universidad Diego Portales.
—— (2016a). "Principales hitos jurisprudenciales en causas DDHH en Chile 1990–2015". Centro de derechos humanos – Universidad Diego Portales.
—— (2016b). "Informe anual sobre derechos humanos en Chile – 2016". Santiago de Chile: Centro de Derechos Humanos – Universidad Diego Portales.
Richard, Nelly (2010). *Crítica de la memoria. Santiago.* Ediciones Universidad Diego Portales.
Sierra, Lucas (2005). "Informe de la CNPPT, y respuestas institucionales". *Estudios Públicos* no. 97: 297–531.
Zalaquett, José (1999). "La reconstrucción de la unidad nacional y el legado de violaciones de los derechos humanos". *Perspectivas*: 385–401.
—— (2000). "La mesa de diálogo sobre derechos humanos y el proceso de transición política en Chile". *Estudios Públicos* no. 79: 5–30.
—— (2002). "Introduction to the English Edition". In *Report of the Chilean National Commission on Truth and Reconciliation*, United States Institute of Peace (ed.). Available at: https://www.usip.org/sites/default/files/resources/collections/truth_commissions/Chile90-Report/Chile90-Report.pdf.
—— (2003). "'No hay mañana sin ayer'. Análisis de la propuesta del Presidente Lagos sobre Derechos Humanos". *Estudios Públicos* no. 92: 29–75.

Internet Sources:

ciperchile.cl
dag.un.org
defensoresydefensoras.indh.cl
derecho.uahurtado.cl
pdh.minjusticia.gob.cl
www.aerchipro.com
www.archivochile.com
www.bcn.cl/
www.camara.cl
www.cepchile.cl
www.defensa.cl
www.freedomcollection.org
www.indh.cl/
www.institutodechile.cl/
www.leychile.cl
www.memoriaabierta.org.ar
www.memoriachilena.cl
www.ombudsman.cl/
www.uchile.cl/
www.vicariadelasolidaridad.cl

ANNEX: LIST OF INTERVIEWEES

María Luisa Sepúlveda Edwards, Valech Commissioner, Chairman of the board of the *Museo de la Memoria y los Derechos Humanos* (Museum of Memory and Human Rights), Santiago, Chile, September 12, 2016.

Roberto Garretón, Human Rights attorney, Santiago, Chile, September 12, 2016.

Álvaro Varela Walker, Valech Commissioner, private business law attorney, Santiago, Chile, September 12, 2016.

Luciano Fouillioux, Valech Commissioner, Human Rights attorney, Santiago, Chile, September 13, 2016.

Elizabeth Lira, Valech Commissioner, Dean of the School of Psychology at the Alberto Hurtado University, Santiago, Chile, September 13, 2016.

Lucas Sierra Iribarren, Valech Commissioner, Director of the *Centro de Estudios Públicos* (Center for Public Studies), Santiago, Chile, September 14, 2016.

Alicia Lira, President of the *Agrupación Familiares de Ejecutados Políticos* (Family Members of Political Execution Victims Group), Santiago, Chile, September 14, 2016.

Margarita Romero, ex political prisoner, President of the *Asociación por la Memoria y los Derechos Humanos Colonia Dignidad* (Dignity Colony Association for Memory and Human Rights), board member of the *Instituto Nacional de Derechos Humanos* (National Institute of Human Rights), Santiago, Chile, September 15, 2016.

Boris Hau, attorney for the *Observatorio de Derechos Humanos de la Universidad Diego Portales* (Human Rights Observatory at the Diego Portales University), Santiago, Chile, September 15, 2016.

URUGUAY'S COMMISSION FOR PEACE

An Unfulfilled Experience?

Federico GHELFI, Sol HOURCADE, Luz PALMÁS ZALDUA, and Marcela PERELMAN*

---

* This chapter was written by researchers from the *Centro de Estudios Legales y Sociales* (Center for Legal and Social Studies, CELS), Buenos Aires. The general analysis and writing is a collective work by Sol Hourcade, Federico Ghelfi, Luz Palmás Zaldua and Marcela Perelman. Fieldwork was conducted in Montevideo by Hourcade and Ghelfi, the systematization of sources was in charge of Hugo Goeury. Andrea Rocha Granados participated during the project preparation phase, in 2015.
The authors wish to express their gratitude for the valuable input of Gabriela Fried to a prior version of this text.

1. INTRODUCTION

This chapter examines the experience of the Uruguayan Commission for Peace (*Comisión para la Paz*), created 15 years after the end of the military dictatorship (1973–85). The Commission began its work in the context of the ongoing memory, truth and justice process in Uruguay, a context very different from that which prevailed in the first years after the reintroduction of democracy. We shall concentrate on an aspect rarely explored in scholarly studies of this truth commission: the recommendations drafted upon the conclusion of the Commission's work. Focusing on the eight recommendations in the final report of the *Comisión para la Paz*, we examine the specific factors and processes that affected their formulation, as well as the actors involved and the challenges encountered in their implementation.

This chapter combines documentary analysis of the Commission's final report with semi-structured interviews with relevant actors in Montevideo during the month of October 2016.[1] We also draw on secondary material, including academic articles, organizational communiqués and CELS' historical archives in our analysis of the Commission. In the chapter, before examining the recommendations, we begin by discussing the nature of the Uruguayan transition. Then, we examine the post-transitional context of the Commission's creation and operation, placing particular emphasis on the role played by human rights organizations, as well as the points of view of the different actors involved in the truth commission process. Access to monitoring reports, specialized articles, library material from the Luz Ibarburu Observatory in Montevideo, and UN reports have been useful in our assessment of the formulation and impact of the *Comisión para la Paz* recommendations.

2. THE URUGUAYAN TRANSITION: NEGOTIATION AND DEMOCRATIC AFFIRMATION

The context in which the Uruguayan Commission for Peace operated in 2000, 15 years after the conclusion of the dictatorship in 1985, should be understood in light of the transition. The political agreements negotiated in the transition from military rule to electoral democracy have to this day laid the foundations for the human rights agenda and the judiciary's ability to prosecute the perpetrators of human rights violations.

During the final years of the military dictatorship, the regime made various attempts at re-legitimizing and institutionalizing itself. These initiatives failed,

1 See the end of chapter for a complete list of the public officers and ex-officers, human rights activists, victim family members, and academics who were interviewed for this project.

although the conditions for liberalization (especially in terms of political rights) and electoral competition had been in place since 1983 (Corbo 2007, 32–33). It was a complex process, with progress and setbacks, forged in the heat of growing political, social, and union mobilization. This period was characterized by a series of disruptive events: widespread power outages; the "pots and pans" protests (*caceroleadas*); the ceremony of May 1, 1983; the Student Week which culminated in a massive student protest in September 1983; the ceremony at the Obelisk of Montevideo in support of a more democratic and less exclusionary Uruguay in November of the same year;[2] and the civic strike in January 1984 organized by the Inter-Union Workers' Plenary Meeting (*Plenario Intersindical de Trabajadores*, PIT), marking the first general strike in 11 years.

The increasingly isolated regime responded by deepening its repression. As early as 1984, records show that this fear-inducing strategy was effective in shaping public preferences over the best path to democracy. A conciliatory policy became the preferred mode of transition. This hurt the *Partido National* (National Party), which centered its strategy on mobilizing the people against the regime. Civil society strategies also changed. The disruptive tactics of the early 1980s were *Intersectorial* (intersectoral organization), including unions such as the PIT, social organizations such as the *Asociación Social y Cultural de Estudiantes de la Enseñanza Pública* (Social and Cultural Association of Public Education Teachers, ASCEEP), and human rights groups such as *Servicio de Paz y Justicia* (Peace and Justice Service, SERPAJ). State repression led to the pro-democracy movement shifting its strategy from mobilization of street protests against the dictatorship to less confrontational tactics. This period, known in Uruguay as the *Multipartidaria* (Multi-party organization), included the active participation of political parties that wished to capitalize on the popular preference towards a strategy of conciliation.

The 1985 democratic transition was the culmination of careful political negotiations between the leading political parties and the military authorities, who wielded considerable power at the time.[3] Negotiations were secretly conducted at the Parque Hotel, Montevideo, in 1983 and concluded with the Naval Club Treaty the following year. The treaty, signed by military authorities and representatives of the *Partido Colorado* (Red Party), *Frente Amplio* (Broad Front), and the *Unión Cívica* (Civic Union), established the framework for

---

2 This event, popularly known in Uruguay as *Río de la Libertad* (the River of Liberty) constituted the largest popular mobilization in the country's history.

3 Charles Gillespie (1995) and Daniel Corbo (2007) suggest that, although resistance groups were essential to the process of mobilizing society against the regime and rebuilding opposition groups, their role in democratic re-institutionalization was subordinated to party strategy and structurally dependent on the left-leaning parties included in the Broad Front, who were seeking to regain legitimacy in the political system after being outlawed.

elections, which took place during the final months of 1984.[4] The agreements involved a "negotiated retreat" by the military authorities, which would define their new institutional role of relative subordination to civilian authorities. Electoral bans and political imprisonment restricted political participation in the elections.[5] This favored politicians and parties that supported a conciliatory policy toward the military, including the *Colorado* Party's Julio María Sanguinetti, who participated in the negotiations and eventually became the first post-dictatorship president in 1985. Lastly, although parties to the Naval Club Treaty have denied it, academics, Uruguayan human rights activists, and opposition politicians agree that a commitment to avoid investigating the criminal liability of members of the dictatorship for their role in human rights violations was also an explicit part of the agreement (Corbo 2007, 34; Caetano 1998, 205; Errandonea 2008, 17). Their belief is reinforced by the subsequent passage of the Amnesty Law by the Uruguayan Parliament two years later.

3. WHAT SHOULD BE DONE ABOUT PAST HUMAN RIGHTS VIOLATIONS?

Burning questions at the time of the transition to democratic rule included human rights and how political actors would deal with the dictatorial past in a framework of "stable equilibrium" between military and civil power. As stated by Lessa and Skaar (2016, 79), the new government headed by Julio María Sanguinetti tended to downplay human rights violations in the public arena. Nonetheless, several issues prompted by re-democratization made it impossible to fully ignore the past. Those who had fled the country wanted to return. There was talk of amnesty for political social prisoners, and reparation for public employees dismissed during the military dictatorship. Moreover, during the final year of the dictatorship and, more insistently, during the first years of democracy, victims, family members, and human rights organizations began filing reports of disappearances, torture, and political assassination in the civil courts. One government response was the Amnesty Law 15.737[6] covering political prisoners convicted under the regime, which was enacted in March 1985.[7] Second, two parliamentary investigative commissions were

[4] No National Party representatives participated in the negotiations because their leader was in prison and the party remained committed to confronting the dictatorship.

[5] The National Party and the Broad Front were particularly harmed by the electoral ban on 5000 citizens and the continued detention of 300 political prisoners (Corbo 2007, 35).

[6] This is different from the Amnesty law (*Ley de Caducidad*) from the Uruguayan government mentioned in section 2: 15.848 (1986).

[7] On the same day, the Uruguayan government ratified the Inter-American Convention on Human Rights.

established in April 1985: one to specifically investigate the kidnapping and murder of ex-legislators Héctor Gutiérrez Ruiz and Zelmar Michelini (who had disappeared in Argentina); and a second to investigate the situation of disappeared persons more generally.[8] The latter, more general, commission's activities were centered in the House of Representatives between April and November 1985. It resulted in the filing of 164 reports of disappearances that had taken place in Uruguay, Argentina, Chile, and Paraguay between 1973 and 1978. In its final report, this Commission concluded that:

> The Parliament must speak out on behalf of the people, who, silenced by force, were unable at the time to report these facts to the legal authorities (…) is confident that the Judicial Branch, which is ideally, technically and constitutionally empowered, will be able to swiftly and effectively achieve full clarification of the facts, as well as process and sentence the guilty parties.[9]

The Commission proposed that the judiciary take action to ensure "the full clarification of the facts, as well as to process and sentence the guilty parties." The Commission's suggestion to Parliament was to remit the information to the Supreme Court of Justice and to the Executive Branch. A dispute followed over which courts – military or civil – should have jurisdiction over the cases of disappeared persons reported by the Commission. Two legislative initiatives attempted to channel the reports to civilian courts, although both failed as a result of the military supporting the *Colorado* Party's firm refusal to make them viable.[10] On September 2, 1986, the Executive Branch, which did not hold a majority in the legislature, presented the *Ley de Pacificación Nacional* (National Pacification Law) to the Parliament, proposing full amnesty to the military and the police for the crimes committed during the dictatorship. This proposal was rejected in the Senate by the *Partido Nacional* and the *Frente Amplio*. On November 24th, the Supreme Court ruled that jurisdiction lay with the civil legal authorities. Two days before the deadline for the military authorities to surrender to legal authorities, the Commander in Chief of the Army, Hugo Medina, stated that he had kept the legal summons for his subordinates locked in his safe, which was interpreted as contempt of court (Bucheli, Curto et al. 2005, 57–58; De Giorgi 2014, 104–105). In the early hours of that same day,

---

8 The full name in Spanish of the second commission was *Comisión Investigadora Parlamentaria Sobre la Situación de Personas Desaparecidas y Hechos que la Motivaron* (Investigative Commission on the Situation of Disappeared People and its Causes).

9 *Informe Final de la Comisión Investigadora Parlamentaria Sobre Situación de Personas Desaparecidas y Hechos que la Motivaron.* Translation by Diana Valori.

10 These efforts to promote accountability in civilian courts were known as the Zumarán Batalla project, dated December 12, 1985, supported by the National Party and the Broad Front, and the "In Defense of Democracy and Human Rights" project, dated September 22, 1986, supported by sectors of the National Party.

December 21, faced with the Executive's argument of a possible institutional breakdown,[11] the House of Representatives voted in favor of Law 15.848 on the Expiration of the Punitive Claims of the State (*Ley de Caducidad de la Pretensión Punitiva del Estado* (popularly called *Ley de Caducidad*).[12]

4. DOES JUSTICE HAVE AN EXPIRATION DATE?

The *Ley de Caducidad* has been the main legal instrument used to preclude the investigation and prosecution of military and police authorities involved in human rights violations during the dictatorship in Uruguay. The Law is justified as consistent with the 1984 Naval Club Agreement. Article 1 clearly states:

> It is hereby acknowledged that, as a logical result of facts set forth in the agreement entered between political parties and the Armed Forces in August of 1984, and for the purpose of concluding the transition and entering full effectiveness of constitutional order, the punitive claims of the State have expired in regards to any crimes committed by military and police authorities up to March 1, 1985 (...) (Law 15.848/1986).

Article 3 granted the Executive Branch, not the Judiciary, authority to determine whether the Law was applicable to reported violations and, in applicable cases, implement the resulting decision to close and file the matter. According to data compiled by the Luz Ibarburu Observatory, 44 reports of disappearances, kidnappings, deaths and other incidents were reported to legal authorities in 1985–86, the period stretching from the creation of the Parliamentary Commission to the approval of the Amnesty Law (Olivera 2016). All reports pending at the time of approval of the Amnesty Law were closed and filed (UN General Assembly 2014, 5). Article 4 of the Amnesty Law would later become a significant source of controversy in terms of its meaning and scope:

> Beyond what the previous articles say, and without affecting them, the judge in charge of the case will send to the Executive the testimonies of the denunciations that have been presented until the enactment of the law in question, regarding people who – seemingly – have been detained during military or police operations and also regarding missing people and children who – seemingly – have been kidnapped in similar circumstances. The Executive will immediately order the investigation of these events, in order to clarify them. Within 120 days of the judicial communication

---

11 Argentina's Full Stop Law (*Ley de Punto Final*), which restricted statutory limitation period for filing reports against State agents for crimes committed during the dictatorship, was approved two days after the Uruguayan Amnesty Law (*Ley de Caducidad*).

12 According to Ana Aguerre, member of SERPAJ Uruguay, it is not unreasonable to assume that the Amnesty Law had already been planned by the Executive Branch before the establishment of the Parliamentary Commission of 1985.

> of the denunciation, the Executive will inform those who made the denunciation about the outcome of the investigation and will give them access to the information gathered. (translation by Roberto Gargarella, cited in Skaar (2002, 163–164)).

Article 4 of the *Ley de Caducidad* has continued to shape the Uruguayan truth and justice process, not only by legally preventing criminal prosecution of alleged perpetrators of human rights abuses,[13] but also by hampering new social and political initiatives seeking to review the dictatorial past.

In view of the lack of initiatives from official institutions, civil society organizations led the efforts to establish truth-seeking mechanisms. The *Uruguay Nunca Más* (Uruguay Never Again) report published in March 1989 by the human rights organization *Servicio Paz y Justicia* (Peace and Justice Service, SERPAJ), was the most comprehensive attempt at the time to provide a systematic account of what had happened during the dictatorship, based on the experiences of victims and their family members. The SERPAJ report analyzed patterns of repression in cases of executions, murders, disappearances, arbitrary detainment and exile, as well the restrictions imposed on political rights, work and freedom of speech.

According to Sempol (2013, 112–113), mobilization around past human rights violations diminished considerably during the first part of the 1990s, although a favorable environment for a "moment of truth" began to develop around the middle of the decade. The March of Silence in support of "Truth, Memory and Never Again", was organized by multiple organizations.[14] In addition, several proposals emerged during this time that sought an official clarification of the meaning of Article 4 of the Amnesty Law in terms of determining the fate of disappeared persons. However, there was no political will to go beyond the "closure" of the transition. Toward the end of the 1990s, the human rights movement renewed its efforts to achieve justice, hand in hand with the emergence of new human rights organizations such as *Hijos Uruguay* ("Children of murdered, imprisoned and exiled individuals", founded in 1995), *Familiares de Asesinados por Razones Políticas*, "Family members of individuals

---

13 Since 1986, any activist or political effort attempting to challenge the Amnesty Law has been blocked. Setbacks include the defeat of the 1989 referendum seeking to revoke the amnesty and the interruption of the constitutional plebiscite in 2009. In the judicial arena, the Supreme Court declared the Amnesty Law constitutional in 1988. In 2013, the Court declared unconstitutional a law that attempted to reinstate punitive claims. For details, see Skaar (2002).

14 Every May 20 for the past 23 years (since 1996), the *Marcha de Silencio* (March of Silence) has mobilized thousands of Uruguayans to march silently in the streets in support for human rights. The slogan of many years, "*Por verdad, memoria y nunca más*" ("For truth, memory, and never again") was recently changed to "*Impunidad: Responsabilidad del Estado, ayer y hoy*" ("Impunity: State responsibility, yesterday and now"), signalling a shift in claims towards the State.

murdered for political reasons", and the *Asociación de ex presos y presas políticos/as del Uruguay* (Association of Ex Political Prisoners of Uruguay, CRYSOL).

5. THE *COMISIÓN PARA LA PAZ*

The emergence of an environment favorable to the creation of the Commission for Peace (*Comisión para la Paz*) can be traced to three factors, according to Gerardo Caetano (2008, 215). First, mobilization of organizations of family members of disappeared persons and human rights groups had kept pressure on politicians by maintaining a certain level of visibility for their human rights demands. The development of a regional context increasingly supportive of overcoming impunity for dictatorship crimes was a second factor. Third, President Jorge Batlle (2000–05) adopted a different attitude towards human rights violations and transitional justice compared to his predecessor, who had been from the same political party (*Partido Colorado*), and which caused internal conflict in the party.

A series of events during the first three months of Batlle's presidency prepared the grounds for the establishment of the *Comisión para la Paz.* Only a week after he assumed office, the new President ordered DNA tests to be carried out on the girl whom the well-known Argentine poet and left-wing activist, Juan Gelman, believed to be his granddaughter, Macarena.[15] She was one of the many children who had "disappeared" together with their detained mothers (either as small children, or in most cases, unborn) during the dictatorship, in Argentina and Uruguay. The tests were positive. Through this unexpected move, President Batlle recognised the need for the State to seek the resolution of forced disappearance cases, particularly disappeared children (Skaar 2011, 159–161). At the beginning of April 2000, the Joint Chief of Staff of the Armed Forces stated his opposition to any initiative to review the authoritarian past, prompting Batlle's order to dismiss him from his position. A few days after this decision, for the first time, the *Asociación de Madres y Familiares de Uruguayos Detenidos Desaparecidos* (Association of Mothers and Family Members of Detained Disappeared Uruguayans, FAMIDESA) was received by the Uruguayan President. A second meeting with organization delegates took place in June the same year. Soon after, Batlle announced the formation of the *Comisión para la Paz.*

The *Comisión para la Paz* was formally established by Presidential Resolution no. 858 on August 9, 2000. It was given a mandate to take "all possible steps to determine the situation of detainees and people disappeared during the de

15 Macarena is the daughter of Marcelo Gelman and María Claudia García Irureta Goyena, who both disappeared in Argentina during the military dictatorship (1976–1983).

facto regime, as well as minors disappeared under similar circumstances." Batlle declared that he was committed to going

> as far as I can and as far as they let me (...) that I must achieve these results in peace, without triggering a war and with the acquiescence of all parties involved. (...) What I can say is that I've noticed a good attitude from the armed forces, an opening (Caetano 2008, 215).

According to the resolution, the goal was to "consolidate national pacification and forever seal the peace among Uruguayans." The resolution stated that the *Comisión para la Paz* would possess "the broadest authority to receive documents and testimony and would be required to maintain the strictest confidentiality of its actions and absolute privacy of the sources of collected information." This guarantee of confidentiality ended up hindering the real impact of the Commission from its inception. Finally, the resolution required the drafting of a final report with conclusions that had to include "suggestions regarding legislative measures appropriate to repair the victims and concerning relationship status, as well as an individual summary of each detainee-disappeared person case considered by the Commission." This was the earliest official allusion to the recommendations' design.

Table 1. Members of *Comisión para la Paz*

Name	Background Information
Monsignor Nicolás Cotugno (M)	Archbishop of Montevideo. President of the Commission.
José D'Elía (M)	Long-standing union representative, Honorary President of the *Plenario Intersindical de Trabajadores* (Inter-Union Worker Plenary Meeting) – National Worker Convention, PIT-CNT.
Luis Pérez Aguirre (M)	Catholic priest, human rights activist. Founder of SERPAJ of Uruguay. Included in the Commission in his capacity as spokesperson of the group *Asociación de Madres y Familiares de Uruguayos Detenidos Desaparecidos* (FAMIDESA).[16]
Jorge Osorio (M)	Catholic priest. Replaced Pérez Aguirre following his death in January 2001.
Dr. José Claudio Williman Ramírez (M)	Prominent *Partido Nacional* politician and a close personal friend of President Batlle.
Dr. Gonzalo Fernández (M)	Attorney. Legal expert and advisor to Tabaré Vasques of *Partido Encuentro-Progresista – Frente Amplio* (Batlle's principal opponent in the presidential campaign)
Dr. Carlos Ramela Regules (M)	*Partido Colorado*. Advisor to President Batlle.

Source: Compiled by the authors.
Note: M = Male. There were no female commissioners.

---

16 FAMIDESA was the only human rights organization that had direct influence over the Commission members and ex-President Batlle. Interview with Ana Aguerre of SERPAJ, Montevideo, October 20, 2016.

The Commission was composed of seven individuals, some of whom were political figures and others were activists (see Table 1 for a background on the commissioners). It had no punitive powers; that is, it was purely an investigative body. The Commission's efforts mainly centered on the collection of materials and testimonies, primarily to try to identify the location of human remains. Its purpose was simply to determine how and when the forced disappearances had taken place and to draft a list of verified victims. All information was to be confidential, and no information was to be used for legal purposes later. The report does not record if any official minutes were kept of the Commission's meetings and actions, which continued for two and a half years, until April 2003, when it presented its Final Report.

In relation to financing, the Final Report details the expenses in the logistics of official trips, general travel expenses, and operating costs during the three years of work, for a total of $5,397 US dollars and 53,937.89 Uruguayan pesos. According to Errandonea (2008, 45) and the Special Rapporteur of the report on the promotion of truth, justice, reparation and guarantees of non-repetition of the UN, Pablo De Greiff, (UN General Assembly 2014, 9), the financial resources at the Commission's disposal have not been adequate to carry out its tasks.[17]

6. BETWEEN EXPECTATIONS AND THE STATUTE OF LIMITATIONS BOUNDARIES

The positive aspects of the historical role of the Commission for Peace are quite clear. This was the first governmental public acknowledgment of persons who had been victims of forced disappearance in Uruguay, thus ending a period of sustained institutional silence (FAMIDESA 2003). In addition, it had a catalyzing effect by promoting the visibility and legitimacy conferred upon the subject of disappeared individuals (UN General Assembly 2014, 10). In an environment of little progress and very challenging obstacles put in place during the transition period, the *Comisión para la Paz*'s work contributed to reduce the marginalization of the human rights agenda in the country.

The Final Report, issued in April 2003, elicited numerous criticisms. Although some of these criticisms were known from the start, others became apparent with the report's reception.

---

17 This amount in Uruguayan pesos is equivalent to a relative value between 1,800 and 4,900 US dollars. Due to the economic crisis linked to the ups and downs of its commercial partners in the region, including Argentina, and the crisis of the banking system that marked the period 2000–2003, there was a strong devaluation of the Uruguayan peso, which went from an average exchange rate of 11 pesos per dollar in 2000 to 29 pesos per dollar in 2003.

6.1. THE COMMISSION'S WORK AND THE QUALITY OF THE INVESTIGATION

A range of objections were voiced against the limitations of the Commission's work and the quality of its investigations. In general, the Commission was strongly criticized for the secrecy with which it conducted its work. There are no public records, which undermines transparency. In particular, the Commission was faulted for failing to disclose the military sources consulted during its investigation.[18] The strongest reaction to the report was reserved for the Commission's seemingly blind acceptance of the story from these anonymous sources that the bodies of the disappeared had been exhumed, cremated and their ashes thrown into the River Plate in 1984. The report failed to provide clear evidence to support such an important conclusion. This skepticism was reinforced years later, when other specific conclusions by the Commission were also found to be incorrect (Errandonea 2008, 46).

Activists and victims' families also were disappointed that the Commission did not act upon data they had provided. FAMIDESA had transmitted information on more than 200 cases of disappearance to the Commission. Nevertheless, the Commission was only able to confirm the detention and disappearance of 26 persons in Uruguay and 146 Uruguayan nationals in Argentina, Paraguay and Chile. Moreover, it only determined the location of the remains of a single disappeared person. Following the publication of the final report, FAMIDESA stated that the *Comisión para la Paz* had "failed to obtain relevant information from more than a hundred reports" (*La República* 2003).

6.2. FRAMING DISCOURSE ABOUT THE PAST

Efforts to officially frame the contribution of the *Comisión para la Paz* as closing a chapter in Uruguay's history were powerfully challenged. Decree 146 on the formal acceptance of the Commission's conclusions explicitly stated:

> It should be considered that the Commission for Peace, with its arduous, serious and responsible work and its trustworthy and grave conclusions, has fulfilled the task it was assigned, even beyond expectations, thus contributing to *a definitive truth that should hereafter be considered the official version* regarding the fate of detainees and disappeared persons (Decree 146/2003. Emphasis added).

---

18 Interview with Mirtha Guianze, Montevideo, October 19, 2016.

In the same sense, Article 6 of the Decree intended to explicitly use the truth procedure provided in Article 4 of the Amnesty Law of 1986 as a pretext to close the investigation into the past. The resolution that created the *Comisión para la Paz* did not make an explicit connection to the amnesty. The linking of these two highlighted the tension between the official desire to achieve definitive closure and civil society's expectation that the Commission would be a new starting point.[19] FAMIDESA responded in a communiqué that the statements in the Decree were "untenable", since the Commission did not enjoy the broad investigative authority required for the effective fulfilment of the investigation ordered by Article 4 of the Amnesty Law. SERPAJ, PIT-CNT and sectors of *Frente Amplio* issued similar statements.[20] In particular, they emphasized that the *Comisión para la Paz* did not satisfy the State's responsibility to investigate with respect to the Amnesty Law (*El Observador* 2003; PIT-CNT 2003). Finally, many representatives of human rights organizations believed that the limited dissemination and circulation of the Final Report also undermined a valuable opportunity to expand the public debate regarding the recent past to broader segments of Uruguayan society.[21]

7. THE *COMISIÓN PARA LA PAZ* RECOMMENDATIONS: A TIMELINE FOR CLOSURE

The Report's "Final Suggestions", summarized in Table 2, can be divided into the categories of specific and general. The specific recommendations are tied to the Commission's original mandate ("measures appropriate to repair the victims and concerning relationship status") in accordance with Article 5 of Presidential Resolution no. 858/2000. By contrast, the general recommendations appear to be those items for which there was a consensus among commissioners that the Executive Branch should consider. This established a clear hierarchy between the two categories.

---

[19] Researcher Diego Sempol (2013: 116–122) describes the *Comisión para la Paz* as a "failed full stop."

[20] Point IX of the lengthy resolution of the Executive Secretary of PIC-CNT (2003) illustrates the contradiction: "Now, President Batlle states that he has fulfilled Article 4. He refused to do that at the judicial level. In order to avoid it, he filed an appeal against the right of Tota [María Almeida de] Quinteros [mother of Elena Quinteros, disappeared in 1976] before an Appeals Court. In order to avoid it, he fought against the family's petition in the Administrative Courts and ordered proceedings to get Tota and the PIT/CNT to waive a favorable sentence. He also failed to empower the Commission for Peace to investigate, thus removing any possibility to act in accordance with the procedures governing administrative investigation, such as those set forth by Article 4 of the Amnesty Law".

[21] Interviews with Ana Aguerre and Fabiana Larrobla.

Table 2. Recommendations of the *Comisión para la Paz*

	Specific suggestions
REC 1 Follow-Up Secretariat	The Commission suggests maintaining a strictly administrative follow-up secretariat tasked with performing monitoring and support of pending proceedings and processes (pending fingerprint comparisons and expert evaluations, correction of death certificates, exhumation of bodies buried in anonymous graves and possible repatriation of mortal remains).
REC 2 Legal definition of absence due to forced disappearance	The Commission suggests to the Honorable President of the Republic the promotion of a legal initiative for the purpose of creating a specific and unique legal definition for the crime of absence by forced disappearance, declarable by means of a summary procedure accepting the conclusions of this Committee as sufficient proof (for the purpose of allowing the family members of the victims to overcome a series of formal obstacles pertaining to their marital status and inheritance rights).
REC 3 Redress criteria	**3a** Acceptance by the Honorable President of the Republic of the conclusions of this Final Report as the official version regarding the fate of persons reported as disappeared.
	3b Dissemination and public declaration of the contents of this Final Report and its Addenda, except for private documents addressed to each reporting family.
	3c Promotion of a legal initiative for the purpose of financially redressing, at the judicial level and by summary proceedings, any damage resulting from the illegal actions of State agents, for the benefit of families of persons deceased in our country who, to this date, have not collected any indemnification for the facts acknowledged in the Final Report.
	General Suggestions[22]
REC 4 (Education I)	Promotion and encouragement, at every level – with special emphasis on general study curricula and docent and educator training processes in particular – of an objective and global analysis of the sad reality experienced by the country from the 1970s to the mid-1980s for the purpose of rescuing and appreciating a full and truthful reality, thus allowing full understanding, acceptance and acknowledgment of the multiple and complex causes and factors leading to one of the harshest and most tragic periods in our national history.
REC 5 (Education II – Measures promoting non-recurrence)	Also teach and stimulate at every level, based on the critical analysis suggested in the prior recommendation, values and principles that strengthen our essence as a nation and embody the best guarantee against any type of violence and arbitrariness, such as the following (among others): democracy as the sole, formal and substantial instrument for coexistence; dialogue and non-violent resolution of conflicts and disagreements; tolerance and respect for the rights of others as a vehicle to define common national goals, without prejudice to the diversity that characterizes us as a free and pluralistic society; full consolidation of the rule of law; absolute compliance of the State and its agents with a strict framework of legality; and, finally, the genuine promotion and protection of the fundamental rights of mankind.

(continued)

22 Because the report only enumerates and does not label each one of the five general suggestions, we have included suggested titles in parenthesis intending to keep the structure of the specific suggestions and to facilitate their identification.

Table 2 *continued*

	General Suggestions
REC 6 (Update of the legal code in alignment with international law)	Review and update our current legal regulations in order to contemplate crimes (such as, for example, torture, crimes against humanity, genocide, forced disappearance, etc.) which have been acknowledged and penalized by comparative law, and even by multi-lateral treaties, for the purpose of avoiding and repressing any excess and deviation of the State itself and its agents.
REC 7 (Treaties, Agreements and Conventions)	Ratification and approval of international treaties, agreements and conventions promoted internationally by societies who share our humanistic and liberal vision.
REC 8 (Institutionalization of Human Rights)	Development of an adequate environment to analyze and solve the creation of a suitable and autonomous institutional structure empowered to permanently monitor and control regulations and laws tending to more effectively protect individual human rights.

Source: Final Report of the *Comisión para la Paz* (2003).

Due to the confidentiality of the process and the lack of access to records, it is difficult to reconstruct the process through which recommendations were formulated. From the establishment of the Commission, FAMIDESA had access to its labor.[23] Other victims' and human rights organizations such as SERPAJ Uruguay were not invited to participate, though they expressed a willingness to collaborate. According to Ana Aguerre of SERPAJ, "They were very unwilling to accept outside proposals."[24]

In an addendum to its 2004 report *A todos ellos. Informe de madres y familiares de uruguayos detenidos desaparecidos*, FAMIDESA provides an extensive list of proposals, dated June 29, 2002, 10 months before the presentation of the Commission's Final Report, under the label "*Recomendaciones para un Nunca Más de Madres y Familiares entregadas a la Comisión para la Paz*". This extensive document, which presents 64 recommendations across 22 pages, was apparently in the possession of the *Comisión para la Paz* as its own report was under construction. FAMIDESA grouped its proposals into five thematic chapters:

- Consequences of repression. Full redress;
- Human rights education;
- Proper adjustment of the legal framework;
- Armed Forces and National Police;
- Follow-up of recommendations.

23 Interviews with Elena Zaffaroni and Ana Aguerre.
24 Interview with Ana Aguerre.

As elaborated in Appendix 1, a detailed comparison between the FAMIDESA suggestions and the final *Comisión para la Paz*'s recommendations reveals that the Commission seemed to base many of its recommendations on items put forward by FAMIDESA.

In general, recommendations suggested by victims' and human rights organizations go further and are more precise than those set forth by the *Comisión para la Paz*. The reforms are more ambitious, involve more institutions, and set higher expectations for broader society's participation in the defense and protection of the proposed measures. They place greater emphasis on the need to disseminate the Commission's work and propose more extensive regulatory reforms. Finally, they include a variety of measures to guarantee non-recurrence and maintain a permanent focus that explicitly refers to the notion of "human rights", in clear contrast with the recommendations of the *Comisión para la Paz*. Thus, our analysis confirms that the Final Report diluted the content of FAMIDESA's recommendations made available to the Commission for Peace.

8. IMPLEMENTING THE RECOMMENDATIONS: BALANCE AND CHALLENGES

The extent of implementation can be assessed from different points of view. A cursory comparison with other truth commissions in the region suggests that the Commission's recommendations are quite limited, both in the way they are formulated and with respect to the goals that they seek to achieve. That is, comparatively, the recommendations made by the *Comisión para la Paz* are expressed in a manner are likely to result in more limited impact, even with full implementation. However, viewed on its own terms, which we do in this section, the recommendations show more potential. As summarized in Table 3, we find evidence of movement to enact the vast majority of recommendations, though progress has been fitful and there has been notable backsliding.

According to the general and specific objectives set forth by the *Comisión para la Paz*, several patterns are apparent. First, the *Comisión para la Paz* did not propose any recommendations to achieve criminal accountability. Therefore, judicial activity about past abuses cannot be directly linked to the implementation of its recommendations. Second, the specific recommendations, which the *Comisión para la Paz* prioritized, were implemented at a higher level than the general recommendations. Third, the greatest progress has been achieved on those recommendations calling for the creation of new institutions and legal reforms. Fourth, redress measures (reparations) were only moderately implemented. Finally, measures connected to human rights training and education were the least implemented, although recent events could portend a change in the future. Below, we discuss each of these patterns in greater depth by chronicling the steps taken on each of the recommendations.

Table 3. Recommendation Implementation Summary

No.	Recommendation	Type	Main implementation milestones
1	Follow-Up Secretariat	Specific	Follow-up Secretariat, Ministry of Human Rights for the Recent Past, Truth and Justice Task Group
2	Legal definition of absence due to forced disappearance	Specific	Law 17.894/2005
3 a	Redress criteria / Acceptance of the conclusions	Specific	Decree 146/2003
3 b	Redress criteria / Disseminate report and communication with family members	Specific	Limited dissemination of report. Ongoing private communication with families. Declaration of "official and final truth" highly controversial and discussed in public.[25]
3 c	Redress criteria / Reparations	Specific	Law 18.033/2006 Law 18.596/2009
4	Education I	General	National Human Rights Education Plan
5	Education II – Measures promoting non-recurrence	General	
6	Update of the legal code in alignment with international law	General	Law 17.914/2005 Law 18.026/2006
7	Treaties, Agreements and Conventions	General	
8	Institutionalization of human rights	General	*Institución Nacional de Derechos Humanos y Defensoría del Pueblo* (National Institution of Human Rights and the People's Ombudsman) (INDDHH)

Source: Compiled by the authors.

8.1. CREATION OF INSTITUTIONS (RECOMMENDATIONS 1 AND 8)

The Follow-Up Secretariat (*Secretaría de Seguimiento*) of the *Comisión para la Paz* is an exceptional example of implementation. It was conceived as a strictly administrative entity, intended to execute and conclude the mandate to investigate the cases evaluated by the Commission. However, its institutional design changed with the passage of time and currently it is a complex organization the purposes of which actually exceed the Commission's recommendation.

As set forth in the recommendation, the office of the Follow-up Secretariat was created on the date of presentation of the Report (April 10, 2003) by

[25] We thank Gabriela Fried for pointing this out to us. Email communication of 25 February 2019.

Presidential Resolution no. 449. The body was tasked with completing a series of pending procedures explained in the recommendation: completing fingerprint comparisons and expert evaluations; the correction of death certificates; and the exhumation of bodies buried in unmarked graves and possible repatriation of mortal remains. Implementation through this office followed the boundaries previously set by the *Comisión para la Paz* in its mandate.

Investigations subsequently went further. In 2005, a General Agreement of Cooperation between the President of the Republic and the University of the Republic (UDELAR) created two research teams; a forensic anthropology group and a group of historians. These teams were tasked with continuing the search and study of data on "Human rights and detainees and disappeared persons" based on the work initiated by the Commission for Peace.

Things progressed further during the first term of the *Frente Amplio* led government. In September 2007, the government established the Follow-up Secretariat for the Commission for Peace (*Secretaría de Seguimiento de la Comisión para la Paz*) to replace the original Follow-up Secretariat. The creation of this new institution reframed the Agreement with the two UDELAR teams, thus allowing them to continue their work. Since then, the university teams have published and updated a series of research reports on the subject of individuals disappeared or murdered for political reasons.[26] The last update includes a total of 192 cases of recorded disappeared individuals (both within Uruguayan territory and elsewhere), 20 cases more than the 172 cases documented by the Commission for Peace. Overall, this investigation was an independent and empirically-based research project that involved a diverse professional interdisciplinary team of historians and scientists that tackled tasks that the Commission was never intended to address.

In 2013, the Secretariat was once again reformed, this time being upgraded to ministerial status. The Ministry of Human Rights for the Recent Past was established by Presidential Resolution no. 463. In May 2015, the Truth and Justice Task Force was created within the Ministry's institutional framework (Decree 131) to provide victims, family members, and Uruguayan society with

---

[26] Presidency of the Republic (2007) *Investigación histórica sobre Detenidos-Desaparecidos*, Montevideo, IMPO; Presidency of the Republic (2007) *Investigación arqueológica sobre Detenidos-Desaparecidos*, Montevideo, IMPO; University of the Republic (2008). *Investigación sobre la dictadura y el terrorismo de Estado en el Uruguay* (1973–1985), Montevideo, FHCE–CSIC; Presidency of the Republic (2011) *Actualización de la Investigación Histórica sobre Detenidos-Desaparecidos*. Digital publication; Presidency of the Republic (2011) *Actualización de la Investigación Arqueológica sobre Detenidos-Desaparecidos*. Digital publication; "*Actualización de la investigación histórica sobre detenidos desaparecidos*" (1971–1982); Presidency of the Republic (2015) "*Investigación histórica sobre asesinados políticos por responsabilidad o aquiescencia del Estado*" (1973–1985) (Available at: http://www.fhuce.edu.uy/index.php/institucional/ddhh-sociedad/pasado-reciente).

"mechanisms to achieve essential Truth, Justice and Memory to guarantee non-recurrence." The scope of the Task Force exceeds anything that came previously. According to one of its members, the above-mentioned Macarena Gelman, the group is the result of society's persistent demands regarding matters related to Truth and Justice, especially the perception of actors committed to human rights that, in spite of progress, "there is still a lot to do" and that these issues "are not settled" in the country.[27] Article 1 of the decree creating the Task Force establishes that its main purpose is to:

> Investigate crimes against humanity committed by agents of the State or others who, although not such, enjoyed the authorization, support or acquiescence of the State, domestically or internationally, in the framework of illegal actions by the State and State terrorism, during the period between June 13, 1968, and June 26, 1973, and June 27, 1973, and February 28, 1985.

In conclusion, this recommendation on follow-up has generated momentum for significantly expanding discussion and investigation of past human rights violations in subsequent years. Particularly since 2007, the scope and purpose of these bodies have grown considerably and has resulted in greater emphasis on the construction of historical truth. Thus, what began as a strictly technical and administrative Secretariat eventually grew into a ministry tasked with being an active promoter of the advancement of the memory, truth, and justice process.

The second recommendation that mentions the creation of institutions is recommendation 8. This recommendation is the most ambitious and largest in scope since it promotes the establishment of "autonomous environments and institutions in charge of following-up and monitoring regulations and laws for the protection of individual human rights." Organizations such as SERPAJ had already insisted on the need to create institutions of this nature during the late 1980s.[28] While Uruguay has certainly introduced human rights institutions in the intervening years, there is no evidence that the creation of the *Institución Nacional de Derechos Humanos y Defensoría del Pueblo* (the National Institution for Human Rights and the People's Ombudsman, INDDHH) in 2008 by Law 18.446, in particular, was based on the recommendation of the *Comisión para la Paz*. However, its institutional and operational features are consistent with the Commission's goals. Since its inception, the INDDHH has made important contributions to developing regulations to protect human rights, specifically, its recommendations regarding reparations, *habeas corpus*, and the administration of justice. Among the pending issues are the need for the institution to possess adequate tools to guarantee its autonomy, a larger budget, and a stronger

27 Interview with Macarena Gelman.
28 Interview with Ana Aguerre.

commitment of "State agencies to take steps to implement its recommendations" (UN General Assembly 2014, 17–21).

8.2. OFFICIAL ACCEPTANCE, DISSEMINATION AND COMMUNICATION (RECOMMENDATIONS 3A AND 3B)

The decree accepting the 2003 Final Report set forth that the Commission had fulfilled its duty to provide "a definitive truth that must, from now on, be considered the official version regarding the fate of the detainees and disappeared persons" (Decree 146/2003). While some victims and human rights activists were unsatisfied with how this was framed, we consider the recommendation fully implemented. Another recommendation merely pointed out the need to publish the report. While this did happen, the Final Report has not been widely disseminated.

Finally, regarding communication, the *Comisión para la Paz* decided that some materials were "documents of a confidential nature." For that reason, during the course of its work, information regarding victims was communicated verbally and personally to family members and, after the report was presented, through a written summary of the cases.[29]

8.3. LEGAL REFORM (RECOMMENDATIONS 6 AND 7)

In terms of the approval and ratification of treaties, agreements and conventions that "are driven at an international level by societies that share our humanist and liberal vision," it should be noted that such generic and imprecise formulation makes it difficult to precisely determine its impact. However, overall, fulfilment of this recommendation is relatively advanced. Law 17.914/2005, for example, approved the Optional Protocol of the Convention Against Torture. Another example is the approval of Law 18.026 on Cooperation with the International Criminal Court on the issue of the fight against genocide, war crimes and crimes against humanity. Nonetheless, according to Errandonea, despite legislative action and the ratification of human rights treaties, "Uruguay has made no effort to develop a legal-institutional architecture to ensure non-recurrence" (Errandonea 2008, 55).

---

29 Interview with Silvia Bellizi, member of FAMIDESA.

8.4. REPARATIONS (RECOMMENDATIONS 2 AND 3c)

The *Comisión para la Paz* recommended creating a new legal definition of "absence due to forced disappearance" (recommendation 2). In principle, this required the government to take relatively simple steps to implement it. Two years after the presentation of the Commission's final report and after a change in government, Law 17.894 was approved in 2005. It established that:

> Persons whose forced disappearance was confirmed by Addendum 3.1 of the Final Report of the Commission for Peace are hereby declared absent. Art. 1: Declare the absence by reason of forced disappearance of persons whose disappearance within the national territory was confirmed in Addendum 3.1 of the Final Report produced by the Commission for Peace (…). In addition, include any cases initiated by the Commission for Peace resolved by the Executive Branch following a report from the Follow-up Ministry (…) The above statement of absence allows the opening of the succession process in respect of the absent individual (Article 1037 of the Civil Code).

Although a series of laws restoring the rights of victims of the dictatorship had been approved since 1985, there were no regulations specifically acknowledging the situation of family members of the disappeared. Recommendation 3 did not specifically formulate the type of "indemnification" established, other than stating that it should be processed "at the administrative level and through summary proceedings." In 2006, following the strong push from the CRYSOL Association (mentioned in section 4 above), Law 18.033 restored retirement and pension rights to the victims and explicitly included the acknowledgment of "survivor pension" rights for family members of individuals declared absent by Law 17.894. Three years later, in 2009, Law 18.596 was approved. According to the Special Rapporteur on the promotion of truth, justice, reparation and guarantees of non-recurrence of the United Nations (UN General Assembly 2014, 12), this law was the first piece of Uruguayan legislation that explicitly acknowledged the right to full reparation of victims and the State's responsibility with regards to the human rights violations. A special Commission to indemnify the victims – including political prisoners, minors born in captivity, as well as disappeared persons and torture victims – was created for this purpose. As of December 2017, the *Comisión Especial de Reparaciones* (Special Commission for Reparations) created within the Ministry of Education and Culture had issued 439 procedures for financial reparation, although the situation of family members of disappeared persons is not specified therein.[30]

---

[30] Available at: https://www.gub.uy/ministerio-educacion-cultura/politicas-y-gestion/comision-especial-reparacion.

Current provisions require victims to choose between the right to reparation and pension and retirement benefits. This situation "blurs the notion of reparation as a legal matter, making it seem like a favour or kindness conferred by the State to the victims" (UN General Assembly 2014, 13–14). In addition, the UN report faults the government for failing to provide the special commissions created to follow-up on reparation laws with sufficient resources and technical personnel to effectively perform their duties.

8.5. TRAINING AND EDUCATION (RECOMMENDATIONS 4 AND 5)

Until recently, these recommendations have attracted comparatively little attention. Around 2014, a UN report concluded that "the study of the dictatorship and human rights violations continues to be marginal notwithstanding the wide variety of available bibliography and didactic resources" (UN General Assembly 2014, 18). The Human Rights Board of the Ministry of Education and Culture was created in 2006. This office produced the National Plan for Human Rights Education in 2007.[31] However, we were only able to verify the first step in the continuity of this plan in 2017. According to information obtained from the government's website, the *Plan Nacional de Educación en Derechos Humanos* (National Plan for Education on Human Rights), was the first of its kind in Uruguay, resulting from a lengthy process of advisory efforts and agreements, and was officially launched in August of that year. The Plan was formulated by the *Comisión Nacional para la Educación en Derechos Humanos* (National Commission for Human Rights Education), constituted by the National Administration of Public Education, the Ministry of Education and Culture, the University of the Republic and the Ministry of Human Rights of the Presidency of the Republic. Currently, we do not have sufficient evidence to assess the real impact of the Plan within the educational system.

9. EVALUATING THE RECOMMENDATIONS OF THE *COMISIÓN PARA LA PAZ*

Evaluating the work of the *Comisión para la Paz* and the implementation of its recommendations poses significant challenges. The Commission was instrumental in bringing about the first official acknowledgment of the disappearances perpetrated by agents of the State. However, public opinion in

---

31 Available at: http://www.ohchr.org/Documents/Issues/Education/Training/actions-plans/uruguay.pdf.

Uruguay has never considered the Commission a fundamental milestone in the process of national memory, truth, and justice.[32]

Official awareness of the issue of disappearances and the acceptance of the right to reparation after a lengthy period of silence undoubtedly feature among the main achievements of the *Comisión para la Paz*. However, it has never captured the broader public's imagination. This lack of public awareness is in part a consequence of the secrecy with which it worked and the limited resources allocated for its investigations. Equally importantly, through the construction of the Commission and its mandate, the government attempted to restrict the activation of a public debate regarding the dictatorial past for the purpose of finding a "definitive truth". These factors resulted in a series of unambitious recommendations that did not generate much expectation at the time.

In general terms, the recommendations set forth by the *Comisión para la Paz* in its 2003 Final Report are in an advanced state of implementation. The steps taken, particularly since 2005, during a series of progressive governments, have generated progress on reparations and legal advances for the protection of human rights. It is difficult to disentangle how much credit the recommendations should be given for these achievements, however. As we have noted, many of these recommendations were claims made by human rights groups and the Left well before *Comisión para la Paz*. This is most clear in the demands articulated by FAMIDESA. Thus, it is not surprising that these ideas were resurrected and advanced once the Left took power in 2005. It is possible that these measures would have been enacted even if the Commission had never existed. Moreover, it is somewhat surprising that the Commission did not implement more of the original nuanced demands when the opportunity arose. In addition, while there has been some progress in truth-seeking efforts regarding military-era abuses, it would be problematic to claim that the Commission was the driving force behind these advances.

Finally, although comparatively limited in scope and with serious setbacks along the way, the growing number of judicial investigations into human rights violations committed by the dictatorship and determination of criminal liability constitutes a new development in the Uruguayan truth and justice process. Note, though, that judicial investigations were underway by 2002 – that is prior to *Comisión para la Paz* – and increased in scope during the period 2005–2010 (Burt, Fried and Lessa 2013; Lessa and Skaar 2016). It is thus difficult to trace these developments to the *Comisión para la Paz*, except in noting the absence of a call for criminal accountability among its recommendations.

---

[32] A cursory examination of the general Uruguayan media coverage of this subject upon the death of ex-President Jorge Batlle in October 2016 is notable for the significant absence of a connection between his political career and the historical-political relevance of the *Comisión para la Paz*. There was scant mention of the Commission as a milestone of his government.

BIBLIOGRAPHY

Amnesty International (2007). *Verdad, justicia y reparación. Creación de una comisión de la verdad efectiva*. London: Amnesty International Publications.

Bohoslavsky, Juan Pablo (2012). "El Eslabón Financiero en la Justicia Transicional Uruguaya". *Revista Uruguaya de Ciencia Política*, no. 21 (SPE): 153–179.

Bucheli, Gabriel, Valentina Curto, et al. (2005). *Vivos los llevaron: historia de la lucha de Madres y Familiares de Uruguayos Detenidos Desaparecidos (1976–2005)*. Montevideo: Trilce.

Burt, Jo-Marie, Gabriela Fried Amilivia, and Francesca Lessa (2013). "Civil society and the resurgent struggle against impunity in Uruguay (1986–2012)." *International Journal of Transitional Justice* no. 7 (2): 306–327.

Caetano, Gerardo (2005). "Introducción general. Marco histórico y cambio político en dos décadas de democracia. De la transición democrática al gobierno de izquierda". In Caetano, Gerardo (ed.), *20 años de democracia. Uruguay 1985–2005: miradas múltiples*. Montevideo: Taurus.

Caetano, Gerardo (2008). "Hacia un 'momento de verdad' en el Uruguay reciente. Las investigaciones sobre el destino de los detenidos desaparecidos (2005–2007)". *Sociohistórica: Cuadernos del CISH*, nos. 23–24: 199–249.

Comisión Investigadora Parlamentaria Sobre la Situación de Personas Desaparecidas y Hechos que la Motivaron (1985). *Informe Final de la Comisión Investigadora Parlamentaria Sobre Situación de Personas Desaparecidas y Hechos que la Motivaron*. Spanish version available at (only pp. 1–25): http://archivo.presidencia.gub.uy/_web/noticias/2007/06/tomo4.pdf.

Comisión Para la Paz (COMIPAZ/ComiPaz) (2003). *Informe Final de la Comisión para la Paz*. Montevideo. Spanish version available at: https://www.usip.org/sites/default/files/file/resources/collections/commissions/Uruguay-Report_Informal.pdf.

Corbo, Daniel (2007). "La transición de la dictadura a la democracia en el Uruguay. Perspectiva comparada sobre los modelos de salida política en el Cono Sur de América Latina". *Humanidades* no. VII (1): 23–47.

Costa, Mario, et al. (October 2006). "Pérez Aguirre y la educación en derechos humanos". Red de Amigos de Pérez Aguirre. Available at: http://www.debateducativo.edu.uy/aportes/Perez%20Aguirre%20y%20la%20ed.htm.

De Frouville, Olivier (2016). "La question de la justice et de la vérité en Uruguay devant les Nationsunies". *ILCEA* no. 26. Available at: http://ilcea.revues.org/3895.

De Giorgi, Álvaro (2014). *Sanguinetti. La otra historia del pasado reciente*. Montevideo: Fin de Siglo.

De Giorgi, Ana Laura (2013). "El Frente Amplio y su laberinto. La izquierda uruguaya frente a la ley de caducidad". In Marchesi (ed.), *Ley de Caducidad, un tema inconcluso. Momentos, actores y argumentos (1986–2013)*, 61–102. Montevideo: Ediciones Trilce.

Decreto 448/2003.

Errandonea, Jorge (2008). "Justicia transicional en Uruguay". *Revista Instituto Interamericano de Derechos Humanos* no. 47: 13–69.

FAMIDESA (2004). *A todos ellos. Informe de madres y familiares de uruguayos detenidos desaparecidos*. Montevideo: Caligráficos.

Fried, Gabriela and Lessa, Francesca (eds.) (2011). *Luchas contra la impunidad. Uruguay 1985–2011*. Montevideo: Ediciones Trilce.

Galain, Pablo (2014). "El proceso de justicia transicional en Uruguay". *Verba Iuris* no. 32 (July–December 2014): 33–44.

Garretón Kreft, Francisca, Marianne González Le Saux and Silvana Lauzán (2011). *Políticas públicas de verdad y memoria en 7 países de América Latina (Argentina, Bolivia, Brasil, Chile, Paraguay, Perú y Uruguay)*. Santiago: Universidad de Chile-Centro de Derechos Humanos.

Gillespie, Charles (1995). *Negociando la democracia. Políticos y generales en la salida uruguaya*. Montevideo: ICP-FCU.

Guianze, Mirtha (2016). "La impunidad más allá de la Ley de Caducidad. Construcción de un marco jurídico nacional de derechos humanos vs. persistencia de la cultura de impunidad". *ILCEA*, no. 26. Available at: http://ilcea.revues.org/3916.

Inter-American Court of Human Rights (Corte IDH) (2011). *Caso Gelman vs. Uruguay. Fondo y Reparaciones*. Sentencia de 24 de febrero de 2011.

La República (April 22, 2003). "Familiares rechazó el decreto del gobierno que enmarca investigación en la Ley de Caducidad".

Lessa, Francesca (2016). "¿Justicia o impunidad? Cuentas pendientes a treinta años del retorno a la democracia". *ILCEA* no. 26. Available at: http://ilcea.revues.org/3874.

Lessa, Francesca and Elin Skaar (2016). "Uruguay. Halfway towards accountability". In Skaar, Garcia-Godos, Collins (eds.), *Transitional Justice in Latin America: The Uneven Road from Impunity towards Accountability*. New York: Routledge.

Marchesi, Aldo (2001). *Las lecciones del pasado, memoria y ciudadanía en los informes 'nunca más'. Informe final del concurso: Culturas e identidades en América Latina y el Caribe*. Programa Regional de Becas CLACSO.

Observatorio Luz Ibarburu (2015). *Informe Anual – 2015*. Montevideo: Observatorio Luz Ibarburu.

Olivera, Raúl (2016). "Memoria, verdad y justicia en Uruguay: la gestión del pasado en un escenario de luces y sombras", *ILCEA* no. 26. Available at: http://ilcea.revues.org/3905.

PIT/CNT (April 23, 2003). *Resolución del Secretariado Ejecutivo sobre el Informe Final de la Comisión para la Paz*. Montevideo.

Polack, Ana (2004). "Ciudadanía y Derechos Humanos en el período de transición a la democracia. Un estudio comparado de los casos de Argentina y Uruguay". e-l@tina *Revista electrónica de estudios latinoamericanos* no. 3 (9): 21–39. Facultad de Ciencias Sociales Universidad de Buenos Aires, Buenos Aires, Argentina.

Sanguinetti, Julio María (1991). *El temor y la impaciencia. Ensayo sobre la transición democrática en América Latina*. Buenos Aires: Fondo de Cultura Económica.

Sempol, Diego (2013). "A la sombra de una impunidad perenne. El movimiento de derechos humanos y la ley de caducidad". In Marchesi, Aldo (ed.), *Ley de caducidad: un tema inconcluso: momentos, actores y argumentos (1986–2013)*. Montevideo: Trilce.

Skaar, Elin (2011). *Judicial independence and human rights in Latin America: Violations, politics, and prosecution*. New York: Palgrave Macmillan.

Sputnik Mundo (March 10, 2017). "Impunidad al acecho: amenazan de muerte a activistas de derechos humanos de Uruguay". Available at: https://mundo.sputniknews.com/americalatina/201703101067488118-amenazas-militares-derechos-humanos-uruguay/.

United Nations, General Assembly (August 28, 2014). *Informe del Relator Especial sobre la promoción de la verdad, la justicia, la reparación y las garantías de no repetición,* Pablo de Greiff.
United Nations, Human Rights Committee (March 1, 2013). *Examen de los informes presentados por los Estados partes en virtud del artículo 40 del Pacto - Uruguay.*

ANNEX 1: LIST OF INTERVIEWEES

Fabiana Larrobla, Political Scientist, Universidad de la República. Member of the teams in charge of the historical research of the dictatorship. Montevideo, October 18, 2016.

Mariana Mota, Judge. Montevideo, October 18, 2016.

Mirtha Guianze, ex Prosecutor, ex Director of *Institución Nacional de Derechos Humanos y Defensoría del Pueblo* (INDDHH). Montevideo, October 19, 2016.

Elba Rama, *Asociación de Funcionarios Judiciales del Uruguay* (Association of Judicial Authorities of Uruguay). Montevideo, October 19, 2016.

Silvia Bellizzi, *Madres y Familiares de Uruguayos Detenidos Desaparecidos.* (Mothers and Family Members of Uruguayan Detainees and Disappeared) Montevideo, October 19, 2016.

Macarena Gelman, *Grupo de Trabajo por Verdad y Justicia* (Task Force on Truth and Justice). Montevideo, October 20, 2016.

Elena Zafaronni, *Madres y Familiares de Uruguayos Detenidos Desaparecidos* (Mothers and Family Members of Uruguayan Detainees Disappeared). Montevideo, October 20, 2016.

Isabel Wschebor Pellegrino, Ex-Director of *la Secretaría de Derechos Humanos del Pasado Reciente* (Secretariat of Human Rights of the Recent Past). Montevideo, October 20, 2016.

Ana Aguerre, *Servicio de Paz y Justicia* (SERPAJ). Montevideo, October 20, 2016.

Aldo Marchesi, Historian. Online interview Buenos Aires–Montevideo, December 6, 2016.

ANNEX 2: COMPARING THE *COMISIÓN PARA LA PAZ*'S RECOMMENDATIONS (2003) WITH THE RECOMMENDATIONS FORMULATED BY FAMIDESA (2004)

***Comisión para la Paz* Recommendations**	**Balance of present differences / similarities** in the text of "Recomendaciones para un Nunca Más de Madres y Familiares entregadas a la Comisión para la Paz"[33] – dated 29 June, 2002.
REC 1 Follow-Up Secretariat	Much broader suggestion regarding establishment of a "Follow-up Commission" which, after publication of the Final Report and for a limited time, monitors the recommendations of the Commission for Peace until a National Commission for Human Rights and a People's Defender or Ombudsman is established with much more ambitious structures and attributions.
REC 3 Redress Criteria (3b and 3c)	It particularly emphasizes the sense of advertising the results: "Publicly and truthfully report the forced disappearances, the facts which motivated such activities and their consequences, acknowledging responsibility and clearly and emphatically committing to take any steps necessary to guarantee non-recurrence of these incidents, which are contrary to human dignity." (FAMIDESA 2004). The features of this policy are expanded by enumerating a lengthy list of other specific measures for full reparation, including not only to direct family members but also the victims of forced disappearance (both children and adults).
REC 4 Education I REC 5 Education II – Measures promoting non-recurrence	Suggests a group of recommendations on education characterized by their more precise formulation and their focus on human rights terminology. It is interesting to note how a sentence-by-sentence comparison verifies that this passage of text from FAMIDESA was reworded by the *Comisión para la Paz* and included as its recommendation no. 5 in the Final Report. The product of such final version indicates an adaptation and a reduced weight placed on certain phrases and definitions. The FAMIDESA passage states: "the Commission recommends a thorough revision and adaptation of academic curricula and plans at all levels of the entire national educational system on the basis of the following principles: the appreciation of democracy and non-violent conflict resolution; the integration of the different sectors of society, thus generating participation mechanisms in a framework of respect for differences and solidarity; the consolidation of the Rule of Law as a resource against authoritarianism, arbitrariness and impunity; and the respect, promotion and protection of human rights as the integrating and driving principle for the prior goals." (FAMIDESA 2004).

(continued)

33 "Recommendations for Never Again from Mothers and Family Members Delivered to the Commission for Peace". Translated by Diana Valori. The set of recommendations are reproduced in FAMIDESA 2004.

continued

Comisión para la Paz **Recommendations**	**Balance of present differences / similarities** in the text of "Recomendaciones para un Nunca Más de Madres y Familiares entregadas a la Comisión para la Paz"[33] – dated 29 June, 2002.
REC 6 Update of the legal code in alignment with international law	FAMIDESA's suggestion is more specific and larger in scope: it suggests creating a legal definition for the crimes of torture and forced disappearance, establishing criminal penalties according to severity of the crime in question. In addition, FAMIDESA's suggestion includes regulatory reforms regarding matters not addressed by the recommendations of the *Comisión para la Paz*: – Creation of a legal definition and punishment for crimes committed with direct or indirect State support (if a type of criminal offense already exists, its inclusion as special aggravating circumstance). – Creation of a legal definition for the crime of failing to inform the fate of detainees-disappeared persons and possible location of the remains as aggravating circumstance for the crime of *False Testimony*. – Express incorporation of behaviour promoting or justifying human rights violations or defend past incidents of such nature in an existing type of criminal offense, such as justification of facts considered crimes – Regulation of the institution of *Habeas Corpus*. – Regulation of the operation of State intelligence agencies – regulation of the promotion of military and police officers for the purpose of hindering the promotion of anybody who participated in facts considered grave human rights violations.
REC 7 Treaties, agreements, conventions	The text more deeply develops this aspect and even highlights a recommendation which was not included in the final report: "The Commission has decided to leave for the end (...) a recommendation considered essentially relevant to the process of reaffirming democracy and respect for human rights in Uruguay. (...) considered a historical step in the development of institutions at the service of the maximum promotion of human persons, to reform the current National Constitution by regularly established mechanisms, to grant constitutional hierarchy to any treaty, agreement or convention on human rights entered, signed or ratified in the future by our Republic." (FAMIDESA 2004).
REC 8 Institutionalization of Human Rights	As stated for REC 1, the text seeks to develop institutionality through the Follow-up Ministry, which would act as precedent for the future establishment of a National Commission on Human Rights and an office of the People's Defender or Ombudsman. It focuses on an aspect not addressed by recommendation 8 of the *Comisión para la Paz*: "Uruguayan society must possess, as soon as possible, one of the most efficient international resources for the protection, promotion and defense of human rights: the Ombudsman or People's Defender. The Commission understands, (...) that it is unacceptable, considering the development of this institution, especially in Latin America, that our country has not yet approved a law establishing the office of the People's Defender, thus ignoring several recommendations from, among other agencies, the Human Rights Committee and the United Nations Committee on Children's Rights." (FAMIDESA 2004).

Source: Authors' analysis based on FAMIDESA 2004.

PARAGUAY'S TRUTH AND JUSTICE COMMISSION

Recommending Justice without Political Change

Félix Reátegui Carrillo, Tania Gómez, and Eduardo Hurtado*

---

* All authors are affiliated with Instituto de Democracia y Derechos Humanos Pontificia Universidad Católica del Perú. The authors wish to thank Cath Collins and Onur Bakiner for helpful comments on earlier drafts of this chapter.

1. INTRODUCTION

In 2003, the Paraguayan State responded to society's demands for truth about the Stroessner dictatorship (1954–89) by creating the Truth and Justice Commission (*Comisión de Verdad y Justicia* – CVJ). These demands had been expressed in different ways after the end of the dictatorship of Alfredo Stroessner in 1989. Institutions such as the Paraguayan branch of the American Association of Jurists and the Ethical Tribunal Against Impunity, created in 1993, promoted public denunciation of human rights abuses, providing a space to listen to the victims and dictating symbolic sentences against perpetrators. These initiatives prepared the political context for the creation and public acceptance of the CVJ years later (Arellano 2012).

The Commission of Truth and Justice was created with the mandate to investigate the crimes and abuses committed by the 35-year-long dictatorship of Alfredo Stroessner. The creation of the CVJ was preceded by some initiatives towards memorialization and the discovery of the "Archives of Terror" in a facility of the Police Investigative Department in 1992. The archives gather a massive amount of documentation from the dictatorship era containing information about detainees; confidential reports of individual surveillance; surveillance of opposition political parties, students' groups and labor unions; immigration records; as well as telephone and other forms of domestic surveillance.

The creation of a truth-seeking body was also anticipated by the establishment of a mechanism to give monetary reparations to the victims through the Ombudsman Office, and the question arose as to whether the victims would lose interest in demands for truth and justice once economic reparations were paid (Arellano 2012). However, international pressure in favor of human rights policies would not allow the demand for truth to disappear. The Inter-American Commission on Human Rights reiterated a recommendation to create a commission to work with the database built from the "Archives of Terror" and other sources. The UNESCO mission in Paraguay asked for the creation of a truth commission, and a National Movement of Victims of the Stronist Dictatorship (*Movimiento Nacional de Víctimas de la Dictadura Stronista* – MNVDS) emerged.[1]

Active in the mid-2000s, the CVJ conducted its operations without significant obstacles and produced a comprehensive report. The report contained a section of 176 recommendations for reparations, justice, and institutional reform designed to address the consequences of authoritarianism and its root causes.[2] However, the truth-seeking process and its aftermath were overshadowed by the past. The CVJ operated in the context of a transition where the old political power structures had not completely faded and where the political culture and institutions remained unreformed from authoritarian times.

As a result, the recommendations made by Paraguay's Truth and Justice Commission have achieved a low degree of implementation, despite the institutional steps that were taken to realize them. In effect, shortly after the Commission released its report, a Directorate was established within the Ombudsman Office with the mission of following up on the recommendations. However, this agency remains underfunded and has not been able to lead an effective process of implementation.

2. HISTORICAL BACKGROUND

The official truth-seeking process undertaken by the Truth and Justice Commission in Paraguay started 14 years after the demise of the 35-year-long dictatorship of General Alfredo Stroessner (1954–1989). The CVJ was created in 2003 as a response to the demands of a coalition of victims and human rights organizations who had been working for the preservation of historical memory since the earliest stages of the political transition.

It is an important feature of the Paraguayan transition that the end of the dictatorship did not translate immediately into a change of regime. "Stronism" continued in place many years after Stroessner stepped down, through successive governments built upon the alliance between the military and Stroessner's Colorado Party.

---

1 *Stronism* is a term derived from the dictator's last name, Stroessner, meaning "in connection with Stroessner", "belonging or related to the Stroessner's rule".

2 The section on recommendations contains 177 items. However, item 177 is not a recommendation but a general remark about the rationale and the importance of the previous recommendations.

General Alfredo Stroessner rose to power through a military coup in 1954 after a long period of political instability. A *New York Times* obituary reported that "[i]n the 27 years before his coup, this small landlocked nation had had 22 presidents, and no experience of a democratic transition of power in its 143-year history".[3] Right after seizing power, Stroessner managed to forge an alliance with the Colorado Party, which became the regime's political machine, facilitating control over the country and the organization of murky electoral processes that gave the regime the trappings of democracy.

The Stroessner regime is usually described as a mixture of personal autocracy, military institutional dictatorship, and one-party exclusionary authoritarianism.

> (T)he *stronato* was based upon a triangular relationship of power between the armed forces, the government and the Colorado Party, with Stroessner as the unifying axis in his role as President, Commander in Chief of the Armed Forces and Honorary President of the Colorado Party (Lambert 2000).[4]

As an example of this conflation of government and party during Stroessner's rule, membership in the Colorado Party became mandatory for public servants. The Party functioned as a political machine that enabled Stroessner to stage and win eight rigged presidential elections during his 35 years in power, five of them with at least 90 per cent of the vote. The lowest vote share he ever received was 70.9 per cent. The whole period was characterized by systematic repression against political opponents through a vast structure of police surveillance. The CVJ established that the regime used the attempts to organize armed resistance against the dictatorship as an excuse to systematically violate the human rights of the Paraguayan civilian population (Comisión de Verdad y Justicia 2008).[5]

Any public expression of dissension or criticism was punished through measures oscillating from police harassment to arbitrary detention.

---

3 Jean Schemo, D. (August 16, 2006). "Stroessner, Paraguay's Enduring Dictator, Dies". *The New York Times*.

4 The term *stronato* refers to the period of Stroessner's rule and to the regime organized during that period. Lambert cites Benjamin Arditi, (1992). *Adiós a Stroessner. La reconstrucción de la política en el Paraguay*. Asunción: CDE.

5 Literally, in Spanish: "El régimen utilizó los distintos intentos de organizar resistencia armada contra la dictadura como una excusa ante la población y la comunidad internacional, para realizar múltiples violaciones de derechos humanos a sus miembros y a grandes sectores de la población civil, considerando como enemigo interno incluso a las bases sociales de apoyo y las propias comunidades donde se alojaron los intentos insurgentes." Comisión de Verdad y Justicia (2008). *Conclusiones y recomendaciones del Informe Final de la Comisión de Verdad y Justicia del Paraguay*, p. 21. Retrieved from: http://www.dhnet.org.br/verdade/mundo/paraguai/informe_cv_paraguay_conclusiones_y_recomendaciones.pdf.

Repression included widespread human rights violations such as arbitrary detention, torture, summary execution, and forced exile. On the other side, the dictatorship put in place a system of reward for loyalists, which included vast opportunities for corruption and land acquisition. The problem of abusive land-grabbing, which severely altered the economic structure of the country and threw people into poverty, would be one of the most ominous legacies of the dictatorship to be addressed after the transition. Among its conclusions, the CVJ established that land adjudication during the dictatorship had taken place in an arbitrary manner and in clear violation of the law (Comisión de Verdad y Justicia 2008).

The definition of transition in Paraguay could be a matter of dispute. Stroessner was deposed by a military coup in February 1989. The coup was led by General Andrés Rodríguez – a relative of Stroessner's by marriage – who felt that his position as Stroessner's successor was in jeopardy because of internal disputes and shifts of power within the Colorado Party. While Rodríguez claimed the coup was intended to introduce democracy,

> it was the reunification of the Colorado Party in government and the restoration of the dignity of the armed forces that were perhaps the real aims of the coup. General Rodríguez was not renowned for his democratic credentials. He had been a loyal servant of Stroessner, had long been the strongman of Paraguay and had amassed a fortune from corruption, contraband, narcotics trafficking and money-laundering. Rodríguez, the military and the *tradicionalista* faction of the Colorado Party, had long supported Stroessner, and for all of them a transition to electoral politics represented a mechanism to safeguard their personal, corporate and institutional interests (Lambert 2000).[6]

According to Collins (2016), although

> (t)he new constitution in 1992 certainly marked a limited political opening (…) the shift from military to party dominance required little more than a change of emphasis for Colorado elites. Formal political alternation and the first successful handover from one uninterrupted presidency to another did not take place until 2008.

Thus, the change of regime did not represent a transition in terms of restoring free and competitive elections or confronting authoritarianism, corruption, and past abuses. The Colorado Party and the military establishment maintained control of Paraguayan political life.

---

6 Lambert (2000) cites R.A. Nickson (1989). "The overthrow of the Stroessner regime. Reestablishing the status quo?". *Bulletin of Latin American Research* no. 8(2), 185–209, and M. Riquelme (1994). "Bases para la discusión de las relaciones Fuerzas Armadas/Sociedad Civil en el Paraguay". In L. Bareiro, T. Escobar and S. Sosnowski, *Hacia una cultura para la democracia en el Paraguay*. Asunción: CDE.

This transition without democratization left open the possibility of a resurgence of authoritarianism, particularly through the rise of General Lino Oviedo. As late as 2003, the Colorado Party candidate, Nicanor Duarte, still handily won the presidential election. Nevertheless, the combined pressure of domestic social demands and the international community led to the establishment of transitional justice measures. The Inter-American Commission on Human Rights (CIDH) had recommended the establishment of an official truth-seeking body to investigate "deaths, disappearances, torture and other human rights violations committed during the dictatorship of Alfredo Stroessner", making use, among other things, of the information gathered in the "Archives of Terror".[7]

The transitional justice measures in Paraguay were not considered to be an exchange of justice for peace. After the transition, ordinary criminal law was applied to cases of past wrongdoings and international criminal law was invoked to impede the application of a statute of limitations for prosecution of crimes committed during the dictatorship (Alfonso 2009). In March 1996 Law 838 was passed, providing economic compensation to victims who applied for it.[8] Under the same law, the National Congress was permitted to give symbolic reparations in the form of medals and documents of recognition as a token of official recognition.

3. THE TRUTH AND JUSTICE COMMISSION (CVJ)

Prior to the establishment of the CVJ two attempts were made to create a truth-seeking body. In 1993–94 a commission was created within the Public Ministry, but it was never properly funded. Another attempt took place in 1996–97, but it stalled in Congress. According to María Stella and Martín Almada, the CVJ was made possible because of the victims' demands and due to diplomatic pressure. José Carlos Rodríguez argues that the new international context created favorable conditions for the victims and some foreign actors to push for truth seeking.[9]

Since the first years of the transition, civil society organizations had been demanding a truth commission as part of the whole democratic transition

7 The archives are now kept at a public agency named the Documentation Center and Archive for Human Rights Protection. The demands for truth and justice spurred by this finding led to the establishment of the "Museum of Memories – Dictatorship and Human Rights" in 2002.

8 Law N° 838 that gives compensation to the victims of human rights violations during the dictatorship 1954–1989, March 29, 1996: http://www.hacienda.gov.py/code/documentos/ley_838_1996.pdf.

9 Interviews with Maria Stella, Martin Almada and José Carlos Rodríguez, February 2017.

package. Among them were human rights organizations and victims' groups. However, a concrete initiative emerged only in October 2002 when civil society organizations assembled at the Roundtable for Memory Initiative and Archives of the Repression. They proposed to declare 2003 the Year of Memory and to convert a detention facility into a museum for memory of the repression. They also demanded the creation of a truth commission. This roundtable was composed of eight organizations and one institution of the Judicial Power: the Committee of Churches for Aid in Emergencies (CIPAE), the Paraguayan Human Rights Coordinator, the National Movement of Victims of the Dictatorship, the National Commission of Human Rights and Never Again to State Terrorism, the Ethical Tribunal Against Impunity, the Journalists' Union of Paraguay, the Celestina Pérez de Almada Foundation, the Catholic University Nuestra Señora de la Asunción, and the Documentation and Archive Center for Human Rights (later to be known as Archives of Terror).

The Truth and Justice Commission of Paraguay was created by Law 2225 in October 2003 with a mandate to investigate crimes and human rights violations perpetrated by State or "para-State" agents from the year 1954 until the issuance of the enabling law. As such, the period covered mainly the years of Stroessner's dictatorship, but also beyond. The Commission was asked to recommend measures to ensure non-recurrence and to make proposals in order to consolidate democracy and peace and to guarantee full respect for human rights in the country.

The Commission was assigned a wide range of tasks. It was in charge of investigating violations and abuses during the period mentioned above and analyzing the conduct of State agents and institutions who committed the abuses or permitted them to take place. It was also asked to collaborate with judicial institutions so that the evidence collected would guarantee the rights of the victims and prevent impunity. The Commission was also asked to contribute to the preservation of the memory of the victims and to identify the whereabouts of those who had been disappeared. In addition, the CVJ was charged with collecting and preserving evidence of the crimes and to establish the responsibilities of State agents and institutions. At the end of its operations, the mandate called upon the Commission to make recommendations for institutional reform and non-recurrence measures, and for reparations for the victims. Finally, the Commission was charged with producing a final report that should be made public.

The Truth and Justice Commission was not granted any judicial powers. Instead, it was empowered to conduct several investigative activities such as receiving testimony from victims and officials who might be knowledgeable about the matters under investigation; to collect documentation; to hold public hearings; to visit facilities relevant to the investigation, to organize public participation in the process; and to take necessary measures to protect witnesses.

State institutions and agencies were ordered by Law 2225 to collaborate with the truth commission.

The mandate ordered the Commission to focus on a specific list of crimes: forced disappearance, arbitrary execution, torture and serious injuries, and exile. Notwithstanding this list, the mandate charged the Commission with investigating "other human rights violations". To perform its duties, the Commission received a temporal mandate of 18 months, which could be extended for six additional months. After the 24 months, including the extension, were completed, Congress gave a further 24-month extension for the CVJ to complete its work.

The members of the Commission were selected on a representative basis and chosen by the President. The mandate established that there would be nine commissioners: one from the Executive Branch, one from the Legislative Branch, and four from the Commissions of Victims of the Dictatorship. The remaining three would be selected from civil society organizations who were working in favor of historical memory, the creation of the truth commission, and the Museum of Memory.

Table 1. Composition of Paraguay's Truth and Justice Commission

Function	Name	Backgrounds
National commission member and President	**Monsignor Mario Melanio Medina Salinas (M)**	Theologian and Philosopher. Director of the magazine *Nuestro Tiempo*. First diocesan bishop of Benjamín Aceval. Residential Bishop of San Juan Bautista de las Misiones. Founder of several organizations such as the Citizen Comptrollerships.
National commission member	Miguel Ángel Aquino Britos (M)	Lawyer, member of numerous legal organizations. Exiled 1971–1989. Congressman in the period 1989–93, member of the National Movement of Victims Commission of the Stronist Dictatorship.
National commission member	Luis Casablanca Rodríguez (M)	Lawyer. Participated in the founding of the National Commission of Human Rights and Never Again to State Terrorism. Leader of the Paraguayan Communist Party and member of its Central Committee.
National commission member	Yudith Rolón Jacquet (F)	Specialist in Accounting and Administrative Sciences. Founding member and member of the Human Rights and Victims Commission of the Stronist dictatorship of the Misiones department. Also supported the founding of the Victims' House in 2002. Has been a delegate of the San Ignacio Guazú Office of the Ombudsman from March 2002 to date. Member of the National Commission of Victims of the Dictatorship

(continued)

Table 1 *continued*

Function	Name	Backgrounds
National commission member	Margarita Durán Estragó (F)	Historian. Belonged to the Congregation of Dominican sisters from where she began her work with the peasantry. Worked with the agrarian leagues, especially from 1969 to 1974. Professor at the Catholic University. Author of numerous investigations. A member of the Paraguayan Academy of History.
National commission member	Jorge Rolón Luna (M)	Lawyer, doctor in law, electoral judge from 1996 to 2002. Worked for new penal legislation. Professor of the Catholic University.
National commission member	Juan Enrique Díaz Bordenave (M)	Educator and communicator. Consultant at UNESCO, UNICEF; UNFPA, World Bank, Inter-American Development Bank, USAID; IICA. Sunday columnist for the newspaper *Noticias*.

Source: Equipo Nizkor (2004).
Note: M= male, F=female.

Although the CVJ was created in October 2003, financial constraints delayed its commencement until July 2004. Thus, its working period ran from July 2004 until August 2008. During its operations, the Commission relied heavily on the information contained in the Archives of Terror and in interviews with victims and relatives. The CVJ held six public hearings in Paraguay and, in order to collect testimonies from exiles, two in Argentina. With this information and the analysis of specific cases, the CVJ was able to establish the individual responsibility of dictator Stroessner and his closest collaborators: state ministers and members of official institutions such as the Congress, the police, the military, and the judiciary. The Colorado Party was found responsible as well as the Catholic Church, in particular for events that occurred during the first decade of the dictatorship (Martínez et al. 2014).

In total, the Commission received reports that during the Stroessner regime 58 persons were victims of arbitrary execution, 337 were victims of forced disappearance, 19,862 suffered arbitrary detention, 18,772 were tortured, and 3,470 were victims of forced exile.

The CVJ also documented another aspect of the repression; namely the violence suffered by peasant communities, particularly during the 1970s. This violence was exerted in the context of land-grabbing by members of the ruling coalition. In particular, the Commission explained in detail the repression suffered by the *Ligas Agrarias Cristianas* (Agrarian Christian Leagues), a collective practicing peaceful resistance to the dictatorship.

The Commission explained in detail the repressive nature of the dictatorship, focusing on two separate dimensions: the "repressive model" and the "repressive apparatus". The first alluded to the societal dimension of repression and sought to establish the "totalitarian" nature of "Stronism". Repression as a cultural model was imposed on the entire Paraguayan society through the school system, cultural institutions and civil society organizations (such as labor unions). The "repressive apparatus" is more directly linked with the crimes committed. It refers to the operational system and its practices, the enabling structures and supporting groups, and the institutions that cooperated.

The Final Report, entitled "*Informe Final. Síntesis y caracterización del régimen*", included 176 recommendations. It was presented to President Fernando Lugo, the first Paraguayan president who was not from the Colorado Party, in 2008. Lugo apologized to victims on behalf of the Nation.

4. THE CVJ RECOMMENDATIONS

The law that created the CVJ mandated it to recommend the adoption of measures to prevent the recurrence of human rights violations, to consolidate democratic rule of law, and to foster a culture of peace and harmony among Paraguayans (Comisión de Verdad y Justicia 2008).[10] The recommendations appear in Chapter 1 of the first volume of the Final Report. The chapter starts with the conclusions reached by the Commission and continues with the list of 176 recommendations.

The CVJ recommendations are organized along five different themes or categories: satisfaction, restitution, compensation, rehabilitation, and guarantees of non-repetition. The first category, *satisfaction*, includes the recommendation that a Human Rights national secretariat at the ministerial level should act as a follow-up mechanism and elaborate a Human Rights National Plan. The CVJ also recommends that the government continue the disclosure of police and military archives and seek classified information in other countries to clarify the abuses committed during the dictatorship. It also recommends that (the state) provide psychosocial support to the relatives of disappeared persons in order to help them to get involved in the search for their relatives, and that it create a national forensic-anthropologic team and a National Genetic Database. The CVJ further demands official apologies, public rectifications, memorialization sites and education for collective memory. It also recommends that the General Prosecutor and the General Attorney receive a copy of the Final Report in order to start prosecutions of the alleged perpetrators. Another measure of satisfaction

---

10 See in particular, *Conclusiones y recomendaciones del Informe Final de la Comisión de Verdad y Justicia del Paraguay*, p. 71. Available at: http://www.dhnet.org.br/verdade/mundo/paraguai/informe_cv_paraguay_conclusiones_y_recomendaciones.pdf.

recommended is to ask the Public Ministry to prosecute public servants who have been involved in violations and to ask the Procurator to investigate the activities of the Central Electoral Board and those involved in Operation Cóndor.

The second category of recommendations is *restitution*. The Commission recommends that the state give back full rights to those who were exiled and displaced and to their relatives. Also, the state should provide jobs with dignity and give compensations. The CVJ recommends that the State ask the General Prosecutor and the Attorney General to start investigations into the illegal appropriation of land, to return stolen property to victims and exiles, and to retrieve collective properties, communal land and other spaces that were unlawfully occupied. The CVJ also recommends the creation of a mechanism for restitution and protection of the land belonging to indigenous communities.

The third category of recommendations refers to *compensation and material reparations*. The CVJ recommends that the state expand the existing Compensations Law to include compensation to exiles. It also recommends that the compensation should be paid monthly in the form of minimum salary to help the victims afford their basic needs. The Commission recommends the creation of a National Fund for Reparations, to be funded by specific annual budget allocations earmarked in the National General Budget. Other important recommendations in this category are compensation to those who were impeded in their access to education, and payments for income loss, for damage to life projects, moral damage and legal loss or damage caused by judicial rulings.

The fourth section of recommendations refers to *rehabilitation* measures. The CVJ recommends an integral plan that includes medical and psychosocial assistance to the victims. This plan should include the victims of torture who suffer physical and psychological consequences, those who were under illegal arrest and their relatives, and other types of victims. The Commission recommends: that health services be made available (to all); education and other public services for indigenous peoples; and respect for their cultures. It also recommends the state to organize and provide legal advice and social assistance to the victims.

Finally, among *guarantees of non-repetition*, the CVJ includes a set of measures dealing with institutional reform. The Commission recommends measures to ensure the control of civilian authorities over the military and security forces, to ensure that trials in civilian or military courts guarantee correct procedures, equity and impartiality. The Commission recommends the strengthening of judicial independence; that legal personnel be protected from vulnerabilities and risks; that training in human rights law be provided to judicial officers, the military and security forces; and to ensure that public servants follow ethical rules. It also recommends measures to guarantee labor rights and to promote social peace. Another important recommendation is to introduce constitutional reforms in order to harmonize the domestic legal framework on human rights with international law.

Table 2. Summary of Paraguay's Truth and Justice Commission Recommendations

Five areas	Recommendations by themes and types
Satisfaction	**Follow-up** Creation of a National Secretary of Human Rights of ministerial rank to follow up on progress and create a National Plan for Human Rights.
	Psychosocial support National team of forensic anthropology and national bank of genetic data.
	Criminal Opening and preservation of archives, and prosecution of cases of human rights violations in women, children and adolescents, indigenous people and others. Judicial sanction of those responsible for human rights violations.
	Symbolic reparations Official declarations and public apologies; creation of places of memory by the State.
	Symbolic reparations/ institutional Human rights education and truth telling.
Restitution	**Reparations [material]** Restitution of rights to exiles and all victims who have suffered material damage.
	Reparations [material]/ criminal Promotion of restitution of assets (ill-gotten land, assets taken from exiles and others).
	Intercultural approach to land restitution for indigenous peoples.
Compensation	**Legal/ reparations [material]** Modification of the Compensations Law.
	Reparation [non-material] Education and other public services for the victims.
Rehabilitation	**Reparation [non-material]** Specific health care and psychological support for the victims.
	Free legal counselling for victims.
Non-repetition	**Non-recurrence / institutional** Effective control of authorities over armed and security forces – Powers to the Ombudsman to investigate and punish excessive use of force. – To adapt the legal framework of the armed forces to ensure observance of human rights. – To prohibit party affiliation of members of the armed forces and police.

(continued)

Table 2 *continued*

Five areas	Recommendations by themes and types
Non-repetition	**Non-recurrence/ institutional** Procedural guarantees, fair and impartial civil and military processes. – Military criminal justice reform to control the use of force. – Respect for women's rights. – Reform for due process in military justice.
	Non-recurrence/ institutional Reform for the independence of the Judiciary. – Constitutional and legal reforms for independence and efficiency. – That the Supreme Court and the Ethics Council promote the ethical conduct of judges. – *Habeas corpus* non-derogable. – Courses on due process, judicial guarantees and international standards in these matters.
	Non-recurrence/ institutional Protection of professionals in situations of special risk. – Protection program of the Human Rights Secretariat for witnesses, human rights defenders and journalists. – Protection for people who give testimony to the CVJ.
	Non-recurrence/ institutional Human Rights training for officials, armed forces and security forces.
	Non-recurrence/ institutional Promotion of compliance with codes of conduct and ethical standards of officials, journalists and company personnel. – Manuals of ethics and education in human rights for agents of the State, and media. – Norms for transnational companies so that they respect human rights of indigenous peoples and others. – Respect for human rights of prisoners.
	Non-recurrence/ institutional Mechanisms to protect labor rights and social peace. – That the Legislative Branch and Ministry of Justice improve conflict resolution. – Promote the work of Justices of the Peace. – Strengthen the Public Defender's Office to provide defense lawyers for people. – Supervise contracts of indigenous peoples in livestock, forestry, etc.
	Non-recurrence/ Constitutional/Legal Constitutional and legal reforms to adapt human rights legal framework to international law. – Ratify international treaties on human rights. – Measures to comply with recommendations and judgments of international courts and other institutions. – Adapt domestic legislation to international treaties.

Source: Comisión de Verdad y Justicia (2008).
Note: Elaborated by the authors.

5. THE PROCESS OF FORMULATING RECOMMENDATIONS

The set of recommendations presented by the CVJ was partially the result of a consultation process with the victims and human rights organizations. Although the process was not sufficiently participatory, it nevertheless permitted the CVJ to take into account the demands made by the victims in their testimonies before the Commission as well as the recommendations presented by the human rights organizations (Valencia 2011).

A CVJ technical team elaborated the recommendations, classifying them into several categories.[11] The participation of local experts such as Alberto Alderete (from the National Institute of Rural Development and Land, INDERT); Óscar Ayala (from *La Coordinadora de Derechos Humanos del Paraguay* CODEHUPY), and Julia Cabello proved helpful. These experts made contributions to the recommendations on agrarian reform, ill-gotten land and indigenous peoples, while Edwin Sokol and Carlos Portillo contributed to recommendations on gender and the search for disappeared persons. Foreign experts such as the Spanish psychologist Carlos Martín Beristain also played an important role in this task group.[12]

The CVJ submitted a questionnaire to the victims in order to receive their demands. As a result, the fight against impunity, the retrieval of land, and the fight against oblivion were incorporated among the recommendations. The most critical demands by the victims were comprehensive reparations, the search for disappeared persons, and the restitution of assets to victims of land-grabbing.[13]

The international standards developed within the United Nations system were also a factor contributing to the formulation of recommendations. These standards were laid out in documents such as the "Updated Set of Principles for the Protection and Promotion of Human Rights through Action to Combat Impunity" and the "Basic Principles and Guidelines on the Right to a Remedy and Reparation for Victims of Gross Violations of International Human Rights Law and Serious Violations of International Humanitarian Law", both established in the mid-2000s.

According to Valencia (2011), the pre-existence of these international tools motivated the CVJ to organize the recommendations into distinctive sections: satisfaction, restitution, rehabilitation, compensation and guarantees of non-repetition, reflecting thus the international standards. However, according to José Carlos Rodríguez, in order to elaborate the recommendations, the CVJ

11 Interviews with María Stella and Martin Almada, February 2017.
12 Interviews with María Stella and Martin Almada, February 2017.
13 Interview with Lourdes Giubi, lawyer at the DGVJR. February 2017.

paid attention to the country's "urgent issues" understood in terms of structural (or historical) problems, but not necessarily bearing in mind their viability.[14]

6. STATUS OF IMPLEMENTATION

In the remaining parts of this chapter, we provide an overview of the status of implementation of the recommendations made by the CVJ. We have chosen a thematic structure for this account, given the interrelationship between recommendations across the five categories used by the CVJ.

6.1. INSTITUTIONAL FRAMEWORK AND OTHER MEASURES

The *Dirección General de Verdad, Justicia y Reparación de la Defensoría del Pueblo* (DGVJR) (General Directorate for Truth, Justice and Reparations) was created on January 23, 2009 to secure the documentation produced by the Commission, disseminate the Final Report and implement the recommendations. The DGVJR was conceived as a body in charge of safeguarding human rights, implementing reparations and continuing the CJV's work.[15] However, since it was created as an agency within the Ombudsman Office, this Directorate lacked full autonomy to fulfil its duties. On the other hand, the DGVJR did not necessarily coincide with the CVJ's approach.[16] The body lacked ministerial status and the necessary competences pertaining to a State agency which was itself dependent on the National Congress. The DGVJR was born with many limitations stemming from the institutional and political context. These limitations were made evident in some critical aspects, such as funding and acting capacity. Other limitations, however, originated in the DGVJR's design. Following the 2012 removal from power of Fernando Lugo, the will to continue the CVJ's work and to promote human rights policies collapsed. To overcome this situation, the Ombudsman, Manuel Páez Monges, offered to absorb the DGVJR within that agency. This means that the Directorate was not established by the Executive Power nor by Congress, both of which were controlled by *Stronism.* To fund the reparations, the DGVJR asked for contributions from the Paraguayan State as well as from international actors, in particular the European Union and private corporations such as Itaipú and Ycayretá.

---

14 Interview with José Carlos Rodríguez, commissioner of the CVJ. February 2017.

15 Portal Guaraní (2015). *Informe final de la Comisión de Verdad y Justicia de Paraguay (CVJ). Antecedentes y normativa.* Retrieved from: http://www.portalguarani.com/detalles_museos_otras_obras.php?id=60&id_obras=1185&id_otras=174.

16 Interview with Martín Almada and María Stella Cáceres. February 2017.

There have been complaints about bureaucratic problems within the Directorate and about its issuing confusing information regarding the documents or procedures that the victims need to produce or to follow in order to receive reparations. Even worse, there have been some accusations of officers demanding bribes in order to facilitate these procedures.[17]

The DGVJR was initially directed by Yudith Rolón, who had been Executive Secretary of the CVJ; it is staffed with a small team with low managerial capacities.[18] So, even though the DGVJR opened several international channels to disseminate the report and tried to promote the implementation of the recommendations,[19] its results were partial. Since it has no effective power over other State institutions, the Directorate functions primarily as an information center.

Another issue is that the Human Rights National Plan, approved on March 6, 2003 and adopted by the Executive Power Human Rights Network,[20] has not yet been fully implemented either, and there are no signals that its original objectives will be pursued (CODEHUPY 2015).

There has not been substantial progress on declassification and disclosure of information archives, except for the Archives of Terror. This has impeded further investigations into gross human rights violations. Even though the State has made some progress regarding institutionalization and new judicial procedures, investigations and prosecutions remain stalled.

6.2. SYMBOLIC REPARATIONS

The main activities regarding symbolic reparations have focused on establishing museums and organizing memorialization activities; the inclusion of texts about violence in educational programs; the memorialization of significant events such as the Discovery of the Archives of Terror; and some gestures towards a State apology. Regarding the museographic activity, even though there is an important precedent in the systematization of the Archives of Terror, there is no clear policy for historical memory that links this effort with other efforts to preserve the victims' memory. Consequently, this has caused some efforts to

---

17 Paraguay.com (December 11, 2014). "CODEHUPY insta a elegir a nuevo defensor del Pueblo". Retrieved from: http://www.paraguay.com/nacionales/codehupy-insta-a-elegir-nuevo-defensor-del-pueblo-120645.

18 Interview with Lourdes Giubi, lawyer at DGVJR, February 2017.

19 Interview with María Stella Cáceres, November 2016.

20 Ministerio de Justicia. (March 6, 2013). "Decreto N 10.747 por el cual se aprueban las políticas públicas en materia de derechos humanos y se pone en fase de implementación el Plan Nacional de Derechos Humanos". Retrieved from: http://www.mre.gov.py/v1/DDHH/DECRETO10747.pdf.

transform some sites of violence into memory sites to fail due to the lack of an institutional framework and weak commitment from the State.

6.2.1. *Implementation of Memorial Sites*

Among museographic initiatives we would like to mention the following: the *Museo Memorias. Dictadura y Derechos Humanos* (LaTécnica); the *Museo de Justicia de la Corte Suprema*; the *Centro de Documentación de San Ignacio Guasu* (Garretón, Gonzales and Lauzán 2011), and the *Museo Meves: Memoria y Verdad sobre el Stronismo*, which gathers stories, testimonies, images, videos and audio-recordings of the history of violence in Paraguay. In addition, the Historical Sites Network, promoted by the Latin American and Caribbean Memorial Sites Network, has been created[21] with the support of the Ministry of Interior.[22] More than five historical and conscience sites have been officialized, among them the former Police Investigations Department of Asunción, the Emboscada Concentration Camp, the *Comisaría 3ª Metropolitana*, the *Comisaría 1ª de San Juan Bautista*, the *Departamento de Misiones* (former Abraham Cué Penitentiary) and the facilities of the *Instituto Técnico Superior en Derechos Humanos Germán Orellano Flores*,[23] which currently bears the name of one of the martyrs of the *Ligas Agrarias Cristianas*.[24] The police and the Ministry of Interior[25] partially demolished the *Comisaría 3ª* and La Emboscada Penitentiary, which shows their lack of political will to maintain memorialization sites.[26]

6.2.2. *Human Rights Education*

With regard to education, it was possible to include in the school curriculum for the third grade of High School the material entitled "Authoritarianism in

---

21 Red de Sitios de Memoria Latinoamericanos y Caribeños. "¿Quiénes somos?" Retrieved from: http://sitiosdememoria.org/es/quienes-somos/.

22 Dirección General de Verdad, Justicia y Reparación de la Defensoría del Pueblo. (2011). *Informe de cumplimiento de las recomendaciones de la Comisión de Verdad y Justicia. Audiencia Pública Nacional Junio 2011*. Asunción: Defensoría del Pueblo.

23 *Diario Última Hora* (May 2, 2014). Declaran a la Comisaría 3a como "Sitio histórico y de conciencia". Retrieved from: https://www.ultimahora.com/declaran-la-comisaria-3-como-sitio-historico-y-conciencia-n791351.html.

24 *ABC Color* (January 16, 2014). "El Estado tiene que devolverle su dignidad al pueblo." Retrieved from: http://www.abc.com.py/blogs/testimonios-para-no-olvidar-142/el-estado-tiene-que-devolverle-su-dignidad-al-pueblo-2429.html.

25 *Blog de Red de Sitios de Memoria Latinoamericanos y caribeños* (2015). "Policía y Ministerio del Interior de Paraguay demuelen Sitio Histórico y de Conciencia." Retrieved from: https://redlatinoamericanadesitiosdememoria.wordpress.com/pronunciamientos-de-la-red/policia-y-ministerio-del-interior-de-paraguay-demuelen-sitio-historico-y-de-conciencia/.

26 *Resumen Latinoamericano* (August 6, 2015). Paraguay: Víctimas de la dictadura rechazan demolición de la Comisaría Tercera. Retrieved from http://www.resumenlatinoamericano.org/2015/08/06/paraguay-victimas-de-la-dictadura-rechazan-demolicion-de-la-comisaria-tercera/.

Paraguay Recent History". This material was designed through consultation workshops with teachers from the educational system and local leaders to introduce a human rights perspective (Garretón, Gonzales and Lauzán 2011). The material introduces the term "State terrorism" to refer to the Stroessner regime's violent actions and includes fragments of oral testimonies from victims, who tell explicitly about human rights violations. This kind of material had never been present in the school textbooks before (D'Alessandro 2014). However, these issues have not been incorporated extensively in the school system. Schools can decide whether to incorporate them or not.[27] Progress can also be observed in the publication of the document "*Próceres de al libertad: una mirada a los héroes y a las gestas de resistencia a la dictadura stronista*", which was based on the CVJ's final report, and the implementation of the School Calendar "*Todas y todos vivimos valores*", presented as a tool to plan and schedule activities throughout the year.[28]

6.2.3. *Memorialization and Public Apologies*

Regarding the establishment of symbolic days and memorialization acts to honor victims, some actions have been made, but they are mostly associated with some public figures and not with a sincere State commitment to give symbolic reparations to the victims. Every December 22 the country commemorates the day when the Archives of Terror were discovered. The day is marked as the "National Dignification Day". Several acts of public recognition take place during the "Human Rights Week", which is linked to the International Human Rights Day on December 10.

When the CVJ's final report was presented, President Fernando Lugo made public acknowledgment of the State's responsibility for human rights violations during the Stroessner regime. In addition, the name of a city – "Port President Stroessner" – was restored to its former name, "East City" (Garretón, Gonzales and Lauzán 2011), after a plebiscite.[29] However, despite public apologies, prominent figures from the Partido Colorado still hold public office. The reason for this is that the acts of acknowledgment have been made by the Judicial Branch and by the Legislative Branch, but not by the Executive Branch. While the former two state branches have gone through a transformation process after the pact for democratic governance of 1993, the Executive branch continues to be controlled of the Partido Colorado (Garretón, Gonzales and Lauzán 2011).

---

27 Interview with María Stella Cáceres. November 2016.

28 Dirección General de Verdad, Justicia y Reparación de la Defensoría del Pueblo (2011). *Informe de cumplimiento de las recomendaciones de la Comisión de Verdad y Justicia. Audiencia Pública Nacional Junio 2011.* Asunción: Defensoría del Pueblo.

29 Gobernación del Alto Paraná. Ciudad del Este. Retrieved from: http://www.altoparana.gov.py/v0/index.php/ciudad-del-este.

6.3. PROSECUTIONS OF ALLEGED PERPETRATORS

One of the weakest aspects of the transitional justice process in Paraguay is the prosecution of those responsible for human rights violations. The judicial processes have stalled or focus only on obsolete police structures (TELESUR 2014) or on members of the Partido Colorado who no longer belong to the upper echelons of the power structures (Collins 2016). Ninety-three per cent of the perpetrators identified by the CVJ have so far not been punished, and a significant number are now dead (CODEHUPY 2014).

However, there has been some progress in the international sphere. The most important precedent has been the judgment of the Inter-American Court of Human Rights condemning the Paraguayan State for the arrest and forced disappeareance of Agustín Goiburu, the Ramírez Villalba brothers, and Amílcar Oviedo as part of Operación Cóndor (Martinez 2014). However, the Paraguayan State has not complied with the judgment: it has not built a memorial site for the four victims; nor has it implemented ordinance n° 6/1993 of the Municipal Junta of Asunción which orders the state to register the names of the victims in the Plaza de los Desaparecidos (CODEHUPY 2014). This is different in other countries, like Argentina, where prosecutions against perpetrators have been initiated.[30]

The progress made in some cases depends mainly on the ability to produce evidence and in response to public demands. The cases that depend on the public prosecutors have not made any progress. In 2011, 50 cases derived from the CVJ Final Report were brought before the Prosecutor, but no action has been taken to produce evidence (CODEHUPY 2014). Disputes within the Partido Colorado and the predominance of some factions over others allowed some prosecutions to take place before the existence of the CVJ. The clearest example of that was the proceedings against Pastor Coronel, the most feared agent of State terrorism during the regime.

The main factor hindering criminal prosecutions is the institutional weakness of the judiciary and the DGVJR, the agency in charge of monitoring the implementation of reparations. In practical terms, the Prosecutor's Office does not have autonomy to conduct investigations (Zorrilla 2014). According to the DGVJR the number and capacity of the prosecutors are inadequate to fulfil the task (Collins 2016). CIPAE shares this perception and adds that, since there are no amnesties or international obstacles to the prosecution of crimes against humanity, the main problem is not the judiciary but the prosecutors and the poor performance of the DGVJR following up on the cases (Collins 2016). This agency has not been able to move forward with the cases due to lack of funds and human resources (Countrywatch 2015).

---

[30] Interview with Martin Almada and María Stella Cáceres, February 2017.

Another obstacle has been the inadequate legal framework which demands proof of too many elements to demonstrate some crimes such as torture and forced disappearance. In the latter case, the Ombudsman demands that the solicitor obtains from a civil court a declaration of absence with presumption of death and that the solicitor demonstrates that the claimant is the heir of the disappeared person. The relatives must pay the costs associated. These are excessive requisites that show a lack of understanding among the public agencies (CODEHUPY 2014).

The difference in the status of the victims and their capacity for agency has been another factor promoting or hindering judicial proceedings. There are some early cases in favor of victims of high economic status, with education and contact networks, while other victims from impoverished and rural areas have not received much attention. Due to this, the proceedings that have been promoted have concentrated on cases of disappearance and arbitrary execution despite the fact that in Paraguay the majority of human rights violations took the form of illegal detentions and torture (Collins 2016).

The lack of information in rural areas increases this gap in judicialization. One third of the 117 disappearance case files that ENABI (*Equipo Nacional para la investigación, búsqueda e identificación plena de personas detenidas-desaparecidas y ejecutadas extrajudicialmente, durante el periodo 1954–1989*; see below) has studied in-depth contain only basic information. In some cases, only the name of the victim is available without any additional information. Rural isolation and absolute poverty remain very high and expectations about democratic change are very low (Collins 2016).

In general, there has been no political will to resolve these cases and prosecute the perpetrators (TELESUR 2014). Monsignor Mario Melanio indicates that successive governments have avoided promoting processes of judicialization for fear of being found responsible or that some close members are found involved. Thus, even though Lugo assumed the presidency, he could not do much because in Congress there were still no representatives of factions other than the Partido Colorado.[31] This has generated a wide sense of impunity related to the period when that party was in control (Collins 2016).

6.4. SEARCH FOR DISAPPEARED PERSONS

The search for missing persons in Paraguay began during the dictatorship and has taken different paths after the delivery of the Final Report. The works were

---

[31] BBC Mundo. (March 11, 2015). "Por qué Paraguay tardó casi 30 años en identificar a sus desaparecidos?" Retrieved from: http://www.bbc.com/mundo/noticias/2015/03/150305_paraguay_desaparecidos_vs.

initiated by the Unit for the Investigation of Enforced Disappearances and Extrajudicial Executions of the CVJ, and then went on to depend on the DGVJR of the Ombudsman's Office until March 2013, and finally to depend on the Directorate of Historical Memory and Reparation of the Ministry of Justice and Labor (CODEHUPY 2016). In the interval, in August 2011, the National Team for the Investigation, Search and Identification of persons detained, disappeared and extrajudicially executed (known as ENABI), coordinated by the DGVJR, was established by Decree No. 7.101 and later, in April 2013, also transferred to the Ministry of Justice and Labour.

The team works with a limited budget and insufficient staff to perform its mandate, to the point that they have required the support of foreign institutions to undertake the search for missing persons. The results, in that framework, reflect these shortcomings. By 2017, 27 exhumations had been carried out and the remains of just four victims had been returned to their families.[32]

Other actions in this line have been the campaign "Jajoheka Jajotopa – National Campaign for the Identification of Missing Persons between 1954 and 1989" promoted in 2015 by the Peace and Justice Service Paraguay (Serpaj-Py) and the Department of Reparation and Historical Memory of the Ministry of Justice, among others. This campaign included the installation of a Blood Bank and the use of its records for the identification of missing persons, as well as the continuity of the genetic studies of bodies recovered to date (CODEHUPY 2015).

Among the factors that have facilitated the search for missing persons, we should consider the participation of external actors both nationally and internationally. Within the country, there is an agreement between the Ombudsman's Office and the Ministry of the Interior to support the search for, exhumation and identification of the victims, installation and declaration of historical sites of places of repression, and compliance with recommendations in general. This has allowed progress in the search for and location of people, as well as in the training of police personnel. There is also support from the Ministry of Public Health, although there is no indication that it is substantial support.[33]

In 2009, by decision of the First Meeting of High Authorities on Human Rights and Foreign Ministries of MERCOSUR and Associated States (RAADH), the Working Group on the Right to Memory, Truth and Justice became the Permanent Commission on Memory, Truth and Justice, with the aim of

---

32 Interview with Lourdes Giubi, lawyer at DGVJR, February 2017.

33 Dirección General de Verdad, Justicia y Reparación de la Defensoría del Pueblo (2011). *Informe de cumplimiento de las recomendaciones de la Comisión de Verdad y Justicia. Audiencia Pública Nacional Junio 2011.* Asunción: Defensoría del Pueblo.

consolidating regional cooperation in memory policies and truth, through the exchange of information and documents on serious human rights violations, and the search for and identification of the remains of victims of forced disappearances (RAADH 2013).

Beyond the support received, the search for missing persons faces two major problems that considerably undermine the Permanent Commission's ability to act: the lack of its own budget and the absence of trained personnel to perform the tasks of searching for, identifying and delivering remains. At the level of human resources, only the salary of the director of the ENABI is covered, and the rest of the collaborations are voluntary. The staff also do not have vehicles or work or office tools. The ENABI has identified 12 places in which there are mass graves with missing persons who were disappeared during the Stroessner regime, which cannot be exhumed due to lack of resources for operational work (CODEHUPY 2014).

In 2013, the Paraguayan State budgeted a fund of 150,000 US dollars to finance an identification program. 50 per cent of this fund should have been transferred to the *Equipo Argentino de Antropología Forense* (EAAF) (Argentine Forensic Anthropology Team), due to the lack of trained personnel. However, the funds were never transferred, government alleging impediments in domestic legislation related to public procurement and the lack of transparency of alternative procedures. These resources were destined for a National Bank of Genetic Data of the relatives of the 336 victims of enforced disappearance during the dictatorship, and to develop the genetic profile of the Paraguayan population in addition to starting work with the identification of 20 of the disappeared.[34] It is in the face of this lack of resources that the work of the relatives of the victims has become vital to develop specific actions and, in general, to sustain the entire process (CODEHUPY 2016).

6.5. RIGHTS OF EXILES

The situation of the exiled during the dictatorship is complex and involves different problems, which in turn means that the degree of implementation of recommendations is also varied. A 2012 study revealed that the fall of Stroessner did not mean substantial changes in the structural situation of the exiles, given that although they were allowed to return to the country, the situation of uprooting continued to be a problem (Wellbach 2009).

Although slow, progress has been made in making agreements for the provision of social and health assistance through cross-border cooperation with Argentine provinces. Examples of these processes are the agreement signed

34 Dirección General de Verdad, Justicia y Reparación de la Defensoría del Pueblo (2011).

between the Ministries of Health of the Province of Misiones (Argentina) and the Department of Itapúa (Paraguay) for the medical assistance of Paraguayan residents in Misiones, or the Agreement of Cooperation in Health celebrated between the Department of Misiones (Paraguay) and the Province of Corrientes (Argentina) for health care programs, exchange of national and border epidemiological information, coordination of programs for HIV-AIDS, STDs, maternity and childhood, livestock diseases, joint strategies in situations of catastrophe or emergencies in the border area, etc (Arellano 2011).

Another important advance has been observed in the recognition of the right to vote of Paraguayans abroad. On October 9, 2011 a referendum was held to approve or reject the proposed amendment to Article No. 12022, first amendment to the National Constitution of 1992, to grant the right to vote for Paraguayan citizens living abroad. Although the electoral participation was very low, the electoral expression in favor of the reform was overwhelming, despite a huge electoral demobilization operation by the main opposition parties who, far from interpreting the reform as an extension of citizen rights and as historical reparation for the exiles and migrants, considered it an "expansion of the register" and an official maneuver that would give a clear electoral advantage to the then President Fernando Lugo (Arellano 2011).

In political terms, the referendum revealed a general political scenario in which President Lugo had social support but lacked political organization and capacity for mobilization – a consequence of the deep fracture within the presidential alliance that deprived Lugo of the organizational capacity of the Liberal Party, the strongest actor in his coalition – and in which the opposition had capacity to demobilize electorally. Months later, similar factors would make possible the removal of Lugo by a parliamentary coup. Beyond this, a new political and social actor is constituted by the hundreds of thousands of Paraguayans living abroad, both because of political persecution during the dictatorship (exiles) and for economic reasons (Paraguayan migrant workers of the democratic period) (Arellano 2011).

Family reintegration and restitution of property for those in exile are the areas where the advances or the impact has been substantially less. Regarding the first point, the CVJ recommended promoting "public policies and programs that promote family reintegration through the meeting of fathers, mothers, sons and daughters who were separated as a consequence of human rights violations". During all this time, in the absence of initiatives from the State, the families of Paraguayan political exiles have found the material means to meet with relatives using their own social networks (Arellano 2011).

Regarding restitution of assets, there is a political cost in complementing repatriation with the return of property. The economic crimes related to exile, perpetrated decades ago, such as the illegal appropriation of property, have involved successive sales of the same asset; as a result, in many cases, the current owners have no link whatsoever with the initial misappropriation. The criminal land-grabbing scheme was developed in such a way that after the appropriations the sites and companies officially changed their name in an operation to eliminate the geographical references to towns and colonies. The repatriation of the Paraguayan exiles exceeds the simple process of return and even social, economic, labor and cultural reintegration. It necessarily implies the expropriation and return of real estate in the vast majority of cases, which entails high political costs for the State. It is a confrontation between legitimate owners and legal owners, and that implies great tension for the current political system (Arellano 2011).

6.6. COMPENSATION AND MATERIAL REPARATIONS

The material compensations have an important antecedent prior to the formation of the CVJ. Law 838/96 was motivated by the magnitude of the discovery of the Archives of Terror in 1992.[35] Then, after the formation of the CVJ, a modification of this law was recommended so that the politically exiled could be recognized as victims, thus implying the recognition of their right to compensation, and also that of their heirs, wives or husbands, and descendants (CODEHUPY 2014).

Currently, the balance is that compensation has been granted to 16 victims of enforced disappearance. The amount has been US$43,000 and has not been complemented by other measures such as medical and psychological assistance. The victims criticize this lack of integrity, as well as the slowness of the processes and the lack of transparency of the adjudications (CODEHUPY 2014). For example, there is a health care law for victims, Law 4793/12,[36] but that does not fully implement the recommendation since there are too many requirements.[37]

In another type of reparation, the Healthy Homes strategy has been adapted for the community of Santa Rosa, Department of Misiones, where 45 community agents have been trained, through the Ministry of Education and Culture, in Health Promotion and Human Rights to be health agents in their respective communities as part of the social reintegration of the victims.[38]

---

35 Interview with María Stella Cáceres, November 2016.

36 *ABC Color* (August 2, 2013). Ley de atención gratuita a las víctimas. Retrieved from: http://www.abc.com.py/edicion-impresa/politica/ley-de-atencion-gratuita-a-las-victimas-602460.html.

37 Interview with Martin Almada and María Stella Cáceres, February 2017.

38 Dirección General de Verdad, Justicia y Reparación de la Defensoría del Pueblo (2011). *Informe de cumplimiento de las recomendaciones de la Comisión de Verdad y Justicia. Audiencia Pública Nacional Junio 2011.* Asunción: Defensoría del Pueblo.

In terms of rehabilitation, a Mental Health Mobile Unit was implemented, which visits four localities once a month (Choré, Repatriación, General Morinigo and Ayolas). Another service offered is the issuance of mental health certificates. These have been issued since 2008 also for victims of the dictatorship in connection to the procedures to obtain victim status before the Ombudsman's Office. During 2011, 614 certificates were delivered (17 per cent were victims of the dictatorship). In 2009, a total of 1140 certificates were issued (47 per cent were victims of the dictatorship). One year later, of the 1,233 certificates, 34 per cent, or 411, were issued for victims of the dictatorship.[39]

6.7. ILLEGAL APPROPRIATION OF LAND

The situation of ill-gotten land in Paraguay, or the illegal appropriation of peasant and indigenous lands, has been one of the main causes of inequality not only during the dictatorship, but even today. Indigenous peoples continue to be dispossessed of their lands and suffer delays in the processes to acquire land titles and to access ancestral lands. To this day, peasant groups demand clarification of the situation of ill-gotten lands, which is the main cause of the unequal distribution of land in the country, and an agrarian reform that is long overdue (Silvero 2013).

However, there is currently no agrarian reform policy that responds to this need. On the contrary, there is a repressive policy towards peasant leaders and human rights defenders,[40] while land expropriations have not ceased (Stabilli 2012). An example of this is the 2012 Curuguaty massacre where 11 peasants and six policemen died. CODEHUPY (2014) records that between 1989 and 2013, 115 leaders and members of peasant organizations were executed and disappeared, in the context of systematic and planned attacks against rural communities with the aim of forcing their displacement to appropriate their territories. There are three rulings by the Inter-American Court of Human Rights for violations of community rights to ancestral lands. These rulings correspond to the following cases: *Yakye Axa Indigenous Community v. Paraguay*, judgment of June 17, 2005; *Sawhoyamaxa Indigenous Community v. Paraguay*, judgment of 29 March 2006; and *Xákmok Kásek indigenous community vs. Paraguay*, judgment of August 24, 2010 (Turner 2014).

Even though there has been some progress in the institutional framework, these advances have not necessarily translated into a real transformation around land tenure. The Attorney General of the Republic has created the Specialized

---

39 Dirección General de Verdad, Justicia y Reparación de la Defensoría del Pueblo (2011).

40 *ABC Color* (January 16, 2014). "El Estado tiene que devolverle su dignidad al pueblo". Retrieved from: http://www.abc.com.py/blogs/testimonios-para-no-olvidar-142/el-estado-tiene-que-devolverle-su-dignidad-al-pueblo-2429.html.

Unit for the defense and recovery of properties of the Paraguayan State in order to focus on the implementation of the agrarian reform. It promotes the regulation and recovery of badly adjudicated lands, through judicial actions or administrative actions in cooperation with the enforcement agency, INDERT.[41] To date, there are 100 administrative files with complaints under analysis and study.[42] The Unit is carrying out a Draft Law on the Restitution of Land, concerning land awarded by the Rural Welfare Institute (currently INDERT) during the dictatorship to persons not subject to the agrarian reform.

Additionally, the Interinstitutional Coordinating Committee was set up to recover land plots in favor of the beneficiaries of the agrarian reform, at the settlements of San Juan and San Isidro located in the department of Canindeyú. The promotion of the judicial measurement on the aforementioned settlements has been achieved in order to determine the area in conflict. Cabinet work is carried out within INDERT in order to identify the titles issued and determine the legality in each case.[43]

Multiple factors come into play on the issue of ill-gotten lands. As mentioned, despite the end of the dictatorship, the structures of Stronism are still present in state institutions or exercising power over them. The perpetrators are landlords with corporate interests linked to agribusiness who have built alliances with traditional political leaders to guarantee protection (CODEHUPY 2014). This means that the institutions responsible for prosecuting the perpetrators of land-grabbing are dominated by representatives of the Colorado party, or are weak.

A second factor, also present in other reparation policies, is the lack of funds. The bodies in charge of land policy are INDERT, and the Instituto Paraguayo del Indígena (INDI) in the case of land restitution for indigenous peoples. But the budget for land restitution assigned to the INDI is very limited and in 2017 it decreased to less than 20 per cent in relation to the previous year.

Thirdly, the land claimed has a legal holder, added to the fact that, due to the intervening expansion of the cultivation of soy and meat production, the price of land would be too high for someone to afford it.[44]

At the institutional level, the DGVJR, in charge of monitoring the implementation of recommendations, has not focused its work on land issues.[45] Although the CVJ had a comprehensive perspective on the issue and had a

---

41 Dirección General de Verdad, Justicia y Reparación de la Defensoría del Pueblo (2011). *Informe de cumplimiento de las recomendaciones de la Comisión de Verdad y Justicia. Audiencia Pública Nacional Junio 2011*. Asunción: Defensoría del Pueblo.

42 Dirección General de Verdad, Justicia y Reparación de la Defensoría del Pueblo (2011).

43 Dirección General de Verdad, Justicia y Reparación de la Defensoría del Pueblo (2011).

44 Interview with Nilo Damián, director of Centro de Estudios Antropológicos de la Universidad Católica Nuestra Señora de la Asunción and Daisi Amarilla, Vice President of Asociación Indigenista del Paraguay, February 2017.

45 Interview with Jorge Vera, General Coordinator of Gente, Ambiente y Territorio, February 2017.

public hearing that presented emblematic cases of indigenous peoples, the subsequent implementation has focused mainly on reparation to victims of political persecution. There is more intensive work undertaken regarding the political rights of city dwellers, since they constitute the population more apt to raise demands about those issues.

Peasants, on the other hand, were not organized on a legal or political level; their organization was dismantled by the dictatorship. Those resisting the dictatorship were the parties and thus the resistance became an urban phenomenon.

6.8. INSTITUTIONAL REFORM

6.8.1. Authorities' Effective Control Over Armed and Security Forces

The recommendations to ensure future civilian control over security forces include the empowerment of the Ombudsman to punish the indiscriminate use of force, the inclusion of a human rights approach within the armed forces, and the prohibition of party affiliation by members of those institutions as well as the police. The main advances have been made in institutional terms. Military Commissions formed by jurists and military officers were created to adapt the military legislation to the mandates of the National Constitution and international treaties and conventions, emphasizing human rights principles, subordination to the constitutional powers, and restricting military jurisdiction over civilians.[46]

Additionally, an Office of the Special Prosecutor for Human Rights was created, with the function of updating the files that were subject to judicial default, providing the necessary procedural impetus.[47] A resolution was passed on January 13, 2011 to assign exclusive functions to prosecutors with specific competences in crimes of torture, bodily injury in the exercise of public functions, coercion to obtain statements, forced disappearance, persecution of innocent individuals, genocide and war crimes.[48] Finally, the State recognizes the Protocol against Torture and the creation of the National Mechanism for the Prevention of Torture.[49] However, in practice, what has been produced is rather a continuation of violations of human rights by the security forces due to a permissive regulatory framework and a subordination of respect for

---

46 Dirección General de Verdad, Justicia y Reparación de la Defensoría del Pueblo. (2011). *Informe de cumplimiento de las recomendaciones de la Comisión de Verdad y Justicia. Audiencia Pública Nacional Junio 2011*. Asunción: Defensoría del Pueblo.

47 Dirección General de Verdad, Justicia y Reparación de la Defensoría del Pueblo (2011).

48 Dirección General de Verdad, Justicia y Reparación de la Defensoría del Pueblo. (2011).

49 Interview with María Stella Cáceres, November 2017.

human rights to other interests such as the promotion of economic activities. The enactment of Law 5036 on National Defense and Internal Security in 2013 allowed the Army to be used in situations of "internal aggression", such as terrorism, and threats or violent actions "against the authorities, without the need to impose a state of emergency that is approved by the Executive Power in the departments of San Pedro, Concepción and Amambay." The consequences already begin to be noticed in reports of cases of people tortured by the Joint Task Force (FTC), the contingent of soldiers and police responsible for fighting guerrilla groups operating in the area.[50]

What lies behind these developments is a pattern of militarization of social conflicts to promote economic activities using as justification the fight against guerrilla groups such as the Paraguayan People's Army (*Ejército del Pueblo Paraguayo* – EPP) and instrumentalizing fear to make use of force (CODEHUPY 2014). Thus, the idea that those who question agribusiness, the advance of soybean and the contamination of communal lands sympathize or support the EPP in some way begins to gain greater traction.[51]

Human rights violations cannot be prosecuted, the most obvious case being the Curuguaty massacre in 2012. No one has been accused of the deaths of the peasants, which raises doubts about the impartiality of the investigation. The process in which the peasants are being prosecuted for alleged invasion of property, criminal association and attempted intentional homicide is already in the stage of oral trial. However, the deaths of the peasants, which occurred at the same time and place, despite the allegations made, have not been subject to an investigation by the Prosecutor's Office because they are assumed to be legally justified. The lack of political will of the State, the lack of operational capacity of the Specialized Unit of Human Rights and the absence of economic resources contribute to perpetuate the impunity of those committing serious violations of human rights (CODEHUPY 2015).

6.8.2. *Reforms to Ensure the Independence of the Justice Administration*

The institutions that administer justice in Paraguay are discredited and are perceived as having little independence to undertake judicial investigations.[52]

---

50 *EFE* (April 21, 2016). "Piden declarar inconstitucional una ley que autoriza a intervenir a los militares en el norte paraguayo". Retrieved from: http://www.efe.com/efe/america/cono-sur/piden-declarar-inconstitucional-una-ley-que-autoriza-a-intervenir-los-militares-en-el-norte-paraguayo/50000553-2904188.

51 *Resumen Latinoamericano* (July 21, 2015). Paraguay: la política de seguridad del gobierno de Cartes alimenta la violencia. Retrieved from: http://www.resumenlatinoamericano.org/2015/07/21/paraguay-la-politica-de-seguridad-del-gobierno-de-cartes-alimenta-la-violencia/.

52 *ABC Color*. (January 16, 2014). "El Estado tiene que devolverle su dignidad al pueblo". Retrieved from: http://www.abc.com.py/blogs/testimonios-para-no-olvidar-142/el-estado-tiene-que-devolverle-su-dignidad-al-pueblo-2429.html.

The Supreme Court has not been able to gain independence from political parties even 20 years after the dictatorship ended. The corrupt logics have intensified and become more sophisticated through the involvement of more actors. This has allowed Paraguay to be one of the first countries in Latin America to present lower levels of judicial independence and at the same time high levels of judicial corruption (Basabe-Serrano 2015).

Although the Supreme Court has presented two bills (retirement law and judicial career law) that could give a strategic direction to the Judiciary, both projects have been ignored by Parliament.[53] On the contrary, there continues to be an influence on the part of representatives of the Legislative Power in the selection of members of the Judicial Power and of the Prosecutor's Office.[54]

6.8.3. Protection of Professionals in Special Risk Situations

In November 2016, the Paraguayan State signed a Letter of Intent addressed to UNESCO for the establishment of a permanent security mechanism for journalists. For its implementation a National Inter-Institutional Commission should be created with representatives of the three branches of the State, representatives of the press and civil society organizations.[55] However, other social actors such as human rights defenders (peasant leaders, trade unionists and activists) do not have a specific protection framework. This has meant that attacks, harassment and sometimes cases of torture of peasant leaders detained during land conflicts remain unpunished, which reflects a marked tendency towards militarization in response to insecurity and the social and political crisis.[56] A report of the Inter-American Commission on Human Rights highlighted that an element that promotes risks is extractive operations and the power of the operating companies which is sometimes even superior to the authority of the States in which they carry out their activities.[57]

---

53 Aguirre, M. (September 30, 2015). Algunos aspectos de la independencia judicial. ABC Color. Retrieved from: http://www.abc.com.py/edicion-impresa/suplementos/judicial/algunos-aspectos-de-la-independencia-judicial-623058.html.

54 Corrales. H. (September 9, 2014). Análisis de la situación del sistema judicial paraguayo. Retrieved from: http://www.unida.edu.py/blog/2014/09/19/analisis-de-la-situacion-del-sistema-de-justicia-paraguayo/.

55 UNESCO (November 28, 2016). Paraguay firmó compromiso pionero sobre seguridad de periodistas. Retrieved from: http://es.unesco.org/news/paraguay-firmo-compromiso-pionero-seguridad-periodistas.

56 Pelli, A. (2002). *Garantías para la lucha por los derechos humanos.* Clacso. Retrieved from: http://biblioteca.clacso.edu.ar/ar/libros/paraguay/cde/cde2002/defensores2002.pdf.

57 CODEHUPY (2016). *Derechos humanos en Paraguay.* Asunción. Retrieved from: http://www.codehupy.org.py/upload/pdf_bibliotecas/Informe%20derechos%20humanos%202016.pdf.

6.8.4. *Education Reform for All Sectors of Society*

The recommendations related to human rights in the education sector have been incorporated in terms of capacities in the area of social sciences, in the disciplines of History and Geography, and Art and Citizen Training, and are addressed as a discipline in the Optional Plan for Education Media, a proposal that is open to consideration by educational institutions across the country.[58]

With regard to indigenous education, progress has been made through the creation of the General Directorate of Indigenous School Education, while the Ministry of Education and Culture has incorporated representatives of indigenous peoples within the technical staff of the Directorate.[59]

In gender equality, different projects have been implemented in different locations such as Ñeembucú and Canindeyú. One of them, "A gender perspective for our teacher training", consisted of sensitization and information on gender issues, aimed at managers, teachers, technicians, administrative staff, students and service staff of the Higher Institute of Education, benefiting 1,842 people. An analysis was made about the possibility of including the gender perspective in the Curricular Mesh of Initial Teacher Training of the Higher Institute of Education. Likewise, a chapter on gender perspective has been prepared within the educational programs of the third year of Elementary school by the Directorate General of Curriculum, Orientation and Educational Evaluation of the Ministry of Education and Culture.[60]

6.8.5. *Training in Human Rights for Officials and Members of the Armed and Security Forces*

There have been some advances in human rights training, but they have not gone beyond the publication of manuals and guides for personnel, without considering a complete re-engineering of the training system to include the human rights approach. In 2010, the manual on the intervention in large-scale evictions was approved. Another manual on the use of force by the Commander of the National Police was also approved in 2011. For its part, the Ministry of the Interior prepared and published the "Basic Guide to Human Rights for police personnel", managing to distribute more than 4,000 copies throughout the country, while the armed forces have a "Manual of Humanitarian Human Rights Standards and International Humanitarian Law", which is a teaching instructional material for military personnel.[61]

---

58 Dirección General de Verdad, Justicia y Reparación de la Defensoría del Pueblo (2011). *Informe de cumplimiento de las recomendaciones de la Comisión de Verdad y Justicia. Audiencia Pública Nacional Junio 2011*. Asunción: Defensoría del Pueblo.

59 Dirección General de Verdad, Justicia y Reparación de la Defensoría del Pueblo (2011).

60 Dirección General de Verdad, Justicia y Reparación de la Defensoría del Pueblo (2011).

61 Dirección General de Verdad, Justicia y Reparación de la Defensoría del Pueblo (2011).

Institutional efforts have been made to bring together State institutions and civil society organizations committed to respecting human rights. There is an agreement signed between the Ministry of the Interior, the Commander of the National Police and the International Committee of the Red Cross, whose purpose is the training of instructors in human rights, the mainstreaming of human rights in all professional technical subjects through the institutes in charge of training and specialization dependent on the Higher Institute of Police Education (ISEPOL).[62] Despite this, the armed forces do not have yet a school of trainers in human rights and international humanitarian law. Nevertheless, it has created a Department of Human Rights and International Humanitarian Law, which with the support and collaboration of the International Committee of the Red Cross (ICRC), the United Nations Information Center (UNIC), the Office of Cooperation of the Embassy of the United States. On some occasions, the Ombudsman's Office has developed workshops, courses and conferences as part of an Integration, Teaching, Promotion and Dissemination of Human Rights and International Humanitarian Law Program within the armed forces of Paraguay.[63]

6.8.6. Ethical Standards of Officials, Journalists and Company Personnel

The situation of the media and journalists in the country includes different forms of subjection and violence. Since the fall of the dictatorship, 17 journalists have been killed without there being any real commitment to investigate the crimes or to endorse a security protocol that protects them. The media outlets are concentrated in few hands after the emergence in the market of the business group of President Horacio Cartes, who in a short time became owner of several national media through his sister, Sarah Cartes. In this way, Cartes, in addition to holding political and economic power, is the owner of a media oligopoly dedicated to promoting his figure and disparaging dissent, especially social organizations critical of its management, using the use of qualifiers and methods of government propaganda befitting of a dictatorship.

Transnational corporations have also been strongly criticized for not knowing how to adapt their activities to the characteristics of the population in the areas where they operate, mainly indigenous peoples. In Paraguay, the rights of indigenous people and their lands have been violated by the expansion of agricultural corporations, such as soy and sugarcane plantations and cattle ranches. Although the Inter-American Court of Human Rights has ruled in

---

62 Dirección General de Verdad, Justicia y Reparación de la Defensoría del Pueblo (2011). *Informe de cumplimiento de las recomendaciones de la Comisión de Verdad y Justicia. Audiencia Pública Nacional Junio 2011*. Asunción: Defensoría del Pueblo.

63 Dirección General de Verdad, Justicia y Reparación de la Defensoría del Pueblo (2011).

favor of indigenous peoples, its recommendations are not being complied with by the State. To this is added the dispossession of lands from communities and peasants.[64] The state policy has been rather to protect and incentivize the *latifundio* and monoculture of soy, neglecting the rights of the indigenous peoples.[65]

The harsh prison conditions, on the other hand, have also motivated expressions of concern on the part of the Inter-American Commission on Human Rights, which has denounced the improper use of preventive detention in the country, after CODEHUPY reported that 7 out of 10 persons in prison are incarcerated without a sentence.[66] Prison conditions in Paraguay are below international standards and endanger the lives of prisoners, who are exposed to overcrowding, abuse by the staff, poor infrastructure and unhealthy living conditions.[67]

The perspective is not encouraging when the highest judicial authority, the Supreme Court of Justice, instructs criminal judges to limit the application of alternative measures to pretrial detention in cases classified as aggravated robbery, especially serious robbery, aggravated robbery in concert, robbery, aggravated robbery, robbery resulting in death or serious injury and theft followed by violence. The Supreme Court affirms, without any concrete evidence, that such a decision and instruction may reduce insecurity (CODEHUPY 2016).

6.8.7. *Constitutional and Legal Reforms to Adapt Laws on Human Rights to International Law*

An Inter-Institutional Commission responsible for the execution of the necessary actions for compliance with the international judgments issued by the Inter-American Court of Human Rights and the recommendations of the CIDH was created in 2009 (Decree No. 1.525). In this context, the Ministry of Foreign Affairs, together with other State institutions, has worked in a coordinated manner with the specific objective of clearing the obstacles and guaranteeing

64 *Info literas* (November 10, 2016), "Transnacionales agrícola, mineras y energéticas violan derechos humanos de pueblos indígenas en AL dice ONU." Retrieved from: http://www.infolliteras.com/articulo.php?id=34582.

65 Hager, K. (2016). *Informe sobre la situación de los pueblos indígenas en Paraguay.* Retrieved from: http://infoindigena.servindi.org/attachments/article/550/2016-GIZ-Hager.K-Situacion-PPII-Paraguay.pdf.

66 Paraguay.com (March 30, 2015). "Denuncian 'privaciones sistemáticas' de derechos en cárceles." Retrieved from: http://www.paraguay.com/nacionales/denuncian-privaciones-sistematicas-de-derechos-en-carceles-125955.

67 Oficina de Democracia, Derechos Humanos y Trabajo de Estados Unidos (2014). *Informe sobre derechos humanos, Paraguay 2014.* Retrieved from: http://photos.state.gov/libraries/paraguay/231771/PDFs/HR%20Report%20Spanish%202014.pdf.

the adoption of effective criteria and actions to comply with the Judgments and Recommendations of the competent institutions of the Inter-American Human Rights System. The Commission is an alternative to the Paraguayan judiciary, which has not performed satisfactorily in terms of executing judgments.[68]

The Ministry of Foreign Affairs coordinates inter-institutional work meetings related to the adoption of measures to comply with the recommendations issued by the different organs and procedures of the United Nations. In this regard, one can cite as an example the responses prepared by the State regarding the follow-up report to the visit of the Subcommittee on the Prevention of Torture, held in September 2010.[69]

Another step forward in institutional terms has been the creation of an inter-institutional body within the Women's Secretariat to monitor compliance with the Convention on All Forms of Discrimination against Women (CEDAW). However, the Convention still needs to be incorporated into the legal practice and legal framework of the institutions.[70]

All these initiatives and changes in the regulatory framework had as their starting point the approval of Law 1160/97 of 1997, which established the principles of legality, reproachability (or blameworthiness), and proportionality, as well as incorporating the presumption of innocence. Criminal offense types were introduced such as family violence, incest, sexual coercion, sexual abuse in defenseless people and children, and trafficking in persons, among others. These types were modified in 2005 and 2008 through subsequent legislation.[71]

7. CONCLUSIONS

The record of implementation of the recommendations made by the Paraguayan Truth Commission is mixed. There has been more progress in memory issues, mainly through museographic initiatives, and the critical study of the dictatorship and the period of violence in the educational system, while the prosecutions of high-level perpetrators and the restructuring of land tenure in the hands of large economic groups with political networks have been largely neglected.

At the institutional level, the DGVJR was set up to carry out follow-up actions on the implementation of the recommendations, but it is an entity dependent on the Ombudsman's Office, which is prone to political interference and lacks the

68 Dirección General de Verdad, Justicia y Reparación de la Defensoría del Pueblo (2011). *Informe de cumplimiento de las recomendaciones de la Comisión de Verdad y Justicia. Audiencia Pública Nacional Junio 2011*. Asunción: Defensoría del Pueblo.

69 Dirección General de Verdad, Justicia y Reparación de la Defensoría del Pueblo (2011).

70 Dirección General de Verdad, Justicia y Reparación de la Defensoría del Pueblo (2011).

71 Dirección General de Verdad, Justicia y Reparación de la Defensoría del Pueblo (2011). Specifically, Decree No. 5.093/05 of 2005 and Law 3440/08 of 2008.

necessary funds and human resources, thus fulfilling rather a purely informative function. The results can be seen in the degree of progress in some actions that fall to the Directorate (such as the search for missing persons, with only 27 exhumations and four restitutions of bodies) and in how much it relies on external organizations such as the Argentine Forensic Anthropology Team to carry out the exhumations.

Regarding memory, there have been advances in the preservation of places of detention and torture as memorial sites for victims. However, the sustainability of these places is not secured and they do not satisfy the requirements of a public policy of memory with specific, long-term goals and guidelines. This has meant that despite the partial political will of State institutions such as the Ministry of the Interior, the interventions have suffered setbacks.

Judicialization is another area where progress has been limited due to political factors. The few sentences that have been passed have fallen on low-ranking members of the armed and security forces and on representatives of factions of the Colorado party that are no longer at the top of the organization. The Prosecutor's Office is not perceived as strong, independent and able to carry out the collection of evidence. This situation has generated a wide sense of impunity among the victims, who have not found in the DGVJR an organization capable of promoting prosecutions.

As for deep reforms, the restitution of lands through the execution of agrarian reform is the greatest debt with the peasant communities and indigenous peoples of the country. In the absence of a coalescing organization such as the Christian Agrarian Leagues, the indigenous communities and peoples have not found a way to influence the State in relation to the restitution of their lands or even to have a better position as victims.

The balance of the implementation process suggests that the democratic transition has been inconclusive and that it is primarily guided by particular political interests rather than by the search for truth, justice and reparation for the victims of state violence. Despite the fact that there was a reconfiguration of the political forces after the fall of Stroessner, the leading actor in national politics has continued to be the Colorado Party. In consequence, the advances in transitional justice are mediated by the interests of those leading this hegemonic political group.

That is why the establishment of the CVJ, as well as the follow-up of the implementation of the recommendations, have depended on national and international human rights organizations and especially on victims and civil society, which in turn are weak and lack the capacity to influence the decision-making processes. As a result, not only have there been limited advances, but the respect for human rights and democratic values by the State in general has been neglected. The Curuguaty massacre evidences the continuation of State practices of repression and violence.

BIBLIOGRAPHY

ABC Color (August 2, 2013). "Ley de atención gratuita a las víctimas." Retrieved from: http://www.abc.com.py/edicion-impresa/politica/ley-de-atencion-gratuita-a-las-victimas-602460.html.

Aguirre, Manuel (September 30, 2015). "Algunos aspectos de la independencia judicial." *ABC Color*. Retrieved from: http://www.abc.com.py/edicion-impresa/suplementos/judicial/algunos-aspectos-de-la-independencia-judicial-623058.html.

Alfonso, César (2010). "Paraguay". In Ambos, K. and Malarino, E. (eds.), *Justicia de Transición. Con informes de América Latina, Alemania, Italia y España*. Bogotá: Temis-Konrad Adenauer Stiftung.

Arellano, Diana (2011). *Reparar lo irreparable: Las víctimas de exilio frente a las políticas de reparación social en Paraguay. En Jornadas de Trabajo: Exilios políticos del Cono Sur en el siglo XX*. Retrieved from: http://jornadasexilios.fahce.unlp.edu.ar/i-jornadas/ponencias/ARELLANO.pdf.

—— (2012). *Proceso de Transición a la Democracia y Políticas de Reparación Social: La Comisión de Verdad y Justicia del Paraguay*. Tesis para obtener el grado de Maestría en Antropologia Social. Universidad Nacional de Misiones. Available at: http://argos.fhycs.unam.edu.ar/bitstream/handle/123456789/476/Tesis_Maestria_ARELLANO_12_Dicatadura_Democracia_Justicia.pdf?sequence=1.

Basabe-Serrano, Santiago (2015). "Informal Institutions and Judicial Independence in Paraguay 1954–2011." *Law and Policy*, no. 37 (4): 350–378. Retrieved from: https://onlinelibrary.wiley.com/doi/full/10.1111/lapo.12038.

BBC Mundo (March 11, 2015). Por qué Paraguay tardó casi 30 años en identificar a sus desaparecidos. Retrieved from: http://www.bbc.com/mundo/noticias/2015/03/150305_paraguay_desaparecidos_vs.

Blog de Red de Sitios de Memoria Latinoamericanos y caribeños (2015). Policía y Ministerio del Interior de Paraguay demuelen Sitio Histórico y de Conciencia. Retrieved from: https://redlatinoamericanadesitiosdememoria.wordpress.com/pronunciamientos-de-la-red/policia-y-ministerio-del-interior-de-paraguay-demuelen-sitio-historico-y-de-conciencia/.

CODEHUPY (2014). *Informe Alternativo Paraguay. Asunción: Presentado ante el Comité contra las desapariciones forzadas en vista del Informe presentado por Paraguay.*

—— (2015). *Derechos Humanos Paraguay 2015*. Asunción: Informe Anual de CODEHUPY.

—— (2016). *Derechos humanos en Paraguay*. Asunción. Retrieved from: http://www.codehupy.org.py/upload/pdf_bibliotecas/Informe%20derechos%20humanos%20 2016.pdf.

Collins, Cath (2016). "Paraguay: Accountability in the shadow of Stroessner". In Skaar, Elin, García Godos, Jemima, and Collins, Cath (eds.), *Transicional Justice in Latin America: The Uneven Road from Impunity towards Accountability*. New York: Routledge, 151–177.

Comisión de Verdad y Justicia (2008). *Conclusiones y recomendaciones del Informe Final de la Comisión de Verdad y Justicia del Paraguay*. Retrieved from: http://www.dhnet.org.br/verdade/mundo/paraguai/informe_cv_paraguay_conclusiones_y_recomendaciones.pdf.

—— (2008). *Informe final. Tomo I. Síntesis y caracterización del régimen*. Asunción. Retrieved from: http://www.dhnet.org.br/verdade/mundo/paraguai/cv_paraguai_tomo_01.pdf.

Corrales, Hugo (September 9, 2014). "Análisis de la situación del sistema judicial paraguayo". Retrieved from: http://www.unida.edu.py/blog/2014/09/19/analisis-de-la-situacion-del-sistema-de-justicia-paraguayo/.

Countrywatch (2015). *Paraguay: 2015 Country Review*.

D'Alessandro, Sandra (2014). "Las representaciones del pasado reciente en los textos escolares de Historia en Paraguay". *Discurso y Sociedad* no. 8 (1): 37–56.

Diario Última Hora (May 2, 2014). "Declaran a la Comisaría 3a como 'Sitio histórico y de conciencia'". Retrieved from: https://www.ultimahora.com/declaran-la-comisaria-3-como-sitio-historico-y-conciencia-n791351.html.

Dirección General de Verdad, Justicia y Reparación de la Defensoría del Pueblo (2011). *Informe de cumplimiento de las recomendaciones de la Comisión de Verdad y Justicia. Audiencia Pública Nacional Junio 2011*. Asunción: Defensoría del Pueblo.

—— (2014). *Informe referente a las desapariciones forzadas y ejecuciones extrajudiciales en el Paraguay*. Asunción: Defensoría del Pueblo.

EFE (April 21, 2016). "Piden declarar inconstitucional una ley que autoriza a intervenir a los militares en el norte paraguayo". Retrieved from: http://www.efe.com/efe/america/cono-sur/piden-declarar-inconstitucional-una-ley-que-autoriza-a-intervenir-los-militares-en-el-norte-paraguayo/50000553-2904188.

Equipo Nizkor (March 16, 2004). "Designan a los integrantes de la sociedad civil en la Comisión Verdad y Justicia". Retrieved from: http://www.derechos.org/nizkor/paraguay/doc/cvyj1.html.

Garretón, Francisca, Gonzales, Marianne and Lauzán, Silvana (2011). *Políticas públicas de verdad y memoria en America Latina: Paraguay*. Centro de Derechos Humanos de la Facultad de Derecho de la Universidad de Chile.

Gobernación del Alto Paraná. Ciudad del Este. Available at: http://www.altoparana.gov.py/v0/index.php/ciudad-del-este.

Hager, Katharina (2016). *Informe sobre la situación de los pueblos indígenas en Paraguay*. Retrieved from: http://infoindigena.servindi.org/attachments/article/550/2016-GIZ-Hager.K-Situacion-PPII-Paraguay.pdf.

Info literas (November 10, 2016). "Transnacionales agrícola, mineras y energéticas violan derechos humanos de pueblos indígenas en AL dice ONU". Retrieved from: http://www.infolliteras.com/articulo.php?id=34582.

Jean Schemo, Diana (August 16, 2006). "Stroessner, Paraguay's Enduring Dicator, Dies". *The New York Times*.

Lambert, Peter (2000). "A decade of electoral democracy: continuity, change and crisis in Paraguay." *Bulletin of Latin American Research* no. 19 (3): 379–396.

Ley N° 838, que indemniza a víctimas de violaciones de derechos humanos durante la dictadura de 1954 a 1989, March 29, 1996. Retrieved from: http://www.hacienda.gov.py/code/documentos/ley_838_1996.pdf.

Martínez, Maitane et al. (2014). "Paraguay: de las violaciones a los derechos humanos a la justicia transicional". *Salud & Sociedad* no. 5 (1): 98–114.

Ministerio de Justicia (March 6, 2013). Decreto N 10.747, por el cual se aprueban las políticas públicas en materia de derechos humanos y se pone en fase de implementación el Plan Nacional de Derechos Humanos. Retrieved from: http://www.mre.gov.py/v1/DDHH/DECRETO10747.pdf.

Oficina de Democracia, Derechos Humanos y Trabajo de Estados Unidos (2014). *Informe sobre derechos humanos, Paraguay 2014*. Retrieved from: http://photos.state.gov/libraries/paraguay/231771/PDFs/HR%20Report%20Spanish%202014.pdf.

Paraguay.com (March 30, 2015). Denuncian "privaciones sistemáticas" de derechos en cárceles. Retrieved from: http://www.paraguay.com/nacionales/denuncian-privaciones-sistematicas-de-derechos-en-carceles-125955.

—— (December 11, 2014). *CODEHUPY insta a elegir a nuevo defensor del Pueblo*. Retrieved from: http://www.paraguay.com/nacionales/codehupy-insta-a-elegir-nuevo-defensor-del-pueblo-120645.

Pelli, Aldo (2002). *Garantías para la lucha por los derechos humanos*. Clacso. Retrieved from: http://biblioteca.clacso.edu.ar/ar/libros/paraguay/cde/cde2002/defensores2002.pdf.

Portal Guaraní (2015). *Informe final de la Comisión de Verdad y Justicia de Paraguay (CVJ). Antecedentes y normativa*. Retrieved from: http://www.portalguarani.com/detalles_museos_otras_obras.php?id=60&id_obras=1185&id_otras=174.

RAADH (2013). Reunión de Altas autoridades en Derechos Humanos y Cancillerías del Mercosur y Estados asociados. Retrieved from: http://www.raadh.mercosur.int/comisiones/memoria-verdad-y-justicia/.

Red de Sitios de Memoria Latinoamericanos y Caribeños. "¿Quiénes somos?" (n.d.) Available at: http://sitiosdememoria.org/es/quienes-somos/.

Resumen Latinoamericano (July 21, 2015). "Paraguay: la política de seguridad del gobierno de Cartes alimenta la violencia". Retrieved from: http://www.resumenlatinoamericano.org/2015/07/21/paraguay-la-politica-de-seguridad-del-gobierno-de-cartes-alimenta-la-violencia/.

—— (August 6, 2015). "Paraguay: Víctimas de la dictadura rechazan demolición de la Comisaría Tercera". Retrieved from: http://www.resumenlatinoamericano.org/2015/08/06/paraguay-victimas-de-la-dictadura-rechazan-demolicion-de-la-comisaria-tercera/.

Riquelme, Marcial (1994). "Bases para la discusión de las relaciones Fuerzas Armadas/Sociedad Civil en el Paraguay." In L. Bareiro, T. Escobar and S. Sosnowski, *Hacia una cultura para la democracia en el Paraguay*. Asunción: CDE.

Stabilli, Maria Rosaria (2012). "Opareí. La justicia de transición en Paraguay." *América Latina Hoy* no. 61: 137–162.

Silvero, Rocío (2013). *La voz de los "vencidos": Análisis de la representación de la memoria del campesinado dentro del Informe de la Comisión de verdad y Justicia*. Retrieved from: http://www.grupoparaguay.org/L_Rojas_2013.pdf.

TELESUR (February 2, 2014). "Víctimas del régimen Stroessner en Paraguay exigen justicia". Retrieved from: http://www.telesurtv.net/news/Victimas-del-regimen-Stroessner-en-Paraguay-exigen-justicia-20140202-0006.html.

Turner, Brian (2014). "Paraguay: La vuelta del Partido Colorado al poder." *Revista de Ciencia Política* no. 34 (1): 249–266. Retrieved from: http://revistahistoria.uc.cl/index.php/rcp/article/view/6000/5622.

UNESCO (November 28, 2016). "Paraguay firmó compromiso pionero sobre seguridad de periodistas". Retrieved from: http://es.unesco.org/news/paraguay-firmo-compromiso-pionero-seguridad-periodistas.

Valencia, Alejandro (2011). "Memorias compartidas: las comisiones de la Verdad de Paraguay y Ecuador". In *Contribución de las políticas de verdad, justicia y reparación a las democracias en América Latina*. Instituto Interamericano de Derechos Humanos, 216–245.

Wellbach, Evelin (2009). *El Paraguay exiliado: memorias de la resistencia 1970–1989*. Retrieved from: http://www.cedema.org/uploads/Wellbach_2012.pdf.

Zorrilla, Elvira Olmedo (January 16, 2014). "El Estado tiene que devolverle su dignidad al pueblo". *ABC Color*. Retrieved from: http://www.abc.com.py/blogs/testimonios-para-no-olvidar-142/el-estado-tiene-que-devolverle-su-dignidad-al-pueblo-2429.html.

ANNEX 1: LIST OF INTERVIEWEES

- María Stella Cáceres, Director of *Museo de las Memorias* (Museum of Memories), Dictatorship and Human Rights of Asuncion, February 2017.
- Martín Almada, victim and Director of *la Fundación Celestina Pérez de Almada* (the Celestina Pérez de Almada Fundation), February 2017.
- Rosa Palau, Director of *Museo de la Justicia del Poder Judicial* (Museum of the Judiciary), Judiciary, April 2017.
- Nilo Damián, Director of *Centro de Estudios Antropológicos de la Universidad Católica Nuestra Señora de la Asunción* (Center of Anthropological Studies, Catholic University Our Lady of Asunción), February 2017.
- Daisi Amarilla, Vice-President, *Asociación Indigenista del Paraguay* (Indigenous Association of Paraguay), February 2017.
- Jorge Vera, general coordinator, *Gente, Ambiente y Territorio* – GAT (People, Environment and Territory), February 2017.
- José Carlos Rodríguez, CVJ commissioner, drafting director for the CVJ's Final Report, February 2017.
- Lourdes Giubi, lawyer, *La Dirección de Verdad, Justicia y Reparación de la Defensoría del Pueblo* (DGVJR-DP), February 2017.

ANNEX 2: RECOMMENDATIONS OF THE *COMISIÓN DE VERDAD Y JUSTICIA DE PARAGUAY* (CVJ)

1. To create a National Human Rights Secretariat, attached to the Presidency of the Republic [...].[72]
2. Request the President of the Republic, as Commander in Chief of the Armed Forces and responsible for the National Police, to continue the disclosure of all the police and military archives with the purpose of contributing to the clarification of the gross human rights violations, safeguarding the information that affects the privacy of the people.
3. Request foreign Governments to declassify the documents in their power related to human rights violations against Paraguayans during the Stroessner regime and to make them available to the Paraguayan society through the National Secretariat of Human Rights promoted by the Commission for Truth and Justice.
4. Preserve and guard all the archives related to the cases of human rights violations, obtain certified copies of all the documents related to human rights violations that are in other national and international archives and make their access unrestricted and public, also using modern instruments to disseminate the content of social interest, safeguarding the information that affects the privacy of people.
5. Analyze and investigate, through the institution proposed to follow-up on the recommendations of the Commission for Truth and Justice, the damage caused by the agreements of Itaipu and Yacyreta in environmental matters and human rights violations committed by the Paraguayan dictatorship.
6. Instruct the National Secretariat of Human Rights and the National Indigenous Institute to conduct research about the cases of killings and other human rights violations against indigenous people during the dictatorship, with the purpose of clarify the dates, locations, offenders and victims, and proposing alternatives for reparation, including the situation of the rights of indigenous children that were sold as servants.
7. Promote through the National Secretariat of Human Rights research about the cases of sexual violence, particularly those that were against children and adolescents, including sexual slavery; the research must be accompanied by an awareness campaign about the topic.

---

72 According to the description of this body in the recommendations chapter, this Secretary would be the mechanism in charge on following up on the CVJ's recommendations. See CVJ, *Comisión de Verdad y Justicia. Informe final. Tomo I. Síntesis y caracterización del régimen.* Asunción, 2008, p. 92.

8. Promote an investigation by the National Secretariat of Human Rights about human rights violations that affected the press and the culture, with the participation of journalists and cultural workers.

Search for Disappeared Persons

9. Continue with the search for the missing people, work that will begin in the Commission for Truth and Justice, including psychosocial support, with two objectives: to facilitate the grieving process and avoid revictimization in different aspects that are involved in the search. To that end, form a National Forensic Anthropology Team with professionals who have experience in similar work. This team must be incorporated into the structure of the National Secretariat of Human Rights proposed in this Final Report.
10. Involve, through the State, representatives of social movements, political parties that were in opposition during the dictatorship and victims' movements in the official creation of a National Genetic Data Bank, in order that the identification of victims of the human rights violations will be tangible and given full legal effect, on the basis of the research of the Commission for Truth and Justice detailed in this report.
11. Promote, through the State, mechanisms to encourage people who hold data and information about disappeared detained people, places or events that may lead to clarifying the violations, to give that information to the National Secretariat of Human Rights proposed in this report, granting them all guarantees of personal safety.

Official Statements

12. Grant full support and legitimacy by the State to the work of individuals and institutions that defend human rights and to victims' organizations.
13. Declare as memory spaces, after an inventory, various places attached to human rights violations, like places of detention and torture, where corpses were disposed of, and exhumation places of human remains, among others, with the participation of civil organizations society and victims' movements.
14. Provide support for collective memory initiatives proposed by local institutions, social organizations or affected communities.
15. Declare through the ministries, to the Governorates and the Municipalities as historical places of repression of the Stroessner dictatorship, such as the Department of Investigation of the Police, Security Guard, Central Police Department, "Abraham Cué", the police unit of Paraguarí and others, according to the final report of the Truth and Justice Commission.

16. Dismantle public monuments and remove names of public places, of people that are considered responsible for human rights violations.
17. Give public recognition, through the State, to the people, the foreign states and national and international organizations that defended and welcomed the victims of the dictatorship.
18. Give public recognition, through the State, to the fighters and victims of the dictatorship to the memory of the resistance of terror and defense of human rights.
19. Entrust to the National Secretariat of Human Rights the development of an inventory of the organizations and entities that disappeared or were severely affected by the repression during the Stroessner regime (newspapers, cultural groups, professional associations, trade unions, peasant associations and other social organizations), with the purpose of publicly honoring them.
20. Promote, through the State, programs for the reintegration into social and political life of the victims of the dictatorship that are still stigmatized because of their social and political struggle, removing from the National Archives and the Department of Identifications all criminal records and/or stigmatization inserted during the dictatorship.
21. Ensure the participation of the communities and indigenous peoples in the proposals and implementation of the initiatives that affect them, complemented by the requirement of free and informed prior consultation.

Public apologies

22. See that the State officially declares their responsibility for human rights violations that occurred during the dictatorship and to apologize to the victims and Paraguayan society, therefore pledging not to repeat such aberrant situations, implementing for that all kinds of the resources needed to do it. Arrange for this statement to be made by the presidents of the Executive, Legislative and Judicial branches, as well as the Commanders of the Armed Forces and the Police, with recognition of the responsibility that corresponds to each one following the conclusions of the investigation of the Truth and Justice Commission.
23. Exhort the State to offer apologies to each indigenous people, accepting the responsibility for human rights violations.
24. Request the State to offer apologies for the grave violations to the victims of sexual violence, especially women and girls, as well as other people of different sexual orientations.

25. Insist that the State offer apologies to other sectors that were victims: children and adolescents, political parties, students, farmers, union workers, journalists, church members, members of the Army, among others.
26. Call for the parties and political groups, or other organizations and institutions that supported or collaborated directly and indirectly with the regime of Alfredo Stroessner, in particular the Colorado Party, to make a recognition of responsibility for human rights violations and offer apologies to the victims.
27. Insist that political parties and other civil society organizations depose those members that were responsible for human rights violations and withdraw from them any distinction or honorary position that has been granted.
28. Exhort the governments of other States, that supported the Stroessner regime, to offer apologies to the Paraguayan people and accept their responsibility for human rights violations contained in this report.
29. Offer apologies from the Paraguayan State to the societies of foreign countries who suffered human rights violations perpetrated in Paraguay or outside the country with the support from the Stroessner regime.
30. Insist that the alleged individual perpetrators of human rights violations who are alive accept their responsibility for the acts committed and offer apologies to the victims.

Applying sanctions

31. Give the Report of the Truth and Justice Commission to the Prosecutor General of the Republic and the Attorney General of the State so that they investigate the complaints of human rights violations contained in the report and to continue the corresponding legal action.
32. To request the Attorney General of the State to continue with the judgments against the perpetrators initiated by the Truth and Justice Commission.
33. Start, reopen or continue, by the judicial authorities, the outstanding process to investigate the criminal responsibility of all the people named as alleged perpetrators in the report of the JVC, given the non-application of statute of limitations of the crimes against humanity that occurred in Paraguay.
34. Promote prosecutions by the Public Ministry against public officials allegedly involved in serious human rights violations, including those magistrates who have not properly fulfilled their duties of protecting fundamental rights.
35. Fortify the prosecution unit charged with investigating human rights violations with enough human and budgetary resources.

36. Urge the Public Ministry and the national judicial authorities to investigate diligently cases of human rights violations that have been decided or are being processed in intergovernmental human rights organizations in order to identify, prosecute and punish those allegedly responsible.
37. Request the Public Ministry to take appropriate measures in order that the victims, their families or their heirs may, individually or collectively, have access to justice to ensure their rights. It also must ensure wide participation in the judicial process for all injured parties and for any person or nongovernmental organization that has a legitimate interest in the process.
38. Suspend from their official duties, during the penal and disciplinary intervention, the people legally accused as responsible for human rights violations.
39. Disqualify from any public charge, any person convicted of human rights violations, including any person involved in the illegal allocation of land.
40. Vetting through the Ombudsman those who bear political responsibility for and those who were perpetrators of human rights violations, to hold elective offices or positions in the public administration.
41. Exhort the Armed Forces and the Police to dismiss members responsible for human rights violations, and to remove from them any distinction or honorary position which has been granted.
42. Proceed with the investigations tending towards the identification, trial and punishment of those responsible for human rights violations committed against the recruits who served in the compulsory military service during the *Stronista* regime.
43. Urge the State's Attorney General to investigate the members of the Central Electoral Commission during the *Stronista* regime, for their suspected responsibility in electoral crimes.
44. Establish legal, judicial and administrative mechanisms that permit the State to take the necessary actions against those responsible for the human rights violations, directed to obtaining the necessary economic resources to pay the reparations of human rights violations' victims.
45. Publish through the State, the identity of offenders and collaborators, who have been declared as such at trial, at a national level and especially in their community and surroundings, as an exemplary and moral measure, aiming for the end of impunity.
46. Urge that the Ministry of Foreign Affairs propose, in the framework of MERCOSUR, an analysis from the point of view of human rights of "Operation Condor" and present their results to the pertinent authorities for them to conduct trials against those bearing intellectual and material responsibility in that operation.

47. Insist that the State in the extradition and punishment of the identified offenders located abroad, making use of all legal and diplomatic means, and hold Congress accountable for the actions being carried out for this purpose. In this sense, recommend the competent Judge to immediately request the extradition of Sabino Augusto Montanaro, Antonio Campos Alum and others responsible for human rights violations, according with the many testimonies received by the Justice and Truth Commission.
48. Request the governments of foreign States where, under any legal condition, Paraguayans responsible for human rights violations reside, to notify the Paraguayan State for the purpose of appeal to the extradition, and enable the judgment of this presumed responsible, or, on the contrary, to judge them under the principle of universal jurisdiction.
49. Include in every extradition treaty in which Paraguay will participate, as one of the causes to not allow the extradition, the justified presumption of danger to the individual's life or that he will be subject to cruel, inhumane or degrading treatment, or that he will not enjoy the guarantees of a proper and impartial legal procedure, for political reasons.
50. Stop paying salaries and pensions by the State, to those who committed torture and other human rights violations, that find themselves sentenced.

Memorialization of victims

51. Establish a nationwide commemorative date in the annual calendar in honor of the fighters and victims of human rights violations.
52. Sign agreements, through the Ministry of Foreign Affairs, with Argentina, Uruguay and Brazil, to establish in the cities where the Paraguayan exile was higher, Museums of the Paraguayan Exile Memory.
53. Assign through Central Government, the Governments and Local Governments, the names of the victims and defenders of human rights to streets, squares, monuments, places and public building, on the basis of the final report of the Justice and Truth Commission, and with the participation of victims and relatives.
54. Place nameplates in public places in memory of the victims of human rights violations.
55. Denominate schools, at national and municipal levels, with names of children who were victims during the dictatorship, such who were born in prison, who were left unprotected because their parent suffered violations of human rights, and who suffered all types of adversity.
56. Recognize, through the realization of commemorations and homages, the communities that were victims of collective attacks, such as Jejuí, Simbrón,

Sangre del Drago, and others mentioned in the report of the Justice and Truth Commission, activities that will be agreed with the communities themselves, promoting their participation in this process.

Human Rights education

57. Guarantee that the subject "Authoritarianism in recent history of Paraguay" is taught in all educational establishments of the country, in both Spanish and Guarani.
58. Train, qualify and evaluate the teachers who must teach the subject "Authoritarianism in recent history of Paraguay".
59. Include in the school texts a pedagogical summarized version of the course "Authoritarianism in recent history of Paraguay", in both Spanish and Guarani, according to the report of the Justice and Truth Commission.
60. Edit texts and broadcast radio programs with a summary of the report of the Justice and Truth Commission in Spanish, Guarani, and other indigenous languages from Paraguay.
61. Promote radio and television programs, both in Spanish and Guarani, about the results of the investigation carried out by the Justice and Truth Commission.
62. Establish, through the Ministry of Education and Culture, an educational calendar in commemoration of the paradigmatic facts of human rights violations, according to the final report of the Justice and Truth Commission, in order to prevent their repetition.
63. Promote, through the National Fund of Education and Culture (FONDEC), the life stories of civil heroes who fought for human rights during the *Stronista* dictatorship and the transition, and republish the out-of-print works referring to the subject, that reinforce the democratic process.

Restitution of Rights

64. Approve a regulatory law of the National Constitution, with the aim of accelerating the access to Paraguayan nationality of the children and grandchildren of Paraguayans born abroad as a consequence of the exile.
65. Maintain close relationships between the State and the Paraguayan exiles of the dictatorship, that still reside abroad.
66. The State must sign agreements with other States for cooperation and assistance to exiles.
67. Promote through public policies, programs that encourage family reintegration by the gathering of fathers, mothers, sons and daughters who were separated because of the human rights violations.

Return to previous residences

68. Encourage by public policies the voluntary, honorable and safe return of exiles and internally displaced people, including their descendants up to the third generation, who abandoned their home or habitual workplace because of the human rights violations.

Restitution to former positions

69. Establish by law that the public servants who lost their positions because they were victims of the violation of their human rights, can be reinstated in them, if they so wish or, alternatively, receive compensation.
70. Establish by law that the citizens who have been deprived of the right to employment and social security, because they were victims of the violation of their human rights, can access an honorable position or, alternatively, receive compensation.

Restitution of property

71. Hand over to the Prosecutor General of the Republic, and the Attorney General of the State, on the part of the Executive Power and the Judicial Power, the report of the Justice and Truth Commission about "illegally gained lands" in Paraguay, with the aim to investigate the allegations about illegally allocated lands, initiate the actions of invalidation of titles, revoke the allocation resolutions and promote actions of reclamation or other actions, when appropriate, for the recuperation of those lands and their institutional allocation to the subjects of the land reform and other beneficiaries. Urge the Judicial Power to actively process those files.
72. Drive the trials about illegally allocated lands already promoted by the Prosecutor General of the Republic and continue the procedures until their finalization, in order to restore the legal and legitimate order of the nation's lands.
73. Modify Law Nº 1863/02, in its article 49, which establishes the order of preference for the adjudication of lands, so that the dictatorship's victims or their relatives who meet the requirements established by the Agrarian Statute to benefit from this law, are to be included in the subparagraph c) of the order of preference.
74. Proceed in a similar way to the recuperation of illegally allocated lands with the other illegally allocated property by the dictatorship's officials that can be identified according to an investigation from the Public Ministry and the Attorney General's Office of the Republic, with the aim that the State can recuperate them and enter them in the General Revenues of the Nation.

75. Initiate the procedures of restitution of the family inheritance divested from the exiles, above all their real estate properties.
76. Adopt by national legislation the legislative and administrative measures, and those of any other kind, including the necessary budget lines, to create an effective mechanism of restitution of ancestral lands to the communities and indigenous peoples for them to access according to their culture and traditional way of life, guaranteeing the protection of biodiversity, according to the articles 62 to 67, Chapter V, "Concerning the indigenous peoples", of the National Constitution.
77. Promote by the Attorney General of the Nation and the Ombudsman office the pertinent judicial and legal actions for the recuperation of the collective and communal properties, communal fields and public spaces that were misappropriated.

Physical or mental harm

78. Modify Law N° 838/96 in the following aspects:
79. Take into account the jurisprudential criteria of the Inter-American Court of Human Rights in order to establish the reparation to the victims of the human rights violations.
80. Anticipate annually in the General Budget of the Nation's Expenditure a specific, nominated and easily identifiable line item, for the payment of reparations to the victims of human rights violations.
81. Anticipate annually in the General Budget of the Nation's Expenditure a specific, differentiated, nominated and easily identifiable line item, for the payment of reparations ordered by judgments and reports of the international bodies of human rights.
82. Create by law a National Fund of Compensations for the payment of compensations to the victims of human rights violations and the payment of reparations ordered by the judgments and reports of the human rights' international bodies. The Fund will be financed with specific, nominated and identifiable annual line items of the General Budget of the Nation's Expenses, as well as the goods and money taken away from those responsible for human rights violations and from the contribution of the international cooperation.

Loss of opportunities such as education and other public services

83. Grant scholarships and other facilities for access to basic, technical and university education for the victims of human rights violations and relatives of lineal consanguinity in all the degrees and collateral until the second degree.

84. Facilitate the access to housing rights for the victims of human rights violations that have scarce resources, through mechanisms that promote it as a part of the compensation.
85. Instruct the National Reparations Fund to carry out a study on the feasibility of other recommendations regarding compensation related to damages for material damage, including loss of earnings, consequential damage, damage to the life project, moral damages and damages for medical care expenses, psychological or legal.

Medical and psychological attention

86. Create an integral reparation program of medical and psycho-social assistance for the victims of human rights violations. This program will have an appropriate legal origin and coverage and will be equipped with adequate economic resources for the number of beneficiaries and a training system for health personnel for care and treatment in cases of human rights violations. Besides it should be articulated with the Ministry of Health and other state institutions and should promote agreements with civil society's organizations for the integral attention to the victims. This program will be free at the basic level of attention, including medicine supply.
87. Include as beneficiaries of the integral compensation program of medical and psycho-social assistance to the torture victims with physical and psychic consequences; to the people who were illegitimately deprived of their liberty, to the relatives of the missing and/or extrajudicially executed, as well as the victims of torture and/or cruel and degrading treatments or sentences, exiles, including the surviving spouse and consanguineous descendants in all degrees, with special attention to children victims.
88. Enlarge in an appropriate amount by the National Congress the increase of the budget for the National Institution of the Indigenous (INDI), for that the indigenous peoples' access, according to their culture, to decent conditions on health, education, as well as other basic services, following the principles and rights contained in the United Nations Declaration on the rights of indigenous peoples.

Legal and social services

89. Create within the entity to be created by recommendation of this Commission a team for free legal assistance for all the victims who are beneficiaries and their direct relatives, on restitution, compensation, rehabilitation, satisfaction and non-repetition.

Effective civilian control over military and security forces

90. Grant by law to the Ombudsman Office the faculty to investigate and impose administrative and disciplinary sanctions on the Armed Forces and Police members involved in human rights violations.
91. Align the legislation of the Nation's Armed Forces, in the aspects which have not yet been, to the mandates of the National Constitution, incorporating in its intern normative the human rights' principles and the subordination to the State's powers (article 173 of the National Constitution).
92. Establish in the organic laws of the Public Force of the Nation (Armed Forces and Police Force) the absolute prohibition of partisan affiliation and to carry out political-partisan works under penalty of automatic destitution or retirement with dishonorable discharge.
93. Establish that in order to enter the member institutions of the Public Force present with the request of admission a sworn statement before the notary public of not being affiliated to any political party.

Guarantee that all civilian and military proceedings are in accordance with international standards

94. Carry out substantive reforms to the military penal justice, adjusting it to the National Constitution, guaranteeing its independence and impartiality, with exclusive competency for crimes directly related with the service and where it is clearly established that it is not competent to investigate and judge civils nor to know the human rights violations.
95. Demand that the Armed Forces fully respect and guarantee women's rights under military jurisdiction.
96. Modify the procedures of military justice in order to incorporate to them the norms of the due process.
97. Implement the pertinent constitutional and legal reforms that guarantee an independent and efficient justice administration, in accordance with the international law of human rights, avoiding the influence of partisan policy and other powerful sectors.
98. Urge the Superintendence and the Ethical Council of the Supreme Court of Justice to dedicate special attention to the ethical conduct of the judges so they guide themselves by the principles of independence and impartiality.
99. Regulate in a special way the Penal Code and the Criminal Procedural Code consecrating with the fullest extent possible the habeas corpus noting, among other, its irrevocable character.
100. Urge that judges, when dictating their resolutions in case of human rights violations, have in consideration the international law of human rights.

101. Create auxiliary laboratories of judicial investigations that, besides having independence conditions, look for evidence about criminal facts, applying methods based in scientific principle, without resorting to privileged probative evidence of what happened to the confession obtained in the interrogations.
102. Organize by the Judicial Power and the Public Ministry periodic training courses in human rights for every employee in the judicial branch, particularly about the due process, the judicial guarantees and the international standards on this subject.
103. Create a school for formators in human rights and humanitarian law in the interior of the Judicial Power and the Public Ministry preferentially conformed by judiciary members and independent experts.

Protection for professionals in situation of risk

104. Create a protection program in the charge of the National Secretary of Human Rights for which is recommended its creation for sectors in particular condition of vulnerability and risk, such as witnesses, human rights advocates, journalists, among others.
105. Provide the necessary protection to the people who testify before the Justice and Truth Commission, by the program that is suggested to be created in the previous recommendation.

Human rights education for all social sectors

106. Include the subject of human rights in the syllabuses of elementary, high-school and higher education through modern and active methods that make it interesting for the students.
107. Introduce human rights content in a transversal manner in subjects as history, geography, ethics and citizen formation, art and literature, as well as in the social sciences subject of the Common Plan of Secondary Education.
108. Promote as an educational policy that in every scholastic environment the presence of a non-authoritarian, human rights culture which avoids violence, and is supported not only in the syllabus, but also in the relationship between the members of the educational community (teachers, directors, students and parents).
109. Arrange for the Ministry of Education and Culture to distribute audiovisual game material to schools, with text in Spanish and Guarani, about the promotion of citizens' rights.
110. Implement, through the Ministry of Education and Culture, free online courses for schools for students on the theme of human rights.

111. Form and actualize teachers, through the Ministry of Education and Culture, the National Board of Education and the National Board of Universities, for the teaching of human rights and for the "Authoritarianism in early history of Paraguay" subject.
112. Entrust the Ministry of Education and Culture and the National Institute of the Indigenous (INDI) the design and realization of specialized training programs in indigenous peoples' rights for the public functionaries and civil society's organizations.
113. Include in the educational programs, by the Ministry of Education and Culture and the Secretariat of Women's Affairs, the rejection of gender discrimination, in the political, economic, social and cultural, the recognition of the fundamental role of women in the national life and the enforceability of women's right of a life free of violence.
114. Incorporate in the educational programs from the Ministry of Education and Culture and the National Institute of the Indigenous (INDI), the right to non-ethnic discrimination, in the political, economic, social and cultural, the recognition of the fundamental role of the pre-Columbian people in the national life and the enforceability of their right to autonomy, dignity and development of their own cultures.
115. Carry out programs of human rights promotion for groups in particular situation of vulnerability and risk, such as women, children, indigenous people, elderly persons, people with other sexual identities, AIDS sufferers, exiles, displaced persons and refugees, people deprived of liberty, migrant laborers, among others.
116. Promote through State activities the knowledge of human rights among social organizations for mutual defense against possible abuses and arbitrariness from the authority.
117. Promote by the State the training of civil society's observers referring to pedagogical practices to monitor the application of human rights in the educational field.
118. Establish an obligatory chair of human rights international law in law departments.
119. Stimulate that the different law departments include optional chairs or seminars about humanitarian international law and penal international law.
120. Motivate in schools and universities events and investigations about human rights.
121. Entrust the Ministry of Education and Culture and the, to be created, National Secretariat of Human Rights, with the publication of specialized materials on human rights, human rights' international law, humanitarian international law and international penal law for all education programs.

122. Publish in the "Official Gazette" all the judgments dictated by the intergovernmental bodies and by the national courts of the cases of human rights violations, occurring in the country.
123. Eliminate the influence of political/partisan criteria in the appointment of schoolteachers and the selection of educational texts, and impede the partisan use of educational personnel in elections and the political instrumentalization of education. Urge the Churches, both in their doctrine and their actions, to persist and include in their pastoral work the promotion and protection of human rights.

Human Rights training for state employees

124. Design and implement training programs and permanent regular courses of education in human rights and humanitarian international law in the formation of the Military, Police and security forces, at all hierarchical levels.
125. Instruct the public force in the respect of human rights and in particular in the Code of Conduct for functionaries in charge of law enforcement and on the basic Principles about the use of force and firearms by functionaries in charge of law enforcement, both in individual and mass interventions.
126. Design publications on human rights and humanitarian law for members of the Police and Military Forces.
127. Create a school for trainers in human rights and humanitarian law inside the Armed Forces and the Police staffed by members of this institution and with the participation of other state and non-governmental sectors.
128. Publish specialized materials in human rights, human rights' international law, humanitarian international law and penal international law for the different education programs of the Police and the Armed Forces.
129. Introduce in the different training programs this section deals with, including in its publications a gender perspective.

Promote respect for codes of conduct

130. Design manuals about the public function of State agents in which it is highlighted the transparence in the public function exercise and the respect of human rights, and that their violation generates disciplinary and administrative consequences that can entail destitution and impediments for the exercise of public charges.
131. Urge the media to promote an editorial line concordant with human rights and to encourage in the public opinion a culture of respect for human dignity, sensitive to the victims of human rights violations.

132. Implement training programs and permanent regular education courses on human rights for journalists.
133. Ensure that the ethics manuals for journalists and communicators promote a culture of respect for human rights.
134. Establish by the competent State entities norms for the transnational companies and other commercial companies in the sense that they have the obligation to promote, ensure that they are enjoyed, respected, enforce and protect the human rights, as well as the rights and interests of the indigenous peoples and other groups in a vulnerable and risky situation.
135. Request the Ministry of Justice and Labor to establish more effective controls so that the human rights of people deprived of liberty are respected and guaranteed, and train the functionaries of penitentiary establishments and especially prison guards about the rights and treatment of people deprived of liberty.

Promote mechanisms to guarantee labor rights and social peace

136. Establish by Legislative Power and the Ministry of Justice and Labor norms that improve the existing mechanisms in matter of conciliation, arbitration, mediation and conflict solution, as well as guaranteeing the fulfilment of the approved agreements.
137. Entrust the Supreme Court of Justice and the National Congress promote the work of the judges of Peace and introduce the legal reforms that permit its adequate functioning.
138. Strengthen the Public Ombudsman with greater staffing and budget resources with the aim to assign more lawyers to the defense of people's rights.
139. Control, by the Ministry of Justice and Labor, the contracts and labor conditions of the indigenous people who work in livestock, forest, agriculture and other areas.

Promote legal and Constitutional reform

140. Approve [...] treaties of human rights and humanitarian law to which the Paraguayan State is not a party.
141. Mediate through the State, by the National Secretariat of Human Rights proposed in this Report, legislative, judicial and administrative measures which allow the fulfillment of sentences of the international jurisdiction bodies of human rights in the treaties in which Paraguay has acknowledged jurisdiction, that establish that the victim can sue the State for the fulfillment of the sentence by the established sentence enforcement procedure stated in the Civil Code.

142. Implement by the Paraguayan State, through efficient mechanisms, the recommendations of the OAS's Inter-American Commission on Human Rights and the conventional and specialized organisms of the United Nations on human rights.
143. Establish mechanisms to fulfil the precautionary and preventive measures on the human rights' intergovernmental organisms.
144. Promote actions to incorporate to the internal legislation the principles, guarantees and rights contained in the United Nations Declaration on the rights of Indigenous Peoples of September 2007.
145. Align the national law according to the dispositions of article 27 on the Rome Statute, that says that the "Statute will apply equally to all without any distinction based on the official position. In particular, the official position of a person, so be chief of State or head of government, member of a government of a parliament, chosen representative or government functionary, in no case will be exempt from penal responsibility nor will such position constitute a motive per se to reduce the sentence. The immunities and norms of special procedures that entail the official charge of a person, in accordance with the national or international law, will not prevent for the Court to exert its competence upon it." In consequence, the regional codes of law which protect impunity are eliminated.
146. Promulgate legislation to harmonize our domestic law with the provisions in the articles 6 (genocide), 7 (crimes against humanity) and 8 (war crimes) of the Rome Statute of the International Penal Court.
147. Dictate a law that establishes the mechanisms of judicial cooperation with the International Criminal Court.
148. Introduce the necessary legal reforms to allow that the courts exert the universal competence regarding the serious violations of human rights in agreement with the international law, the applicable principles of the customary law and the law of treaties.
149. Promptly align, by the State, the national legislation in terms of enforced disappearances and extrajudicial executions contemplated in the international documents of the United Nations and the Organization of American States, including the recommendations of the Special Rapporteurs.
150. Categorize as punishable facts in the penal legislation the deprivation of life that constitutes an extrajudicial or arbitrary execution.
151. Reform the civil legislation for the purpose of recognizing enforced disappearance as a cause of a declaration of presumed death.
152. Reform the civil legislation for the purpose of recognizing enforced disappearance as a cause of a declaration of presumed death.

153. Align article 236 of the current Penal Code to the international categorization on enforced disappearance, punishing the act per se independently that it is carried out with political purposes or to frighten the population.
154. Align article 309 of the current Penal Code to the international categorization of torture, including physical and mental pressure, and include the specific reference to "other cruel, inhumane or degrading behaviors" as is established in the international legislation which Paraguay is part of. Likewise, necessary the necessary presence of injuries should be excluded as a typical element.
155. Encourage the bill that creates an independent national mechanism for torture prevention, in conformity with the mandate of the Facultative Protocol to the Convention against torture and other cruel, inhumane or degrading treatments and sentences, to which the Paraguayan State is a party.
156. Categorize as a punishable fact in penal legislation all acts of discrimination and justifications, directed against people on grounds of race, color, sex, language, religion, political opinion or of other nature, sexual option, national, ethnic or social origin, economic position, birth or any other social condition.
157. Enshrine in the Paraguayan penal law the non-applicability of statute of limitations of actions and sentences for all the serious human rights violations and humanitarian law infractions.
158. Introduce in penal legislation, the guarantee that the victims or their heirs, have the ability to act in a direct manner before the justice (*jus standi*) with the purpose of protect their rights.
159. Establish by law penal sanctions to impede the removal, destruction, dissimulation or falsification of files which contain documents related to human rights violations.
160. Adapt the Military Penal Code according to the National Constitution of 1992 and the international treaties ratified by the Paraguayan State abolishing the death penalty.
161. Abolish or modify national legislation contravening to the international documents of human rights and humanitarian international law which Paraguay has supported or ratified.
162. Include in all constitutional and legal reforms a gender perspective that includes in a particular way the rights of women and of other sexual identities.
163. Establish by the conventions of the eventual national constituent assembly, to give constitutional status to the international law, humanitarian international law and international penal law treaties of human rights.
164. Motivate a constitutional reform that allows the election of the Ombudsman in a more impartial manner, that he is empowered to interpose judicial

actions and resources in favor of the human rights protection, that he is in charged with the promotion and diffusion of human rights and that he is assigned enough personal and financial resources for the compliance of his functions.

165. Approve a law that regulates the intelligence services of the Public Forces, contemplating the unconditional respect to the human rights and defense of national sovereignty, establishing sanctions to the functionaries who violate them.
166. Enable by a constitutional reform the right to vote of the Paraguayans who are abroad.
167. Promote a constitutional reform that allows that the descendants of the Paraguayans that live abroad to acquire the Paraguayan nationality (dual nationality) as well.
168. Restore to the indigenous peoples' victims of the violations of their rights as people, through legal reforms that provide them with lands, health and education centers, as well as basic services, recognizing their autonomy and own governments.
169. Reincorporate the indigenous labor rights that were abolished in the last legislative reform of the Labor Code.
170. Disapprove any counter-terrorist bill that threatens the validity of human rights and criminalizes the social demands.
171. Impede the installation of any foreign military or intelligence service base in Paraguay that threatens the national sovereignty and human rights as happened in "Operation Condor".
172. Discourage any initiative that tends to the promulgation of laws or judicial measures under the cover of "Full Stop" that can give rise to the use of prescription, amnesty, right of asylum, denegation of extradition, non bis in idem, the due obedience, the official immunities, the laws on the reformed, the military courts' competence, as well as the non-removability principle of judges that promotes impunity or contributes to it.
173. Guarantee by the State the fulfilment of the dispositions expressed of the National Constitution of 1992, in Chapter V, articles 62 to 67, so that attacks against life, physical integrity and the right over their habitat against indigenous peoples, do not continue.
174. Modify the current electoral system for closed lists that restricts the political rights of the elector.
175. Consider in case of constitutional reform the possibility for a recall referendum for the elected authorities.

BRAZIL'S NATIONAL TRUTH COMMISSION

Recommendations for a Pending Democratic Agenda

Federico GHELFI, Sol HOURCADE, Luz PALMÁS ZALDUA, and Marcela PERELMAN*

---

* This chapter was written by researchers from the *Centro de Estudios Legales y Sociales* (Center for Legal and Social Studies, CELS), Buenos Aires. The general analysis and writing is a collective work by Sol Hourcade, Federico Ghelfi, Luz Palmás Zaldua and Marcela Perelman. Fieldwork in Sao Paulo was conducted by Ghelfi and Camila Barreto Maia. Systematization of sources was completed by Hugo Goeury. Andrea Rocha Granados participated during the project preparation phase, in 2015.
The authors wish to express their gratitude for the comments of Elin Skaar, Jemima García-Godos, Eric Wiebelhaus-Brahm, and Nina Schneider on prior versions of this text.

1. INTRODUCTION

Twenty-six years after the conclusion of the Brazilian military dictatorship (1964–85), the creation of the National Truth Commission (*Comissão Nacional da Verdade*, CNV) provided a historical opportunity to realign Brazil's difficult project for memory, truth and justice. Created in 2011 and effectively established in May 2012, the CNV launched an intense effort that lasted over two years, culminating with the delivery of a voluminous final report to the Executive Branch, drafted for the purpose of clarifying the circumstances of the disappearance of persons during the period 1946 to 1988. While this recent commission has attracted significant attention, like elsewhere, its recommendations remain underexplored.

Following the framework of the *Beyond Words* project, we conduct a focused analysis of the report's recommendations. Specifically, we track their formulation as well as the concrete factors and processes affecting this task. Furthermore, we examine the challenges in implementing the recommendations. To do so, we combine documentary analysis of the Commission's final report, the processing and classification of the 29 recommendations and semi-structured interviews with relevant parties in Sao Paulo during September 2016.[1] We also used secondary material, such as academic articles and press reports, for the purpose

1 Annex 1 to this chapter is a list of interviewed CNV members and collaborators, human rights activists, dictatorship victim family members, public officers and ex public officers.

of reconstructing the context of the Commission's work, the nature of the Brazilian transition, the role of human rights issues, the country's recent history, and the stance taken by the parties involved. In reviewing the formulation and impact of these recommendations, we also drew from human rights reports, specialized articles, CNV public documents available on its website, and archival material of the *Universidad Estatal Paulista Júlio de Mesquita Filho* (Sao Paulo Julio de Mesquita Filho State University).

Organizationally, the next section describes Brazil's long, drawn-out transition from military rule. Next, Section 3 provides an overview of the Commission's work. Section 4 presents a summary of the CNV's recommendations. Section 5 explains the criteria used to define implementation and formulates a tentative typology to analyze the impact of the Brazilian case. We conclude by reflecting upon the implications of the CNV's recommendations for Brazil's social and political development.

2. A PROTRACTED TRANSITION: THE ROLE OF THE HUMAN RIGHTS AGENDA

To understand the conditions that led to the creation of the National Truth Commission in Brazil, one must begin with the end of the dictatorship in 1985 and trace activism through the approval of the law that created the Commission in 2011. The portrayal of this period can be structured using two interrelated dimensions: the complex transition from dictatorship to democracy, and the characteristics of the socio-political disputes surrounding human rights demands.

Brazil's transition period is much longer than the transfer of power to an indirectly elected civilian president in 1985. In fact, some trace the starting point for the "co-management" of the protracted Brazilian transition to 1974. This point of view assumes that, along with military prominence, the transition involved a broader group of elites who later led the first democratic phase (Marenco 2007; Quinalha 2015). Born in official discourse, the beginning of the transition was characterized as a "slow, gradual and safe opening up" and a "relaxation" of repressive policies.[2] Although we can affirm that it was a re-institutionalization process guided by the military (Corbo 2007, 26), we must also consider that the erosion of the regime, albeit not abrupt, also was driven "from below" (Schneider 2013, 151; Montero 2006). Even under the dictatorship, civil society successfully

2 Among the most significant measures and events that took place between 1974 and 1985 are the repeal of the Institutional Actions via Constitutional Amendment 11/1978; the end of censorship of certain media; the introduction of partisan activity, the *Diretas Já* campaign; and indirect elections held in 1984, which resulted in the victory of Tancredo Neves (Paiva Carvalho et al., 2016).

mobilized to demand amnesty for political prisoners.[3] These demands led to the approval of the 1979 *Ley de Amnistía* (Amnesty Law) 6.683/1979, which brought freedom to a very limited group of politically persecuted persons, allowed the return of some exiles, and introduced the possibility of exonerating military and police personnel. The latter was interpreted by some sectors as a sort of self-amnesty and, with the passage of time, it became the core of the dispute over prosecuting the dictatorship's crimes.[4]

Unlike many other countries in the region, human rights were not a priority in the agendas of the first democratic governments in the 1980s. In this context, starting with the incipient political opening up 10 years before the end of the dictatorship, the demands for human rights were almost exclusively propelled by the persistent civil society struggle for truth and justice. The creation of the Sao Paulo Commission for the Family Members of the Persons Killed or Disappeared for Political Reasons (CFMDP) at the beginning of the 1980s and Rio de Janeiro's *Tortura Nunca Mais* Group were important events. The investigation carried out by the Sao Paulo Archdiocese and the World Congress of Churches beginning in 1979 and its 1985 report, *Brasil: Nunca Mais*, documented human rights violations based on records of military justice proceedings against political prisoners (Comissão da Verdade do Rio 2015).

The year 1995 marked an important turning point in public transitional justice awareness and debate. Law 9.140, the first official acknowledgment of state responsibility for human rights violations, was enacted that year. The legislation was framed by a rhetoric of reconciliation (Mezarobba 2007), thus exhibiting continuity with the "conciliated transition" to democracy. A central component of the Law established economic reparations for family members

---

3 According to Moreira da Silva Filho (2015), it is convenient to differentiate "three amnesty phases", each with a specific standardized expression. The dictatorship's amnesty, in 1979, which "at the same time as it hindered investigation and responsibility for their crimes, (…) also represented a conquest for the social movements struggling for the country's re-democratization, the release of political prisoners and the return of exiles, in the light of the enormous popular mobilizations of the seventies held under the Amnesty flag. Second, the Constitutional Amendment 26/1985, which, in the context of a civil government, although elected indirectly, (…) repeated the terms of the 1979 Law with some changes, extending reparations and omitting the definition of 'connected crime'. Lastly, with the promulgation of the 1988 Constitution, the term 'amnesty' underwent an evident modification of its legal meaning, since it is only addressed in two instances in the constitutional text. (…) Article 5, XLIII, which records torture as a crime not susceptible to amnesty (…) [and] Article 8 of the *Acto de las Disposiciones Constitucionales y Transitorias* (Constitutional and Transitory Provisions Act), where amnesty is presented as a right of reparation for those affected by acts of the State during times of suspension of constitutional rights between 1946 and 1988 implemented for political reasons".

4 For a reconstruction of the context of the Law's approval, the underlying debates that guided the drafting process, and legislative debate about the meaning of amnesty, see Schneider (2016).

of deceased and disappeared persons.[5] The *Comissão Especial de Mortos e Desaparecidos Políticos* (Special Commission on the Dead and Disappeared for Political Reasons – CEMDP) was established as the state's agency to manage the reparations program as well as to facilitate the search for and identification of the bodies of disappeared persons.[6] CEMDP has been working in coordination with the Ministry of Human Rights since 2004. Together with *Brasil: Nunca Mais* published in 1985, the 2007 report published by the CEMDP, *Direito à verdade e à memória*, constituted the most comprehensive documentary sources for the investigation developed later by the National Truth Commission.

In 2002, the government went further. Law 10.559 created a reparations scheme to grant symbolic and economic reparations for people subject to "political amnesty", that is, people whose civilian lives, and professional careers had been affected by political events in the period 1946 to 1988.

An important step with regards to truth seeking was taken in 2009 with the third National Plan for Human Rights (*Programa Nacional de Direitos Humanos*, PNDH-3). Coordinated by the Special Ministry of Human Rights, a department of the Presidency, the plan was organized around the central concept of the "Right to memory and truth". Among other things, it recommended the creation of a National Truth Commission.[7]

Subsequently, the PNDH-3 proposal underwent substantial changes. Although these modifications are not directly connected to the creation of a commission, they conditioned some of the important attributes of the CNV three years later. The main differences between the first and second versions of the third Plan resulted from resistance both internal and external to the state. In particular, the Ministries of Defense and Foreign Relations opposed introducing a path towards criminal justice in the human rights agenda. In addition, the presidents of three civil society organizations that include active and reserve members of the military (the Military, Naval and Air Force Clubs) criticized the plan by stating that it would cause "division among Brazilians" (Quero January 6, 2010) because it would disrupt the "atmosphere of conciliation" produced by the 1979 Amnesty Law.

As suggested by Schneider and Almeida (2018), the introduction of changes finally allowed political consensus on the plan. Among the most significant differences recorded between Decree 7.037 of 2009 and Decree 7.177 of 2010,

---

5 For the purpose of civil reparations, the Law acknowledged as deceased any person disappeared as a result of participation or being charged with participation in political activities during the period between September 2, 1961 (the beginning of the last democratic government before the dictatorship) and August 15, 1979. Seven years later, this regulation was modified by Law 10.536 of 2002, which extended the term to October 5, 1988, the date of enactment of Brazil's latest constitution.

6 By the end of the first stage of its work in 2006, CEMDP had extended its analysis and acknowledgment from the 136 initial cases in 1995 to 362 cases.

7 Interview with Rogerio Sottili; Comissão da Verdade do Rio, 2015.

aimed at implementing the plan, is the avoidance of the use of the following terms and passages: "dictatorial repression"; "regime of 1964–1985"; "popular resistance to repression"; "individuals who committed crimes against humanity" and "criminal liability for cases involving actions connected to the 1964–1985 regime".

The next milestone in the constitution of the CNV was the formation of a working group in January 2010 to develop draft legislation. Under the presidency of Erenice Guerra, Executive Secretary of the Civil House of the Presidency (Chief of Staff), the group included Paulo Vannuchi, Secretary of Human Rights; Paulo Abrão, president of the Amnesty Commission; Vilson Vedana, legal advisor to the Minister of Defense; Marco Antônio Rodrigues Barbosa, of CEMDP; and Paulo Sérgio Pinheiro, representative of civil society and future CNV commissioner. In May, the resulting legislative proposal was sent by Brazilian President Luiz Inácio Lula da Silva to the National Congress.

There is wide agreement that two judicial decisions also were important in setting the stage for the creation of the CNV.[8] First, the Federal Supreme Court of Brazil (*Supremo Tribunal Federal*, STF) upheld the Amnesty Law on April 29, 2010. This confirmed the decision to exempt from criminal prosecution state agents who had committed grave human rights violations (Judgment regarding the Accusation of Constitutional Non-conformity of Legislation - ADPF 153). Second, on November 24 of the same year, the Inter-American Court of Human Rights (IACtHR) entered judgment in the case *Gomes Lund et al. vs. Brazil*, The Court found the Brazilian state liable for the disappearance of Araguaia Guerrillas during military operations in the 1970s. The IACtHR's judgment held that the provisions of the 1979 Amnesty Law were manifestly incompatible with the American Convention on Human Rights. Therefore, it had no legal effects and could not continue to hinder the investigation of grave human rights violations, nor the identification and punishment of perpetrators

3. THE NATIONAL TRUTH COMMISSION (CNV): A HISTORICAL OPPORTUNITY

On December 18, 2011, the National Congress enacted the Law creating the National Truth Commission for the purpose of examining and clarifying human rights violations committed between 1946 and 1988,[9] "seeking to implement the historical right to memory and truth and promote national reconciliation" (Law 12.528, December 18, 2011).

---

8 Interview with Marlon Weichert and Maria Amelia Teles; Comissão da Verdade do Rio, 2015.

9 The following section examines the meaning of this temporal delimitation and its role in the initial phase of the organization of the CNV's internal work.

Among its mandates, the Commission was assigned the task of clarifying the facts and circumstances concerning the torture, death, forced disappearance and concealment of bodies, as well as determining the identity of the perpetrators. It was granted the power to request collaboration from other public agencies. According to the legislation, its specific goals were: to identify and make public the structures, locations, institutions and circumstances surrounding the violations and their possible ramifications within various state agencies and society; to remit any information obtained capable of aiding the location and identification of individuals disappeared for political reasons to the competent public agencies; to collaborate with all instances of public authority for the purpose of clarifying human rights violations; to recommend the adoption of measures and public policy to prevent further violations, thus ensuring they would not be repeated, promoting an effective national reconciliation and driving the reconstruction of the history of cases of grave human rights violations (Law 12.528, November 18, 2011).

The CNV had seven members, who were appointed by the President, Dilma Rousseff. They were selected based upon their identification with the precepts of defense of democracy, institutionalization of the constitution and respect for human rights.[10] Lastly, it was established that, upon termination of their activities, members were required to present a descriptive report of the facts investigated, including conclusions and recommendations.

The members of the Commission were attorneys José Carlos Dias, José Paulo Cavalcanti and Rosa Cardoso; the ex-chief of the Federal Attorney General's Office, Claudio Fonteles; the Supreme Court Judge Gilson Dipp; psychoanalyst María Rita Kehl, and professor and political scientist Paulo Sergio Pinheiro. Dipp and Fonteles stepped down in 2013, and the latter was replaced by attorney Pedro Dallari. The members were in charge of directing the task of investigating and producing the Final Report.

---

[10] According to Gonzalez and Varney (2012), most Latin American truth commissions have had commissioners who serve in a personal capacity, having been selected for their notoriety and moral leadership. The Brazilian case appears to follow this pattern. According to the authors, "this method of appointment is quick and can transfer the legitimacy and prestige of the individual to the commission. However, the risk of appearing to be elitist must be considered, as this would result in mistrust". In order to guarantee legitimacy and independence, González and Varney suggest criteria for the appointment of commissioners; one of them being that members "must be selected by means of a transparent and preferably consultative process that considers the opinion of different sectors of society, especially those of the victims and marginalized groups. In some commissions, the process of selection was performed by means of public nominations and the creation of a selection panel in charge of reviewing such nominations, interviewing the finalists and supporting public scrutiny of the candidates, as well as recommending a list to the highest authorities". This was absent in the Brazilian case.

The CNV was in operation between May 16, 2012, and December 2014, including the extension granted in May 2014 to conclude its work. Thus, in total, it operated for two years and seven months. The Commission worked throughout the entire country. It collected more than a thousand statements from victims, military personnel, and witnesses, and inspected military and police facilities (Dallari 2015).

During its operation, the CNV developed active transparency measures.[11] It maintained an official website with current information about its work. Relevant documentation also was available there. It actively engaged the media, including by holding press conferences and making its members available for interviews.

Neither the website nor the public reports offer detailed information regarding the Commission's financing, which was sourced from the public budget. There is official data for fiscal years 2013 and 2014, but not for the first eight months of work in 2012. According to the annual statements of the Civil House of the Presidency of the Republic, in 2013 the CNV had a budget of 8,826,809 *Reales*, about 4,100,000 U.S. Dollars at the average exchange rate for that year. The report reveals that 79.3 per cent of the budget was used for the purpose of hiring investigators, administrative assistants for investigation support activities and other activities for the purpose of drafting the final report; 12.2 per cent for travel tickets; 5 per cent for daily expenses; and 3.3 per cent for the payment of outsourced services and events.[12] For 2014, the expected budget from the Presidential Unit to the CNV was 8,300,000 *Reales*, about 3,500,000 Dollars (average exchange rate for 2014).[13]

During 2014, the CNV produced its Final Report. It presented it to President Dilma Rousseff on December 10, International Human Rights Day. The official ceremony at the Government House was widely broadcast at the national and regional levels. The CNV had investigated a total of 434 cases of assassinated and disappeared persons: 191 assassinated persons, 210 disappeared persons, and 33 cases of disappearance where the bodies have been located. On the other hand, it disclosed the names of 377 perpetrators responsible for the repression, including five members of the armed forces who headed the dictatorship during its different phases and the three members of the military *Junta* that governed during the year 1969.

The Final Report contains three volumes totaling 4,325 pages. Volume I was drafted for the purpose of complying with the legal mandate of the CNV and contains 18 chapters. It describes the activities performed by the Commission

11 The recommendations section mentions limitations and criticism of the adopted information and communication policies.

12 Available at: http://www.casacivil.gov.br/acesso-a-informacao/relatorios-de-gestao/relatorio-de-gestao-2013/relatorio-de-gestao-2013-versao-final.pdf.

13 Available at: http://www.secret ariadegoverno.gov.br/acesso-a-informacao/auditorias/secretaria-de-controle-interno/auditorias-anuais-de-contas/casa-civil/relatorio-de-gestao-casa-civil-2014.pdf.

and the results of data refinement and the circumstances surrounding the cases of illegal detention, torture, execution, forced disappearance and concealment of bodies. In addition, it identifies victims, perpetrators, modalities of violence, and describes the institutional structures which promoted them and the location of such events. This volume ends with a group of conclusions and recommendations.

Volume II is divided into nine thematic sections that describe and more deeply examine the human rights violations against specific social groups. For example, it highlights abuses within the military, against workers, peasants, Christian churches, indigenous peoples, and universities. It further discusses collaboration of civilians with the dictatorship and resistance within civil society. Lastly, Volume III is the lengthiest part of the report. It includes profiles of the 434 deaths and disappearances it investigated. The entirety of the data collected during the investigation is presented.

3.1. INTERNAL WORK AND DIFFERENCES OF OPINION

The Commission was constituted five months after the enactment of the Law ordering its creation. During those months and the whole first year of work, those interested in a strong investigation remained expectant and significantly concerned. A variety of interviewees agree that this first stage of the CNV "operated by inertia" and "had a hard time getting started with its work".[14] Very skeptical about those first months, one interviewee depicts the situation: "The first year was almost entirely lost to internal arguing. That period ended, and we were left open-mouthed thinking it would be a failure (...) The end of the first year was pretty hopeless."[15]

The discussions surrounding the appropriate focus for the early stage of the CNV can be summarized into three subjects: the period to be investigated; how to face the pressures to investigate the responsibility of resistance groups; and the publicity and transparency of the Commission's work.

3.1.1. The Temporal Delimitation of the State Activities to be Investigated

Although the Parliament had determined the period to be investigated as that between the two most recent democratic Constitutions in Brazil, 1946 and 1988, the CNV, as reconstructed by commissioner Pedro Dallari,

> ended up concentrating its efforts on more precisely establishing and verifying the grave violations committed during the dictatorship period, wherein such violations were considered as a condition for the country's national state policies (Dallari 2015).

---

14 Interview with Maria Amelia Teles.

15 Interview with Marlon Weichert.

That is, they focused on the dictatorship period, between 1964 and 1985. Anivaldo Padilha, a collaborator of Commissioner Paulo Sergio Pinheiro, stated that the parliamentary mandate had included the period between 1946 and 1988 as a result of a negotiated draft, and confirmed that the CNV focused on the dictatorship period.[16]

3.1.2. *Pressures to Investigate the Responsibility of Groups Resisting the Dictatorship*

According to one of the Commission's advisors, there was a second point of conflict resulting from "right-wing political sectors, the press and the National Congress" regarding the need to investigate "both sides". Although two of the commissioners supported this initiative, only one of them maintained this stance throughout the discussions:

> The Commission decided to investigate crimes of the State. The argument was very clear: first, there were no "two sides"; it was not a war with equality of arms, but rather a dictatorship that used violence against its opposition. The victim cannot be equated to the perpetrator. This was the prevailing argument.[17]

3.1.3. *The Publicizing of CNV Activities*

The last point of debate, regarding the methods used to communicate the CNV's work, had minor political repercussions. However, it sheds light on the different perspectives regarding the essence of a truth commission and the type of contribution it must make.

Some members alleged that the CNV was required to perform its activities discreetly and only disclose its activities at the end, with the publication of its Final Report. Another faction, which prevailed in the end, maintained the opposite: "Some of us said no; for us, the Commission's strength was its requirement to regularly disclose information. This had to have a pedagogical purpose for society."[18] In June 2013, these differences of opinion became publicly known following a meeting between the CNV and members of the Sao Paulo Commission for the Families of Persons Killed or Disappeared for Political Reasons. There, family members emphasized the importance of "producing a public discussion about the dictatorship, working with public testimonies and providing greater visibility of all the steps of the Commission's task forces" (CartaCapital, June 24, 2013).

---

16 Interview with Anivaldo Padilha.

17 Interview with Anivaldo Padilha.

18 Interview with Anivaldo Padilha.

3.2. GENERAL IMPACT AND OPPORTUNITIES

The interviewed parties share an ambivalent view of the CNV. While many perceived it to be a "new starting point", the lack of progress in achieving truth and justice in Brazil more than 30 years after the end of the dictatorship generated deep skepticism.

Interviewees appreciated the place occupied by the CNV's voice in the public arena as an official truth-seeking exercise. A positive assessment predominated regarding the quality of the investigation, its Final Report, the collection of documentary material essential for truth seeking[19] and even the diversity of its recommendations.[20] The interviewees also highlighted the strong impulse to create and/or strengthen truth commissions at a municipal, state and union level and within universities. Victim and family member organizations[21] appreciated the social repercussions and public interest generated by the Commission, when the broadcasting of testimonies and the significant thrust to make the subject of state crimes visible became prominent in public discussion.[22]

The interviewees also mention some of the obstacles to progress. In particular they lamented the lack of accountability of the military. They posited that this was the result of the scant cooperation offered by the Armed Forces and the Ministry of Defense to the process. According to one of the commissioners, this problem should have been addressed more forcefully both by the CNV and the government.[23] Objections were also raised, both by human rights activists and other sectors driving judicial investigations, to the absence of an autonomous examination of the most pervasive repressive method used by the dictatorship, that of imprisonment and torture. Consequently, the victims of those practices were denied acknowledgment.[24] Although it is widely considered that the CNV provided a valuable contribution to truth in general, some subjects received less attention, such as the human rights violations perpetrated against indigenous peoples and peasants.[25] In addition, there were disputes regarding interpretation and assessment of certain facts with other investigative commissions, as was the case with the conclusions of the *Comissão da Verdade of the Municipal Council of Sao Paulo* regarding the circumstances surrounding the death of the ex-President of Brazil, Jucelino Kubitschek, in 1976 (Schneider and Almeida, 2018).

19 Interview with Maria Rita Kehl.
20 Interview with Marlon Weichert and Anivaldo Padilha.
21 Interview with María Amelia Teles.
22 Interview with Anivaldo Padilha.
23 Interview with Maria Rita Kehl.
24 Interview with Marlon Weichert.
25 Interview with Marlon Weichert.

Finally, organizations such as the CFMDP complained that the CNV should have established a stronger and more permanent link with the family members of the victims.[26]

4. FINAL REPORT RECOMMENDATIONS

In Volume I of the Final Report, the CNV describes four general conclusions, presented as actual findings resulting from its investigative work. These are: (i) verification of the occurrence of grave human rights violations between 1946 and 1988, especially during the period of military dictatorship between 1964 and 1985; (ii) verification of the generalized and systematic character of such violations; (iii) the portrayal of the occurrence of crimes against humanity; and, finally, (iv) the persistence of a framework of grave human rights violations (CNV Report 2014).

The section following these conclusions formulates 29 mutually agreed Commission recommendations, formally grouped as "Institutional Measures", "Constitutional and Legal Reforms", and "Action and Recommendation Follow-up Measures". Many of these proposals contain a description, or diagnosis of sorts, of the problem addressed and the background regarding the issue. Below, we reproduce the general headings presented in the CNV's Final Report and outline the recommendations and sub-recommendations identified for the purposes of this research, not necessarily following the document's numbering structure. Excluded from this presentation are those descriptive sections that do not add information or specify the propositional character or mode of implementation of each recommendation.[27] In some cases, we have summarized the content for brevity.

4.1. INSTITUTIONAL MEASURES

[1] Acknowledgment, by the Armed Forces, of their institutional responsibility for grave human rights violations during the military dictatorship (1964 to 1985).

[2] Determination, by the competent organisms, of the legal liability – criminal, civil and administrative – of the public officers responsible for the grave human rights violations occurring during the period investigated by the CNV, removing for such agents the application of the amnesty-granting means included in the

---

26 Interview with María Amelia Teles.

27 The CVN report was written in Portuguese. This English translation is made by Diana Valori, based on the Spanish translation of the official text, partly done by the authors, partly the NGO *Brasil Conectas* (available at: http://www.conectas.org/arquivos/editor/files/CNV%20conclusiones%20y%20recomendaciones%20-%20Espanhol.pdf).

articles of Law No. 6.683, of August 28, 1979, and other constitutional and legal provisions.

[3] Proposal, by the public administration, of administrative and judicial indemnification measures against public officers who perpetrated actions resulting in the condemnation of the state as a result of grave human rights violations.

[4] Prohibition of all commemorative events of the military coup of 1964.

[5] Reformulation of the selection processes governing admission into and continuous evaluation of the Armed Forces and the public security sector for the purpose of assessing knowledge regarding principles inherent to democracy and human rights.

[6] Modification of curricular content of military and police academies for the promotion of democracy and human rights.

[7] Rectification of the cause of death recorded on the death certificate of persons killed as a result of grave human rights violations.

[8] Rectification of information in the *Red Infoseg* (Network of National Integration of Public Security, Justice and Tax Information) and, in general, in public registries.

   [8a] Exclusion of information involving records of political persecution and Military Justice sentencing during the period between 1964 and 1988 from the *Red Infoseg* as well as from other registries connected to the field of public security.

   [8b] Procedures for the development of systems contributing to the promotion of human rights, such as the maintenance of a data bank containing DNA samples of every person buried without identification, must be adopted to allow family members to locate the remains.

[9] Creation of mechanisms to prevent and combat torture. The creation of mechanisms, even committees, for the prevention and struggle against torture in all the states of the Federation, with participation of civil society, is recommended, in accordance with the provisions of Law No. 12.847/2013.

[10] Disengagement of legal medical institutes, as well as forensic expert agencies, from the Secretariats of Public Security and civil police departments. The creation, within the states of the Federation, of advanced forensic anthropology centres and the performance of forensic investigations independent from those carried out by the Secretary of Public Security and with full autonomy from police structure, for the purpose of generating better quality technical evidence and improve the ability to detect torture cases.

[11] Strengthening of Attorney General Offices. The Attorney General Offices were created constitutionally to assist low-income individuals and were provided with institutional resources necessary to support greater protection of detainees. Personal contact between the attorney general and the prisoner within the police districts and the jail system is the best guarantee for the full exercise of the right to receive defense assistance and the prevention of fundamental right abuses and violations, especially torture and mistreatment.

[12] Increase the dignity of the jail system and the treatment of prisoners.

[12a] It is necessary to abolish, with reinforcement from the legal mandate set forth, all degrading and humiliating processes experienced by children, the elderly, women and men when visiting their imprisoned family members. Visitors can no longer be forced to be fully stripped of clothing and have their genitalia inspected. This practice must be prohibited throughout the national territory.

[12b] Special attention is recommended to be given to the adoption of measures dignifying jails, promoting respect for human rights and avoiding the adoption of measures – for example, the privatization of such structures – resulting in departure from the principle asserting that punitive power is exclusive to the state and must be exercised within the democratic rule of law.

[13] Legal institution of external auditing of the penitentiary system and of any bodies connected to it. The audits must operate as a fiscal and social control of the penitentiary system and of bodies connected to same, such as police officers, public defenders, the Attorney General and judicial bodies. It must be adopted as a public policy seeking to perfect institutions and their governance. The auditors must be selected with the participation of civil society, must be functionally independent and possess the necessary prerogatives and structure to exercise their powers.

[14] Strengthening of Community Councils for the monitoring of penal establishments (as already provided by Law No. 7,210 of July 11, 1984 (Law of Penal Enforcement).

[15] Guarantee of permanent medical and psycho-social assistance for the victims of grave human rights violations.

[17] Support for the establishment and operation of an organism protecting and promoting human rights.

[17a] The creation of Secretariats of Human Rights must be promoted, and their operation supported within states and municipalities, thus allowing them to operate within the public administration to develop and coordinate actions tending to protect and promote human rights.

[17b] Existing bodies, such as the *Conselho Nacional de Direitos Humanos* (National Council for Human Rights, CNDH), the *Comissão Especial sobre Mortos e Desaparecidos Políticos* (Special Commission for Political Deaths and Disappearances) (CEMDP) and the *Comissão de Anistia* (Amnesty Commission), must be assessed within the specific scope of the investigation of the grave human rights violations that occurred during the history of Brazil, thus promoting reforms to the regulatory framework governing such bodies for the purpose of improving conditions for their operation.

[17c] Public administration at its different levels must support the activities of state, municipal and sectoral truth commissions created during the period of operation of the CNV, which should continue operating even after the end of the National Commission.

4.2. CONSTITUTIONAL AND LEGAL REFORMS

[18] Revocation of *the Lei de Segurança Nacional do Brasil* (Law of National Security) (Law No. 7.170 of December 14, 1983).

[19] Improvement of Brazilian legislation for the purpose of categorizing the penal definition of crimes against humanity and the crime of forced disappearance.

[20] Demilitarization of state police organisms (a model born from the structure defined for public security activities within the Constitution of 1988). It is necessary to promote constitutional and legal changes ensuring the disassociation of state military police bodies from the Armed Forces and resulting in full demilitarization of such police bodies, seeking their unification within each state.

[21] Extinction of state Military Justice. A constitutional reform must be adopted for this purpose, resulting solely in the provision of a system of federal Military Justice, whose jurisdiction, as highlighted in the following item, must apply only to members of the Armed Forces.

[22] Exclusion of civilians from the jurisdiction of the federal Military Justice system.

[23] Suppression of discriminatory references to homosexuality in legislation.

[24] Modification of procedural penal legislation for the purpose of eliminating the concept of resistance to authority. Modification for the purpose of having injuries and deaths resulting from police operations or confrontations recorded as "bodily injury resulting from police intervention" and "death resulting from police intervention", in substitution for the existing terms "act of resistance" and "resistance resulting in death", respectively.

[25] Introduction of the detention control hearing, for the prevention of torture and illegal imprisonment.

4.3. ACTION AND RECOMMENDATION FOLLOW-UP MEASURES

[26] Establishment of a permanent body empowered to follow up on the CNV's actions and recommendations.

Establishment of a body with administrative duties, whose members are designated by the Presidency of the Republic, representing civil society, whom, together with similar existing bodies, such as the CNDH, the CEMDP and the Amnesty Commission, must continue the activities of the CNV, especially for the purpose of:

a) continuing the investigation of the facts seeking truth regarding illegal and arbitrary detentions, torture, executions, forced disappearances and the concealment of bodies;
b) completing investigation of events and behaviors which the CNV was unable to complete, such as the case of worker massacres during the military regime and the support provided by companies and business owners to the creation and operation of structures used to perpetrate grave human rights violations;

c) cooperating with, complementing and coordinating documentary investigation with persons, and public and private institutions and bodies, for the purpose of assessing, exchanging and disclosing information;
d) organizing, coordinating and promoting information activities regarding the grave human rights violations in the country and abroad;
e) monitoring the fulfilment of the CNV's recommendations, with unlimited access and powers to demand information, data and documents from public authority bodies and entities, including those classified as confidential, by implementing work and investigation groups and establishing offices within federated units, where necessary;
f) supporting collective reparation measures for the grave violations perpetrated against the peasant population during the period investigated by the CNV, with emphasis on extending public policy to guarantee access to the land and agrarian reform;
g) supporting collective reparation measures for the grave violations perpetrated against the indigenous peoples during the period investigated by the CNV, with emphasis on regularization, termination of occupation and environmental recovery of land;
h) supporting public policy measures created for the purpose of preventing human rights violations and avoiding their recurrence.

[27] Continuation of activities oriented to the location, identification and delivery to family members or authorized persons of the human remains of individuals who disappeared for political reasons, for the purpose of providing them with a proper burial.

[28] Preservation of the memory of grave human rights violations.

[28a] Preservation, restoration and promotion of custodianship or creation of memory markers within urban or rural properties where grave human rights violations were perpetrated; establishment and installation of the Memory Museum in Brasilia.

[28b] revocation of measures which, during the military dictatorship, were implemented for the purpose of honoring the authors of grave human rights violations. Among other things, measures must be adopted for the purpose of: removing any honors bestowed on public or private agents associated with these instances of grave violations, as was the case with many individuals decorated with the *Medalla del Pacificador* (Peace-Maker Medal); promoting the changing of street names, transportation routes, buildings, and public institutions of any type, either federal, state or municipal, which refer to public or private agents who were notoriously involved with the perpetration of grave violations.

[29] Continuation and strengthening of the policy of locating and opening the files of the military dictatorship.

[29a] The files of the Armed Forces, including those belonging to their information centers – *Centro de Informaciones del Ejército* (Army Information Center) (CIE), *Centro de Informaciones de la Marina* (Naval Information Center) (Cenimar) and *Centro de Informaciones de*

Seguridad de la Aeronáutica (Center for Air Force Security Information) (CISA), as well as the *Centro de Informaciones del Exterior* (Center for Foreign Information) (Ciex), which operated within the Ministry of Foreign Relations (MRE), must be integrated within a sole platform for the whole country, including any documentation generated by the agencies of the *Sistema Nacional Desinformaciones y Contra Informaciones* (National System of Disinformation and Counter Information) (Sisni). The same must be done with the files of all the *Divisiones de Seguridad e Informaciones* (Security and Information Divisions) (DSI) and the *Asesorías de Seguridad e Informaciones* (Security and Information Consultancy) (ASI) established by the military dictatorship within the bodies of the Federal government with links to the *Servicio Nacional de Informaciones* (National Information System) (SNI).[28]

[29b] Within the states of the Federation, any archives belonging to the agencies connected to political repression must be located and opened, especially the documents of the political and social order departments or delegations (DOPS), thus promoting their collection and technical processing within public archives and their availability in the National Archive data bank. In addition, such data bank must be enlarged and improved by the incorporation of digital copies of documentary and oral files still in possession of public authorities and by the installation of technical resources implemented for the purpose of optimizing investigative tools and universalizing access, including Internet archive availability.

[29c] Continue locating documentation connected to the military dictatorship period by means of diplomatic missions and Brazilian Consular branches and remitting these documents to the National Archive. It is also recommended to continue international cooperation oriented to the identification of documentation about the period under investigation by the CNVin foreign archives and international organizations.

[29d] The establishment of lines of investigation, content production and statement taking, information recording and collection and technical processing of files about not yet known or clarified facts regarding the military dictatorship period must be stimulated and supported.

[29e] In terms of current legislation, any private business and individual archives with the potential of contributing to the thoroughness of the investigation of grave human rights violations in Brazil must be considered of public and social interest.

---

28 The essence of this recommendation is that the files of the Armed Forces, including those belonging to their information centers as well as the ones operated within the Ministry of Foreign Relations, must be integrated within a single platform for the whole country, including any documentation generated by the agencies of the National System of Disinformation and Counter Information (Sisni). The same must be done with the files of all the security services established by the military dictatorship within the bodies of the Federal government.

The law creating the CNV provided for the drafting of recommendations Specifically, it was mandated to "Recommend the adoption of measures and public policies to prevent new violations, thus ensuring they will not recur and promoting an effective national reconciliation." The text implies a mandate oriented towards the construction of truth. Beyond the reference to "clarification of the facts and violations", the legislation did not stipulate that the documentation was to be remitted to the penal justice system for the purpose of investigating responsibilities.

The introduction to the recommendations in the Final Report expands the perspective of the law creating the CNV:

> Considering the conclusions set forth above and for the purpose of preventing grave human rights violations, avoiding their recurrence and *promoting the strengthening of the democratic rule of law*, the CNV recommends the adoption of a group of [recommendations] (...) (emphasis added) (CNV Report 2015).

The incorporation of "the reinforcement of the democratic rule of law" is the way the introduction foresees the expansion of the human rights agenda connected to the dictatorship to an agenda focused on strengthening democracy. As we shall see, the diversity and range of recommendations are not directly relevant to the strict purpose established by law for the CNV. This reformulation demonstrates the human rights agenda adopted by the CNV and the reform agenda it intended to prompt.

4.4. THE TRAIL OF THE RECOMMENDATION DEVELOPMENT PROCESS

As the diverse list of recommendations indicates, the CNV delved into subjects not provided in its original mandate. Such broadening conditioned, as we shall see, the CNV's ability to influence the implementation of the recommendations by competent authorities or bodies. Knowledge regarding the process of formulating recommendations is important to understand the underlying logic behind the CNV's decision to make wide-ranging recommendations.

Official sources, mainly the Final Report and the CNV website, offer very little information regarding the process of formulating recommendations. Although a description is provided for the formal reception mechanism for civil society suggestions regarding recommendations, there is no explanation of the selection, discussion and drafting criteria used for the internal organization of the commission's work. As a result of this difficulty, we were able to reconstruct their formulation process based on the documents and testimonies collected during the present investigation.

The Commission did not set forth a pre-established method to formulate the recommendations, since such subject was not included in the commissioners' meeting guidelines, as verified by the response of the CNV to an inquiry made by the *Instituto de Estudos da Religiao* (Religious Studies Institute, ISER) in May 2014.[29] However, some of the commissioners were clear from the start regarding the content of some of the recommendations they wished to elaborate, in particular, about the need to investigate penal responsibility for the dictatorship's crimes (Rosa Cardoso in *Globo.com*, May 21, 2013). We find a marked contrast between the absence of a previously established methodology and some premises that were very clearly defined, at least by some commissioners.

The actual recommendation drafting process began during the last months of the Commission's work,[30] at least as pertains to certain themed internal work groups. The results were included in Volume II of the report.

In August 2014, the CNV set up a form on its website to receive suggestions for the elaboration of recommendations. The portal was open from August 11 to September 30, 2014. 399 suggestions were received, and the Commission considered that 307 were valid due to their pertinent subject matter. The CNV did not create a record of who submitted the suggestions due to the design of their reception system[31] (CNV website; CNV Report 2014; Westhrop, Simi, Chernicharo 2015). We lack sufficient information to characterize the way in which the CNV reviewed external suggestions or how commissioners viewed them in light of recommendations they had already planned.

The absence of planning and prior decisions regarding categories for the recommendations to be formulated, together with the participative mechanism set up on-line, serve to explain the wide range and diversity of the resulting list. Outside input allowed for the incorporation of multiple recommendations for reforms in the fields of the public security, policing and penitentiary systems. Such suggestions are not directly connected with the investigation set forth in the report about the clarification of human rights violations during the period indicated in the mandate (1946–88). Rather, they demonstrate the CNV's desire to highlight current human rights issues and connect them to the persistence of impunity. According to Marlon Weichert,

> there is a very interesting technical point: many recommendations do not show a connection with the investigation. A criticism of methodology and argumentative coherence could be pointed out. It's very interesting that nobody in the opposition has done it (…) It's very curious, but, on the other hand, it demonstrates that the Commission has had the desire to make a difference and move forward, and I really liked this a great deal.[32]

---

29 Official document no. 13 to the CNV; CNV – response to official document no. 57 /2014.

30 Commissioner Kehl stated that, in the case of recommendations regarding indigenous peoples and peasants, of which she was in charge, these were formulated during the final days of work. Interview with María Rita Kehl.

31 Official document no. 57 of the ISER dated November 5, 2014.

32 Interview with Marlon Weichert.

A CNV collaborator stated: "Our intention was to promote discussion about the recommendations. We knew that some of them (…) demanded extensive reforms".[33] The quality and precision of many of the recommendations on institutional reforms, for example in the field of the security system, are worth noting. They are evidence of the confluence of parties working on the "historical" human rights agenda and what is customarily called the "extended agenda" in connection to the problems and institutions of present-day democracy. Among some commissioners, the implementation of some recommendations set an agenda for more difficult reforms. In short, the expansiveness of the recommendations can be read as commissioners' attempt to leverage this opportunity to advance political debate about human rights.

4.5. THREE SOURCES

We have identified three influences on the formulation of recommendations based on their content. Some recommendations seem to have been on the commissioners' minds from the beginning, as shown by the advance notice that the CNV would include some reference to penal responsibility for the dictatorship's crimes, but it would not include a suggestion to reform the Amnesty Law. The CEMDP was a second important factor. Finally, we identify the influence of the IACtHR ruling in the Araguaia case.

4.5.1. The Unexpected Inclusion of Criminal Responsibility

The issue of criminal responsibility for the crimes committed during the dictatorship was eventually included in the Final Report. As we have seen, this perspective was not among the official expectations for the Commission. Rather, it resulted from pre-existing tensions over the National Plan for Human Rights and the law creating the CNV itself.

On May 21, 2013, in the midst of an assessment of the first year of work, Commissioner Rosa Cardoso anticipated that the Commission would draft a recommendation regarding the need to impose penal sanctions on agents responsible for the crimes against humanity committed during the military dictatorship. In addition, she indicated the possibility of a new interpretation of the Amnesty Law, although she made it clear that the CNV would not send a proposed law to the Congress to revoke such legislation: "As far as the Commission is concerned, we will not participate in a social movement" (*Globo.com*, May 21, 2013). CNV advisor Anivaldo Padilha confirms internal discussions about retributive justice: "We knew that, as soon as the Commission

---

33 Interview with Anivaldo Padilha.

made the information public by means of its work, there would be a demand for a punitive response." Among the commissioners "except for one member [who expressed his disagreement in the report], it was clear that the matter of justice was indispensable" (ibid.).

A year and a half later, when the report was published, Commissioner Dallari presented analogous reasoning:

> That issue of legal responsibility must be investigated by the competent institutions, the Judicial Branch and the Attorney General's Office. It is not the CNV's place to affirm that the Amnesty Law should be revoked or reinterpreted. We point out that the facts are very serious, that they constitute criminal acts and, therefore, there must be responsibility, and we must distance ourselves from any rule that hinders the trial of the perpetrators. It is not a fundamental duty of the CNV to determine if such distance must be achieved by the Judicial Branch reinterpreting the Amnesty Law, or by the Legislature by changing legislation (*La Nación*, December 10, 2014).

The way this was finally worded in the report was:

> Determination, by the competent organisms, of the legal liability – criminal, civil and administrative – of the public agents responsible for the grave human rights violations occurring during the period investigated by the CNV, removing the application of the amnesty-granting means included in the articles of Law No. 6.683, of August 28, 1979, and other constitutional and legal provisions for such agents (CNV Final Report 2014).

The development of the basis for recommendations records the disagreement of a commissioner based on his assessment of the Amnesty Law:

> The CNV considered that extending amnesty to the public officers who caused illegal and arbitrary detentions, torture, executions, forced disappearances and concealment of bodies was incompatible with Brazilian legislation and international rule of law, since such illicit actions, given the scale and systematic nature with which they were committed, constitute crimes against humanity, which are not subject to statutes of limitation or amnesty. We record the dissenting position of council member José Paulo Cavalcanti Filho regarding this recommendation exclusively within the larger group of recommendations, based on the same reasons stated by the Federal Supreme Court, which on April 29, 2010, during the trial of the Accusation of Constitutional Non-conformity of Legislation in 153, which, based on the rigid clauses of the Brazilian Constitution, led to the rejection of this thesis by a large majority (seven votes against two) (CNV Final Report, 2014).

4.5.2. The Influence of the Comissão Especial sobre Mortos e Desaparecidos Políticos

On November 6, 2014, one-month prior the finalization of the Final Report, the CEMDP submitted a lengthy document to the CNV suggesting a series of recommendations. The CNV reviewed these proposals but used only its general ideas.[34] For example, the CEMDP suggested the need to extend the jurisdiction and power of the institution itself, as well as the creation of a National Secretariat of Transitional Justice. While the CNV did propose the creation of a permanent state agency with duties similar to those suggested by the CEMDP, the recommendation states a need to implement reforms to optimize the performance of existing bodies, including the CEMDP itself.

4.5.3. The Momentum Provided by the 2010 Inter-American Court of Human Rights Ruling

The judgment entered by the IACtHR in the Araguaia case influenced four recommendations considered "institutional measures", those numbered 4, 5, 6 and 8 in section 4.1 above (Dóro de Oliveira 2016). In addition, recommendations 15 and 19 also evidently revisit the ruling's content. In fact, the Final Report frames some recommendation within the context of Brazil's international obligations under the American Convention on Human Rights (CNV Report 2014; IACtHR, November 24, 2010).

5. IMPLEMENTATION: CURRENT SCENARIO AND ONGOING CHALLENGES

Below, we analyze actions, policies and projects which can be used to trace the implementation of the CNV's recommendations. Implementation should be understood as a continuous process and not mere cause-effect relation. In the Brazilian case, due to the proximity of the formulation of recommendations to the present, we can establish with greater certainty the relationship between the recommendations that were formulated and the accepted measures as forms of implementation.

The difficulties encountered when tracing the recommendation's methods of implementation result mainly from the wide scope and diverse nature of their formulation. The brief time that has elapsed since the presentation of the report is a second factor. Since 2015, Brazil has been roiled by political and economic crises as the economy slowed and politicians have become enmeshed in corruption scandals.

In total, we find evidence for implementation of 17 of the 38 recommendations. For identifying "implementation events", we especially benefited from data

---

34 Secretary of Human Rights of the Presidency of the Republic, 2015.

taken from the monitoring work performed by the Religious Studies Institute (*Instituto de Estudos da Religião*, ISER) of Brazil (ISER 2014, 2015a, 2015b; Westhrop et al. 2015, 2016a, 2016b) and by the *Rede Latino-Americana de Justiça de Transição* (Paiva Carvalho et al. 2016).

Table 1 summarizes the factors that have impeded and promoted implementation in the ensuing years. Below, we highlight certain attributes that we propose as explanatory of these general tendencies.

Table 1. Trends regarding implementation of CNV recommendations

	Tending to implementation	**Tending to non-implementation**
Factors explaining the tendency	Deepening or strengthening of existing internal regulations and/or institutional devices	Structural limitations
	Progress in the field of truth and memory	Lack of drive in the legislative branch
	Linkage to the development of a thematic agenda	Absence of institutional mechanisms needed to drive the recommendations and follow up on them

Note: Compiled by the authors.

In the cases where we have available data and according to the type of recommendation, we complement information regarding implementation with the conditions that could explain why the situations and/or actors favor or hinder the tendency towards implementation.

The fieldwork completed in 2016 suggests several things with respect to implementation. First, an air of pessimism predominated regarding the prognosis for implementation in the near future. This is connected to certain aspects of the Brazilian human rights agenda and a less receptive political environment following Dilma Rousseff's removal from office. When asked about the recommendations, the Regional Prosecutor of the Federal Attorney General's Office, also a human rights activist and former advisor of the CNV, said "they were put away in a drawer."[35] A member of the Sao Paulo CFMDP pointed out a structural aspect that conspires against progress: the reproduction and normalization of human rights violations in multiple circles in Brazil establish a "climate of impunity" which impedes effectively address of the dictatorship's human rights violations.[36]

35 Interviews with Marlon Weichert and Anivaldo Padilha.

36 Interview with Maria Amelia Teles.

5.1. RECOMMENDATIONS TENDING TOWARDS NON-IMPLEMENTATION

5.1.1. Due to Limiting Structural Factors

Recommendations

#1: Acknowledgment of institutional responsibility by the Armed Forces.
#2: Determination of criminal, civil and administrative responsibility of public officers.
#19: Legislate for the purpose of categorizing the penal definition of "crimes against humanity" and the "crime of forced disappearance".
#29: Continuation and strengthening of the policy of locating and opening the files of the dictatorship.

This group of recommendations contributes to the debate regarding the need to achieve justice for the victims of the crimes of the dictatorship. Due to their subject matter, they depend on structural transformation as a condition for their implementation. In terms of the more innovative content of the recommendations, it clashes with the status quo, which, based upon the Brazilian mode of transition, insulated those who were responsible for past abuses. These obstacles include, among others, the institutional behavior of the Armed Forces, the effectiveness of the Amnesty Law, and the predominance of juridical interpretation that prioritizes domestic laws over international human rights laws.

(#1) There has been no concrete progress in terms of an institutional acknowledgment by the Armed Forces of the grave human rights violations committed between 1964 and 1985. The CNV Report stated that the military's position of "not denying" past violations is insufficient as an acknowledgment. On May 28, 2015, the *Serviço de Informações ao Cidadão* of the Ministry of Defense responded to a state inquiry about this recommendation stating, "the best way to implement it is under study" (ISER, 2015b).[37] In response to a request by the Commission, the Ministry of Defense stated that the state's acknowledgment of responsibility regarding disappearances during the military dictatorship and the "exceptional acts committed during periods of suspension of constitutional rights" during the 1946–1988 period "is already incorporated in the Brazilian regulatory system" (Ministry of Defense 2014a). Some media

[37] Three civil lawsuits have been brought against the CNV by, respectively, family members of an ex-military attaché of the Army in the Brazilian Embassy of the Republic of Argentina, a former police commissioner, and members of the *Federação Nacional de Entidades de Oficiais Militares Estaduais* (National Federation of State Military Official Entities – *Feneme*) to demand the exclusion of references to members of the armed forces and police officers in the Final Report (Paiva Carvalho et al., 2016).

sources interpreted that response as the first official acknowledgment of torture and death by the Armed Forces (State of Sao Paulo, September 20, 2014). However, such an interpretation is exaggerated, since it was the state, not the Ministry of Defense, that had acknowledged the fact in providing reparations in 1995.

(#2) The difficulties hindering progress on penal judicial actions still persist, regardless of the claims of those who insist that the Federal Attorney General's Office is making progress. The prevailing position among members of the judiciary is that international human rights laws undermine national sovereignty. This sentiment hinders the process of establishing the universal and Inter-American system standards as hierarchically superior to domestic laws. This is particularly important regarding the Amnesty Law and the supposedly binding effect of the decision of the Federal Supreme Court (interview with Marlon Weichert, September 14, 2016; Paiva Carvalho et al. 2016). Concretely, at the judicial level, the complaints and their actions experienced the following developments during 2015 (based on Paiva Carvalho et al. 2016 and Westhrop et al. 2016a, 2016b):

- In January and March, different civilian courts dismissed two complaints against five ex-members of the military by stating the applicability of the Amnesty Law. In June, another court also dismissed a complaint against seven members of the military forces on the same grounds, although the Federal Attorney General's Office appealed the decision.
- In June, the Superior Court rejected a judicial action filed against Colonel Carlos Alberto Brilhante Ustra based on the Amnesty Law. In addition, the Federal Attorney General's Office filed a judicial action against service member Arrechea Andrade for crimes against humanity committed during the Argentine dictatorship (1976–1983), after the Supreme Court's May denial of the extradition requested by the Republic of Argentina. This was the first time the Attorney General's Office had filed an action of this nature.
- In November and December, the Federal Attorney General's Office filed two complaints against seven agents and two medical examiners.

(#19) There was a bill being discussed in the Senate (245/2011) to classify the crime of forced disappearance in the Penal Code. On August 29, 2013, the bill was sent to the House of Representatives, under the name 6.240/2013. The House of Representatives modified it substantially by restricting the scope of the agents included in this penal violation.

As a result of counter-pressures from the Human Rights and Minorities Commission (*Comissão de Direitos Humanos e Minorias*) and the Ministry of Defense, exemptions were incorporated regarding the absence of a statute of limitations for the crime of forced disappearance, in accordance with the Amnesty Law: "The crime of forced disappearance is not subject to a statute of limitations, except for the cases affected by the Amnesty Law 6.683/79" (Dóro de Oliveira 2016; House of Representative website, December 27, 2013). At the time of writing, the modified bill was being evaluated by the Commission for Public Security and against Organized Crime.

5.1.2. Due to Lack of Legislative Action

Recommendations

- #10: Disassociation of legal medical institutes, as well as forensic expert agencies, from the Secretariats of Public Security and civil police departments.
- #18: Revocation of the Law of National Security (Lei de Segurança Nacional do Brasil) of 1983.
- #24: Modification of procedural penal legislation for the purpose of eliminating "resistance to authority". Substitution of the terms "act of resistance" and "resistance resulting in death" to "bodily injury resulting from police intervention" and "death resulting from police intervention".
- #25: Introduction of the detention control hearing, for the prevention of torture and illegal imprisonment.

We identified four recommendations that resulted in bills being discussed in Parliament. Although this might be considered a favorable indication, the bills were drafted prior to the Commission's work.

(#10 and #18) With respect to the recommendation to disassociate legal medical institutions and criminal forensic entities from Public Security Secretariats and civil police, on May 9, 2015, the Office of the Secretary of Human Rights mentioned a bill for the disassociation of police criminal forensic activities (PEC 499 of 2010) that was being discussed in the National Congress (Office of the Secretary of Human Rights, 2015, at the request of ISER). In the same document and in connection with the National Security Law, the Office detailed the status of a bill for the reform of the security model and the demilitarization of police structures (51 of 2013). This legal document, due to its nature, also required a constitutional amendment that also was under discussion in the Congress (Office of the Secretary of Human Rights, 2015). As of November 26, 2015, it was being assessed by the Constitution, Justice and Citizenship Commission (*Comissão de Constituição e Justiça*, CCJC).[38]

(#24 and #25) Bill PLS 554 of 2011, on the regulation of detention hearings (control), was approved by the Senate in December 2016 and sent to the House of Representatives. However, it has not progressed since that time. Bill 4471 of 2012,

[38] Available at: https://www25.senado.leg.br/web/atividade/materias/-/materia/114516.

which proposes changes to the Brazilian Code of Penal Procedure regarding the recording of injuries or deaths resulting from the use of police force, was pending for plenary discussion by the House of Representatives as of March 2018.[39]

5.1.3. Due to the Absence of Institutional Support for Follow-Up

Recommendations

#26: Creation of a permanent body empowered to follow up on the CNV's actions and recommendations.

#17a & #17b: Support for the establishment and operation of institutions to protect and promote human rights (a – support the work of Municipal and State Secretariats for Human Rights; b – improve conditions for the performance of existing bodies: CNDH, CEMDP and Amnesty Commission).

(#26) The CNV proposed a body with ample authority and scope to follow-up on its recommendations. The Public Hearing of the 154th Period of Sessions of the Inter-American Commission on Human Rights (CIDH) "The Right to Truth and the Report of the National Brazilian Truth Commission" was held in March 2015. The hearing was requested by the organizations *Conectas Direitos Humanos de Brasil*, the Washington Office on Latin America (WOLA) of the United States, the *Centro de Estudios Legales y Sociales* (Center for Legal and Social Studies) (CELS) of Argentina, and the *Comissão Justicia e Paz* of Sao Paulo. These organizations pointed out the CNV's value in terms of guaranteeing the right to memory and truth in Brazil and cautioned regarding the need to continue working and creating mechanisms of implementation and following up on the recommendations of the CNV (CELS et al. March 20, 2015; Departamento de Direitos Humanos e Cidadania 2015).

Six months after the conclusion of the CNV's work, the Office of the Secretary of Human Rights of the Presidency indicated that a national law was needed for the creation of a follow-up body (Office of the Secretary of Human Rights, 2015, upon a request for information by ISER). One year later, in the context of the impeachment procedure against President Rousseff,

> An inter-ministerial work group in charge of defining, within a term of 120 days, the structure and operation of the organism in charge of CNV follow-up, as well as the establishment of the monitoring mechanisms for its recommendations, was established by request of the Office of the Secretary of Human Rights (inter-ministerial Decree number 4, dated May 11, 2016).

[39] Available at: http://www.camara.gov.br/proposicoesWeb/fichadetramitacao?idProposicao=556267.

The Decree was published in the newspaper *Unión* on May 12, 2016, the same date on which the Senate approved the process of *impeachment* whereby President Rousseff was suspended from office while it considered her permanent removal. The timing of the inter-ministerial decree suggests the cabinet was trying to make progress while the Workers' Party remained in power. However, the effort has languished ever since.

(#17) The Amnesty Commission of the Ministry of Justice – the referral organ for reparations – experienced two setbacks in terms of the strengthening recommended by the CNV. First, the federal justice system responded to a petition by military clubs against the indemnification of family member of a victim, Carlos Lamarca, one of the leaders of the resistance against the dictatorship who was assassinated in 1971. As a result, the family members were ordered to return the sums received to the public treasury. The measure was appealed, and the Amnesty Commission criticized the judicial order. In the second setback, three days after Rousseff's removal from office, the Ministry of Justice replaced 19 of the 25 members of the Amnesty Commission. Among them, they appointed Paulo Lopo Saraiva, an ex-Sergeant of the Army during the military dictatorship, who is recorded in documents of the National Information System (SIN) as a suspected collaborator of the dictatorship. This action was opposed by human rights activists and the Truth Commission of the Federal University of Rio Grande do Norte (*Comissão da Verdade da Universidade Federal do Rio Grande do Norte*) (Éboli, E. September 2, 2016).

5.2. RECOMMENDATIONS TENDING TOWARDS IMPLEMENTATION

5.2.1. Deepening or Strengthening of Existing Laws and Institutions

Recommendations

#7: Correction of the registry of causes of death on victim death certificates.
#9: Creation of mechanisms to prevent and combat torture at the state level and application of Law 12.847/2013 (System, Committee and Mechanism for the Prevention and Struggle against Torture).
#15: Guarantee of permanent medical and psycho-social assistance for the victims.

Significant progress has been made on each of these recommendations. First, a number of death certificates have been corrected. The Minister of the Office of the Secretary of Human Rights, Ideli Salvatti, stated:

> Most were implemented by judicial decision, but we already concluded a debate regarding the matter with the *Comissão Especial sobre Mortos e Desaparecidos* and

> we have prepared a draft of the [ministerial] decree that will facilitate the corrections. We were already working on this before the CNV released its recommendations (Westhrop, Simi and Chernicharo 2015, response to ISER's inquiry on February 4, 2015).

Second, the Office of the Secretary of Human Rights of the Presidency of the Republic highlighted the creation, within that institution, of the National System for the Prevention and Combat of Torture (*Sistema Nacional de Prevenção e Combate à Tortura)* (Secretary of Human Rights 2015). However, it did not make any statements regarding the creation of state mechanisms or committees, as emphasized by the precepts of said National System (response to ISER inquiry on May 29, 2015). Finally, the Latin American Network of Psychological Reparation (*Rede Latino-Americana de Reparação Psíquica* – RLARP)) was created in November 2015 within the existing structure of Testimony Clinics of the Ministry of Justice's Amnesty Commission (Paiva Carvalho et al. 2016).

5.2.2. Progress in Terms of Truth and Memory and the Development of a Thematic Agenda

Recommendations

#17c: Support for the establishment and operation of an organism protecting and promoting human rights (support State, Municipal and sectoral truth commissions created during the CNV's operation).
#23: Suppression, in legislation, of discriminatory references to homosexuality.
#27: Continuation of activities oriented to the location, identification and delivery to family members or authorized persons of the human remains of individuals who were disappeared for political reasons.
#28: Preservation of the memory of grave human rights violations.

These recommendations have experienced the greatest progress, partly as a result of the dynamic generated by the CNV itself during its time of operation.

(#17c) During and after the CNV's operations, about 90 more specialized truth commissions were created within very diverse sectors: unions, social movements, universities and legislative bodies, for example. These entities have increased the visibility of the subject (Ocariz 2015). Also worth emphasizing is the establishment of forums for the filing of complaints for the protection of human rights since the return of democracy, such as the *Comissão da Verdade da Democracia "Mães de Maio"* (CVDMM) ("May Mothers" Democracy Truth Commission) created in May 2006 to investigate 494 deaths that occurred in the City of Sao Paulo.

(#23) Regarding the elimination of discrimination based upon sexual orientation, we cite the decision of the Federal Supreme Court dated October 28, 2015, one month before the presentation of the CNV report, regarding the unconstitutionality of Article 235 of the Penal Military Code.

(#27) In terms of identifying remains, in 2015, courses were organized to standardize forensic anthropology procedures. In addition, 385 boxes of evidence were identified for analysis at the lab of the Federal University of Sao Paulo (UNIFESP). Moreover, samples were collected from family members of disappeared persons in three cities (Paiva Carvalho et al. 2016).

(#28) Lastly, in terms of memory building and preservation, initiatives occurred at the state and local levels. In March 2015, the State of Maranhao implemented measures to replace the "names of all the schools honoring dictators" (Westhrop et al. 2016a). The program *Ruas de Memória* of the Prefecture of Sao Paulo, implementing the changing of the names of streets, avenues, bridges, viaducts and plazas honoring persons connected with the military dictatorship repression, was launched in August 2015. In the same month, the Federal District of Brasilia changed the name of a bridge that honored Marshal Costa e Silva, who headed the dictatorship's government between 1967 and 1969, to Honestino Guimarães, the name of the student militant who was disappeared in 1972.

Furthermore, in November 2015 negotiations began between the Federal Attorney General's Office and the car manufacturer Volkswagen to offer reparation due to its participation and financing of the dictatorship's repression. We argue this is evidence of partial progress in the preservation of memory (#28). According to Paiva Carvalho et al. (2016), the company was preparing to sign a collective reparation agreement and build a memorial.

6. CONCLUSIONS

The implementation status of the CNV's recommendations issued at the end of 2014 is limited. The parties interviewed for this study generally agree that the CNV's impact on the memory and truth agenda was positive, since the Commission's solid investigation work contributed to placing the military dictatorship's crimes (1964–85) on the public agenda after decades of relative silence.

However, the prospects for further progress on implementation of its recommendations are bleak. Evidence for this is that very few measures for the purpose of guiding, propelling and monitoring the recommendations have been enacted. Therefore, the reasoning for the recommendations articulated by the CNV is at risk of being lost. As the state moves on, it will once again fall to the human rights movement to apply pressure for action. There seems to be a consensus among the political party system, the military, and the judiciary that criminal investigation of crimes committed during the dictatorship is not legally or politically viable.

Circumstances soured with the political crisis beginning in 2014. While the crisis peaked with Rousseff's removal at the beginning of 2016, continued corruption scandals and instability remained. With the 2018 election of former military officer Jair Bolsonaro, there is little prospect of further addressing the past, promoting rights, and addressing deeper structural inequities that persist in Brazil. It is yet to be determined if this adverse dynamic will eventually completely dilute the value of the CNV's recommendations; whether the Commission will prove to have been an important turning point or a forgotten exercise.

BIBLIOGRAPHY

Campos Melo, Carolina (n.d.). "Das comissões de verdade à Comissão Nacional da Verdade Revista". Taken from: http://www.revistavjm.com.br/artigos/das-comissoes-de-verdade-a-comissao-nacional-da-verdade/.

Carta Capital (June 24, 2013). "Familiares de mortos e desaparecidos dão ultimato à Comissão da Verdade" Taken from: http://www.cartacapital.com.br/politica/familiares-de-mortos-e-desaparecidos-dao-ultimato-a-comissao-da-verdade-8086.html.

Comissão Especial sobre Mortos e Desaparecidos Políticos (2007). *Direito à verdade e à memória*. Brasilia: Office of the Special Secretary of Human Rights.

Corbo, Daniel (2007). *La transición de la dictadura a la democracia en el Uruguay.* Perspectiva comparada sobre los modelos de salida política en el Cono Sur de América Latina. *Humanidades* no. VII (1): 23–47.

CELS et al. (March 20, 2015). The Inter American Commission on Human Rights analyzes the Report issued by Brazil's Truth Commission. Taken from: http://cels.org.ar/agendatematica/index.php?info=detalleDoc&ids=3&lang=es&ss=&idc=1917.

Comissão Especial sobre Mortos e Desaparecidos Políticos (2014). *Sugestões da Comissão Especial sobre Mortos e Desaparecidos Políticos para o capítulo do relatório final da Comissão Nacional da Verdade que versa sobre as recomendações ao Estado brasileiro.* Brasilia: Comissão Especial sobre Mortos.

Comissão da Verdade do Rio (2015). *Comissão da Verdade do Rio. Relatório.* Rio de Janeiro: Comissão da Verdade do Rio.

Dallari, Pedro (October 22, 2015). "La Comisión Nacional de la Verdad de Brasil: algunas notas sobre su trabajo, informe final, conclusiones y recomendaciones con un enfoque en el sistema de justicia", *Revista Sistemas Judiciais* no. 19: 46–54.

Departamento de Direitos Humanos e Cidadania (2015). *Comissão Nacional da Verdade na OEA*. Taken from: http://www.dedihc.pr.gov.br.

Contexto Journal (May 27, 2015). "Lo importante es que el Estado demuestre que fue responsable y lo reconoce". Taken from: http://www.diariocontexto.com.ar/2015/05/27/lo-importante-es-que-el-estado-demuestre-que-fue-responsable-y-lo-reconoce/.

Dóro de Oliveira, Carla (2016). "Cinquenta anos despois: O relatório da Comissão Nacional da Verdade e a ADPF 320", presented at *XII Seminário nacional de demandas sociais e políticas públicas na sociedade contemporânea & II Mostra nacional de trabalhos científicos* (Santa Cruz do Sul: May 19–20, 2016).

Éboli, Evandro (September 2, 2016). "Nomeado para Comissão da Anistia aparece como colaborador da ditadura". *O Globo*. Taken from: http://oglobo.globo.com/brasil/nomeado-para-comissao-da-anistia-aparece-como-colaborador-da-ditadura-20043410.

Globo.com (May 21, 2013). "Comissão recomendará que agentes da ditadura respondam judicialmente". Taken from: http://g1.globo.com/politica/noticia/2013/05/comissao-recomendara-investigacao-criminal-contra-agentes-da-ditadura.html.

González, Eduardo and Howard Varney (eds.), (2013). *En busca de la verdad. Elementos para la creación de una comisión de la verdad eficaz.* Taken from the International Center for Transitional Justice (ICTJ) website: https://www.ictj.org/sites/default/files/ICTJ-Book-Truth-Seeking-2013-Spanish.pdf.

Interministerial Decree No-4 (May 11, 2016). *Official Journal of União de Brasil.*

Inter-American Court of Human Rights (November 24, 2010). *Gomes Lund et al. ("Guerrilha Do Araguaia") vs. Brasil.*

ISER (2014). Document No. 57/2014 to Mr. Pedro Dallari Coordenador da Comissão Nacional da Verdade.

—— (2015a). Ministério da Defesa: Consulta sobre as Recomendações da CNV.

—— (2015b). Relatório de Pedido de Informação ao Ministerio de Defensa.

Law No. 12.528 (November 18, 2011). Cria a Comissão Nacional da Verdade no âmbito da Casa Civil da Presidência da República.

Marenco, André (2007). "Devagar se vai ao longe? A transição para a democracia no Brasil em perspectiva comparada". In Melo, C.R. and Sáez, M.A. (eds.), *A democracia brasileira: balanço e perspectivas para o século 21.* Belo Horizonte: Editora UFMG.

Mezarobba, Glenda (2007). *O preço do esquecimento: as reparações pagas as vítimas do regime militar (uma comparação entre Brasil, Argentina e Chile).* PhD Dissertation, University of Sao Paulo.

—— (2016). "Brazil. The tortuous path to truth and justice". In Skaar, Elin, García-Godos, Jemima, Collins, Cath (eds.), *Transitional Justice in Latin America: The Uneven Road from Impunity towards Accountability.* New York: Routledge.

Ministerio da Defesa (2014a). Oficio nº 10944 a CNV, de 19 de setembro de 2014. Brasilia.

Montero, Alfred (2006). *Brazilian Politics. Reforming a Democratic State in a Changing World.* Cambridge: Polity Press.

Moreira da Silva Filho. Jose Carlos (2015). *Justiça de Transição da Ditadura Civil-militar ao Debate Justransicional.* Porto Alegre: Livraria do Advogado.

Notícias STF (October 28, 2015). "STF mantém no Código Penal Militar crime de ato libidinoso". Taken from: http://www.stf.jus.br/portal/cms/verNoticiaDetalhe.asp?idConteudo=302782.

Ocariz, M. Cristina (2015). *Violência de estado na ditadura civil-militar brasileira (1964–1985): efeitos psíquicos e testemunhos clínicos.* Sao Paulo: Escuta.

Oliveira, Mariana (March 23, 2013). "MPF pode denunciar 170 casos de violação de direitos durante ditadura". *O Globo.* Taken from: http://g1.globo.com/politica/noticia/2013/03/mpf-pode-denunciar-170-casos-de-violacao-de-direitos-durante-ditadura.html.

Osmo, Carla (2016). "Judicialização da justiça de transição na América Latina." *Brasília: Ministério da Justiça, Comissão de Anistia, Rede Latino-Americana de Justiça de Transição (RLAJT),* 44.

Paiva Carvalho, Claudia, José Nogueira Guimarães, and María Pia Guerra (2016). "Justiça de transição na América Latina. Panorama 2015". Brasilia: Ministério da Justiça, Comissão de Anistia, Rede Latino-Americana de Justiça de Transição (RLAJT).

Passarinho, Nathalia (May 21, 2013). "Comissão recomendará que agentes da ditadura respondam judicialmente". *O Globo*. Taken from: http://g1.globo.com/politica/noticia/2013/05/comissao-recomendara-investigacao-criminal-contra-agentes-da-ditadura.html.

Quinalha, Renan (2015). "Reflexões sobre a Comissão Nacional da Verdade no Brasil". Presented at the VII International Seminar of Politics of Memory. *Memoria. Verdad. Justicia. Debates y políticas de memoria en Argentina*, Buenos Aires: September 24–26, 2015.

Quero, Caio (January 6, 2010). "Para clubes militares, investigação causará 'divisão'". BBC Brasil. Taken from: http://www.bbc.co.uk/blogs/portuguese/br/2010/01/para-militares-apuracao-de-cri.html.

Schneider, Ann M. (2018). "Legislative Efforts against Impunity in the 1979 Amnesty Debate in Brazil." *Bulletin of Latin American Research* no. 37 (1): 18–32.

Schneider, Nina (2011). "Impunity in post-authoritarian Brazil: The Supreme Court's recent verdict on the Amnesty Law." *European Review of Latin American and Caribbean Studies* no. 90: 39–54.

—— (2013). "'Too little too late' or 'Premature'? The Brazilian Truth Commission and the Question of 'Best Timing'." *Journal of Iberian and Latin American Research* no. 19 (1): 149–162.

Schneider, Nina, and Gisele Iecker de Almeida (2018). "The Brazilian National Truth Commission (2012–2014) as a State-Commissioned History Project." In B. Bevernage and N. Wouters (eds.), *The Palgrave Handbook of State-Sponsored History After 1945*. London: Palgrave Macmillan, 637–652.

Secretaria de Diretos Humanos da Presidência da República (Office of the Secretary of Human Rights of the President of the Republic) (2015). *Reposta à solicitação de acesso a informações*. Brasilia.

State of Sao Paulo (September 20, 2014). Pela 1ª vez, Forças Armadas reconhecem tortura e morte na ditadura. *Estadão*. Taken from: http://politica.estadao.com.br/noticias/geral,pela-1-vez-forcas-armadas-reconhecem-tortura-e-morte-na-ditadura,1563487.

Vermelho.org (January 20, 2015). "Propostas das comissões da verdade esão temas de mudanças legislativas. Portal Vermelho". Taken from: http://www.vermelho.org.br/noticia/257476-1.

Westhrop, Amy Joe, Ayra Guedes Garrido, and Carolina Genovez Parreira (2016a). "Um processo inacabado e as permanências autoritárias: Uma Análise sobre as Experiências de Comissões da Verdade na América Latina". Presented at the *IX Seminario Internacional de Políticas de la Memoria, 40 años del golpe cívico-militar: reflexiones desde el presente*. Buenos Aires, Argentina, Centro Cultural de la Memoria Haroldo Conti, Buenos Aires, November 3, 4 and 5, 2016.

—— (2016b). *Pelos Caminhos da Verdade: Uma Análise sobre as Experiências de Comissões da Verdade na América Latina*. Rio de Janeiro: ISER.

Westhrop, Amy Joe, Simi Gustavo and Luciana Chernicharo (2015). *As Recomendações da Comissão Nacional da Verdade ao Estado*, ISER.

ANNEX: LIST OF INTERVIEWEES

Full name	Institution/Agency	Location	Date
Marlon Weichert	Regional Prosecutor of the Attorney General Office Federal Department of Justice	Sao Paulo	July 14, 2016
Anivaldo Padilha	Advisor to Commissioner Paulo Sergio Pinheiro (CNV)	Sao Paulo	July 14, 2016
Maria Amélia de Almeida Teles	União de Mulheres de São Paulo, Comissão de Familiares de Mortos e Desaparecidos Políticos and Advisor to the Truth Commission of the State of Sao Paulo	Sao Paulo	July 15, 2016
Rogerio Sottili	Ex Special Secretary of Human Rights (October 2015-May 2016)	Sao Paulo	July 15, 2016
Maria Rita Kehl	CNV Commissioner	Sao Paulo	July 16, 2016

PART II

THE ANDES

ECUADOR'S TRUTH COMMISSION

Official Support, Weak Compliance

Félix Reátegui Carrillo with Diego Uchuypoma
and Eduardo Hurtado*

1. INTRODUCTION

The Truth Commission of Ecuador, *Sin verdad no hay justicia*, was established in May 2007, with a mandate to investigate human rights violations committed between 1984 and 1988 and other special cases. Although the period investigated was extended up to 2008, with Rafael Correa as President, the core focus of the Commission's investigations was this first period of time established by the mandate when León Febres-Cordero's administration crushed the guerrilla group known as *Alfaro Vive Carajo!* (AVC), as well as different social movements,

* All authors are affiliated with the *Instituto de Democracia y Derechos Humanos Pontificia Universidad Católica del Perú*.
We would like to thank specially the work team of the National Direction of Victims' Reparation from the Ombudsman Office, the General State Prosecutor Office and the Ministry of Justice, Human Rights and Beliefs of Ecuador, as well as all the stakeholders who were interviewed for their support during the fieldwork. The authors also wish to thank Sebastián Yerovi and Onur Bakiner for helpful comments on earlier drafts of this chapter.

including human rights organizations. The Commission's final report, released in September 2010, offered information about 456 victims including 365 victims of torture, 269 victims of illegal detention, and 68 victims of extrajudicial execution (Comisión de la Verdad 2010, 53).

The Ecuadorian Truth Commission had some salient features around the truth-seeking process. One was the high degree of support from President Rafael Correa's administration, despite several extensions in its functioning. At the same time, the Commission worked under strong supervision from the victims, who were represented through a Committee of Support and had a multidisciplinary, although very young, work team. In addition, the Commission considered a large list of recommendations organized in a well-defined structure according to existing international human rights instruments. Because of this, the Ecuadorian Truth Commission shows some of the patterns that define contemporary truth-seeking mechanisms noticeable in the more recent Latin American truth-seeking commissions such as the Paraguayan one (Valencia 2011).

The Commission formulated 155 recommendations dealing with reparations, justice and institutional reform. After the Commission closed its operations, several State agencies were in charge of following-up and fulfilling its recommendations. The main agencies involved were the Ombudsman's Office, the Ministry of Justice, Human Rights and Beliefs, and the General State Prosecutor's Office.

This chapter seeks to provide an assessment of the level of implementation of the recommendations formulated by the Truth Commission, examining some actors and factors that either have impelled the process or have hindered it. To do this, we present a brief account of the scenario in which the Truth Commission was created, as well as the social and political context that motivated the investigation. This allows us to comprehend the reconstruction of the events that characterized the period from 1984 to 2008 in Ecuador, but also to understand the role of actors such as Correa's government during the creation of the Commission and later during the implementation of the recommendations.

The legal framework for the creation of the Truth Commission is then presented, which ideally defined its mandate, scope and the duration of its function. This section also addresses the difficulties faced within the Commission and the interests of the different actors that were part of the work of the Commission; interests that will continue to prevail after the end of the Commission's work, influencing the perception of the State performance on the implementation of recommendations.

Before describing and analyzing the implementation level of the recommendations, we discuss the formulation process of the measures recommended by the Truth Commission, examining the influence of different elements and actors. Thus, our evaluation of the implementation process is carried out based on all these elements.

Finally, it is important to mention that the present study followed a qualitative methodology comprising archival and documentary work between 2016 and 2017 that included compiling information about the Ecuadorian context and on the level of implementation of the recommendations. At this stage, it was necessary to establish contact with public entities in charge of achieving the implementation of the recommendations in order to have documentary evidence that would indicate whether there was compliance with the recommended measures. Later, in a second stage, fieldwork was carried out in Ecuador at the beginning of 2017 where in-depth semi-structured interviews were conducted with different social and political actors, such as victims' organizations, commissioners, the technical team of the Truth Commission, researchers and public officials, to know the post-conflict situation in the country as well as the factors that they consider have influenced the implementation process. This strategy compares what the official and communication media have disseminated about the practical application of these measures and, above all, with victims' perception about State institutions. The findings of this case study should be understood within the framework of the advantages and limitations of our methodology.

2. THE CONTEXT

The process of transitional justice in Ecuador, which includes the creation of a truth commission, a reparations process, and criminal justice measures, was initiated due to the State's recognition of human rights violations that had taken place between the 1980s and 2000s. Even though Ecuadorian society did not suffer from a full-fledged armed conflict or from a dictatorship, it experienced a period of State violence during a democratic government, giving way to numerous human rights abuses.

Human rights violations in Ecuador can be divided in two different periods. The first period corresponds to President León Febres-Cordero's administration (1984–88). During this period the abuses were connected to the administration's tactics to control or repress political opposition, including the military's actions against armed groups, the above-mentioned AVC organization and the *Montoneras Patria Libre* organization (MPL), but also human rights organizations. The second period of human rights violations was during the 1980s and 1990s, as several administrations countered social mobilization against economic reform and measures aiming to favor private investment in some regions, through State violence.

A right-wing politician elected in August 1984, Febres-Cordero's candidacy gathered a wide array of right-wing sectors under the umbrella of the *Frente de Reconstrucción Nacional* (National Reconstruction Front) to confront left-wing parties. Febres-Cordero's administration made various attempts to overhaul the economic system in Ecuador by introducing sweeping liberal (or neoliberal) measures and controlling or eliminating every social movement or institution that criticized the government's program (Krupa 2013). According to Krupa (2013) this synergy between Febres-Cordero's neoliberal program and the use of State force was produced through the construction of a chaotic national reality, with an economic crisis and social violence provoked by previous administrations (mainly by Osvaldo Hurtado), and the characterization of organizations such as AVC, MPL, and civil society institutions as terrorists or violent. In this way, Febres-Cordero portrayed a national reality full of violence and backwardness, delineated by the incompetence of previous governments and by the threat of subversive groups. At the same time, he positioned himself and his government plan as the only option for society to overcome that situation. The introduction of these neoliberal measures was accompanied by other decisions designed to stabilize the economy: taming inflation, stabilizing the exchange rate, and reducing the deficit. These measures provoked intense mobilizations and social unrest, to which the government responded with police repression.

Febres-Cordero's and his successors' responses to social mobilization were framed by a legal norm inherited from the previous military dictatorship (1976–79): the *Doctrina y Ley de Seguridad Nacional* (National Security Doctrine and Law). This doctrine introduced the theory of "internal enemies", referring to those nationals inside the country who could be deemed hostile to the national interest on account of their acts of political opposition (Aguirre and Paula 2015). This was an approach strongly marked by the ideology of "anticommunism", which led the State to consider strikes, political meetings and demonstrations as potentially threatening to social order and therefore dangerous (Peñafiel 2013). The prevalence of the *Doctrina y Ley de Seguridad Nacional* during the new democratic administrations led them to inherit authoritarian methods to deal with political opposition and with social protest when "social order" was deemed to be in peril. According to the Truth Commission, under this doctrine, Febres-Cordero's regime repressed many civil society sectors, including Christian groups identified with Liberation Theology (Comisión de la Verdad 2010). The disproportionate use of force was legitimized thanks to a legal framework and an administration that maintained a conception of respect and guarantee of human rights only for those who did not represent opposition to the national government (Valencia 2011).

During this period, armed groups such as AVC and MPL began using violence to publicize their political agendas. They also carried out bank robberies to obtain resources for launching an armed revolution. The administration responded with harsh measures, committing human rights abuses that amounted to "State terrorism" (Peñafiel 2015). These included arbitrary executions, torture and ill-treatment, arbitrary arrest, and sexual violence. On the other side, the administration instrumentalized the AVC potential threat to justify repression against political and social leaders in the opposition.

Human rights abuses continued after the end of Febres-Cordero's government in a context of high political instability during the 1990s. The ensuing period was characterized by new attempts by subsequent administrations to enforce neoliberal measures or to put in place new ones, which often provoked intense social unrest. After Rodrigo Borja's (1988–92) and Durán Ballén's (1992–96) administrations, a profound political crisis settled in and prevented three elected presidents from finishing their mandates: Bucaram (1996–97), Mahuad (1998–2000) and Gutiérrez (2003–05).[1] A common feature underlying these different periods was the Government's resolve to impose liberal reforms and the use of the National Security Doctrine and Law to repress social protest.

Repression of social movements targeted labor unions, indigenous movements, university students and NGOs, who were deemed "internal enemies" under the National Security Doctrine (Peñafiel 2013). To respond to the protests, the Government used special task groups created within the police and the armed forces. The most important was the Criminal Investigation Service – SIC-10 that operated during the administration of Febres-Cordero as a clandestine unit within the National Police, responsible for stopping the progress of groups and organizations classified as subversives, through methods of investigation and repression that violated human rights, from enforced disappearances to acts of torture. The SIC-10 was later transformed in 1989 into the Special Investigations Unit, in the charge of Edgar Vaca, who had also been the director of SIC-10. This evidenced that despite the administration of Febres-Cordero having finished, in practice these offices continued operating within the police institution under the same logic, independently of the government administration.

Homicides or arbitrary execution, torture, arbitrary arrest and forced disappearance were some of the worse crimes committed during 1984–88. By the end of this period, there existed widespread impunity regarding these human rights abuses. In the cases where some action was taken, judicial processes went to military tribunals, where the defendants were usually exonerated.

During these years, several groups of victims and human rights organizations had expressed demands for truth, justice, and reparations to the government. The creation of the Truth Commission was thus mainly a State response to claims from victims' organizations for truth (Valencia 2011). Among them were the *Comité de Familiares de Presos Políticos* (Committee of Relatives of Political Prisoners), the *Comité de Familiares contra la Impunidad* (Committee of Relatives against Impunity), and the *Comité Ecuatoriano contra la Impunidad* (Ecuadorean Committee against Impunity). The role of victims' organizations was crucial in the creation of the Truth Commission.

The presidential elections of 2006, which Rafael Correa ended up winning through the political organization *Alianza PAIS – Patria Altiva I Soberana*

1 During the period 1988–2006, Ecuador had 19 presidents; however, not all of them were democratically elected. Due to the impeachment of Abdala Bucaram, Fabián Alarcón was made acting president in 1997. After Jamil Mahuad's resignation, due to a coup d'état, Vice President Gustavo Noboa assumed the presidency until 2003, when Lucio Gutiérrez won the elections. Gutiérrez was dismissed after going through a serious crisis that involved acts of corruption. Alfredo Palacio, Vice President during Gutiérrez's administration, assumed the presidency until 2007.

(PAIS Alliance Movement) opened a floodgate to victims' groups (especially those that identified themselves as political victims) to present their demands in matters of justice and reparation to the State. Correa, a former finance minister during Alfredo Palacio's administration, won the elections using a strong discourse opposing the neoliberal policies established during the 1980s in Ecuador, as well as elsewhere in Latin America, that govern country's economic and political system. During elections, Correa proposed the formation of a Constituent Assembly and sought to establish a socialist model for Ecuador. However, Correa constructed a discursive strategy in which he placed neoliberalism and its promoters as the cause of instability and the prevalence of corruption in the country. At the same time, he positioned his administration as the one that would engender "not a change of epoch, but an epoch of changes" (Krupa 2013).

3. THE ECUADORIAN TRUTH COMMISSION

The Truth Commission was created by Executive Order 305 (Decreto Ejecutivo) on May 3, 2007. The Commission received a mandate to "investigate and clarify and prevent impunity regarding the violent acts and human rights violations that took place between 1984 and 1988, and in other periods" (Article 1°, Decreto Ejecutivo 305, 2007). Due to this open-ended phrasing of its substantive mandate, the Commission was able to consider and investigate crimes or abuses committed as late as 2008, at the beginning of Correa's administration.

To this general purpose the mandate added some specific objectives (Article 2° Decreto Ejecutivo 305, 2007):

a. To conduct a detailed independent investigation about the human rights abuses that took place between 1984 and 1988 and other special cases such as the one known as the "Fybeca Case", and about the factors and circumstances that made them possible.
b. To demand the declassification of State archives bearing confidential status or related to national security.
c. To promote the recognition of the victims and to design reparation policies.
d. To recommend the necessary legal and institutional reforms and effective mechanisms to prevent and to punish human rights violations; and
e. To establish the existence of probable evidence of civil, criminal and administrative responsibilities in order to present them to the pertinent authorities to address them.

In order to fulfil its mission, the Commission was granted the following functions: to interview and collect information from whomever it considered pertinent, including State agents, and to have access to official archives, even if they were confidential or related to national security; to organize the participation of the population, in particular those affected by past violence, in the truth-seeking process; to visit official facilities in order to conduct its investigations; and to hold private or public hearings to collect information from individuals, among others (Article 4°, Decreto Ejecutivo 305, 2007). However, like most truth commissions, the Truth Commission of Ecuador did not possess judicial powers.

The Truth Commission had four members designated by Executive Order: Elsie Monge Yoder (President), Julio César Trujillo, Luis Alberto Luna Tobar and Pedro Restrepo Bermúdez. In addition, the Truth Commission included a Support Committee, composed of victims' relatives, an expert from the civil society and a representative from the government.[2] The Committee's function was to advise the Truth Commission on how it thought the process should be organized and conducted.

The Truth Commission's operations were organized and managed by an Executive Secretary.[3] The Commission's multidisciplinary staff included lawyers, psychologists and social scientists. It had 30 in-house researchers in charge of the ordinary operations and also worked with national and international consultants, such as Carlos Beristain.

Table 1. Composition of the Ecuadorian Truth Commission

Function	Commissioner	Background
National commission member and Chair	**Elsie Monge Yoder (F)**	Teacher, nun and human rights activist. Executive Director of the Ecumenical Human Rights Commission in Ecuador (CEDHU) since 1981.[4]
National commission member	Julio César Trujillo Vásquez (M)	Ecuadorian lawyer and politician. Participated in the Constitutional Assembly of 1998, which recognized the collective rights of indigenous people and afro-descendants.[5]
National commission member	Monseñor Luis Alberto Luna Tobar (M)	Catholic priest. Archbishop of Quito in 1977 and Archbishop of Cuenca in 1981. In 2007, led the Special Commission to Investigate the Foreign debt.[6]

(continued)

2 The Support Committee was composed by Mireya Cárdenas, Clara Merino, Francisco Acosta, Ramiro Ávila and Gabriela Espinoza, who represented the Ministry of Government. However, this last function was initially developed by Juio César Quiñónez until October 2008. Later, Quiñónez was replaced by Iván Granda until February 2009. Finally, Gabriela Espinoza assumed the position which she held until the end of the Commission work (Comisión de la Verdad 2010, 22).

3 Across the two years of its work, the Commission had two Executive Secretaries, Mr. Romel Jurado in 2008 and Mr. Cristhian Bahamonde in 2009 (Comisión de la Verdad 2010, 22).

4 https://www.fidh.org/IMG/pdf/bio-elsie_monge-en.pdf.

5 http://www.expectativa.ec/julio-cesar-trujillo-50-anos-de-trayectoria-en-el-ambito-juridico/.

6 http://www.elcomercio.com/tendencias/fallecimiento-monsenor-lunatobar-iglesiacatolica-cuenca.html.

Table 1 *continued*

Function	Commissioner	Background
National commission member	Pedro Restrepo Bermúdez (M)	Colombian engineer, father to Carlos and Pedro Restrepo, disappeared during the Febres-Cordero administration.[7]
Executive Secretary	Cristhian Bahamonde Galarza (M)	Director General on Public Policy at the Ombudsman Office[8]
General Counsellor	Alejandro Valencia Villa (M)	Colombian lawyer. Advisor for the UNOHCHR and expert witness at IACtHR. Participated in the truth commissions of Peru, Paraguay and Guatemala[9]
Counsellor	Francisco Terán Hidalgo (M)	–

Sources: See footnotes.

Note: Table elaborated by the authors. M = male, F =female.

The mandate granted the Commission a working period of nine months, which could be extended for three additional months if necessary (Comisión de la Verdad 2010, 21). After these 12 months were over, the Commission received further extensions, amounting to one additional year.[10] Thus, the Commission started its operations in January 2008 and closed them in December 2009 with the release of its Final Report. After some delays, its Final Report was published in September 2010. The main reason behind these extensions was the delay in the distribution of the budget by the government and organizational problems (Caicedo 2012, 46).

The Truth Commission was based in the capital, Quito, where it carried out the largest part of its investigations. However, commissioners and researchers travelled across the country to receive testimonies from witnesses and to collect relevant documentation in other provinces. Commissioners also travelled abroad with the same purpose (Comisión de la Verdad 2010, 22).

The investigation relied on a variety of sources. Among them, testimonies collected from victims and/or witnesses had particular relevance. The Truth Commission was able to collect more than 700 testimonies, which were registered in a database and analyzed in order to document criminal cases (Comisión de

7 http://webcache.googleusercontent.com/search?q=cache:lbjn2zscNlEJ:www.pichinchauniversal.com.ec/index.php/desayunando-con-el-personaje/item/14918-pedro-restrepo+&cd=3&hl=es&ct=clnk&gl=pe.

8 https://www.mininterior.gov.ar/prensa/prensa.php?i=11416.

9 http://www.icdhcolombia.org/cursointernacional/index.php/es/ponentes-curso?showall=&start=6.

10 First, the Commission received six more months through Presidential Order 1514, December 2008; later, three more months through Presidential Order 1794, June 2009; and a final extension through Presidential Order 81, September 2009 (Comisión de la Verdad 2010, 22).

la Verdad 2010, 23). One important source, as anticipated in the mandate, was declassified documents relating to national security. The Commission's Final Report states that they were able to collect and analyze 300,000 documents originated in the National Security Council, the National Defense Ministry and the National Police. Other important sources used by the Commission were judicial records and press records.

At the end of its working period the Truth Commission produced a Final Report comprising five volumes. The Final Report describes the social and political context surrounding the human rights abuses, presents documentation and analysis of the serious abuses committed, makes an assessment of the consequences and impact of abuses on victims, and analyzes the role played by official institutions involved or associated with the dynamics of abuse by those responsible. The Report also presents 155 recommendations dealing with reparations for the victims, institutional reforms, and non-recurrence measures. In addition, the Commission also formulated a bill of follow-up guidelines in order to continue the efforts to combat impunity.

The Commission documented 118 cases over the period 1984–2008, involving human rights violations (right to life and to individual freedom), forced disappearance, arbitrary executions, torture and ill-treatment, and sexual violence. In the Commission's terminology, a "case" does not refer to one single event involving one single victim; it means a complex unit of events with similar characteristics. The decision to group human rights violations around cases would give the Commission not only a historical or archival character, but also an analytical one. The Commission identified 456 victims distributed across the following six main types of human rights violations:

(i) Illegal imprisonment: 269 victims
(ii) Torture: 365 victims, of whom 301 were men and over 30 suffered from psychological torture
(iii) Forced disappearance: 17 victims
(iv) Attacks against life: 26 victims
(v) Arbitrary execution: 68 victims
(vi) Sexual violence: 48 victims

According to most of the sources interviewed for this research, the real universe of victims around the country in the study period reach over 1,000 people. This can be explained by the methodological approach used by the Commission, which prioritized compilation of voluntary testimonies and relied on victims' capability to go to the Commission to report their experiences. Even the level of knowledge of the victims about the work of the Commission and its objectives could influence the gap between the actual number of victims and the victims identified by the Commission.

Even though many of these abuses occurred throughout the entire period, the Commission established that 68 per cent of the violations were perpetrated under Febres-Cordero's presidency where most of the visible victims were members of AVC. The Commission further established that the crimes committed were crimes against humanity (Peñafiel 2015). The Support Committee, some of whose members were relatives of AVC leaders, exhorted the Commission to focus on the Febres-Cordero period, as if the violence concerned only (or principally) the AVC organization. Nevertheless, this proposal was not followed because of the commissioners' insistence on considering not only the Leon Febres-Cordero administration, but also the subsequent governments and even Correa's administration. That way, the Commission could consider victims that weren't related to political or armed organizations. In its interpretation of the factors permitting State violence and abuse, the Commission highlighted the role played by the National Security Doctrine and Act and the willingness of several administrations to apply the status of "internal enemy" to political opponents and social protesters. The Commission called upon the General State Prosecutor to investigate and punish for the crimes documented during its work.

Finally, it is worth mentioning that the Final Report got a positive reception by the government, but not by the entire Ecuadorean society. One particular criticism of the Commission was that it failed to focus on the crimes committed by non-State violent organizations, such as AVC (Caicedo 2012, 42). The Commission identified 459 perpetrators, of whom almost 80 per cent were officers and members of the National Police and Armed Forces. For some political groups, especially for the Febres-Cordero-led Social Christian Party and its supporters, the Commission did not fully expose the nature of AVC and other armed groups and their actions. In addition, for some people there is a perception that the Commission functioned as a revenge mechanism against Febres-Cordero's political party (Caicedo 2012, 44).

Besides the variety of perceptions, for victims' relatives, whether they were members of AVC, civilians or military (*Comandos Taura*), the Truth Commission's Final Report represented a way of revealing truth about a period of Ecuadorian history where the State used different types of mechanism – legal and illegal – to suppress any organization or social movement that represented opposition to the government. For some of the relatives and victims interviewed, this process of truth seeking had to be accompanied by a set of integrated reparations such as judicial processes, institutional reforms and symbolic measures. Such measures were concentrated in the list of recommendations of the Final Report.

4. FORMULATION OF THE TRUTH COMMISSION'S RECOMMENDATIONS

The formulation of the recommendations was the result of a consultative process involving groups of victims, non-governmental organizations and public institutions. At first, the Commission organized meetings in Quito, Guayaquil and Loja in order to decide what kind of reparations would be ideal according to the victims' needs. After this, the Truth Commission began a systematization process that produced a preliminary list of recommendations to be debated and improved at meetings with public institutions' representatives. Finally, the Commission organized meetings with non-governmental human rights organizations in order to obtain their points of view about the preliminary list (Valencia 2011). The commissioners also organized visits to other Latin American countries such as Argentina, Chile and Peru in order to learn about previous experiences in transitional justice and how to implement the reparations program. In addition, the Commission received directly the counsel of international experts like Carlos Beristain and Alejandro Valencia that had wide experience in transitional justice processes in Latin America.

Besides the Commission's work itself, another important influence in the recommendations formulation came from the United Nations (UN). Between 2005 and 2006, it released two instruments related to the promotion of human rights and the right of victims to obtain reparations. Both of these instruments determined a structure that member states should consider in reparations formulation. The *Updated Set of Principles for the Protection and Promotion of Human Rights Through Action to Combat Impunity* adopted by the United Nations on February 8, 2005, urges States to include not only groups of victims, but also social organizations in the elaboration and enforcement of reparations programs (Principle 32). It also mentions that the right of victims to obtain reparations should include restitution, compensation, rehabilitation and satisfaction measures (Principle 34), which must be complemented with non-repetition guarantees such as the implementation of public institutional reforms: removal of functionaries who are responsible for human rights violations; guarantee the functioning of independent courts; civil control of army forces; civil complaint procedures; among others (Principle 36).

The other instrument, Basic Principles and Guidelines on the Right to a Remedy and Reparation for Victims of Gross Violations of International Human Rights Law and Serious Violations of International Humanitarian Law, adopted by the United Nations General Assembly on 16 December 2005, reaffirmed the categories adopted previously, but emphasized what kind of actions should be considered in each of these measures. Restitution should aim to restore the victim's identity, family life, citizenship, place of residence, among other things, in a way that restores, whenever possible, the original situation of the victim before the human rights violations were produced. Compensation has to be given proportionally to the magnitude of the human rights violations, considering physical and mental harm, loss of opportunity, material damage, and so on. Rehabilitation refers to the provisioning of psychological and medical attention, but also of social and juridical services. Finally, the satisfaction should include measures related to public and complete disclosure of the truth, search for the disappeared, official declarations restoring dignity, public apologies, among others.

The Truth Commission considered this structure as well as the guidelines formulated by the United Nations. Most of the recommendations were classified by the same categories adopted previously, except the last two, which had to do with the creation of a reparation program in charge of executing the measures considered by the Truth Commission. Table 2 shows the final classification of the recommendations made by the Ecuadorian Truth Commission:

Table 2. Summary of Ecuador's Truth Commission's Recommendations

Type of Recommendation	Measures
1) Satisfaction	– To obtain official public apologies to restore the dignity of victims. – Full and public disclosure of truth. – To seek victims of forced disappearance and the bodies of those who were arbitrarily executed.
2) Restitution	
3) Rehabilitation	– Mental and physical health. – Education. – Employment.
4) Compensation	
5) Non-Recurrence Guarantees	– Human Rights education for all different sectors of society. – Strengthening the Judicial Branch. – Strengthening judicial investigations into human rights issues. – To apply judicial or administrative sanctions to those responsible for human rights violations. – To ensure effective civilian control over the military and security forces. – To give human rights training to law enforcement agencies and to the military. – To promote human rights protection mechanisms and the compliance with codes and ethical norms. – To foster public policies and other administrative measures related to human rights. – To develop legal reforms in order to adapt the existing human rights framework to International Human Rights Law.
6) Reparations through Administrative Channels	

Source: Truth Commission Final Report 2010.

Note: Elaborated by the authors.

The consideration of these guidelines was not only an Ecuadorian matter. In Paraguay, where a Truth Commission was created in 2004, the formulation of recommendations followed the same structure, as if it was a standard determined by international organizations and an essential part in the new model of truth commissions. According to some of the members of the technical team, most of the work in the formulation process rested on the commissioners or was principally an internal product, which means that the information from participatory spaces was not always mandatory for the Commission. On the other hand, some of the victims interviewed did not perceive the formulation of the recommendations as something they were consulted on or which was discussed with them, but as a part of a bigger package of information provided by the Truth Commission.

5. IMPLEMENTATION OF RECOMMENDATIONS

An assessment made by the United Nations Human Rights Committee in 2016 acknowledges some relevant progress on human rights protection through a diversity of measures adopted by the Ecuadorian government. Although many of those measures are not directly related to the Commission's recommendations, they are relevant to address the problems that were highlighted in the Final Report. These are:

Legal measures:

- Adoption of an Organic Penal Code.[11]
- Law for National Councils for Equality.
- National Plan for Well Being.
- Organic Law for Intercultural Education.
- Integral National Plan to eradicate sexual abuses from the education system.
- Plan to Eliminate Racial Discrimination and Ethnic and Cultural Exclusion.

Ratification of treaties:

- Protocol to the Convention against Torture and Other Cruel, Inhuman or Degrading treatment.
- Protocol to the International Covenant on Economic, Social and Cultural Rights.
- International Convention for the Protection of all Persons from Enforced Disappearance.

However, assessing the above measures is problematic given the fact that they are part of a comprehensive plan proposed by the Correa Government, rather than the result of compliance with the recommendations forwarded by the

[11] The official name is *Código Orgánico Integral Penal.*

Truth Commission. In the same way, most of the recommendations actually implemented, especially those that are neither specifically related to the violence period nor to the victims, do not make explicit reference to the Truth Commission.

Formally, the first step taken by the Government in terms of truth commission recommendations was the approval of the Law for Reparations for victims and prosecution of severe human rights violations and crimes against humanity occurring in Ecuador between October 4, 1983 and December 31, 2008 (published in 2013). The law stablished the guidelines for victims' reparations such as the following:

- To create an administrative reparation program in charge of the Ombudsman Office
- The definition of the beneficiaries: victims documented by the Truth Commission and their relatives to the second degree
- The recognition of the right of victims to receive by way of reparation:
  - Physical rehabilitation, psychosocial counselling and job training
  - Deletion of police records
  - The search for, finding and release of bodies of missing persons by the General State Prosecutor
  - Certification of death and definitive title to property of victims of enforced disappearance
- Restoration of full last names to those children of victims who were registered in the Civil Register with different names to prevent being targeted by the perpetrators of human rights abuses against their parents. The compensation for material and immaterial damage is the responsibility of the Ministry of Justice, which must establish the compensation amount according to the Inter-American Human Rights System parameters.
- The judicial reparation is the responsibility of the General State Prosecutor, who must investigate not only the cases reported by the Truth Commission, but also those crimes that couldn't be analyzed.

In practice, although there is not a mandatory sequence of administration, the reparations follow the chain of steps (below) to be followed by different public institutions:

Figure 1. Principal institutions responsible for implementing recommendations

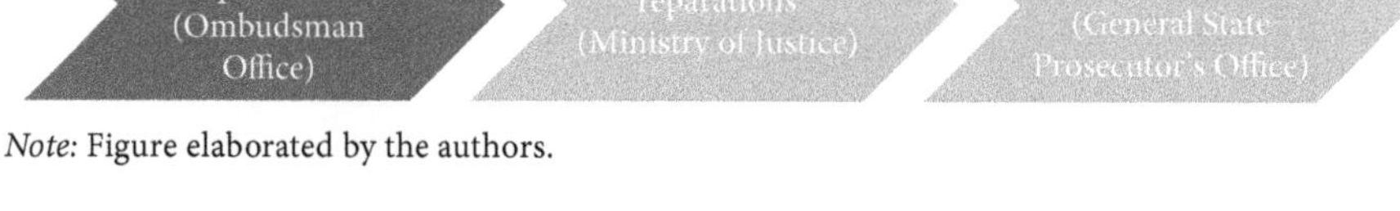

Note: Figure elaborated by the authors.

The first institution to make contact with the victims is the Ombudsman Office, based on the registers of the Truth Commission, through the Directorate for Victim Reparation and Protection Against Impunity. This institution is in charge of managing psychosocial support for the victims and setting up case files for victims according to their needs and demands. The office works also as a nexus between victims and the other two responsible institutions: The Ministry of Justice, Human Rights and Beliefs, and the General State Prosecutor's Office.

The second institution to intervene is the Ministry of Justice, which is in charge of the material compensation. The Ministry receives the information from the Ombudsman Office and starts negotiations with victims in order to compensate them financially.

The third step involves the General State Prosecutor's Office, which is responsible for the judicial procedures. Of the three steps, this part is the most autonomous due to the information collected by the Truth Commission. Thus, the judicial sanction depends more on the Prosecutor's work rather than on the information flow from the Ombudsman Office. In this last institution, a specific unit has been created: the Directorate for the Truth Commission and Human Rights, although, not necessarily with a special group of prosecutors specialized in human rights issues.

None of the three steps of the "reparations system" functions as a padlock. They are conceived as an ideal sequence, but in practice victims' interests and necessities are what matters. According to representatives of the Ombudsman Office, some victims are more interested in getting compensation rather than receiving symbolic, immaterial reparation, while other groups of victims privilege the full disclosure of truth and judicial sanctions, giving less importance to compensation.

The main problem around the design of this reparation system is that measures of non-recurrence do not lie with one specific responsible institution, because of the variety and complexity of the measures. It is therefore very difficult not only to track the implementation of those recommendations, but also for the Government to address them. In the next sub-sections we provide a brief review of some of the most important advances made with regard to implementing the recommendations.

5.1. SATISFACTION

Symbolic reparations have been provided in the form of restoration of the victims' dignity. The President and some ministers who were involved in the abuses have made official apologies.[12] For victims interviewed, however, the

12 See: http://www.presidencia.gob.ec/wp-content/uploads/downloads/2014/01/07-06-10-presentacion-Informe-de-la-Comision-de-la-Verdad.pdf.

statements are perceived as individual, isolated efforts rather than a complete recognition by the State of the human rights violations. In terms of full disclosure of truth, an archive has been created to preserve the documentation of the Truth Commission. These archives were originally in the Ombudsman Office but have been transferred to the National Archive. However, there has not been an official request for the declassification of police records. This is problematic because most of the perpetrators identified by the Truth Commission were either members of Armed Forces or the National Police. Members of this latter institution led and managed the SIC-10, a center of detention focused on conducting surveillance actions around AVC members and every opponent to the national government.

Concerning the search for disappeared persons, as part of the International Convention for the Protection of All Persons from Enforced Disappearance, Ecuador was due to present in 2013 a report to the Committee on Enforced Disappearances (CED), which monitors implementation of the Convention by the States Parties. The report was presented in 2015 yet without the participation of civil society organizations. At the same time, Ecuador has introduced the criminal offense of enforced disappearance in the Organic Integral Penal Code since 2014. This crime refers only to State agents, not to other actors, who are still dealt with by an administrative process. Procedures to follow-up cases of disappearance have not been established.[13]

The issue of forced disappearance exceeds the period of violence in Ecuador and situates it in a contemporary context where involuntary disappearance of people does not receive adequate treatment. The Judicial Council published a protocol, but it coexists with other guidelines from other public institutions without certainty as to how they complement each other.[14]

Another important measure was the creation of the National Directorate of Crimes against Life, Violent Deaths, Disappearance and Kidnappings, attached to the National Police, in 2013. This Directorate, previously called the Anti-kidnapping and Extortion Unit, was created to incorporate a specialized and well-formed technical team on a permanent basis. In practice, according to social organizations, the prosecutors in this unit are not specialized and have received insufficient training on the topic. For the victims' relatives, especially for those who have suffered the involuntary disappearance of family members, the procedures have passed from being incomplete to being a long-delayed, wide-open process with several administrative steps, triggering re-victimization processes.[15]

13 See ASFADEC and INREDH (2015). *Informe sobre la situación de personas desaparecidas de forma involuntaria y sus familiares en el Ecuador*. Quito, September 4, 2015. Retrieved from: http://tbinternet.ohchr.org/Treaties/CED/Shared%20Documents/ECU/INT_CED_ICO_ECU_24748_S.pdf.

14 ASFADEC and INREDH (2015).

15 ASFADEC and INREDH (2015).

5.2. REHABILITATION

In this group of recommendations, the Truth Commission considered measures related to health care, education, and employment. In the area of health care, the Ombudsman Office has had a central role, coordinating measures with different Ministries addressing victims' needs through the Reparations Program. Victims have received health care and legal support, and State functionaries have received training on how to attend to victims of human rights abuses. However, there is so far no national health care policy to respond to victims' needs. The victims interviewed for this project revealed that the attention in public hospitals does not distinguish between regular patients and those who are victims from the violence period and suffer the delayed effects from human rights violations. The health care personnel is the same regardless of whether the patient has suffered from arbitrary detention or is affected by a particular illness. Victims therefore perceived that there is a general lack of sensibility in the health system regarding victims' backgrounds and the difficulties involved in dealing with physical or mental illness resulting from a traumatic past. This causes, again, re-victimization processes and a feeling of disappointment among the victims.[16] Victims therefore demand that the Ombudsman Office play a more active role in the process and to be more than a nexus institution regarding rehabilitation.

In the area of education, the Ombudsman Office has attempted to include victims and their relatives in a scholarship program. However, the government has not formulated a clear public policy that could integrate a scholarship strategy specifically for the victims. The victims perceived the Ombudsman Office's role in a very similar light to that which it plays in health care, namely just as a nexus. Some of the victims interviewed perceived the Ombudsman to be in charge of coordinating with the Ministry of Education, but not of ensuring that victims of the violence period can obtain a scholarship.[17]

One clear achievement of the Ombudsman Office was the dissemination of the Final Report in the public education system in order to show how this past period has affected the present context. Due to the close relation between members of the Truth Commission and members of the Reparation Program, commissioners such as Pedro Restrepo have occasionally participated in meetings and presentations with school students to talk about the political and social context in the past and to explain the importance of knowing about and respecting human rights.

---

16 See Mesa Nacional de víctimas de graves violaciones de derechos humanos y delitos de lesa humanidad ocurridos en Ecuador 1983–2008 et al. (2015). *Informe para la audiencia. Estado de cumplimiento de las recomendaciones del Informe Final de la Comisión de la Verdad del Ecuador*. Washington DC, October 19, 2015.

17 Ibid.

In the area of employment, the Reparations Program has coordinated with the Employment Network of the Ministry of Labor in order to provide victims with employment in public institutions. In addition, some victims have received training in the search for labor opportunities. Similarly to victims' perceptions of special reparatory measures in health care and education, victims do not perceive the government to take a genuine interest in bringing victims back into the workforce.[18] Existing benefits, such as training or employment, are aimed only at specific groups composed by some of the leaders of AVC or their relatives. The link between some of the old members of guerrilla group AVC and Rafael Correa caused criticism from different social and political groups, but also from other members of AVC, who adopted a more critical position, politically speaking, and demanded more than a key governmental position: a real compromise to the Truth Commission's recommendations.

5.3. COMPENSATION

Concerning financial compensation to victims, the Ministry of Justice, Human Rights and Beliefs created a formal procedure to implement payments. Although the level of progress is quite low, at an institutional level, the efforts of the Ministry in the elaboration of institutional guidelines are quite substantive. The most relevant issue around compensation measures is the gap between the high expectations of the victims and the real capacity of the State to respond. One of the factors that influenced that expectation was the compensation level that the relatives of some iconic victims such as teenaged Pedro Restrepo[19] and schoolteacher Consuelo Benavides[20] received. Both cases were revisited by the Inter-American System of Human Rights, where it determined the State's responsibility for the human rights violations, setting an important precedent in the country. Yet the Ministry cannot negotiate with victims on the basis of the compensation amounts applied in those two cases by the IACtHR. In the present context, the compensation received by the Restrepo and Benavides families are considered more exceptional rather than mandatory.

5.4. NON-RECURRENCE

Non-recurrence measures constitute the largest group of recommendations listed by the Commission. The level of progress in implementation varies considerably

18 Ibid.

19 Report n°99/00, Case 11.868, *Carlos Santiago and Pedro Andrés Restrepo Arismendy, Ecuador*, October 5, 2000, IACtHR.

20 *Benavides Cevallos vs. Ecuador*, Decision June 19, 1998, IACtHR.

between different kinds of measures. Human rights education is the area in which there has been most progress. The upgrade of the 2016 school guidelines has included a human rights approach. In social science education, the curriculum includes an analysis of the Ecuadorean historical context with a human rights perspective.[21] Intercultural bilingual education has been introduced in 63 per cent of schools, and an Organic Law for Intercultural Education has been passed.[22] In addition, the Ministry of Justice and the Ombudsman Office have started human rights training programs for functionaries. The Ombudsman has launched a library with human rights publications. However, the Ministry of Education has not organized human rights training for teachers.

Regarding a gender approach, the most important measure has been the adoption of guidelines for the inclusion of the gender approach in the organization of technical training programs.

Concerning strengthening of the legal system, an ethical code for workers has been adopted, which is mandatory and aims to foster human rights values among workers. Since 2014, the National Assembly has been preparing a law to strengthen the Ombudsman; the law seeks to improve legal representation of victims, in particular to work in human rights co-defense before international bodies.

The General State Prosecutor has implemented a system to protect victims and witnesses from risk situations. In the judicial training schools, they have included human rights information, but only at the primary level additional training programs.

With regard to strengthening judicial investigations into human rights violations, progress has been minimal. In cases of gender violence or sexual crimes, the procedures have been centralized in one office, where victims undergo all procedures and tests, both physical and psychological. A camera system has been implemented to prevent re-victimization, to reduce excessive time of the expert work, and to create better conditions for the presentations of criminal complaints.[23]

The implementation of judicial and administrative sanctions represents another topic where there has been limited progress. The Ecuadorian Truth Commission did not proceed with formal judicial complaints, but delivered every case file, accompanied by guidance, to the General State Prosecutor's Specialized Unit for the Truth Commission. The Unit was in charge of dealing with the cases resulting from Truth Commission's investigation. The Unit was transformed into a Directorate of Human Rights and the Truth Commission, which is currently in charge of the cases.

---

21 See: https://educacion.gob.ec/wp-content/uploads/downloads/2016/08/CCSS-completo.pdf.

22 See https://educacion.gob.ec/pde/#ejes.

23 See: http://www.fiscalia.gob.ec/index.php/sala-de-prensa/boletiness/72-2016/noviembre-2016/302-fiscalia-entrega-un-servicio-integral-a-las-victimas.

Although the creation of this specific office represented the starting point of a judicial process, as of 2014, the majority of the cases were still at the stage of preliminary investigation. One year later, of 118 cases reported by the Commission, only six had advanced.

Concerning human rights training, two proposals are highlighted: (i) a Sustained Program for Integral Capacity-building organized by the Ministry of Interior,[24] and (ii) a Gender Policy for the Armed Forces.[25] The first one attempts to provide police officers with training on human rights and administrative procedures involving the Ministries of Justice and Interior, as well as the International Committee of the Red Cross. The Gender Policy attempts to prevent gender discrimination and to strengthen gender equality within the Armed Forces.

Other public policies have been implemented during Correa's administration, but as part of government plans. The creation of a new Constitution in 2008, which also was an electoral promise, represented a turn in the application of human rights in Ecuador. The Constitution incorporated the "*sumac kawsay*" concept (*buen vivir* in Spanish) from the Kichwa people and declared a new form of social co-existence based on the recognition of the cultural diversity in the country, the construction of a harmonic relationship with nature, and the search for a sustainable way of living. The National Development Plan formulated in 2017 adopted this approach and included it as its main guideline.[26]

Despite this attempt to build a new way of co-existence in contemporary Ecuador, the appropriation of an indigenous traditional concept has not necessarily led in practice to a complete embrace of the cultural diversity in the country, or to full respect for different groups' human rights. In fact, in 2015 Correa's government received several complaints for its indiscriminate use of force against protesters, including members of indigenous peoples. Thus, the inclusion of a human rights approach both in the Constitution and in the National Development Plan does not necessarily reflect the influence of the Commission, but rather, a mere starting point for a new political and economic period.

6. CONCLUSIONS

The transitional justice process in Ecuador is characterized by lack of information and lingering prejudices against victims. According to Aguirre and Paula (2015),

24 See http://www.ministeriointerior.gob.ec/programa-de-capacitacion-integral-fortalece-la-practica-del-servicio-policial/.

25 See http://www.defensa.gob.ec/wp-content/uploads/downloads/2013/03/politicas-texto-final.pdf.

26 See http://www.planificacion.gob.ec/wp-content/uploads/downloads/2017/10/PNBV-26-OCT-FINAL_0K.compressed1.pdf.

the victims are still treated as "terrorists" by a significant sector of the society and the State, which makes it more difficult for people to believe in the validity of the whole process.

The work of the Truth Commission had been used by President Correa to distance himself from previous administrations regarding their record on human rights issues. By revealing how the Febres-Cordero administration – and the subsequent national governments – used State power and the police forces to keep any kind of opposition away from the public sphere, Correa directly confronted his political, ideological contenders with testimonies and actual facts. With public support, Correa could pose his political, national program as the key to rebuilding the country, while giving also certain degree of legitimacy to AVC and other political actors that were persecuted during the Febres-Cordero regime. On this basis, the support given by Correa to the Truth Commission is noteworthy. However, there has been little progress in the implementation of recommendations, with scant participation of the victims.

Regarding the implementation of institutional measures, the Ombudsman Office and the General Prosecutor have established special agencies to address the victims' needs and demands. The Ministry of Justice does not have a specialized unit to this effect; however, it has established a protocol to facilitate the implementation of the reparations agreements. This can be considered an advance, considering that formal mechanisms or specialized institutions to deal with human rights violations did not exist. Thus, the reparation process starts with the Ombudsman and continues through the General Prosecutor, the Ministry of Justice and the rest of the institutions involved directly in reparations, such as the Ministry of Education, the Ministry of Public Health and the Ministry of Labor. Although the process appears to be well designed, for victims the link between the Ombudsman and the other public institutions does not produce a reduction in the number of requirements and procedures that they have to go through to obtain reparations. The perspectives offered on the reparations process by the victims and analysts we interviewed do not match the government's intention of a cohesive process.

The main criticism is that the government's reparation plan does not have a holistic or integrated approach. On the contrary, the process for receiving reparations is dispersed through many different institutions, which makes every step of the process like starting from the beginning. For non-recurrence measures this is even more evident since there are several subcategories of recommendations that involve different types of institutions for their implementation. The consequences of this dynamic are re-victimization, excessively lengthy processes, and inefficient use of resources.

Our overall impression is that the State has not done enough to repair the damage suffered by the victims. This is especially true in the area of criminal justice. At the time we conducted our fieldwork, there were only six cases (of a total of 118) that reported some level of judicial progress, and only one compensation agreement between the Ministry of Justice, Human Rights and Beliefs and the victims. These low numbers capture the main concern of victims; a sense of impunity and the slow implementation of the reparations program.

The process of constructing a collective memory about the violent past is still ongoing and has proven hard to achieve. Efforts have been limited to the construction of a memory museum, which, notwithstanding its significance is not sufficient to allow the victims to experience an authentic process of memory. If we consider that the Truth Commission's Final Report has not been internalized by society, this leaves the goals of transitional justice still unaccomplished and with limited possibilities to enter into the public agenda.

BIBLIOGRAPHY

Aguirre, Andrés and Paula Christian (2015). *Justicia transicional en contextos democráticos: caso Ecuador*. Retrieved from: http://www.unsam.edu.ar/ciep/wp-content/uploads/2015/10/Justicia-Transicional-en-Democracia-Analisis-del-Caso-Ecuatoriano.pdf.

Caicedo, Danilo (2012). *Experiencia de la Comisión de la Verdad Ecuador. Perspectivas de judicialización de las graves violaciones de derechos humanos y crímenes de lesa humanidad* (Tesis de Programa de Maestría en Derecho). Quito: Universidad Andina Simón Bolívar. Retrieved from: http://repositorio.uasb.edu.ec/bitstream/10644/3058/1/T1117-MDE-Caicedo-Experiencia.pdf.

Comisión de la Verdad para Impedir la Impunidad (2010). *Informe de la Comisión de la Verdad Ecuador 2010: Sin verdad no hay justicia*. Spanish version available at: https://issuu.com/triguero/docs/ecuador._sin_verdad_no_hay_justicia (English version not available). See also *Resumen Ejecutivo*. Quito. Retrieved from: http://www.alfonsozambrano.com/comision_verdad/cdv10-informe_final.pdf.

Decreto Ejecutivo 305 (May 3, 2007). Se creó la Comisión de la Verdad "para impeder la impunidad". Retrieved from: http://www.legal-tools.org/doc/fba04f/pdf/.

Krupa, Christopher (2013). "Neoliberal reckoning. Ecuador's Truth Commission and the mythopoetics of political violence". In M. Goodale and N. Postero (eds.), *Neoliberalism interrupted: social change and contested governance in contemporary Latin America* (pp. 169–194). Stanford, CA: Stanford University Press.

Ley para la reparación de las Víctimas y la Judicialización de Graves Violaciones de Derechos Humanos y Delitos de Lesa Humanidad ocurridos en el Ecuador entre el 4 de Octubre de 1983 y el 31 de Diciembre de 2008, 13 de Diciembre de 2013.

Peñafiel, Diego (2015). *El terrorismo de Estado en Ecuador: autoritarismo, seguridad y derechos humanos (1984–1988)* (Trabajo de Fin de Máster. Facultad Latinoamericana de Ciencias Sociales, sede Ecuador). Retrieved from: http://repositorio.flacsoandes.edu.ec/bitstream/10469/8940/1/TFLACSO-2015DFPV.pdf.

United Nations (2005). *Updated Set of Principles for the Protection and Promotion of Human Rights Through Action to Combat Impunity*. E/CN.4/2005/102/Add.1, February 8, 2005. Retrieved from: http://www.derechos.org/nizkor/impu/principles.html.

United Nations General Assembly (2005). *Basic Principles and Guidelines on the Right to Remedy and Reparation for Victims of Gross Violations of International Human Rights Law and Serious Violations of International Humanitarian Law*. A/RES/60/147, December 16, 2005. Retrieved from: https://undocs.org/A/RES/60/147.

United Nations Human Rights Committee (August 11, 2016). *Observaciones finales sobre el sexto informe periódico del Ecuador*. CCPR/C/ECU/CO/6. Retrieved from: https://www.refworld.org.es/docid/58763f004.html.

Valencia, Alejandro (2011). "Memorias compartidas: Las Comisiones de Verdad de Paraguay y Ecuador." In Instituto Interamericano de Derechos Humanos, *Contribución de las políticas de verdad, justicia y reparación a las democracias en América Latina* (pp. 215–245). San José: IIDH. Retrieved from: https://www.iidh.ed.cr/IIDH/media/1583/contribucion-de-las-politicas-vjr-2011.pdf.

ANNEX 1: LIST OF INTERVIEWEES

Name	Institution	Place and date of interview
Hna. Elsi Monge Yoder	President Truth Commission Executive Director of the Ecumenical Human Rights Commission in Ecuador (CEDHU)	Quito, February 14, 2017
Pedro Restrepo Bermúdez	Commissioner, Truth Commission	Quito, February 15, 2017
Cristhian Bahamonde Balarza	Executive Secretary, Truth Commission Former Director General on Public Policy at the Ombudsman Office	Quito, February 13, 2017
Clara Merino	Member of Truth Commission Support Committee President, Committee for Victims of Human Rights Violations in Ecuador	Quito, February 14, 2017
Yolanda del Pilar Galarza Yáñez	National Director, Directorate for Victim Reparations and Protection against Impunity, Ombudsman Office	Quito, February 13, 2017
Diego Rodríguez Mayorga	National Victim Reparations Program, Ombudsman Office	Quito, February 13, 2017
Diego Peñafiel Valencia	Advisor to the Directorate for the Truth Commission and Human Rights, General State Prosecutor (*Fiscalía General del Estado*)	Quito, February 14, 2017
Jeny Vargas Yangua	Advisor to the Directorate for the Truth Commission and Human Rights, General State Prosecutor (*Fiscalía General del Estado*)	Quito, February 14, 2017
Juan Pablo Albán Alencastro	Director, Legal Counselling (*Consultorio Jurídico*) Lecturer, University of San Francisco de Quito	Quito, February 16, 2017
Gina Benavides	Coordinator, Andean Human Rights Program, Andean University Simón Bolívar – Campus Ecuador	Quito, February 14, 2017
César Duque	Legal advisor to the Ecumenical Human Rights Commission in Ecuador (CEDHU)	Quito, February 14, 2017
Telmo Pacheco	Representative, Association of the Families and Friends of Disappeared Persons in Ecuador (ASFADEC)	Quito, February 15, 2017
Diego Betancourt	Former leader of AVC Leader, National Victims Board	Quito, February 13, 2017
Víctor Bolaños	Former military officer	Quito, February 13, 2017

ANNEX 2: RECOMMENDATIONS MADE BY THE ECUADORIAN TRUTH COMMISSION[27]

SATISFACTION RECOMMENDATIONS

Measures related to obtaining official statements that offer public apologies and restore the dignity of victims

1. To offer victims and the Ecuadorian society a declaration in the name of the State, made by the President of the Republic accompanied by the Minister of Defense and Government, and by the Commanders of the Armed Forces and the Police; that recognizes the facts and accepts the responsibility of the State in the violation of human rights established in the Final Report of the Truth Commission, asks forgiveness for what happened and commits to prevent such regrettable events from happening again, as well as to promote their clarification and investigation when necessary.
2. To call on those responsible for the violation of human rights to voluntarily accept their responsibility for the violations committed, provide the information they have available so that cases can be solved, and apologize publicly to the victims.
3. To exhort the Attorney General of the State, the President of the Supreme Court of Justice, and the President of the Judiciary, to accept the responsibility of their offices and functionaries in the denial of justice and the violation of human rights established in the Final Report of the Truth Commission and apologize to the victims and the Ecuadorian people.
4. To urge the National Memory Center of the Ministry of Culture and the Human Rights Under Secretary of the Ministry of Justice and Human Rights, through different programs in different scenarios and according to particularity of the victims and violations, to dignify publicly the honor of the victims. In addition, to provide the facilities so the mentioned elements of memory can be established, if there is a social demand, in a local setting.
5. To request the media to implement dissemination strategies directed to point out the conclusions and recommendations of the Final Report of the Truth Commission, in order to restore the dignity of the victims and prevent any repetition of the facts.

---

27 *Source:* Comisión de la Verdad para Impedir la Impunidad. *Informe de la Comisión de la Verdad Ecuador 2010: Sin verdad no hay justicia.* Spanish version available at: https://issuu.com/triguero/docs/ecuador._sin_verdad_no_hay_justicia Translation of recommendations by authors.

6. To require the Ministry of Government and the Ministry of Defense to close and dismantle all of the places that were used as centers for illegal deprivation of liberty and torture, so they can never again be used for these ends and can be declared as places for memory. Require the Ministries of Culture, and Justice and Human Rights to manage the places for memory, make them public, and articulate them through the national policy for social memory.
7. To exhort the National Memory Center of the Ministry of Culture and the Under Secretary for Human Rights to support the initiatives for collective memory proposed by the victims, the decentralized autonomous governments (such as rural parishes, cantons, provinces, regions, metropolitan districts, indigenous or pluricultural territories), social organizations or the affected communities.
8. To urge the Central Government and decentralized autonomous governments to dismantle public monuments and eliminate the names of public places, including schools, related to those responsible for human rights violations. For such ends, legal reforms and administrative actions must be promoted by the National Government and the decentralized autonomous governments.
9. To determine national, provincial, and local commemorative dates in honor of the victims of human rights violations. The Permanent National Commission for Civic Commemoration, with the participation of the victims and the decentralized autonomous governments, should establish the necessary mechanisms to set such dates.
10. To urge local governments to place plaques or names in relevant or symbolic public places in memory of the victims of human rights violations. The State and regional or local authorities should provide the means and facilitate the necessary consensus to make this happen as part of the duty of memory and prevention of future human rights violations.

Measures related to the public and complete disclosure of truth

11. To create a "Memory of Human Rights Violations in Ecuador Archive", which has as its starting point the set of declassified official documents and other evidence held by the Truth Commission. This registry must be articulated in accordance with the national policy of social memory and should involve the participation of the National Archive of Ecuador, the National Memory Center of the Ministry of Culture and the Ombudsman Office, among others. The Archive should be orientated to preserve this memory for researchers, relatives of victims and civil society interested in

the knowledge of these violations, establishing standards of access and use of information.

12. To request the President, through the Ministries of Government and Defense, to continue with the declassification and opening of all police and military archives, to contribute to the clarification of human rights violations, in accordance with the constitutional and legal rules governing the matter. In particular, archives related to the Special Investigations Unit and Public Security Office of the National Police, the National Security Council and the Special Group of Military Intelligence Operations of the Armed Forces and the Presidency.
13. To request the governments of other states, for example the United States of America, Peru, Panama, Colombia to declassify their own documents linked to the human rights violations that occurred in Ecuador or against Ecuadorian people, and to make them available to the public, through the "Memory of Human Rights Violations in Ecuador Archive".

Measures orientated to the search for missing people and the bodies of executed people

14. To design, within the Attorney General of the State, a Program for finding people who were forcibly disappeared a Search Committee with the participation of families of the victims, non-governmental human rights organizations, the Ombudsman Office and the Attorney General of the State.
15. To promote the creation of a team of anthropologists and forensic and psychosocial doctors within the Attorney General of the State to lead the search for persons who were forcibly disappeared, and search for other evidence tending to establish the facts and responsibilities in other cases of people who were executed.
16. To establish special protocols for burial and exhumation of the bodies to facilitate the identification of missing and executed people, according to the handbook on the effective prevention and investigation of extra-legal, arbitrary and summary executions, or "Minnesota Protocol".
17. To urge the Ministry of Foreign Affairs to promote the realization of agreements with specialized professionals in anthropology and forensic medicine from other countries, to train, advise, and accompany the Attorney General of the State and the Committee of Missing People in the search for and identification of missing people and the bodies of those executed.

RESTITUTION RECOMMENDATIONS

18. To rectify and eliminate judicial and police records that appear in the personal background certificate and in the judicial, police, military or other files, of people who were arrested, prosecuted or convicted when their human rights were violated or denied due process.
19. To request the National Secretary for Migrants (SENAMI) to provide conditions for the voluntary, safe and dignified return of people who were exiled or forcibly displaced as a result of human rights violations covered by this report.
20. To urge the President of the Republic and the Minister of Defense to make effective the decision of the National Constituent Assembly of June 13, 2008, in which amnesty was granted to 62 commands of Taura who participated in the events of January 16, 1987, and to captain Oswaldo Cevallos Terán, who participated in the taking of the bases of Manta and Quito, related facts to the "Taurazo".

REHABILITATION RECOMMENDATIONS

Physical and psychosocial health

21. To articulate a policy of physical and psychosocial care for victims of human rights violations and their families. To provide adequate care for victims of human rights violations contained in the Truth Commission report, and by extension for victims of human rights violations that still occur in the country, it is necessary to have a policy that takes into account health and social aspects, for health care from an interdisciplinary perspective needs to be structured.

    This policy should make visible the importance of recovering (or restoring) a democratic culture as a means to overcome the stigma and the culture of silence around human rights violations which has extended in Ecuador in the last three decades.

    It is necessary that public institutions give relevance to the problem and establish the resources and mechanisms in order to implement this recommendation in a coordinated way with existing initiatives concerning the violence problem in the country that must consider the human rights approach.

    The dissemination of the Truth Commission Final Report, as a social and political sensibilization instrument, is a fundamental tool to develop the recommended measures. The rupture of a history of normalization history or the silencing of violations, as well as overcoming the fear of speaking and the recovery of the capability to defend human rights are key tools for public health and prevention.

22. To create an integrated framework of specific State policies. It is necessary to articulate the actions for care and prevention under guidelines, providing a specific treatment and integration into the mechanisms of interagency coordination on existing violence. The integral treatment must consider specific health problems as a consequence of human rights violations and wide health necessities of the victims and their families. The care should be based on criteria such as availability, accessibility, acceptability and adaptability in the different regions of the country. The public and complementary network should favor the punctual, continued and appropriate care.

    Considering the existence of several plans related to this topic that also have interinstitutional mechanisms, it is necessary to integrate specific mechanisms to treat victims of human rights violations. This articulation is especially important in a local level, where they are trying to establish care networks and professionals. It requires a different point of view from the health system in these cases but articulated with the rest of institutions that play a role in the interdisciplinary care.

23. Assessing health needs. Creating an interdisciplinary team to diagnose and assess the health status of the people named as beneficiaries by the Truth Commission. The team should make a diagnosis to identify the beneficiaries and determine the treatment in each case with an individual and familiar approach. For this purpose, referral centers will be established to overcome the usual difficulties of repeated consultations, to access secondary or tertiary services, examinations or diagnostic tests.

    The initial assessment should provide treatment for different health problems considering welfare criteria, as well as specific reparations criteria orientated to the acknowledgment of the damage produced by the violations, the dignity of the victims and the respect of the measures as forms of reparation. The treatment would be costless for victims of human rights violations.

    Considering the existence, fragmentation or lack of unity in the treatment criteria, it is necessary to establish regionally treatment networks at different levels, to attend formation and experience criteria, available and commitment in monitoring, establishing a diagram of victims' treatment.

    A victims' treatment protocol will be created that collects objectives, routes and indicators of treatment and assessment, and that coordinates these protocols with other existing guidelines such as gender violence.

24. To establish networks and routes of health care. Create a network (in coordination with the existing ones linked to issues of sexual violence or childhood) of professionals, especially in the cities of Quito, Guayaquil, Cuenca and Lago Agrio, where more cases have been identified by the Truth Commission, with capacity to cover different parts of the territory that offers comprehensive care in mental health and psychological impacts to the victims of human rights violations. In order to determine the

members of this network, consultation will take place with the existing health services, social organization and universities. The members of the network should receive elemental training in topics related to the consequences of torture and other human rights violations, which will allow united criteria and the preparation of periodical reports that can make it possible to evaluate the impact of programs and the network. These should have a territorial vision and should establish, create, organize rapid response teams whenever required. For the definitive elaboration of this measure the victim's opinion will be considered.

25. Training of health care staff to treat victims of human rights violations. These teams will receive the necessary resources and equipment, and will be staffed with the professionals required to work properly.
26. Care management. A personnel or reference team for actions in health care needs to be established, in order for them to be agile and efficient in response, and a coordination of interventions in health care for victims. The State must provide the resources necessary to provide treatment without delay.
27. Social participation in self-help groups. Hold meetings of groups of victims at realistic and suitable intervals (e.g. quarterly during the first year), including meetings of specific groups by age, gender, ethnicity or disability status. Responsible functionary and professionals of the integral health network should be present in these meetings in order to achieve monitoring of the Final Report recommendations.
28. Actions aimed at prevention. Given the frequency of human rights violations in detention centers, mechanisms must be established for the prevention, proper medical and legal intervention, and resources and mechanisms for proper care. Intervention should involve independent professionals unrelated to State security forces. For cases that might arise in the future, an intervention protocol needs to be established, to be applied by independent professionals with knowledge of the Istanbul Protocol, for comprehensive care for victims of torture.
29. Psychosocial support in the judicial investigation. Provide victims and their families with psychosocial assistance from the submission of complaints to the stage of prosecution of their cases. Justice officials should be trained on issues related to the care of victims and the investigation of human rights violations. The training should be established via agreements with universities and civil society organizations with experience in this field. These actions should provide psychosocial support through public or complementary networks, and with the support of sectors of civil society network should focus on:
    1) accompanying victims who are involved in judicial processes,
    2) providing security for victims in their demands and protect witnesses, and
    3) continuing the search for missing victims. Such support should have sufficient means and resources to ensure their effectiveness.

30. Specific attention in cases of sexual violence. For the prevention of sexual violence, psychosocial care and interdisciplinary, immediate and specialized health for victims of sexual violence must be strengthened. The standards of comprehensive care for gender-based violence that already exist must be socialized with the institutions that are handling this in populations such as children and adolescents, with forensic experts involved in court cases, etc.

Education

31. To grant (if wanted) scholarships for higher education, university or technical college, or scholarships for professional, social or leadership development, for the sons and daughters of people executed or forcibly disappeared and the surviving victims of illegal deprivation of liberty, torture or other cruel, inhuman or degrading punishment, including victims of sexual violence. The beneficiaries of the grant may transfer the benefit to their sons or daughters, grandsons and granddaughters, without prejudice to the duty of the State to guarantee free public education to all people, including victims, to the third level of higher education, according to Article 28 of the Constitution.

Work

32. To create specific job training programs, technical training or assistance and support for the development of economic inclusion initiatives for women and men whose partners were executed or disappeared and the surviving victims of illegal deprivation of liberty, torture and other cruel, inhuman or degrading punishment, including victims of sexual violence.
33. To have job opportunities for people with permanent disabilities who were victims of torture and other cruel, inhuman or degrading punishment.

COMPENSATION RECOMMENDATIONS

34. It is recommended to assign unique compensation amounts for victims of illegal or arbitrary detention, torture and sexual violence, and other injuries not resulting from torture, extrajudicial executions and enforced disappearances. Such compensation should be granted to victims recognized as such by the report of the Truth Commission, and to the new ones that will be recognized by the reparations program through administrative channels that is recommended to be created. The consultation process which carried out the Truth Commission with victims suggests the adoption of compensation as single sums of money, instead

of pensions. It is also recommended to grant additional compensation to victims considering that, in the context of illegal deprivation of freedom, torture, sexual violence, extrajudicial execution or enforced disappearance, they could have suffered great destruction or loss of property and housing, as reflected in the report of the Truth Commission.

35. When compensation is given to relatives of the direct victim, in cases of forced disappearance and extrajudicial execution, it is recommended that it should be distributed as follows: 50% for children, distributed among them in equal amounts, 25% for the father and mother, and 25% for the surviving spouse, or to whomsoever had been cohabiting, with or without prior marriage union or same-sex partnership, for at least three years at the time of the death or disappearance of the direct victim, if a notary declares it.
36. If the victim has not had a spouse, cohabitated with or without prior marriage union or had a same-sex partner at the time of his or her death or disappearance, nor has sons or daughters, it is recommended that compensation should be distributed as follows: 50% to the father and mother, and 50% to the brothers and sisters.

NON-RECURRENCE MEASURES

37. To formulate an Education Plan on Human Rights to the National Education Plan, by the Ministry of Education, with the participation of all sectors of education.
38. To incorporate into the relevant subjects of school and high school, a vision of Ecuadorian history according to the Final Report of the Truth Commission, which contributes to an understanding of the facts, in which the dignity of the victims is restored, and oriented to generate awareness about the demands for human rights and the importance of social commitment in preventing violations.
39. To modify educational texts so students can visualize the human rights violations that occurred throughout the history of Ecuador since the Spanish conquest, and to incorporate the teaching of history according to the Report of the Truth Commission, restoring the dignity of the victims.
40. To guarantee by the National Directorate of Intercultural Bilingual Education of the Ministry of Education that the education in elementary, high school and university has a multicultural perspective.
41. To integrate the gender equity approach in institutional practices and promoting it to be a crosscutting issue in all levels of education, as mandated by the Law for Educational Democracy.
42. To request the Ministry of Education, in coordination with the equality council, to periodically train teachers in human rights issues with an age, gender and multicultural perspective.

43. To urge the Ministry of Education and the Public Defender to conduct training in non-formal education to community leaders about the human rights approach with an age, gender and multiculturalism perspective.
44. To include in the various programs of human rights education with a gender perspective, the issue of sexual and reproductive rights from a preventive and restorative perspective.
45. To promote educational activities aimed at critical awareness of human rights violations, facilitating possibilities for visits to memory spaces that are created (e.g., those that in the past were used as center of illegal deprivation of liberty and torture).
46. To urge the Office of the Public Defender, the Ministry of Education and the Ministry of Justice and Human Rights to promote, with the National Council of Higher Education (CONESUP) or the public agency for planning, regulation and internal coordination mentioned in the article 353 of the Constitution of the Republic, research on human rights in schools and universities.
47. To urge the Ministry of Education and the National Council of Higher Education (CONESUP) or the public agency planning, regulation and internal coordination mentioned in article 353 of the Constitution of the Republic, to produce publications specializing in human rights for students of elementary, high school, college, and groups particularly vulnerable and at risk, for programs of formal and non-formal education.
48. To encourage the Ministry of Education and the Ministry of Culture to promote radio and television programs as well as educational texts and audio-visual materials in both Spanish and languages of indigenous nationalities, according to a human rights approach with an age, gender and multiculturalism perspective.
49. To undertake programs to promote human rights of indigenous peoples, Afro-Ecuadorians and *Montubios*, by the Council for Ethnic Equality in coordination with the National Directorate of Intercultural Bilingual Education of the Ministry of Education, the Ministry of Culture and the Ministry of Justice and Human Rights.
50. To urge the Ministry of Justice and Human Rights to permanently train the suppliers, conciliators and mediators in human rights issues with an age, multicultural and gender perspective.
51. To incorporate into the law faculties of public and private universities a major specialized in human rights that includes aspects of international law of human rights, international humanitarian law and international criminal law.
52. To request the National Council of Higher Education to promote university programs in various subjects of anthropology and forensic medicine.
53. To encourage the participation of citizens and different organizations of civil society in the design and implementation of the various programs

of human rights education. The State should have opportunities for participation of human rights organizations that play an important role in research, reporting and work in defending victims of human rights violations.

54. To strengthen the judicial career path stipulated in the Organic Code of the Judiciary, through the integration of the members of the Judicial Council, in accordance with the Constitution and the Organic Code of the Judicial Function.
55. To incorporate the human rights approach as an indicator for evaluating the actions of the judicial system, as a condition of entering and remaining in the judiciary.
56. To arrange that the Judicial Council, in accordance with the Organic Code of the Judicial Function, issue and update codes of ethics or conduct for judicial officers, prosecutors, public defenders and lawyers, according to the principles of professional ethics, of the Constitution of the Republic and international standards.
57. To request the Ministry of Justice and Human Rights to strengthen the Public Defender Office to put it on equal administrative, technical and operational term with the State Attorney General Office, and the Ministry of Finance to provide it with the necessary financial resources to develop effectively in the different regions of the country.
58. To strengthen the Public Defender Office in the legal representation of victims of cases of human rights violations.
59. To strengthen with a human rights approach and the necessary means for effective operation, the program for protection and assistance to victims, witnesses and other participants of criminal proceedings, by the General Attorney General.
60. To allocate additional resources to penal institutions to improve detention conditions in local judicial police, remand centers, and social rehabilitation centers.
61. To set as mandatory interdisciplinary training regarding human rights in every major in the Judicial School, such subject should cover constitutional and international aspects in this field, with emphasis on the subjects of fair trial and due process. The gender variable and differential approach will be incorporated in judicial decisions and the analysis of evidence, through training by a permanent group of human rights trainers, composed of the different operators of justice.
62. To require the Judicial School to trains justice operatives in due consideration, registration and processing of complaints of human rights violations.
63. To request the Judicial School to provide specialized training to prosecutors and judges responsible for investigating and prosecuting crimes that constitute human rights violations, crimes of aggression, genocide, and

crimes against humanity against persons and property protected by the international humanitarian law.

64. To urge the Constitutional Court and judges, courts and the judiciary, when issuing statements that are mandatory precedents, to incorporate the application of international law of human rights.
65. To form a body of specialized professionals enrolled in the Judicial Council for conducting medical and psychological assessments that have specialized protocols, specifically in line with the Istanbul Protocol, for the determination of torture and sexual violence.
66. To strengthen technically, economically and scientifically the Judicial Police, with professional corps of civilian experts in criminal research and forensic science, trained and sensitized on human rights issues.
67. To urge the State Attorney General Office and the National Police to improve the coordination of plans and related activities with the Judicial Police.
68. To request the State Attorney General Office to provide victims of sexual violence, as well as children who are victims of crime, with psychosocial care during the judicial process, establishing a single interview about the facts of such cases. Strengthen existing mechanisms and expand its coverage in hospitals or reference centers in different regions of the country.
69. Redesigning a research protocol of sexual violence in accordance with international standards such as the Istanbul Protocol, which would allow the State Attorney General Office to evaluate the hypothesis of occurrence of sexual violence prior to murder, in which the psychological expert report is taken into account as evidence of sexual violence.
70. To implement disciplinary sanction mechanisms included in the Organic Code of the judiciary, in particular to impose the dismissal of prosecutors who do not initiate investigations promptly.
71. To require the State Attorney General Office to take measures to facilitate the investigation and punishment of officials of the institution who participated, acquiesced or permitted human rights violations, as illustrated in this report.
72. To request the State Attorney General Office to investigate the acts of violence perpetrated by individuals or illegal armed groups linked to the dispossession of indigenous territories and the invasion and / or illegal appropriation of land.
73. To require the State Attorney General Office to appoint a special investigation team on the murders in the province of Sucumbios, related in this report, called the Shushufindi case.
74. To request the State Attorney General Office to appoint a specialized human rights unit, to boost investigation of cases of human rights violations contained in this report.

75. To start, reopen or continue the necessary investigations, by the judicial authorities, to determine the criminal liability of the persons named as alleged perpetrators of human rights violations in the report of the Truth Commission.
76. To urge the judicial authorities to investigate diligently cases of human rights violations that have been decided or are being processed by intergovernmental human rights bodies, in order to identify, prosecute and punish those allegedly responsible.
77. Ask the judicial authorities diligently to bring forward the investigations against persons mentioned in this report and located abroad, responsible for human rights violations as crimes enshrined in criminal law, so that once legal requirements are met, to play their respective parts for the extradition of those people to Ecuador.
78. To require the Ministry of Foreign Affairs to request the governments of foreign states – under any legal status, Ecuadorian responsible for violations of human rights reside – to notify the Ecuadorian State for the purpose of resorting to the process of extradition and prosecution of those allegedly responsible or – otherwise – that they should be investigated and prosecuted under the principle of universal jurisdiction.
79. Reforming the internal regulations of the National Police and the Armed Forces to suspend from duty those against whom investigations for human rights violations have been started'.
80. Grant the Ministry of Government and the Ministry of Defense the authority to investigate and punish, administratively and disciplinarily, members of the police and the armed forces involved in human rights violations.
81. To request the creation of specialized processes of citizen oversight at the Council of Citizen Participation and Social Control, so that appropriate accountability mechanisms can be established for the National Police and the Armed Forces, especially on human rights, as set out in the National Human Rights Plan of Ecuador.
82. To establish and/or strengthen specialized bodies at the level of the Armed Forces and Police, responsible for receiving complaints of human rights violations and to refer them for investigation to the competent authorities.
83. Clearly define the procedures regarding the conduct of members of the Armed Forces in states of emergency, to ensure that they respect and guarantee – in all cases – constitutional and international human rights standards.
84. To prohibit the use of police or military facilities as detention centers.
85. Confirm the need to develop a new security doctrine and policies that are based on respect for human rights and the participation of all state institutions and citizens.
86. To maintain and strengthen permanent educational programs in human rights and international humanitarian law in the education, training and specialization of members of the military, police and security forces at

all hierarchical levels, establishing a permanent evaluation system of its impact and results.

87. To strengthen training programs for the members of the police or those acting in their stead in the Code of Conduct for officials responsible for enforcing the law, the basic principles on the use of force and firearms for officers who enforce the law, the set of principles for the protection of all persons under any form of detention or imprisonment, and the code of professional ethics.
88. To incorporate into education programs and training of the Armed Forces, National Police and Security, content on the prevention of sexual and gender-based violence, and its operation in cases involving children, and adolescents. Its fulfilment must be evaluated.
89. Design publications and material for promotion of human rights and international humanitarian law, specifically aimed at members of the Police and the Armed Forces.
90. To urge the ministers of National Defense and Government and the Police to refuse authorization of attendance of members of the Armed Forces and National Police at training courses or training in schools or institutions that have a history of teaching practices contrary to human rights.
91. To urge the Ministry of Public Administration of the President of the Republic to incorporate in the various manuals on public function, a human rights perspective that emphasizes the duties of respect and guarantees by the State.
92. To require various professional organizations to include human rights as a transversal issue in their different codes of ethics. And that advance internal professionals who have failed in their duties to respect and guarantee human rights investigations.
93. Demand the inclusion of the classes of human rights as a subject in university courses on social communication.
94. Demand the National Council of Radio and Television (CONARTEL), the Ecuadorian Association of Television Channels, the Ecuadorian Association of Newspaper Editors and the Ecuadorian Broadcasting Association, to place human rights as its own specialized subject on the agenda of the media, including adopting this perspective in their style manuals or other existing procedures.
95. To instruct the Public Defender's Office and the Ministry of Justice and Human Rights to implement codes of behavior on human rights, taking into account existing international commitments in the field, for transnational corporations and other business enterprises, working with populations affected by their projects or operations.
96. To request the Ministry of Justice to design a scheme of incentives for compliance with good practices in the respect of human rights for the public and private sector, of national or international origin.

97. Order the Ministry of Justice and Human Rights to establish permanent training to all staff in the prison system.
98. To request the Ministry of Justice and Human Rights to observe strict compliance with the rights of children and adolescents who are in detention centers for juvenile offenders in accordance with the Standard of Minimum Rules for the Administration of Juvenile Justice of 1985, the Guidelines for the Prevention of Juvenile delinquency of 1990, and the Rules for the Protection of Minors Deprived of Freedom of 1990.
99. Promote alternative dispute resolution mechanisms such as mediation and strengthen mediation centers.
100. Promote the use of the Mediation Center of the Judiciary and the Department of Labor Mediation of the Ministry of Labor Relations and strengthen it with human and material resources. In addition, other mechanisms should be promoted for arbitration, mediation and conflict resolution such as mediation and arbitration centers of bar associations and chambers of commerce.
101. To urge the Judicial Council to appoint, as soon as possible, justices of peace under the Constitution of the Republic and the Organic Code of the Judiciary, so that their decisions on an equitable basis can resolve individual, community, neighborhood and eliminate misdemeanors respecting human rights.
102. To request the Ministry of Labor Relations to guarantee, in accordance with international standards, the right to organize, without additional requirements that hinder the effective enjoyment of this right.
103. To urge the current transitional unit of the Criminal Public Defender to fulfil its constitutional mandate of not having prisoners without trial in Ecuador by October 2009.
104. To implement human rights as one of the priority areas of free legal clinics and community legal assistance, in accordance with the Organic Code of the Judicial Function.
105. Motivate citizens and civil society groups to protest in cases of human rights violations.
106. Include the human rights approach as an axis of the different constitutional functions of the Ecuadorian State, as well as a cross-cutting theme of the different ministerial and sectoral agendas.
107. Incorporate human rights as a cross-cutting issue in the Development Plan, which is established as a priority in the Millennium Development Goals of the United Nations organization.
108. Reformulate the National Human Rights Plan of Ecuador, in order that:
    1. it is constructed in a comprehensive manner with the participation of different sectors of civil society with an indivisible and interdependent perspective,

2. it articulates the issues of human rights embodied in other national plans, and
3. the rights enshrined in the Constitution are implemented in accordance with the standards of international law of human rights.

109. Urge the Ministry of Justice and Human Rights, with the Ministry of Foreign Affairs and the State Attorney General, to coordinate the implementation of the recommendations of the rulings of the Inter-American Court of Human Rights, the reports of the Inter-American Commission Human Rights, and interim or provisional measures ordered by these same agencies in the Organization of American States.

110. Encourage the Ministry of Justice and Human Rights, with the Ministry of Foreign Affairs and the Attorney General, to give effect to the recommendations made by the organs of the universal human rights system of the United Nations bodies, among others, of the Council of Human Rights; special rapporteurs, independent experts and working groups as well as the various committees established by human rights treaties.

111. Require the government to make the following statements in which the competence of international bodies is recognized, in order to strengthen the respect of human rights:
1. The declaration referred to in Article 90 of additional Protocol I of 1977 to the Geneva Conventions whereby the competence of the International Commission of Inquiry for Ecuador is recognized.
2. The declaration that, under Article 77 of the International Convention on the Protection of all rights of migrant workers of 1990, can submit individual cases to the Committee on the Rights of Migrant Workers.
3. The declaration that, under Article 31.1 of the International Convention for the protection of all persons against enforced disappearance of 2006, allows individual cases to be submitted to the Committee against enforced disappearance.

112. Urge the Executive, when declaring states of emergency, to do so in accordance with international law of human rights without suspending or limiting the rights considered non-derogable and without affecting the core of all human rights.

113. Urge the National Council of Social Rehabilitation to strengthen and promote in the different places of detention in the country actions about the respect of the rights of persons deprived of liberty, in accordance with the Standard of Minimum Rules for the Treatment of Prisoners of the United Nations, taking gender, sexual diversity and multiculturalism into account.

114. Require the Ministry of Economic and Social Inclusion and all State ministries and secretariats to incorporate human rights, gender and

multiculturalism as cross-cutting themes in the generation of public policies and the implementation of programs and projects with groups in particular situations of discrimination and inequity: women, children, adolescents, indigenous people, Afro-Ecuadorian and *Montubios*, people with disabilities, senior citizens, people with other sexual identities, people living with HIV, exiles, displaced persons and refugees, persons deprived of liberty, migrant workers, people living in poverty and extreme poverty, among others.

115. Include in both the National Development Plan and in the reformulation of the National Human Rights Plan a transversal approach to the human rights of nationalities, indigenous peoples, Afro-Ecuadorians and *Montubios*, to generate or formulate public policies that favor these peoples, recognized as collective subjects.
116. Fulfil the right to consent and to prior consultation of indigenous and tribal peoples on projects and policies that affect them, in accordance with the Convention 169 of the International Labour Organization and the Declaration of the United Nations on the rights of indigenous peoples.
117. Ensure that same-sex couples are beneficiaries of all remedies under the same conditions as heterosexual couples.
118. Incorporate public policies that favor non-discrimination based on sexual orientation and gender identity incorporating the active participation of civil society organizations in their formulation.
119. To urge the Public Defender Office to elaborate:
    1. annually, a report on the situation of human rights in Ecuador in which specific recommendations to overcome the problems and identified obstacles are made;
    2. periodically, reports on the situation of human rights of different peoples and nationalities in Ecuador such as indigenous peoples, Afro-Ecuadorians and *Montubios*, including an analysis of the human rights violations perpetrated in the past;
    3. current and periodic reports on the situation of human rights of persons deprived of liberty, including recommendations and a work plan to improve respect and guarantee their rights.
120. Urge the Ministry of Justice and Human Rights to issue a decree on the prevention and punishment of torture, in which the prohibition of any interrogation technique amounting to torture and other cruel, inhuman or degrading punishment is underlined.
121. Create within the Human Rights Department of the Ministry of Justice and Human Rights a National Observatory of Human Rights Violations involving victims' organizations and non-governmental organizations, which serve both to monitor the human rights situation and to formulate public policies on the matter.

122. Order the Ministry of Justice and Human Rights to design a system of public recognition of the good practices for respect and guarantee of human rights of the entities and organizations that respect, protect, promote and fulfil human rights.
123. Request the government to submit to the National Assembly draft legislation aimed at approving the following treaties on human rights and humanitarian law:
    1. Convention on the Prohibition of using environmental modification techniques for military or other hostile ends of 1976.
    2. Additional Protocol to the Geneva Conventions of August 12, 1949, concerning the adoption of an additional distinctive emblem, Protocol III of 2005.
    3. Optional Protocol to the International Covenant on Economic, Social and Cultural Rights of 2008.
124. Regulate the enforcement action provided in Article 93 of the Constitution of the Republic to ensure compliance with judgments, rulings, decisions and reports of agencies and the Inter-American system of universal human rights, related in recommendations 106 and 107.
125. Support the definition of crimes of aggression, genocide, crimes against humanity and against persons and property protected by international humanitarian law in internal and international armed conflicts, as well as the forced disappearance and torture, stated in the criminal guarantees bill. Urge the National Assembly for their total approval, in accordance with their definition in international law of human rights.
126. Criminalize the use, trade and production of equipment specifically designed to inflict torture or other cruel, inhuman or degrading treatment, and implement monitoring mechanisms for proper compliance by the Office of the Public Defender and the Ministry of Justice and Human Rights.
127. To incorporate in the law of criminal guarantees the applicability of the action and punishment not only for the crimes of genocide, war crimes against humanity, enforced disappearance and aggression stated in Article 80 of the Constitution of the Republic, but for all serious human rights violations and breaches of humanitarian law.
128. Create specialized units of prosecutors and judiciary that have permanent and exclusive powers to investigate and prosecute crimes that constitute human rights violations and crimes of aggression, genocide, crimes against humanity and against persons and property protected by international humanitarian law.
129. Promote a reform of criminal procedures in which the victim is an active part in criminal proceedings, including simple and expeditious mechanisms that allow them to get comprehensive reparation and apply protective measures in case they are required.

130. Support mechanisms for judicial cooperation with the International Criminal Court included in the bill of penal guarantees.
131. Create by law the independent national mechanisms that are necessary for the prevention of torture at national level, as mandated by the Optional Protocol to the Convention against Torture of 2002.
132. Reform civil code in order to introduce the status of permanent absence in cases of forced disappearance with the same effects of the alleged death.
133. Promote a penal reform in which an adequate and complete definition of crimes of sexual violence and other gender-based crimes is made, incorporating rape, other abusive sexual acts, sexual slavery and forced prostitution, forced pregnancy, forced sterilizations, forced nudity, sexual mutilation, forced marriage or cohabitation, servitude or domestic slavery, persecution based on gender, sexual harassment, trafficking for sexual exploitation and other behaviors of comparable gravity.
134. Reform the criminal procedure law to align with the Statute of the International Criminal Court, its rules of procedure and evidence and the definition of the crimes listed there under the elements of the crime.
135. Reform the criminal procedural law to incorporate measures to ensure the confidentiality of the proceedings – in cases of sexual violence and crimes affecting children and adolescents – and measures to avoid confrontation of victims of sexual crimes with their assailant, for which it is recommended the use of mechanisms such as evidence given behind closed doors, pre-recorded testimonies or through a Gesell chamber.
136. Incorporate in criminal legislation the possibility for psychological expertise to be accepted as evidence in cases of sexual violence and other evidentiary standards stated in the Istanbul Protocol in reference to torture.
137. Decriminalize abortion in cases where the pregnancy is the result of sexual violence, when the life or health of the woman is in danger or when there is severe fetal malformation incompatible with life outside the womb.
138. Reform the civil registration law to allow the restoration of the full names of people who were registered at birth with other names that do not correspond to their natural parents, and filiation, namely, the rights and obligations of persons concerned, since for reasons of political persecution or human rights violations the registration was made with the name of another person.
139. Regulate the right of repetition enshrined in the Political Constitution against the persons responsible for the damage produced, in which the persons convicted in national and international judgments of cases of human rights violations are considered responsible. In this sense, the action of repetition regulated in the bill of jurisdictional guarantees and constitutional control is supported.

140. State by law the impediment, to any person who has been convicted for committing human rights violations in national or international rulings, to be a candidate for public office and to hold public office.
141. Reform laws and regulations at the level of the Armed Forces and the National Police so that any distinction or honorary position that has been granted is removed, and that internal administrative processes are initiated from the conclusions of the Report of the Commission, so those accountable for human rights violations are dismissed.
142. Modify the Public Safety Act to include measures that enable the declassification of official documents and the opening of public archives that allow the clarification of human rights violations.
143. Incorporate into the public and the State safety bill the limits of states of emergency, based on Articles 164 through 166 of the Constitution and on international law of human rights.
144. Approve a new Organic Law of the Office of the Public Defender under the Constitution of the Republic, international law of human rights and the principles of Paris.
145. Create by law a system of legal medicine and forensic science attached to the State Attorney General Office.
146. To reform the judiciary police to place it under the authority of the Attorney General office regarding matters of discipline. In cases which involve members of the National Police, the investigation will be conducted by an independent body attached to the prosecution.
147. Ensure that in the reformatory laws of the Criminal Code and Code of Criminal Procedure, it is stated that any violation of human rights must be investigated and judged in accordance with the common Penal Code, regardless of who the alleged offender is.
148. Report by law that mediation should become a stage in legal proceedings with the exceptions established by other laws according to the subject matter.
149. Regulate the right to strike guaranteed in the Constitution according to the standards of international law of human rights, particularly based on the doctrine of the International Labour Organization. Also, regulate the right to resist stated in Article 98 of the Constitution, and anticipate that this right can be exercised via provincial, regional or national strikes by workers and communities, peoples and nationalities.
150. Reform the Law of Education for Democracy with the purpose of including an obligatory subject of human rights in elementary school and high school.
151. Develop constitutional norms through laws and regulations that establish non-discrimination based on sexual orientation and gender identity and ensure the participation of LGBTI people and women in the Equality Councils.

152. Implement, based on the constitutional framework and international law, the content of the Declaration on the Rights of Indigenous Peoples of 2007, in order to strengthen the protection of the rights of indigenous peoples. Regulate, with the participation of different nationalities and indigenous peoples, rights to free, prior and informed consent, and consultation and cooperation. Promote reforms aimed at protecting indigenous self-government, land and water and environmental resources of these peoples, food sovereignty, and participation, among others.
153. Push a bill to officially create indigenous justice in accordance with the principles established in the Constitution, the Organic Code of the Judiciary, with the participation and decision of different peoples.

Administrative Reparations Plan

154. In order to guarantee the right of victims to effective, prompt and adequate reparation it is recommended to establish an administrative reparations program, operating in administration offices (or agencies) and government channels, and responsible for the implementation of remedial measures recommended by the Truth Commission, including restitution, compensation, satisfaction and guarantees of non-repetition.
155. The reparations program by administrative means, should be responsible for comprehensively compensating the victims of the events that occurred between October 4, 1983 and December 31, 2008. It is also recommended that the program processes applications for the recognition of victims who did not submit their case to the Truth Commission, as well as those cases in which the Truth Commission could not come to the conviction that the violation occurred or that it was the direct responsibility of the State.

PERU'S TRUTH AND RECONCILIATION COMMISSION

Recommending a Piecemeal Approach to Transitional Justice

Félix Reátegui Carrillo and Diego Uchuypoma*

* The authors are affiliated with IDEHPUCP – Instituto de Democracia y Derechos Humanos PUCP in Lima, Peru. The authors are thankful to Diego Uchuypoma and Augusto Rosas for providing valuable research assistance. The authors also wish to thank Rebecca Root and Onur Bakiner for valuable comments on earlier drafts.

1. INTRODUCTION

In 2000, a transition to democracy started in Peru after Alberto Fujimori's regime collapsed under serious accusations of corruption. Fujimori had ruled the country since he was democratically elected in 1990. His regime turned authoritarian in April 1992, when he staged a *coup d'état*, closing down the Parliament and the Judicial Branch. In that same year, the founder and leader of the Shining Path (*Sendero Luminoso*) was captured by the police, enabling Fujimori to neutralize the illegal armed organization which had launched a communist revolutionary war with terrorist methods in 1980. The success in defeating the Shining Path and a strong Peruvian economy driven by economic liberalization allowed him to enjoy strong public support despite the widespread human rights abuses and authoritarian ways that characterized his administration. When the transition began at the turn of the millennium and democratic forces reasserted themselves, the government decided to establish an independent investigative body to address the demands for truth and justice that victims and human rights organizations had been making, without success, since the early 1980s (Root 2012, 52–53).

The creation of an investigative body to document the abuses carried out during the period of violence was a key element of the Peruvian transitional context. This decision was made possible, in part, due to the fact that the Peruvian transition was not a negotiated process. As Eduardo Gonzalez (2006, 74) points out, "Peru's transition would not be the result of a negotiated arrangement, like the Spanish or the Chilean transitions that were the paradigm for many Peruvian democratic politicians". The Fujimori regime had crumbled under a stream of revelations of corruption; the military lost legitimacy due to its subordination to Fujimori's collaborator, Vladimiro Montesinos. At the same time, the Shining Path no longer presented an armed challenge to the State. As a result, the Peruvian transition did not need peace negotiations and the inevitable compromises implied in such political processes (Gonzalez 2006).

This situation permitted the government to make some important decisions. One was to shed light on past human rights abuses committed not only by the Shining Path but also by the military and the police. Second, prior to the decision to create the truth commission, was the return in 2001 to the Inter-American system of human rights (Root 2012, 69).[1] According to Rebecca Root these were "(t)he first crucial steps toward a comprehensive transitional justice process" (Root 2012, 69). According to the same author, other key steps were "an end to amnesties, new civilian trials for alleged terrorists, a truth commission, plans for wide-reaching reforms, and prosecutions of those accused of grievous crimes" (Root 2012, 69). However, it does not appear that there was a comprehensive

[1] Peru withdrew from the Inter-American system of human rights in July 1999. See http://www.corteidh.or.cr/tablas/R06838-3.pdf.

transitional justice strategy. Leaving aside the truth commission, no other decision was taken at that moment regarding the creation of other extraordinary mechanisms for accountability, such as special jurisdiction for certain kinds of crimes or sweeping institutional reforms. Moreover, one important decision dealing both with peace-building and with transitional justice was neglected: a demobilization strategy. According to Jemima García-Godos (2016, 234),

> (i)n terms of transitional justice, the Repentance Law (...) is possibly the closest one gets to a state-sponsored demobilisation process in Peru. The law was effective until November 1994, and the number of people registered as *arrepentidos* (repentant) reached several thousand.

Basically, the Repentance Law allowed members of the illegal armed organizations to go free after surrendering their weapons and providing information about other cadres.

The Peruvian Truth and Reconciliation Commission (*Comisión de la Verdad y Reconciliación*, CVR) conducted an investigation into the violence that had taken place in Peru during the period 1980–2000. The investigation focused on the human rights violations committed by two armed organizations – the Shining Path and the Tupac Amaru Revolutionary Movement – and by the State security forces, including armed civilian patrols supported by the military. As a result of its investigations, the CVR concluded that crimes against humanity had been committed by both the illegal armed organizations and by the State. It asserted that almost 70,000 people had been killed or disappeared during the conflict.

As part of its mandate, the CVR assessed the factors underlying violence, human rights abuses, and impunity, and the consequences of the abuses for the victims. This information led to the formulation of a wide-ranging set of 84 recommendations designed to overcome the legacy of violence in Peru. These recommendations included measures of reparation for the victims and institutional reform intended to ensure non-repetition and to build upon the lessons learned in order to strengthen Peruvian democracy.

In this chapter, we document the types of recommendations made by the CVR and provide an analysis of their implementation record. This chapter is divided into six sections. Following this brief introduction, the next part provides a short description of the historical background of conflict and transition in Peru. The third section gives a short description of the Truth and Reconciliation Commission. In the fourth section, we describe the different types of recommendations (the full list of recommendations is presented in an annex), also commenting on how these recommendations were elaborated and formulated. In the fifth section, we analyze the implementation of the recommendations before we present some conclusions in the final section of the chapter.

The main point we wish to make is that, in the 16 years that have elapsed since the CVR issued its final report in August 2003, the Peruvian State has achieved a mixed record in terms of implementing the recommendations made by the CVR. Positive achievements include the national reparations program created in 2004, following the proposal made by the Commission. In addition, some State agencies have made valuable efforts to include elements of human rights in their design. Institutional reforms, by contrast, have been limited.

2. HISTORICAL BACKGROUND

The political transition that led to Peru's transitional justice process started in 2001, when the administration of Alberto Fujimori (1990–2001) collapsed under serious charges of corruption. This political transition overlapped with an older war-to-peace transition. In 1980, the Maoist Shining Path launched a revolutionary war against the Peruvian State and society. After a special branch of the Peruvian police arrested its founder and leader, Abimael Guzmán, in September 1992, the Shining Path was defeated over the next several months. Nevertheless, violence associated with the internal armed conflict continued during the Fujimori administration, mainly in the form of political repression of opponents whom the government portrayed as so-called "fellow-travellers of terrorism". Thus, the Peruvian transition should be understood as (i) a transition from armed violence to peace, and (ii) a transition from authoritarianism to democracy. Even though violence and authoritarianism were conflated processes during the 1990s, we will consider them separately in order to clarify the dilemmas faced by the government as the transitional process started in 2001.

In 1980, Peru's democracy was restored after 12 years of military rule. The "Revolutionary Government of the Armed Forces" (*Gobierno Revolucionario de la Fuerza Armada*, 1968–1980) was a leftist authoritarian regime that had sought to impose a wide range of social reforms inspired by socialism and nationalism, designed to dismantle the oligarchy that had ruled Peru since its inception as an independent Republic. One of the most substantial transformations was a sweeping land reform program, the likes of which had been proposed by different political groups since the 1930s. Peruvian historians and social scientists agree that this measure put an end to the remnants of the oligarchic regime and brought about many political and economic changes with important consequences for rural Peruvian society.

The Shining Path started its armed insurrection on May 17, 1980, the same day that Peruvians voted to elect a new President and restore democracy. The Shining Path was a radical offspring of the left-wing movement that had existed in Peru since the early 1930s. By 1980, almost all political parties that comprised the Peruvian left had decided to take part in democratic and legal political life.

The Shining Path, by contrast, chose to stay apart from this democratization process and instead start a revolutionary war.

From the beginning, the period of armed struggle initiated by the Shining Path was characterized by brutal violence against the civilian population. The Shining Path engaged in acts of terrorism and massacres with an aim to prevent the rural population from collaborating with State forces. At the same time, the Shining Path carried out assassinations against police and military officers. Over time, terrorism and different types of crimes against international law were extended to the largest cities and to the Amazonian territory, where, among other things, the Shining Path held captive the Ashaninka people. The State's response to Shining Path violence was almost equally ruthless. After the State briefly tried to confront the Shining Path through policing, it quickly resorted to a full-fledged military response. In this context, State crimes against civilians became increasingly frequent in rural and urban areas. Forced disappearance, sexual violence, and arbitrary detention were some of the most common abuses by the State.

During the 1980s, widespread violence and a deep economic crisis took its toll on the country. Unable to consolidate itself after its rebirth in the wake of the military dictatorship of the 1970s, the party system was discredited and gave way to the "independents". Alberto Fujimori was elected in April 1990 (beating the favorite, Mario Vargas Llosa, a world-class writer supported by two of the main traditional right-wing parties). Fujimori started his term in a period of acute social distress and deep mistrust of the *partidocracia* (the traditional political parties). This situation permitted Fujimori to stage a *coup d'état* (misleadingly often referred to as *auto-golpe* or "self-coup") against the Legislative and Judicial Branches of government in 1992. The subsequent capture of Abimael Guzmán and the rapid defeat of the Shining Path strengthened the regime's prestige and allowed it to stay in power until 2000 through winning local and national elections. Fujimori's success was principally due to his tremendous popularity, but he also profited from the control of State resources used to gain advantage during electoral campaigns. During the 1990s, Fujimori's regime continued to commit serious human rights abuses such as forced disappearance and arbitrary incarceration. The use of "invisible judges", for example, led to the incarceration of thousands of innocent people. The creation of a death squad (*Grupo Colina*) and the unchecked actions of the President's aide Vladimiro Montesinos compounded the human rights situation during this period. Moreover, widespread corruption persisted, including bribing TV stations and newspapers to use them as political tools against the opposition. Nonetheless, the public exposure of corruption finally brought about the collapse of the regime. Fujimori resigned the Presidency while attending an international summit. However, his resignation was not accepted by Congress, which removed him from office on the grounds of "moral incapacity" to be President and a transitional government was appointed for eight months. The President of Congress, Valentín Paniagua, assumed the Presidency with the task of restoring the rule of law and organizing new elections.

As a result, by the year 2000, when democracy was restored, a large number of human rights violations and other international crimes had accumulated without receiving a proper response from the State. Victims' demands for truth and justice had been ignored for the most part, both by the judiciary and by the government. Even though the government severely punished the Shining Path, this pursuit of justice was not associated with providing answers to victims.

Thus, as the recovery of the rule of law was taking place and extraordinary mechanisms were being established to cope with Fujimori's legacy of corruption, human rights also became an important part of the transitional agenda. Human rights organizations, victims' groups, and the international community pushed for the creation of transitional justice mechanisms to give a swift and proper response to victims' demands. In this context, the new government decided to create a truth commission following the example of Argentina, Chile, Guatemala, and El Salvador.

3. THE PERUVIAN TRUTH AND RECONCILIATION COMMISSION (CVR)

The Truth and Reconciliation Commission of Peru was created in the context of this political transition. Since the early 1980s, civil society organizations, such as human rights NGOs and victims' groups had been demanding a response to the thousands of human rights violations committed (Hayner 2011). When the transition took place, these organizations found the opportunity to place this issue on the agenda, with the support of the international community, chiefly the United States Embassy and the European Union. However, this did not mean that there was a strong commitment from the State to public exposure of truth and its consequences (Gianella Malca 2015).

The interim government of Valentín Paniagua created the Truth Commission in June 2001, by Supreme Decree 065-2001-PCM. In July, newly elected President Alejandro Toledo confirmed the creation of the truth-seeking body with two modifications. First, the number of commissioners was increased from seven to 12 plus a Presidential observer. Second, the body's name was changed to Truth and Reconciliation Commission – adding the word "reconciliation" (Root 2012). The CVR's mandate, unchanged by Toledo, was broad. The CVR was charged with performing the following tasks:

a) To analyze the political, social and cultural conditions, as well as the behaviors, of society and State institutions, that contributed to the tragic situation of violence through which Peru has passed;

b) To contribute, when appropriate, to the justice system's clarification of the crimes and violations of human rights committed by terrorist organizations or State agents, seeking to determine the whereabouts and situation of the victims and identifying, to the extent possible, those who were allegedly responsible;
c) To draw up proposals for reparation and dignification of the victims and their family members;
d) To recommend institutional, legal, educational and other reforms, as preventive guarantees, so that these may be processed and attended to through legislative, political or administrative initiatives; and
e) To establish mechanisms to follow up on its recommendations (CVR 2003).

The mandate ordered the Commission to address the crimes "imputable to terrorist organizations, State agents or paramilitary groups" and presented an open-ended list of the crimes to be investigated. The list included murders and abductions, forced disappearances, torture and other serious injuries, violations of the collective rights of the country's Andean and native communities, and other crimes and serious violations of the rights of individuals.

The CVR did not receive any judicial powers in order to fulfil its mission. Nonetheless, it was granted some resources with which to interview functionaries and public servants, to request the cooperation of State agents, to carry out visits and inspections of relevant facilities, to hold public hearings, and to adopt security measures for the protection of persons relevant for its investigation.

Table 1. Composition of the Peruvian *Comisión de la Verdad y Reconciliación* (CVR)

Function	Commissioner	Background
President	**Salomón Lerner Febres (M)**	Philosopher. Rector of the Pontificia Universidad Católica del Perú.
Member	Sofía Macher Batanero (F)	Sociologist. Human rights activist. Former executive secretary of the *Coordinadora Nacional de Derechos Humanos.*
Member	Carlos Iván Degregori (M)	Anthropologist. Former director of the *Instituto de Estudios Peruanos.*
Member	Carlos Tapia García (M)	Agronomist engineer. Former congressman from *Izquierda Unida.*
Member	Rolando Ames Cobián (M)	Political scientist. Professor at the *Pontificia Universidad Católica del Perú.* Former senator from *Izquierda Unida.*
Member	Enrique Bernales Ballesteros (M)	Constitutionalist. Former senator from *Izquierda Unida.* Former Special Rapporteur to the United Nations Human Rights Commission.

(continued)

Table 1 *continued*

Function	Commissioner	Background
Member	Beatriz Alva Hart (F)	Lawyer. Former deputy minister of Labor during the Fujimori administration and congresswoman from the Fujimori organization.
Member	Monseñor José Antúnez de Mayolo (M)	Former apostolic administrator of the Archdiocese of Ayacucho during the period 1959–61. Member of the Salesian community.
Member	Inspector General (retired) Luis Arias Graziani (M)	Former Inspector General of the Air Force; chief of the Major Estate; general of the FAP (Peruvian Air Force) and President of the Joint Command of the Armed Forces and Minister of the Air Force.
Member	Padre Gastón Garatea Yori (M)	Member of the *Congregación de los Sagrados Corazones*. Former prelate of Ayaviri (Puno). Former *Padre Provincial de los Sagrados Corazones.*
Member	Pastor Humberto Lay Sun (M)	Architect. Member of the *Grupo de Iniciativa Nacional Anticorrupción*; of the *Junta Nacional de la Alianza Cristiana y Misionera.*
Member	Alberto Morote Sánchez (M)	Chemical engineer. Former dean of the *Filial Departamental de Ayacucho del Colegio de Ingenieros del Perú* and technical advisor to the *Instituto Nacional de Desarrollo de Comunidades Campesinas y Nativas*. Professor, deputy administrative rector, and former Rector of the *Universidad Nacional de San Cristóbal de Huamanga.*
Presidential Observer	Monseñor Luis Bambarén Gastelumendi S.J. (M)	Jesuit Priest. Former Prefect of the *Colegio Inmaculada* in Lima and Rector of the *Colegio San Ignacio de Piura*. Former Auxiliary Bishop of Lima, vice-president of Caritas Internationalis and vice-president of the United Nations Convention of the Child. Former bishop of Chimbote, Secretary General of the *Conferencia Episcopal Peruana* and former President of the *Conferencia Episcopal Peruana.*

Source: Truth and Reconciliation Commission of Peru website: http://www.cverdad.org.pe/lacomision/nlabor/comisionado13.php.
Note: M=male, F=female.

The 12 commissioners, two women and 10 men, were appointed by the President and were not selected as representatives of any particular group or organization (see Table 1). Rather, they were appointed as individuals who had a sound moral standing in Peruvian society. The President of the Commission was Dr. Salomón Lerner Febres, a philosopher who was Rector of the Pontifical Catholic University of Peru at the time of his appointment (Root 2012). The CVR made its most important strategic and political decisions through its Assembly of Commissioners, presided over by the Commission's Chairman. Its operations were managed by an Executive Director.

The CVR was established for a working period of 18 months, which could be extended for five additional months. In the end, the Commission's operation took 26 months, ending in August 2003. During its inception phase, the Commission adopted a decentralized organization. To cover the territory affected by violence, it established five regional offices in addition to its headquarters in Lima. Another goal of this organization was to build trust with victims and to efficiently collect their testimony.

The CVR operations were funded by several sources. A large part of the Commission's budget came from public resources, particularly from funds recovered from the money illegally obtained through corruption under Fujimori's regime. The CVR approached representatives of the international community who had supported human rights organizations during the Fujimori regime and who had been supportive of the democratic transition. One key actor was the office of the United Nations Development Program (UNDP) in Peru, which served as an intermediary between the Commission and other potential international collaborators. The CVR developed a strategic plan, which it presented to the international community. As a result, an important part of the budget was funded by international cooperation, mainly from the European Union (EU), United States Agency for International Development (USAID), and UNDP.

The strategic planning of the Commission was multifaceted. It included the organization of statement-taking operations. In addition, legal studies were conducted to assess patterns of criminality and to investigate specific cases of human rights violations. Furthermore, the CVR instigated social science investigations into the historical and cultural context of violence and the political and institutional factors underlying the violence and human rights violations. Regional offices also conducted investigations into local histories of violence. Moreover, the Commission organized psycho-social work to provide support to victims and to assess the mental-health-related consequences of violence. Finally, the Commission established a Gender Unit, which sought to streamline the gender approach in the other CVR units.

In addition to the investigative units, the CVR established a strong outreach unit in charge of (i) reaching out to victims' groups; (ii) managing communications with the press and stakeholders; and (iii) managing relations with civil society organizations relevant to the investigations.

During its work, hearing testimonies became the most important task. The CVR was able to collect 16,985 testimonies from victims and their relatives over a period of approximately 12 months. This information was registered and analyzed in a database that allowed the Commission to produce information about the demographics of victimhood during the period. The Commission received reports of 24,000 deaths and disappearances and estimated that the most likely total number of victims was 69,280 (CVR 2004, 16). This information also permitted the CVR to identify patterns of victimhood. One of the most striking findings was that 75 per cent of the victims had been people of indigenous descent (*Quechua, Aimara, Ashaninka*). This overrepresentation of indigenous victims combined with qualitative research led the Commission to highlight the role of racism during the period of violence. Regarding the responsibilities of armed actors, the CVR established that the Shining Path bore the largest responsibility: 54 per cent of casualties reported to the Commission were attributed to the Shining Path, while 38 per cent were caused by State security forces (i.e. police and military).

Legal studies allowed the CVR to establish broader patterns of violations. The CVR established that both non-State (terrorist organizations) and State (police, military) had engaged in crimes against humanity. The Commission established the prevalence of nine other types of human rights abuses: assassinations and massacres; arbitrary executions; forced disappearance; torture and ill-treatment; violence against children; sexual violence against women; violations of due process rules; kidnapping and hostage-taking; and violations of collective rights.

The CVR's Final Report, released on August 28, 2003, was presented to the President of the Republic and to the Presidents of the Congress and the Judiciary. It also was presented to the Peruvian public in Ayacucho on August 29. The Final Report comprises nine volumes plus 12 annexes. The CVR also produced an abbreviated version of the Report in one volume (*Hatun Willakuy*) and shorter versions for dissemination in three different languages. The Report describes the context of violence, the behavior of the armed actors during the period, the role played by several State institutions or systems (such as the Judiciary, the Congress, and the education system) and by social actors (such as the Catholic and Evangelical churches), and the patterns of criminal behavior. It also presents the history of violence in each region and reconstructs emblematic cases from both an ethnographic and forensic perspective. The report also contains an assessment of the consequences of violence and the recommendations for justice, reparations, and non-recurrence.

The CVR made 1000 copies of the complete Final Report in Spanish, which were distributed among authorities and public institutions such as ministries, agencies of the justice system, members of Parliament, public libraries, public and private universities, and regional authorities. Furthermore, 20,000 copies of a *quechua* language translation of *Hatun Willakuy* (roughly translated as "the grand story" in *quechua*) were distributed in 2004. The CVR also distributed short explanations of its final report in journal articles and made other versions in local indigenous languages, *quechua* and *ashaninka* in particular.

The Final Report was well received by the government, Congress, and the judiciary. They all professed at least some formal commitment to enact the report's recommendations. Victims also expressed acceptance of the report. However, political controversy soon emerged regarding the statistics presented by the Commission. Right-wing politicians accused the Commission of deliberately exaggerating the number of victims to accentuate the responsibility of the State. Nevertheless, the general atmosphere in this initial period, as reflected in the press, was that of acceptance and positive reception of the report as an invitation to critical reflection on the nation's historical debts towards marginalized communities (Barrantes and Peña 2006).

In the following years, though, the situation changed and criticism of the Commission (indeed, against the whole idea of truth and memory) grew louder among politicians and different sectors of society. Nevertheless, victims, academics, artists, and NGOs continue to consider the Final Report as the cornerstone for memory and democratization. Struggles over memory are a visible aspect of political debate today, 16 years after the Final Report was released.

4. RECOMMENDATIONS MADE BY THE CVR

The 84 recommendations made by the Truth and Reconciliation Commission appear in the ninth and last volume of the Final Report. Their presence was a result of the stipulation in its mandate (Supreme Decree N° 065-2001-PCM) that asked the Commission to "make proposals for the reparation and dignification of the victims and their relatives"; to "recommend institutional, legal, educational and other types of reforms as a means to prevent recurrence and to be processed and addressed through legislative, political or administrative initiatives"; and to "establish mechanisms to follow-up on its recommendations" (article 2). Accordingly, the chapter of recommendations (volume VIII, chapter 2) is organized in four sections: institutional reforms, a comprehensive reparations plan, a national forensic-anthropologic investigations plan, and follow-up mechanisms. We discuss each group of recommendations in turn.

4.1. INSTITUTIONAL REFORMS

The recommendations on institutional reform rest on the assumption that, to overcome the legacy of armed violence, it is necessary to transform the relationship between State and society. This means that these recommendations are oriented towards addressing the root causes of the conflict and of human rights violations. It also reflected the Commission's approach to reconciliation, which it saw as a societal process rather than an individual one. Therefore, for the CVR, institutional reform amounted to a concrete manifestation of a reconciliation process.

The institutional reform proposals were broad and varied, and can be grouped into four general areas: measures to develop democratic authority and public services uniformly across the country in a way that respects social diversity; building democratic accountability in the military and security services; strengthening the administration of justice and the protection of citizens' rights and the constitutional order; and transforming the educational system in order to promote democratic values. This classification arose from the CVR's interpretation regarding the historical factors leading to violence and also to the contemporary conditions that had permitted human rights violations and impunity. Its legal mandate asked the Commission to produce an explanation of the process of violence and to conduct an evaluation of the role of the main armed actors. The commissioners paid special attention to understanding the institutional and cultural framework underlying the process of violence. The most general institutional factor was the absence of State authority in whole areas of Peru, whereas elsewhere the State's presence was highly authoritarian. That is why the Commission considers establishing democratic authority a priority. Recommendations related to institutional reform can also be seen as non-recurrence measures. The police and the military must be able to effectively maintain social order and security, but they must do so while respecting human rights. Justice administration is another important institutional factor. Educational reforms are meant to address historical aspects of violence, namely the lack of engaged citizenship and democratic values. It is important to add that, according to the CVR and to scholarly research, the Shining Path was able to expand across the country, using the collapsed school system to recruit among schoolteachers and students, mostly in rural areas (Degregori 2016).

The institutional reform proposals were elaborated in two stages. First, the commissioners asked one commissioner, Enrique Bernales, to take the lead. Commissioner Bernales assembled a group of experts who produced several thematic papers. These papers were then discussed in a plenary session, which decided that the proposals should be more specifically linked to the Commission's findings and its interpretation of the process. Therefore, the proposals were referred to another commissioner, Rolando Ames, who worked together with a political scientist, Martín Tanaka. This revised set of proposals was then discussed and approved by the commissioners and incorporated into the Final Report. While no specific public consultations on institutional reform were conducted as the proposals were being formulated, the general approach to institutional reform, and to the recommendations more broadly, was influenced by consultations by the CVR team in charge of proposing a general approach to reconciliation.

The recommendations related to ensuring the presence of democratic authority across the territory contained specific proposals dealing with, among other things, strengthening collaboration between the police and local authorities; strengthening and regulating civilian self-defense organizations; strengthening the role of local judges (these are authorities who administer justice, but do not have professional legal training); establishing special units within the police, the judiciary and the Public Ministry in charge of protecting human rights; and creating a public institution at the national level to look after indigenous rights. All these recommendations aimed to transform the State, particularly those aspects of the State that interact with the citizens on a daily basis. The underlying assumption was that if the population has a concrete experience of the benefits of democracy, their loyalty to the system will increase and citizenship will be strengthened.

The second group of recommendations were related to the security sector. Among other things, recommendations contained proposals to rearrange the functions related to defense and the military so that all those issues fall under the Ministry of Defense; to develop a national security proposal that includes a strategy for national pacification; to cultivate a civilian elite specialized in security and defense; to ensure democratic control over the military intelligence services; to distinguish clearly between national defense and domestic order; to transform the education of the military; and to establish a new ethics code.

Problems in the administration of justice appear as a major factor explaining human rights violations during and after the period of armed violence. According to the Commission, impunity permitted State abuses to increase. At the same time, the weakness of tribunals and their difficulties in prosecuting and sentencing members of the Shining Path undermined the credibility of democratic institutions and legitimized authoritarian methods used by the State. To strengthen the justice system, the Commission recommended staffing courts with tenured judges (instead of interim ones). It advocated placing the military justice system under the authority of the Supreme Court. The CVR urged the State to establish an autonomous Victims and Witnesses Protection Program, and a special temporary system to prosecute human rights violations committed during the armed conflict. It also called upon the State to incorporate the international human rights instruments into the national legal framework. Further, it identified the importance of strengthening human rights knowledge among judges, attorneys and lawyers, including training in Human Rights Law, International Humanitarian Law and aspects of democratic culture. Lastly, the Commission recommended several reforms to the Penal Code and institutional changes in the prison system.

Finally, the CVR paid special attention to the educational system, in particular the school system. These recommendations were intended to ensure high-quality education that promotes democratic values, including respect for human rights and cultural diversity, and more sophisticated interpretations of the Peruvian social reality. The Commission emphasized that these reforms were particularly important for the rural areas, where the Shining Path had instrumentalized the schools for its revolutionary plans in the 1970s and 1980s. These recommendations were general, and often more focused on goals to be attained than in actions to be undertaken. For example, the first recommendation was to emphasize education policies aiming to transform the schools into places where the human condition of the students is respected and where the integral development of their identities is fostered. Other recommendations were to establish programs that prevent students from being attracted to violence and to change simplistic approaches to Peruvian history and reality; to promote respect for cultural diversity and to adapt the schools to the linguistic and ethnic diversity of the country; to reinforce participation and democratization in schools; to pay urgent attention to the most vulnerable population; and to redefine the contents and methods of education in order to meet the demands and opportunities of the labor market. Once again, the rural areas were regarded as a special problem. The Commission recommended restoring dignity and quality to the rural schools.

These recommendations were addressed to the government in general. The Commission did not identify particular agencies responsible for any specific set of recommendations. Some of them required action from the Congress, such as those regarding normative or legal reforms. Other recommendations required decisions from the Executive Branch, such as those related to introducing human rights as part of military education and those demanding changes in the school system. The beneficiaries of many recommendations were the general population and future generations, though, in some cases, the rural population were targeted in particular (CVR 2003, 220–246).

4.2. REPARATIONS

In its Final Report (volume IX, section 4), the Truth and Reconciliation Commission presented a proposal to establish a *Plan Integral de Reparaciones* (PIR). This comprehensive reparation plan contained six components: symbolic reparations; a health program; an education program; a citizens' rights restitution program; an economic reparations program; and collective reparations programs. This plan was conceived of as a means to "heal the wounds caused by violence, to prevent the repetition of the past and to create the conditions necessary for reconciliation" (CVR 2003, 146).

The elaboration of the comprehensive reparations proposal was the result of several activities conducted by the Commission. First, when taking testimony, victims were asked about what they expected in terms of reparation for the abuses suffered. This was an input to the unit in charge of reparations, which was established by the Plenary of Commissioners. Another source of information was the interviews and analysis of the Public Hearings conducted by the team in charge of elaborating a reconciliation proposal. This team found that among those harmed by the conflict, the notion of reparations was a key component for reconciliation (CVR 2003, 30–32). A third important source for the formulation of PIR was a document submitted to the CVR by the International Center for Transitional Justice (ICTJ), which explained the international standards for reparations and showed how these could be applied to the Peruvian situation. Finally, the Commission sustained ongoing conversations with victims' groups and with human rights NGOs. With these four main sources, the Reparations Unit elaborated the PIR, which was submitted to the Plenary and approved as a component of the Final Report.

The PIR explains the ethical and legal dimensions of reparations and emphasizes the legal obligation of the Peruvian State to provide reparations. It also explains the objectives to be accomplished by a reparations plan. The general objective is to "repair and compensate for the human rights violations as well as losses and social, moral and material harms suffered by the victims as a consequence of the internal armed conflict". This general objective is specified by the Commission in three separate objectives:

- To recognize the condition of victims of those who suffered the violation of their human rights during the internal armed conflict in order to restore their citizens' rights and to contribute to the reestablishment of civic trust and social solidarity.
- To contribute to the moral, mental and physical recovery of the victims who have survived the human rights violations (…) as well as the recovery of the relatives of those who died or were disappeared (…).
- To repair the social and economic harms to individuals, families and communities caused by the internal armed conflict (CVR 2003, 154–155).

The Commission defines the notions of "victim" and "beneficiary". Victims will be considered to be all those who suffered human rights violations as a result of the conflict. These violations include forced disappearance, kidnapping, arbitrary execution, forced displacement, arbitrary arrest and due process violations, forced recruitment, torture, sexual violence, injuries or death. The beneficiaries are all those who will receive any type of benefit, symbolic or material, individual or collective. The Commission establishes that the beneficiaries will be not only direct victims but also their relatives and members of collectives that have been severely harmed by violence. This last provision means that the beneficiaries can be individual as well as collective.

Before we describe the various components of the PIR, it is important to mention that, according to the Commission, the PIR should incorporate five cross-cutting perspectives: psycho-social, participative, intercultural, gender equality, and symbolic.

The first component of the PIR is the Symbolic Reparations Program, whose beneficiaries should be the victims of violations and violence whose dignity and rights were affected, and the citizens of the territories affected by the conflict. This component includes, first, public gestures such an official endorsement of the CVR's Final Report; apologies by the Presidents of the Executive; Legislative and Judicial Branches; letters to the victims; and public ceremonies dedicated to acknowledging the truth. Other symbolic reparations include acts of recognition; restoration of civic trust dedicated to innocent persons who suffered unjust imprisonment; recognition of social leaders and civilian authorities; recognition of members of the armed forces and the police; and recognition of the local governments. Another component recommended the creation of memorial sites. Yet another involved symbolic acts that the Commission believed would advance reconciliation, such as the closure of military facilities where human rights violations had occurred.

The second component of the PIR is the Health Program. Its purpose was to contribute to the mental and physical recovery of people affected by the conflict and to rebuild social support networks to ensure social and individual development. The beneficiaries would be individuals suffering from physical or mental illness, and affected communities. This program focused on training health care personnel; promoting recovery through community intervention (including rebuilding networks of communitarian support, recovering historical memory and the creation of instances or facilities for communitarian interaction); promoting recovery through clinical intervention; promoting access to health care services; and promoting preventive medicine.

Access to education is the third component of the comprehensive reparations plan. Violence prevented tens of thousands of Peruvians from attending school because they were either deserted by teachers, children and their families were displaced, or their families fell into extreme poverty when one or both parents were killed or disappeared. The beneficiaries of this program, according to the CVR, should be all those who had their studies interrupted, children of women who were raped, and people who were members of *rondas campesinas* (self-defense committees) when they were of school age. This program included eliminating fees in public schools and universities for beneficiaries; integral scholarships; and the creation of education programs for adults.

The fourth component of PIR is the program to restore citizens' rights. This program aimed to solve several problems emerging from the conflict. The first was the legal status of the victims of forced disappearance and their relatives. The second was the problem of people who had unjust arrest warrants against them for terrorism charges. The third problem was the lack of national identification and other documentation among people from territories where the public registries had been destroyed. To address these problems, the Commission proposed to regulate the situation of those with arrest warrants; to annul police, judicial, or penal records; and to address the problem of people without official documentation.

The fifth component of the reparations plan is the program for economic reparations. The objective of this program was to compensate for the material and moral harm suffered by victims. The commission established a list of beneficiaries: relatives of victims of death and disappearance; people suffering from (total or partial) permanent disability; innocent people who had been unjustly incarcerated; victims of sexual violation; and children of parents who had suffered sexual violence. The program included pensions and indemnification and economic reparations in the form of services such as access to jobs and housing.

Finally, the reparations plan included a collective reparation program, the beneficiaries of which would be the peasant communities; native communities and other populations affected by the conflict; and organized groups of non-returning displaced people, who would receive benefits in their new places of residence. Collective reparations also included strengthening local institutions, rebuilding infrastructure, rebuilding and extending public services (schools, health care facilities, communal facilities, electricity networks), and providing access to employment and sources of revenue.

4.3. THE NATIONAL FORENSIC ANTHROPOLOGY INVESTIGATIONS PLAN

During its operations, the CVR received reports of 4,644 clandestine burial sites (including individual graves and mass graves) and was able to confirm the information in 2,200 of those cases (CVR 2003, 211). The Commission's proposal intended to set the guidelines for a comprehensive plan to recover human remains through an adequate process, in a legal context respectful of human rights. The plan also aimed to identify the victims, to establish the facts surrounding the causes of death, and to identify alleged perpetrators. The proposal demanded the development of an adequate legal and institutional framework that should lead to the establishment of a National Commission for Persons Disappeared during the Internal Armed Conflict. It also described the basic stages to be contemplated by a national effort to recover and identify human remains: preliminary investigation and registration of burial sites; exhumations; analysis and identification of the victims.

4.4. FOLLOW-UP MECHANISM

The last and shortest section of recommendations deals with the follow-up mechanisms. The CVR recommended in the first place having a period for an orderly closing of technical as well as administrative operations. The second recommendation asked for the creation of an Inter-institutional Working Group, which would be in charge of producing a plan for the implementation of recommendations, identifying the agencies responsible for implementing each part of the recommendations. This group would also draft and propose legal norms necessary for addressing the recommendations. It further proposed a dissemination plan for the Final Report. Finally, the Commission proposed the establishment of a centralized unit in charge of the recommendations, which would be named the National Reconciliation Council. The Commission even presented, as part of this section of the Final Report, a draft bill for the creation of the proposed Council. The Commission carried out consultations with agencies of the Executive Branch, members of Parliament and representatives of civil society organizations as it drafted the legislation. The Commission emphasized that, in its view, the only way to secure an adequate approach to implementing the recommendations would be through a centralized unit created by law (CVR 2003, 278).

5. STATUS OF IMPLEMENTATION

The four types of recommendation mentioned above – institutional reform, reparations, forensic-anthropologic investigations, and follow-up mechanisms – were not addressed to specific institutions or State agencies. Rather, the CVR explicitly stated that its recommendations were addressed to "all the Peruvian population, starting with those holding public office" (CVR 2003).

Nevertheless, before describing the four types of recommendations, the CVR made some recommendations addressed to specific institutions. For instance, it recommended that, within a period of 30 days, the Public Ministry should start investigations into the criminal cases referred to it by the CVR. Before closing its operations, the CVR submitted 43 files containing documentation about human rights violations. During its work, the Commission had already submitted four cases (Defensoría del Pueblo 2004, 23). The Public Ministry responded by establishing a commission in charge of analyzing the information contained in each file during a period of 45 days. Three months later, the Public Ministry sent 40 cases to *Fiscales Provinciales* (regional attorneys) and three to the courts (Defensoría del Pueblo 2004, 23).

Another preliminary recommendation was for the Ombudsman Office to make available all the documentation obtained or produced by the CVR during its operations. The Ombudsman Office responded to this recommendation by establishing a documentation center where academic researchers and ordinary citizen can access the materials of the CVR (García-Godos 2016).

It is important to consider that some of the recommendations identified by the CVR overlapped with other reforms made by other State agencies in order to transform Peruvian society after the experience of authoritarianism under Fujimori. One of these efforts was the (still existing) *Consejo Nacional de Educación* (National Council for Education). Established in 2002 (parallel to the CVR), this Council received the mandate to elaborate a proposal for an integral transformation of the education system and to follow up on its implementation. The Council was ratified by a new *Ley General de Educación* (General Education Law), passed by Congress in 2003. The Council presented its proposal in 2007, under the name of *Proyecto Educativo Nacional* (National Educational Project).[2] Although the Project made no specific references to the CVR's Final Report, it shared the Commission's approach regarding the importance of education for democracy and human rights' protection, and its proposals about those issues were more specific from a pedagogical perspective (Consejo Nacional de Educación 2007). By 2017, the National Educational Project had been only partially implemented. However, its formulation as a national policy proposal after the Final Report illustrates the difficulties (and the necessity when examining implementation) to distinguish between reform initiatives undertaken as a response to the Commission's recommendation and those emerging from other initiatives.

The same could be said about the most serious attempt to reform the justice administration system. In effect, another important effort for institutional transformation was the Special Commission for Integral Reform of Justice Administration (CERIAJUS). The CERIAJUS was established by Congress in October 2003 (Law 28083), two months after the CVR's Final Report was delivered, but with no direct connection with it. The CERIAJUS received a mandate to elaborate and propose a comprehensive plan for justice reform (*Plan Integral de Reforma de la Justicia*). The CERIAJUS released its proposal in April 2004.[3] It is a massive and very detailed document, which is still considered by many experts as the most serious effort made in that field. However, the plan has not been implemented.

Another important aspect worth considering when evaluating the status of implementation is the process of decentralization. Many efforts have been made since the end of the last military dictatorship (1968–1980) to correct the extreme centralization of Peruvian political and economic life. Currently, these efforts have led to a structure of 25 regional governments. Leaving aside the discussion of the merits and flaws of this model, each of these governments has authority and responsibility to implement the recommendations. Therefore, implementation varies across the country. For example, even though the Ministry of Education is considered the highest authority in the educational sector, educational policies are decentralized. Each region has its own *Dirección Regional de Educación* (Regional Education Directorate, DRE) elaborating its own educational policy. Even though they follow the general guidelines elaborated by the Ministry of Education, they have relative autonomy.

Regarding the implementation of the recommendations, the State arguably gave an early promising response, even if the Executive Branch, under President

2 http://www.cne.gob.pe/somos/.
3 http://www4.congreso.gob.pe/comisiones/2004/ceriajus/Plan_Nacional_ceriajus.pdf.

Toledo, was not fully engaged in the task at hand. In effect, in his first official response to the Final Report and its recommendations, President Toledo proposed to include the reparations agenda as part of the government's policy for the development of impoverished territories (Laplante and Theidon 2007). This proposal was criticized by several actors who felt that such an approach neglected the particular rights of the victims of human rights violations. The proposal was not mentioned again or revisited by the President (which illustrates in an oblique way the scant attention paid by the Presidency to the recommendations).

However, two important decisions were made. First, in February 2004, the government approved Supreme Decree 011-2004-JUS, which created the *Comisión Multisectorial de Alto Nivel Encargada del Seguimiento de las Acciones y Políticas del Estado en los Ámbitos de la Paz, la Reparación Colectiva y la Reconciliación Nacional* (High-Level Multisectorial Commission, CMAN). It is charged with following up on public policies regarding peace, collective reparations, and national reconciliation. This special body appears as an agency in charge of overseeing the implementation of the recommendations, although it is different from the centralized and highly empowered agency envisioned by the Commission in its recommendations. For example, CMAN is in charge of only collective reparations, as opposed to individual economic reparations, and it is not involved in fulfilling, facilitating, coordinating, proposing, or overseeing institutional reform.

The second important legislative decision came in July 2005, when Congress approved the law creating the PIR (Ley 28592) (APRODEH-ICTJ 2008).

However, soon after this promising start, the momentum to implement the recommendations weakened. The Reparations policy, notwithstanding its insufficiencies, remains to this day the clearest response from the State to the recommendations.

5.1. INSTITUTIONAL REFORMS

The implementation of institutional reforms is arguably the weakest area when it comes to implementation. The four administrations that have followed the release of the Final Report have not specifically addressed this group of recommendations.

One general response, although not directly linked to the recommendations, was the elaboration of a *Plan Nacional de Derechos Humanos* (Human Rights National Plan). The *Plan Nacional de Derechos Humanos* is a policy tool designed to disseminate a human rights approach across the State structure, organization and policies in different areas. The process of elaborating this plan is led by the Ministry of Justice, but it follows a participative methodology. Civil society organizations are invited to submit proposals and to discuss the contents of the plan. As mentioned, the plan is not focused on the transitional justice agenda. However, the State is committed to this agenda, in particular regarding reparations and the introduction of human rights education in different sectors of the State structure, including domestic security. The first Plan, for the period 2006–10, was approved in 2005 by Supreme Decree 017-2005-JUS.[4] It contained provisions regarding the implementation of the recommendations. It specifically mentioned State obligations in four areas: reparations, education, institutional reform, and military justice. Two additional plans have since been approved. The second plan was elaborated for the period 2014–16 and the third for the period 2018–21. The latter has been severely criticized by the human rights community because the government excluded some important issues from the final version – such as and gender-based policies, and an official strategy to protect human rights defenders, which had been previously agreed on. The *Coordinadora Nacional de Derechos Humanos* declared that the plan was "a fraud".[5]

One important intention of the recommendations was to ensure democratic accountability across the territory. According to the CVR, this transformation would in turn strengthen the sense of citizenship among the whole population. The State should be perceived as a structure in charge of guaranteeing rights, which implied that it should be strong enough to effectively enforce the law and sufficiently democratic to do so while respecting human rights.

In relation to democratic authority, domestic security has been and still is perceived as a major concern by the population. In the urban areas, this perception is related to ordinary forms of crime, whereas in some rural areas the concern is provoked by organized crime, ranging from drug-traffickers to tiny remnants of the Shining Path still active in isolated areas. However, the government has so far not come up with a coordinated plan to organize collaboration between the police, municipalities, and citizens. We see this as a major failure in terms of implementing institutional reform.

One important condition for ensuring democratic authority throughout the country is to transform the structure of State power in a geographical-administrative sense. This idea is implied in the notion of *decentralization*. According to the CVR, one major factor explaining the extreme vulnerability of the regions most affected by armed violence was their disconnection from the centers of effective power and the State's institutions' inability to effectively govern indigenous territories (CVR 2003, 117). In response to this, the State should develop an effective decentralization strategy whereby regional governments would be more effective guarantors of legal democratic order and collaborate with the rural population to rebuild political institutions ravaged by violence.

---

4 https://www.mindef.gob.pe/informacion/documentos/Plan%20Nacional%20de%20DD.HH%202006-2010.pdf.

5 http://derechoshumanos.pe/2018/02/nuevo-plan-nacional-de-derechos-humanos-simulacion-y-fraude/.

Even though decentralization policies have been popular since the transition,[6] they have failed to incorporate institutional policies to ensure the participation of the under-represented population in municipal planning and budgets as recommended by the CVR.

However, one important area of progress relates to the rights of indigenous people. At least at the institutional level, the government provided some clarity regarding official responsibility by the creation, under the authority of the Ministry of Culture, of a secretariat in charge of indigenous affairs. The main task of this agency is to ensure that the State's obligations regarding indigenous rights are met. In the current social-political context in Peru these obligations are concretized in two main aspects. The first one is related to the exploitation of natural resources and the conflicts this provokes with indigenous people's rights to territory. The second one is related to the State's obligation to develop and adopt an intercultural approach in all its policies. The deputy-ministry of indigenous affairs has not been a sufficient response to these necessities; however, it provides a concrete institutional location to which demands can be addressed and engage in dialogue with indigenous groups and other actors holding stakes in these issues.

The limitations of this agency in enforcing its official agenda illustrate, once again, the difficulties involved in implementing the recommendations in the absence of a centralized body empowered for the task. When dealing with issues related to territorial rights and indigenous communities' right to be consulted about investments in their ancestral areas, the agency often finds itself contradicted by other (more powerful) State agencies such as the Ministry of Economy and the agencies related to production and mining. Meanwhile, the issues related to intercultural policies must be coordinated, for instance, with the decentralized educational authority, which is dispersed across a national Ministry of Education and 25 regions that have their own powers to elaborate their own educational policy.

Another set of recommendations asked for a reform of the military (in charge of national defense) and of the police (in charge of domestic order). The CVR's recommendation was that staff in these two bodies should be educated in human rights and trained to perform their duties effectively while simultaneously respecting human rights. To achieve these goals, it has been important to adopt two notions: first, that the military should not be summoned to restore domestic order since its logic and training are associated with national defense; second, that the police should not be conceived as a militarized force, but rather as a body

---

6 Decentralization policies existed prior to the Fujimori regime. During the authoritarian period, regional governments were replaced by a centralized structure composed of *Consejos Transitorios de Administración Regional* (Temporary Regional Administrative Councils, CTAR).

associated more with the civilian government than with the armed forces. This general idea has not been implemented so far. The police remain unreformed. The institution still reflects a militarized model and has not built a collaborative relationship with municipalities and civil society.

One interesting development, however, is revision of the laws regulating states of emergency to redefine the use of force and the rules of engagement with the civilian population. There are some provisions that nevertheless open the door to impunity in cases where the military and the police use force against civilian protesters. However, it can be counted as an advance directly connected with the CVR's recommendations that the military and the police have included courses on human rights and humanitarian law in their curricula.

There have been some attempts at introducing reforms of the administration of justice, although these have not necessarily been in direct response to the CVR's recommendations. As noted above, the most ambitious and coherent of these attempts was the CERIAJUS, a temporary body established by Congress. The proposal made by CERIAJUS was disregarded, though, and has not been followed by other relevant proposals.

We note that some progress has been made in terms of staffing the courts with permanent judges instead of temporary and interim substitutes. During the Fujimori regime, the overrepresentation of temporary and interim judges made it possible for the Executive Branch to manipulate the courts. Since the judges were insecure in their positions, they were prone to government pressure and often were "rubber stamps". Increasing the proportion of permanent judges is, therefore, an important element in strengthening judicial independence.

Educational reform is another important area of recommendations. As mentioned above, some attempts have been made, but not in connection with the recommendations. In 2007 the State adopted the National Education Project elaborated by the National Education Council. This project incorporated (or coincided with) many of the recommendations made by the Commission. The Project has not been fully implemented, although it has provided guidance for the development of educational plans at the local level.

Progress has been made on intercultural bilingual education in compliance with the CVR's recommendations. The Ministry of Education has made efforts in staffing and training schools for intercultural bilingual education. We note, though, that there are budgetary constraints limiting the progress of this policy.

Education curricula have been updated in order to include general aspects of civic education. Courses dealing with memory of the conflict have not yet been included, however. Although the official curriculum includes references to this, there are many constraints hindering the achievement of this goal. Structural constraints include the generally poor quality of teachers in Peru; teacher training, particularly regarding pedagogy on memory, remains lacking. There are also social constraints. Teachers, particularly in rural areas, are still fearful of speaking of this subject since this could cause problems for them in terms of stigmatization and even criminalization. There is still a law about "apology of terrorism" (defense or justification of terrorist acts) that can be used to penalize schoolteachers who promote a critical discourse about the State's role during the conflict, or who seek to explain the period of violence in terms of "structural causes", which is interpreted by right-wing groups as a form of legitimizing the Shining Path's war.[7]

This tendency to impede the incorporation of critical perspectives on Peru's history of violence is deeply rooted in the school system and is responsible for the lack of significant advances in implementing the recommendations. After the CVR released its Final Report and presented educational materials to discuss the subject in schools, the government rejected the educational materials due to a veto by the Ministry of Defense. In recent years (2016–17), the materials have been accepted by the State, but have not yet been deployed in schools.

5.2. INTEGRAL REPARATIONS PLAN (PIR)

The recommendations on reparations feature among the most implemented recommendations. Several successive administrations have been involved in this process. The first response to recommendations for reparations came very early, in 2004, when Congress passed the law creating the Plan of Integral Reparations. This law adequately adopted the proposals made by the CVR. The only contentious issue was article 4 of the law, which excluded from reparations all the persons linked to terrorist organizations and their relatives. Although this provision goes against international standards on reparations, it was not vehemently contested by the human rights movement.

The prompt response to the recommendations on reparations by Congress was due to the presence of lawmakers who shared the human rights agenda. In 2004, a socialist congressman, Henry Pease, was President of Congress. This situation would end after the 2006 general elections, which ushered in a more conservative Parliament. In this new environment, Alejandro Toledo's Government created a body in charge of implementation, the Multisectorial Commission for Reparations (CMAN). The CMAN did not really reflect the CVR's follow-up proposal. Some of the problems of the CMAN are that it has to coordinate with too many different ministries and State agencies. Moreover, it lacks the authority to enforce its plans.

7 See the law of apology of terrorism at: http://busquedas.elperuano.pe/normaslegales/ley-que-modifica-el-articulo-316-e-incorpora-el-articulo-316-ley-n-30610-1545774-2/.

The government also created the Council of Reparations in charge of registering the victims entitled to receive reparations. The Council of Reparations has created a registry of individual victims and a registry of collective victims (Ruiz Caro 2017). The government started with collective reparations. This program has been in place since 2005 and has benefited many communities. Some criticisms have been made, however. In particular, the program is said to lack a true reparation message and is mostly associated with development measures. According to Ruiz Caro, the government only offered two types of collective reparations: small productive or infrastructure projects and basic services projects (Ruiz Caro 2017, 87). Another problematic aspect of the program has been the lack of coordination with and participation of communities and local governments in the process of decision-making and implementation (Aprodeh-ICTJ 2008).

The same coordination and consultation problems have affected the individual economic reparations program. This program was started several years after the collective reparations program. The first list of beneficiaries entitled to economic reparations (30,000 persons) was sent to CMAN by the Council of Reparations in 2009. However, Alan García's Government did not take action until, without any consultation, it determined that the amount allocated for each "family group" would be 10,000 Nuevos Soles (around US$3,000). Furthermore, it established December 31, 2011 as the deadline to apply for inclusion in the economic reparations program, leaving thousands of prospective beneficiaries without support due to the short time-frame. After protests by the victims and human rights groups, the deadline was cancelled. The economic reparations program is still working.

One important aspect of reparations is access to education. A program of granting scholarships has been in place and many victims have received scholarships. The programs need to be expanded and improved, though. One criticism is that victims who receive such scholarships are discriminated against in the universities that they attend. Another problem was that the right to scholarship could not be passed on from the victim to his or her children. This deficiency was fixed in 2016.

5.3. IMPLEMENTATION OF THE NATIONAL PLAN FOR FORENSIC-ANTHROPOLOGICAL RESEARCH

The CVR received information about over 4,000 burial sites and presented a list (elaborated through a joint effort with other institutions, such as the International Red Cross Committee (ICRC), the *Coordinadora Nacional de Derechos Humanos*, and the Ombudsman Office) of almost 15,000 disappeared persons. These findings led the Commission to recommend the establishment of a national policy to search for disappeared persons, and to make a detailed proposal to this end.

Nevertheless, until 2016 there was no national policy on what to do about the disappeared. Forensic interventions and the possibility to identify buried remains and to return them to their relatives were limited to judicial processes. Only if a criminal investigation against alleged perpetrators was in progress as part of a judicial process would a forensic team be deployed. This approach denied the majority of victims, who for a variety of reasons could not advance their cases through the courts, the right to know the truth about the fate suffered by their loved ones. This had psychological consequences in terms of interfering with the mourning process. Legally, it denied relatives the possibility of exercising many rights because of the uncertain legal status of the disappeared person.

For many years, victims' groups, human rights organizations, and international actors (such as ICRC) have demanded the delinking of the search for the disappeared from criminal prosecutions. This approach has been called a "humanitarian approach" as opposed to a "criminal approach". Finally, in 2016 the Law for the Search for Disappeared Persons was passed by Congress and signed by the President. This law introduced the humanitarian approach, which means that forensic investigations would no longer depend on a judicial process. Perhaps as important was the way in which the legislation was to be implemented. The national policy adopts gender-sensitive and intercultural approaches (which is very important due to the indigenous background of the majority of potential beneficiaries) and includes a participatory perspective.

As suggested above, the Law was made possible by a convergence of efforts both from civil society and from some State agencies, such as the Ministry of Justice, that were open to dialogue about this critical issue. The Ombudsman Office also played an important role. We emphasize that in this process victims' groups found a significant opportunity to act in a coordinated fashion and to get involved in negotiations with the State to obtain a very concrete response. The association between NGOs, international actors such as ICRC, and victims' groups proved very effective in this particular case.

Memory forms part of symbolic reparations (CVR 2003). In its report, the Commission presents memory as a national necessity but, more specifically, as a reparation for the victims of human rights violations. As of yet, there is no official national policy for memory. It is not present in education curricula, and the government has failed to establish special commemoration dates. Nevertheless, the State has created a national memory site under the name of *Lugar de la Memoria, la Tolerancia y la Inclusión Social* (LUM) in the Peruvian capital city of Lima. This site was created after a debate started when, in 2009, the German government offered two million Euros to build a permanent place for the CVR's photographic exhibition *Yuyanapaq*. The Government of Alan García rejected the offer, saying that Peru did not need a memory museum. This negative response provoked harsh criticism from Peruvian civil society organizations. Finally, after a critical op-ed piece published by renowned author Mario Vargas Llosa (2009), the García Government reconsidered and accepted the German offer under the condition that Vargas Llosa presided over a commission to create the memory site. The creation of the LUM followed a long process during which it became disassociated from *Yuyanapaq* and was conceived as a national museum for memory. The museum was inaugurated in 2015. Even though it has been well received by victims' groups and civil society, since its inauguration it has been criticized by right-wing political parties and by groups closely associated with human rights violations, such as the *fujimorismo*.

Besides this national memory initiative, some local governments have also created or endorsed memorial sites. One of the more important sites is Yalpana Wasi, in Huancayo, region of Junín.

A general interpretation of the implementation of CVR recommendations is that the area with the most progress is the PIR. However, even it has faced important criticisms. Victims consider it too slow and underfunded. There are serious coordination problems between the different agencies involved. The amounts of economic compensation are too low. Furthermore, victims do not find a truly "reparative" meaning in the Plan due to the lack of symbolic content in the different activities.

By contrast, the institutional reforms appear to be the weakest component in terms of implementation. Despite the lack of political will to undertake reforms, some progress has been made in the fields of education and justice. However, there is not a clear connection to the CVR. The Peruvian case illustrates the difficulty of isolating the effect of a truth commission recommendation from other factors. The lack of a centralized agency in charge of following up on these recommendations makes it very difficult for civil society to address concrete demands and for observers of the process to determine when a recommendation can be considered implemented.

6. CONCLUSIONS

To conclude, the recommendations of the CVR have been partially implemented by the State. The lack of greater progress is due to an absence of political will. This situation also can be explained, though, by the structural limitations of the Peruvian State to carry out social policies. It is important to acknowledge the scope and complexity of the recommendations. They do not deal exclusively with the direct consequences of armed conflict, but also more broadly with deep structural problems in Peruvian society.

As a result, it is not easy to pinpoint when a State action is intended to respond to the CVR recommendations and when it forms part of more general development policies. During the democratic transition following Fujimori's departure, specific institutions were established to propose reform in particular areas. This situation makes it more difficult to distinguish the actions undertaken as a response to the CVR and those responding to other reform-oriented initiatives. One such institution was the National Education Council, which proposed the National Education Project. Another was CERIAJUS, established by Congress to propose an integral reform of the justice administration system.

One particular limitation for the implementation of CVR recommendations was the State's failure to create a centralized body that is sufficiently empowered to take overall responsibility for overseeing and following up on the implementation process. The Government of Alejandro Toledo created CMAN, but this body is mainly in charge of reparations and does not have the power necessary to coordinate with other ministries tasked with the implementation of other types of recommendations.

The recommendations that have the highest implementation rate are reparations. However, the institutional framework established to implement reparations is very complex and has proven to be somewhat dysfunctional over the years. Overall, victims have been deeply unsatisfied with both the material as well as the symbolic aspects of the reparations process. By contrast, institutional reform has been largely neglected by the State, except in some cases where human rights education has been adopted as part of the training of public servants.

Two important contextual factors explain these rather unsatisfactory results in the Peruvian case. First, Peru's political party system is underdeveloped. Second, victims' organizations are weak. In the absence of highly institutionalized political parties, it is very difficult for victims and other civil society actors to find a secure path to set an agenda and to bring transitional justice issues to the public agenda. In some cases, the collaboration between victims' groups, human rights organizations, international actors and sympathetic State agencies has resulted in positive responses to the transitional justice agenda. The most significant case is the process of developing the law for disappeared persons and the negotiations leading to legislative action on the matter.

BIBLIOGRAPHY

Aprodeh-ICTJ (2008). *Escuchando las voces de las comunidades. Un estudio sobre la implementación de las Reparaciones Colectivas en el Perú.* Lima: Aprodeh-International Center for Transitional Justice.

Barrantes, Rafael, and Peña, Jesús (2006). "Narrativas sobre el conflicto armado interno en el Perú: la memoria en el proceso político después de la CVR." In IDEHPUCP, *Transformaciones democráticas y memorias de la violencia en el Perú.* Colección Documentos de Trabajo/Serie Reconciliación N.° 2. Lima: IDEHPUCP.

Comisión de la Verdad y Reconciliación (CVR) (2003). *Informe Final. Tomo IX: cuarta parte. Recomendaciones de la CVR. Hacia la reconciliación.* Lima: CVR.

—— (2004). *Hatun Willakuy. Versión abreviada del informe final de la Comisión de la Verdad y Reconciliación.* Lima: CVR.

Comisión Nacional para la Reforma Integral de la Administración de Justicia (2004). *Plan Nacional de Reforma Integral de la Administración de Justicia.* Lima, April 23, 2004: http://www4.congreso.gob.pe/comisiones/2004/ceriajus/Plan_Nacional_ceriajus.pdf.

Consejo Nacional de Educación (2007). *Proyecto Educativo Nacional hacia el 2021.* Lima: Consejo Educativo Nacional.

Defensoría del Pueblo (2004). *A un año de la Comisión de la Verdad y Reconciliación. Serie Informes Defensoriales.* Informe Defensorial N°86. Lima: Defensoría del Pueblo.

Degregori, Carlos Iván (2016). *El surgimiento de Sendero Luminoso. Ayacucho 1969–1979.* Obras escogidas VII. Lima: Instituto de Estudios Peruanos, Segunda parte, caps. III and IV.

García-Godos, Jemima (2016). "Peru: beyond paradigmatic cases". In Skaar, Elin, García-Godos, Jemima, and Collins, Cath (eds.), *Transitional Justice in Latin America: The Uneven Road from Impunity towards Accountability.* New York: Routledge.

Gianella Malca, Camila (2015). "Peru: changing contexts for transitional justice". In Skaar, Elin, Gianella Malca, Camila, and Eide, Trine (eds.), *After violence. Transitional Justice, Peace and Democracy.* New York: Routledge.

González Cueva, Eduardo (2006). "The Peruvian Truth and Reconciliation Commission and the Challenge of Impunity". In Naomi Roht-Arriaza and Javier Mariezcurrena (eds.), *Transitional Justice in the Twenty-First Century. Beyond Truth versus Justice.* Cambridge University Press.

Hayner, Priscilla (2001). *Unspeakable truths. Transitional Justice and the Challenge of Truth Commissions.* Second edition. New York: Routledge.

Laplante, Lisa J. and Theidon, Kimberly (2007). "Truth with Consequences: Justice and Reparations in Post Truth Commission Peru". *Human Rights Quarterly*, no. 29 (1): 228–250.

Root, Rebecca K. (2012). *Transitional Justice in Peru.* New York: Palgrave.

Ruiz Caro, Marusia (2017). "Reparaciones a las víctimas de la violencia: insensibilidad y postergación". In DESCO, *Perú Hoy. Desarrollo con derechos. Acceso a la dignidad.* Lima: DESCO.

Vargas Llosa, Mario (2009). "El Perú no necesita museos". *El País*, March 8 2009: https://elpais.com/diario/2009/03/08/opinion/1236466813_850215.html

ANNEX: RECOMMENDATIONS OF THE PERUVIAN TRUTH AND RECONCILIATION COMMISSION (CVR)

(I) Institutional Reforms

1. To develop policies and standards for the vital collaboration between the Police, municipalities and citizens.
2. To strengthen the institutional framework and adequate regulation of self-defense committees. Examine the potential for a rural police force.
3. To strengthen the accessibility of justice services through Justices of the Peace (*Jueces de Paz*).
4. To improve access to justice by increasing the availability of government-provided legal aid.
5. To establish a system for the defense of human rights through specialized branches of the police, the justice system, and the prosecutor's office in zones where violence had a greater impact.
6. To establish short-term goals for the application of Government policies set out in the *Acuerdo Nacional*, prioritizing their application in zones most affected by violence.
7. To establish institutional policies at the local level to ensure the incorporation of the needs and necessities of marginalized groups in municipal planning and budgets.
8. Recommend to regional governments in rural areas, particularly in those most affected by violence, the participation of municipalities in urban planning projects to ensure that the needs of populations in sparsely populated areas are taken into account.
9. To provide incentives to public officials assigned to remote locations affected by violence.
10. Recognition and integration of the rights of Indigenous Peoples and their communities in the national legal framework.
11. Creation of an institution or official body in charge of indigenous issues and policies.
12. To draft a new law of political parties and to modify the system of political representation.
13. To strengthen efforts aimed at combatting poverty and to promote development.
14. To incentivize the participation of youth in all spheres of life (education, local governance, higher education, labor market) aiming to encourage leadership.

(II) *Reform of National Defense Systems and Domestic Order*

15. To specify the scope of the concept of national defense and the meaning of relevant policies, so that all the issues that are named "defense" and rely on military personnel and military bodies that are the responsibility of the Ministry of Defense.
16. To develop a national security policy that includes a national strategy for pacification and aims at reconciliation and State presence across the territory.
17. Formation of civilian expertise on security and defense.
18. Regulation of states of emergency.
19. Civilian control of military intelligence.
20. To establish at the Constitutional level – as well as at lower-levels – the distinction between National Defense, on the one hand, and internal order and public security, on the other.
21. To define at the Constitutional and legal levels the National Police as a non-militarized civil institution. To modernize the Police profession according to the definition of the National Police as a civilian institution.
22. To strengthen, with an explicit mention in the Constitution, the role of Interior Minister as the political and administrative authority that organizes and leads the police in accordance with the law and for the purposes of guaranteeing public order, crime prevention and law enforcement.
23. To reform military education and its curriculum.
24. A new ethics code.
25. Create the Military Ombudsman.
26. To modernize education and training in ethics and human rights for police officials/officers as members of a civil institution.

(III) *Reform of the Administration of Justice*

27. To strengthen the independence of the system of administration of justice.
28. A Judicial Branch staffed by permanent (tenured) judges instead of interim judges and temporary substitutes.
29. To establish at the Constitutional and legal levels that the Military Court is subordinate to the Supreme Court of Justice.
30. To establish a temporary special system in charge of processing cases of crimes and violations of human rights.
31. To promote an integrated system to address the issue of victims of forced disappearance during the internal armed conflict between 1980 and 2000.

32. To incorporate into the national legal framework innovations in international law related to justice administration and due process; in particular, to establish the constitutional status of human rights treaties in the Constitution.
33. To start a sustained training program in human rights, humanitarian law and democratic culture for judges, prosecutors and lawyers.
34. It is essential to establish in the Prosecutor's Office (*Ministerio Público*) a unit specialized in investigating human rights issues.
35. Permanent application of *control difuso* by judges in situations of *regimenes de excepción* [exceptional regimes].
36. To define a specialized institution for policy on prisons.
37. Modernize the Criminal Procedural Code adapting it to the real situation of the prison system.
38. To make effective the regulation for the Code of Criminal Enforcement DS N. 023-2001-Jus.
39. To establish procedures and the institutional framework necessary for evaluation and resolution of clemency requests from persons convicted of terrorism who claim innocence.
40. To maintain at the Constitutional level that the purpose of the prison system is the re-education, rehabilitation and reintegration of convicted persons to society.
41. To stop arbitrary transfers of male and female inmates, as this impedes visits from their relatives; in the case of persons in prison for terrorism, to promote their concentration in few places for better treatment and safety.
42. To consider, for purposes of specific treatment, the different situations and comportments of those inmates who renounced the PCP-SL and MRTA; those who were sent to prison under the "repentance law"; and those who claim to be innocent. To promote alternative measures such as the restoring of penitentiary benefits and access to sentence commutation.[8]
43. To improve prison conditions in terms of access to basic services such as nourishment and health care.

(IV) Education Reform

44. Emphasize educational policies aimed at transforming school into a place where students' human rights are respected and that contributes to the development of the whole person. Promote the value of peace and assert education as a tool for peace.

---

[8] People serving sentences for terrorism were not eligible for some ordinary measures to reduce their time in jail on account of their behavior or other factors. We call these measures "beneficios penitenciarios". This recommendation calls for restoring "beneficios penitenciarios" for those types of inmates.

45. Establish a curriculum that stimulates and orients knowledge with a focus on non-violence and that corrects distorted understandings of Peruvian history.
46. Promote an education respectful of ethnic and cultural differences. In all respects, schools should be sensitive to the ethno-linguistic, cultural and geographical diversity of the country.
47. Strengthen mechanisms of participation and democratization in schools.
48. Discipline.
49. Give urgent attention to the most vulnerable population: start with the youngest children in the most needy areas.
50. Promote a literacy plan prioritizing adolescent and adult women in rural areas.
51. Redefine education in terms of content, methodologies and coverage, depending on the capabilities of the labor market, with emphasis on the rural population.
52. Restore dignity and improve the quality of rural schools.

*(V) **Integral Reparations Plan***

Symbolic

53. Public gestures. Among them, Presidential endorsement of CVR recommendations and incorporation the Integral Reparations Plan (PIR) as policy in the National Agreement.
54. Acts of recognition of all victims of the armed conflict, including restoring public respect for those who were illegally imprisoned and expressing public recognition for social leaders and civilian authorities who were killed or disappeared during the conflict.
55. Memorialization sites in cemeteries, parks or public squares and preservation of the photographic exhibition Yuyanapaq.
56. Acts that lead to reconciliation including the transformation or re-signification of symbols associated with violence and human rights violations in the affected territories.

Health Care

57. To implement an education, training and support program for professionals from public entities such as the Ministry of Health and the health organizations associated with the armed forces, and to promote the participation of personnel from private entities, non-governmental organizations, churches and universities in those programs.
58. Integral recovery through communitarian intervention and restoration of social ties. This component should be based on a community intervention

that seeks to address the entire recovery process, taking into account the cultural differences and the needs of the victims, and facilitating the intervention of personnel external to the community. It will focus primarily on the reconstruction of the social fabric and community support networks as a fundamental element for the emotional and physical recovery of the people affected by the conflict.

59. Integral recovery through clinical intervention; designing a model of clinical health care.

    This component aims to understand the specific effects caused by violence, the social reintegration of the person, the development of personal autonomy and the restoration of the project of life truncated by violence. The CVR also recommends addressing this type of recovery by a comprehensive approach, including the psychological, family, physical, work and social participation dimensions. The therapeutic modalities may be individual, family and group.

60. Access to health care. The CVR recommends that people included in the universe of individual beneficiaries who suffer from physical problems and those who are permanently disabled, partially or totally, whose disability is the product of sexual violations, torture, or injuries typified by the CVR, are considered within the scope and coverage of the already existing Comprehensive Health Insurance.

61. Health promotion and health prevention. This component seeks to provide elements of analysis on the way in which the internal armed conflict provoked negative consequences for those who were directly affected and for the rest of society. It will allow the community and society to become aware of the damage to the overall health of the population and will provide guidelines for action to strengthen resilient behaviors to face the conflict situation.

Education

62. Exemption of education fees. The CVR recommends that the Executive Branch establish through a Supreme Decree the exemption for the victims from tuition and accommodation fees, including entry examination fees, in elementary and high schools, Universities and the other higher-education institutions of the State.

63. Implementation by the Ministry of Education and through the National Institute of Scholarships and Educational Loans (INABEC) of a comprehensive scholarship program for higher education in education centers located outside the applicant's place of residence. This benefit includes both national and international scholarships.

64. Expansion or establishment by the Ministry of Education of adult education programs through its National Literacy Program, in those areas with the

highest incidence of violence, both urban and rural, in coordination with local educational institutions that have experience in this type of program and that can develop methodologies and specific contents for this sector, taking into consideration the cultural and linguistic differences of each zone.

Restoration of civil rights

65. Regularize the legal status of the missing to solve the legal problems generated by forced disappearance and to determine a firm legal status for those who were the object of disappearance. This measure must allow their relatives to fully exercise their rights. To this end the CVR recommends amending the Civil Code to establish a special legal status which must recognize by judicial declaration the "absence by disappearance" of the person who was forcibly disappeared.
66. Regularizing the legal status of persons under arrest warrants. The CVR recommends to continue and finalize the revision of the list of arrest warrants for the crimes of terrorism and treason by the National Counter-Terrorism Chamber in order to eliminate those lacking legal basis.
67. Cancellation of police, judicial and criminal records of people who were pardoned as a means to achieve full reintegration into the social life of those persons acquitted, released by serving a sentence, or who have obtained a pardon or have benefited from the right of grace.
68. Regularize the situation of undocumented citizens through the creation of a massive documentation and documentation regularization program for people who, as a consequence of the armed conflict, are undocumented, in order to allow them access to their identity and citizenship rights, as well as to PIR programs in which are recognized as beneficiaries.
69. Providing legal counselling for the beneficiaries of the Citizen Rights Restitution Program considering that, although in many cases the normative framework (regularization of the situation of requisition, cancellation of criminal records, regularization of the undocumented, etc.) already exists, people do not have sufficient information to apply and to navigate the system. It also recommends that advice be given to all potential beneficiaries of the Integral Reparations Plan (PIR).
70. Exemption from fees. The CVR recommends that the access to the measures proposed in the Citizen Rights Restitution Program should not constitute an additional burden for the beneficiaries' finances.
71. Economic repairs in the form of pensions and compensations for relatives of persons dead or disappeared and for persons who have suffered disabling damage, whether physical or mental, for victims of arbitrary imprisonment, for victims of sexual violation and for the children of women who have been victims of sexual violation.

Collective Reparations Program

72. Institutional consolidation measures aiming to restore local institutions, authority and leadership within the traditional organizations of local governance, both peasant and native, in the high Andean territories and in the Amazon. Likewise, the CVR recommends the recovery of the local government and the strengthening of the technical and management capacity of the municipalities, communities and other relevant local organizations (governorates, courts of peace, communal boards, boards of irrigation users, etc.).
73. Reconstruction of production infrastructure through initiatives aiming to have an impact on income, commercial dynamism, job creation and capacity development. The initiatives may include funds destined for: training (internships), technical assistance, livestock capitalization, recovery of lands and pastures, contribution (complementary) of inputs for innovation of crops, agricultural intensification or improvement of techniques or varieties adapted to the demand of the markets, etc.
74. Reconstruction and expansion of basic services. This component must support projects for the reconstruction and development of the infrastructure of services and communications, identified by the communities and local institutions themselves. The commitment of complementary contribution by local governments and the insertion of the works within concerted strategic plans of local development will be especially valued.
75. Implementation of the National Plan for Forensic-Anthropological Research, including the following aspects: to propose an integral National Forensic Anthropological Investigations Research Plan in accordance to Human Rights standards; to apply internationally established technical and scientific criteria for forensic-anthropological intervention, appropriate to the national reality, both for the recovery of information regarding victims, events and spaces, as well as for the recovery of the remains, their analysis, identification and restitution, considering the different contexts in which they may be found; to have a multidisciplinary team of forensic experts, professionally qualified, with extensive experience in the field, but also properly trained to assume the moral responsibility involved in the execution of the work; to establish a program of psychological and legal support for families who have suffered forced disappearance and / or extrajudicial executions, establishing mechanisms to keep them constantly and appropriately informed about the status of the investigations and the results reached; to guarantee the restitution of the remains as well as the victim's belongings, when they exist, to the respective families, allowing them to carry out the relevant

rites and commemorations within the mourning process, according to the individual and community beliefs.

76. Establishment of a follow-up mechanism. To this effect the Commission presented a draft law creating a National Reconciliation Council designed as a decentralized public body of the Presidency of the Council of Ministers, with legal status in public law and technical, administrative, economic and financial autonomy, in order to centralize decisions aimed at developing and implementing the recommendations of the CVR.

(VI) Justice

77. To encourage the Prosecutor's Office to open without delay (30 days maximum) the investigations against alleged perpetrators of the crimes investigated by the CVR. To this effect the CVR submitted files containing 43 cases of crimes.
78. Refer to the Ombudsman, custodian of the archives of the CVR, to make public the names of those who in the opinion of the CVR merit criminal investigation if the Prosecutor's Office fails to act on the matter within the period established above.
79. Recommend the National Counter-Terrorism Chamber of the Superior Court of Lima to take into account the findings made by the CVR regarding crimes committed by members of the PCP-SL and the MRTA.
80. To urge the Government branches to refrain from applying amnesties, pardons and other Presidential pardons beyond the framework established by the Inter-American Court of Human Rights.
81. To recommend to the authorities in charge to adopt administrative measures against public servants responsible for serious violations of human rights, including those judges who did not fulfil properly their duties to protect fundamental rights.
82. Recommend the provision of necessary safety measures to witnesses and victims of serious crimes and violations of human rights through a system that integrates the resources of the judiciary, the Prosecutor's Office, the Ministry of Interior and the Ombudsman. It is especially important to respect confidentiality rules regarding the identity of witnesses who have provided valuable information for investigations.

(VII) Memory

83. To promote decisively the dissemination of the final report of the truth commission so that all Peruvians can access complete knowledge of our recent past, preserve the historical and ethical memory of the nation, and

draw lessons to prevent the repetition of moments as painful as those experienced.

84. To suggest that the Ombudsman Office, custodian of the CVR's archives, implement a system for wide dissemination, promoting scientific and academic research on the issues outlined therein, while giving due consideration to the safety of victims and witnesses.

PART III

CENTRAL AMERICA AND THE CARIBBEAN

EL SALVADOR'S TRUTH COMMISSION

Recommending Peace in Exchange for Justice

Elena Martínez-Barahona, Sonia Rubio-Padilla, Héctor Centeno-Martín, and Martha Gutiérrez-Salazar*

* Institutional affiliation of authors: Elena Martínez-Barahona, Sonia Rubio-Padilla, and Héctor Centeno-Martín are at *Universidad de Salamanca*. Martha Gutiérrez-Salazar is affiliated to *Universidad de Bogotá Jorge Tadeo Lozano*. The authors wish to thank Patricia Valdez, Onur Bakiner, and Stener Ekern for constructive comments on earlier drafts of this chapter.

1. INTRODUCTION

The transition to democracy in El Salvador after 12 years of internal armed conflict (1980–92) between the State and the left-wing *Frente Farabundo Martí para la Liberación Nacional* (Farabundo Martí Front for National Liberation – FMLN) was based on a peace agreement negotiated by the United Nations and signed in1992 in Chapultepec, Mexico. The peace agreement set the premises for the institutional reforms required in the country's transition from internal armed conflict to democracy. As in the rest of Latin America, a truth commission was put in place to address past abuses. Neither the peace agreement nor the truth commission discounted the possibility of future prosecutions for atrocities, yet criminal investigation and prosecution were postponed until the country had a more developed justice system able to perform the task (Martínez and Gutiérrez 2016).

El Salvador received the direct support of the United Nations in its process of ending the conflict and establishing the Truth Commission of El Salvador (*Comisión de la Verdad Para El Salvador*; the "CVES" or "the Commission"). The CVES's recommendations, which are examined in this chapter, were one of the key points of the Commission's mandate. At the time the CVES delivered its report, the recommendations offered hope for a structural change in the country and its institutions. However, the scant acceptance of the report by the national population, its rejection by the State's official institutions, and the maintenance of political balance required by the distribution of power between the two main political parties who signed the peace agreements, did not only hinder the possibility of making deep structural changes. These power dynamics have also, in fact, distorted the reforms that have been achieved (Gutiérrez 2015).

2. HISTORICAL BACKGROUND: INFORMATION ON CONTEXT AND TRANSITION

Since its independence from Spain in 1821, El Salvador has been a country where politics, violence and the economy have been combined to guarantee the predominance of a landed economic elite (Dunkerley 1982; Hume 2014). There have been numerous dictatorships in the country's history, with a predominant role of the Armed Forces in politics, acting in favor of the economic elites (Guidos et al. 1980; Stanley 1996).

The personalist dictatorship of General Maximiliano Hernández-Martínez lasted from 1931 until 1944 and set the basis for a political arrangement between the military and the oligarchy to guarantee the institutionalization of military dictatorship thereafter (Artiga 2015, 52). This became evident in various political shifts, such as when the success of Napoleón Duarte, the candidate for the *Unión Nacional Opositoria* (National Opposition Union), was not recognized in the 1972 elections and Colonel Armando Molina (1972–76) instead took control of the government, followed by General Carlos Humberto Romero (1977–78). Both Molina and Romero used force to suppress social dissent. In October of 1979, Romero was overthrown by a Revolutionary *Junta* that included civilian and military members, which remained in power for three months before being restructured to include Napoleón Duarte himself and other officers who supported continuing the repression (Chinchón 2007).

In 1980, in the midst of a national political context of exclusion and repression, with institutions unable to guarantee basic human needs for the population, and in the international context of the Cold War, various organizations formed the FMLN. The FMLN launched a military offensive in 1981, thus sparking civil war in El Salvador (Córdoba et al. 2007).

As stated by the United Nations, the Salvadorian conflict "was the result of social and economic inequalities and of many decades in El Salvador where life was dominated by the country's repressive armed forces and the repressive public security forces" (UN 1995b, 7). Although there is no consensus on the number of victims produced by the conflict, the conflict was clearly among the most intense in Latin America at the time. While the 1981–82 Annual Report of the Inter-American Commission of Human Rights states that there were more than 35,000 victims between 1978 and 1981 (CIDH 1982), Sieder (2002) indicates the total number of victims to be 50,000 people killed during the entire civil war, 42,000 of whom were civilians who lost their lives at the hands of state agents between 1978 and 1983. According to Seligson and McElhinny (1996), that number is even higher, estimating between 80,000–94,000 deaths, of whom between 50,000 and 60,000 were civilians. Wood (2003) estimates that the civil war caused more than 75,000 deaths, a number with which both the United Nations (1992) and Buergenthal (1996) agree.

A new Constitution was enacted in 1983 seeking to open a path towards a process of democratization (Córdoba et al. 2007). José Napoleón Duarte, the first civilian candidate (for the *Unión Nacional Opositora*, UNO party) to win the elections in more than half a century, was elected President in 1984. After that, Alfredo Cristiani (1989–94), of the opposition party *Alianza Republicana Nacionalista* (Nationalist Republican Alliance, ARENA) became President.[1] Due to multiple international and domestic factors at the time, an end to the conflict was negotiated during Cristiani's government.

Following three years of negotiations between the government and the FMLN, a peace agreement was signed on January 16, 1992 in Chapultepec,[2] Mexico, establishing the conditions for the reintegration of the FMLN into civil and political life in El Salvador. The signing of the peace agreement was preceded by multiple agreements in which the intervention of the United Nations was fundamental. Earlier agreements, signed in Geneva and Caracas in April and May 1990 respectively, were designed to establish a framework for negotiation and to create a general agenda for the peace talks; while the San Jose agreement, in July 1990, established the parties' obligation to guarantee respect for human rights.

The Mexico agreement was reached in April 1991 by the negotiating parties, foreseeing the need for a constitutional reform to insure the subordination of the Armed Forces of El Salvador (FAES) to civilian power, the reform of the justice administration system and the establishment of the CVES. In September

1 This party was founded by Major Roberto D'Abuisson, who, according to the CVES, was directly responsible for the assassination of Monsignor Oscar Arnulfo Romero, reasoning that he was the person who gave the order to commit the crime.

2 This agreement contains the following nine chapters: 1) Armed Forces, 2) National Civil Police, 3) Judicial System, 4) Electoral System, 5) Socio-economic Issues, 6) Political participation of the FMLN, 7) Ceasefire of the armed conflict, 8) Verification by the United Nations, and 9) Implementation timetable.

of that same year in New York City, the creation of the *Comisión Nacional para la Consolidación de la Paz* (National Commission for the Consolidation of Peace, COPAZ), the reform of the FAES, the creation of an *ad hoc* commission for the purging of the Armed Forces, the establishment of the National Civil Police (PNC) and an agrarian reform were agreed upon.

During the two decades following the international-sponsored peace accords, the Presidency of the Republic was uninterruptedly occupied by candidates from ARENA.[3] The first political change occurred in 2009, with the election of Mauricio Funes for the FMLN,[4] and later in 2014, with the election of Salvador Sánchez Cerén, an old-time member of the FMLN.

3. THE SALVADORIAN TRUTH AND JUSTICE COMMISSION (CVES)

The CVES was established as the central axis for the measures in favor of the victims of the conflict (Martínez, Gutiérrez and Rincón 2012), with a mandate to investigate the violent events that had occurred since 1980 and that had severely impacted society. Only the most serious events were to be investigated. As stipulated in the Peace Accords, the CVES would be constituted by three persons to be designated by the UN Secretary General after hearing the opinions of the parties.

The 1991 Mexico Agreement had established the mandate of the Commission and granted it the authority to issue binding recommendations. The CVES was requested to make an effort to adopt its decisions by unanimous agreement, which, if not possible, could be overcome with the vote of two of its three members, and it was granted the authority to remit criminal cases to the Attorney General of the Republic for their judicial investigation. It was clearly stipulated that the Commission's action would not be jurisdictional.

The Commission was granted the authority to organize its own work and operations, foreseeing the confidentiality of its actions and granting it the power to collect information. The 1991 Agreement established that the Final Report was to be delivered within a six-month term to the parties and the UN Secretary General, who would be in charge of making it public. The delivery of the Report was to officially conclude the Commission's mandate.

In 1992, the Commission's mandate was expanded by Article 5 of Chapter I of the Chapultepec Agreements, entitled "overcoming impunity." This article

---

3 The ARENA candidates were Armando Calderón (1994–99), Francisco Flórez (1999–2004), and Antonio Saca (2004–09).

4 Recognized for his work as a journalist, he was not historically connected to the party, and he also received support from figures and groups outside of the party.

assigned it the additional duty to clarify the facts connected with human rights violations committed by the Armed Forces of El Salvador, without this limiting the option to prosecute the perpetrators of such events within the justice system.

The Commission was established on July 15, 1992, and it took eight months to issue its report. The CVES was composed of former Colombian President Belisario Betancur (elected president of the CVES); Reinaldo Figueredo, former Minister of Foreign Relations of Venezuela and Thomas Buergenthal, ex-President of the Inter-American Court of Human Rights. The CVES team further included between 12 and 20 persons, all of them foreigners, due to the country's extreme polarization (Buergenthal 1996).[5]

The Commission's budget was US$2.5 million, fully financed by international donors through a special United Nations fund (Hayner 2010). The main donors were the United States, the European Union, the Netherlands and Scandinavian countries (Buergenthal 1996).

The final report, entitled *De la locura a la esperanza: la guerra de 12 años en El Salvador* (From Madness to Hope: the 12 Year War in El Salvador), was delivered on March 15, 1993. According to the report, there were approximately 22,000 reports of human rights violations committed during the conflict, mostly disappearances, executions and torture.

Although the CVES stated that the Armed Forces of El Salvador and paramilitary forces were responsible for 85 per cent of human rights violations committed during the conflict, the report focused on only 33 emblematic cases committed by different actors in the conflict, thus leaving "information regarding many other cases up in the air" (Lazo and Rey Tristán 2011, 211; Sieder 2002). The commissioners structured the pertinent information in eight sections, the five first containing most of the report's weight. The 33 emblematic cases were included in the fourth and longest section of the Report following the same methodology and pattern.[6]

After its publication, the government, the Armed Forces of El Salvador and the Judicial Branch rejected the Report. President Cristiani criticized it for failing to contribute to national reconciliation. The FMLN was also dissatisfied with the Report's findings. In other sectors, the Commission was accused of protecting rich civilians who financed death squads[7] and for failing to mention the role

---

5 Méndez (2011, 201) points out that, in spite of its international presentation as a successful experience, "the fact that the members and the team of the Commission were exclusively foreign [has caused] the different sectors of Salvadorian society to consider the final document as merely another external "report", leading them to ignore the report's findings".

6 The selection of only emblematic cases assumes current relevance given the institutionalization of the 2016 Amnesty Law, which only allows the re-opening of cases included in the CVES report, ruling out all other cases.

7 Whatever the case, "it was believed that the [CVES] had received many more names than those it published, that it lacked clarity in terms of the criteria used to determine which names to publish and which not" (Méndez 2011, 206).

played by the United States as a supporter of repressive governments (Hayner 2001). With regard to the Report's dissemination, Douglas Cassel[8] has pointed out that the Central American University (UCA) was the only institution that made an effort to publicize it, in contrast with the FMLN and the government (Sanz and Martínez 2012).

One week after the Commission delivered the Report, a broad amnesty law was approved by the Salvadorian Legislative Branch, effectively guaranteeing the impunity of the parties responsible for serious violations committed during the conflict. This law prevailed over time and no judicial decision limited its scope until 2016. In September of 2013, the Constitutional Court admitted a new application from representatives of Salvadorian NGOs seeking a ruling of unconstitutionality of the law. On July 13, 2016, the Constitutional Court declared the Amnesty Law unconstitutional, thus opening a new stage in the fight against impunity and the prosecution of cases investigated by the CVES, among others. The case of the El Mozote massacres, involving the killing of approximately 1,000 people by military personnel in 1981, was re-opened in March 2017.

Table 1. Main institutional characteristics of the CVES

Commission's Name	***Comisión de la Verdad para El Salvador* (Truth Commission for El Salvador - CVES)**
Mandate Term	Inaugurated on July 13, 1992 and report completed on March 15, 1993
Period covered	January 1980 to July 1991
Created by	Chapultepec Peace Agreements in 1992
Composition	3 members
Commissioners	Belisario Betancur (Ex-President of Colombia) Reinaldo Figueredo Planchart (Ex-Minister of Foreign Relations of Venezuela) Thomas Buergenthal (Ex-President of the US Inter-American Court of Human Rights Court)
Budget	US$2.5 million
Total Number of Cases Presented	22,000 reports
Public Hearings	No
Name of the Report	"*De la locura a la esperanza: Informe de la Comisión de la Verdad para El Salvador*" (From Madness to Hope: Report of the Truth Commission for El Salvador)

Sources: The final CVES report (1993); Buergenthal (1996); Hayner (2006).

8 Attorney specializing in human rights and international humanitarian law subjects recruited by the United Nations' Peace Maintenance Operation Department to provide support to the CVES during its final months of work.

4. RECOMMENDATIONS OF THE SALVADORIAN TRUTH COMMISSION

The CVES issued 43 recommendations, classified in five main categories. The first group contained nine recommendations designed to penalize and disqualify the persons who had committed and/or were accomplices in human rights violations, while the second group, consisting of 16 specific recommendations, sought to eliminate the structural causes which had set the stage for the violence. The third section, consisting of 38 recommendations, aimed to avoid the recurrence of violent acts by means of institutional reforms. Finally, the last group contains 12 recommendations, designed to provide reparations to the victims of the conflict.

The most numerous recommendations are of a legal nature (70 per cent), institutional (47 per cent), and constitutional (26 per cent), which starkly contrast to the very few recommendations dealing with criminal prosecution (2.33 per cent). Our analysis of the CVES recommendations allows us to state that the Salvadorian Transitional Justice Process was mainly focused on institutional reform of the State. The CVES' recommendations apparently confirm Teitel's evaluation of the Commission, in the sense that "the primordial purpose of the [Commission] was not to achieve truth, but rather peace" (2003, 79). In other words, it was a race to the future designed to avoid prosecution, centering efforts on the creation of a new state structure, more democratic and committed to human rights. Furthermore, 60 per cent of the recommendations may also be classified as "non-recurrence", suggesting measures intended to avoid similar events in the future.

The Commission formulated the recommendations with clear purposes and recipients, identifying institutions that would end up being the implementing actors. Most of the recommendations were addressed to the Legislative and Executive Branches of the state.

5. STATUS OF IMPLEMENTATION OF THE RECOMMENDATIONS

The combined effect of the Salvadorian Transitional Process with the process of societal "pacification" generated a context of extreme political polarization and strong mistrust between actors, which greatly conditioned the implementation of the recommendations, mainly in a negative way. In this section we analyze the processes of implementation of the CVES' recommendations, identifying both the actors and the factors that influenced the implementation processes. We further verify the current compliance status of the recommendations. We have structured our discussion according to the list of 43 recommendations presented in the Report (as numbered by ourselves for the purposes of our analysis).[9] Our analysis shows that approximately 41 per cent of the recommendations had been implemented by the end of data collection. As for the remaining 59 per cent, almost no attempt had been made at implementation (in 28 per cent of the cases) or, if an attempt was made, it had failed to materialize (14 per cent).

5.1. RECOMMENDATIONS INFERRED DIRECTLY FROM INVESTIGATION RESULTS

The first recommendations, classified as pressing and requiring urgent fulfilment, were designed to purge state institutions. Clearly, this group of recommendations sought to remove from state institutions any persons who, according to the CVES investigations, were responsible for, or had contributed to the serious human rights violations.

5.1.1. Dismissal from the Armed Forces of El Salvador (FAES)

Despite the fact that many active military personnel stepped down from their positions, we interpret this recommendation as not implemented because most of the dismissals did not result from implementation of CVES recommendations, but rather because these individuals "retired after fulfilling their required active duty legal term within the Armed Forces of El Salvador" (UN 1994a, §148). Since these army officers were not dismissed as recommended by the CVES, many of them ended up occupying positions within the government's structure, such as consular representatives.

Due to the nature of the Salvadorian transitional process, it is important to point out that this recommendation is intimately connected to the compliance mechanisms of other obligations accepted within the framework of the Peace Agreement. Ten military officers appearing in the report of the Ad Hoc Commission presented on September 23, 1992 were also mentioned by the CVES six months later (March 15, 1993),[10] out of the total 62 officers directly named in the CVES Report (Fiumara 2004; UN 1993a, 2).

However, naming those responsible did not yield the expected results. It has been documented that, from September 1992 to March 1993, President Cristiani attempted to protect the military commanders in chief, constantly postponing

9 See Annex 1 for a complete list of the recommendations.

10 The Peace Agreements set forth that the CVES would appoint a representative to observe the sessions of the Ad Hoc Commission.

their dismissals and giving them the option to retire instead. Cristiani's actions caused multiple interventions from people in high positions in the United Nations. However, it was not the UN's pressure but rather pressure from the United States that allowed the establishment of a definitive action plan for the dismissals from the FAES (Spence et al. 1994, 15).

The opposition of other high-ranking state officials was added to the climate of confrontation. There is evidence that, after the presentation of the CVES Report, the President of the Supreme Court, upper government officers and some political leaders, as well as media sectors, vehemently and publicly rejected the conclusions and recommendations of the Truth Commission regarding the Salvadorian Armed Forces purge. The UN was heavily criticized, and anonymous threats were once again made against the UN Mission for El Salvador (UN 1993a).

5.1.2. *Dismissal from the Public Service*

Following the above logic, this recommendation, which sought to dismiss public servants and members of the judiciary mentioned in the Report's conclusions from their positions, was also never implemented. There are no records of any dismissals. In July of 1993, in a letter addressed to the UN Secretary General, President Cristiani stated that he was not prepared to apply this recommendation (UN 1993b, §10). This same unwillingness was seen when one of the civilians mentioned in the Report represented the government at a public event (UN 1993b). As for the three judicial officers mentioned in the Report, there also is no record of their dismissal from their positions at the judiciary.

5.1.3. *Disqualification from Holding Public Office*

This recommendation involved the disqualification of people identified by the CVES as responsible for human rights violations, from holding any public post or office for a period of not less than 10 years, and permanent disqualification from any activity related to public security or national defense. The COPAZ did not draft any legislative project recommended by the Commission. As a matter of fact, some of the persons mentioned in the Report have occupied lower and higher public positions within the government, demonstrating the degree of impunity in El Salvador.

This recommendation resulted in an active exchange of opinions and communications between the Office of the Secretary General of the United Nations, the government, the FMLN and the COPAZ. Based on the communications of the COPAZ *pro tempore* coordinator to the Secretary General of the United Nations, between August of 1993 and January of 1994, the consensus was to not apply this recommendation (UN 1993b, §11 and

UN 1994b, §65). The then Secretary General of the United Nations legitimized the consensus within the COPAZ by alleging that

> although (...) the signatories are required to fulfil the commitments accepted pursuant to the agreements, I have already pointed out that, if they and the Salvadorian society as a whole (represented, for example, by the COPAZ) should agree that certain specific provisions should not be fulfilled, I would be willing to recommend that the Security Council exempt default on such provisions from being considered a violation of the Agreements (UN 1993b, §13).

5.1.4. *Judicial Reform: Resignation of the Supreme Court Judges*

The 1989–94 Supreme Court magistrates did not resign, thus failing to comply with the provisions of the CVES. This recommendation was immediately rejected by all of them, especially its president. Specifically, during an event organized as a reaction to the Final Report, the Supreme Court refuted the CVES' conclusions and recommendations, alleging that their true purpose was to "subvert the order established by the Constitution, the international treaties or the current Salvadorian legislation" (Corte Suprema de Justicia (CSJ) 1993). Later, Mauricio Gutiérrez Castro, then president of the Supreme Court, stated that the signing of the Agreement to establish the CVES in the Salvadorian peace process had been a "stupidity" (Spence et al. 1993, 6). For this reason, although the recommendation sought to facilitate the prompt establishment of a new magistrate selection model, this was not put in place until 1994, the date of expiration of the magistrates' terms.

5.1.5. *Judicial Reform: Removal of the Members of the Judicial Council*

The Commission also recommended the modification of the system of removal for members of the National Judicial Council (*Consejo Nacional de la Judicatura* – CNJ) to one where they could only be dismissed for precise legal reasons verified by the Legislative Assembly. Although this recommendation apparently introduced significant improvements to the CNJ's independence, it generated certain criticism from the independent expert for El Salvador designated by the UN Human Rights Commission, Pedro Nikken, who felt that the exclusive participation of the Assembly increased the risk of politicizing the body (UN 1995a, §65).

However, the changes suggested by the CVES were implemented. First, those regarding dismissal cases were fulfilled through a legal reform of the CNJ Law's Article 11, effective in March of 1994. Second, a Constitutional reform of Article 187, paragraph 3, was necessary in order to implement the recommendation related to transferring the power to regulate the dismissal of a CNJ member to the Legislative Assembly. The constitutional reform was started in 1994 but was not completed until 1996, following the complex process required for constitutional reform. This reform was ratified in 1996 in a tense and confrontational political context. Legislative agreement was only reached thanks to the mediating intervention of Álvaro Soto, sent by the Secretary General of the United Nations (UCA, 1996).

5.1.6. *Judicial Reform: Judicial Evaluation*

In evident violation of the CVES' recommendations, the *Ley de la Carrera Judicial* (Law for the Judicial Career, LCJ) was never amended to provide that only judges demonstrating judicial dedication, efficiency, concern for human rights, independence, judicial criteria, honesty and impartiality – as per the rigorous evaluation of the CNJ – could remain in the judicial system. This, despite the fact that the Legislative Assembly had established a technical commission to draft this reform project in 1993 (UN 1993b). There is currently no evidence of the drafting and discussion of a bill in the Legislative Branch. The only verifiable reform to the LCJ at the time of writing was made in December 1994 and referred to a different matter.

5.1.7. *Penalties*

Last in the CVES' set of recommendations designed to penalize and disqualify the persons who, according to the investigation, had committed or been accomplices in human rights violations, the CVES established the need to criminally punish such persons mentioned in the Report. However, due to the shortcomings of a judicial system that lacked the independence and trust required to prosecute the offenders, the prosecution of the cases was postponed until the institutional changes recommended for the Judicial Branch were completed.

Notwithstanding this, as a result of the blanket amnesty enacted in March 1993,[11] the prosecution of the parties responsible for the human rights violations mentioned in the Report continued to be postponed. With the 2016 declaration of the unconstitutionality of the Amnesty Law, a renewed opportunity was established for the victims of those serious crimes to seek justice.

---

11 The "General Amnesty Law for the Consolidation of Peace", approved by Legislative Decree no. 486, on March 20, 1993, published in the Official Gazette no. 56, Volume no. 318, dated March 22, 1993, substituted a general for a partial amnesty which had been approved in 1992, shortly after the signing of the Chapultepec Peace Agreements. A characteristic feature of the latter was that it excluded any persons included in the CVES Report (although the Commission didn't yet exist and the cases to be investigated had not been selected). One year later, when the Commission issued its report, the political and military elites of the time exerted pressure to inhibit any criminal prosecution derived from the CVES' investigations, resulting in the enactment of the 1993 Amnesty Law (Popkin 1998).

5.2. ERADICATION OF STRUCTURAL CAUSES LINKED DIRECTLY TO ABUSES

The second block of recommendations refers directly to the Armed Forces of El Salvador. These recommendations have not been uniformly implemented. While some of them have indeed been implemented (i.e. the reform of the educational system of the Armed Forces of El Salvador), others have been subjected to deliberate neglect (i.e. the removal of the Armed Forces of El Salvador from tasks related to public security and intelligence operations). The lack of follow-up of the Peace Agreement following the withdrawal of the United Nations from El Salvador, the scant commitment of post-war governments to professionalize the Armed Forces and the lack of accountability mechanisms to control and audit the military institution have hindered any progress towards greater institutionalization of the Armed Forces (Aguilar 2016, 70).

5.2.1. Reform of the Armed Forces of El Salvador: Special Legislative Commission

The Peace Agreement negotiations envisioned a series of constitutional reforms regarding military subordination to civilian authorities. Although it is often said that Alfredo Cristiani and the Armed Forces of El Salvador provided fundamental support for compliance with the Peace Agreement, the fact is that the reforms agreed during negotiations not only lacked political backing from the President but also had to overcome his government's and the Armed Forces' efforts to hinder progress in this regard (Aguilar 2016, 63).[12] This government's resistance at the negotiating table regarding the dissolution of the National Guard, the Treasury Police, the National Intelligence Office (*Dirección Nacional de Inteligencia* – DNI) and the Atlacatl Battalion, and the purge of the Armed Forces of El Salvador, held back the negotiations and prevented the signing of the ceasefire before the proposed date (Costa 1999, 133).

Finally, the subordination of the Armed Forces of El Salvador to civil authorities materialized with the reform of two articles of the Constitution at the time, included in "Agreement for Constitutional Reform no. 1", dated April 29, 1991. This Agreement contained, firstly, Article 213, which provides that "[t]he Armed Forces are part of the Executive Branch and are subordinated to the authority of the President of the Republic, who is the Commander in Chief" and, later, Article 82, which establishes that "[t]he ministers of any religion, the active members of the Armed Forces and the members of the National Civil Police may not belong to political parties or run for positions

---

12 According to Call (2002, 561), the Armed Forces of El Salvador were always skeptical about the FMLN's commitment to laying down its arms, thus always significantly hindering the government's ability to fulfil its commitments.

elected by the people." Subordination to civilian authorities is, as these articles show, understood simply as subordination to the President only.

Democratic control was also established over central military promotions and postings by means of constitutional changes and secondary laws. Furthermore, military careers and democratic controls were regulated by changes to the National Defense Law. In the same manner, there is accuracy in military budgetary records (Article 167, Ordinal 3° – executive control – and Article 131, Ordinal 10° – legislative control –, both from the Constitution; Article 25, paragraph 4° of the Law of National Defense). The changes to the education system and professionalization of the Armed Forces of El Salvador were made by means of the Organic Law of the Armed Forces (Article 59 and Chapter II) like the Law of Military Careers (Article 20).

5.2.2. *Reform of the Armed Forces of El Salvador: Legislative Reform*

The entire regulations of the Armed Forces were enacted after the Peace Agreement, and therefore included revision of earlier policies and new laws created under modern precepts, including the Organic Law of the Armed Forces (1998), the Law of the State Intelligence Body (2001), the Law of National Defense (2002), the Law of Military Careers (1995) and the Law of Armed Forces Military Service and Reserve (1992). Only the Military Code of Justice from 1964 remained unrevised, although with three modifications: one in 1985, another in 1992, and a judgment of unconstitutionality in 2014 (final part of the Code).

5.2.3. *Integral Reform of the Armed Forces of El Salvador*

Article 211 of the Constitution states that the Armed Forces of El Salvador are not a "deliberative" institution and there is jurisprudence from the Constitutional Court, specifically on unconstitutionality (Judgment no. 4-2012), which sets forth the governing principles of democratic military morals: legality, due obedience, respect for human rights and rule of law.

In the same manner, the Law of Military Careers regulates the system of dismissal on the grounds of bad public or private behavior. Regarding the military curricular system, courses on human rights, the rule of law and sociology are included in military academic plans starting in military school and continuing all the way up to the courses for joint chiefs of staff. The Law of Military Careers and its regulations include the method of education within the Armed Forces of El Salvador, although it does not specifically mention human rights. It also establishes training courses to be taken overseas by officers of the Armed Forces. According to Schultze-Kraft (1998), "the modification of the military education system was the reform area that encountered least resistance from the Armed Forces of El Salvador."

Finally, the Armed Forces of El Salvador also published in the printed media their new doctrine of respect for the rule of law and for human rights, as well as the exclusion of internal security activities and the differentiation between such activities and external defense (Call 2002, 565). With regard to the Court of Honor of the Armed Forces, created by the Peace Agreements to hear cases on actions violating the military code of honor, the United Nations Observer Mission in El Salvador (ONUSAL) has not found any institutional relationship between the members of the Armed Forces of El Salvador and paramilitary or illegal groups (UN 1993b).

5.2.4. *Demilitarization of the Police*

Although Article 159 of the Constitution establishes the separation of public security from national defense, controlled by different Ministries, there was a great deal of resistance to this notion, both inside and outside the Armed Forces of El Salvador as a result of strong interests connected to the *status quo* (Aguilar 2016, 63). Notwithstanding this, the Armed Forces of El Salvador accepted most of the institutional changes:

> the dissolution of the three police forces under its control [CUSEP], the delimitation of its duties of internal security, the dismantling of the paramilitary civil defense forces, the suspension of forced recruitment activities, and the modification of its doctrine and training under an Academic Council which included civilians from different political backgrounds (Call 2003, 835).

In the same way, Call indicates (2003, 835) how the FAES also reduced their numbers earlier than expected "going from 63,170 in 1992 to about 30,500 in 1994", although he points out that "this dramatic reduction was probably exaggerated due to the thousands of 'ghost soldiers' in the original lists, whose salaries were taken by corrupt officers."

However, "the military kept many of their prior roles and their sense of institutional autonomy" (Call 2002, 565). In addition to its regular participation in the so-called *Joint Task Forces*, this continuation is also the result of the approval of the deployment of essentially military patrols known as Task Forces (*Fuerzas de Tareas*), which operated outside the jurisdiction of the National Civil Police (PNC). In November of 2009, by means of Executive Decree no. 70, the President authorized the launching of military commandos, who were granted authority to establish control, inspection and detention posts on roads and with the power to arrest people and later put them at the disposal of the PNC. The same decree further allowed the military access to the penitentiary system. With this, the operational subordination of the military to civilian authorities during joint patrols which had prevailed since 1995 was interrupted in a context of greater operational autonomy of the Armed Forces (Aguilar 2016, 74).

The military commandos and public security autonomous territorial intervention plans were created during this period, as well as the formulation by the military of the strategic security plan known as "*Plan de Campaña Nuevo Amanecer*" (New Dawn Campaign Plan). The participation of the Armed Forces in the public security plans went from being marginal activities by the military to becoming every-day and strategic roles (IUDOP, 2014[13]).

5.2.5. *Investigation of Illegal Groups*

Little or nothing has been done to dismantle military-like organizations parallel to the state, which enjoyed a certain degree of support from the government and the Armed Forces and were accustomed to exterminating political enemies and committing all sorts of illicit acts for the purpose of achieving "state stability". Also, no serious investigations have been performed on the fully verified actions of the death squads which operated during the war; nor were there any attempts at prosecuting their members and commanders. On the other hand, the transfer of these perverse paralegal security group structures that existed during the war into the "new" National Civil Police was promoted or at least allowed. According to Morales (2006, 3), at no point was there any attempt to dismantle these groups, much less punish their members. Further, according to Morales, there was never a serious judicial investigation "due to the enormous political power of their financial sponsors and leaders."

Broad queries performed by the UN Mission in El Salvador and directed by the Under-Secretary General of Political Matters, Marrack Goulding (November 1993), had resulted in the establishment of a Joint Group tasked with the investigation of politically-motivated illegal armed groups. The members of the Joint Group were two independent representatives from the Salvadorian government designated by the President, the Attorney for the Defense of Human Rights, and the Director of the Division of Human Rights of the ONUSAL.

The Joint Group's Report was made public in July of 1994. As recorded by Amnesty International, President Calderón Sol "received a confidential attachment listing the names of presumed perpetrators and promised to investigate all the charges supported by sufficient evidence." However, the

---

13 According to Aguilar (2016, 78) we can verify the participation of the Armed Forces of El Salvador in at least 12 security plans between 1992 and 2015: Plan grano de Oro (Grain of Gold Plan) (1992–93); Plan vigilante (Vigilante Plan) (1993); Plan guardián (Guardian Plan) (1995); Plan mano dura (Strong Hand Plan) (2003); Plan Super Mano dura (Super Strong Hand Plan) (2004); Plan de operaciones Zeus (Zeus Operation Plan) (2009–14); Plan de prevención y apoyo a la comunidad (Prevention and Community Support Plan) (2009–14); Plan de operaciones San Carlos (San Carlos Operations Plan) (2010–14); Plan de operaciones Sumpul (Sumpul Operations Plan) (2011–14); Plan Barrios (Barrios Plan) (2011); Plan de Seguridad Escuela Segura (Safe School Security Plan) (2012); Plan Grupo Conjunto Cuscatlán (Joint Cuscatlan Group Plan) (2012–15).

"management of discourse" was exquisite, but without concrete results. Despite the report and promises, no investigation was carried out to charge and punish the members of these illegal/criminal structures. The public reception of the Report of the Joint Group was foreseeable: The ex-Minister of Defense, General Humberto Corado Figueroa, "vehemently criticized the report as confusing and not at all conclusive, echoing the reaction of the military to the 1993 report of the Truth Commission" (Amnesty International 1996, 4).

5.3. INSTITUTIONAL REFORMS TO PREVENT RECURRENCE

The goal of the third group of recommendations was to undertake institutional reforms to avoid the recurrence of the Salvadorian civil war experiences. This group of recommendations had been previously identified in the Peace Agreement. However, the Commission believed it was necessary to reiterate them, since the country's ability to achieve "a modern and democratic institutional framework as required by the rule of law" rested on the implementation of these recommendations (CVES Final Report 1993, 192). Of the 17 recommendations included in this section, seven refer to the reform of the justice system (17–23), 10 refer to the protection of human rights (24–33) and one affects the police institution (34). These will be discussed in that order.

5.3.1. *Administration of Justice*

The CVES issued a series of recommendations for the purpose of transforming the authoritarian Salvadorian institutional system into a more democratic model. This reformist spirit was especially important in the judicial field, because the CVES' investigation work had uncovered the judicial system's lack of independence, due mainly to the high concentration of duties of a "politicized" Supreme Court; and, especially, to the serious shortcomings of the Salvadorian justice administration system, which had recently allowed some of its history's worst atrocities against human dignity (Popkin 2004, 410; Díaz and Linares 2005, 54).

5.3.1.1. Justice Administration: Decentralization of Supreme Court Powers

The first recommendation regarding judicial reform was intended to overcome, in the CVES' words, "one of the most notorious deficiencies of the Salvadorian Judicial System", that is, the high concentration of judicial powers granted to the CSJ, and to its president as leader of the Judicial Authority. In order to implement this recommendation, it was necessary to modify the Constitution.

However, a simple review of the constitutional legislation verifies that the Supreme Court, and its President, continue to hold a great number of administrative powers (Article 182 of the Constitution). This might be explained by various factors, but mainly, it was the result of the vehement opposition of the Supreme Court to the idea of losing control over the judges and, of course, due to the unconditional support of its political allies in the Legislative Assembly (Popkin et al. 1994). Instead, at that time of reformist effervescence, several sectors showed their support and began the procedures needed to implement such recommendation, but those efforts never materialized. Although several constitutional reforms were agreed in April 1994, only one of them intended to reduce the authority of the Supreme Court,[14] and it was never ratified.

5.3.1.2. Justice Administration: Appointment and Removal of Judges and Magistrates

The CVES considered that "the judges should not be appointed [or] removed by the [CSJ] but rather by an Independent National Judicial Council." However, the current Salvadorian system does not reflect such a change.[15] This recommendation required a constitutional reform. In spite of a favorable environment to make this change in the years immediately following the signing of the Peace Agreements (Popkin et al. 1994, 1), no Legislature has been able to proceed with the amendment process. This recommendation had the support of several sectors (i.e. political parties, COPAZ, etc.), but the Supreme Court's resistance to change and the absence of political will to transfer judicial career control duties to the Supreme Court have been difficult to overcome (UN 1994b, §51; Spence et al. 1994, 8).

5.3.1.3. Judges' Responsibility Regarding the National Judicial Council

Another recommendation related to the reduction of the Supreme Court powers, which has not been strictly implemented, was that "[e]ach judge should take responsibility for managing the resources of the court under his[her] charge, answering to the National Judicial Council." As reported by the United Nations, this recommendation entailed a modification of the Organic Judicial Law and the approval of reforms to the Law of Judicial Careers (UN 1993a, 7). However, these reforms were never implemented (Villavicencio 1996). Currently, the assets and salaries of the courts are entirely managed by the Supreme Court,

---

14 Related to the creation of the *Consejo Nacional de la Abogacía y Notariado* (National Legal Profession and Special Notary Public Council), examined below.

15 Currently, Article 182, Ordinal 9° of the Constitution still attributes the authority to appoint and remove magistrates and judges to the CSJ. Article 6 of the Law of Judicial Careers expands along these same lines.

causing the centralization of services and supplies, from physical infrastructure to basic operational service payments, under the Financial Department of the Supreme Court (Díaz and Urquilla 2000, 8).

5.3.1.4. Creation of the National Legal Profession and Special Notary Public Council

The CVES also recommended removing the CSJ's authority to approve, punish and suspend the exercise of the legal and special notary public professions, as established in Article 182, Ordinal 12° of the Constitution. Although procedures were initiated in 1994 to transfer this duty to another body, it is still entrusted to the Supreme Court. Compliance with this recommendation required reform of the Constitution, both in order to create a new institution and to transfer functions connected to the practice of the notary public professions. However, although a reform agreement was adopted in April of 1994, including the creation of a "National Law and Notary Public Professional Council", which would be tasked with sanctioning and suspending the exercise of these functions (however, not the power to authorize such exercise, as fully recommended by the CVES), this reform was never ratified. Specifically, instead of ratifying this agreement, the Legislature amended it. In July of 1996, the Legislative Assembly modified the institutional design of the "National Law and Public Notary Profession Council", granting it all the functions mentioned by the CVES in its recommendation. However, this modification was once again converted into a "constitutional reform agreement," waiting for a ratification that never came.

5.3.1.5. Budgetary Allowance: Court and Salary Increases

One of the recommendations that did get implemented was connected to the constitutional guarantees of a certain proportion of the state budget earmarked for the judiciary,[16] to ensure the creation of new courts and to improve the salary conditions of judges. According to the United Nations, the Supreme Court had been creating new courts and improving the judges' salaries before the CVES report was published. During the period 1989–93, the number of lower instance courts had actually increased significantly. In addition, it is possible to verify the increase in number of courts by examining the multiple reforms undergone by the Organic Judicial Law during the following three years. During the

16 As a result of the constitutional reform of Article 172, paragraph 4, made in the framework of the Peace Agreements, the Judiciary's budget cannot be lower than 6% of the State's General Budget.

period 1994–96, there were more than five reforms mentioning the creation of Second Instance Chambers, First Instance Courts, and Peace Courts in several municipalities. The judicial salaries similarly experienced an increase in the same period (Villavicencio 1996, 92).

5.3.1.6. Due Process

This recommendation issued by the CVES addressed four measures created to strengthen the effectiveness of due process. They are addressed in the following sub-sections.

5.3.1.7. Extrajudicial Confessions Deprived of Any Effect

This recommendation could be implemented by means of either legal reforms or constitutional reforms, although the latter would establish the principle of a "prohibition of extrajudicial confession." Possibly for this reason, Salvadorian political actors opted for constitutional reform, but this has not yet been completed. Up to the present, at least two constitutional reform agreements addressing this subject have been issued, neither of which have been ratified to become fully effective constitutional amendments. Although there were hopes that the Criminal Procedural Code of 1998 would comply with the recommendations of the CVES and the Human Rights Division of ONUSAL, in regard to "depriving extrajudicial confession from any effectiveness", this has not happened (Villavicencio 1996). Article 222 of the Criminal Procedural Code (repealed in 2009) continued to validate evidence acquired through extrajudicial confessions, when fulfilling certain requirements described in the Code. Other legal statutes reformed at that time followed a similar path (UN 1995a). They addressed the subject tangentially, but none of them deprived extrajudicial confession of all validity.

5.3.1.8. Guaranteeing the Presumption of Innocence

This recommendation was positively received. During the period when the CVES report was issued, there were a great variety of institutional and legislative changes that centered their efforts, *inter alia*, on breaking with existing inquisitorial and authoritarian institutions. The main contribution to the implementation of measures guaranteeing the presumption of innocence was the criminal justice reform implemented in the same period for the purpose of changing from an inquisitorial criminal system into an adversarial system. As a result, the Criminal Procedural Code issued in the years following the Peace Agreement (now revoked) incorporated many of the recommendations issued by, respectively, the CVES, the Division of Human Rights of the ONUSAL, and the UN's Independent Expert for El Salvador (Villavicencio 1996, 95).

5.3.1.9. Use of Police and Judicial Detention

This recommendation was also implemented in connection with the broader institutional and legal reforms undertaken during the 1990s. However, the administrative mechanisms for verification of the conditions of detainees and administrative processes for violators of police and judicial detention – created as a result of the establishment of institutions such as the Office of the Attorney for the Defense of Human Rights of El Salvador (*Procuraduría para la Defensa de los Derechos Humanos de El Salvador*, PDDH) and the Office of the Inspector of the PNC – are not at all negligible. Essentially, the criminal system reform allowed substantial implementation of this recommendation. The 1998 Penal Code incorporated the crime of "deprivation of freedom by a public officer or employee, law enforcement agent or public authority", which punishes failure to comply with the maximum police/administrative detention terms (see Article 13 of the Constitution) with a three-to-six-year sentence and a special disqualification from holding office for the same term.

5.3.1.10. Strengthen the Right to Defense

The implementation of this recommendation was also made possible due to the establishment of new democratic institutions. Its compliance came in connection with reform of the criminal justice system, which transitioned from inquisitorial to adversary. Thus, these new regulations introduced the following crime in Article 298 of the Penal Code: "Attack on the right to defense", designed to regulate the behavior of public officers and employees.

5.3.1.11. Judicial Training School

In fulfilment of this recommendation, the *Escuela de Capacitación Judicial* (School of Judicial Training) became a department of the National Council of the Judiciary, CNJ). According to the reports of the UN Secretary General, the CNJ made an effort to improve and strengthen the institution. During the first few years, it managed international technical assistance with governmental support (UN 1993b), but the task was not easy. When the CNJ attempted to perform its constitutional responsibilities, it was met with great resistance from the Supreme Court of Justice. By contrast, the judicial training school now operates fully within the CNJ, where they offer courses and train not only the members of the judicial body but also members of the Attorney General's office, private attorneys and government officers.

5.3.2. *Protection of Human Rights*

Another group of 10 recommendations explicitly addressed the protection of human rights.

5.3.2.1. ONUSAL Recommendations

The first CVES recommendation on the protection of human rights sought to promote the fulfilment and implementation of ONUSAL's recommendations with regard to human rights. However, these recommendations were not strictly addressed by the government. Among other things, ONUSAL recommended (i) the ratification of international treaties on human rights; (ii) organic and functional reform of the Judiciary; (iii) the creation of an Ad Hoc Commission to investigate extrajudicial executions; (iv) the modification of statutes on *habeas corpus* and constitutional protections; (v) the creation of a fund to indemnify the victims of serious human rights violations; (vi) the categorization of torture and enforced disappearance as crimes; (vii) measures for the purpose of regulating the behavior of public officers entrusted with law enforcement, reversing the practice of arbitrary detentions, and acknowledgment of the legal capacity of associations and unions (UN 1993c); as well as (viii) measures to reinforce control over minor detainees rehabilitation centers (UN 1992a).

ONUSAL's Division of Human rights assessed the compliance with the institution's recommendations in its tenth report (UN 1994c). It concluded that the implementation of the creation of an Ad Hoc Commission to investigate extrajudicial executions did not satisfy the criteria required to guarantee an effective and impartial investigation of such facts. The report lamented the government's inactivity in terms of the creation of a compensation fund (UN 1994c), which had never materialized. Concerning the detention of minors, the Task Force on Arbitrary Detention (*Grupo de Trabajo Sobre Detención Arbitraria*) pointed out in 2013 that sentenced minors are placed together in regular cells and that there is no special place for female minors or girls (UN 2013, §102).

5.3.2.2. Strengthening the Office of the Attorney for the Defense of Human Rights

In order to strengthen the Office of the Attorney for the Defense of Human Rights – PDDH, an institution created within the framework of the Peace

Agreement, three measures were implemented.[17] The first Attorney was Carlos Mauricio Molina Fonseca (1992–95), who, starting in 1994, was accompanied by ONUSAL in an effective collaboration to conduct human rights investigations (Holiday and Stanley 1997).

5.3.2.3. Resource Base

The first recommended measure was to carry out assessment of the PDDH's current situation and its most immediate priorities and needs, in order to secure the means, including international cooperation, to achieve those objectives. This recommendation was not fulfilled. No structural reforms were made to the Office of the Attorney for the Defense of Human Rights[18] in the short term, and collaboration between institutions decreased over time:

> In spite of its success and acceptance by the newly elected (and widely respected) Attorney of Human Rights, Victoria de Avilés [in March 1995], the program was suspended when ONUSAL transitioned to MINUSAL, to a great extent due to inadequate follow-up and internal struggles among United Nations personnel (Holiday and Stanley 1997, 19).

5.3.2.4. Territorial Deployment

The CVES further recommended extending the Office of the Attorney for the Defense of Human Rights' presence throughout the country. This was gradually done. There were five regional offices by June 1994 and, by 1995, the PDDH already had an office in each of the country's departments (Johnstone 1997). The PDDH has 17 departmental and/or local delegations offering legal training and receiving reports. Nevertheless, the PDDH's authority is limited, as acknowledged by the institution itself (PDDH 2012, 81).

5.3.2.5. Penitentiary Surveillance

Thirdly, the CVES recommended that the PDDH make more frequent use of its powers to inspect any site or installation in the country, especially where places of detention are concerned. The Office of the Attorney for the Defense of Human Rights has fulfilled this recommendation regarding penitentiary monitoring, especially for detention centers. The PDDH carries out this work through its "Department for Penitentiary Verification" and monitoring delegations.

---

17 During the Mexico 1991 Agreement, the parties agreed on the creation of the PDDH as a constitutional entity within the framework of the Office of the Attorney General. The constitutional reform allowing the creation of this institution became effective on November 30, 1991.

18 The decree creating the Office of the Attorney for the Defense of Human Rights (no. 183 of 1992) was not reformed until February 2001, by means of Legislative Decree no. 269.

5.3.2.6. Constitutional Protections and *Habeas Corpus*

The CVES recommended adopting measures to make constitutional protection (*recurso de amparo constitucional*) and *habeas corpus* complaints truly operational. The idea was to make every first instance judge competent to hear these complaints within his or her territorial jurisdiction. This recommendation has not been implemented.

Habeas corpus continues to be applicable exclusively by the Constitutional chamber of the Supreme Court and in the second instance Chambers located outside the country's capital, while constitutional protection is the exclusive responsibility of the Constitutional Court.

In addition, the CVES recommended the explicit provision that constitutional protections, *habeas corpus* and due process rules cannot be suspended under any circumstance, not even during states of emergency. This recommendation was not implemented either, since Article 29 of the Constitution does not explicitly establish what specific guarantees are not subject to suspension.

5.3.2.7. Constitutional Standing of Human Rights

The Commission stated that it was necessary to reaffirm the constitutional standing of human rights, including those that are not explicitly mentioned in the Constitution, but which appear in international treaties ratified by El Salvador. This recommendation was never implemented. Even as of now, in accordance with Article 144 of the Constitution, international human rights treaties in El Salvador are subordinate to the Constitution but have standing if ratified. This creates an unclear situation for the courts.

5.3.2.8. Administrative Detention

With regard to administrative detentions,[19] the Commission set forth three recommendations, which are discussed in turn.

5.3.2.9. Define the System of Administrative Detention

The CVES stated that the system of administrative detentions needed to be reformed in three ways, according to which they must be precisely outlined, with restrictive standards: (i) what are the causes supporting administrative detention, (ii) who are the competent public officers who order it and (iii) who are competent to enforce it? Strictly speaking, this recommendation has not

19 Original in Spanish, *detención administrativa*. Term commonly used for holding people without trial, usually for security or terrorism reasons.

been fulfilled, since the legal description continues to be very broad. Specifically, Article 14 of the Constitution establishes the possibility of administrative detention without requiring precise and restrictive criteria.

5.3.2.10. Duration of Administrative Detention

The Commission's recommendation was to restrict administrative detentions as much as possible. However, Article 13, paragraph 2 of the Constitution establishes a maximum of 72 hours, "during which time, the detainee must be put at the disposal of a competent judge, in compliance with any provisions applied." In 2010, the UN Committee of Human Rights stated its concern in this regard, reminding the State of its duty to

> review legislation regarding provisional detention in order to make it compatible with the provisions of the Agreement, to guarantee such detention does not exceed 48 hours, and, in any event, not exceed beyond the time when the person is put at the disposal of a judge.[20]

Thus, neither the CVES recommendation nor the request of the UN Human Rights Committee has been fulfilled.

5.3.2.11. Limit the Power to Impose Administrative Detention

The recommendation to limit the administrative authorities' competence to impose freedom-restricting penalties has not been fulfilled. Currently, the Constitution, Article 14 (added to the Constitution in 1996), authorizes administrative authorities to impose freedom-restricting penalties, i.e. arrest orders of up to five days.

5.3.2.12. Information on Detainees

The CVES recommended extending the detainee information system and centralizing an updated list of detained persons, their location and their legal status through the Office of the Attorney for the Defense of Human Rights. This recommendation has been partially fulfilled. As of 2017, detainee information records are managed by the Supreme Court and its Department of Detainee Information (*Departamento de Información sobre Personas Detenidas*). According to the PDDH, the department possesses detainee data recorded by the Supreme Court itself.

---

[20] Concluding Observations ICCPR, UN Human Rights Committee, November 18, 2010, 94.

5.3.2.13. Criminal Law Reform

The Commission pointed out that the criminal law system needed to be reformed in the future in order to adequately consider crimes committed with direct or indirect support from the State. This recommendation has been gradually implemented, both through reform of the criminal law in 1998, and later in 2001, when provisions on aggravating circumstances were added to the Penal Code for situations where the active subject is a public officer, authority or law enforcement agent (Article 30, Ordinal 17°).

In addition, the criminal law reform of 1990s also included crimes that could only be committed by the authorities or public officers, for example, torture (Article 297), which requires a qualified active subject: "The public officer, employee, law enforcement agent or public authority". The crime of enforced disappearance committed by public officers (Article 364) was also made an offense with a sentence of four to eight years, and the crime of genocide, with the aggravating circumstance of commission by a civil or military authority (Article 361), which customarily carries a 10 to 25-year prison sentence, can be increased by up to 30 more years.

In any case, it is noteworthy that genocide is the only crime which appears to carry sentences that are proportional to the gravity of the offense, if we consider, for example, that the sentence for embezzlement can be up to 15 years (Article 325).

5.3.2.14. Access to Remedies

In addition, the CVES recommended granting every victim of a human rights violation a simple, quick and readily accessible recourse to obtain material reparation for any damage incurred. This recommendation was not fulfilled either, since, although certain mechanisms exist, these are not expeditious. The report on the application of the Commission's recommendations issued by the Secretary General of ONUSAL stated that, in this regard, it would be advisable to "enact laws to distinguish the indemnification proceedings set forth in the codes and indemnification proceedings resulting from human rights violations" (UN 1993b, §69). This has not yet occurred.

5.3.2.15. Ratify Human Rights Treaties and Accept the Contentious Jurisdiction of the IACtHR

Undoubtedly, one of the recommendations that improved human rights protection in El Salvador was the recommendation to accept the contentious jurisdiction of the Inter-American Court of Human Rights and to ratify seven international human rights treaties. All of these treaties were ratified between 1994 and 2006, except one: the Convention on the Non-Applicability of Statutory Limitations to War Crimes and Crimes Against Humanity. One plausible explanation for this lack of compliance is the systematic absence of State commitment (both governmental and legislative) to prosecute and try the crimes of the past, which was made most evident by the passing of a general and unconditional Amnesty Law a few days following publication of the Commission's report. In other words, the Salvadorian government had no intention of ratifying an international treaty mandating prosecutions for human rights violations of the past.

Table 2. El Salvador's Ratification of Human Rights Treaties

Human Rights Treaties	Date of Ratification	Date of Filing
Inter-American Convention to Prevent and Punish Torture	July 8,1994	December 5, 1994
United Nations Convention Against Torture and Other Cruel, Inhuman or Degrading Treatment or Punishment	May 19, 1994	June 17, 1996
Additional Protocol to the American Convention on Human Rights in the Area of Economic, Social and Cultural (Protocol of San Salvador)	May 5, 1995	June 6, 1995
Optional Protocol to the International Covenant on Civil and Political Rights (OP-ICCPR)	May 5, 1995	June 6, 1995
Acceptance of Contentious Jurisdiction of the Inter-American Court of Human Rights	May 5, 1995	June 6, 1995
Agreement 87 of the International Labor Organization	August 29, 2006	September 6, 2006
Agreement 98 of the International Labor Organization	August 29, 2006	September 6, 2006
Convention on the Non-Applicability of Statutory Limitations to War Crimes and Crimes Against Humanity	Not ratified	Not ratified

Source: Prepared by the authors based on data supplied by OHCHR and OAS.

Note that the treaties were ratified at three different points in time. In 1994, two torture-related treaties were ratified. In 1995, El Salvador ratified the San Salvador Protocol and the OP-ICCPR and accepted the contentious jurisdiction of the Inter-American Court of Human Rights. The government was initially reluctant to assume the responsibility resulting from its international adherence to the Inter-American Convention and the Convention against Torture (UN 1993b, §52 and ss. 52–56), but it later found a legal strategy to escape the control of the bodies of these international treaties. In the documents it filed, the Salvadorian State limited the jurisdiction of both control bodies, the Committee and the Court, to "exclusively those situations, events, cases, omissions, facts and legal acts occurred after the date of filing of the ratification document."

Thus, it extracted all incidences of serious human rights violations committed during the armed conflict. So, although "the Optional Protocol [of the ICCPR] was effectively ratified, and the contentious jurisdiction of the Inter-American Court of Human Right was accepted", as had been recommended by the CVES, we cannot confirm fulfilment of the Commission's purpose of guaranteeing the effectiveness of human rights for the victims of crimes against humanity and for the serious war-time human rights violations in El Salvador, since all attempts to obtain justice made by international bodies were obstructed. Finally, a decade later, El Salvador ratified two fundamental conventions regulating international labor standards (Conventions no. 87 and no. 98).

5.3.3. *National Civil Police*

The Commission required the reform of the National Civil Police (*Policía Nacional Civil* – PNC); the institution in charge of defending citizens and preventing situations leading to human rights violations. Although the National Civil Police became the only public security institution in El Salvador as of January 12, 1995, with the goal of becoming a "democratic" police force and a necessary tool to ensure the protection of human rights, the implementation of this recommendation has seen both progress and setbacks over the years.

5.3.3.1. Establishment of National Civil Police

The CVES recommended the establishment and functioning of the National Civil Police, in accordance with the model defined in the peace agreements, for defending the population and preventing human rights violations. In 1995, the creation of the PNC marked a transcending event in the history of El Salvador since it was assumed that, for the first time in the country's history, internal public security matters would be handled by a sole police body including mostly civil personnel. The PNC sought to end the military monopoly over internal security. However, this recommendation has been inconsistently implemented.

Even before its creation, the government did not seem inclined to develop a solid National Civil Police and supply it with the resources required to perform its responsibilities, notwithstanding the help received form ONUSAL's Police Division.[21] Despite initial lack of support from Cristiani's government, some

[21] ONUSAL's Police Division, in response to a petition presented by the government and in close coordination with the international technical team that advises the General Director of the PNC, performed an evaluation of the new police agency's operations in the field between April 1 and September 30 of 1993 and provided it with technical advice and logistic support. On July 27, 1994, the National Civil Police and ONUSAL signed a framework agreement and later signed memorandums of understanding regarding technical cooperation both with the Police Division and the Human Rights Division of ONUSAL.

improvements have been made in the police institution. In 2000 the National Civil Police underwent the most thorough purge ever, which resulted in the removal of more than 1500 members, among them, 20 sub-commissioners, inspectors and sub-inspectors. The General Inspectorship of the National Civil Police was created the following year, under the authority of the General Director, although in 2014, by means of a legislative reform, authority over the General Inspectorship was transferred to the Ministry of Justice and Public Security.

However, police reform suffered several setbacks between 2009 and 2014, since the Armed Forces of El Salvador, under the command of General Munguía Payés temporarily recovered full control of the country's public security sector, while the General held the position of Minister of Defense. The President extended his authority and marginalized other actors in the public security sector. General Munguía Payés was appointed Minister of Security, and General Francisco Salinas, who had been his Vice Minister of Defense, was appointed Director of the PNC. This allowed the military to recover certain control over civilian institutions, such as security and State intelligence. A court ruling of unconstitutionality in 2013 (Judgment no. 4-2012) declared these two senior position appointments illegal on the grounds that they violated Article 159 of the Constitution, which establishes the separation of national defense functions from public security functions.

Additionally, between October 2009 and March 2014, seven executive decrees and one legislative decree were issued authorizing the participation of members of the Armed Forces in a variety of tasks and activities connected with public security. This more than tripled the number of soldiers working in public security, from 1975 to 6500 (Aguilar 2016, 74).

5.3.3.2. Investigation of Crime/Dissolution of the CIHD

The CVES further recommends that every effort be made to put into practice as soon as possible the criminal investigation mechanism decided on in the peace agreements, which entails joint action by the National Civil Police and the Office of the Attorney General of the Republic.

It also recommends that the *Comisión Investigadora de Hechos Delictivos* (Commission for the Investigation of Criminal Acts – CIHD) be dissolved (since it was through its omissions that serious human rights violations during the period under investigation were covered up).

The constitutional reform of 1996 and the 2001 Organic Law of National Civil Police both mention the criminal investigative powers of the PNC and the need to decentralize criminal investigations by way of departmental delegations or sub-delegations. The also propose strengthening the PNC by specializing the police career and improving the availability of material resources.

However, the non-fulfilment of this recommendation became evident already in 1993, when the CIHD and the *Unidad Ejecutiva Antinarcotráfico* (Executive Anti-Drug Trafficking Unit – UEA), both military in nature, were incorporated to the PNC.[22] This is especially so because the CIHD was singled out by the PDDH due to its involvement in human rights violations and procedural faults (PDDH 2003, 27). The Human Rights Division of ONUSAL was highly critical of this, leading to several changes in the organization of the CIHD over the years.

Throughout the life of the PNC, many of its members who were part of the CIHD have been dismissed due to crimes committed before the creation of the PNC or perpetrated during the implementation of the new security force, thus violating police professional codes. In 2001, the UN Secretary General reported the growing number human rights violation reports and of the existence of criminal groups within the PNC (Morales 2006). Thus, the existence of criminal structures infiltrated in the PNC continues to be a problem in El Salvador.

5.4. STEPS TOWARDS NATIONAL RECONCILIATION

The fourth group of recommendations made by the CVES aimed to facilitate national reconciliation. The Final Report highlights the importance of measures such as material and moral reparations. The last two recommendations address the operation of COPAZ and the follow-up efforts by the international community.

5.4.1. Material Reparation Measures for Victims of the Conflict

The Commission established four specific recommendations regarding material reparations to victims. First was the creation of a special fund for the material compensation of victims of the conflict. In spite of some initial efforts, the fund's creation was postponed, as neither the government of El Salvador nor the international community demonstrated sufficient enthusiasm for the implementation of this recommendation (Hayner 2010).

The first tangible efforts towards implementation materialized in 2009, when the FMLN stepped into power. In 2013, President Mauricio Funes launched the "Program for the reparation of victims of serious human rights violations occurring in the context of the internal armed conflict", and in 2016, President

22 Members of the Commission for the Investigation of Criminal Acts (CIDH) and the Executive Anti-Drug Trafficking Unit (UEA) were inappropriately admitted to the PNC after completing a course that lasted only five days (See report on PNC irregularities and the Academia Nacional de Seguridad Pública (ANSP) operation presented by ONUSAL on July 15, 1994 in compliance with the Complementary Agreement of May 19, 1994.

Salvador Sánchez Cerén established the "Program for monetary transfers to victims of human rights violations during the armed conflict." Although the reparation programs set forth by these governments had earmarked funds for this purpose, a fund was created in combination with a previously existing fund, the *Fondo de Inversión Social para el Desarrollo Local* (Fund for Social Investment for Local Development – FISDL).[23] This recommendation can thus be considered partially implemented, since there is indeed a fund dedicated to the payment of reparations to victims, though not quite as set forth in the CVES report.

The Commission also ordered the creation of a Board of Directors to run the reparations fund and established selection criteria for the Board. The three-member Board was to be composed of one appointed by the government of El Salvador, one by the United Nations, and the third by mutual agreement between the first two appointed members (CVES Final Report, 1993). This selection methodology was not followed by President Cerén's administration. Instead, the Board of Directors was composed of government representatives and representatives of victims' organizations. Regarding the financing of the fund, it did not receive appropriate financial support from the State. Therefore, this recommendation was not implemented in accordance with the terms set forth by the CVES.

Lastly, we observe that the FMLN governments are the only ones that have made some effort to contribute to material reparations. The time gap between the publication of the Final Report in 1993 and the FMLN's ascent to power in 2009 partly explains the delay in compliance and follow-up of this recommendation.

5.4.2. *Moral Reparation Measures for Victims of the Conflict*

Recommendations seeking to provide moral reparation (also known as symbolic reparations) experienced a higher degree of implementation. This group contains three specific recommendations. First, the CVES recommended that the Salvadorian State build a monument to commemorate the victims of the armed conflict. This recommendation was not implemented by the government but rather by a civil society group;[24] the Committee for Monuments to Civilian Victims of Human Rights Violations (*Comité Pro Monumento de las Víctimas Civiles de violaciones de Derechos Humanos*), which included 10

---

23 This institution was created in the year 1990 with the name *Fondo de Inversión Social* (Social Investment Fund – FIS). Its purpose was to decrease existing inequalities in El Salvador.

24 In the year 2003 Amnesty International urged the political parties to heed the claims of civil society and acknowledge the Memory and Truth Monument as a national monument (Barrero 2014).

non-governmental organizations.[25] The monument, located in the Cuscatlán Park (San Salvador) was built by Julio Reyes and consists of an 85-meter black granite wall bearing the names of 25,626 victims (Sanfeliu 2011). It was inaugurated on December 6, 2003 and was declared a "protected cultural asset" in 2013 (LPG 2013). Other places of remembrance have been inaugurated in recent years, such as the "Reconciliation Park" and the "Piedras Coloradas Memorial Plaza", both inaugurated in 2017. Thus, the recommendation concerning symbolic reparation has been fulfilled in the terms set forth by the CVES' Final Report.

Regarding the second recommendation, acknowledging the honor of the victims, the Salvadorian State only began implementation after FMLN took over the government. Thus, on January 16, 2010, on the eighteenth anniversary of the Peace Agreements, President Mauricio Funes acknowledged, on behalf of the State, the responsibility of the Salvadorian Armed Forces, the public security forces, and other armed actors involved in human rights violations committed during the Salvadorian conflict. The President apologized to the victims and their family members (OEA 2010). This act was also recognized by the Organization of American States, which stated that "the acknowledgment of responsibility and the apology are important reparation measures and evidence a commitment to avoid the recurrence of the serious violations" (OEA 2010).

The third CVES recommendation for moral reparations involves the establishment of a national day to commemorate the victims of the conflict and affirm national reconciliation. This recommendation has not been implemented. Although commemorative acts have been organized on specific dates, there is yet no official date recognized by the State, as requested by the CVES. While there is a Peace Day to commemorate the Peace Agreements (January 16) (UN 1993b, §73), the closest to a national day of remembrance is a yearly commemoration organized by human rights organizations and the victims' families on November 1 at the Cuscatlán park, the location of the Monument for the Victims.

---

[25] The organizations were the following: *Asociación de Mujeres por la Dignidad y la Vida* (Association of Women for Dignity and Life), *Museo de la Palabra y la Imagen* (The Words and Images Museum), *Oficina de Asociación de Pro-Búsqueda de niñas y niños desaparecidos* (The Office of the Association for the Search for Disappeared Boys and Girls), *Centro para la Paz* (the Center for Peace), *Centro para la Promoción y Defensa de los Derechos Humanos "Madeleine Lagadec"* (the "Madeleine Lagadec" Center for the Promotion and Defense of Human Rights), *Comisión de Derechos Humanos* (the Commission of Human Rights), *Comité de Familiares de Víctimas de Violaciones a los Derechos Humanos Marianela García Villas* (the Marianela Garcia Villas Committee of Families of Victims of Human Rights Violations), *Comité de Madres de Desaparecidos y Asesinados Políticos "Monseñor Oscar Arnulfo Romero"* (the "Monseñor Oscar Arnulfo Romero" Committee of Mothers of Persons Disappeared and Assassinated for Political Reasons). Gloria Guzmán, also a member of this Committee played an important role in the implementation of this recommendation (Hernández Rivas 2015, 212).

5.4.3. Measures Regarding the Operation of COPAZ

The Commission thought it would be useful if the conclusions and recommendations and progress towards national reconciliation in its Final Report were to be analyzed not only by the Salvadorian people but also by a special forum comprising the most representative sectors of society to monitor strict compliance with the recommendations. However, this was never implemented, and the possibility for civil society to positively influence the fulfilment of the Commission's recommendations was blocked (Cuellar 2005, 155).

5.4.4. International Follow-Up of Recommendation Compliance

The last recommendation of the CVES addresses international follow-up of the process. Specifically, the Commission requested that the Independent Expert for El Salvador in the UN Commission of Human Rights present a report including an evaluation of the fulfilment of CVES recommendations. The Expert, Professor Pedro Nikken, did indeed perform a follow-up on the fulfilment of the Commission's recommendations and delivered a report on January 1995 (UN 1995a, §14). Consequently, we consider this recommendation implemented.

6. THE ROLE OF INSTITUTIONAL ACTORS IN IMPLEMENTATION

In concluding this chapter, we want to reflect on the role of various institutional actors regarding the implementation of the CVES recommendations. As is evident, the Salvadorian case cannot be understood without considering the presence of international actors in exerting pressure in support of the implementation of the recommendations. On the one hand, we have the United Nations, tasked with the mission to provide technical support and monitor implementation of the recommendations and Peace Agreement and, on the other we have the external actors whose pressure responded to economic interests. Regarding the latter, there are two exemplary cases. The first one is the Clinton Administration, which conditioned its military assistance to the State upon the fulfilment of the recommendations connected with the dismissal of members of the Armed Forces of El Salvador. The second is the European Union, which conditioned its renewal of tariff benefits upon the ratification of international treaties recommended by the CVES.

The participation of the Salvadorian Executive Branch was more ambiguous, since its performance was conditioned by the political parties in power at any one time: ARENA (1989–2009) and FMLN (2009 to date). Thus, two periods can be distinguished in the Salvadorian transitional justice process. The first is demarcated by the ARENA governments and the second by the coming to power of the FMLN. During the ARENA governments, some of the recommendations experienced a poor rate of implementation. The position of ARENA in terms of how to deal with the past armed conflict favored institutionalized oblivion and perpetrator impunity. Therefore, their efforts were centered on implementing institutional recommendations designed to prevent recurrence of similar events. Many of these institutional recommendations were implemented only due to international pressure. Notably, after FMLN took over power in 2009, efforts were more focused on the implementation of recommendations concerning material and moral reparations for the victims. However, the Executive Branch is responsible for the setbacks experienced in the field of implementation before the FMLN came to power.

The behavior of the Legislative Branch has been similarly ambivalent, probably as a direct result of the shifting interests of parliamentarians at different points in time. Undoubtedly, the parliamentary ARENA group refused to honor governmental commitments. For example, it has been verified that the recommendations focusing on reforming state institutions for the future without assigning responsibility for past events were usually processed without much resistance. We see this clearly in the recommendation regarding the ratification of international human rights treaties. Commitments were made to the Convention against Torture, but the Convention on the Non-applicability of Statutory Limitations to War Crimes and Crimes Against Humanity was thoroughly ignored. Another negative development was the issuance of the Amnesty Law a few days after the publication of the CVES Report. It became apparent that political will could be galvanized when the actors' interests were at stake.

At the outset there was no commitment whatsoever in the judicial sector to accept the CVES Report and fulfil its recommendations. A few days after the publication of the truth commission report, the Supreme Court and its President expressed their condemnation and alleged that the CVES' efforts were examples of international meddling in national sovereignty. However, later, they changed their strategy from downright rejection to more strategic behavior with the aim to retain control of the Supreme Court functions. With time and changing court members, the attitude has significantly changed. The judgment on the unconstitutionality of the Amnesty Law in 2016 proves this change and opens a window of opportunity to prosecute exemplary cases of human rights violations documented in the CVES Final Report.

The Salvadorian Armed Forces were among the actors who opposed implementation of many recommendations of the CVES. This is due to its hegemonic position within the Salvadorian political system, which they practically governed uninterruptedly "since independence and between 1932 and 1979" (Costa 1999, 77). Due to this, the process of re-composition of the Armed Forces of El Salvador turned out to be highly traumatic for the military sector at the time. Thus, the "imposed" military reform faced strong resistance both within the military sector and in more radical conservative sectors, which had been benefited by the autonomy and power held by the military up to the end of the civil war, and who clearly knew that this was the *de facto* end of their privileges and power (Aguilar 2016, 62). To this initial resistance, we should add in later years the successive attempts of the military high command, in alliance with some ex-military, to reconquer civil arenas, such as the public security sector, by alleging the emergence of new security threats.

Human rights organizations played a role in the quest for truth, the prosecution of alleged human rights perpetrators, and seeking both moral and material reparations. The Salvadorian case included participation of both international NGOs, such as Amnesty International, and national NGOs, such as the Committee for the Monument to Civilian Victims of Human Rights Violations. In addition, the country received the support of foreign non-governmental organizations such as *Solidaridad Extremeña* (Extremaduran Solidarity). The greatest success was the construction of the Monument for Victims of the Salvadorian armed conflict at the Cuscatlán Park. In this case, they operated as implementing actor for one of the recommendations set forth in the Report by fulfilling tasks that, to a large extent, should have been assumed by the State.

7. CONCLUSIONS

The Salvadorian process has several features that makes it different from other transitional processes in the region, of which we highlight two: First, El Salvador went through a negotiated transition from internal armed conflict to peace, parallel to the national process of democratization and reconciliation, with the intervention of external actors in addition to those usually included in transitions from authoritarianism to democracy (Kumar 1997; Azpuru 2007). As a result, following the signing of the Peace Agreement, the Salvadorian process was marked by distrustful political actors, and significant political polarization, still noticeable today in Salvadorian society. This contributed to the rigidity of the political actors when it came to developing "cooperation and consensus" mechanisms, which are essential in order to implement all of the CVES recommendations.

This dynamic established a complicated environment for the implementation of the recommendations. This is more so if one considers that just before the issuance of the Report the military trenches had been exchanged for political arenas and, thus, the environment of confrontation and mistrust between the main political parties, who in the recent past had confronted each other militarily, was reproduced within institutional spaces which, par excellence, are designed for debate and agreement (Córdova et al. 2007, 265).

Logically, these conditions became real obstacles for the materialization of many of the institutional reforms recommended by the Commission.

The second characteristic feature, just as important as the first, is the international community's unusual degree of participation in the Salvadorian process. Indeed, this peace process was supported by the United Nations starting with the negotiations, and later, enjoyed UN follow-up and monitoring of the Agreements and recommendations set forth in the process. This peculiarity made all the representatives of the UN system – from its Secretary General to the Commission of Human Rights' Independent Expert for El Salvador – become important actors for the compliance with the Commission's recommendations. In other words, the mission performed by the United Nations in El Salvador was extremely complex, since it not only was in charge of keeping the peace but also participated in verifying the fulfilment of the peace agreement; that is, performing "*peace-building*". According to Costa, El Salvador has been "the most successful among missions of this type" (2013, 34). It should be highlighted that, purely as a result of the United Nations' reporting mechanisms, it has been possible for us to obtain detailed information on the implementation of many recommendations.

Third, to understand the role of the CVES and the implementation of its recommendations, one must also understand the scope of the Peace Agreement and the role of the other institutions that were created or who acted within the framework of the Peace Agreement. Concerning the latter, we can mention the *Comisión Ad Hoc para la depuración de las FAES* (Ad Hoc Commission for the Purging of the Salvadorian Armed Forces) (1992) or the cooperation and verification of ONUSAL through its specific Human Rights, Police or Military divisions (1991–95).

Although all the Commission recommendations were binding for the signatories of the Peace Agreement, most of them were not fulfilled, even with the pressures exerted by ONUSAL and the United Nations Secretary General. The first setback for the CVES occurred a mere five days after the publication of its Report, when the Assembly approved the Amnesty Law as a strategy to guarantee impunity for the parties involved in cases of serious human rights violations committed during the conflict.

Successive ARENA governments did little to drive implementation of the Commission's recommendations, until political power changed hands in 2009. That year marked the end of ARENA's 20 years in power and the inauguration of the first FMLN Presidency, allowing the rearrangement of the Salvadorian political system. Thus, a window of opportunity was opened, generating expectations and also causing frustration to those who expected great changes regarding the country's endemic impunity for human rights violations. In this context, leveraging the Eighteenth Anniversary of Peace, the State acknowledged responsibility for the first time and issued an apology to the victims of human rights violations perpetrated by the Salvadorian Armed Forces, public security forces, and parallel organizations. Since then, some progress has been made to implement the recommendations (especially those related to justice and reconciliation), for example, the declaration in 2016 of the unconstitutionality of the Amnesty Law. However, the country has also suffered some setbacks in the field of public security. The lack of follow-up of the Peace Agreement after the United Nations left the country, combined with strong power elites and serious insecurity and violence issues in the country, within a context of strong political polarization, hinder implementation of many of the recommendations even to this day, 25 years after the signing of the Peace Agreement.

BIBLIOGRAPHY

Aguilar, Jeannette (2016). "El rol del ejército en la seguridad interna en El Salvador: lo excepcional convertido en permanente". In Argueta, Lorena (ed.), *Re-conceptualización de la violencia en el Triángulo Norte*. San Salvador: Fundación Heinrich Böll.

Amnesty International (1996). *El Salvador: El espectro de los "escuadrones de la muerte". Diciembre de 1996*. Resumen índice de AI: AMR29/15/96/s.

Artiga, Álvaro (2015). *El sistema político salvadoreño*. San Salvador: United Nations Development Program and UCA Editores.

Azpuru, Dinorah; Blanco, Ligia; Córdova Macías, Ricardo; Loya Marín, Nayelly; Ramos, Carlos; Zapata, Adrián (2007). *Construyendo la democracia en sociedades posconflicto: Guatemala y El Salvador, un enfoque comparado*. Guatemala: IDRC.

Buergenthal, Thomas (1996). "La Comisión de la Verdad para El Salvador". In Buergenthal, Thomas and Cançado Trindade, Antônio (eds.), *Estudios especializados de Derechos Humanos* I. San José: IIDH, 11–62.

Call, Charles T. (2002). "*Assessing El Salvador's Transition from Civil War to Peace*". In Stedman, Stephen; Rothchild, Donald & Cousens, Elisabeth (eds.), *Ending Civil Wars*. Boulder CO: Lynne Rienner Press, 543–602. Available at: https://www.wiltonpark.org.uk/wp-content/uploads/el-salvador-assessing-transition.pdf.

—— (2003). "Democratisation, War and State-Building: Constructing the Rule of Law in El Salvador". *Journal of Latin American Studies* no. 35 (4): 827–862.

Chinchón, Javier (2007). *Derecho internacional y transiciones a la democracia y la paz. Hacia un modelo para el castigo de los crímenes pasados a través de la experiencia iberoamericana*. Madrid: Ediciones Parthenon.

CIDH (Inter-American Commission of Human Rights) (1982). *Informe Anual, 1981–1982*. OEA/Ser.L/V/II.57, doc. 6 rev.1, 20 de septiembre de 1982, Capítulo V, El Salvador.

—— (1992). Informe Anual de la Comisión Interamericana de Derechos Humanos 1991–1992. OEA/Ser.L/V/II.81, Doc. 6 Rev.1, 14 febrero 1992, Capítulo IV: El Salvador.

—— (1995). Informe Anual de la Comisión Interamericana de Derechos Humanos 1994–1995. OEA/Ser.L/V/II.88. Doc. 9 rev. 17 febrero 1995. Original: Español.

—— (2012). *Caso Masacres de El Mozote y lugares aledaños vs. El Salvador*. Fondo, Reparaciones y Costas. Sentencia de 25 de octubre. Serie C No. 252.

Collins, Cath (2010). *Post-transitional Justice. Human Rights Trials in Chile and El Salvador*. University Park, PA: Editorial Penn State Press.
Comisión de la Verdad para El Salvador (CVES) (1993). *De la locura a la esperanca. La guerra de 12 años en El Salvador.* Spanish version available at: http://www.derechoshumanos.net/lesahumanidad/informes/elsalvador/informe-de-la-locura-a-la-esperanza.htmand https://www.scribd.com/document/137504386/De-la-locura-a-la-esperanza-La-guerra-de-12-anos-en-El-Salvador.
English version available at: http://www.usip.org/sites/default/files/file/ElSalvador-Report.pdf.
Córdova-Macías, Ricardo (1996). "El Salvador. La nueva agenda de posguerra". *Nueva Sociedad*, no. 145: 9–15.
Córdova Macías, Ricardo; Ramos, Carlos and Loya, Nayelly (2007). "La contribución del proceso de paz a la construcción de la democracia en El Salvador (1992–2004)". In *Construyendo la democracia en sociedades posconflicto. Guatemala y El Salvador, un enfoque comparado*. Guatemala: F&G editores and IDRC.
Corte Suprema de Justicia (1993). *Pronunciamiento de la Corte Suprema de Justicia de El Salvador sobre el informe de la Comisión de la Verdad para El Salvador y sus anexos.* San Salvador, marzo 1993.
Costa, Gino (1999). *La Policía Nacional Civil de El Salvador (1990–1997)*. San Salvador: UCA Editores.
—— (2013). "El papel de Naciones Unidas en la construcción de la paz: el caso salvadoreño". Lima: Mimeo.
Cuellar, Benjamín (2005). "Los dos rostros de la sociedad salvadoreña". In Pacheco Oreamuno, Gilda; Acevedo Narea, Lorena and Guido Galli (eds.), *Verdad, justicia y reparación. Desafíos para la democracia y la convivencia social*. San José: Instituto Internacional para la Democracia y la Asistencia Electoral e Instituto Interamericano de Derechos Humanos (IIDH).
Díaz, Francisco and Urquilla, Carlos (2000). *Informe sobre Independencia Judicial en El Salvador* [online]. Available at: http://www.dplf.org/uploads/1192409584.pdf.
Díaz, Borja and Linares, Sebastián (2005). *Fortalecimiento de la independencia judicial en Centroamérica: Un balance tras veinte años de reformas. América Latina Hoy* no. 39 (abril): 47–96.
Dunkerley, James (1982). *The Long War: Dictatorship and Revolution in El Salvador.* London: Junction.
Fiumara, María Paz (2004). "Éxitos y fracasos: las Fuerzas Armadas y de Seguridad en El Salvador y Haití". El papel de las fuerzas armadas en América Latina y el Caribe. Programa Regional de CLACSO. At: http://bibliotecavirtual.clacso.org.ar/ar/libros/becas/2003/mili/fiumara.pdf.
Guidos Béjar, Rafael and Roggenbuck, Stefan (1980). *El ascenso del militarismo en El Salvador*. San Salvador: UCA Editores.
Gutiérrez-Salazar, Martha Liliana (2015). "El Salvador: paradigma de una democracia imperfecta". *Revista Latinoamericana de Política Comparada* no. 10: 149–172.
Hayner, Priscilla (2001). *Unspeakable Truths. Confronting state terror and atrocity.* New York: Routledge.
—— (2010). *Unspeakable Truths. Transitional Justice and the challenge of Truth Commissions*. New York: Routledge.

Holiday, David and Stanley, William (1997). "En la mejor de las circunstancias: ONUSAL y los desafíos de verificación y desarrollo institucional en El Salvador". *Estudios Centroamericanos* (584): 1–30.

Hume, Mo (2014). "El Salvador". In Sánchez-Ancochea, Diego, and Martí i Puig, Salvador (eds.), *Handbook of Central American Governance*. New York: Routledge.

Johnstone, Ian (1997). "Rights and reconciliation in El Salvador". In Doyle, Michel W., Johnstone, Ian, and Orr, Robert C. (eds.), *Keeping the peace. Multidimensional UN operations in Cambodia and El Salvador*. Cambridge: Cambridge University Press, 312–341.

Kumar, Krishna (1997). *Rebuilding Societies after Civil War*. Boulder, CO: Lynne Rienner Publishers.

Lazo, Xiomara and Rey Tristán, Eduardo (2011). "¿Es la justicia el precio de la paz? Logros y limitaciones en el proceso de paz salvadoreño". In Rey Tristán, Eduardo and Cagiao Vila, Pilar (eds.), *Conflicto, memoria y pasados traumáticos: El Salvador contemporáneo*. Santiago de Compostela: Universidad de Santiago de Compostela, 211–240.

Martínez-Barahona, Elena and Gutiérrez-Salazar, Martha (2016). "El Salvador: The difficult fight against impunity". In Skaar, Elin; García-Godos, Jemima and Collins, Cath (eds.), *Transitional Justice in Latin America: The Uneven Road from Impunity towards Accountability*. New York: Routledge.

Martínez-Barahona, Elena; Gutiérrez-Salazar, Martha and Rincón-Fonseca, Liliana (2012). "Impunidad en El Salvador y Guatemala: De la Locura a la Esperanza: ¿Nunca Más?". *América Latina Hoy* no. 61: 101–136.

Méndez, Juan (2011). "Responsabilización por los abusos del pasado". In Reátegui, Félix (ed.), *Justicia Transicional. Manual para América Latina*. Brasilia: Comisión de Amnistía, Ministerio de Justicia. New York: International Center for Transitional Justice, 195–225.

English language version: (1997) "Accountability for Past Abuses", *Human Rights Quarterly* no. 19 (2): 255–282.

Morales, David (2006). *Los Acuerdos de Paz, su agenda pendiente y los derechos humanos en El Salvador de hoy*. San Salvador: ASDI.

Orgambides, Fernando (1993). "Cristiani jubila a los generales responsables de la muerte de los jesuitas en El Salvador". *El País*, July 2, 1992. Retrieved from: http://elpais.com/diario/1993/07/02/internacional/741564012_850215.html.

PDDH (Procuraduría para la Defensa de los Derechos Humanos de El Salvador) (2012). *Informe Especial sobre la situación de los derechos humanos a la luz de los acuerdos de paz de El Salvador, 2012*. At: http://www.pddh.gob.sv/menudocs-7/publicaciones/send/6-infesp/150-informe-especial-sobre-la-situacion-de-los-derechos-humanos-a-la-luz-de-los-acuerdos-de-paz-de-el-salvador.

—— (2003). *La Policía Nacional Civil y el respeto a los derechos humanos en El Salvador*. Informe del 3 de diciembre.

Popkin, Margaret (1994). *Justice Delayed: The Slow Pace of Judicial Reform in El Salvador*. Washington Office on Latin America.

—— (1998). *La Amnistía Salvadoreña: una perspectiva comparativa ¿se puede enterrar el pasado? Revista Eca* nos. 597–598 (53): 643–656.

—— (2000). *Peace without justice: Obstacles to building the rule of law in El Salvador*. University Park, PA: Pennsylvania State University Press.

—— (2001). "Building the Rule of Law in El Salvador". In Studemesiter, Margarita (ed.), "El Salvador implementation of the peace accords". *Peaceworks* No 3. Washington: United States Institute of Peace.

—— (2004). *Fortalecer la independencia judicial*. In Pásara, Luis, *En busca de una justicia distinta. Experiencia de reforma en América Latina*. First edition. México: Instituto de Investigación Jurídicas de la UNAM, 409–448.

Popkin, Margaret; Spence, Jack and Vickers, George (1993). *Justice Impugned. The Salvadoran Peace Accords and the Problem of Impunity*. Cambridge, MA: Hemisphere Initiatives.

Sanfeliu, Alba (2011). "Monumentos conmemorativos y memoria". In Artes and Paz. *Escola de cultura de Pau*. Available at: http://escolapau.uab.cat/img/programas/musica/monumentos.pdf.

Sanz, José and Martínez, Carlos (2012). "En un juicio, la información que recabamos habría resultado en la condena de D'Aubuisson". *El Faro*, Interview with Douglas Cassel, February 8. Retrieved from: https://elfaro.net/es/201202/noticias/7525/.

Schultze-Kraft, Markus (1998). "Pacificación, relaciones cívico-militares y democracia en El Salvador de posguerra: Apuntes para el debate". *Revista Electrónica Theorethikos* no. 2.

Seligson, Mitchell and McElhinny, Vincent (1996). "Low-intensity warfare, High-intensity death: The Demographic Impact of the Wars in El Salvador and Nicaragua". *Canadian Journal of Latin American and Caribbean Studies*, no. 21 (42): 211–241.

Sieder, Rachel (2002). "Políticas de Guerra, Paz y Memoria en América Central". In Barahona de Brito, Alexandra, Aguilar Fernández, Paloma, and González Enríquez, Carmen (eds.), *Las políticas hacia el pasado. Juicios, depuraciones, perdón y olvido en las nuevas democracias*. Madrid: Ediciones Istmo, 247–284.

Spence, Jack, Vickers, George and Popkin, Margaret (1994). *A Negotiated Revolution? A Two Years Progress Report on the Salvadoran Peace Accords*. Cambridge, MA: Hemisphere Initiatives.

Stanley, William (1996). *The Protection Racket State: Elite Politics, Military Extortion, and Civil War in El Salvador*. Philadelphia, PA: Temple University Press.

—— (2003). "¿Protectores o Perpetradores? La crisis institucional de la Policía Nacional Civil salvadoreña". Boston, MA and Washington DC: Hemisphere Initiatives and Washington Office on Latin America.

UCA. *Semanario PROCESO del 26 de junio de 1996*. Número 715, año 17.

United Nations (UN) (1991). Segundo Informe ONUSAL. A/46/658 S/23222. 15 de noviembre de 1991: 40.

—— (1992a). Tercer Informe ONUSAL. A/46/876 S/23580. 19 de febrero de 1992: 39.

—— (1992b). *Informe del Experto Independiente, Profesor Pedro Nikken, sobre la evolución de la situación de los derechos humanos en El Salvador*, A/47/596. 13 de noviembre de 1992.

—— (1993a). *Informe del Secretario General sobre la Misión de Observadores de las Naciones Unidas En El Salvador (anexo)*. UN DOC. S/25812/Add.3, del 25 de mayo.

—— (1993b). *Informe del Secretario General sobre la misión de observadores de las Naciones Unidas en El Salvador*. UN DOC. S/26581, del 14 de octubre.

—— (1993c). *Informe del Director de la División de DDHH de ONUSAL*. A/47/968 S/26033. 2 de julio de 1993: 60–61.

—— (1994a). *Informe del Experto Independiente, Profesor Pedro Nikken, sobre la evolución de la situación de los derechos humanos en El Salvador, elaborado de conformidad con la resolución 1994/62 de la Comisión de Derechos Humanos*. UN DOC. E/CN.4/1994/11, del 3 de febrero.
—— (1994b). *Informe del Secretario General sobre la misión de observadores de las Naciones Unidas en El Salvador*. UN DOC. S/1994/561, del 11 de mayo.
—— (1994c). *Décimo informe del Director de la División de Derechos Humanos de la Misión de Observadores de las Naciones Unidas en El Salvador (1 de noviembre de 1993 a 28 de febrero de 1994)*. UN DOC. A/49/116- S/1994/385, de 5 de abril.
—— (1995a). *Informe del Experto Independiente, Profesor Pedro Nikken, sobre la evolución de la situación de los derechos humanos en El Salvador, elaborado de conformidad con la resolución 1994/62 de la Comisión de Derechos Humanos*. UN DOC. E/CN.4/1995/88, de 13 de enero ONU.
—— (1995b). *Las Naciones Unidas y El Salvador, 1990–1995*. Serie de Libros Azules de las Naciones Unidas [Volumen IV]. Nueva York: Sección de Reproducción de las Naciones Unidas.
—— (2000). Observaciones finales del Comité Contra la Tortura: El Salvador. A/55/44. 15 de mayo de 2000.
—— (2013). Informe del Grupo sobre Detención Arbitraria, ONU. A/HRC/22/447Add.2. 11 de enero de 2013.
Villavicencio Terreros, Felipe (1996). "Proceso de paz y administración de justicia en El Salvador". *Jueces para la democracia* no. 27: 91–95.

ANNEX 1: LIST OF RECOMMENDATIONS MADE BY THE TRUTH COMMISSION OF EL SALVADOR[26]

RECOMMENDATIONS INFERRED DIRECTLY FROM THE RESULTS OF THE INVESTIGATION (1–7)

[1.] The findings on the cases investigated by the Commission on the Truth and published in this report give the names of officers of the Salvadorian armed forces who are personally implicated in the perpetration or cover-up of serious acts of violence, or who did not fulfil their professional obligation to initiate or cooperate in the investigation and punishment of such acts. [A] For those officers who are still serving in the armed forces, the Commission recommends that they be dismissed from their posts and discharged from the armed forces. [B] For those now in retirement or discharged, the Commission recommends application of the measure described in paragraph C below.

[2.] The findings on the cases investigated by the Commission on the Truth also give the names of civilian officials in the civil service and the judiciary. These officials, acting in their professional capacity, covered up serious acts of violence or failed to discharge their responsibilities in the investigation of such acts. For these persons, the Commission recommends that they be dismissed from the civil service [A] or judicial posts they currently occupy [B]. For those who no longer occupy such posts [C], the Commission recommends application of the measure described in paragraph C below.

[3.] Under no circumstances would it be advisable to allow persons who committed acts of violence such as those which the Commission has investigated to participate in the running of the State. The Commission therefore believes that the persons referred to in the preceding paragraphs, as well as any others equally implicated in the perpetration of the acts of violence described in this report, including [A] the civilians and [B] members of the FMLN Command named in the findings on individual cases, should be disqualified from holding any public post or office for a period of not less than 10 years, and should be disqualified permanently from any activity

---

26 *Source:* Comisión de la Verdad Para El Salvador (CVES). 1993. *De la locura a la esperanca. La guerra de 12 años en El Salvador.* Spanish version available at: http://www.derechoshumanos.net/lesahumanidad/informes/elsalvador/informe-de-la-locura-a-la-esperanza.htm and https://www.scribd.com/document/137504386/De-la-locura-a-la-esperanza-La-guerra-de-12-anos-en-El-Salvador. English version available at: http://www.usip.org/sites/default/files/file/ElSalvador-Report.pdf.
The list includes all 43 recommendations enumerated from 1–43. Where applicable, paragraphs indicate the original number or letter given in the CVES report.

related to public security or national defence. While the Commission does not have the power to apply such a provision directly, it does have the power to recommend to the National Commission for the Consolidation of Peace (COPAZ) that it prepare a preliminary legislative draft on this issue, offering proper guarantees in accordance with Salvadorian law, and that it submit such draft to the Legislative Assembly for early approval. It also has the power to recommend to the bodies authorized to make appointments to public office that they refrain from appointing the persons referred to above.

[4.] (a) Reform of the Supreme Court of Justice. The constitutional reform approved as part of the peace process provided a new procedure for the election of judges to the Supreme Court of Justice, the body which heads the judicial branch. Those innovations cannot be put into effect until the current judges' terms expire, with the result that the Court continues to consist of persons elected in accordance with the rules that applied before the constitutional reform and the peace agreements. Given the tremendous responsibility which the judiciary bears for the impunity with which serious acts of violence such as those described in this report occurred, there is no justification for further postponing the appointment of a new Supreme Court of Justice, whose current members should make way for the immediate implementation of the constitutional reform by resigning from their posts.

[5.] (b) National Council of the Judiciary. The peace agreements provided for the establishment of a National Council of the Judiciary independent from the organs of State and from political parties (Mexico Agreements: "Political agreements elaborating on the constitutional reform", A (b) (1); Chapultepec Peace Agreement, chap. III (1) (A)). However, the National Council of the Judiciary Act, adopted in December 1992 by the Legislative Assembly, contains provisions which, in practice, leave the dismissal of some members of that Council to the discretion of the Supreme Court of Justice. The Commission recommends that this system be changed and that it be possible to dismiss members of the Council only for precise legal causes, to be weighed by the Legislative Assembly which, being the body constitutionally authorized to appoint such members, should, logically, also be the one to decide on their dismissal.

[6.] The Career Judicial Service Act, the amendment of which, the Commission understands, is under discussion for the date on which this report will be submitted, should establish that only those judges who, according to a rigorous evaluation made by the National Council of the Judiciary, have demonstrated judicial aptitude, efficiency and concern for human rights and offer every guarantee of independence, judicial discretion, honesty and impartiality in their actions may remain in the career judicial service.

[7.] One of the direct consequences of the clarification of the serious acts which the Commission has investigated should, under normal circumstances, be the punishment which those responsible for such acts deserve. However, in view of current conditions in the country and the situation of the administration of justice, the Commission is facing insurmountable difficulties which it will describe below.

It is not within the Commission's powers to directly impose penalties on those responsible: it does not have judicial functions and cannot therefore decide to impose a particular penalty on a person. That is a function which, by its nature, properly belongs to the courts, a question which raises serious problems for the Commission. Accordingly, the problem and possible solutions to it cannot be discussed in isolation from the current situation in the country.

One painfully clear aspect of that situation is the glaring inability of the judicial system either to investigate crimes or to enforce the law, especially when it comes to crimes committed with the direct or indirect support of State institutions. It was because these shortcomings were so apparent that the Government and FMLN agreed to create an instrument such as the Commission on the Truth to perform tasks which should normally be undertaken by the bodies responsible for the administration of justice. Had the judiciary functioned satisfactorily, not only would the acts which the Commission has had to investigate have been cleared up at the proper time, but the corresponding penalties would have been imposed. The inability of the courts to apply the law to acts of violence committed under the direct or indirect cover of the public authorities is part and parcel of the situation in which those acts took place and is inseparable from them. This is a conclusion which emerges clearly from most of the cases of this kind examined in this report.

We must ask ourselves, therefore, whether the judiciary is capable, all things being equal, of fulfilling the requirements of justice. If we take a detached view of the situation, this question cannot be answered in the affirmative. The structure of the judiciary is still substantially the same as it was when the acts described in this report took place. The reforms of the judicial system agreed on during the peace process have been implemented to only a limited extent, so that they have yet to have a significant impact which translates into a transformation of the administration of justice. What is more, the judiciary is still run by people whose omissions were part of the situation which must now be overcome, and there is nothing to indicate that their customary practices will change in the near future.

These considerations confront the Commission with a serious dilemma. The question is not whether the guilty should be punished, but whether justice can be done. Public morality demands that those responsible for the crimes described here be punished. However, El Salvador has no system for the administration of justice which meets the minimum requirements of objectivity and impartiality so that justice can be rendered reliably. This is a part of the country's current reality and overcoming it urgently should be a primary objective for Salvadorian society.

The Commission does not believe that a reliable solution can be found to the problems it has examined by tackling them in the context which is primarily responsible for them. The situation described in this report would not have occurred if the judicial system had functioned properly. Clearly, that system has still not changed enough to foster a feeling of justice which could promote national reconciliation. On the contrary, a judicial debate in the current context, far from satisfying a legitimate desire for justice, could revive old frustrations, thereby impeding the achievement of that cardinal objective, reconciliation. That being the current situation, it is clear that, for now, the only judicial system which the Commission could trust to administer justice in a full and timely manner would be one which had been restructured in the light of the peace agreements.

ERADICATION OF STRUCTURAL CAUSES LINKED DIRECTLY TO THE ACTS EXAMINED (8–16)

[8.] 1. The transition to the new model of the armed forces outlined in the peace agreements and in the constitutional reform should be made rapidly and transparently, under the close supervision of the civilian authorities. It is recommended that a special committee of the Legislative Assembly be appointed for that purpose, comprising the various political forces represented in the Assembly. Special attention should be paid to [A] the subordination of the military establishment to the civilian authorities, [B] democratic control over promotions to senior ranks and positions of command, [C] rigorous budgetary management, [D] greater decentralization of the military structure, [E] application of the new doctrine and [F] new educational system of the armed forces and steady professionalization of officers.

[9.] 2. The comprehensive review of the military legislation in force should be completed without delay, in order to bring it fully into line with the new Political Constitution, the new doctrine of the armed forces and the requirements of respect for human rights.

[10.] 3. Among the reforms referred to in the preceding paragraph, a simple and practical mechanism must be established to resolve the situation of subordinates who receive illegal orders, so that they are protected if they refuse to obey. The provision of article 173 of army regulations which requires a subordinate to obey, at all times and irrespective of risk, the orders he receives from a superior, should be repealed, and the pledge so to obey should be eliminated from the formula used when swearing the solemn oath of allegiance to the flag as part of military ceremonial. It must be made clear, in any case, that so-called "due obedience" does not exonerate a person who carries out an order which is clearly illegal.

[11.] 4. The above-mentioned reforms should also provide that all actions whereby members of the armed forces take advantage of their status to commit abuses of power or violations of human rights are to be regarded as serious offences against the military institution and should stipulate the administrative and legal penalties to which the perpetrators are liable, including discharge, without prejudice to the imposition of the corresponding criminal penalties, where appropriate. A strict system of discharges should not allow persons who have been discharged for the type of conduct described, or for other reasons which adversely affect the service or the institution, to be readmitted to the institution.

[12.] 5. Military curricula, from the Military College to General Staff courses, should include thorough training in human rights. The assistance of a highly qualified civilian teaching staff will be required for this.

[13.] 6. In selecting advanced training courses for officers of the armed forces to follow abroad, care will have to be taken to ensure that such courses are based on a doctrine of democracy and respect for human rights.

[14.] 7. The armed forces Court of Honour created by the peace agreements should give priority to the eradication of any vestige of a relationship between serving and retired members of the armed forces and now-disbanded paramilitary bodies or any illegal armed group.

[15.] One of the prominent features of the peace agreements was the decision to disband the former public security forces (CUSEP), which were organically linked to the armed forces, and to entrust civilian security to the National Civil Police, a new and absolutely civilian entity. The Commission recommends most emphatically that the guidelines for the new body be scrupulously observed. The demilitarization of the police is a big step forward in El Salvador and it must be ensured that there are no links between the National Civil Police and the former security forces or any other branch of the armed forces.

[16.] One of the most horrendous sources of the violence which swept the country in recent years was the activity of private armed groups which operated with complete impunity. All necessary measures must be taken to ensure that they are disbanded. Given the country's history, prevention is essential in this area. There is always a risk that such groups may become active again. The Commission recommends that a thorough investigation of this issue be undertaken immediately and that, since the newly established National Civil Police is still in its early stages, assistance be sought, through channels which the confidentiality of the issue requires, from the police of friendly countries which are in a position to offer it.

INSTITUTIONAL REFORMS TO PREVENT THE RECURRENCE OF SUCH ACTS (17–34)

[17.] 1. One of the most glaring deficiencies which must be overcome in the Salvadorian judicial system is the tremendous concentration of functions in the Supreme Court of Justice, and in its President in particular, as the body which heads the judiciary. This concentration of functions seriously undermines the independence of lower court judges and lawyers, to the detriment of the system as a whole. The formal origin of this problem is constitutional, with the result that solving it requires analysing whether the relevant provisions should be amended, through the procedure provided for in the Constitution itself, so that the Court, without losing its status as the country's highest court, is not also the administrative head of the judiciary.

[18.] 2. Judges should not be appointed and removed by the Supreme Court of Justice, but by an independent National Council of the Judiciary.

[19.] 3. Each judge should be responsible for administering the resources of the court under his jurisdiction and should be accountable for them to the National Council of the Judiciary.

[20.] 4. The functions of granting authorization to practice as a lawyer or notary and suspending or penalizing members of those professions should be attributed to a special independent body and not to the Supreme Court of Justice.

[21.] 5. The budget allocation for the administration of justice provided for in the Constitution should be used to create new courts and improve judges' salaries.

[22.] 6. The Commission recommends the adoption of the following measures to reinforce the application of the right to due process: (a) Invalidate extrajudicial confessions. (b) Ensure that accused persons, in all circumstances, exercise their right to be presumed innocent. (c) Ensure strict compliance with the maximum time-limits for police and judicial detention, establishing immediate penalties for violators. (d) Reinforce exercise of the right to defence starting from the very first actions in a proceeding.

[23.] 7. The utmost priority should be given to the proper functioning of the Judicial Training School, conceived as a study centre not only for professional training but also to establish bonds of solidarity among judges and a coherent overall vision of the function of the judiciary in the State – to quote the peace agreements. There is also a short-term need to train new, sound human resources to staff new courts or to replace members of the judiciary who, according to the evaluation which the Commission has recommended, should not remain in the judiciary. This is an area susceptible to constructive, tangible international cooperation. The Commission calls on those in a position to offer such assistance to do so without delay, as part of an accelerated programme of implementation, and even ventures to appeal first and foremost to the European Economic Community, because of the similarities between the Salvadorian legal system and that of several of its member countries.

[24.] Many agreements were reached on this issue during the peace negotiations, including constitutional and legal reforms and the deployment of a United Nations human rights verification mission, something unprecedented in the history of the Organization. The Commission's first recommendation is that these agreements should be complied with strictly and that ONUSAL recommendations on human rights should be implemented.

[25.] 1. The Office of the National Counsel for the Defence of Human Rights must be strengthened: (a) It would be desirable if the Counsel, with the support of ONUSAL and the participation of all governmental and non-governmental sectors concerned, made an assessment of the Office's current situation and its most immediate priorities and needs, in order to secure the means, including international cooperation, to achieve those objectives. (b) The Office's presence should be extended throughout the country through offices in the various departments. (c) The Office should make more frequent use of its powers to inspect any site or installation in the country, especially where places of detention are concerned.

[26.] 2. Measures must be taken to make the remedies of *amparo* and *habeas corpus* truly effective. To that end, the Commission recommends the following: (a) Competence to hear these remedies should be broadened in order to make them more accessible to the population. All judges of first instance should be competent, within their sphere of jurisdiction, to hear remedies of [A] *amparo* or [B] *habeas corpus*, and [C] this competence could be extended to justices of the peace. The Supreme Court of Justice should only be the final instance in such proceedings. (b) [D] Express provision should be made that the remedies of *amparo* and *habeas corpus*, like the rules of due process, cannot be suspended under any circumstances, including during a state of emergency.

[27.] 3. The constitutional force of human rights provisions should be reaffirmed, including those not set forth expressly in the Constitution but in other instruments such as human rights conventions binding on El Salvador.

[28.] 4. The system of administrative detention also warrants a number of changes. This is a matter of prime importance, since violations of integrity of person and even disappearances can occur during such detention: (a) The restrictions as to which officials can order administrative detention, which officials can carry it out and for what reasons should be spelled out. (b) The duration of administrative detention should be kept to the absolute minimum. (c) The administrative authorities should be stripped of their power to impose penalties involving deprivation of liberty. Such penalties should be imposed only by the law courts, in the context of due process.

[29.] 5. It is recommended that the current system of information on detainees should be expanded. Through the Office of the National Counsel for the Defence of Human Rights, a centralized, up-to-date list should be kept of all persons detained for any reason, indicating their location and legal status. The competent authorities must inform the Office of any detention that is carried out and the personnel involved in the arrest.

[30.] 6. Any future reform of criminal legislation should give due consideration to crimes committed with the direct or indirect support of the State apparatus, either by establishing new categories of crimes, modifying existing ones or introducing special aggravating circumstances.

[31.] 7. Legislation should be passed granting a simple, swift and accessible remedy to anyone who has been a victim of a human rights violation enabling them to obtain material compensation for the harm suffered.

[32.] 8. Certain decisions should also be taken at the international level to reinforce the country's adherence to global and regional systems for the protection of human rights. To that end, the Commission recommends that El Salvador:

(a) Ratify the following international instruments: Optional Protocol to the International Covenant on Civil and Political Rights, Optional Protocol to the American Convention on Human Rights (Protocol of San Salvador), Conventions Nos. 87 and 98 of the International Labour Organization, Convention on the Non-Applicability of Statutory Limitations to War Crimes and Crimes against Humanity, United Nations Convention against Torture and Other Cruel, Inhuman or Degrading Treatment or Punishment and the Inter-American Convention to Prevent and Punish Torture.

[33.] (b) Recognize the compulsory jurisdiction of the Inter American Court of Human Rights established by the American Convention on Human Rights, as all the other Central American Republics have done.

[34.] The Commission emphasizes the importance of [A] the establishment and functioning of the National Civil Police, in accordance with the model defined in the peace agreements, for defending the population and preventing human rights violations. In addition to making a general recommendation to this effect, it wishes to emphasize criminal investigation, an issue closely linked to the impunity which accompanied the serious acts of violence described in this report. [B] First, it recommends that every effort be made to put into practice as soon as possible the criminal investigation mechanism decided on in the peace agreements, which entails joint action by the National Civil Police and the Office of the Attorney General of the Republic. This is also an area where international technical and financial cooperation can make a substantial contribution. [C] Second, it recommends that the Commission for the Investigation of Criminal Acts be dissolved: it was through its omissions that serious human rights violations during the period under investigation were covered up.

STEPS TOWARDS NATIONAL RECONCILIATION (35–43)

[35.] 1. It is recommended that a special fund be established, as an autonomous body with the necessary legal and administrative powers, to award appropriate material compensation to the victims of violence in the shortest time possible. The fund should take into account the information on the victims reported to the Commission on the Truth contained in the annexes to this report.

[36.] 2. The fund should receive an appropriate contribution from the State but, in view of prevailing economic conditions, should receive a substantial contribution from the international community. Therefore, without prejudice to the obligations of the State and of FMLN, the Commission urgently appeals to the international community, especially the wealthier countries and those that showed most interest in the conflict and its settlement, to establish a fund for that purpose. It also suggests that the United Nations Secretariat promote and coordinate this initiative. It further recommends that not less than 1 per cent of all international assistance that reaches El Salvador be set aside for this purpose.

[37.] 3. The fund could be managed by a board of directors consisting of three members: one appointed by the Government of El Salvador, one appointed by the Secretary-General of the United Nations and a third chosen by mutual agreement between the two appointed members.

[38.] 4. The fund must be free to establish its own rules of procedure and to act in accordance with the Commission's recommendations, Salvadorian law, international law and general legal principles.

[39.] 1. The construction of a national monument in El Salvador bearing the names of all the victims of the conflict.

[40.] 2. Recognition of the good name of the victims and of the serious crimes of which they were victims.

[41.] 3. The institution of a national holiday in memory of the victims of the conflict and to serve as a symbol of national reconciliation.

[42.] The Commission thinks it would be useful if this report and its conclusions and recommendations and progress towards national reconciliation were analyzed not only by the Salvadorian people as a whole but also by a special forum comprising the most representative sectors of society which, in addition to the above-mentioned objectives, should strive to monitor strict compliance with the recommendations. It is not for the Commission to indicate how such a forum should be established.

However, a National Commission for the Consolidation of Peace (COPAZ) was established under the peace agreements as "a mechanism for the monitoring of and the participation of civilian society in the process of change resulting from the negotiations". It therefore seems appropriate that the task referred to by the Commission should be entrusted primarily to COPAZ. However, given the scope [and] the importance of the subject-matter dealt with in this report, the Commission would like to suggest to COPAZ that, to this end, it consider expanding its membership so that sectors of civilian society that are not directly represented in COPAZ can participate in this analysis.

Moreover, COPAZ is the body entrusted by the agreements with preparing preliminary legislative drafts related to the peace process. In this sphere, it has a crucial role to play in the implementation of the recommendations in the present report that call for legal reforms.

[43.] The Commission has carried out its mandate as part of an extraordinary process which is a milestone in the history of United Nations operations for the maintenance of international peace and security. The tragedy in El Salvador absorbed the attention of the international community. As a result, the current peace process continues to arouse expectations throughout the world. The United Nations is also responsible for verifying all the agreements, which includes ensuring that the recommendations of the Commission on the Truth, which the Parties undertook to carry out, are implemented.

The Commission requests the Independent Expert for El Salvador of the United Nations Commission on Human Rights, in the report he is to submit to the Commission on Human Rights pursuant to his mandate and to the extent allowed by that mandate, to make corresponding evaluation of the implementation of the recommendations of the Commission on the Truth.

ANNEX 2: ACTORS SUPPORTING OR OBSTRUCTING IMPLEMENTATION

Actors Supporting or Obstructing Implementation the Implementation of Recommendations made by the CVES in El Salvador

Recommendation Name	Actors in Support	Actors Obstructing
I.A. Dismissal from the Armed Forces	– Secretary General of the UN, and his Special Representative for El Salvador – Human Rights Division of ONUSAL – Clinton Administration – Independent Expert on El Salvador of the UN Commission on Human Rights – Human Rights Committee (UN)	– President (1989–94) – ARENA – The High Command of the Army – "La Tandona" – Media
I.B. Dismissal from Public and Judicial Administration	– Secretary General of the UN – Human Rights Division of ONUSAL – Independent Expert on El Salvador of the UN Commission on Human Rights – General Coordinator of the FMLN (1993) – Human Rights Committee (UN)	– President (1989–94) – Supreme Court (1989–94) and its President
I.C. Disqualification from Holding Public Office	– Secretary General of the UN – Human Rights Division of ONUSAL – Independent Expert on El Salvador of the UN Commission on Human Rights	– COPAZ – Executive Branch (1989–94) – The High Command of the Army – Media
I.D. Judicial Reform	– Secretary General of the UN, and his Special Representative for El Salvador – Human Rights Division of ONUSAL – Independent Expert on El Salvador of the UN Commission on Human Rights – Supreme Court (1994–1997) – National Judiciary Council – Some opposing parliamentary groups – National NGO	– Supreme Court (1989–94) – Executive Branch (1989–94) – Legislative Branch – ARENA

(continued)

continued

Recommendation Name	Actors in Support	Actors Obstructing
I.E. The Judges	- Secretary General of the UN - Human Rights Division of ONUSAL - Independent Expert on El Salvador of the UN Commission on Human Rights - COPAZ	- Legislative Branch - Supreme Court (1989–94) and its President
I.F. Penalties	- Organized Civil Society - National and International Human Rights Institutions	- Legislative Branch - Supreme Court (1994–2009)
II.A. FAES Reforms	- Secretary General of the UN, and his Special Representative for El Salvador - Human Rights Division of ONUSAL - Military Division of ONUSAL	- Executive Branch - Legislative Branch - The High Command of the Army
II.B. Public Security Reforms	- Police Division of ONUSAL - Director General of NCP - Supreme Court	- Executive Branch - The High Command of the Army
II.C. Investigation of Illegal Groups	- Under-Secretary General for Political Affairs (1993) - Joint Group for the Investigation of Illegal Armed Politically Motivated Groups	- The High Command of the Army - ARENA - Executive Branch (Minister of Defense 1993)
III.A. Justice Administration	- Secretary General of the UN, and his Special Representative for El Salvador - Human Rights Division of ONUSAL - Independent Expert on El Salvador of the UN Commission on Human Rights - National Judiciary Council - Some opposing parliamentary groups - National NGO - USAID	- Supreme Court (1989–94) - Executive & Legislative Branches - ARENA's parliamentary group
III.B. Protection of Human Rights	- Human Rights Division of ONUSAL - Independent Expert on El Salvador of the UN Commission on Human Rights - Salvadoran Ombudsperson - European Union	- Executive & Legislative Branches - ARENA & FMLN[27]

(continued)

continued

Recommendation Name	Actors in Support	Actors Obstructing
III.C. National Civil Police	– Secretary General of the UN, and his Special Representative for El Salvador – Human Rights Division of ONUSAL – Police Division of ONUSAL	– Executive Branch – The High Command of the Army
IV.A. Material Reparation	– Human Rights Commission for El Salvador – Human Rights Division of ONUSAL – Executive Branch (starting in 2009)	– International Community – Executive Branch (1989–1994)
IV.B. Moral Reparation	– *Comité Pro-Monumento de Víctimas Civiles de violaciones de Derechos Humanos (Committee in Support of the Monument for Civil Victims of Human Rights Violations)* – Secretary General of the UN – The Mayor of San Salvador [FMLN] (2000–03) – International Cooperation – National and International Human Rights Institutions	– Executive Branch (1989–2099) – ARENA
IV.C. Truth and Reconciliation Forum	– Secretary General of the UN – Human Rights Division of ONUSAL – Independent Expert on El Salvador of the UN Commission on Human Rights	– COPAZ
IV.D. International Follow-Up	– UN	

Source: Comisión de la Verdad para El Salvador (CVES) (1993). *De la locura a la esperanca. La guerra de 12 años en El Salvador* and a wide range of other sources referenced in the chapter. See Bibliography. Table prepared by authors.

[27] This was a "veiled obstruction" reflected in a lack of implementation and political will, but these two organizations have fully controlled political power in the country since the transition to peace and have had the opportunity to make reforms. Thus, they are responsible for failing to do so.

GUATEMALA'S COMMISSION OF HISTORICAL CLARIFICATION

The Memory of Silence or the Silence of Memory?

Héctor Centeno-Martín*

When politics enter the temple, justice flees through the window and returns to heaven.

Francesco Carrara

* Héctor Centeno-Martín is JCyL-FSE fellow at the *Universidad de Salamanca*, Spain. The author wishes to thank Elena San José (*Universidad de Salamanca*) for helping to build the database that supports this work, and Raúl Gutiérrez Canales and Ivette Cardona for research assistance. The author also wishes to thank Ruth del Valle at the Office of the Guatemalan Attorney of Human Rights for her availability and services for the analysis of the CEH recommendations. Thanks to Stener Ekern for helpful comments on an earlier draft.

1. INTRODUCTION

The negotiation of peace agreements in Guatemala marked the end of a bloody war that lasted more than three decades (1960–1999). Truth commissions have been established as a key mechanism to promote transitional justice in such contexts of political transition. The documentation, analysis, and explanation of the structural factors that caused the violence in Guatemala were undertaken by the Commission for Historical Clarification of Guatemala (*Comisión para el Esclarecimiento Histórico de Guatemala*, hereafter the CEH or the Commission). The Commission concluded its work in 1999 with the publication of its Final Report entitled *Guatemala: Memoria del Silencio* ("Guatemala: The Memory of Silence"). The Report included the CEH's recommendations for restructuring the systemic defects which had allowed past human rights violations to take place. As this chapter shows, civil society organizations, rather than the Guatemalan State, have been the main political drivers for the implementation of the Commission's recommendations.

This chapter examines the fate of the CEH's 84 recommendations. The next section provides a brief overview of Guatemala's recent history. Section 3 provides a general summary of the establishment of the CEH and its recommendations. The main section, section 4, studies the relative progress toward implementation of these recommendations. The chapter concludes by briefly analyzing the role of each of the main actors in this process.

2. HISTORICAL BACKGROUND

The history of Guatemala is characterized by the virtual absence of civilian governments. From its independence from Spain in 1821 until 1996, the country has experienced a number of dictatorships and *coups d'état* (Blanco and Zapata 2007, 292–338). Following the dictatorships of the first half of the twentieth century,[1] the "October Revolution" ended with Juan José Arévalo as President. He initiated reformist policies that were continued by his successor Jacobo Arbenz,

[1] Manuel Estrada Cabrera (1898–1920) and Jorge Ubico (1931–44).

when he achieved his electoral victory in 1950. The agrarian reform implemented by Arbenz adversely affected the interests of the Guatemalan elite and the United States government. Consequently, Arbenz was forced to resign on June 27, 1954. From then until 1986 (except for the period between 1966 and 1970, when the civilian government of Julio César Méndez Montenegro ruled), the history of Guatemala features the prohibition of social democratic, socialist and communist parties, and frequent *coups d'état* (Poitevin 2004, 18).

On November 13, 1960, the failed *coup d'etat* against Ydígoras Fuentes ignited a 36-year-long civil war between the Guatemalan government and a variety of guerrilla groups. The conflict resulted in over 200,000 deaths and "disappearances", which, according to the CEH, were mostly perpetrated by the government and allied paramilitaries and civilian self-defense patrols. A total of 626 massacres affecting Mayan communities were attributed to the Army (CEH 1999a). Most of the deaths and disappearances occurred between 1981 and 1983, in the context of the "scorched earth" offensive perpetrated by the Generals Benedicto Lucas García and Efraín Ríos Montt. Ríos Montt took power through a *coup d'état* in March 1982 and was President until August 1983, when he was overthrown by his defense minister Óscar Mejía Víctores in yet another *coup d'etat*. Mejía swiftly issued Decree Law 3-84 calling the National Constituent Assembly to elections. The Constitution of 1985 was created in this environment and in 1986, Christian Democrat Marco Vinicio Cerezo Arévalo's civilian government was elected.

Five years later, during the general elections of 1990–91, Jorge Serrano Elías from the *Movimiento de Acción Solidaria* (Movement of Action in Solidarity) was elected President. The democratization process that had begun in 1985 was disrupted, however, by President Serrano Elías himself who implemented a "self-coup" in May 1993. After returning to democratic normalcy in June 1993, Congress elected human rights attorney Ramiro León Carpio as Guatemala's new President of the national government. Carpio himself was replaced in 1996 by Álvaro Arzú of the *Partido de Avanzada Nacional* (National Progress Party, PAN), which also won control of the legislature.

These latter years of free and democratic elections in Guatemala occurred in an international context featuring the end of the Cold War. Whereas Central American democracy had once posed a national security problem for the United States, democratic governance was now deemed necessary for economic liberalization. Negotiations for peace began in the context of the Cold War thaw, beginning in October 1987 with a meeting between the government and the *Unión Revolucionaria Nacional Guatemalteca* (Guatemalan National Revolutionary Union, URNG) in Madrid. The peace process concluded with the signing of the Firm and Lasting Peace Agreement on December 29, 1996.

3. THE CEH'S CREATION, ITS OPERATION, AND THE RECEPTION OF ITS FINAL REPORT

The CEH was created by the UN-brokered Peace Agreement between the Guatemalan government and the URNG guerrillas, signed in Oslo on June 23, 1994. The Commission operated from August 1997 until February 1999. The Commission was given a period of six months, which was extendable, to investigate violent acts connected to the armed conflict that occurred from January 1962 until the signing of the peace accords on December 29, 1996. The CEH's objective was to explain the individual and structural causes of violence, seek the truth regarding human rights violations and prevent the recurrence of these incidents by enacting measures for reconciliation.

The composition of the Commission was mixed: two Guatemalans and one German. The foreign commissioner was Christian Tomuschat, a professor of international law and well-known independent expert on Guatemala for the UN Human Rights Commission (1990–93). The Guatemalan nationals were Otilia Lux de Cotí, Kiché, indigenous leader and future Secretary of Culture and Sports of Guatemala (2000–04) and attorney Edgar Alfredo Balsells Tojo.

The CEH had a total budget of approximately US$9.5 million, financed by the Guatemalan government and international donations.[2] The funds were used to manage the investigations and to pay the salaries of approximately 200 foreign and national staff. The workforce included different profiles, featuring attorneys, sociologists, anthropologists, social workers, and logistics experts (Ibáñez 2017).

One of the key tasks entrusted to truth commissions is accessing information, understood as access not only to official documents, but also to different regions of the country. In Guatemala, the CEH hired translators for the various Mayan languages to better understand what had happened in the regions. Access to official documents presented greater obstacles, as the Commission received little cooperation from the Armed Forces. However, the Commission enjoyed great support from civil society and the Church, which drafted the report *Nunca Más* ("Never Again") through the *Proyecto Interdiocesiano de Recuperación de la Memoria Histórica* (Interdiocesan Project for the Recovery of Historical Memory, known as REMHI). In addition, the Commission worked tirelessly providing exhumation, medical, and psychological services. Over 40,000 violations were documented by the CEH (Simon 2002; Hayner 2006, 16). The victims were able to communicate

[2] Of its US$9,796,167 total budget, Guatemala provided US$800,000, with the rest provided by the governments of Germany, Austria, Belgium, Canada, Denmark, the United States, Italy, Japan, Norway, the Netherlands, the United Kingdom, Sweden, Switzerland, and the European Union.

their testimonies in Spanish or in the Mayan languages used by the majority of victims. The process of providing testimony was strictly confidential, as no public audiences were held. Of the cases documented, the CEH only investigated 80 cases in depth (Hayner 2006). Following this difficult task, the CEH issued its Final Report of over 3,000 pages, *Guatemala: Memoria del Silencio* ("Memories of Silence"), on February 25, 1999. Although the conclusions were devastating, responsibility focused on the institutional and collective levels. Perpetrators were not individually identified, because the peace agreements stipulated that responsibility would not be individually assigned. Rather, violations were investigated from a holistic point of view by documenting massacres, disappearances, extrajudicial executions, killings, torture, displacements, forced recruitment and violent economic power struggles.

The Report received a fair amount of publicity and enjoyed domestic and international coverage (Ceballos 2009). The commissioners put forward recommendations aimed at finding the truth, obtaining justice, providing reparations to the victims, and obtaining guarantees of non-recurrence. First, the CEH called upon the State and the URNG to apologize to victims. Recommendations highlight the need to preserve the victims' memory through the construction of spaces for remembrance and the acknowledgment of the multicultural nature of Guatemalan society. Second, reparation measures are organized into three groups. One is a package known as the *Programa Nacional de Reparación* (National Reparation Program, PNR). Another was related to the search for disappeared persons, particularly children who disappeared or were illegally separated from their parents or adopted. The final group was an active policy of reparations. The third set of recommendations was created to support a culture of mutual respect and observance of human rights. It advocated several measures to do so, including broadcasting and teaching the findings of the Report; education programs to promote a culture of mutual respect and peace; the adoption of international human rights law; raising awareness about international humanitarian law; the protection of advocates for human rights; and the vetting of public officers to exclude those responsible for the violations that occurred during the armed conflict. A fourth set of recommendations focused on strengthening the democratic process and promoting peace and harmony. Although the variety of measures is dealt with in greater depth later in the chapter, they include reforms to promote civilian control over security and intelligence services, to strengthen the rights of detained individuals, and to address the historical marginalization of indigenous people, among other things.

In quantitative terms, most of the recommendations deal with reparations (44 per cent) and non-recurrence (36 per cent). By contrast, recommendations related to criminal accountability constitute merely 7 per cent of the Report's corpus. Lesser importance was granted to the reform of current laws and institutions, since these constitute only 28 per cent and 25 per cent of the Report's recommendations respectively. However, one feature that stands out is that none of the recommendations was geared directly to reforming the Constitution. These quantitative differences indicate that, overall, the commissioners were more focused on solving immediate problems, specifically those directly concerning victims, rather than reforming the systemic defects that caused the human rights violations.

4. IMPLEMENTATION OF THE RECOMMENDATIONS

4.1. MEASURES TO PRESERVE THE MEMORY OF VICTIMS

The purpose of the first set of recommendations is to repair the dignity of victims and to honor their memory. The first recommendation referred to the importance of the State apologizing and accepting responsibility for past human rights violations before Guatemalan society, particularly victims, their family members and their communities (CEH 1999, 61). Following the inadequate apologies issued by Presidents Álvaro Arzú Irigoyen (1996–2000) and Alfonso Portillo (2000–04) (MINUGUA 2004a), President Álvaro Colom (2008–12) did accept responsibility and accepted that the crimes during the civil war amounted to genocide (AFP-REUTERS 2009). Two subsequent events kept the issue on the agenda. First, the First Court of Criminal Sentencing, Drug Trafficking Activities and Crimes Against the Environment ruled that genocide had occurred (Council of Ancestral Mayan Authorities of the Region of Ixil 2013), and encouraged the State to apologize to the Mayan Ixil people (EFE-Guatemala 2013). Second, in a historical 2016 judgment, the *Sepur Zarco* case saw the prosecution of sexual slavery as a war crime for the first time in history (UN Women 2018). More recently, the tide has turned as President Jimmy Morales (2016–19) denies the occurrence of a genocide (EFE-Guatemala 2016), marking an interesting example of how compliance with recommendations can be reversible. The Commission also, in its third recommendation, recommended that the ex-commanders of the URNG apologize publicly to society, the victims, family members and communities, and that they acknowledge responsibility for past violent incidents (CEH 1999, 61). This was fulfilled by ex-commander Jorge Ismael Soto, who spoke on behalf of the URNG on March 12, 1999 (MINUGUA 2004a).

In its second recommendation, the CEH encourages the National Congress to issue a solemn declaration reaffirming victims' dignity and honoring them (CEH 1999, 61). While it is true that some specific actions were taken, these have been limited in scope. For example, Congress made an appeal for peace and showed solidarity with the bereaved families in the case of the 1980 occupation of the Spanish Embassy in Guatemala City[3] through Resolution No. 6-98.[4] Nonetheless, according to United Nations Mission for the Verification of Human Rights and of Compliance with the Commitments of the Comprehensive Agreement on Human Rights in Guatemala's verification report (MINUGUA 2004a), the National Congress has not fulfilled this recommendation.

In its fourth recommendation, the CEH issued several sub-recommendations regarding honoring victims. In the first place, it proposed celebrating a "National day of remembrance of victims of violence" in collaboration between the State and civil society organizations. This has proven to be a source of contention in Guatemalan politics. Initially, Congress issued Legislative Agreement No. 15-2000, which designated February 25 as the day of the victims of violence, at the behest of civil society organizations such as *Frente Democrático Nueva Guatemala* and the Myrna Mack Foundation. However, three weeks later, the President introduced a bill prepared by the Secretariat of Strategic Analysis that proposed April 26, the day of the assassination of Monsignor Gerardi,[5] as a day for the commemoration of victims (MINUGUA 2004a). Two years later, Congress issued Legislative Decree 61-2002, which declared March 31 as the National Day of Victims of Violence. Later, in 2004, Decree 06-2004 established February 25 as the National Day for Victims. Article 1 of this decree was modified by Decree 48-2008, to legislate for the procedure for the day of commemoration. In this procedure the Ministries of Culture and Sports and Education would be present and would be in charge of promoting the commemorative activities. For all these reasons, this recommendation is considered as implemented.

The second sub-recommendation on remembrance refers to the construction of monuments and public parks in memory of the victims at the national, regional, and municipal levels (CEH 1999, 62). Although several monuments have been

---

3 On January 31, 1980, under the dictatorship of Fernando Romeo-Lucas García, the Guatemalan Police invaded the embassy, murdering 37 people. In successive days other bloody events occurred in which two more people died. Among the victims are Ixil and Kiche peasants, members of the Campesino Unity Committee, members of the Robin García Student Front (FERG) or officials and employees of the Spanish embassy, among others. From this event, Spain broke diplomatic relations with Guatemala. This massacre was a starting point for the bloody decade of the 80s in Guatemala.

4 The resolution stated, in part, "Historical memory is part of social culture and that it must be an inspiration for reconciliation and peace, so that the events that have occurred will never recur in Guatemalan society …" and resolved: "To be in solidarity with the relatives of those who gave their lives to find the way to a better future and to achieve a firm and lasting peace … [and] To exhort Guatemalan society to commemorate these events that are part of the history of Guatemala …" (MINUGUA 2004a).

5 For four years, Guatemalan Bishop Juan José Gerardi had led a serious effort by the Catholic Church to document the effects of a brutal government counterinsurgency campaign through the Project for the Recovery of Historical Memory (REMHI), the results of which were published in the report, "Guatemala: Never Again", mentioned in section 3 above. Two days after the report was publicly released on April 24, 1998, Monsignor Gerardi was brutally assassinated.

created with the support of the Ministry of Peace (SEPAZ) and civil society, authors such as Hoelscher (2008, 201) point out the scant presence of these monuments in general terms. Because they are scarce, this recommendation is considered only partially implemented.

A third sub-recommendation, regarding naming educational institutions, buildings, and public roads after victims (CEH 1999, 61), has not been as widely implemented as the prior recommendation. Although there are *lieux de mémoire*, such as those honoring Irma Flaquer (a journalist assassinated on October 16, 1980) and Myrna Mack (an anthropologist assassinated on September 11, 1990) (Garranzo and Climent 2006, 173), these were *ad hoc* initiatives. The government has no coherent policy to implement this recommendation (MINUGUA 2004a). For this reason, it's consider partially implemented for the purposes of this research.

The fifth recommendation is divided into two sub-recommendations. The first refers to the creation of monuments by the national government and local authorities to honor the multicultural nature of Guatemala. According to MINUGUA'S report (2004a), SEPAZ financed the construction of two ceremonial centers located in the Llano del Coyote community, in Aguacatán, Huehuetenango. With regard to the second sub-recommendation, the creation of communal cemeteries appropriate to the Mayan collective memory customs, MINUGUA (2004a) verifies the construction of one cemetery and niches built with the financial support of SEPAZ in the community of Río Blanco de la Vega (Aguacatán, Huehuetenango). Thus, although there is some progress on these recommendations, it is thoroughly insufficient given the large number of Mayan victims.

The sixth and last recommendation in this group supports the rescue of sacred Mayan sites. The *Unidad de Lugares Sagrados y Práctica de la Espiritualidad Maya* (Unit of Sacred Mayan Sites and Spiritual Practices), created under Ministerial Agreement No. 510-2003 and located within the *Consejo Nacional de los Acuerdos de Paz* (National Council for Peace Agreements, CNAP), acknowledges the historical value of ceremonial centers of Mayan cultural, historical and spiritual heritage. For these reasons, this recommendation is considered implemented.

4.2. REPARATION MEASURES

The second set, comprising 24 recommendations, focused on reparations, aiming to repair the damage inflicted on victims and their families. The CEH Report divided reparation measures into three main groups: those dealing with (A) a national reparations program; (B) enforced disappearance; and (C) exhumations.

4.2.1. *National Reparation Program*

In the first place, the Commission recommended that the government and the National Congress urgently create a National Reparation Program (*Programa de Reparación Nacional*, PNR) (CEH Report 1999, 62). On May 7, 2003, President Portillo approved Governmental Agreement number 258-2003, creating the National Compensation Program (reformed by Governmental Agreement 43-2005 in order to adopt the model proposed by the CEH) (Gómez 2011, 31). Portillo's government used this program for clientelist purposes by granting a large amount of funds to ex *Patrullas de Autodefensa Civil* (PAC) paramilitaries. However, since the reparations were collective in nature, other sectors of society also benefited from them. Notwithstanding this fact, many victims and affected communities have not benefited from the program.

The next recommendation contains two sub-recommendations. The first encourages the government to "urgently present to the National Congress a legislative project regarding reparations to the victims of the armed conflict to support the National Reparation Program" (CEH 1999, 62). The PNR was established by a Governmental Agreement instead of a Legislative Agreement, which is significant because legislative action would have represented a democratic commitment to victims. Victims and civil society organizations tried to ameliorate this by presenting the Bill of Reparation, known as the 3551 initiative, in Congress in September 2006. The purpose was to institutionalize the PNR (CAFCA 2015, 19), but they were unsuccessful. Thus, although some steps have been taken on this eighth recommendation, the shortcomings noted lead to the conclusion that it has not been fully implemented. As a result of the non-compliance with this sub-recommendation, the subsequent one regarding its content, structure, beneficiaries, procedures and financing mechanisms (CEH 1999, 62) was not implemented either.

Along these same lines, the Commission next recommended creating individual and collective measures within the PNR, including material restitution, financial compensation, psycho-social rehabilitation and reparation (community medical and mental health attention and legal and social services), and satisfaction and dignity-building measures, all according to the principles of equity, social participation and respect for cultural identity (CEH 1999, 63). With regard to material restitution, a total of 2,009,999 housing units were delivered, with 3,000 others under construction as of 2009 (Gómez 2011, 44–45). In as much as financial restitution is concerned, this began during Colom's government. Regarding psycho-social rehabilitation and reparation, they have not been emphasized. While there were pilot plans, such as SEPAZ's "Assistance and Compensation Plan", which involved regional collective reparations measures, none emphasized psycho-social reparation (MINUGUA 2004a). Finally, with regards to measures aimed at satisfaction and building dignity, it is true that these have been applied, although scantily, by building spaces for remembrance (Gómez 2011, 44–45). Overall, while some progress has been made, the measures have not followed the terms laid out in the Report. Therefore the ninth recommendation can be considered only partially implemented.

In line with the CEH Report's tenth recommendation, according to the MINGUA Report (2004a), projects executed within the framework of the Assistance and Compensation Plan of the SEPAZ did have a regional and collective approach, although they failed to focus on psycho-social reparation. This recommendation is therefore considered partially implemented.

On the other hand, Guatemalan society and the Mayan people were urged to participate in the design, execution, and evaluation of the PNR (CEH 1999, 63). According to Ruth del Valle (2018), an expert from the Guatemalan Human Rights Ombudsman's Office, the National Compensation Commission (CNR), which is in charge of the direction and execution of the PNR, was headed by one Mayan-Ixil and Francisco Calí, and included representatives of victims' and human rights organizations. During the early years of its existence, civil society worked well with government bodies. However, Rosalina Tuyuc, the second CNR president, proposed that the President of the Republic eliminate the representation of victims' and human rights organizations, in favor of a purely governmental body. In this context, during the Colom government (2008–12), a National Council of Victims was created within the PNR in order to serve as a counterweight. When right-wing parties (*Partido Patriota* and *Frente Convergencia Nacional*) came to power, the CNR was chaired by Ladino people who were far removed from the social movement. This did not promote the participation of indigenous peoples or promote the spirit of the PNR. During Patriot Party rule (2012–15), the governmental agreement was changed and the possibility of compensating the victims of the genocide was eliminated. The fact that the PNR had been established by a Governmental Agreement instead of through legislation meant that there were consequently no checks on an administration's ability to alter the plan as it wished (Valle, 2018).

The CEH outlined recommendations to determine eligibility for reparations. According to the commissioners, the beneficiaries of the moral and material reparations needed to be the victims of violations of international human rights and humanitarian law, or their family members (CEH 1999, 63). This twelfth recommendation was implemented through article 1 "Objective" (Book I "General Provisions", Chapter I "General") of the Manual of Basic Criteria for the Application of Reparation Measures Granted by the National Reparation Program. As the PNR manual indicates,

> its fundamental objective to establish the criteria, guidelines and basic procedures to determine the measures of integral reparation, linked to violations of Human Rights committed during the internal armed conflict, which are to be applied after

the processes have been completed of qualification of beneficiaries of the National Reparation Program (Resolution CNR-001-2015, 4).

Furthermore, the Commission in its thirteenth recommendation suggested considering "those who personally and directly suffered the human rights violations and the violent events connected to the internal armed conflict" as the victims (CEH 1999, 64). Paragraph G of the aforementioned Manual defines a victim as "any person who directly or indirectly, individually or collectively suffered the human rights violations committed during the Internal Armed Conflict" (CNR 2015, 3). Therefore, this recommendation also was implemented. Finally, the Commission recommended establishing priorities for the beneficiaries of individual financial indemnification based on the severity of the violation, their economic condition, and social weakness (CEH 1999, 64). These compensation criteria are included in Article 2 of Governmental Agreement 258-2003, modified by Governmental Agreement 539-2013 and Resolution CNR-001-2015.

In the Report, commissioners address issues surrounding the management of the PNR. With regard to the identification of PNR beneficiaries, the commissioners requested that the process be "governed by the principles of transparency, justice, equity, accessibility and participation" (CEH 1999, 64). Article 4 of Resolution CNR-001-2015 does highlight basic principles laying the foundation for compensation criteria and measures. Although some of these may be questioned, this recommendation is considered implemented. On the other hand, management of the PNR worsened over time. Recommendations outlined a Board of Directors that included nine specific and representative members (CEH 1999, 64). In the beginning, Article 4 of Governmental Agreement 258-2003 stipulated it would include 10 members (five representatives of civil society and five government representatives). However, after the reforms in Governmental Agreement 619-2005, civil society representatives were transferred to a mere advisory board, without decision-making authority. Further, the Commission detailed the functions of the Board of Directors (CEH 1999, 64). In this regard, point a) of Article 9 of Governmental Agreement 539-2013 includes 10 items that advance the recommended functions. In addition to governmental agreement 539-2013, Resolution CNR-001-2015 (Approval of the Basic PNR Criteria) which is based on its Title II (procedure to apply compensation measures) and the "General Definitions" section also regulates what recommendation 7.18 requests. In addition, the commissioners called on the Attorney of Human Rights to appoint a person to manage the process of designating representatives from victims', human rights, Mayan and women's rights organizations (CEH 1994, 64). However, Article 4 of Governmental Agreement 619-2005 indicates that the organizations themselves will be in charge of such designations. Therefore, this recommendation was not implemented either.

The Commission established recommendations regarding the PNR's financing by means of a progressive fiscal reform and, in addition, through the reorientation of social investment expenses and a reduction of military spending (CEH 1999, 65). In its implementation, the State provided the funds for PNR. However, it was not done by means of a progressive fiscal reform. Moreover, the government resisted significant pressure from the international community about this during the post-war period.

Along the same lines, the Commission recommended that the State manage the international cooperation of countries that provided financial and military help during the civil war (CEH 1999, 65). The State has not managed international cooperation funds with an eye to addressing the past. The United States Agency for International Development (USAID) projects, for example, have no relationship to the matter of "compensation" (Valle 2018). Thus, this recommendation was not implemented.

Lastly, the Commission recommended that the PNR's effective term be at least 10 years (CEH 1999, 65). In line with the recommendation, a term of 10 years was established, and the PNR is currently operating under a 10-year renewal granted in accordance with Governmental Agreement 539-2013.

4.2.2. Enforced Disappearance

The Commission put forward several measures to address the practice of forced disappearance during the war. First, it recommended that the government and Judicial Branch initiate as quickly as possible investigations regarding forced disappearances to establish the location of disappeared persons and, in the event of their being found to be dead, deliver the remains to their families (CEH 1999, 65). By and large, civil society organizations such as *Fundación de Antropología Forense de Guatemala* (Guatemalan Forensic Anthropology Foundation, FAFG), with support from the United Nations Development Program (UNDP) and Sweden, have substituted for the government in the performance of this work. In fact, neither the government of Guatemala nor the Judicial Branch have initiated investigations or independently delivered remains to family members. Second, the Commission recommended that the Army and URNG provide information regarding disappearances (CEH 1999, 65). Although the Army has not delivered such information, the former-URNG has largely cooperated with this request (Castañón 1999).

Third, a few recommendations dealt with the disappearance of children. The CEH urged the government to create a National Commission for the Search for Disappeared Children to coordinate this effort (CEH 1999, 66). While the government has not taken this step, civil society organizations unsuccessfully attempted to institutionalize such an effort by lobbying Congress to enact Law 3590 in 2002. The CEH further called for the promulgation of legislative measures to obtain information about children given up for adoption or illegally separated from their families during the armed conflict (CEH 1999, 66). No law to this effect was found in the course of researching this chapter. Besides, the archives of the Army, the Foreign Relations Ministry, Immigration authorities, Embassies, and children's homes may contain information on the location of these children, but these records have not been unsealed (Amnesty International 2009) due to the lack of interest by successive governments (SEPAZ 2010). A further suggestion to enact an information campaign to raise awareness about the search for disappeared children has been disregarded (Valle 2018).

Finally, there has been no action on three other recommendations related to adoptions. The Commission urged the "communication media [to] actively collaborate with initiatives for the search of children" (CEH 1999, 66). Commissioners further called for the utilization of extraordinary legislative measures to review child adoptions made without the knowledge or against the will of the natural parents, the adopted persons or their relatives, and always taking into account the opinion of the person who was adopted at the time (CEH 1999, 66–67). Another failed recommendation outlined a bill to create a legal designation of absence due to enforced disappearance (CEH 1999, 67).

4.2.3. Active Policy of Exhumation

A last area of focus with respect to reparation is a set of recommendations (numbered 28–31 in the report) designed to implement an active policy of exhumation. The first recommendation regarding this matter exhorted the government to urgently present to Congress a bill addressing the subject of exhumations (CEH 1999, 67). Reports from MINUGUA in 2000 and Amnesty International in 2009 each point to the absence of any such law and the State's failure to provide financing for this activity. The Commission also recommended the exhumations be carried out in accordance with cultural values and respecting the dignity of victims and their family members (CEH 1999, 67). MINUGUA's report on the exhumations (1997–2000) concluded that the PNR's content in this regard did not fully comply with the recommendations of the CEH. Psycho-social work resulting from this recommendation was taken on by the UNDP through the *Programa de Dignificación y Asistencia Psicosocial a Víctimas del Enfrentamiento Armado* (Program for the Dignity and Psychosocial Assistance of Victims of Armed Conflict) (DIGAP), financed by USAID and the Netherlands. The Ministry of Health and Social Assistance (MSPAS) adhered to this program as of 2002. So, this recommendation has been partially implemented by the State.

In addition, the CEH recommended that the bodies and remains of the victims be delivered to their family members to allow burial in accordance with the culture of the victim (CEH 1999, 67). According to the International Committee of the Red Cross (CICR) mission for Guatemala, forensic organizations draft a report of exhumed bodies that they deliver to the Public

Prosecutor's Office, who delivers the identified remains to family members and non-identified remains to forensic organizations for their burial (CICR 2010, 26). These facts demonstrate that the recommendation was implemented. Lastly, the Commission recommended *State* support for the work of forensic anthropology organizations (CEH 1999, 67–68). This has not only failed to happen, but statements by Alfonso Portillo and Álvaro Arzú have actually been made against these organizations (CICR 2010, 26). It also recommended that these organizations work cooperatively with the Attorney of Human Rights, whose office was to be "the holder of the corresponding data bank" (CEH 1999, 68). As stated by Ruth del Valle (2018), the Office of the Attorney of Human Rights was never the holder of such information and has been excluded from the process, even though its mandate is sufficiently broad to include this follow-up.

4.3. MEASURES TO SUPPORT A CULTURE OF MUTUAL RESPECT AND HUMAN RIGHTS OBSERVANCE

The third group consisting of 13 recommendations (numbered 32–45) aimed to develop a human rights culture in Guatemala, through both (A) teaching people what human rights are, and (B) adopting legal protection measures.

4.3.1. Culture of Mutual Respect

The seven recommendations in this area were divided into two groups: dissemination and teaching of the Report's content, and education within a culture of mutual respect and peace. In the first group, the CEH requested the State to acknowledge the content of the Report (CEH 1999, 68). This has never happened, since the signatories themselves, other than the URNG in its public apology, have denied such content after its publication (Impunity Watch 2012). Another recommendation urged the State to support any initiative put forth for the purpose of disseminating and promoting the Report (CEH 1999, 68). However, in 1999, during the administration of Álvaro Arzú Irigoyen, 285,000 copies of the Conclusions and Recommendations of the CEH Report were printed (MINIGUA 2004). During the Colom administration, some attempts were made to disseminate the Report, like the broadcasting of documentaries such as *Monseñor Gerardi* or *The Massacre of Panzós*. These steps were motivated by the mandatory nature of judgments of the Inter-American Court of Human Rights. In this manner, the recommendation was only partially implemented. The CEH also urged the government to promote a massive campaign for the Report, together with civil society organizations and in accordance with the social, cultural and linguistic context of Guatemala (CEH 1999, 68). Furthermore, the commissioners recommended several translations of the Report, which are featured in two specific recommendations (CEH 1999, 69). The Commission recommended the translation of the entire Report into at least five major Mayan languages. In addition, it recommended the translation of the Report's conclusions and recommendations into the 21 existing Mayan languages. Even more specifically, commissioners urged the government to support and finance the translation of the conclusions and recommendations into the Garifuna and Xinca languages. Although it is true that the Report was translated into some Mayan languages, it did not cover the entire linguistic scope of Guatemala and no massive dissemination campaign was organized (MINUGUA 2004a). In particular, translations were made into only seven languages, though Garifuna and Xinca were not among them.

Another group of recommendations dealt with education. For example, the Commission recommended that primary, secondary, and university education should include age-appropriate discussion of the causes, development and consequences of the armed conflict and the content of the Peace Agreements (CEH 1999, 69). While the transformation of public education curricula (basic and diversified levels) has been unsuccessful (Board of Education for Peace in 2009), these were applied in the private education sector (Universidad Rafael Landívar) (Impunity Watch 2012). Two other recommendations were created for the purpose of supporting education within a culture of mutual respect and peace. One encouraged the State, together with national human rights NGOs, to develop a peace culture and mutual respect campaign (CEH 1999, 69). It further called for educational reform to support tolerance and respect. No evidence of implementation has been found for either recommendation.

4.3.2. Observance of Human Rights

One emphasis of the recommendations was to bring Guatemalan law into alignment with international norms. Since the CEH, Guatemala has ratified the First Optional Protocol to the International Covenant on Civil and Political Rights (on June 19, 2000); the Additional Protocol to the American Convention on Human Rights in the Area of Economic, Social and Cultural Rights – San Salvador Protocol (ratified on May 30, 2000); the Inter-American Convention on the Enforced Disappearance of Persons (ratified on July 27 1999); and the Statute of the International Court of Justice (ratified on March 22, 2012). All of this was done as recommended by the Commission (MINEX 2017). With respect to international humanitarian law (IHL), the Commission made two specific recommendations (CEH 1999, 70–71). The first one urged the government to fully incorporate IHL into national legislation. This occurred with the creation of the Guatemalan Commission for the Application of International Law (Governmental Agreement no. 948-99). The second IHL-related measure urged the government to provide periodic IHL training for State personnel, especially the Army (CEH 1999, 71). These efforts materialized through training workshops for magistrates of the Constitutional Court, organized by the Office of the United Nations High Commissioner for Human Rights (Impunity Watch 2013, 35). With regards to the Army, Ruth del Valle (2018) points out that is an inter-institutional commission coordinated by the Ministry of Foreign Relations, that incorporates the Army, which conducted a course.

The Commission recommended other measures to promote human rights domestically. One proposal was that the government should promote legislative measures specifically oriented to the protection of human rights advocates, following consultation with human rights organizations (CEH 1999, 71). The government has created several human rights bodies over the years, including a Governmental Commission and a Special Prosecutor's Office; a Coordinating Unit for the Protection of Human Rights Advocates, Administrators and Justice Operators, Journalists and Social Communicators; and the Institution for the Analysis of Attacks against Advocates of Human Rights in Guatemala. Nonetheless, international organizations continue to issue warnings about the vulnerability of Guatemalan human rights advocates (ONU 2010).

Other recommendations formulated by the CEH were connected to administrative measures regarding public officers. In this sense, the Commission recommended that the President of the Republic establish a commission to examine the behavior of officers of the Army and various bodies and security forces of the State active during the Internal Armed Conflict (CEH 1999, 71). Commissioners provide specific guidelines about the commission's membership and its operative practices. Both MINUGUA's report (2004a) and the report of the Special Rapporteur on the Independence of Magistrates and Attorneys, Mr. Param Cumaraswamy, have verified a situation of impunity when it comes to human rights. The last recommendation regarding administrative measures involved the adoption of the content of the UN Human Rights Commission's "Set of Principles for the Protection and Promotion of Human Rights through Action to Combat Impunity" (CEH 1999, 71).[6] In this regard, some partial efforts have been made, such as the creation of the *Comisión Internacional contra la Impunidad en Guatemala* (International Commission Against Impunity in Guatemala, CICIG) in 2006. However, they do not entirely fulfil the Commission's recommendations.

4.4. MEASURES TO STRENGTHEN THE DEMOCRATIC PROCESS

Another set, numbering 32 recommendations, is designed to promote Guatemala's democratization process.

6 Equipo Nizkor – Updated Set of principles for the protection and promotion of human rights through action to combat impunity. Access here: http://www.derechos.org/nizkor/impu/principles.html.

4.4.1. *Justice Administration System and Traditional Conflict Resolution Methods*

One group of proposals dealt with the justice system. In the first recommendation, the commissioners advocated for the fulfilment of the justice commitments made in the Agreement on the Strengthening of Civil Authority and the Purpose of the Army in a Democratic Society, and for the fulfilment of the recommendations issued by the *Comisión de Fortalecimiento de la Justicia* (Commission for the Strengthening of Justice) (CEH 1999, 72). Although partial efforts have been made in this direction, such as the approval of the Judicial Career Law or the creation of community magistrate courts, among others, this recommendation has only been partially implemented (Orozco and Gramajo 2016; MINUGUA 2004a). The Commission also recommended the fulfilment of the Law for National Reconciliation by prosecuting, sentencing, and punishing crimes for which criminal responsibility is not extinguished pursuant to Article 8 of such Law (CEH 1999, 72). Despite multiple efforts, as of early 2019, there have been few trials and rarely have guilty verdicts been issued. The "Myrna Mack Chang" case in particular stands out in this group of cases (Impunity Watch 2014). The abuse of motions for the protection of constitutional rights or motions based on unconstitutionality is a clear obstacle for the fulfilment of this recommendation.

Further, the CEH called for a clear legal distinction among different levels of responsibility, particularly to identify the promoters and instigators of the human rights violations (CEH 1999, 73). Deficiencies in the Guatemalan Penal Code prohibit the clear determination of degrees of participation and responsibility in terms of the crimes (Impunity Watch 2014), which has resulted in a smaller number of charges against the intellectual authors of the crimes (for example, in Myrna Mack's case) compared to the material perpetrators. Over the years, prosecutorial efforts have experienced advances and setbacks.

Other recommendations called for strengthening the protection of Guatemalans' rights. One urges the government to present a bill to the National Congress seeking to regulate the right to *habeas data* (CEH 1999, 73). The Law of Access to Public Information (Legislative Decree no. 57-2008) only regulates *habeas data* in the administrative field and, therefore, the motion for appeal included in Decree 1-86 of the National Constituent Assembly is applied in the judicial field (Valdiviezo 2014). Due to these grave deficiencies, this recommendation is not considered implemented. Another proposal argued that the government should implement the constitutional right acknowledged in Article 31 of the Constitution granting access to any information contained in any type of State or private registry and penalizing any unauthorized storage and concealment of information (CEH 1999, 73). This recommendation was implemented by means of the above-mentioned Law of Access to Public Information (Decree no. 57-2008) (Alamilla 2017).

The CEH also requested the integration of common law into the Guatemalan juridical system, in order to prevent the violation of the rights acknowledged in the Constitution and in International Human Rights Treaties (CEH 1999, 73). Some authors, such as Schwank (2005) and Sosa (2017), argue that common law has not been integrated into the juridical system following the suppression of indigenous courts in 1987. Nonetheless, legal pluralism has been gradually reintroduced as a result of the new law of municipalities of 2002, projects of the *Instituto de Defensa Pública Penal* (Criminal Public Defender Institute, IDPP) and a 2012 Supreme Court decision (01004-2012-01525), granting the same level of authority to both justice systems. However, there remains a lack of a clear State policy on the issue.

Still other proposals advocated for the promotion of conflict resolution measures. For example, the Commission advised State universities and other institutions to include a course on traditional conflict resolution systems within law school curricula (CEH 1999, 74). In this regard, there are different academic plans in institutions such as the School for Judicial Studies, the Rafael Landívar University or the San Carlos of Guatemala University that include programs that align with this recommendation (MINUGUA 2004a; UNIVERSIA 2018). Along the same lines, the Commission recommended that the Ministry of Education support the publication of material to show the progress of research on practices included in common law (CEH 1999, 74). To date, however, only NGO and research and education institutions such as the Rafael Landívar University, the Social Research and Study Association (ASIES) and the Latin American School of Social Sciences (FLACSO) have completed work in this regard.

4.4.2. Priority of Civil Authority and Purpose of the Armed Forces

Another set of 20 recommendations (numbered 53–72 in the CEH Report) aimed to ensure civilian control over the military and redefine the role of the military in a democratic context. The first batch of these recommendations urged the National Congress to present legislative reforms to promote civilian control over the military (CEH 1999, 74). For example, the Commission called for the elimination of the positions of Presidential and Vice-Presidential Chiefs of Staff (CEH 1999, 74). On October 30, 2003, pursuant to Law 50-2003, the Presidential Chiefs of Staff were dissolved, and the 564 Army officers were discharged (MINUGUA 2004a). The CEH also urged the drafting of a new Military Code in accordance with the Constitution and with the reforms resulting from the Peace Agreements (CEH 1999, 75). Currently, the Military Code effective in Guatemala dates from 1878 (Decree no. 214) and, although it has been modestly reformed, it continues to adopt old patterns that meddle in civil affairs. In addition, the inclusion of new concepts of discipline and obedience in the Military Code, to the detriment of the concept of "due obedience" for all types of orders was recommended (CEH 1999, 75). Article 5 of the Military

Code exempts members of the armed forces from liability when they commit a crime while complying with an order from a superior, while Article 65 requires absolute vertical obedience, without exception (Decree no. 214). Thus, it is clear that this recommendation has not yet been implemented.

Another recommendation was for the elimination of the death penalty for military crimes of disobedience (CEH 1999, 75). The death penalty in Guatemala is in a state of legal ambiguity, since it has not been eliminated from part of its jurisdiction (Article 18 of the Constitution; Articles 41 and 43 of the Penal Code; Article 63 of the Military Code, which MINUGUA states has been repealed by a reform), but cannot be applied due to the absence of opportunities to take shelter in legal recourses (as set forth by Article 43) such as amnesty, pardon (the law was repealed by Congress in the year 2000) or commutation of sentence (Article 4.6 of the American Convention on Human Rights, ratified by Guatemala). In addition, the Constitutional Court declared capital punishment unconstitutional. Commissioners further urged the drafting of legislation to define the structures, tasks, and jurisdiction of civil and military intelligence organs, limiting the actions of the latter to military purposes (CEH 1999, 75). Although it is still in its development phase, the 2008 Framework Law of the National Security System (Decree no. 18-2008) effectively satisfies the recommendation. The CEH further called on Congress to establish clear control over State intelligence bodies (CEH 1999, 75). Although Chapter VII of the Framework Law for the National Security System adpots these controls from the National Security System, specialists caution us about the irresponsible use of such controls and their lack of application (Capó 2016).

With regards to the commitments contained in the Agreement on the Strengthening of Civil Authority and the Purpose of the Army within a Democratic Society, the Commission recommended prompt compliance with commitments connected to intelligence matters (CEH 1999, 75). To do so, it recommended the approval of the Law of Supervision Modalities for State Intelligence Organisms. MINUGUA (2004a) reported that this law was pending and no specific law regarding this issue has been approved subsequently. The Commission recommended the creation of a Law Regulating Access to Information on Military or Diplomatic Matters connected with National Security (CEH 1999, 75). Currently, although Article 23 of the Law of Access to Public Information (Decree no 57-2008) states that information regarding military or diplomatic matters classified as concerning national security is to be kept confidential, Article 24 establishes that under no circumstances can information regarding investigations of fundamental human rights violations or crimes against humanity be classified as confidential or reserved (CERIGUA 2012). However, no specific legislation deals with Military or Diplomatic Matters relating to Military Security. The third commitment required the limitation of the competency of the Director of Intelligence of the National Defense Chiefs of Staff, adjusting it to the new duties of the Army (CEH 1999, 75).

This recommendation has been implemented through the General Regulation for the Organization and Operation of the National Defense Chiefs of Staff (Ministerial Agreement no. 14-2006) (which superseded the 1988 one). Chapters IV and V regulate the Director of Intelligence and provide guidelines for the Chiefs of Staff. The last intelligence-related recommendation referred to the fulfilment regarding the configuration of the Civil Intelligence and Information Analysis Intelligence Department and the Ministry of Strategic Analysis (CEH 1999, 75). This recommendation was implemented through (i) the creation of the Ministry of Strategic Analysis, (ii) the implementation of the Law of the Presidency's Ministry of Strategic Analysis (Legislative Decree no. 114-97) and its organic regulations (formulated by means of Governmental Agreement no. 633-98), and (iii) the creation of the Law of the General Director of Civil Intelligence (Legislative Decree no. 71-2005) and its regulations (Governmental Agreement no. 203-2008).

With regard to the Armed Forces as an institution, commissioners formulated several recommendations. For example, they called for the creation of a Military Doctrine, born from internal reflection and in consultation with civil society and with a specific content, such as its subordination to civil authority, the Constitution and respect for human rights (CEH 1999, 75–76). By means of a process of discussions, the *Libro Blanco de la Defensa Nacional* (White Book of National Defense) was created in 2002 establishing the State's policies in matters related to National Defense (MINUGUA, 2004a), and in 2004, they approved the new, more modern and democratic Military Doctrine. Thus, this recommendation is considered implemented. In addition, the CEH felt it important that the values of this military institution needed to be based upon fundamental democratic concepts and principles (CEH 1999, 76). It is true that visible progress has been made regarding human rights with Article 1 of the Framework Law for the National Security System (Legislative Decree no. 18-2008), although the independent experts of the United Nations caution about the risk of using the Army for public security tasks (CERIGUA 2012).

With respect to academic programs, the Commission recommended that the government take measures to include democratic values and principles as fundamental subjects in the Guatemalan Army's training (CEH 1999, 77). Despite the efforts made with the 2009 Educational Reform of the Army and the content of the National Defense Ministry's Strategic Plan (MINDEF 2016), we have not identified any specific references to the subject in curricula. A further recommendation was to incorporate the study of the CEH Report within the Guatemalan Army's educational centers (CEH 1999, 77). In 2004, MINUGUA already cautioned on the lack of fulfilment of this recommendation. The 2014 Guatemalan Ministry of Defense magazine regarding the Army, which includes all the Higher Education modules of this institution, contained no plan integrating the study of the CEH Report (MINDEF 2014). Currently, it remains unimplemented. Along the same lines, neither the recommendation regarding a purge of the docent body involved in human rights violations (MINUGUA 2004a) nor the naming of faculty members with a recognized pro-democratic record have been implemented (CEH 1999, 77). Moreover, commissioners urged the revision of the training of forces conceived for the counterinsurgency struggle, such as the Kaibil School (CEH 1999, 77–78). MINUGUA (2004a) deemed the reforms too timid.

Several other proposals dealt with military recruitment. With regard to rules regulating military service, the Commission recommended strict respect for the principles of equality before the law when determining the mechanisms and processes of recruitment. This recommendation was implemented through Article 2c, Chapter I, of the Law of Civic Service (Legislative Decree no. 20-2003), which addresses the issues of equality and universality. The commissioners also recommended the establishment and regulation of the right to conscientiously object to armed service in exchange for some other type of community service (CEH 1999, 77). Although attempts were made in the 1990s to allow conscientious objection, these were rejected by Congress in 1996 (Mazariegos 2009). Other legislation, such as the Law of Civic Service or its regulation, does not even mention the issue. For this reason, this recommendation is considered not implemented. In addition, the Commission called for victims of human rights violations during the civil war and their immediate family members to be exempted from military service and be directly assigned to social services (CEH 1999, 77). The MINUGUA report (2004a) verifies how the Law of Civic Service does not include this recommendation, which has been disregarded by the Guatemalan State.

A few other recommendations dealt with the military's domestic and international standing. For instance, commissioners asked the Armed Forces to discontinue their practice of using Mayan names and symbols to designate military structures and units (CEH 1999, 79). Although apparently the name of the Special Forces is no longer the Mayan word "Kaibil", this name continues to be used unofficially within the military (MINDEF 2018b). Furthermore, the CEH urged military professionals to make an effort to achieve an Army that is at the service of peace and the country's citizens, thus allowing Guatemalans to feel proud of this institution (CEH 1999, 78–79). Nonetheless, several domestic and international watchdogs continue to alert us regarding the Army's deficiencies, and the continued impunity that the military largely enjoys. Finally, the Commission recommended that the Armed Forces participate in UN and Organization of American States (OAS) peace operations (CEH 1999, 79). This recommendation was implemented with Guatemala's execution of a November 12, 2003, Memorandum of Understanding with the UN to contribute military units to peacekeeping efforts. Subsequently, Guatemala has participated in operations in the Central African Republic, the Democratic Republic of Congo, Ivory Coast, Lebanon, and South Sudan, among others (MINDEF 2018a).

4.4.3. *Public Security*

Another institution targeted by the Commission's recommendations was the National Civil Police (PNC). It argued that the institution should be based on the principle of service to the community, without discrimination and respecting the nation's multi-ethnic nature. This is addressed by Article 2 of the Law of the National Civil Police (Legislative Decree no. 11-97), and Point 9c of Chapter 2 of the Institutional Doctrine of the National Civil Police (PNC 2012). The CEH also called for reinforcing the civil character of the PNC and its consequent demilitarization. This has seen both progress and setbacks (Pocasangre 2017), yet Article 244 of the Constitution continues to charge the Army with the maintenance of both internal and external security. In addition, the Commission promoted measures to support the investigation, prosecution, and punishment of human rights violations within the PNC, some aspects of which are addressed in Articles 11 and 34 of the Law of the PNC (Legislative Decree no. 11-97) and in Point 10 of the Institutional Doctrine of the PNC (PNC 2012). A further demand was to instill respect for the rule of law, a point addressed in Articles 12 and 34 of the Law of the PNC. Lastly, the CEH advocated for permanent training for the PNC, an item addressed in Point 4 of the Doctrinal Principles of the Educational Policy of the PNC and in the Personnel Performance Manual of the Civil National Police (SGP 2016). Progress is most clearly manifest in the continuous training program of the Virtual Education Center under the General Assistant Director of Studies of the PNC (SGED 2018a).

Along the lines of reforming the PNC, the commissioners offered several suggestions. It recommended purging the police force and the creation of a new control unit (CEH 1999, 79). The Interior Ministry's Inspector General arrested a total of 1,371 PNC agents between 2012 and 2015 (MINGOB 2015). Another recommendation was for the creation of a new internal inspector's office with the autonomy to punish both individual and institutional behavior, and open to the Human Rights Attorney and to the public. Subsequent reforms brought the PNC's internal control of the Office of Professional Responsibility (ORP) of the Inspector General of the PNC, under the Assistant General Director (OAS 2009).

The commissioners also focused on the relationship between the PNC and indigenous peoples (CEH 1999, 79–80). They made four recommendations regarding this matter. First, the CEH urged the consideration of bilingualism as a favorable element when academically assessing recruits and when deciding where to station personnel. This recommendation largely has been disregarded. In the rare instances where action was taken, like in the case of deciding where to deploy personnel, "this practice did not last more than a year and, very soon, stationing decisions were based on other reasons and priorities" (Hernández 2014). Second, the elimination of discriminatory requirements for applicants and during selection, thus adapting them to the country's multi-ethnic reality, was deemed important. Except for commitment 26c of the Agreement for the Strengthening of Civil Authority and the Purpose of the Army within a Democratic Society (Civil Society Assembly 1994) which only mentions the country's multi-ethnic reality, there is no indication the authorities have acted upon the recommendation. Third, the Commission argued for the importance of education on multiculturalism and inter-cultural co-existence within the PNC Academy. This is addressed in the section "social science knowledge" of the "Study guide for the process of evaluation for the basic training course for police agents – 2018" (SGED 2018b), which includes subjects on Mayan Ethnography, Geography and Culture. Finally, the recommendation of using indigenous languages when the PNC addresses the indigenous population for the development of better relationships between them was put into practice for less than a year and then discontinued.

The CEH also thought it important for the government and the National Congress to increase the PNC budget in order to guarantee its training, equipment provision and proper facilities (CEH 1999, 80). According to data from the Public Finance Ministry (2001–16) the amount assigned to citizen security and, specifically to the PNC, has been dramatically increasing, rising from 24 million Quetzals in 2001 to 2,169 million Quetzals in 2018 (MINFIN 2018). Nonetheless, since line items in the budget change annually, such data must be analyzed with care.

Regarding the maintenance of public order, the Commission recommended the creation of a new Law of Public Order concerning the civil character of the PNC during states of emergency, preventing it from being required to perform tasks traditionally assigned to the Army (CEH 1999, 80). However, as of March 2018, no new Law of Public Order has been drafted. The current law was created in 1965 and has been described as authoritarian and repressive by Alejandro Balsells (who was a member of the CEH) (Crónica 2016). Along these same lines, the Commission called for separating the duties of the Army from those of the Police, in particular limiting the participation of the Armed Forces in matters of public security (CEH 1999, 80). In this sense, in addition to Legislative Decree no. 40-2000, which supports inter-institutional cooperation between the Army and the PNC in tasks of interior security, on Army Day 2016, President Jimmy Morales supported the joint operation of the PNC and the Army during street patrol operations (La Hora 2016). So, this recommendation must be considered not implemented, and demonstrates that progress is indeed reversible.

4.5. OTHER RECOMMENDATIONS TO PROMOTE PEACE AND NATIONAL HARMONY

The commissioners issued five recommendations for promoting national peace and harmony that did not fit into prior categories. For example, commissioners recommended that the "people of Guatemala" continue their efforts to investigate and analyze the past to avoid the errors that caused past violence (CEH 1999, 81). Along these lines, civil society organizations such as the Myrna Mack Foundation and the Forensic Anthropology Foundation of Guatemala have promoted initiatives to investigate and analyze the past, such as the *Instancia Multiinstitucional por la Paz y la Concordia* (Multi-Institutional Agency for Peace and Harmony) and the *Comisión Nacional de Búsqueda de Niñez Desaparecida* (National Commission for the Search for Disappeared Children) (Impunity Watch 2012).

Another set of recommendations sought to promote the participation of indigenous peoples. One called for the inclusion of qualified and experienced indigenous professionals in State institutions (CEH 1999, 81). Currently, indigenous peoples continue to be underrepresented in a variety of areas, including the fields of administration and politics, although they represent more than half of Guatemala's population (IWGIA 2018). Reforms to the Electoral and Political Party Law were discussed in 2017 in an attempt to overcome this problem. However, "parity and equity for women and indigenous peoples were not approved, as was proposed by the Supreme Electoral Court and social organizations" (Valle 2018). A second recommendation urged the State to establish and finance a program of scholarships for the training and specialization of indigenous professionals (CEH 1999, 81). Although progress has been made in this field by other institutions, such as the Rafael Landívar University, the State has made no attempt to implement this recommendation. A third area identified was full compliance with the Agreement on the Identity and Rights of Indigenous Peoples (AIDPI) (CEH 1999, 81). Although some legal progress has been achieved, such as the incorporation of the crime of discrimination into the Penal Code (Article 202*bis*) or the creation of the Presidential Commission against Discrimination and Racism against Indigenous Peoples of Guatemala, both MINUGUA (2004a) and a UNDP report on the Identity and Rights of Indigenous Peoples point out continued severe discrimination experienced by indigenous peoples (Saquec 2016).

A final recommendation in this category urged the government to reinforce the mobilization of national resources through a fair, equitable and globally progressive fiscal reform, as established in the 1996 *Acuerdo sobre Aspectos Socioeconómicos y Situación Agraria* (Agreement on Socioeconomic Aspects and Agricultural Situation) (CEH 1999, 82). In the years since the CEH, both MINUGUA (2004a) and Sandoval (2018) point out the absence of a progressive tax policy, highlighting the increase of VAT and the persistence of tax exemptions that disproportionately benefit the wealthy.

4.6. ENTITY DRIVING AND MONITORING RECOMMENDATION FULFILMENT

The last recommendation considered by the CEH urged the National Congress to establish an entity, the *Fundación por la Paz y la Concordia* (Foundation for Peace and Harmony), to support, drive, and monitor compliance with the CEH's recommendations (CEH 1999, 82). However, successive governments have made no effort to create such a body. To fill the void, civil society organizations and human rights activists established the *Instancia Multiinstitucional para la Paz y la Concordia* (Multi-Institutional Agency for Peace and Harmony) to monitor fulfilment of the recommendation's objectives.

Key actors in the implementation process When it comes to obstacles for implementation, there is a lot of blame to go around. A large percentage of recommendations were addressed to the government of Guatemala and/or Congress. Often, though, there has been a lack of political will to act. In other cases, politicians have interpreted recommendations to suit their own interests, which results in many instances where only partial implementation has occurred. Moreover, there are some recommendations that were implemented and later experienced setbacks. One example that stands out is the recommendation on a State apology, which, contrary to his predecessors, President Morales opposed. Overall, although significant efforts to implement some of the recommendations were made under President Colom, both the Executive and the Legislative Branches were (and are) far from fulfilling the CEH's recommendations.

The former combatants have taken different approaches to the recommendations. Similarly to the State, the Armed Forces are characterized in many ways by their lack of change. Although these institutions have experienced improvements, at least formal ones, many reforms have not been implemented. In practice, the nation's citizens continue to hold the Armed Forces in low esteem. For its part, the URNG adopted a lower profile. Nonetheless, it behaved cooperatively towards the two recommendations that concerned it directly, namely the public apology and the provision of information about disappeared persons. This behavior likely reflects the fact that, after the peace agreements, the URNG sought to transform itself into a political party.

State institutions untainted by civil war violence played a more uniformly positive role. In general, the Office of the Attorney of Human Rights collaborated on the implementation of the recommendations. It had a significant role in reparation measures, since it was present during the negotiations included in the National Compensation Program. It also participated in matters regarding disappearances (specifically, in cases of disappeared children), in the observance of reforms made to the justice system, in investigations of the past, as well as in the fulfilment of CEH recommendations more generally.

Domestic non-State actors also played an important role in the politics surrounding the CEH's recommendations. Unlike the State, Guatemalan civil society has taken the leading role in shaping the Commission's legacy. A variety of organizations, such as the Myrna Mack Foundation, the Multicultural Agency for Peace and Harmony, the Board for Peace and Harmony, and the Forensic Anthropology Foundation of Guatemala have acted as driving forces for the implementation of the recommendations. These organizations have been active in promoting all types of recommendations, including those seeking the truth, compensation, exhumation, educational reform, and even reforming the Army. In Guatemala, circumstances have demonstrated that civil society organizations are indispensable to advancing the peace process. The Catholic Church, too, stands out as a positive force for the implementation of the recommendations. It was very active in truth-seeking processes, as well as in activities pertaining to symbolic reparation of the victims. In addition, it contributed to the Commission's work through its own investigation and report, all of this framed within the *Proyecto de Recuperación de la Memoria Histórica* (Project for the Recovery of Historical Memory, REMHI), directed by the Office of Human Rights of the Archbishopric of Guatemala. Finally, universities participated in driving implementation of recommendations regarding education within a culture of peace and respect for human rights and the integration of the indigenous community. In particular, the University of San Carlos de Guatemala and Rafael Landivar University stand out among institutions that participated in the process.

The role of foreign actors was significant, and largely beneficial. The role of the United States evolved from support of the Cold War doctrine of National Security to the role of agent working for good governance and stability of other countries. After the CEH, the United States remained very active in Guatemala's peace-building process through USAID, and other foreign governments, such as the Netherlands, Sweden and Spain, also collaborated to help fulfil the recommendations. Spain, in particular, provided support for public security operations through its Civil Guard Police. International and regional organizations such as the UN, especially UNDP and UNESCO, and the Inter-American Commission on Human Rights (*Comisión Interamericana de los Derechos Humanos*, CIDH) also were present throughout the process. The United Nations was highly influential in the peace-building process, although not as much as in El Salvador, for example. UNDP played a key role regarding disappearances, exhumations and publicizing reports through its United Nation Programs for the Development of Guatemala (PAJUST, Spanish acronym). UNESCO also participated in promoting the CEH Report. For its part, the

CIDH, through its Task Force against Enforced Disappearance, made significant efforts to implement recommendations connected to enforced disappearance.

5. CONCLUSIONS

One salient feature of the Guatemalan case is that the United Nations itself learned from its past mistakes and, thus, improved its performance during the period when the recommendations were due to be implemented. While the United Nations monopolized the peace process in El Salvador, in Guatemala they shared it with civil society organizations. This point was key in order to avoid leaving the country to its fate once the UN mission left the country.

In addition, during the period when the CEH was formed, representation of the Guatemalan society was a fundamental requirement in order to confer greater legitimacy to the process. In El Salvador's process, by contrast, Salvadorans had practically no representation, since all of the commissioners were foreigners, a fact that decreased social acceptance of the Commission there. For this reason, the Guatemalan experience enjoyed greater social and demographic representativeness. This, in turn, empowered civil society to assume a decisive role in the process.

The CEH's recommendations were directed primarily to the State, principally to the Executive and Legislative Branches. However, the dominant feature when it came time to implement such recommendations was their lack of political will. A high percentage of recommendations saw *some* steps taken toward implementation. In this manner, the elites directed a process where the purpose of the recommendations was reformulated to match the political goals of each period. Moreover, as of early 2019, some of the basic recommendations that had shown some progress during the Colom administration are experiencing setbacks under Morales.

As in any transitional justice process, the passage of time constitutes an obstacle in itself, because, even if it is possible to arrive at the truth, the processes of reparation and retributive justice gradually get lost in the fog of history. The deaths of many of the main perpetrators of human rights violations without having ever experienced any punishment for their actions constitute visible evidence of this fact. Thus, on April 1, 2018, ex-dictator Efraín Ríos Montt died without ever being imprisoned. Although the Guatemalan case reflects a learning process and introduces improvement in terms of transitional justice procedures, such justice has yet to be addressed by political elites in a way that allows for institutional reform and establishes the foundations necessary to implement CEH recommendations. As long as this remains so, many of the efforts to analyze the past and formulate recommendations will be in vain.

BIBLIOGRAPHY

Acuerdo Gubernativo No. 633-98 (October 23, 1998). *Acuerda adscribir al Ministerio de Gobernación una fracción de terreno con el fin de construir el edificio que albergue la Estación de la Policía Nacional Civil en el Municipio de San Pedro Sacatepéquez.* Diario de Centro América. Tomo CCLX. No. 13. Retrieved from: https://leyes.infile.com/index.php?id=182&id_publicacion=44347.

Acuerdo Gubernativo No. 948-99 (January 12, 2000). *Comisión Guatemalteca para la Aplicación del Derecho Internacional Humanitario.* Diario de Centro América, Órgano Oficial de la República de Guatemala, Tomo CCLXIII, Número 23. Retrieved from: https://leyes.infile.com/index.php?id=182&id_publicacion=36974.

Acuerdo Gubernativo No. 258-2003 (May 8, 2003). *Creación del Programa Nacional de Resarcimiento (PNR).* Diario de Centro América, Órgano Oficial de la República de Guatemala, Tomo CCLXXI, Número 63. Retrieved from: https://leyes.infile.com/index.php?id=182&id_publicacion=24492.

Acuerdo Gubernativo No. 43-2005 (February 4, 2005). *Reglamento del Programa Nacional de Resarcimiento.* Diario de Centro América, Órgano Oficial de la República de Guatemala, Tomo CCLXXVI, Número 7. Retrieved from: https://leyes.infile.com/index.php?id=181&id_publicacion=43099&cmd=login.

Acuerdo Gubernativo No. 619-2005 (November 29, 2005). *Se reforma el Acuerdo Gubernativo 258-2003, de fecha 7 de mayo de 2003, Creación del Programa Nacional de Resarcimiento.* Retrieved from: https://leyes.infile.com/index.php?id=182&id_publicacion=49634.

Acuerdo Gubernativo No. 203-2008 (July 30, 2008). *Reglamento de la ley de la dirección general de Inteligencia Civil.* Retrieved from: http://igsns.gob.gt/pdf/Acuerdoguber203-2008.pdf.

Acuerdo Gubernativo No. 245-2010 (November 26, 2010). *Reglamento de la Ley del Servicio Cívico.* Retrieved from: https://serviciocivico.files.wordpress.com/2011/08/ley-del-servicio-cc3advico-y-el-acuerdo-gubernativo.pdf.

Acuerdo Gubernativo No. 177-2011 (June 8, 2011). *Reglamento de la Inspectoría General del Sistema Nacional de Seguridad.* Retrieved from: http://stcns.gob.gt/docs/Legislacion/Reglamento_Inspectoria.pdf.

Acuerdo Gubernativo No. 539-2013 (December 30, 2013). *Acuérdase las siguientes Reformas al Acuerdo Gubernativo No 258-2003.* Diario de Centro América, Órgano Oficial de la República de Guatemala, Tomo CCXCVIII, Número 62. Retrieved from: http://www.minfin.gob.gt/images/downloads/leyes_acuerdos/acuerdogub539_301213.pdf.

Acuerdo Ministerial No. 66-98 (August 23, 1988). *Reglamento general del Estado mayor de la defensa nacional.* Retrieved from: http://igsns.gob.gt/pdf/LeyExterior/LeyesMindef/Ministerial066_88reggraldelEMDN.pdf.

Acuerdo Ministerial No. 510-2003 (September 11, 2003). *Creación de la Unidad de Lugares Sagrado y Práctica de la Espiritualidad Maya.* Retrieved from: http://mcd.gob.gt/wp-content/uploads/2013/10/Acuerdo-Ministerial-510-2003.pdf (Última visita: 1 de abril de 2018).

Acuerdo Ministerial No. 14-2006 (July 12, 2006). *Reglamento general de organización y funcionamiento del Estado Mayor de la Defensa Nacional.* Retrieved from: http://www.mindef.mil.gt/leyes_reglamentos/acuerdos_mdn/2006/14.pdf.

Acuerdo Ministerial No. 04-2011 (June 7, 2011). *Reglamento de organización y funcionamiento del Comando Superior de Educación del Ejército de Guatemala.* Retrieved from: www.mindef.mil.gt/leyes_reglamentos/acuerdos_mdn/2011/04.pdf.

Acuerdo sobre el establecimiento de la Comisión para el Esclarecimiento Histórico de las violaciones a los derechos humanos y los hechos de violencia que han causado sufrimientos a la población guatemalteca (Oslo, June 23, 1994). Retrieved from: http://www.sepaz.gob.gt/Accesoalainformacion/index.php/79-acuerdos-de-paz/93-acuerdo-sobre-el-establecimiento-de-la-comision-para-el-esclarecimiento-historico-de-las-violaciones-a-los-derechos-humanos-y-los-hechos-de-violencia-que-han-causado-sufrimientos-a-la-poblacion-guatemalteca.

AFP-REUTERS (December 30, 1998). "Álvaro Arzú pide perdón a Guatemala". En *El tiempo*. Retrieved from: http://www.eltiempo.com/archivo/documento/MAM-809656.

AFP-REUTERS (February 26, 2009). "Tribunal pide perdón a víctimas de guerra". In *La Prensa*. Retrieved from: http://www.laprensa.com.ni/2009/02/26/internacionales/1356228-colom-pide-perdon-a-victimas-de-guerra.

Alamilla, Ileana (June 22, 2017). "Ley de acceso a la información y sus efectos". En *Prensa Libre*. Retrieved from: www.prensalibre.com/opinion/opinion/ley-de-acceso-a-la-informacion-y-sus-efectos.

Amnistía Internacional – Equipo de América Central (2009). *La Comisión para el Esclarecimiento Histórico de Guatemala, diez años después.* (Índice AI: AMR34/004/2009). Email enviado de "Equipo de América Central" a "Coordinadores/as de Guatemala, Coordinadores/as de la Red de Acción Especial de América Central (CASA) y Red de Coordinación de Justicia Internacional, 30 de enero de 2009.

Arreaga, Aisza (2017). *CPR de la Sierra no es propiedad de un gobierno, es propiedad de su historia. En Memorial para la Concordia Guatemala*, Mapeo de la Memoria (Retrieved from: http://mapeo.memorialparalaconcordia.org/article.php?id=194.

Asamblea de la Sociedad Civil (September 28, 1994). *Fortalecimiento del Poder Civil y la Función del Ejército en una Sociedad Democrática*. Retrieved from: http://biblioteca.clacso.edu.ar/Guatemala/flacso-gt/20120809013001/12funcion.pdf.

Azorín, Jaime (2009). *Derechos Humanos en Guatemala: un compromiso con la Justicia Universal.* Madrid: Confederación Sindical de Comisiones Obreras.

Balsells, Edgar Alfredo (2000). *La memoria del silencio*. Ponencia presentada en las Jornadas sobre Olvido, Memoria y Comisiones de la Verdad, Barcelona.

Blanco, Ligia and Zapata, Adrián (2007). "La contribución del proceso de paz a la construcción de la democracia en Guatemala". In Azpuru, Dinorah et al. (eds.). *Construyendo la democracia en sociedades posconflicto. Guatemala y El Salvador, un enfoque comparado*. Guatemala: FyG editores.

Capó, Grisel (March 3, 2016). "La inteligencia en Guatemala: un nuevo modelo para el siglo XXI". In *República*. Retrieved from: republica.gt/2016/03/03/la-inteligencia-en-guatemala-un-nuevo-modelo-para-el-siglo-xxi/.

Castañón, Francisco (1999). "Conferencia". In *Conferencia y Seminario sobre la experiencia de cultura de paz en Guatemala*. Bilbao: Unesco Etxea.

Ceballos, Marcela (2009). *Comisiones de la Verdad y transiciones de paz. Salvador, Guatemala, Suráfrica y posibilidades para Colombia*. Medellín: La Carreta Editores.

CEH (1999a). *Informe: Guatemala, memoria del silencio. Tomo IV. Consecuencias y efectos de la violencia*. Guatemala: FyG Editores.

—— (1999b). *Informe: Guatemala, memoria del silencio. Tomo V. Conclusiones y recomendaciones*. Guatemala: FyG Editores.

Centro de Análisis Forense y Ciencias Aplicadas CAFCA (2015). *Informe. Auditoría social a la política de reparación del Estado de Guatemala. Red de organizaciones sociales y de víctimas*. Guatemala: Magna Terra editores.

CERIGUA - Centro de Reportes Informativos sobre Guatemala (February 6, 2012). "Congreso discutirá reformas a la ley de Acceso a la Información". In *CERIGUA. Retrieved from*: https://cerigua.org/article/congreso-discutira-reformas-a-la-ley-de-acceso-a-l/.

—— (October 13, 2012). "Relatores especiales de la ONU preocupados por la utilización de la violencia en los actos legítimos de protesta social". In *CERIGUA*. Retrieved from: https://cerigua.org/article/relatores-especiales-de-la-onu-preocupados-por-la-/.

CEH - Comisión para el Esclarecimiento Histórico (1999). *Guatemala: Memoria del Silencio: conclusiones y recomendaciones*. Guatemala: Oficina de Servicios para Proyectos de las Naciones Unidas (UNOPS).

CNR - Comisión Nacional de Resarcimiento (2015). Resolución CNR-001-2015 (January 7, 2015). Gobierno de Guatemala (Programa Nacional de Resarcimiento). Retrieved from: http://www.sepaz.gob.gt/images/PNR/Resolucin-CNR-001-2015.pdf.

Consejo de las Autoridades Ancestrales Mayas de la Región Ixil (Council of Ancestral Mayan Authorities of the Region of Ixil) (May 2013). *Sentencia por genocidio contra el pueblo Ixil*. Boletín informativo 002, mayo de 2013. Retrieved from: http://www.albedrio.org/htm/otrosdocs/comunicados/caamri-006.html.pdf.

Constitución Política de la República de Guatemala (1985) (con la reforma a través de Acuerdo legislativo No. 18-93 del 17 de noviembre de 1993). Retrieved from: https://www.oas.org/juridico/mla/sp/gtm/sp_gtm-int-text-const.pdf.

Contreras, Geovanni (July 5, 2017). "Conmemoran 12 años de hallazgo del archivo de la Policía Nacional". In *Prensa Libre*. Retrieved from: http://www.prensalibre.com/guatemala/politica/conmemoran-12-aos-de-hallazgo-del-archivo-de-la-policia-nacional.

Corte Interamericana de Derechos Humanos - CorteIDH (IACtHR) (2010). *Necesidad de legislar en Materia de Desaparición Forzada. Aprobación de la ley 35–90 que crea la Comisión de Búsqueda de Personas, Víctimas de la Desaparición Forzada y otras Formas de Desaparición, en Guatemala*. Grupo de trabajo contra la desaparición forzada en Guatemala, perteneciente a la Comisión Interamericana de Derechos Humanos.

Convención Americana sobre Derechos Humanos (Pacto de San José) (1969). Retrieved from: https://www.oas.org/dil/esp/tratados_b-32_convencion_americana_sobre_derechos_humanos.htm.

Crónica (October 11, 2016). "Ley de Orden Público: Legislación de 1965, autoritaria y represiva". In *Crónica*. Retrieved from: http://cronica.gt/ley-de-orden-publico-legislacion-de-1965-autoritaria-y-represiva.

De Leon, Quimy (June 30, 2017). "El Diario Militar: Una Historia de Desapariciones y Muerte". Interview with Kate Doyle. *Prensa Comunitaria*. Retrieved from: http://www.prensacomunitaria.org/tag/kate-doyle/.

Decreto Legislativo No. 72-90 (December 13, 1990). *Ley Constitutiva del Ejército de Guatemala.* Recuperado de: http://www.oas.org/juridico/spanish/mesicic2_gtm_decreto_72-90.pdf.

Decreto Legislativo No. 11-97 (February 25, 1997). *Ley de la Policía Nacional Civil.* Recuperado de: http://pnc.edu.gt/wp-content/uploads/2013/07/LEY-DE-LA-PNC.pdf.

Decreto Legislativo No. 114-97 (November 13, 1997). *Ley del Organismo Ejecutivo.* Retrieved from: https://www.mem.gob.gt/wp-content/uploads/2015/06/12._Ley_del_Organismo_Ejecutivo_Decreto_114_97.pdf.

Decreto Legislativo No. 40-2000 (June 16, 2000). *Ley de apoyo a las fuerzas de seguridad civil.* Retrieved from: http://relapt.usta.edu.co/images/2000-Ley-de-Apoyo-a-las-Fuerzas-de-Seguridad-Civil-Decreto-40.pdf.

Decreto Legislativo No. 61-2002 (28 de octubre de 2002). *Ley que Declara el Día Nacional de la Dignidad de las Víctimas de la Violencia.* Diario de Centro América, Órgano Oficial de la República de Guatemala, Tomo CCLXX, Número 31. Retrieved from: https://guatemala.justia.com/nacionales/leyes/decreto-no-61-2002-sep-10-2002/gdoc/.

Decreto Legislativo No. 20-2003. (May 12, 2003). *Ley del Servicio Cívico.* Retrieved from: https://www.unicef.org/guatemala/spanish/LeyServicioCivico.pdf.

Decreto Legislativo No. 06-2004 (March 29, 2004). *Ley que conmemora el 25 de febrero de Cada Año, como el Día Nacional de la Dignidad de las Víctimas del Conflicto Armado Interno.* Diario de Centro América, Órgano Oficial de la República de Guatemala, Tomo CCLXXIII, Número 89. Retrieved from: http://ww2.oj.gob.gt/es/QueEsOJ/EstructuraOJ/UnidadesAdministrativas/CentroAnalisisDocumentacionJudicial/cds/CDs%20leyes/2004/PDFs/Decretos/DECRETO%2006-04.pdf.

Decreto Legislativo No. 71-2005 (November 9, 2005). *Ley de la Dirección de Inteligencia Civil.* Tomo CCLXXVII. No. 98. Diario de Centroamérica. Retrieved from: https://www.congreso.gob.gt/consulta-legislativa/decreto-detalle/?id=12856.

Decreto Legislativo No. 18-2008 (April 15, 2008). *Ley Marco del Sistema Nacional de Seguridad.* Tomo CCLXXXIV. No. 15. Retrieved from: https://www.congreso.gob.gt/consulta-legislativa/decreto-detalle/?id=13040.

Decreto Legislativo No. 48-2008 (September 23, 2008). *Reformas al Decreto 06-04 del Congreso de la República, Ley que conmemora el 25 de febrero de cada año como el Día Nacional de la Dignidad de las Víctimas del Conflicto Armado Interno. Diario de Centro América, Órgano Oficial de la República de Guatemala,* Tomo CCLXXXV, Número 23. Retrieved from: https://guatemala.justia.com/nacionales/modificaciones/decreto-no-48-2008-aug-20-2008/gdoc/.

Decreto Legislativo No. 57-2008 (October 22, 2008). *Ley de Acceso a la Información Pública.* Retrieved from: www.oas.org/juridico/pdfs/mesicic4_gtm_acceso.pdf.

Decreto-Ley No. 106 (September 14, 1963). *Código Civil.* Retrieved from: http://www.wipo.int/wipolex/es/text.jsp?file_id=333379.

Decreto No. 214. *Código Militar Penal y de Procedimientos respectivos* (Secretaría de la Guerra). 1 de agosto de 1878. Retrieved from: https://archivos.juridicas.unam.mx/www/bjv/libros/5/2048/9.pdf.

EFE-Guatemala (May 13, 2013). "Tribunal de Guatemala exige al Estado pedir perdón a los indígenas por genocidio". In *El Diario.* Retrieved from: http://www.eldiario.es/politica/Tribunal-Guatemala-perdon-indigenas-genocidio_0_131937603.html.

—— (December 27, 2016). "El vicepresidente de Guatemala elude tildar de genocidio el conflicto armado". In *Agencia EFE*. Retrieved from: https://www.efe.com/efe/america/politica/el-vicepresidente-de-guatemala-elude-tildar-genocidio-conflicto-armado/20000035-3135017.

Elías, José (May 21, 2013). "El Constitucional de Guatemala anula la condena al exdictador Ríos Montt". En *El País*. Retrieved from: https://elpais.com/internacional/2013/05/21/actualidad/1369101633_290958.html.

Gomez. Ana M.V. (2011). "Reparations in Guatemala: Effects of a Truth Commission Not Recognized by the State". *Asian Journal of Latin American Studies* no. 24 (4): 21–47.

Hayner, Priscilla (2006). "Comisiones de la Verdad: resumen esquemático". *International Review of the Red Cross* no. 862: 1–18.

Hernández Batres, Iduvina (2014). "La Policía Nacional Civil de Guatemala: vida, pasión y muerte de una institución desdeñada". *Perspectivas* no. 7. Retrieved from: http://library.fes.de/pdf-files/bueros/la-seguridad/10873.pdf.

Hernandez, Juan (2005). "'Memoria del silencio': Un informe estremecedor para la memoria de los mártires". In *Terminar la Guerra Traicionar la Paz*. Guatemala: FLACSO Guatemala.

Hoelscher, Steven (2008). *Angels of Memory: Photography and Haunting in Guatemala City. Collective Memory and the Politics of Memory*. Stanford CA: Stanford University Press.

Ibáñez, Jorge Enrique (2017). *Justicia Transicional y Comisiones de Verdad*. Madrid: Instituto Berg.

ICEFI – Instituto Centroamericano de Estudios Fiscales (2007). *Historia de la tributación en Guatemala (Desde los mayas hasta la actualidad)*. Documento preparado para la Superintendencia de Administración Tributaria – SAT. Retrieved from: http://icefi.org/sites/default/files/pags_1-64.pdf.

Impunity Watch-Equipo de Guatemala (2012). *Verdad histórica en Guatemala: un paso al costado*. Retrieved from: http://www.impunitywatch.org/docs/Guatemala verdad_historica_un_paso_al_costado_2012.pdf.

—— (2012). *Monitoreo de la Justicia Transicional en Guatemala. Tomo I: Derecho a la verdad para las víctimas del Conflicto Armado Interno*. Retrieved from: https://www.impunitywatch.org/docs/TomoI_Derecho_a_la_verdad.pdf.

—— (2014). *Monitoreo de la Justicia en Guatemala. Tomo II: Derecho a la Justicia para las víctimas del Conflicto Armado Interno*. Retrieved from: https://www.impunitywatch.org/docs/Research_report_informe_monitoreo_IW_JUSTICIA_Dec_2014.pdf.

Iniciativa de Ley No. 3590 (January 18, 2007). *Iniciativa que dispone aprobar Ley de la Comisión de Búsqueda de Personas, Víctimas de la Desaparición Forzada y otras Formas de Desaparición*. Congreso de la República de Guatemala, C.A. (Dirección Legislativa – control de iniciativas). Retrieved from: http://www.crin.org/en/docs/Guatemala_desparicion.pdf.

IWGIA – Grupo Internacional de Trabajo sobre Asuntos Indígenas (2016). *Indigenous peoples in Guatemala*. Retrieved from: https://www.iwgia.org/es/guatemala.

La Hora (July 16, 2016). "Un Ejército que cuesta Q2 mil 61 millones está en las calles". *La Hora*. Retrieved from: http://lahora.gt/ejercito-cuesta-q2-mil-61-millones-esta-las-calles/.

La Prensa (July 2, 2004). "Guatemala reduce el Ejército y cambia de doctrina". *La Prensa*. Retrieved from: https://www.laprensa.com.ni/2004/07/02/internacionales/949534-guatemala-reduce-el-ejrcito-y-cambia-de-doctrina.

Mazariegos, Waldemar (2009). *Estudio crítico del avance o estancamiento en el cumplimiento del Acuerdo Global de Derechos Humanos en Guatemala enfocado al derecho a la vida*. Tesis Universidad de San Carlos de Guatemala. Retrieved from: http://biblioteca.usac.edu.gt/tesis/04/04_8089.pdf.

Memorial para la Concordia (2017). *Mapeo de la memoria*. Retrieved from: mapeo.memorialparalaconcordia.org.

MINDEF – Ministerio de la Defensa Nacional (2014). *Trascender generacionalmente*. In *Ejército de Guatemala*. No. 1. Retrieved from: www.mindef.mil.gt/pdf/revista2014.pdf.

—— (2016). *Plan estratégico del Ministerio de la Defensa Nacional 2016*. Retrieved from: www.mindef.mil.gt/pdf/2016/PLAN%20ESTRATEGICO%20INSTITUCIONAL%20 2016-MDN.pdf.

—— (2018a). *Direcciones de Operaciones de Paz*. Retrieved from: http://www.mindef.mil.gt/onu/dopaz/historia.html.

—— (2018b). *Brigada de Fuerzas Especiales "General de Brigada Pablo Nuila Hub"*. Retrieved from: http://www.mindef.mil.gt/comandos/kaibil/historia.html.

MINFIN – Ministerio de Finanzas Públicas (2018). *Presupuestos aprobados*. Retrieved from: http://www.minfin.gob.gt/index.php/presupuestos-aprobados.

MINGOB – Ministerio de Gobernación (September 25, 2015). *Fortalecen depuración en la PNC*. Retrieved from: mingob.gob.gt/fortalecen-depuracion-en-la-pnc/.

—— (August 17, 2016). *Agentes son capturados como parte de la depuración de la PNC*. Retrieved from: http://mingob.gob.gt/agentes-son-capturados-como-parte-de-la-depuracion-de-la-pnc/.

MINEX – Ministerio de Relaciones Exteriores, Gobierno de Guatemala (2018). *Consulta de Tratados Internacionales Vigentes*. Retrieved from: http://www.minex.gob.gt/pBase.aspx?ID=/MAYT/MAYT_TRATADO_ACUERDO/MAYT_TRATADO_ACUERDO_VIGENTEWebReport.aspx.

MINUGUA – Misión de Verificación de las Naciones Unidas en Guatemala. (September 2000). Informe de verificación. Procedimiento de Exhumaciones en Guatemala (1997–2000). Guatemala: MINUGUA.

—— (2004a). Informe de verificación. El estado de cumplimiento de las recomendaciones de la Comisión para el Esclarecimiento Histórico. Ciudad de Guatemala.

—— (2004b). Informe de verificación. De la Verdad Histórica a la Reconciliación. Declaración de URNG, 12 de marzo de 1999. Ciudad de Guatemala.

OEA – Organización de los Estados Americanos (2009). *Seguridad Pública y Privada Guatemala*. Retrieved from: https://www.oas.org/dsp/documentos/publicaciones/seg%20publica-%20guatemala.pdf.

ONU – Oficina del Alto Comisionado de las Naciones Unidas (2010). "Defensoras y defensores de los derechos humanos". In *Boletín Derechos Humanos*. Retrieved from: http://ww2.oj.gob.gt/cursos/COMPILACION3/docs/Boletines/boletin_20.pdf.

—— (2018). *Principales tratados internacionales sobre derechos humanos aprobados y ratificados por Guatemala*. Retrieved from: http://ww2.oj.gob.gt/cursos/COMPILACION3/docs/instrumentos/Ratificaciones.pdf.

Orozco, Andre y Gramajo, Jessica (July 26, 2016). "Ley de Carrera Judicial cobra vigencia en noviembre". In *Prensa Libre*. Retrieved from: http://www.prensalibre.com/guatemala/justicia/cambios-a-carrera-judicial-tendran-vigencia-en-noviembre.

Padilla, Luis Alberto (2013). "Guatemala: relaciones internacionales y contexto geopolítico mundial, (1954–1996)". In Álvarez, Virgilio; Figueroa, Carlos; Arturo, Jorge; Taracena, Sergio Visquerra, Thisler; and Urrutia, Edmundo: *Guatemala: Historia reciente (1954–1996). Tomo IV. Proceso de paz y contexto internacional*. Guatemala: Facultad Latinoamericana de Ciencias Sociales-Guatemala.

Palmieri, Luis Arturo (August 2017). "Indulto y pena de muerte en Guatemala". In *brújula.com.gt*. Retrieved from: http://brujula.com.gt/indulto-y-pena-de-muerte-en-guatemala/.

Panneta, Francesco (November 2013): Derecho a la reparación en Guatemala: Por la senda de la negación. Policy Brief Impunity Watch. Retrieved from: http://www.albedrio.org/htm/documentos/IWGuatemalaReparacion.pdf.

PNC - Policía Nacional Civil (2012). *Doctrina Institucional. Guatemala*. Retrieved from: http://pnc.edu.gt/wp-content/uploads/2013/07/DOCTRINA-INSTITUCIONAL.pdf.

PNUD - Programa de Naciones Unidas para el Desarrollo para Guatemala (2014). *Proyecto PAJUST II, Articulación y alianzas entre Estado y sociedad civil para el impulso de la justicia de transición. Plan estratégico PNUD 2014–2017*. Retrieved from: https://info.undp.org/docs/pdc/Documents/GTM/PRODOC%20PAJUST%20II%20DIM%20%20firmado.pdf.

Pocasangre, Henry (December 28, 2017). "Ejército patrullará con la PNC hasta marzo de 2018". *Prensa Libre*. Retrieved from: http://www.prensalibre.com/guatemala/justicia/ejercito-seguridad-ciudadana-apoyo-a-la-pnc-patrullajes-combinados.

Poitevin, René (2004). "Historia Política". In Berganza, Gustavo (Editor General): *Compendio de Historia de Guatemala*. 1ª Edición, 2004. Guatemala: Centro de Impresiones Gráficas - CIMGRA-.

Prensa Libre (December 30, 2013). "Programa de Resarcimiento tendrá vigencia hasta 2023". In *Prensa Libre*. Retrieved from: http://www.prensalibre.com/noticias/justicia/PNR-Resarcimiento-Victimas-Conflicto_Armado_0_1057094384.html.

—— (May 13, 2014). "Aprueban punto resolutivo que niega genocidio en Guatemala". In *Prensa Libre*. Retrieved from: http://www.prensalibre.com/noticias/justicia/diputados-aprueban-punto_resolutivo-negaria-genocidio-Guatemala_0_1137486508.html.

Punto Resolutivo No. 6-98 (1998). *Solicita a la Comisión de Esclarecimiento Histórico, investigación de lo ocurrido en la Embajada de España el día 31 de enero de 1980*. Retrieved from: https://leyes.infile.com/index.php?id=182&id_publicacion=25017.

RESDAL - Red de Seguridad y Defensa de América Latina (2012). *Atlas comparativo de la Defensa en América Latina y Caribe*. Retrieved from: www.resdal.org/atlas/atlas12-18-guatemala.pdf.

Saquec, Daniel (ed.) (2016). *Acuerdo sobre Identidad y Derechos de los Pueblos Indígenas. Avances y desafíos a 20 años de la firma de los Acuerdos de Paz*. Programa Maya - PNUD. Retrieved from: http://onu.org.gt/wp-content/uploads/2017/03/AIDPI-Informe-final-PDF.pdf.

Sandoval, Miguel Ángel (2018). "Las exenciones fiscales son antidemocráticas". *El Periódico.* Retrieved from: https://elperiodico.com.gt/opinion/2016/08/31/las-exenciones-fiscales-son-antidemocraticas/.

Scwank, John (2005). *"La costumbre jurídica de los pueblos mayas". Revista IIDH* no. 41: 253–285.

SEPAZ – Secretaría de la Paz (2010). *Niñez desaparecida en Guatemala como parte de la estrategia de la Guerra. Búsqueda, Casos y Efectos.* Guatemala: Secretaría de la Paz (SEPAZ).

SGED – Subdirección General de Estudios y Doctrina de la Policía Nacional Civil (2018a). *Política educativa.* Retrieved from: https://pnc.edu.gt/politicas-2/.

—— (2018b). *Guía de estudio del proceso de evaluación para el curso básico de formación de agentes de policía 2018.* Retrieved from: http://pnc.edu.gt/wp-content/uploads/2018/01/5.-GUIA-DE-ESTUDIOS-PARA-LAS-EVALUACIONES-2018.pdf.

SGP – Subdirección General de Personal de la PNC (October 24, 2016). *Manual de evaluación del desempeño del personal de la Policía Nacional Civil".* Retrieved from: http://pnc.edu.gt/wp-content/uploads/2017/01/RESOLUCION-14-2016-EVALUACION-DEL-DESEMPE%C3%91O.pdf.

—— (2017). *Manual de Evaluación del Desempeño del personal de la Policía Nacional Civil.* Retrieved from: http://pnc.edu.gt/wp-content/uploads/2017/07/Manual-de-Evaluacion-del-Desempe%C3%B1o.pdf.

Simon, Jan-Michael (2002). *La Comisión para el Esclarecimiento Histórico, verdad y justicia en Guatemala.* Ponencia en el coloquio internacional "Estado de derecho y delincuencia de Estado en América Latina. Procesos de transformación comparados", celebrado del 22 al 24 de febrero de 2002 en la ciudad de Sao Paulo, Brasil, organizado por el Instituto Brasileiro de Ciências Criminais, la Fundación Konrad Adenauer-Programa Estado de Derecho en Sudamérica y el Instituto Max Planck de Derecho Penal Extranjero e Internacional.

Sosa, Lizardo (March 30, 2018). "Derecho consuetudinario". *El Periódico.* Retrieved from: https://elperiodico.com.gt/opinion/2017/03/08/derecho-consuetudinario-2/.

Steinberg, Michael K. and Taylor, Matthew J. (2003). "Public Memory and Political Power in Guatemala's Postconflict Landscape". *Geographical Review* no. 93 (4): 449–468.

UN Women (2018). "Sepur Zarco case: The Guatemalan women who rose for justice in a war-torn nation", Retrieved from: https://www.unwomen.org/en/news/stories/2018/10/feature-sepur-zarco-case.

UNIVERSIA (2018). *Maestría en etnicidad, etnodesarrollo y derecho indígena (Universidad de San Carlos de Guatemala).* Retrieved from: www.universia.com.gt/estudios/usac/maestria-etnicidad-etnodesarrollo-derecho-indigena/st/176568.

Valdiviezo, Nuria (2014). *Procedimiento específico para el Hábeas Data.* Tesis De Grado. Retrieved from: http://recursosbiblio.url.edu.gt/publicjlg/Tesis/2013/02/04/Valdiviezo-Nuria.pdf.

Wallace Fuentes, Myrna (2012). "The Spanish Embassy Occupation and Assault: History and the Partisan Politics of Memory since 1980 in Guatemala". *A Contra corriente. A Journal on Social History and Literature in Latin America* no. 10 (1): 365–412. Retrieved from: https://acontracorriente.chass.ncsu.edu/index.php/acontracorriente/article/view/100/977.

Weber, Sanne and Panetta, Francesco (2013). *¿La hora de la verdad? Monitoreo de la Justicia Transicional en Guatemala.* Informe Impunity Watch. Retrieved from: http://www.impunitywatch.org/docs/IW_La_hora_de_la_verdad.pdf.

INTERVIEWS

Ruth del Valle. Expert from the Commission on Human Rights of Guatemala, March 17, 2018.

HAITI'S TRUTH AND JUSTICE COMMISSION

Forgotten Recommendations, Living Demands

Lisa-Marie Måseidvåg Selvik*

* The author is affiliated to Chr. Michelsen Institute, Bergen, Norway and to the Department of Comparative Politics at the University of Bergen, Bergen, Norway.
I am grateful to all the interviewees (listed in appendix) for their generosity, and to Rachelle Doucet for facilitating my fieldwork in Port-au-Prince. I also want to thank Elin Skaar for trusting me with this assignment, giving me the chance to get to know Haiti and be part of the *Beyond Words* project. Thank you to Joanna Quinn and Onur Bakiner for reviewing the chapter and providing valuable input, and to Eric Wiebelhaus-Brahm for his thorough review. Thanks to the Rights & Legal Institutions and the Gender research groups at CMI for valuable feedback on drafts, especially Monica Kirya and Mari Norbakk. I also thank Jørgen Sørlie Yri for both comments and enthusiasm for this study. Last but not least, I thank the team at CELS for providing me with a copy of Rodolfo Mattarollo's *Rien n'a été en vain* (2013) from their archives.

1. INTRODUCTION

In 1995, a truth commission was convoked in Haiti. The Haitian National Truth and Justice Commission (*Commission Nationale de Vérité et de Justice*, CNVJ) sought to uncover the truth about human rights abuses committed between 1991 and 1994, to end impunity, and to reform the justice system in Haiti. First and foremost, the CNVJ was to uncover and establish the facts surrounding a military regime and the most serious human rights violations committed during the three-year period following a *coup d'état* in 1991.

Completed in 1996, the CNVJ report was entitled "*Si m pa rele*",[1] a contraction of the Haitian Creole expression *Si m pa rele m'ap toufe*, meaning "If I do not cry out I will suffocate". In it, the truth commission listed a great many recommendations. Reforms of Haiti's justice system attracted significant attention, with the hope of safeguarding against a repetition of the violations the commission had uncovered and providing justice to victims. The comprehensive body of recommendations included reparations, institutional and administrative reform, criminal proceedings, and non-repetition measures. Among other things, the final report placed particular emphasis on addressing sexual violence against women, as well as judicial independence and education of the police force.

Today, Haiti is often labelled a "failed" or "weak" state and has, since 1994, had a near-constant presence of United Nations peace operations (McCalpin 2012, 143; Mobekk 2017, 8). The CNVJ arguably addressed all of the issues that the Haitian state and society faced in 1996, aspiring to overall social and political

---

1 This study is based on a reproduction and digitalization of the report made available by the Institute of Haitian Studies at the University of Kansas, in 1998. It contains only minor typographical corrections to the original text.

change. However, many of the issues addressed by the CNVJ are still relevant today. There is still a need to reform the justice system, impunity is still high, the army that was abolished in 1994 has been reinstated, and the issue of sexual violence against women is a growing focus area. These issues are still salient, and the measures the CNVJ recommended remain highly relevant. In other words, while the CNVJ and its report are today largely forgotten, the demand for truth and justice in Haiti still stands.

This chapter examines the implementation of the CNVJ's recommendations. The next section provides the historical backdrop to the creation of the CNVJ and outlines the circumstances under which it operated. The third section presents the CNVJ, its mandate, composition, and other aspects of its work. The fourth section details its recommendations, elaborating on their characteristics and presentation in the report. The fifth section is concerned with the process of formulating the recommendations. The sixth section discusses the implementation of the recommendations and provides a brief account of the political environment in Haiti over the subsequent 20 years in which the implementation of those recommendations has been contemplated. The seventh section sums up Haiti's overall implementation record and discuss the actors and factors affecting it. Finally, conclusions are drawn in the eighth section.

This chapter is written based upon fieldwork conducted in Port-au-Prince in July 2016, in the course of which13 key informants were interviewed, who either had knowledge about the work of the CNVJ or about the key issues addressed in the recommendations. Further, this study is informed by archival sources, situation reports, and analysis and scholarly work on specific issues. The many years that have passed since the CNVJ finished its report presented challenges in gathering information on certain aspects of the commission's work, such as the process of formulating the recommendations. While the two decades that have passed provide ample time to study trajectories of implementation, informants' memory of the process may have faded, and rationales for actions and connections between events may not be recalled accurately, posing a challenge to mapping the implementation of recommendations. I attempt to remedy this by triangulating a vast amount of information from a variety of sources.

2. HISTORICAL BACKGROUND

Haiti has a long, turbulent history. Haiti was "discovered" by European powers in 1492, when Christopher Columbus arrived on the Caribbean island of Hispaniola after his first voyage across the Atlantic. In the centuries to follow, Haiti proved to be a valuable colony, first for Spain (1492–1625) and later for France (1625–1804), based on its slave-based plantation economy. In 1804, however, Haiti was the first slave colony to gain independence.[2] In contrast to the long line of changing governments that represent Haitian political history after independence, the reign of the Duvaliers lasted from 1957 to 1986.[3] The brutal reign of father and son, François Duvalier and Jean-Claude Duvalier,[4] who ruled Haiti as Presidents for life, lasted until the latter was ousted in 1986.

Due to persistent political and civil unrest and violence, in addition to a series of economic crises, several generations of Haitians have fled the country, which has created an extensive Haitian diaspora[5] (Hoogenboom and Quinn 2011, 10; Quinn 2019, 1838). The Haitian diaspora in the late 1980s and early 1990s stretched across North America and the Caribbean, the most prominent communities residing in New York, Boston, Santo Domingo, Miami and Montreal (Quinn 2009, 267). During the Duvalier era, many of Haiti's intellectuals, including much of the legal community, fled (*Si m pa rele*, Annex III, p. 3, in Quinn 2009, 267). After the ousting of Jean-Claude Duvalier from power by popular revolt, the Constitution of 1987, which is still in effect today, was written. This new constitution departed from earlier ones (of which there were several) in that it focused on individual liberty (Lechtenberg 1996, 3). It also was written in Creole rather than French, a first in a country where French fluency symbolized racial and class divisions. After the removal of the dictatorship and the beginning of a new constitutional regime, Haitian politics entered yet another turbulent period, with fraudulent elections and several *coup d'états*. In such an environment, the justice system was dysfunctional, and impunity was high. For many, the election of Jean-Bertrand Aristide in 1991, a progressive Roman Catholic priest adhering to liberal theology, marked a critical turning point in the democratic development of the country (Aristide 2006, 283; Quinn 2010, 57). Those who believed this to be a promise of a better future were deceived, however.

On September 29, 1991, six months into Aristide's term, General Raoul Cédras led a military coup. Aristide and his government were forced into exile in the United States, while the population suffered gross abuses at the hands of the military and its supporters. The military was aided by armed civilian auxiliaries, commonly known as attachés, together with bands of thugs called *zenglendos* (HRW and NCHR 1994). In 1993, these *zenglendos*, armed and nurtured by

2 Freedom proved costly, as the Haitian government was forced to agree to a treaty in which France formally recognized independence in exchange for a payment of 150 million francs in 1825. This debt was a significant economic burden up until the start of the 20th century (Aristide 2006).

3 An unusually long reign in Haitian political history (Lechtenberg 1996, 2).

4 Also known by the nicknames "Papa Doc" and "Baby Doc".

5 A "diaspora" can be defined as "a people with a common origin who reside, more or less on a permanent basis, outside the borders of their ethnic or religious homeland" (Shain and Barth 2003, 452), cited in Hoogenboom and Quinn 2011, 10–11).

the military, formed a quasi-political organization known as the Front for the Advancement and Progress of Haiti (*Front pour l'Avancement et le Progrès d'Haïti*, FRAPH).[6] FRAPH's membership includes long-time Duvalierists, as well as *tontons macoutes*, attachés, and other army supporters. Under François Duvalier, the *tonton macoutes*, a group of Duvalier supporters, acted as his personal army, and several thousands were killed under his command (Quinn 2010, 56). The army has also historically contributed to bloody dictatorships instilling public fear.

The military regime that followed the coup lasted from 29 September 1991 to 15 October 1994, which is the period subject to the CNVJ's investigation. The military installed several provisional governments during this period, but *de facto* rule in Haiti remained in the hands of the military. The coup plunged Haiti into a maelstrom of state-inflicted and state-sanctioned human rights abuses, like political assassinations, arbitrary arrests and detentions, the torture of prisoners, and other means of terrorizing the population (HRW and NCHR 1994, 3). In the three years of military rule, at least 5,000 people were reported killed, and 1,000 or more beaten, tortured, and raped (Quinn 2010, 57). Virtually all constitutionally guaranteed rights and procedures were suspended, and several cases of massacre, forced disappearance, and violent assaults on entire neighborhoods were documented. The December 27, 1993 arson and murders in Cité Soleil and the April 1994 massacre in the Raboteau neighborhood are the most well-known cases (HRW and NCHR 1994, 3). Violations were considerably worse in some regions than others, following a pattern of widespread persecution of Aristide's supporters (Quinn 2010, 57; USAID 1996, 8–9). This caused many, including Aristide, his government, and other outspoken supporters, to flee. Around 300,000 went into hiding within the country, while over 50,000 people attempted to escape by boat to the US (Quinn 2010, 57). A joint peacekeeping effort between the United Nations (UN) and the Organization of American States (OAS), the International Civilian Mission in Haiti (*Mission Civile Internationale en Haïti*, MICIVIH), was deployed in 1993 to monitor and report on conditions in Haiti.[7]

Peace negotiations between Aristide and Cédras were brokered by the US government in 1994. Several actors were involved in order to make this deal, including then-US President Bill Clinton and former US President Jimmy Carter. Although a UN trade embargo had been in place for several years, there was a shift in US policy towards Haiti in 1993 with the election of Bill Clinton, who wanted to reinstate Aristide to end the refugee crisis

---

6 The organization's co-founders were Jodel Chamblain, a former *tonton macoute*, and Emmanuel Constant, the son of an army commander under François Duvalier (HRW and NCHR 1994).

7 The UN peacekeeping mission in Haiti continued until 2019, as will be discussed below.

(Martin 1999; Quinn 2010, 57–58). Subsequently, strict constraints were placed on the Aristide government, which was pressured to make concessions to the bourgeoisie and the military. The US offered the military a handsome settlement to induce cooperation, thus undermining the Aristide government's position, and the military were awarded amnesties in respect of their criminal acts (Quinn 2010, 58). The diaspora community also played a role in shaping the policies and conditions under which Aristide could return to power (Laguerre 1997, 170–177, in Quinn 2011, 267). Under the resulting peace agreement, known as the Governors Island Accord, Aristide was reinstated as President; he returned to Haiti and resumed power on October 12, 1994. The Governors Island Accord was not only a hard peace agreement to negotiate, but also for many Aristide supporters to accept because, despite his return to power, it made it difficult to hold the military accountable in legal proceedings.[8] Furthermore, when Aristide returned to Haiti, he could only finish his original term, which arguably had implications for the follow-up and implementation of the CNVJ's recommendations because he was ineligible for re-election.

Several features can be drawn from this historical narrative that are relevant for considering the CNVJ's recommendations. First, Haiti's economy is chronically weak. Second, the weakness of the Aristide government upon its return and the seemingly constant state of political crisis has persisted. Third, a variety of international actors has long operated in Haiti. Before the CNVJ started, and after it concluded, there was a strong presence of international and regional actors like the UN, the OAS, and the European Union. Other international organizations, like the IMF and the World Bank, have also played a significant part in shaping Haitian politics. The US also has a long tradition of intervening in Haiti, dating back about a century. In addition, there has been strong bilateral involvement by Canada, France, and Argentina, among others. Finally, the Haitian diaspora, primarily in the US and Canada, became influential. As we will see, these features have shaped the implementation of CNVJ recommendations.

3. THE HAITIAN TRUTH AND JUSTICE COMMISSION (CNVJ)

Less than six months after President Aristide returned from exile, he issued a presidential decree on March 28, 1995, which provided for establishing the CNVJ; the decree outlined its mandate and functions, composition and possible

[8] Interview with Florence Elie, Port-au-Prince, July 19, 2016.

sources of funding. The mandate stated that the CNVJ was to "establish the overall truth of the most serious human rights violations committed", both inside and outside of Haiti, during the period in which the military had dislodged Aristide (September 29, 1991 to October 15, 1994), with the aim of reconciling all Haitians. The commissioners were mandated to do so "without prejudice to judicial remedies which may arise from such violations".[9] In the final report, the CNVJ allocates a chapter on elaboration of their mandate and how they interpreted it (see *Si m pa rele* 1996 [1998], Chapter II).

Previous research on the CNVJ is scarce. The most prominent work by far is Quinn (2009; 2010). Other studies have focused on specific aspects of the CNVJ, usually in a comparative perspective (see Chapman and Ball 2001; Hayner 2006; McCalpin 2012). The overall perception of the CNVJ is that it was a largely failed truth commission (Quinn 2009). This section will go into some of the aspects of the truth commission's workings, starting with why a truth commission was established. Further, the composition and work of the CNVJ will be presented, as well as the sources of funding and the distribution of the final report.

3.1. WHY A TRUTH COMMISSION?

The initiative to establish a truth commission started a year before Aristide issued the decree. The initial thought of establishing such a mechanism was born in the Haitian diaspora in Canada. The first proposal for a truth commission, named *The Elements of a Truth Commission in Haiti*,[10] was sent to Aristide's government-in-exile from a Haitian group in Montréal in 1994 (McCalpin 2012, 144). This proposal constituted the framework of what would later become the CNVJ (Quinn 2010, 76–77). In this way, the Haitian diaspora also played a role in shaping the mandate of the commission, as well as providing members once the commission was set up (Quinn 2019, 1842).

Another important element concerning the choice to establish a truth commission was determining the period it would investigate. Due to Haiti's turbulent past with changing political regimes employing varying degrees of repression, there are several *époques* worthy of further investigation.[11]

---

9 Article 2, Presidential Decree on March 28, 1995, Annex I, *Si m pa rele* (1996[1998]) (All translations are done by the author).

10 The original French title was '*Proposition pour une Commission de la vérité en Haïti: Éléments constitutifs*' (Quinn 2010, 76–77).

11 At the time of this study, there was an ongoing effort to examine the Duvalier period, the "Procès Duvalier" (Colette Lespinasse, Port-au-Prince, July 15, 2016). However, the process in the court system has not yet led to a decision (as of July 2020, Avocats sans frontiers Canada, 2020), even though the Court of appeal (Cour d'appel) in Port-au-Prince re-instated the charges against Jean-Claude Duvalier of committing crimes against humanity.

Even though this is beyond the scope of this chapter, it is an intriguing question why Aristide restricted the mandate to a three-year period, and not the brutality of the Duvalier era (Chapman and Ball 2001, 13).

3.2. COMPOSITION OF THE CNVJ[12]

As the question of the truth commission's composition was a key issue in the initial phase, a note is due on who the commissioners were and how they were selected. The commission started out as a seven-member body, later reduced to six people as one member left mid-way (see Table 1). As stated above, the diaspora community had significant influence in selecting the members of the commission (Quinn 2019, 1842). In fact, many of those who ended up being involved in the work of the CNVJ were also involved in the first truth commission initiative developed in Montréal, including two commissioners, the executive secretary, and a consultant on judicial reform (Quinn 2019, 1842). Three foreign members were included in the commission's composition under pressure from international donors, who argued that the commission needed a better balance between "national" and "international" members. The international members were well-respected international jurists, while the four national members represented parts of the government and important non-governmental organisations (Chapman and Ball 2001, 17). The international commissioners lived abroad for the whole working period of the CNVJ, and visited only for brief meetings (Chapman and Ball 2001, 18).

Table 1. Composition of the CNVJ

Function	Name	Background
Chair	Françoise Boucard (F)	Exiled Haitian who spent considerable time in Montreal. Sociologist.
National members	Ertha Elysée (F)	Exiled, living in Montreal. Jurist.
	Freud Jean (M)	Selected from the Haitian NGO community. Social scientist.
	René Magloire (M)	Exiled, living in Montreal. Left mid-way to become Minister of Justice.[13] Jurist.

(continued)

[12] See Articles 13 and 14 of Presidential Decree of March 28, 1995 for comments on composition and nomination of the seven members, and Presidential Decree of April 20 for the subsequent modification of the composition.

[13] René Magloire has served as Minister of Justice in two terms, the first from November 7, 1995–March 8, 1996. The final report was signed by F. Boucard, E. Elysée, O. Jackman, F. Jean, B.W. Ndiaye and P. Robinson on February 5, 1996, and not by R. Magloire (see *Si m pa rele* (1996 [1998], 245)).

Table 1 *continued*

Function	Name	Background
International members	Bacre Waly Ndiaye (M)	From Senegal. Jurist. UN Special Rapporteur on extrajudicial, summary or arbitrary executions (1992–98).
	Oliver Jackman (M)	From Barbados. Jurist. Judge on the Inter-American Court of Human Rights (1995–2001).
	Patrick Robinson (M)	From Jamaica. Jurist. Commissioner of the OAS (1988–95), and UN Special Rapporteur on the Rights of Indigenous Peoples (1991–95).

Sources: Si m pa rele (1996 [1998]); Quinn (2019; 2010; 2009); Hoogenboom and Quinn (2011).
Note: M = male, F = female.

A common feature for many of the commissioners was their juridical background. All were trained lawyers, except two social scientists, including the sociologist Françoise Boucard, who was the commission's chair (Chapman and Ball 2001, 17). According to Chapman and Ball (2001), these disciplinary divides caused major tensions inside the commission and weakened the resulting final report (more on this below).

Another intriguing aspect of the national members of the CNVJ is their links to the Haitian domestic political scene. The Haitian intellectual community was at the time both small and interrelated (Quinn 2009, 269). As one international consultant to the commission phrased it: "[The commissioners] were all either friends, lovers, or associates of people in the Haitian government" (cited in Quinn 2009, 269). To mention the most prominent examples, the CNVJ's chair, Françoise Boucard, was married to the then-Minister of Health; Ertha Elysée's husband functioned at one point as Minister of Justice-in-exile; and René Magloire himself left the CNVJ partway through to become Minister of Justice (for more, see Quinn 2009). Despite the apparent close ties with the government, it should also be mentioned that the commissioners themselves were conscious of the need to remain independent, and to appear so for the public (Quinn 2009, 269).

In sum, this section highlights three interesting features of the CNVJ's composition: (i) the diaspora's importance, (ii) the dominance of lawyers on the commission, and (iii) the commissioners' apparent close relations with the state. All of this might explain some of the claims that have been made concerning how the CNVJ failed to win popular support (see Beidas, Granderson, and Neild 2007; Chapman and Ball 2001; McCalpin 2012; Quinn 2009; Segovia 2006). On the other hand, it could also explain some of the initial support from the government for the CNVJ. However, despite these apparent close links, one of the main challenges identified by Quinn (2010) and Segovia (2006) was precisely a lack of political will and support. This affected the work of the commission, and inevitably the implementation of the CNVJ's recommendations, as will be detailed in the next section.

3.3. THE WORK OF THE CNVJ AND ITS FINAL REPORT

The CNVJ started its work on April 1, 1995. Initially, it was only allocated six months to complete its work; it was later granted a three-month extension. In the end, and due to internal disorganization, poor performance, and lack of financial resources, the period was extended to eleven months (Chapman and Ball 2001; Segovia 2006, 163). The work of the CNVJ concluded on February 5, 1996, when the commission presented its final report to President Aristide, on his last day in office.

For most of its existence, the administration of the CNVJ consisted of only a small team of analysts and support personnel, and the commissioners themselves worked with the daily organization of the work (Chapman and Ball 2001, 19). Florence Elie, who was working closely with the CNVJ in her capacity of representing the Ministry of Justice and Public Security in 1996, explained how lack of funding from the start caused some administrative problems. Among other things, the Chair of the CNVJ had to take on a more administrative role than a "leading" one. Even after the inclusion of Jean-Claude Icart as executive secretary to the staff, the commission's organization suffered from the fact that the Chair could not escape the administrative role and assume her full role as a coordinator and leader of the work.[14] Hayner (2006) notes that, to complete its work, the CNVJ employed between 50 and 100 staff, while Chapman and Ball (2001, 35) narrow the count to approximately 75 staff members. When the data collection was at its most intense, the CNVJ deployed 80 interviewers into the field for less than two months, throughout July and August 1995 (Chapman and Ball 2001, 19; *Si m pa rele* 1996 [1998], xv).

The CNVJ used various sources to uncover human rights abuses. In total, the CNVJ report was based on 8,650 interviews, which identified more than 8,700 victims and alleged 19,308 human rights violations (*Si m pa rele* 1996 [1998]). The CNVJ itself collected some 6,000 semi-structured interviews, which were supplemented with interviews and documentation gathered by other actors, mainly MICIVIH, the Inter-American Commission on Human Rights, the Platform of Haitian Human Rights Organizations, and the National Commission for Justice and Peace (JILAP) (*Si m pa rele* 1996 [1998], xiii, 16–17). The CNVJ also sponsored a series of forensic investigations of mass graves undertaken by a multinational team of experts assembled by the American Association for the

14 Interview with Florence Elie, Port-au-Prince, July 19, 2016.

Advancement of Science (Macilwain 1995), and consulted with morgue records from University Hospital in Port-au-Prince. All the victims and violations were compiled and analyzed systematically in a database, which resulted in a comprehensive and cross-referenced list of the abuses (listed in Annex III of the report).

Many people characterized the work of the CNVJ as hurried and time-constrained, and saw the product as unfinished (Quinn 2010, 59). The final report consists of eight chapters and is filled with detailed analyses of some of the events that took place. The report chose to focus on some selected events, like the Cité-Soleil and Raboteau massacres, highlighting some notorious cases among the many that were reported to the CNVJ. According to Chapman and Ball (2001, 31), the final report submitted was extremely truncated, and much of the work of the CNVJ, which included several regional sub-reports with rich analytical and textual material, was not included. This was due to internal disagreements, stemming from a conflict between legal and social science approaches to investigation and classification of violations. One fundamental disagreement was over the use of qualitative or quantitative data, which resulted in the production of both substantive sub-reports and a large quantitative database. Chapman and Ball (2001, 31) note that the mix of social scientists (two) and jurists (five) in the CNVJ led to repeated conflicts among them, and contributed to a poor outcome, rather than providing an interdisciplinary balance. Even though the Chair was a sociologist, some of the lawyer members "openly disdained social science methods" (Chapman and Ball 2001, 9). This caused both extra work and delays, and, in the end, the hiring of an outside expert, in December 1995, to write the final report (Chapman and Ball 2001, 31).

3.4. SOURCES OF FUNDING

It is difficult to ascertain the total budget of the CNVJ. The commission was initiated by the government but was heavily supported financially by the UN and the OAS (through MICIVIH) and by the European Union (EU). The CNVJ also received bilateral support on specific issues, such as forensic work in examining mass graves (Quinn 2010, 59). In the Presidential Decree of March 28, 1995, Article 24 stated that the Haitian government "may seek the cooperation of the international community and of the countries supporting it in this endeavor" (*Si m pa rele* Annexe I, 1996 [1998], 9). In its acknowledgements, the CNVJ gave thanks to the MICIVIH, the UN Centre for Human Rights (today the Office of the United Nations High Commissioner for Human Rights), the Inter-American Commission on Human Rights, the EU, the United Nations Development Programme, the World Council of Churches, and the Canadian, Swiss, Dutch, and Haitian governments, as well as the Chinese embassy, for their contributions (*Si m pa rele* 1996 [1998], xiii). Nonetheless, the funding was scarce, and the CNVJ complained that the lack of sufficient funds considerably reduced its capacity to complete the assigned task (*Si m pa rele* 1996 [1998], Chapter III). According to some studies, the CNVJ worked with little more than US$1 million (Chapman and Ball 2001), the main share of which came from international aid (Segovia 2006, 167).

Interesting to note, for political reasons, is the international actors' handling of the issue of funding. The behavior of the US stands out. According to Human Rights Watch (HRW 1996), the US government offered US$250,000 to support the CNVJ in May 1995, but later withdrew the offer. In the end, the CNVJ received only US$50,000 from the US government, just a month before the end of its work, and, in the end, these funds were used to pay for supplies that were previously given by other donors (Segovia 2006, 175). In addition, to fund the work of the CNVJ further, the Haitian diaspora community in Montreal asked the International Centre for Human Rights and Democratic Development (ICHRDD), a Canadian government-funded institution, for assistance. According to Quinn (2009), the diaspora's heavy involvement in the work of the CNVJ and unwillingness to compromise caused some disagreement with the ICHRDD. At one point during the establishment of the CNVJ, the Canadians withheld funding until the composition of the commission showed a better balance of national and international members (Quinn 2009, 269).

3.5. DISTRIBUTION OF THE FINAL REPORT

After its submission, the final report was poorly distributed to the Haitian public. As Aristide received the report on his last day in office, he handed it straight over to his successor René Préval. The report was not published until September 1996, over six months after its completion, and then only 75 copies were made and distributed to governmental offices, the parliament, and human rights organizations and other non-governmental organizations. A second edition of 1500 copies was published in March 1997, but these were also circulated only in Haiti (Chapman and Ball 2001, 35). The reason for the delay was never officially explained, though the Ministry of Justice cited the expense of printing the report as one cause (HRW 1996). Florence Elie, who was working at the office of the Minister of Justice and Public Security in 1996, explained that the Ministry had found a solution to the expensive printing problem; by selling the final TC report in a newspaper format, people who were interested in reading the report could buy it.[15] However, this did not include any of the annexes, or the chapter on recommendations. Cost concerns prompted the Haitian government

15 Interview with Florence Elie, Port-au-Prince, July 19, 2016.

as late as 1999 to ask for the MICIVIH's assistance to publish the report, something the MICIVIH allegedly already was intending to do (United Nations 1998, 6). Another accessibility problem related to language. Ironically, despite the title being a Creole expression, the report itself was written in French.[16] This underlines Quinn's (2010) assertion that the report was intended for an international audience.[17]

In addition, interviews conducted for this study uncovered another way of disseminating and popularizing the report not commonly mentioned, namely broadcasting the report on the radio. In a series of 50 radio programs aired in 1999, the *Centre de Recherche et d'Action pour le Développement* (CRAD), a non-governmental organization, translated and produced radio programs, presenting the report in Creole.[18] This was the first (and only) effort to translate the report from French into Creole and then present it to the people in an accessible way. However, this presentation of the report concentrated on the findings of the CNVJ and did not cover the CNVJ's recommendations. In sum, it took several years before the report was presented to the public, and the scope of dissemination was limited. The delay in dissemination arguably severely affected the possibility for popular support (Segovia 2006, 167).

Overall, the sentiment expressed in all interviews conducted for this study, without exception, was that *Si m pa rele*, and especially its recommendations, was put in a drawer and forgotten. As we shall see below, the recommendations vocalized in the report might be largely forgotten, but the demands behind them are still very much alive.

4. RECOMMENDATIONS IN THE CNVJ REPORT

4.1. THE SCHEME OF THE RECOMMENDATIONS CHAPTER

This section describes the CNVJ's recommendations found in the last chapter of the report, namely Chapter VIII entitled "Recommendations". The focus in this section is on characteristics of the recommendations, their subject matter, who they target and who they address. Further, as will be shown, the recommendations often actually represented clusters of sub-recommendations.

---

16 This had meant translating testimonies from Creole into French.

17 The report has a clear international perspective on the period of investigation, exemplified in Chapter IV titled "Chronological analysis of the human rights violations under the *de facto* regime", in which, for each time period, the CNVJ sub-categorized events and reactions i) in Haiti and ii) on the international scene (see *Si m pa rele* (1996 [1998]), 21–38). The CNVJ even directed a few of its recommendations to the international community.

18 Interview with Colette Lespinasse (GARR/CRAD) and Gotson Pierre (Groupe Médialternatif/CRAD), Port-au-Prince July 15 and 20, 2016 respectively.

The mandate to present recommendations was set forth in Article 22 of the Presidential Decree of March 28, 1995. Article 7 calls for measures of reparation to victims, and Article 8 calls for recommendations on legal and administrative measures designed to avoid a repetition of such crimes in the future (*Si m pa rele*, Annex I, 1996[1998], 5). The recommendations in the final report are divided into five sections: A) measures of reparations, B) rape and sexual violence against women, C) reforms of judicial institutions, D) follow-up and sanctions, and E) other recommendations. The recommendations stretch over 46 pages and vary in their length and complexity. The CNVJ also devoted some space to justifying the relevance of their recommendations. The recommendations span across all typologies proposed in the *Beyond Words* project, as they recommend measures concerning institutional reform, such as reform of the courts or the police; legal or administrative reform, such as creating new laws or revising old ones; constitutional amendments; criminal prosecution; reparations for victims; non-repetition measures; and follow-up measures.

In order for a recommendation to be identified as a recommendation in this case study, the CNVJ must have explicitly stated that it "recommended" something. However, there are quite a few exceptions, where the intention behind the formulation has been interpreted in this analysis as a recommendation of something to be done.[19] The targets of the recommendations span from the victims and their families, to police officers on the ground and judges from the highest to the lowest courts, as well as institutions like the Ministry of Justice. The recommendations are at times both broad and general, but at most times they are very specific. Occasionally, the report offers suggested alternative means to implement a recommendation. Many of the recommendations are formulated without specific mention of who or what should implement the recommendation (what the broader *Beyond Words* project calls the implementing actor). However, the CNVJ did call upon international organizations and other states to give assistance to Haiti and to aid in the follow-up of addressing past crimes (see recommendations 64 and 65, or *Si m pa rele* 1996 [1998], 241).

Table 2 gives an overview of the CNVJ's recommendations and their distribution in the chapter on recommendations. In addition, the table provides a numeric presentation of how many recommendations the different sections entail.

19 The identification of recommendations has therefore partly relied on the textual presentation in the final report, and partly on the author's own assessment. More on the methodological issue of counting below.

Table 2. An overview of the recommendations in the CNVJ final report

Chapter VIII	Sections of chapter VIII	Recommendation number	Number of recommendations	Types
Section A	Measures of reparations	1–2	2	Reparations, Criminal, Follow-up
Section B	Rape and sexual violence against women	3–13	11	Institutional, Legal, Criminal, Reparations, Non-repetitive, Follow-up
Section C	Reforms of judicial institutions			
	1. Judges	14–23	10	Institutional, Legal, Criminal, Follow-up
	2. Government commissioners	24–25	2	Legal, Non-repetition
	3. Protector of Citizens	26	1	Institutional
	4. Police	27–39	13	Institutional, Legal, Follow-up
	5. Legal reform	40–45	6	Institutional, Legal, Follow-up
	6. Penal Code and Criminal Instruction Code	46–50	5	Legal, Follow-up
	7. Supreme Judicial Council	51	1	Institutional, Legal
	8. Ministry of Justice		0	
	Implementation of judicial reform	52	1	Institutional, Legal, Follow-up
	Reform of the law on the Bar association	53–58	6	Legal
Section D	Follow-up and sanctions	59–68	10	Legal, Constitutional, Reparations, Follow-up
Section E	Other recommendations	69–75	7	Institutional, Legal, Constitutional, Reparations, Follow-up
In total:			75	

Source: The database compiled for the *Beyond Words* project.

As an overall comment on the report, one might say that, while the report itself focused on bringing the "truth" forth, the recommendations chapter represents a substantially greater focus on reforming the justice system to deal with atrocities committed and to prevent repetition. This is due to how the CNVJ interpreted its mandate, as the CNVJ itself emphasized the necessity of a functioning justice system in order to have either truth or transitional justice in Haiti

(Segovia 2006, 163). This is further discussed in section 5 on formulation of the recommendations.

4.2. METHODOLOGICAL NOTE ON COUNTING RECOMMENDATIONS

For some truth commission reports, recommendations may be long and complex, and multiple sub-recommendations may be listed under what the commission has labeled one recommendation. In the case of the CNVJ report, many of the recommendations are also long and complex. However, when it comes to identifying a recommendation, the reverse is often true. The CNVJ report made several recommendations that together serve a bigger goal, so that what appears as several different recommendations in the presentation of the report should be understood as one recommendation, with more specific sub-recommendations, for the sake of comparability in the broader project. As the recommendations are not numbered (at least not coherently throughout the report), there is no standard answer on the number of recommendations produced. It has been challenging to count how many recommendations the CNVJ actually gives. At the first count conducted by the author, 108 recommendations were counted. This is close to USAID's (1996) count of 111 recommendations. The author later revised the way of counting adopted for this research by distinguishing between main recommendations and sub-recommendations that directly serve the intent of the main recommendation. Through this, the number of 75 recommendations was reached, as shown in Table 2.

Overall, for the purposes of this research, a recommendation exists when the CNVJ explicitly mentions that they "recommend" ("*la Commission recommande*") a measure to be taken, which it does consistently throughout the recommendations chapter. However, not all recommendations and sub-recommendations are identified by the wording "recommend". This is typically the case with sub-recommendations, and, as explained above, when it is evident that different proposed steps or actions are necessary for the main recommendation to be possible, this is included as a recommendation.[20] In addition, a recommendation is made when the CNVJ "urges" ("*La Commission exhorte*") that something be done, which is the case when it is addressing the international community.

Further, some recommendations are explicitly divided into several parts. For instance, the CNVJ calls upon the Haitian government to ratify international

[20] Typical phrases for these sub-recommendations are that it is "necessary" ("*Il est necessaire*") or that something "should" or "could" be done ("*il faudra(it)*" or "*il pourra(it)*").

human rights conventions. Then, three particular conventions are specified. Some other recommendations are clearly contingent upon the implementation of other recommendations; these are counted as sub-recommendations. For instance, the recommendation related to the composition of a new organ necessarily must come after the actual creation of the organ, as is the case with recommendations on the Supreme Judicial Council and the creation of a national bar association.

Another challenge is that some of the recommendations overlap with each other. For instance, this is the case with two recommendations calling for further investigations. While the first recommends further investigations into alleged perpetrators of sexual violence, the second calls for the same concerning human rights abuses, and thus encompasses the first. This illustrates how a recommendation can be encompassed by another but is still counted in this study as its own recommendation. There also are instances where the same recommendation is mentioned twice, with different wording, but with the same recommended measure. This is the case for calls for the development of a computerized register of persons in custody. When this occurs, the recommendations are counted twice, and so will their "implementing events" be, as they are mentioned in different places in the report and were chronologically inserted into the database.

5. FORMULATION OF THE RECOMMENDATIONS

This section is concerned with the process of formulating the recommendations and is intended to give an account of what we know about why the CNVJ gave the recommendations they did. Ideally, this section should provide details about why certain recommendations were included or excluded from the report. Unfortunately, this study has uncovered little exact information on the process of formulating the different recommendations. One reason for this is merely methodological and resides in the challenge of consulting people's memories, in that it is over 20 years since the CNVJ completed its work. Frankly, when asked about the inclusion or formulation of a certain topic or a specific recommendation, with a few exceptions, none of the interviewees had any specific answers. Another reason is the fact that the process of writing the report was extremely hurried and that an external consultant was hired to write the report at the last minute. How much this affected the recommendations set forth is, however, unknown. Regardless, there are some interesting inferences to draw concerning the formulation of recommendations.

First, if we turn to the mandate of the CNVJ, we find most of the CNVJ's justifications for the different focus points of the recommendations. The mandate explicitly states that the CNVJ should give recommendations on reparations and rehabilitation, on legal and administrative measures that can be taken to prevent the repetition of such violations again, by reforming the justice system, the police, and the army, by legal prosecution of identified perpetrators, and by preventing illegal groups from forming anew, and ending impunity (see Articles 7 and 8, *Si m pa rele*, Annex I, 1996 [1998], 5–6). Of special interest, however, is that the CNVJ was mandated to pay particular attention to "crimes against humanity", and, within that, especially female victims of sexual violence with a political motive (see Article 3, *Si m pa rele* Annex I, 1996 [1998], 4). Indeed, Selvik (2021) places the CNVJ at the forefront of the so-called 'gender turn' in the field of transitional justice, as it was the first truth commission worldwide to be mandated to investigate sexual violence in conflict. Why the recommendations in section A on reparations and legal prosecution and section B on rape and sexual violence against women were included in the report can thus be partly explained by the mandate of the CNVJ.[21]

Second there was a seemingly large number of other reports focused on the necessity of justice sector reform published around the same time as the *Si m pa rele* report. This could have implications for the factors and actors that shaped the formulation of the recommendations, as well as their implementation. A review by USAID (1996) of the numerous documents and data at that time, consisted of reports by Haitian organizations, the Haitian Ministry of Justice, and international human rights organizations, in addition to the CNVJ report. The *Si m pa rele* report was treated as a point of comparison to the others in the review, as it was regarded both as an important document, and was the most comprehensive in its recommendations (USAID 1996, 1–2).

There were four other documents included in USAID's review.[22] There was a MICIVIH report on justice sector reform from May 1996, *The Justice System in Haiti – Analysis of Penal Aspects and Penal Procedure*, which also concluded by making recommendations. This report largely overlaps with the CNVJ's report, but does not cover the full range of issues covered by the CNVJ (USAID 1996, 3). Another report of note is the *Xaragua retreat and follow-up reports*, issued by the Ministry of Justice after its retreat at the Xaragua Hotel April 26–28, 1996,

21 There are surely other factors affecting how these priorities came to be stated explicitly in the mandate. It was not just that the report was written to speak to the international community, which was particularly concerned with the rule of law at the time, but the process at large. Furthermore, concerning the formulation of recommendations on specific topics like sexual violence, another significant aspect is how the data collection in the CNVJ's investigation was compiled in a database, and how the quantitative analysis and mapping was influential for how the commissioners became aware of the pervasiveness of sexual violence. Additionally, there was a significant mobilization by both domestic and international women's movements for the CNVJ to address sexual violence (Coté 2014; Selvik 2021).

22 This study has not been successful in locating all of these reports, so this section is relying largely on the review and analysis by USAID (1996).

where Ministry officials discussed the recommendations of the CNVJ report. The Ministry of Justice report was not disseminated to the public at large. According to USAID (1996, 4), it generally seems to adopt the CNVJ's recommendations, and concludes by setting forth its own recommendations for further action on justice reform. This report is even more detailed than the one from the CNVJ, as it takes many of the ideas one step further (USAID 1996, 4). The third report under review wa a report issued by the Lawyers' Committee for Human Rights in 1990, titled *Paper Laws, Steel Bayonets: Breakdown of the Rule of Law in Haiti*. This report addressed the failure of the justice system to safeguard human rights, and USAID (1996, 3) notes how many of the Lawyers' Committee for Human Rights' conclusions were still relevant in 1996. Lastly, a report issued by Human Rights Watch (HRW) in September 1996 was also reviewed. The *Thirst for Justice: A Decade of Impunity in Haiti* (HRW 1996) offers a 10-year retrospective of the problems and progress of human rights in Haiti (see USAID 1996, 4).

The USAID summary of these reports identifies areas of broad consensus and provides an extensive table in which each of the reports are compared to the final report of the CNVJ, to find areas of agreement on which recommendations are set forth. To give an exhaustive overview of where recommendations were first mentioned is impossible, however. The most valuable inference drawn from this is the fact that other reports were written on the same topic, and that many of their recommendations overlap with those of the CNVJ, which says much about the relevance of the recommendations listed in the CNVJ's final report.

Third, and related to the second point, is the fact that the demand for reform of the justice system was not born with the CNVJ. The malfunctioning of the Haitian justice system was a well-known problem, and the demand for justice had been a demand ever since the fall of the Duvalier regime. It is, therefore, essential to underline that the CNVJ itself placed a higher priority in its recommendations on institutional reforms than reparations and reconciliation. According to Commissioner Freud Jean: "for the CNVJ, the reform of the judicial system was of clear importance (…) because it corresponds to justice" (cited in Segovia 2006, 166). Therefore, for the commissioners, reparations and reconciliation could not be separated from justice. Furthermore, since the justice system in Haiti was deeply malfunctioning, they should emphasize judicial and institutional reform, in order to achieve the other goals of truth, reparation, and reconciliation. This is a widely held belief in Haiti, until this day. In prolonging this argument, the idea of reparations should not leave the context of the justice system, as a process independent or outside of the justice system would legitimize the fact that it does not function (Segovia 2006, 166). The CNVJ, therefore, argued that "truth" was inseparable from "justice" – a connection also shown in its name, the "Truth *and Justice* Commission". What implications this might have for the implementation of the recommendations, coupled with the actors and factors involved, will be discussed in the next section.

6. IMPLEMENTATION OF THE RECOMMENDATIONS

The discussion of implementation is divided into several sub-sections below, largely reflecting the structure of the CNVJ's final report. The following discussion will have the same structure, by examining A. measures of reparation and legal prosecution, B. rape and sexual violence against women, C. reform of the justice system, and D. follow-up and sanctions. The implementation of these recommendations is sometimes overlapping, which will be noted where it applies.[23] Although the general perception is that the Haitian government has been entirely unresponsive, the reality is more complex. This section maps out which measures have been enacted, and by which actors.

In fact, in the 20 years since the report was finalized, the conditions affecting the prospects for implementation have varied considerably. To understand the broader political and socio-economic environment in which the implementation of the CNVJ's recommendation was considered, namely 1996–2018, it is necessary to have some knowledge about this 20-year period. The mere fact that Aristide received the report on his last day in office, and that the follow-up thereby fell to his successor Préval, is an important point to consider for the start of the implementation period.[24] Conflicts developed between the supporters of Aristide and the Préval administration, which made the report something of an embarrassment for Préval (Chapman and Ball 2001, 35). The political scene in Haiti was turbulent for both Préval and Aristide, when the latter was re-elected in 2000. Aristide was forced into exile anew in 2004 by a military *coup d'état*, and the UN Stabilization Mission in Haiti, MINUSTAH, was dispatched. MINUSTAH was mandated to assist the transitional government in monitoring, restructuring and reforming the police, and to assist with the restoration and maintenance of the rule of law (Mobekk 2017, 83). The UN presence and its efforts have continued through mid-2018.[25] Other than political turmoil and a dire economic situation, Haiti also has suffered several natural disasters, with social and humanitarian consequences. (The overview in Annex 2 provides a

---

23 Section E on other recommendations transcend the other four and will be included where relevant.

24 Aristide had to step down at the end of his first term, as Haitian law prohibits a President from running for two consecutive terms. Préval was a candidate from the same political party as Aristide, the Lavalas party.

25 The MINUSTAH operation was replaced on October 16, 2017 by a new mission, called UN Mission for Justice Support in Haiti (MINUJUSTH). With this change, the focus shifts from security and stability to the justice sector and institution-building.

brief timeline on major events in Haiti's recent history that are relevant to the implementation of the CNVJ's recommendations).

When examining the "record of implementation", it is important to remember that this "record" is not exhaustive. Despite a thorough mapping, there are bound to be events of importance that have been left out. In addition, some recommendations will have one event that is important for its implementation, while others will have several "implementing events". This does not necessarily signify that the main recommendation is implemented. Non-implementation of a recommendation can also be counted as an implementing event. In addition, as several of the recommendations have many sub-recommendations, some recommended measures, or alternatives of action, can have many possible implementing events. Nonetheless, as will be shown below, tracing the implementation record yields insights on the process of implementation.

With regards to the different actors involved on the Haitian scene, it is useful to make a distinction between the formal act of implementation and whether the recommendation has actually affected norms and behaviors. In particular, the international presence in Haiti cannot be disregarded. The international presence, and the funding and priorities that follow, is impossible to ignore when studying developments in Haiti over the last 20 years. Subsequent peacekeeping missions have followed the first one sent to Haiti in 1993, and a UN presence in Haiti has continued to this day. While the notion of "implementing a recommendation" suggests that actions have been taken in order to meet the demands set forth in the recommendation, this is not always the case in Haiti. Some of the recommended measures have been taken, but these measures might not have been specifically at the recommendation of the CNVJ. The actors and factors influencing the implementation will be discussed along the way, as indicators of the processes that have driven the progress, as well as whether there is a link between the recommendations of the CNVJ and the implemented measures and actions.

6.1. MEASURES OF REPARATION AND LEGAL PROSECUTION[26]

The first section in the chapter on recommendations is entitled "Measures of reparation", and states two main recommendations. First, the CNVJ calls for the establishment of a special commission on reparations for damage caused to victims of the military regime, to "meet legal, moral and material obligations described [in the report]". Second, the government was urged to "take all

26 This part consists of section A 'Measures of reparations' and section D 'Follow-up and sanctions'.

necessary measures" to ensure that minors under 15, orphaned as a result of the coup, could obtain an education and a decent standard of living, "as wards of the nation" (*Si m pa rele* 1996 [1998], 197). In addition, other recommendations concerning reparations are placed in other sections of the recommendations chapter. For instance, in Section B concerning reparations to victims of politically motivated rape, and in Section D on the rebuilding of neighborhoods and the identification of victims not identified by the CNVJ, the commission recommends that these individuals also should be eligible for compensation. As explained above, the CNVJ did not want to separate reparations and justice by legal prosecution. Therefore, they are examined together and viewed as interlinked.

On the implementation of reparations, it must be noted that there was a half-hearted attempt at following-up the work of identifying victims and providing reparations. In 1997, the UN Secretary General's report on Haiti pointed out that the Compensation Committee was not yet established (United Nations 1997, 9). However, a Follow-up Committee, called the *Bureau Poursuite et Suivi*, was created by the Préval government in 1998. This committee was charged with examining the issue of reparations for victims of the military coup, with work in three main work areas: social, economic and legal-medical assistance (United Nations 1998, 6). The office was created by the Ministry of Justice, with a budget of 60 million Gourdes (approximately US$7,000,000 per October 2021) and must be understood as responding to the recommendation to establish a commission on reparation. According to the United Nations (1998, 6), the Follow-up Committee had started a pilot project for the reconstruction of homes destroyed by the military in the southern region of Haiti, which was to be completed shortly after the report was issued. Unfortunately, the Follow-up Committee ceased its activities shortly after its establishment, and without having achieved much on the overall aim of reparations to all victims, both material and symbolic (Segovia 2006, 164).

Subsequently, there has been no nation-wide process of reparation for victims, either material or symbolic. The victims that gave testimony during the work of the CNVJ have received no compensation, and no memorials have been erected.[27] Overall, the sentiment is that the Haitian government has not implemented the recommendations pertaining to reparations (Segovia 2006, 164). As Mattarollo (2013, 108) phrased it: "the issue of reparations is a constant in the Haitian reality".

There was, however, one case of victims seeking reparation by pursuing their case in the courts. The Raboteau trial held in 1999 was the sole event where

[27] Based on interviews in Port-au-Prince 2016, with human rights activist Collette Lespinasse (July 15) and Director of OPC, Florence Elie (July 19).

a group of victims sought a legal prosecution.[28] This trial was an exceptional attempt at bringing the perpetrators of violence during the coup to justice through prosecution.[29] Just before the end of the military regime, in April 1994, there was a massacre of 11 unarmed civilians in the neighborhood of Raboteau in Gonaïves, a city in northern Haiti. The Raboteau massacre in itself became a symbolic event, and a section in the final report of the CNVJ was devoted to it.

Even though the trial was regarded as an overall success (Concannon Jr. 2001a), the lower court's sentence was overturned by the Cour de Cassation in 2005 (Amnesty International 2005). As a result, the victims and their families have received nothing through the court system. When asked why the conviction was overturned, trial judge Justice Napela Saintil exclaimed, "It's all politics!"[30] Under the investigation, requests were made for the extradition of members of the military high command, but these were rejected by recipient countries on legal grounds (United Nations 1998, 7). Still, several of the accused were found guilty *in absentia*. The Raboteau trial process has been praised by international human rights organizations both for its initial prosecution and for its pursuit for justice, as it remains the sole attempt to do so on the basis of the atrocities uncovered by the CNVJ (Mattarollo 2013, 113; Concannon Jr. 2001a, 2001b). However, it also demonstrates the many challenges the justice system in Haiti faces to this day, and the difficulties of achieving justice within the formal justice system for the crimes committed under the military regime (for more on this, see Concannon Jr. 2001a, 2001b, or Mobekk 2017, 147).

6.2. RAPE AND SEXUAL VIOLENCE AGAINST WOMEN

The CNVJ devoted a section of its recommendations to the issue of rape and sexual violence against women (section B).[31] The recommendations address several issues, including the legal classification and status of rape in the Penal Code, the problematic process of reporting and prosecuting defendants for rape in the justice system, popular attitudes and understandings about the phenomenon of rape, and the limited services and social programs for rape

28 There was one other trial related to the military regime, namely the case in 1996 against the killers of the Minister of Justice Guy Malary, killed in 1993. His alleged killers were acquitted (Mobekk 2017, 147).

29 Non-written sources for this account consist of interviews in Port-au-Prince in 2016, with the coordinator of the trial from the Ministry of Justice, Florence Elie (July 19), with the chairing judge, justice of the peace Napela Saintil (July 21), and a lawyer working for the victims through Bureau des Avocats Internationaux (BAI), Mario Joseph (July 25).

30 Interview with Napela Saintil, Port-au-Prince, July 21, 2016.

31 There are also some recommendations concerning the issue of rape and sexual violence in sections on the Haitian National Police and on follow-up measures.

victims. In addition, the recommendations encompass legal prosecution and compensation, and the necessity of ratifying relevant international conventions. In relation to the types set forth in the *Beyond Words* project, the recommendations in section B span most of the typologies proposed, namely "Institutional", "Legal", "Criminal", "Reparations", "Non-repetition", and "Follow-up".

One initial question is why the issue of sexual violence was allocated its own section in the recommendations chapter. The occurrence of sexual violence in Haiti during the coup was widely reported by actors like the MICIVIH, international human rights groups, women's rights organizations, local human rights monitors, and the press. A pattern of rape was used as a political weapon by state agents (military groups, police and their supporters), in order to punish and intimidate women for their actual or assumed political beliefs, or to simply terrorize communities during violent sweeps of pro-Aristide neighborhoods (HRW and NCHR 1994, 3).[32] Although rape also was a part of apparently random violence committed by bands of *zenglendos*, the MICIVIH noted that FRAPH and the Haitian Armed Forces (FAd'H) were implicated in this kind of gender-specific violence that seemed an integral part of the political violence and terror, as they were rapes of a "political nature".[33] This pattern of "political sexual violence"[34] is the reason why the CNVJ allocated a sub-chapter to describe the sexual violence perpetrated against women, and why a section of the recommendations concerned rape and sexual violence.

Even though the sexual violence documented during the coup in most instances was of a political nature, the recommendations in section B also address the overall issue of rape in Haitian society.[35] This highlights the tendency throughout all the recommendations to focus on questions that extend beyond the limited period of investigation of the CNVJ, into the larger faults of Haitian society. Instead of giving recommendations on how to avoid the repetition of politically motivated sexual violence in the future (which is arguably an

---

32 "Terrorizing" due to the nature of the violence, as rape also functions as punishment for the victims' relatives.

33 See UN/OAS International Civilian Mission, Press Release, Ref. CP/94/28, June 17, 1994; Ref. CP/94/20, May 19, 1994; Ref. CP/94/8, March 21, 1994.

34 The term Sexual and Gender Based Violence (SGBV) is used in newer discourse, but I will emphasize that the recommendations in the CNVJ report do not address the full picture of gendered violence, as they only concern violence against women, even though Human Rights Watch (1994) notes that sexual violence affected male victims during the military regime too.

35 This gap between the issue mandated to the CNVJ and the issues the CNVJ actually dealt with becomes evident in the translation of the recommendations in a USAID report, where the USAID (1996) translated a recommendation into "victims of political rape", even though the CNVJ in that instance referred to rape in general.

impossible task), the CNVJ chose to focus on the legal issues relating to sexual violence and the legal status of rape as a crime. The formulation process of the recommendations found in this section is therefore intriguing. On the one hand, the occurrence of sexual violence during the coup is relatively modest in scope.[36] Nonetheless, the use of rape was striking, and it was an issue that Haitian women's organizations mobilized around during the conflict (Coté 2014). On the other hand, an increasing focus on women's rights and sexual violence against women was evoked after the Fourth World Conference on Women in Beijing in 1995 (Bunch and Fried 1996).[37] Examining this further, Selvik (2021) argues that the CNVJ seized the opportunity and provided an opening to address sexual violence as a more structural issue in Haiti, as the CNVJ's approach became a rallying point for the women's movement in their continued demands to end impunity for sexual violence.

Overall, the implementation of the recommendations in section B has been a long struggle for Haitian women's rights organizations, with support from the international community. The first recommendation in section B concerns a modification of the classification of rape in the Penal Code. The classification of rape was modified in 2005, after close to 10 years of lobbying by women's rights and human rights organizations. The modification concerned certain articles dealing with acts of violence against women,[38] and is regarded as one of the most progressive justice initiatives for women, and a success for the feminist movement (Coté 2014).[39] The change in classification entailed a change from rape being classified as "assaults on morals" to "sexual aggression". The problem with the old classification was that rape was regarded as a harm inflicted on the victim's honor and dignity rather than a crime against her physical integrity and well-being (Duramy 2014; HRW and NCHR 1994). The penalty for rape also was changed, from simple imprisonment to 10 years of hard labor. This success was due to a long process of lobbying in the parliament, and collaboration between the then-Minister of Women and civil society organizations including women's organizations gathered in

36 A report conducted by the Americas and Women's Rights divisions of Human Rights Watch documents first-hand nearly a dozen rape and attempted rape cases in the period between August 1992 and February 1994 (HRW and NCHR 1994, 3).

37 The Beijing Conference introduced the concept of human rights as it applies to women, whereas UN women's conferences before this had focused primarily on women and development (Bunch and Fried 1996, 200).

38 "[A]rticle 278 states that anyone who commits a crime of rape or is responsible for any other type of sexual aggression executed or attempted with violence, threats, surprise, or psychological intimidation against an individual of one sex or the other should be punished with ten years of labor" (Duramy 2014, 4).

39 Interview in Port-au-Prince with human rights activist Colette Lespinasse (July 15, 2016) and member of *Solidarité des Femmes Haitiennes* (SOFA) Olga Benoit (July 25, 2016).

the National Coordinating Body for Women's Rights, CONAP. By contrast, international actors often credit pressure from the UN and other international actors working in Haiti for these legal reforms.

The last recommendation related to sexual violence concerns the ratification of three international conventions pertaining to women's rights: the UN Convention against Torture and Other Cruel, Inhuman or Degrading Treatment or Punishment (1985); the Inter-American Convention on the Prevention, Punishment, and Eradication of Violence against Women (1994); and the UN Convention on the Non-Applicability of Statutory Limitations to War Crimes and Crimes Against Humanity (1968). The former two instruments were implemented respectively in 2013 and 1997, while the latter has neither been signed nor ratified by Haiti.

Concerning the other recommendations on sexual violence, the Haitian government has taken no further action. The process of reporting a case of rape to the authorities is still difficult. In order to determine whether a rape has occurred, it is, for legal reasons, necessary to get a medical certificate. Even though the CNVJ recommended expanding the competences of ascertaining rape to health workers, and spreading the knowledge of forensic medicine, the process of acquiring a medical certificate that proves rape is still difficult. Different actors are working to provide services and support to rape victims. Haitian and international NGOs are providing victims with support, following and guiding them through the process of reporting a rape,[40] while the Haitian National Police (HNP) are receiving support and training in order to better investigate rape and accommodate victims.[41] The Haitian non-governmental organization *Unité de Recherche et d'Action Médico-légale* (URAMEL) is teaching and promoting forensic medicine and health law in Haiti.[42] Several organizations are working to educate and to change attitudes towards the issue of rape. There might be some improvements with respect to how Haitian society deals with sexual violence, but the fragmented picture of actors working on the issue of women's rights and sexual violence against women, on the legal, medical, and police levels, makes it difficult to give an assessment of the magnitude of change.

6.3. REFORM OF THE JUSTICE SYSTEM

Concerning the recommendations relating to the demand for justice, the picture is more complex. The larger part of the recommendations focuses on reform

40 Interview with Olga Benoit, Port-au-Prince, July 25, 2016.

41 The UNPOL section of the MINUSTAH has a specialized unit on sexual and gender-based violence, providing special training for the HNP and building one-stop centers where rape victims both can be examined and give testimonies to the police (Caparini and Osland 2016).

42 Interview with Marjorie Joseph, Port-au-Prince, July 25, 2016.

of the justice system (as evident from Table 2). Overall, the lack of progress regarding reforming the justice system in Haiti indicates that few of the recommendations on structural reform have been implemented.

Pressure for justice sector reform is still an important focus for civil society (Forum Citoyen, 2013a, 2013b, 2015). No improvements have been achieved concerning the independence of judges, judges' career prospects, or the material conditions for the courts. However, there are some exceptions that will be elaborated on in this section, concerning the Magistrate School, the Office of Citizen Protection (OPC), the Supreme Judicial Council (CSPJ), and the police. Notably, some of the more "successful" recommendations concerning the justice system were those that supported initiatives that were already underway, such as the establishment of a Magistrate School and the creation of a national police force, the Haitian National Police (HNP), to replace the military.

6.3.1. The Magistrate School

Concerning the Magistrate School (*École de la Magistrature*), the CNVJ notes the opening of the academy in 1995 and recommends strengthening the educational program of the school (see *Si m pa rele* 1996 [1998], section 2.1.2.iii). Today, the school is still up and running, despite some interruptions under different coups since its opening (see timeline in Annex 2). Its main purpose is to provide ongoing education for Haitian magistrates. These seemingly successful implementations may be a coincidence in timing, as the CNVJ gave recommendations linked to already ongoing processes, making it difficult to establish a causal connection. To disentangle the (potential) causal connections, more work needs to be put into analyzing the process of how and why the recommendations were formulated and included in the report in the first place.

6.3.2. The Office of Citizen Protection

Constitutional provisions were made for the creation of an Office of Citizen Protection (OPC), an autonomous, ombudsman-like office, in the Haitian Constitution of 1987. The CNVJ called for the establishment of this constitutional body, which did not exist in the mid-1990s when the commission report was being written. Almost two decades later, the OPC was finally set up in 2005. The OPC receives complaints from citizens claiming to be victims of abuse on the part of state officials. The CNVJ recommended that the OPC's functions should be expanded, which they have been to a large extent. Although the OPC still lacks adequate resources, it is reasonable to say that the recommendation suggested by the CNVJ regarding the enlarging of this office has in fact been implemented. According to Fortin and Pierre (2008, 23), the collaboration between the OPC and the police also has improved. Nonetheless, according to the sitting Protector of Citizens (*Protectrice du Citoyen d'Haïti*), Florence Elie, this expansion is more due to some key people and actors on the Haitian political scene pushing for this to happen, than a result of the recommendations of the CNVJ.[43]

6.3.3. *The Supreme Judicial Council*

Another recommendation dealt with the Supreme Judicial Council. The creation of the Supreme Judicial Council (CSPJ, *Conseil Supérieur du Pouvoir Judiciaire*) in 2007 was a long process,[44] and was in the end a result of the recommendations of the Preparatory Commission for the Reform of Law and Justice (CPRDJ, see below under "Follow-up and sanctions"), which furthered the recommendations of the CNVJ (OPC 2014). However, the establishment of the Supreme Judicial Council was just a small step in the full implementation of the complex recommendations set forth by the CNVJ and the CPRDJ. Despite being in place, the Supreme Judicial Council does not function as the CNVJ's report envisioned. The CNVJ recommended that this organ should be a consulting body for the Magistrate School, that it should be independent in its nomination of judges, and that it should have a code of ethics and abide by international norms and standards. Although the CSPJ serves as advisor in the running of the Magistrate School, it is encountering challenges in its work and does not have the means to fulfil its functions properly (OPC 2014). For one, there are challenges with regards to the nomination of judges, where the CSPJ formulates opinions while political interests dominate impartial nominations. According to former judge Napela Saintil, judicial culture may pose a greater obstacle than institutions themselves. Saintil argues that real change to the judicial system will not occur until a new generation of judges comes to the fore.[45] Further, much of the competence of the CSPJ remains with the Ministry of Justice and Public Security, and has not yet been transferred (OPC 2014).

6.3.4. *The Army and the Haitian National Police*

The area where there has arguably been the highest rate of implementation is recommendations concerning the Haitian National Police (HNP). After military

43 Interview with Florence Elie, Port-au-Prince, July 21, 2016.
44 Interview with member of the CSPJ, Dilia Lemaire, Port-au-Prince, July 25, 2016.
45 Interview with Napela Saintil, Port-au-Prince, July 21, 2016.

rule ended in 1994, the military was dismantled and the HNP was established. In the last 20 years, the HNP has enlarged its role and assumed many of the functions envisioned. It had a surge of public support and was regarded as a trustworthy body with integrity by the majority of Haitians in the late 1990s. At least through 1997, the building of the HNP was a relative success story (Beidas et al. 2007). Yet, there have been ups and downs. Today, the HNP faces many problems, including those pointed out by the CNVJ in 1996 concerning the standards of its prisons, the code of conduct concerning temporary arrest, and the relationship between the police and the investigatory judge (for a comprehensive analysis of the police and security reform in Haiti, see Beidas et al. (2007) and Mobekk (2017)).

Not coincidentally, police reform was a focal point of commitment and investment from abroad. Between 1995 and 2000, US assistance to the HNP totalled US$65,294,000, while the Canadian contribution was US$30 million in aid, and the UNDP gave US$6 million (Beidas et al. 2007, 82). These numbers do not include the costs of deploying the UN CIVPOL mission, which would add many more millions of dollars to the count. Overall, Haiti received massive support for police reform and, despite problems in coordinating the provisions of assistance and some donor competition, donor coordination and cooperation was relatively good (Mobekk 2017, 82). However, the aid was temporarily suspended in July 2000, with significant negative consequences.

The CNVJ also provided numerous recommendations concerning the education of the police force. At the time of this study, there was a comprehensive education system for the HNP, run by the government with major support from the UN mission in Haiti, MINUSTAH. MINUSTAH's UNPOL division contributed to the formation of the police force, especially through facilitating bilateral agreements for donors such as Canada and the United States. The efforts to improve education of the police are a joint Haitian-international effort, although it could be argued that the UN has been indispensable. In its report, the CNVJ issued detailed recommendations and suggestions concerning the education of police, on the content of its curriculum, like human rights and international basic principles on the use of force and firearms, and type of training, like non-lethal methods of crowd control. In addition, the CNVJ detailed what the police's prerogatives and formal function ought to be. Furthermore, and maybe due to the UN being the implementing actor in this regard, there is also a heavy emphasis on sexual and gender-based violence, and thereby also tapping into several of the recommendations in section B of *Si m pa rele*. Thus, many of the ongoing reforms of the police force today are in large part in congruence with the CNVJ's recommendations, even the ones concerning sexual crimes against women, although they are likely to have developed independently from them.

6.4. FOLLOW-UP AND SANCTIONS

Section D on follow-up and sanctions detailed what the CNVJ recommended should follow its report. Throughout the recommendations chapter, the CNVJ called for two follow-up bodies to be created, namely a Follow-up Committee (*Comité de Suivi*) and a Special Reparations Commission (*Commission Spéciale de Réparation*). The functions of these two recommended bodies were seemingly collected in the *Bureau Poursuite et Suivi* (the Follow-Up Committee described in section 6.1 on reparations). In addition, the CNVJ called for the Ministry of Justice to create a Preparatory Commission for the Reform of Law and Justice (the above-mentioned CPRDJ, *Commission préparatiore à la réforme du droit et de la justice*). This was set up in 1997, with the mandate of producing recommendations on reforming of the justice system. In May 1999, the CPRDJ submitted its official report to President Préval, entitled *Document de Politique Générale* (OPC 2014).

The CNVJ recommended that the Government of Haiti refer all cases of human rights violations they had uncovered to judicial authorities for the purposes of investigation, prosecution, and, where appropriate, sanctions. This concerned both those cases where a violation was ascertained and the perpetrator (or perpetrators) identified, and those where violations were ascertained, but where no culprit could be identified necessitating further investigations by the authorities. The CNVJ recommended that investigations be opened against the alleged perpetrators of violations of human rights identified by them within 30 days of the publication of the report. This did not happen, either within the set time limit, or at all. The CNVJ also recommended that all those identified as alleged perpetrators of human rights violations be suspended from all functions they currently occupied in public administration, pending the outcome of criminal investigations, but this has not happened either.

The CNVJ also recommended that the names of people identified as perpetrators should be made public only once legal proceedings were taken. The names of the perpetrators were listed in Annex IV of *Si m pa rele*, and not made public with the rest of the report. This was to avoid people taking justice into their own hands, as summary justice was a both a problem in society and an issue against which Aristide was very vocal (Mobekk 2017, 146). However, as the legal proceedings never occurred, the list remained unpublished for two years. The list was finally published amid much controversy in three consecutive issues of the weekly *Haïti Progrès*, published in Brooklyn, New York, in February 1998 (Freeman 1998 reprint, iii).

Concerning legal prosecution, the CNVJ recommended that further investigations should be carried out to determine the degree of complicity of superior officers of the army and the police in human rights violations documented in their report. They further recommended that the Haitian government should pay special attention to the investigation, prosecution and punishment of crimes against humanity, and to investigate whether certain executions or massacres that took place meet the requirements to call them crimes against humanity.[46] However, as shown by the case of the Raboteau trial, this did not happen (see section 6.1).

Interestingly, the commission also calls upon the international community in two recommendations on follow-up. First, the CNVJ "urges the international organizations and the other states to provide assistance to Haiti in the investigation and prosecution of crimes against humanity" and then "urges the states that have the necessary jurisdiction to open investigations on the perpetrators of political rape and to prosecute and punish crimes against humanity". These recommendations are inevitably hard to ascertain in terms of implementation, but they are an interesting manifestation of the fact that the report was written for an international audience.

Another interesting follow-up recommendation, listed in the section above on "Other recommendations", concerns the retrieval of files from FRAPH headquarters that are in the possession of the US government. These files were confiscated by US military forces in 1993, and the US government refused to return them on the grounds that they contained names of American citizens. The repatriation of the FRAPH documents was seen in Haiti as detrimental to the efforts of legal prosecution and in achieving justice, and there was a huge demand from Haitian civil society to retrieve them (Mattarollo 2013, 115). After much pressure from the MICIVIH and several other states, the US government relented and agreed to return the archive. However, they erased the references to American names, and the Haitian government refused to accept the files in such condition. Therefore, to date no criminal proceedings have been initiated based upon them (Mobekk 2017, 147).

7. HOW TO UNDERSTAND THE RECORD OF IMPLEMENTATION? A SUMMARY DISCUSSION

This analysis of the implementation of the CNVJ's recommendations reveals that their fate has varied depending upon whether the recommendations were championed by international actors or were dependent upon domestic political will for implementation. These factors also ultimately shape whether they have had a significant impact on Haitian society. The general perception is that nothing has happened on the Haitian government's part. There are a few exceptions, but whether these reforms are due to the work of the CNVJ or happened as a result of other circumstances is rather questionable. This is

46 The CNVJ particularly highlighted the assassinations of Antoine lzméry, Guy Malary, and Jean-Marie Vincent, and the Raboteau massacre.

not to say that recommendations rooted in international norms and standards have been implemented successfully, but rather that these are areas where some change has occurred during the last 20 years.

When a common feature of many of the recommendations actually in place is that they encompass international norms, the more pertinent question might be which came first: the chicken or the egg? When the recommendations implemented have occurred at the hands of international actors, this implies that the recommendations set forth by the CNVJ might have been more concerned with its international audience than its national. Second, this spurs the question of whether these events would have happened in any case.

This raises the utility of the distinctions between different actors in the framework proposed by the *Beyond Words* project, namely the distinctions between "implementing actors", "supporting actors" and "obstructing actors". In the Haitian case, one might also make a distinction between *intended* and *actual* implementing actors. While the intended implementing actor for many of the recommendations was the Haitian government and governmental bodies, many of the recommendations are today actually being implemented by actors other than the state, especially MINUSTAH. This is particular true of areas like education and the national police. In addition, the framework provides a separation between "facilitating factors" and "hampering factors". In this regard, the knowledge we have about the actors who influenced the inclusion and elaboration of certain recommendations, might to some extent provide insight as to what forces come into play as either supporting or obstructing the implementation of the recommendations.

The broader political and socio-economic environment in which the implementation of the recommendations was considered also matters. Especially in examining why the recommendations on reparations have largely gone unimplemented, there are several factors that come to the fore (Segovia 2006, 164). For one, the government of Aristide (1994–96) and the government that officially inherited the responsibility to comply with the recommendations set forth by the CNVJ, the Préval government (1996–2001), were chronically weak. The Aristide government particularly suffered due to the way it came to power, by the help of foreign invasion and having accepted an amnesty for individuals involved in the coup. Moreover, it had inherited a profound economic crisis from the military regime. In addition, conflicts between the supporters of Aristide and Préval made the report something of an embarrassment for Préval (Chapman and Ball 2001, 35).

A second important factor that can help explain the lack of implementation on the reparations measures is the lack of importance given to the reparations by the two governments that could implement the recommendations. For most of his term, Préval was preoccupied with a political crisis stemming from allegations of electoral fraud and the resulting resignation of his Prime Minister (Segovia 2006, 165). This crisis had grave repercussions, including the before-mentioned suspension of international aid, which placed the state in jeopardy, and negatively impacted the institutional reform program that the government had pledged to realize (Segovia 2006, 165). Reparations for victims of the coup were not a priority. The lack of importance given to reparations was also reinforced by the international community, who prioritized institutional reform and the achievement of minimal political stability. Further, the second Aristide government (2001–04) was also preoccupied with trying to survive in the midst of a profound political crisis and severe economic limitations. Thus, it had less flexibility in its definition and implementation of public policies, reinforcing the traditional dependence of the country on international aid (Segovia 2006, 164). This has basically been the case for the last 20 years, and it has reduced the margins of action that all subsequent Haitian governments have had to define national policies and priorities. These factors impeding the implementation of recommendations on reparations have arguably been affecting the other recommendations as well.

8. CONCLUSIONS

This chapter claims that, although *Si m pa rele* is largely forgotten, the demands it vocalized through its recommendations are still very much alive. There is a general perception that "nothing has happened" concerning the recommendations, a statement echoed by many of the interviewees for this study. The victims of the military regime are still awaiting compensation; there have not been any major reforms of the justice system; and the overall aims of getting justice and eradicating corruption and impunity have not been achieved. Still, in tracing CNVJ recommendations in this study, one might be surprised by the number of recommendations actually implemented. However, these measures have mostly resulted from the initiatives and efforts of the UN, bilateral donors, and other international organizations, and cannot be said to make this into a "success story". Many of the issues raised by the CNVJ are still of current public concern. Although the demand for reparations has long been overshadowed by subsequent crises, the recommendations concerning reform of the justice sector and the police force represent in many ways goals that the government and international actors are still trying to achieve. The CNVJ's final report has garnered little notice in the 20 years since its submission to the government, either by the government, the UN, or the population writ large, for reasons outlined above.

A key argument here is that, when examining the implementation record of the CNVJ's final report, it is necessary to reflect upon the counterfactual, namely whether these reforms would have happened without the CNVJ. This concern is especially relevant in the realm of legal reform, where in 1996 alone there were at least four comprehensive reports on law reform, one of which, the *Xaragua* report from the Ministry of Justice, followed up on the CNVJ's final report. However, this question of causality is an inherent problem in this project of tracing implementation overall. Interviews conducted for this study highlighted that many of the central recommendations set forth by the CNVJ concerning justice reform, were issues of great public concern long before the commission issued its report (see section 5 above). The CNVJ recommendations, therefore, were not "born" with the CNVJ, but the CNVJ rather used its report to pick them up and flag public concerns over injustice, continued violations, and malfunctioning government institutions.

Another key conclusion that emerges from the analysis is who the actual implementing actors are and are meant to be. As set forth in section 6 on implementation, the 20 years since the report was finalized and the wide range of actors operating on the Haitian scene make determining the "record of implementation" highly complex. It may be difficult, if not impossible, to ascertain whether a recommendation has been implemented due to the CNVJ's final report, or for some other reason. However, what this study of the implementation record has shown is the surprisingly "high" rate of implementation of the recommendations set forth by the CNVJ. At the same time, the implementation itself is faulty, and has not contributed to the overall aims that it was meant to serve. In Haiti, overall, there is a sense of "too many cooks spoil the broth", and, despite benevolent contributions by international donors to build up Haiti's rule of law, these contributions have to some extent lacked coordination and coherence.

This is highly interlinked with who are the supporting and facilitating actors in the process of implementation, and – if we could say more about it – who pushed for the recommendation in the formulation phase. The latter is hard to ascertain. Concerning the supporting and facilitating actors and factors, three things seem to have influenced the likelihood of a recommendation being implemented. First, recommendations that were linked to ongoing processes, like the HNP and the School of Magistrates, were more likely to be implemented. Second, the CNVJ's recommendations appear to have provided additional pressure to implement previous commitments, such as provisions of the Constitution of 1987 on the OPC and CSPJ, which had not yet been enacted. Third, changes that had the backing of international actors or followed international norms, like the focus on sexual violence and different functions of the police, also were more likely to be implemented. In a sense, over 20 years, the recommendations have been kept alive through constant demands from both Haitian civil society and the UN's involvement in Haiti. As one interviewee working with women's rights expressed it when I presented her with section B of the report: "I should probably read this again. It seems useful." The recommendations set forth by the CNVJ are (sadly) still relevant.

A final central explanation for the weak implementation record is that it has simply been a matter of prioritizing. Haiti has been hit by several disasters since 1996, on top of an already severe economic situation. The country was struck by an earthquake of catastrophic magnitude in 2010, followed by a widespread outbreak of cholera in 2011. A country prone to natural disasters, Haiti was again struck hard by Hurricane Matthew in 2016 and another significant earthquake in 2021 with fatal consequences. In such circumstances, scarce resources have been used for survival, not channeled to greater reforms of the system. Haiti's domestic political environment also has been turbulent. A *Junta* carried out another successful military coup in 2004, for the second time sending President Aristide into exile. Haiti spent nearly all of 2016 with an interim government, as there was no agreement on the results from presidential elections, leaving Haiti in a political stalemate. Elections were delayed again and again, the last time in October 2016 when Hurricane Matthew hit. The period under President Moïse, finally beginning in February 2017, was also characterized by a lot of controversy, culminating in the dramatic event of his assassination on July 7, 2021 – followed by the latest earthquake in August 2021. All of these events, some due to the nature of the government and some due to happenstance, have distracted attention from the CNVJ and its ambitious recommendations. Not only the work of the commission but also the period in question, the military regime of the early 1990s, have been overshadowed by more recent calamities.

BIBLIOGRAPHY

Amnesty International (2005). *Haiti: Obliterating justice, overturning of sentences for Raboteau massacre by Supreme Court is a huge step backwards.* Amnesty International, Index No. AMR 36/006/2005. Retrieved from: https://www.amnesty.org/en/documents/amr36/006/2005/en/.

Aristide, Mildred (2006). "A historical and dignity-centred perspective on Haiti's struggle for justice". *International Journal of African Renaissance Studies – Multi-, Inter- and Transdisciplinarity* no. 1 (2): 265–305: https://doi.org/10.1080/18186870608529721.

Beidas, Sandra, Granderson, Colin, and Neild, Rachel (2007). "Justice and Security Reform after Intervention: Haiti". In C.T. Call, *Constructing Justice and Security after War*, 69–112. Washington, DC: US Institute of Peace Press.

Bunch, Charlotte, and Fried, Sandra (1996). "Beijing '95: Moving Women's Human Rights from Margin to Center". *Signs* no. 22 (1): 200–204.

Caparini, Marina and Osland, Kari (2016). "MINUSTAH's Specialized Police Team to Combat Sexual Violence in Haiti." *NUPI Working Paper* 867. Retrieved from: https://brage.bibsys.no/xmlui/bitstream/handle/11250/2424172/_Working_Paper_867_Osland_Caparini.pdf?sequence=3.

Chapman, Ardrey, and Ball, Patrick (2001). "The Truth of Truth Commissions: Comparative Lessons from Haiti, South Africa, and Guatemala". *Human Rights Quarterly* no. 23 (1): 1–43. https://doi.org/10.1353/hrq.2001.0005.

Commission Nationale de Vérité et de Justice (1996a). *Si m pa rele*. Reprinted: Bryant Freeman [1998]. *Si m pa rele: 29 sept. 1991–14 oct. 1994*. Occasional Paper No. 14, pp. xviii–245. Lawrence, KS: University of Kansas. Retrieved from: http://ufdc.ufl.edu//UF00085926/00001.

—— (1996b). *Si m pa rele. Annexes I et II*. Reprinted: Bryant Freeman [1998]. *Si m pa rele: 29 sept. 1991–14 oct. 1994*. Occasional Paper No. 15, pp. xviii–245. Lawrence, KS: University of Kansas. Retrieved from: http://ufdc.ufl.edu//UF00085926/00002.

Concannon Jr., Brian (2001a). "No Reconciliation without Justice". *Criminal Justice Matters* no. 44 (1): 22–24. https://doi.org/10.1080/09627250108552900.

—— (2001b). "V. Justice for Haiti: The Raboteau Trial". *International Lawyer* no. 35 (2): 641.

Côté, Denyse (2014). "Anpil fanm tombe, n'ap kontinye vanse: luttes féministes en Haïti". *Possibles* no. 38 (1): 209–223. Retrieved from: http://hdl.handle.net/10625/54365.

Duramy, Benedetta (2014). *Gender and Violence in Haiti: Women's Path from Victims to Agents*. New Brunswick, NJ: Rutgers University Press.

Forum Citoyen (2013a). *Dossier 1: Indépendance du Pouvoir Judiciaire. Propositions d'amendements à certains actes juridiques* (Plaidoyer pour la reforme de la Justice, des practiques de l'État et de la société civile.), 36. Port-au-Prince: Comité Coordonnateur du Forum Citoyen pour la Reforme de la Justice.

—— (2013b). *Dossier 2: Plaidoyer pour une chaîne pénale efficace dans la lutte contre l'impunité et la corruption, et respecteuse de la dignité humaine. Propositions d'amendements à certains actes juridiques* (Plaidoyer pour la reforme de la Justice, des practiques de l'État et de la société civile.), 47. Port-au-Prince: Comité Coordonnateur du Forum Citoyen pour la Reforme de la Justice.

—— (2015). *Dossier 3: Plaidoyer pour une systeme judiciaire proche de la population dans la lutte contre l'impunité et la corruption et respectueux de la dignité humaine.* (Plaidoyer pour la reforme de la Justice, des practiques de l'État et de la societe civile). Port-au-Prince: Comité Coordonnateur du Forum Citoyen pour la Reforme de la Justice.

Hayner, Priscilla (2006). "Truth commissions: a schematic overview" – ICRC. *International Review of the Red Cross* no. 88 (862): 295–310. Retrieved from: https://www.icrc.org/eng/resources/documents/article/review/review-862-p295.htm.

—— (2011). *Unspeakable Truths: Transitional Justice and the Challenge of Truth Commissions* (2nd edn.). New York and London: Routledge.

Hoogenboom, David A., and Quinn, Joanna (2011). "Transitional Justice and the Diaspora: Examining the impact of the Haitian Diaspora on the Haitian Truth Commission." Presented as a Conference paper at the International Studies Association Annual Convention, March 18, 2011. Now published in (2020) *Griffith Law Review*, no. 29 (1): 134–149. Retrieved from: http://politicalscience.uwo.ca/research/docs/joanna_quinn/TransitionalJustice_Diaspora_haitian_truth_commission_2_.pdf.

Human Rights Watch (1996). *Thirst for Justice: A Decade of Impunity in Haiti*. New York: Human Rights Watch. Retrieved from: https://www.hrw.org/legacy/reports/1996/Haiti.htm.

Human Rights Watch, and National Coalition for Haitian Refugees (1994). "Rape in Haiti. A Weapon of Terror". *Human Rights Watch and National Coalition for Haitian Refugees* no. 6 (8): 1–28.

Laguerre, Michael S. (1997). "The Role of the Diaspora in Haitian Politics". In R.I. Rotberg (ed.), *Haiti Renewed*, p. 170. Washington, DC: Brookings Institution Press.

Lawyers without borders (2020). *Affaire Duvalier. La décision de la Cour d'appel de Port-au-Prince du 20 février 2014: une étape importante pour la justice en Haïti.* Canada: Avocats sans frontiers Canada. Retrieved from: https://www.asfcanada.ca/site/assets/files/7187/affaire-duvalier_haiti.pdf.

Lechtenberg, Sara (1996). *An overview of the Haitian justice system*. Lawrence, KS: Institute of Haitian Studies, University of Kansas. Retrieved from: https://kuscholarworks.ku.edu/handle/1808/12606.

Macilwain, Colin (1995). "Forensic team digs up Haiti's deadly past". *Nature* no. 377 (6547): 278.

Martin, Ian (1999). "Haiti: International Force or National Compromise?". *Journal of Latin American Studies* no. 31 (3): 711–734.

Mattarollo, R. (2013). *Rien n'a été en vain*. Copy consulted from the CELS archive.

McCalpin, Jermaine O. (2012). "Truth and Freedom in Haiti: An Examination of the Haitian Truth Commission". *The Global South* no. 6 (1), 138–155: https://doi.org/10.2979/globalsouth.6.1.138.

Mobekk, Eirin (2017). *UN Peace Operations. Lessons from Haiti, 1994–2016*. London and New York: Routledge.

OPC (2014). Rapport Alternatif sur L'application du Pacte International Relatif aux Droits Civils et Politiques. Office de la Protection du Citoyen. Retrieved from: http://tbinternet.ohchr.org/Treaties/CCPR/Shared%20Documents/HTI/INT_CCPR_NHS_HTI_18091_F.pdf.

Quinn, Joanna R. (2009). "Haiti's Failed Truth Commission: Lessons in Transitional Justice". *Journal of Human Rights* no. 8 (3): 265–281. https://doi.org/10.1080/14754830903110350.

—— (2010). *The Politics of Acknowledgement: Truth Commissions in Uganda and Haiti*. Vancouver: UBC Press.

—— (2019). "Diaspora influence on the thin sympathetic response in transitional justice". *Ethnic and Racial Studies* no. 11 (42): 1830–1849. https://10.1080/01419870.2019.1615629.

Reuters. (December 5, 2016). "Guy Philippe, former coup leader wanted by US, wins Haiti senate seat". *The Guardian*. Retrieved from: https://www.theguardian.com/world/2016/dec/05/guy-philippe-haiti-senate.

Segovia, Alexander (2006). "The Reparations Proposals of the Truth Commissions in El Salvador and Haiti: A History of Noncompliance". In P. de Greiff (ed.), *The Handbook of Reparations* (pp. 154–175). Oxford: Oxford University Press.

Selvik, Lisa-Marie M. forthcoming. "The Unknown Pioneer. The Haitian truth commission (1995–1996) addressing sexual violence against women." *Journal of International Organizations Studies*.

United Nations (1997). *The situation of democracy and human rights in Haiti* (Report of the Secretary-General No. A/51/935). United Nations. Retrieved from: http://dag.un.org/bitstream/handle/11176/215706/A_51_935-EN.pdf?sequence=3&isAllowed=y.

—— (1998). *The situation of democracy and human rights in Haiti* (Report of the Secretary-General No. A/52/986). United Nations. Retrieved from: http://dag.un.org/bitstream/handle/11176/178623/A_52_986-EN.pdf?sequence=3&isAllowed=y.

USAID /Haiti Office of Human Rights and Democracy (1996). *Respect for the Rule of Law in Haiti: Literature and Data Review* (Research and Reference Services Project).

ANNEX 1: LIST OF INTERVIEWEES

Total number of interviews: 13

Full name	Institution	Location	Date
Benoit, Olga	Working at SOFA (*Solidarité des Femmes Haïtiennes/Solidarite fanm ayisyèn*), a Haitian non-governmental organization working on women's rights.	Port-au-Prince	July 25, 2016
Cairn, Pierre	Chief of the Training Section of the Haitian National Police, UNPOL (United Nations Police), MINUSTAH.	Port-au-Prince	July 23, 2016
Colas, Jocelyne Noel	Working at the National Commission for Justice and Peace, JILAP (*Commission Episcopale Nationale Justice et Paix*).	Port-au-Prince	July 18, 2016
Elie, Florence	Director of the Office of Citizen Protection, OPC (*Office de la Protection du Citoyen et de la Citoyenne*), the Haitian Ombudsman office.	Port-au-Prince	July 19, 2016
Esperence, Pierre	Executive Director of National Human Rights Defense Network, RNDDH (*Réseau national de défense des droits humains*).	Port-au-Prince	July 20, 2016
Joseph, Mario	Director at BAI (*Bureau des Avocats Internationaux*), a public law firm committed to the promotion of human rights in Haiti.	Port-au-Prince	July 25, 2016
Joseph, Marjorie	The Medico-Legal Research and Action Unit, URAMEL (*Unité de Recherche et d'action Médico Légale*), a Haitian non-governmental organization promoting and teaching forensic medicine and health law.	Port-au-Prince	July 25, 2016
Lemaire, Dilia	Member of the the Supreme Judicial Council, CSPJ (*Conseil Supérieur du Pouvoir Judiciaire*), where she is the civil society representative.	Port-au-Prince	July 25, 2016
Lespinasse, Colette	Coordinator of GARR (*Groupe d'Appui aux Rapatriés et Réfugiés*), a platform of Haitian NGOs working on migration.	Port-au-Prince	July 15, 2016
Pierre, Gotson	Coordinator of Groupe Médialternatif. Used to work at CRAD (*Centre de Recherche et d'Action pour le Développement*), a Haitian non-governmental organization.	Port-au-Prince	July 20, 2016
Pierre, Raynard	Member of the Judicial Affairs Offices, Unit for the Support of Institutions and Legislative Reforms, Justice Section, MINUSTAH.	Port-au-Prince	July 25, 2016

(continued)

continued

Full name	Institution	Location	Date
Saintil, Napela	Haitian Magistrate, working as a lawyer. Used to work as a judge (justice of the peace) and chaired the Raboteau trial.	Port-au-Prince	July 21, 2016
Thomas, Philippe	Chair of the Board of Directors of GARR (*Groupe d'Appui aux Rapatriés et Réfugiés*), a Haitian non-governmental organization.	Port-au-Prince	July 22, 2016

ANNEX 2: TIMELINE OF POLITICAL EVENTS IN HAITI, 1996–2016

- 1996, February 5: CNVJ handed over its report to President Aristide. 7 February: Préval, a member of Aristide's political party, replaces Aristide as President.
- 1997–1999: Characterized by political deadlock.
- 1999: President Préval declares that parliament's term has expired and begins ruling by decree following a series of disagreements with deputies.
- 2000, November: Aristide is re-elected President, amid allegations of irregularities and low voter participation.
- 2001, July: Presidential spokesman accuses former army officers of trying to overthrow the government. December: 30 armed men try to seize the National Palace in an apparent coup attempt. The government blames former army members.
- 2004, January–February: Violent uprising spreads throughout the country and escalates. February: President Aristide is forced into exile by a *coup d'état* by the military. March: An Interim Prime Minister forms a transitional government. April: The Security Council establishes MINUSTAH. June: The first UN peacekeepers arrive to take over security duties from the US-led force.
- 2004–2005: Rising levels of deadly political violence and gang violence in the capital.
- 2005: Creation of the OPC. Modification of the classification of rape in the Penal Code.
- 2006, February 7: General elections. Préval emerges as the winner of the presidential vote. June: A new government takes office. October: US partially lifts an arms embargo imposed in 1991.
- 2007: Creation of the CSPJ. November: Allegations of sexual misconduct by Sri Lankan peacekeepers leads to repatriation of 108 soldiers (including three commanders).
- 2008, February: Parliamentary vote of no confidence in the Prime Minister fails, protesting the government's economic policies. April: Violent demonstration and riots in several cities as a result of the rising cost of living. Government announces emergency plan to cut price of rice in bid to halt unrest. April: Parliament dismisses the Prime Minister. August–September: Four consecutive hurricanes and storms cause severe damage, an estimated 800 killed and hundreds injured. September: Parliament approves a new government, ending a five-month impasse.
- 2009, May: Former US President Bill Clinton is appointed UN Special Envoy to Haiti. July: World Bank and IMF cancel 80 per cent of Haiti's debt. November: The Senate passes censure motion against the Prime Minister, and a new Prime Minister takes office.

- 2010, January: An estimated 300,000 people are killed by a magnitude 7.0 earthquake. March: International donors pledge US$5.3 billion for post-quake reconstruction. October–December: Cholera outbreak claims some 3,500 lives and triggers violent protests. November: Presidential and parliamentary elections. December: Announcement of inconclusive provisional results of presidential election triggers violent protests.
- 2011, January: Former President Jean-Claude Duvalier returns from exile, faces corruption and human rights abuse charges. March: Legislative and presidential election. May: Martelly is sworn in as President. July: Death toll from cholera outbreak climbs to nearly 6,000.
- 2012, January: President Martelly proposes reviving Haiti's army. February: The Prime Minister resigns in protest at the refusal of many of his ministers. May: A new Prime Minister is appointed. October: Hundreds protest the high cost of living and call for the resignation of President Martelly.
- 2013, September: The first recruits of the new armed forces return from training in Ecuador. November–December: Street protests in Port-au-Prince and other major cities, voicing discontent about the overdue election, unemployment, and corruption.
- 2014, April: Further anti-government protests. December: The Prime Minister is forced to resign.
- 2015, January: A new Prime Minister is appointed. August: First round of delayed parliamentary elections is held. October: Second round of parliamentary elections, first round of presidential elections. Second round is postponed.
- 2016, February: The Prime Minister resigns. President Martelly ends his term without handing over power. Interim President Privert is sworn in. April: Presidential elections are again postponed until October. October: Hurricane Matthew hits Haiti, leaving widespread damage affecting around 1.3 million Haitians.

Sources: Information collected from Mobekk (2017, 199–201), and supplemented with information on implementation collected for this study.

PANAMA'S TRUTH COMMISSION RECOMMENDATIONS

Out of Sight, Out of Mind?

Adriana RUDLING*

---

* The author is affiliated to Chr Michelsen Institute, Bergen, Norway and Instituto Pensar, Bogota, Colombia.
The author wishes to thank Salvador Sánchez, and the members of the Centro de Iniciativas Democráticas (CIDEM) for their invaluable help throughout the fieldwork in 2011. She would also like to thank Elin Skaar, Joanna Quinn, Margaret E. Scranton, and Stener Ekern

1. INTRODUCTION

The Panamanian Truth Commission (PTC) was created by President Mireya Moscoso via Executive Decree No. 2 on January 18, 2001. The decree charged the PTC with contributing to the "clarification of the truth about the violations of the human rights fundamental to life, including enforced disappearance, carried out during the military regime" that governed Panama between 1968 and 1989. The PTC also was tasked with making "recommendations for legal and administrative measures that to their judgement can be adopted to hinder or prevent the [recurrence of similar] events." This feature implies that the very architects of the PTC hoped this body would have an impact beyond the report it produced. This chapter follows the implementation of these recommendations so as to better understand the effects of truth commissions. This is especially critical in the case of Panama, where, besides a follow-up body established in 2003, the PTC has been the only transitional justice mechanism adopted to date.

The chapter finds that the majority of the final report's 11 recommendations have seen limited implementation. The underlying reason, it is argued, is the fact that the creation of the PTC was not part of a sweeping social and political commitment to censure the human rights violations of the military regime. Rather, it was an isolated policy that sought to get the Moscoso administration out of a bind. Therefore, once President Martín Torrijos, leader of the political party created by the military regime to safeguard its legacy, took office in September 2004, implementation was side-lined, at best, and dismantled, at worst. Where some strides towards implementation were made, they were the result of the right civil servant at the right place, acting with the support of the Inter-American Court for Human Rights (IACtHR) and Inter-American Commission on Human Rights (CIDH). At present, the PTC report is regarded as little more than an important historic document, which broaches a topic that many would have preferred to avoid.

The record of implementation was reconstructed through a combination of documentary evidence – that is mainly newspapers, (international) non-governmental organisations' reports, and reports from local authorities – as well as more than a dozen semi-structured interviews and countless informal conversations with victims, human rights activists, commissioners, and government officials. Fieldwork in Panama was undertaken between March and June 2011[1]

for their insightful comments on earlier versions of the chapter. Her deepest appreciation is reserved for the interviewees, and especially the victims of the military regime, who took the time to guide her in better understanding these issues. Without their help, this chapter would not have got this far.

1 The results of this stage of the fieldwork were reported in the author's MSc thesis in Latin American Studies, completed at the Universidad de Salamanca, Spain in July 2011. The aim of the thesis dovetailed with the *Beyond Words* project as it focused on examining the hypothesis that truth commissions established late in relation to the events they analyzed were more successful. For the purposes of the dissertation, success was defined in reference to the implementation of the recommendations, making an analysis of the progress of the implementation of recommendations the centerpiece of the research.

and in October 2016 to guarantee accurate data was collected on each of the recommendations. Three points are worth mentioning in relation to this. First, where a PTC recommendation refers to legal or institutional reform, is difficult to establish a causal link to the body of inquiry unless it is duly mentioned in the text of the resolution or law. States are complex multi-level machineries in which interests are in constant flux and measures are adopted for a variety of reasons. Second, interviewees' views on the scope of implementation vary, as some cited efforts made as being equivalent to implementation, where others saw the same actions as empty promises. The assessment of the effects of implementation was primarily based on whether the aspect flagged by the recommendation improved as a result of state action. When some effort was made, but the matter that the recommendation considered was not resolved the implementation of the recommendation was deemed limited. Where no steps were taken at all, it was deemed not implemented. Third, no source of information was privileged between interviews and documental evidence, with the corroboration of information between the sources being the guiding principle. Where interviewees manifested memory failings, whereby they could not link actions taken to the PTC recommendations or could not recall the outcome of certain proceedings, documentary evidence was sought. Where written sources were absent or incomplete, information was sought through interviews and informal conversations.

This chapter is divided into seven sections. The next section introduces the military regime that governed Panama between 1986 and 1989. The third section presents the PTC, focusing on its mandate, its composition, its work, and its report. While the fourth section comprises a general description of the recommendations, the fifth section addresses their implementation along with the actors and factors influencing this process. The sixth section clarifies the patterns discerned in the implementation of each of the recommendations. The chapter concludes with a brief discussion of future avenues for implementation.

2. HISTORICAL BACKGROUND

Panama is best known in the academic literature for the Panama Canal and its tormented relationship with the US. As stated by President George H. Bush, the aim of the US invasion of December 20, 1989 was to "safeguard American lives, restore democracy, and bring General Noriega to trial, and to protect the integrity of the Panama Canal Treaty." The US and the Panama Canal were also key in the independence of Panama from Colombia in 1903. Backed by the US, Panamanian elites pushed for independence once the Colombian Senate refused to adopt the necessary legislation to provide for the construction of the Canal. Between independence and the 1968 coup, Panamanian politics was controlled by a symbiotic alliance between local urban commercial elites and US interests.

For the former, this alliance meant that they could enjoy the benefits of the Canal and govern by excluding popular sectors. For the latter, it provided the stability needed for a smooth operation of the Canal (Pérez 2011, 7). Towards the end of the 1980s, Noriega increasingly threatened this mutually beneficial arrangement and the US intervened as domestic opposition alone failed to oust him (Pérez 2011, 37).

It was widely expected that the October 11, 1968 takeover would be a fleeting affair once it was broadcast. Not only had the security forces carried out two short-lived coups before (CVP 2002, i), but initially many saw the coup as a backlash against the infringement on the autonomy of the National Guard by newly elected President Arnulfo Arias. Besides Noriega, General Omar Torrijos was the most important actor to shape the regime until his death in 1981 (Ropp 1992, 216). With Torrijos, the regime devised the plan that would ensure its survival: it transformed social inequalities into a base for social support through the application of clientelist programs and policies that supported the emerging working and peasant classes. It also sought to appeal to nationalistic inclinations by re-negotiating its relationship with the US, allowing Panama to eventually gain control over the Canal (Beluche 1994, 65–66).[2] Thus, the military regime survived by effectively redefining the role of the security forces as the exclusive protector of national interests (Pérez 2011, 66).

The PTC and Follow-up Office reports identify 116 victims of the military regime, between extra-judicial executions and forcibly disappeared persons. The majority of victims are concentrated in two periods; that is between 1968 and 1972 and between 1984 and 1989. Repression declined between 1972 and 1984 as the regime deployed an ingenious carrot-and-stick strategy based on a combination of targeted repression and selective co-optation of antagonists. On the one hand, it promoted loyalty by, for instance, adopting programmes of land redistribution, access to basic public services, the implementation of a progressive Labor Code, and giving students influence over the appointment of school and university staff. On the other, it isolated, humiliated and, in some cases, forcibly exiled those who opposed it, mercilessly atomizing opposition and civil society more generally. Such was the case of Major Boris Martínez, who, together with then Lieutenant Omar Torrijos, had led the coup against Arias only to be exiled four months later when he challenged Torrijos' government plan. The heightened repression in these two main periods relates to a higher degree of uncertainty faced by the regime. The in-fighting of the security forces,

---

2 The first of the Torrijos-Carter treaties of September 1977 acknowledged the sovereignty of Panama over the Canal and made provisions for the gradual shift of control from 1979 to 1999. The second, known as The Panama Canal Treaty, made provisions for the use of the Canal under neutrality starting 1979 (Smith III and Hogan 1987, 5). The treaties were hugely celebrated affairs in Panama at the time, but the fact that the US reserved a right to intervene in the country if it believed the security of the Canal was at risk was met with suspicion by some (*El País*, May 13, 1978). The 1989 invasion made use of this clause in the first treaty.

pro-Arias guerrillas, and the lack of a clear ideological orientation produced serious clashes in the first period where half of the fatalities are concentrated. The second period, which includes less than a third of all victims, can be traced to the exhaustion of the foreign loan-based government assistance funds and the implementation of austerity models. Repression expanded as street protests amplified (Guevara 1994, 121).

3. THE PANAMANIAN TRUTH COMMISSION (PTC)

Unlike Chile and Argentina, to give two well-known Latin American examples, the return of democracy did not spell the adoption of policies to deal with the violent past in Panama. This could be explained through shortages of both "supply" and "demand". In terms of social demand, a report by CIVICUS finds that the legal environment in which civil society operates in Panama is not friendly, resources are lacking, and mechanisms of dialogue and collaboration with the government are insufficient (CIVICUS 2015). According to Edwin Wald (Interview, May 2011), it was the startling discovery in 1999 of the first human remains in an area close to Tocumen International Airport, known to have been the headquarters of the Second Infantry Company, the Pumas, during the military regime, that galvanized the demand for justice. It was, thus, not until 1999 that the first victims' organization, namely the *Comité de Familiares de Detenidos y Asesinados de la Dictadura Militar de Panamá Héctor Gallego* (Committee of Relatives of Detained-Disappeared Persons of the Military Dictatorship of Panama Héctor Gallego, COFADEPA-HG), was established. The PTC process was then used by COFADEPA-HG to reach out to victims outside of Panama City, primarily in David, Chiriquí, and found a sister organization (Maestre, Interview, April 2011). The lower death toll registered throughout the regime, comparable only to the cases of Uruguay and Brazil in Latin America, acted negatively on the demands of the victims by reducing the visibility of their plight nationally and internationally. Panamanian victims did not command the same level of attention during the transition because of the date when the takeover occurred, the duration of the military regime, and the fact that the surviving victims, together with their relatives, are generally older, have fewer resources, and are less educated than their counterparts elsewhere (CIVP 2004, 93–95).

In terms of "supply", two main problems arose. On the one hand, the issue was protracted. The focus of Guillermo Endara, inaugurated President – with the help of the US troops as he was widely believed to have won the annulled elections of May 10, 1989 – was national reconciliation, economic recovery, and the modernization of law enforcement. Despite the fact that Endara was the leader of the *Partido Arnulfista* (today *Partido Panameñista*), the party of the deposed Arias, and many expected him to show more interest in victims' matters, his term was primarily devoted to the creation of democratic institutions.

For instance, following the recommendations of the National Reconciliation Commission (Panamá América January 28, 2001), the military was purged and transformed into a police force (Caumartin 2007, 112–114).

On the other hand, and perhaps more importantly, the *Partido Revolucionario Democratico* (Democratic Revolutionary Party, PRD), heir to the military regime, not only survived, but returned to power with President Ernesto Pérez Balladares in 1994 (Scranton 1995). The emblem of the PRD, for instance, is an "11" encircled by an "O" in reference to the day of the coup, October 11, 1968. This is particularly illustrative of the fact that its members, and those associated with it more generally, subscribe to a positive interpretation of the military regime (Loxton 2015, 160). Due to its populist policies, many view the military regime as the reign of progressive caudillos (Rouquié and Suffern 1998, 180). Having emerged in 1978 as the "political arm" of the regime, the PRD protects its legacy at every turn. The continued relevance of the PRD became distinctly consequential for the implementation of several PTC recommendations, as will be shown below. Criminal trials, to take one example, were blocked following the transition not through an amnesty law, but because of presidential pardons, a strategy that finds its origins in the Pérez Balladares administration.

The near absence of social demand and the continued political relevance of the successor of the military regime are decisive factors in explaining the striking lack of transitional justice policies prior to 2001. The following five sub-sections describe the creation of the PTC, emphasizing the contingencies involved in the process, the composition of this body, its sources of funding, and the problems it faced while carrying out its work, as well as the distribution of the report.

3.1. WHY A TRUTH COMMISSION?

Between September 1999 and December 2000, human remains with clear signs of torture emerged on a site known to have been a military base during the regime. While the Public Ministry revealed its lack of interest in pursuing an investigation into the human rights violations of the military regime (La Crítica Libre January 10, 2001), President Moscoso was of the opinion that exhumations had to continue (Panamá América December 28, 2000). As the widow of the deposed Arias, Moscoso had a personal interest in the victims of the regime. Further, as the leader of the *Partido Panameñista*, she had an institutional interest in them. Thus, José I. Blandón, party whip, proposed a debate on a truth commission in Congress before the end of 2000 (Blandón, Interview, April 2011). The main opposition party, the PRD, rejected such a prospect. Omar Torrijos' son, Martín Torrijos, an important figure of the PRD, labelled the prospective truth commission a "Vengeance Commission" and accused it of aiming to present "a bloody and heartless [General] Torrijos who never existed" with the objective of "turning him into a Pinochet, to pass judgement and sentence him" (Panamá América January 15, 2001). Notwithstanding this overt resistance, Moscoso authorized the creation of the PTC before Congress reconvened after Christmas break, with little consultation with civil society.

The PTC was tasked with several goals:

a. establish as complete a picture as possible about the referred events, their background, and their circumstances;
b. gather information that allows the identification of the victims and the establishment of their whereabouts;
c. make recommendations for legal and administrative measures that to their judgement can be adopted to hinder or prevent [the recurrence of similar] events (Executive Decree No. 2 of 2001, article 2).

Executive Decree No. 2/ January 18, 2001 restricted the work of the PTC in a number of ways. First, to avoid clashes with the Public Ministry, the PTC mandate explicitly prohibited its interference in pending judicial proceedings, urging the Commission instead to provide any relevant information it uncovered to the judiciary. Second, the PTC was meant to be in operation for no longer than nine months. Considering the duration of the regime, and the difficulties of obtaining information more than a decade after the fall of the regime, not to mention the funding difficulties addressed below, this raises serious questions about the intentions of the Moscoso administration. Third, much to the frustration of its commissioners, who knew these to be the least common abuses of the period, their investigations were restricted to "the violations of the human rights fundamental to life, including [forced] disappearance" (Tejada Mora, Interview, October 2016).

The seemingly spontaneous way in which the PTC came about, together with the scant support from the Executive throughout its term, led some to conclude that Moscoso only made arrangements for its creation to get out of a bind. De Britton, one of the commissioners who withdrew only months after being appointed, was of the impression that the Moscoso administration "played a bait-and-switch game" with the victims.[3] For de Britton, the PTC was only meant to divert attention from the inaction of the Public Ministry as human remains kept appearing at different sites around the country (de Britton, Interview, April 2011). Once the PTC proved not to be as toothless as expected and as well as something of a political liability for Moscoso, who sought to broker a deal with the PRD to ensure governability, she committed to silencing it.

[3] The expression used by the commissioner was "*el gobierno tiró la bola y escondió la mano,*" which roughly translates to "the government played a 'ring-and-run'/ 'bait-and-switch' game."

3.2. COMPOSITION OF THE PTC

Alberto Santiago Almanza, Juan Antonio Tejada Mora, Fernando Berguido, Osvaldo Velasquez, Otilia Tejeira de Koster, Anglican Bishop Julio E. Murray, and Rosa Maria Crespo Justiniani de Britton were the seven commissioners appointed to the PTC by the decree. While the first four are lawyers, Otilia Tejeira was known for her human rights work and Rosa Maria de Britton was a reputable writer and medical doctor. Further, Berguido was the President of the Panamanian chapter of Transparency International, and, together with Velasquez and Tejeira, had been known critics of the military regime (La Crítica January 18, 2001). Velasquez founded the Panamanian Human Rights Committee in 1978 and was its director two years prior to the fall of Noriega (Panamá América January 9, 2005). Although there was no formal consultation of civil society on the commissioners, there was some overlap with their suggestions. For example, Tejeira was proposed by the *Asamblea de la Sociedad Civil* (Civil Society Assembly), an umbrella organization that demanded a truth commission in a December 2000 open letter to President Moscoso. Bishop Murray was put forward by *Coordinadora Popular de Derechos Humanos Panamá* (Popular Coordinating Committee for Human Rights Panama, COPODEHUPA), a human rights organization that had been working with victims of the regime since 1999 (Panamá América January 9, 2001). Almanza came as a replacement for Catholic Archbishop José Dimas Cedeño, the first choice of the victims (La Nación January 19, 2001).

Table 1. Composition of the Panamanian Truth Commission

Name	Period served	Profession
Alberto Almanza (President) (M)	Until April 18, 2002	*Lawyer* Once the PTC submitted its report, Almanza became the unofficial chief of the Follow-up Office later endorsed by Moscoso
Juan Antonio Tejada Mora (M)	Until April 18, 2002	*Lawyer*
Osvaldo Velasquez (M)	Until April 18, 2002	*Lawyer*
Bishop Julio E. Murray (M)	Until April 18, 2002	*Anglican Bishop*
Fernando Berguido (M)	Until October 18, 2001	*Lawyer*
Otilia Tejeira (F)	Until May 2001	*Public figure and human rights activist*
Rosa Maria de Britton (F)	Until April 2001	*Medical doctor and writer*

Source: Compiled by the author.
Note: M = male, F = female.

3.3. SOURCES OF FUNDING

Information about how the PTC was funded is scarce. What is known is due to Law 6 of January 22, 2002, a transparency law for public entities. Supported by former commissioner Fernando Berguido, this piece of legislation prompted PTC President Almanza to reveal that its budget had fluctuated between USD 350,000 and USD 450,000 (La Prensa February 20, 2002). The majority of this funding came from the Moscoso administration, but the PTC report also mentions the Embassy of the Federal Republic of Germany and the Embassy of Great Britain as additional sources. Together with some support given by Embassy of the Republic of China (Taiwan), international aid was of a more "symbolic" nature rather than a substantive and sustained source of funding for the PTC (Almanza, Interview, April 2011).

President Moscoso justified her reluctance to fund the PTC by saying that she "did not want [this body] to be perceived as being part of the government, and … [its] work being partial [to the government]" (Panamá América February 5, 2001), a claim that had already been made by some opponents of the PTC. She claimed that, prior to their appointment, she had made the commissioners aware that they would be responsible for collecting funds (La Crítica Libre February 6, 2001). While Berguido, the third commissioner to abandon the PTC, passionately disputes this (Berguido 2013, 615), other commissioners believe the funding problems were related to a lack of genuine interest on the part of the administration (Tejeira, Interview, April 2011; de Britton, Interview, April 2011). The PTC became so strapped for cash that it had to stop working several times throughout its operation (Almanza, Interview, April 2011; Tejada Mora, Interview, October 2016; Perez Jaramillo, Interview, October 2016), much to the despair of the victims (Maestre, Interview, April 2011).

3.4. THE WORK OF THE PANAMANIAN TRUTH COMMISSION

Besides the lack of funding, the PTC faced two other main difficulties, namely rapid loss of commissioners and repeated conflicts with the Public Ministry. The PTC lost both Rosa María de Britton and Otilia Tejeira in the first five months of operation. After Tejeira left, it became clear that both departures were related to disagreements with the PTC President about work methodologies and his leadership style (Panamá América May 26, 2001). It did not help the image of the PTC that Tejeira described Almanza as authoritarian and ignorant of the matters at hand (Tejeira, Interview, April 2011). The prologue of Executive Decree No. 268 of October 19, 2001, which extended the term of the PTC to April 18,

2002, references the difficult organizational stage, the resignation of these two members, the large amount of human remains located, and difficulties relating to their identification as the main reasons for the new deadline. Yet, once this extension was granted, Berguido vacated his post because of other work commitments (Tejada Mora, Interview, October 2016). Thus, the PTC final report lists a total of 59 staff, including the President, but excluding Juan Antonio Tejada Mora, Osvaldo Velasquez, Bishop Julio E. Murray, and Fernando Berguido, who appear on the first page.

The biggest headache for the PTC was the General Prosecutor, José Antonio Sossa. Sossa repeatedly accused the PTC of being a "political entity" due to its proximity to the Executive (La Prensa March 2, 2001). COFADEPA-HG, the largest victims' organization in existence at that point, and an ally of the PTC, accused Sossa of aiming to "foster impunity [in] the cases of enforced disappearance and extrajudicial killing of the dictatorship" (La Prensa November 12, 2001). The problems with the Public Ministry worsened when it emerged that Sandra Anderson, one of the foreign forensic anthropologists who had collaborated with the PTC, was accused of planting evidence and obstruction of justice in the US (La Prensa August 22, 2003). Claiming that Almanza, now President of the Follow-up Office of the PTC, had covered up similar practices in Panama, Edwin Wald, the brother of the disappeared Rita Wald, filed a complaint against him (Wald, Interview, May 2011). Although these allegations[4] were not substantiated (Supreme Court of Justice 2003, 103), the reputation of the PTC was damaged, and the findings linked to Anderson's contributions had to be reassessed. Seizing on the opportunity, the PRD used this debacle to discredit the PTC report throughout the 2004 presidential campaign (La Prensa March 28, 2004).

These difficulties notwithstanding, the PTC was a media darling as a result of a combination of the visits of foreign experts, researchers, and academics, the Human Rights Watch director, the field visits of the commissioners as well as the promise made by US representatives to deliver necessary documentation to assist its work (Rudling 2013). As the contentious claims made by Wald only emerged a year later, the report was generally well received upon submission to President Moscoso and Prosecutor General Sossa on April 17, 2002. Moscoso promised the victims reparations (Panamá América April 18, 2002) and work began on setting up a Follow-up Office (La Prensa July 31, 2003). COFADEPA-HG released a statement on May 2, 2002 where it positively evaluated the work of the PTC, especially with regard to "the analysis [carried

---

4 Almanza was pardoned despite the absence of a guilty verdict through Executive Decree 317 of August 25, 2004, making the handling of the Anderson case even more suspicious in the eyes of the public (La Crítica August 28, 2004). This pardon was later revoked (Supreme Court of Justice 2008).

out] by [the] historic … document." It expresses its support for many of the recommendations given by the PTC and urges the Public Ministry to collaborate with the relatives in reopening the cases where new evidence had been uncovered (COFADEPA-HG May 2, 2002).

3.5. DISTRIBUTION OF THE FINAL REPORT

There are, to date, two full printed versions of the PTC report. Both of these versions were published in 2002. The Office of the Ombudsman supported the publication of the first edition's 450 copies, and the 2000 copies of the second edition were produced by the PTC alone.[5] Besides the different covers, there is no substantive difference between these two editions. More information about the whereabouts of these two reports can be found in the evaluation of recommendation 7 below. To improve access, the Office of the Ombudsman also uploaded the report to its webpage, where it can be found today. Furthermore, two shorter reports were produced, one in 2002 for popularization purposes, and the other in 2004 for educational purposes (Tejada Mora, Interview, October 2016). The first, titled *Final Report. Truth Commission*, was produced with the help of the local newspaper *La Estrella de Panamá*. 40,000 copies were printed and distributed free of charge with the newspaper. The 2004 report also was developed by the Department of Education in collaboration with the Follow-up Office to serve as the basis for the implementation of recommendation 6, which pleaded for improving human rights education in schools. Although it was never used (Maestre, Interview, October 2016), 60,000 copies of this volume were printed (Panamá América March 3, 2004) for primary education (CIVP 2004, 82).

4. RECOMMENDATIONS IN THE PTC REPORT

The recommendations emerged as part of the mandate of the PTC set out in article 2 of the Executive Decree. Paragraph c tasked the PTC with providing recommendations for "legal and administrative measures" that can "hinder or prevent" developments like the ones that it analyzed. Although they were the result of consultation amongst the commissioners (Tejada Mora, Interview, October 2016), the writing of the recommendations was a rushed job, as the

5 There is some debate about which of these versions was published first, as Perez Jaramillo (Interview, October 2016) believes the order to be reversed, the 2000 copies coming first. Nevertheless, the inside cover of the 2000 copies volume references this edition as the second one. Perhaps it is worth mentioning that, at the time, the Human Rights Ombudsman was Juan Antonio Tejada Espino, the son of commissioner Juan Antonio Tejada Mora.

PTC focused most of its energy on adjusting the lists of victims to accurately reflect the human rights violations related to the military regimes as mandated, reconstructing the narrative of human rights abuses during the regime, and carrying out exhumations (Perez Jaramillo, Interview, October 2016). The statement released by COFADEPA-HG in May 2002 in support of the PTC explains that some of the recommendations had been "recorded in previous proposals of [the victims' organizations]" (COFADEPA-HG May 2, 2002). Inspiration was also drawn from other truth commissions' reports, mainly the Argentine *Comisión Nacional sobre la Desaparición de Personas* (National Commission on the Disappearance of Persons, CONADEP), and the Chilean *Comisión Nacional de Verdad y Reconciliación* (National Commission for Truth and Reconciliation) (Perez Jaramillo, Interview, October 2016).

The main preoccupation of the Panamanian commissioners was to safeguard the work of the PTC in light of its clashes with the General Prosecutor (Perez Jaramillo, Interview, October 2016) and the upcoming presidential elections (Tejada Mora, Interview, October 2016). Thus, the repeated disputes with Sossa stimulated concerns about the future of the judicial investigations, so that several recommendations refer directly to such investigations, the archives of the PTC, and continuing work on the location and identification of the human remains (Perez Jaramillo, Interview, October 2016). Furthermore, the final recommendation directly refers to the establishment of an office that would monitor the development and implementation of the recommendations.

The report contains 11 recommendations, all listed on page 265. There is no formal division between them; nor are they organized in sections, as has been the case in other reports, although some are directed at different state actors on whose endorsement they depend. The recommendations, together with their type and targeted actor, are summarized in Table 2 at the end of the following section. This table uses quotation marks where the actor charged with implementation is specifically identified in the recommendation. More than one recommendation falls into several types, as well as targeting different potential implementing actors.

5. IMPLEMENTATION OF THE PTC'S RECOMMENDATIONS

This section is entirely devoted to tracking the implementation of the recommendations individually. Whereas these separate evaluations offer concrete reasons why the implementation of the recommendation followed that path, section 6 below addresses the lack of implementation in a general fashion.

5.1. RE-OPENING OF CRIMINAL CASES

1. *To reopen those cases of human rights violations which occurred during the period under investigation, where the investigations of the Truth Commission have contributed new evidence that can support sentencing.*

Relating to criminal investigations and prosecutions, this first recommendation has seen only limited progress. Information on implementation could be obtained from several sources: first, though the records of the Follow-up Office of the PTC; second, a report presented by the Foreign Ministry to the CIDH on January 26, 2005; third, a report presented by the Special Investigative Agent[6] to the relatives of the victims sometime in 2010; and fourth, a document provided by the General Prosecutor dated February 2, 2011 to the Office of the Vice-President. Due to space limitations, this chapter focuses on the most recent report produced by Superior Prosecutor Geomara Guerra de Jones, appointed to these cases in September 2015 (La Estrella September 24, 2015). Presented to the relatives of the victims in March 2016, this report shows that defendants involved in the same case were treated unevenly, as some were pardoned before trial while others were sentenced. Having previously been grouped into 81 cases based on the particular incident of repression, this report shows 47 of them were to be closed due to statutes of limitations or dismissed because of lack of evidence or witnesses. 34 cases could not be accounted for fully (La Prensa April 18, 2016). The main reasons for the lack of advancement on the implementation of this recommendation have been the lapse of time, pardons, and judicial inefficiency.

5.2. REPARATION FOR VICTIMS' FAMILIES

2. *That the relatives of those extra-judicially executed and forcibly disappeared at the hands of the military regime be provided with adequate moral and material compensation proportionate with the damage they suffered.*

Maritza Maestre, President of COFADEPA-HG, claims that representatives of the Moscoso administration assured them that, if a petition was filed with the CIDH, her government would see to it that the victims were granted reparation in accordance with its decision (Maestre, Interview, October 2016). The friendly settlement was reached in 2019 (CIDH 2019) after Petition 882-03 "Victims of the Military Dictatorship", was finally admitted for proceedings on October 27, 2015 (IAComHR 2015). Although the Martinelli administration formalized the talks with the victims through Executive Decree 449 of December 30, 2011, which continued during the following two

[6] See more information about this in recommendation 3.

administrations, no collective reparative measures had been implemented so far (Panamá América September 13, 2021).

The only reparative efforts have been the result of the intervention of the two regional bodies on human rights. On the one hand, the reparative effects in the 2008 IACtHR judgement in *Heliodoro Portugal vs. Panama* aimed to be individual, but the ceremony of acknowledgement of responsibility organized by the Martinelli administration included COFADEPA-HG members (IACtHR 2010a, 4).[7] The Portugal family received material reparation and a plaque bearing the name Heliodoro Portugal, which was unveiled in 2010 in the neighborhood of Santa Ana where he was last seen before his disappearance (IACtHR 2010, 3–4). Following a friendly settlement reached with the Martinelli administration before CIDH on July 26, 2011, the Wald family received material reparation for the disappearance of Rita Wald (Decreto de Gabinete 42 of November 13, 2012). In March 2017, President Varela publicly asked the Wald family for forgiveness (La Prensa March 15, 2017).

Collective and symbolic reparations are long overdue. Outgoing President Martinelli placed the first stone of the *Plaza Monumental en Honor a las Víctimas de la Dictadura Militar en Panamá* on June 23, 2014 on a plot of land where one of the properties of Manuel Noriega once stood. COFADEPA-HG criticized the project, claiming that it diverged from its agreement with the government (La Prensa June 24, 2014) because of its remote location in the fashionable neighborhood of San Francisco, not far from Panama City's largest park which still bears the name Omar Torrijos (COFADEPA-HG June 23, 2014). This project has seen no advancement to date. Furthermore, on April 3, 2017 the Varela administration announced the winner of a competition for the design of a monument dedicated to the victims to be placed in Poinciana Park in Panama City by 2019 in line with the agreement at the Roundtable (El Siglo April 4, 2017). Nevertheless, the tender for the construction of the project has been suspended twice (La Prensa February 23, 2018) and no delivery date is in sight (Panamá América May 19, 2021). Due to the haphazard way in which some victims received reparations, implementation can only be considered limited.

5.3. CREATION OF A SPECIAL PROSECUTOR

3. *To create a Special Prosecutor to investigate the human rights violations and crimes against humanity.*

Aimed at linking the investigations of the PTC to criminal prosecutions, this recommendation has not been implemented in the way specified by the text of

7 The previous public act organized by the Government and Justice Minister, under the Torrijos administration, had been judged as insufficient by the Inter-American Court (IACtHR 2010, 5).

the recommendation. Following a meeting with the IAComHR in early 2005, Ana Matilde Gomez, having been appointed General Prosecutor by President Torrijos that same year, created the position of the "Special Investigative Agent." According to Resolution 2 of March 2, 2005, the task of this new Prosecutor was to follow up on the investigations of the PTC on forced disappearances. Nevertheless, Perez Jaramillo (Interview, October 2016), who worked for this Prosecutor's office, explains that they had little institutional support. First, as a travelling Prosecutor, the post-holder was meant to work in those offices that stored the archives of each of the cases. Second, the functions of this Special Agent were widened by Resolution 51 of November 15, 2006 to include "cases of high social impact" to be determined by the General Prosecutor. It is uncertain when the special prosecutorial body was closed. Gomez stated that she believed it was after February 2010 when she was herself removed from her post by President Martinelli (Gomez, Interview, October 2016).[8] Considering the configuration of this office and the lack of advancement of the cases, the implementation of this recommendation is deemed limited.

5.4. CIVILIAN CONTROL OF THE NATIONAL POLICE

4. *To improve juridically the law that organizes the National Police so as to ensure that the control and development of the National Police and any other organization dedicated to public security stays in the hands of civilian authorities.*

There have been two known modifications to the National Police Act of 1997, both of which are contrary to the letter and the spirit of this recommendation. First, Law 69 of December 27, 2007 established the Judicial Investigations Department of the National Police and transferred the Criminology Services to the Institute of Legal and Forensic Medicine. Then-Prosecutor General Gomez opined that this introduced a double hierarchy into the investigative process. Staff were now part of the National Police's chain of command, while formally following orders from prosecutors (La Crítica April 22, 2007). Contrary to the recommendation's aims, this weakens civilian control of judicial investigations. More concerning is the adoption of several pieces of legislation to protect police agents from disciplinary action following complaints, suits and investigations against them. This was the case of Law 74 of October 29, 2010, declared unconstitutional by the Supreme Court of Justice (2011), which allowed officers to remain on active duty until the probes regarding the legality of their use of force were resolved (La Prensa December 17, 2013). Considering the above,

8 Yet, a report of the Human Rights Network – Panama, submitted to the 2010 UN Universal Periodic Review on Human Rights, asserts that the Special Agent ceased to exist in 2009 (RDH-P 2010).

these officers could influence the outcome of the investigation launched against them if they outranked staff from the Judicial Investigations Department. These ebbs and flows support a negative evaluation of the implementation of this recommendation.

5.5. COMPLIANCE WITH INTERNATIONAL HUMAN RIGHTS OBLIGATIONS

5. *That the Republic of Panama faithfully comply with its international human rights obligations so that the domestic legislation effectively guarantees the enjoyment of those rights.*

The evaluation of the implementation of this recommendation is hampered by the fact that it is itself very cryptic. One possibility is that it was meant as a guarantee of non-repetition and it exhorted the Legislative or the Executive Branch to criminalize human rights violations in domestic legislation. Another possibility is that, like the first recommendation, it referred to prosecution and was directed to the courts. These differences notwithstanding, it targets the same problem, namely the lack of recognition by courts of the crimes of the military regime.

According to the International Covenant on Civil and Political Rights, adopted through Law 15 of October 28, 1976, the Panamanian state was obligated to prosecute acts criminalized by the international community even before the end of the military regime (RDH-P 2008, 6). Moreover, the American Convention on Human Rights entered into force in 1978 (DDP 2006, 88). Despite this, extra-judicial executions, and enforced disappearance were not only not investigated or otherwise punished, but the body responsible for investigations, namely the National Investigations Department, was an active participant in these crimes. This explains why many direct victims and relatives had little option but wait to file their complaints until after the fall of the regime (CVP 2002, 30–31). Problems appeared then too because, although Panama signed the Inter-American Convention on Enforced Disappearance in 1994, ratifying it the following year, it failed to (appropriately) criminalize enforced disappearance until 2011.[9] Furthermore, the new Penal Code, adopted in 2007, and reformed on three occasions, specifically addresses crimes against

9 Law 1 of January 13, 2011 is a response to the ruling of the IACtHR that found Law 63 of August 28, 2008 to be in breach of the standards of the Convention on Enforced Disappearance because it only considered situations where crimes were generalized and systematic (IACtHR 2008a, 14). All crimes where agents of the state are involved either in the cover up of forced disappearance or in involving third parties are covered by the new legislation. It also criminalizes torture as a separate crime, not as an aggravating circumstance of forced disappearance, and establishes higher periods of detention for both crimes.

humanity, including a new segment, Title XV, which incorporates international norms on their criminalization and two articles that define and criminalize forced disappearance.[10]

Since domestic legislation did not criminalize forced disappearance, some legal judgments equated it with ordinary homicide, imposing limitations on the period it was open to prosecution to 20 years. This was the case when the Supreme Court Justice enforced statutes of limitations in two cases in the PTC report. Nevertheless, there was some reason for hope as the Superior Tribunal of the Third Judicial Ward resisted the same practice in two other cases (CIVP 2004, 44). Since the return of democracy, effective prosecution was also frustrated by pardons. President Perez Balladares, of the PRD, uncovered the perfect formula to deal with the past in the absence of an amnesty law: presidential pardons in the name of "national reconciliation". From this point on, both PRD and *Partido Panameñista* presidents handed out hundreds of pardons (Pérez 2011, 120–121). The glimmer of hope offered to victims is the fact that the Supreme Court ruled that pardons applied to individuals not yet sentenced, called to trial, or charged are unconstitutional (Supreme Court of Justice 2008, 42–43). Nevertheless, it is worth acknowledging that, even in the absence of this legal limitation, the simple passage of time affects the capacity for effective prosecution because of the difficulty of establishing facts and responsibilities so many years after the commission of the crimes.

If the recommendation refers to the criminalization of the abuses committed by the military regime, it may be considered implemented, albeit at the insistence of the IACtHR. Alternatively, if this recommendation was aimed at achieving effective prosecution, its implementation can only be considered limited as already outlined above in the evaluation of the first PTC recommendation.

5.6. HUMAN RIGHTS EDUCATION

6. *To strengthen human rights education at all levels of education and in the law enforcement sector.*

Relating to educational reform, this recommendation is only partially implemented, as efforts have been largely in vain. Between May and October 2003, the Follow-up Office of the TC, in collaboration with the *Ministerio de Educación* (Department of Education, MEDUCA), worked on a text for Forms Five and Six. It combined a digest of the PTC report with a series of workshops and exercises to give secondary school students historical and testimonial

10 Prior to this, article 1968-B of Law 27 of May 21, 2008 prohibited the enforcement of "statutes of limitations in the crimes of terrorism, crimes against humanity and enforced disappearance." This legislation had a provisional character until the new Penal Code entered into force on May 23, 2008 (González 2010, 49).

information about the military regime, to acknowledge that citizens are defenseless when public institutions fail to fulfil their assigned roles, and to show the human and moral costs of these violations (MEDUCA 2004). Submitted to the Minister of Education in 2004, this handbook was to be used in History of Panama, Civics III, History of the Relations of Panama, and Ethics and Values (CIVP 2004, 80–82). Nevertheless, it disappeared from the repositories of the Department of Education soon after Martin Torrijos became President (Civil servants MEDUCA, Interview, April 2011).

Two civil servants responsible for the public-school curriculum interviewed in October 2016 argued that human rights have always been a part of education in Panama, as the subjects Ethics, Morals and Values, Civic Education, Geography, and Social Sciences include human rights (Civil servants MEDUCA, Interview, October 2016). Further, upon the invitation of the Foreign Ministry in charge of the Roundtable of Mutual Understanding, the Department of Education was involved in talks with COFADEPA-HG about teaching the history of Panama under the military regime. Despite the fact that COFADEPA-HG had outlined their expectations that the topic would be taught based upon the texts referred to above in 2016 (COFADEPA-HG January 14, 2016), by 2019 there was no progress in this regard as shown by the inclusion of the same demand in the friendly settlement (CIDH 2019).

The only information that could be obtained about human rights training in the security forces originates in the 2008 submission made by Panama for the UN Universal Periodic Review. The National Police offered a practical and theoretical training program of 80 hours, split over 16 courses on human rights and humanitarian principles in police work. By the date of that report, 309 police units had received this training focusing on, amongst other things, the obligations of civil servants pursuant to human rights principles, humanitarian police work, disciplinary rules in police work, and legal due process work (RDH-P 2008, 7). Considering the size of the National Police – that is nearly 30,000 units (La Crítica June 26, 2014) – this is not much to be proud of. Thus, it is easy to conclude that the implementation of this recommendation is limited.

5.7. DISSEMINATION OF THE PTC REPORT

7. That the National Government guarantee the adequate dissemination of the contents of the Final Report of the Panamanian Truth Commission, so that it is made available to all Panamanians and contributes to a better and deeper understanding of the pain suffered by the victims and their relatives.

Serious efforts have been made to implement this recommendation citing dissemination as a guarantee of non-repetition. As explained above, a total of 2,450 copies were published across the two editions of the PTC report. The Follow-up Office of the PTC specifies that 9 per cent of the available copies are in the possession of the relatives of the victims, 4 per cent were acquired by government authorities, 13 per cent were purchased by the general public, 17 per cent are in the possession of NGOs, 2 per cent can be found in school libraries, 10 per cent in university libraries, 7 per cent have been bought by churches, and 21 per cent are in the public sector (CIVP 2004, 81). The PTC, in collaboration with the newspaper *La Estrella de Panamá*, published 40,000 free copies of a digest of the report. The Follow-up Office also produced a CD of the report and carried out activities to give it publicity (CIVP 2004, 80). Further, the original report is available on the website of the Office of the Ombudsman. Nevertheless, in light of the fact that the report is still not widely known in Panama today (Perez Jaramillo, Interview, October 2016; Tejada Mora, Interview, October 2016), the implementation of this recommendation is considered limited.

5.8. NATIONAL DAY OF REMEMBRANCE

8. *To institutionalize through a State organ the National Day of the Forcibly Disappeared as a form of state acknowledgement of those who sacrificed their lives for Panamanian democracy.*

Aiming at non-repetition and symbolic reparation, Maritza Maestre reports there have been five failed attempts to implement this recommendation (Panamá América June 9, 2016). The Follow-up Office presented a draft bill to the Commission on Human Rights of the National Assembly in November 2002 based on three points (CIVP 2004, 84). First, it put forward that June 9 of every year should be declared the Day of the Disappeared. Second, the PTC urged that civic remembrance and reflection activities be carried out in private and public education. Finally, it recommended that, as a measure of reparation, a monument should be erected in the memory of the victims. On June 17, 2003, the first debate of this draft bill took place, but there is no record of it passing to the second stage of debate necessary for its implementation[11] (Panamá América September 30, 2003).

The effort did not end there. Another draft bill was brought by COFADEPA-HG before the same commission on November 20, 2009 (Panamá América November 30, 2009). However, observers are unaware of its fate (Maestre, Interview, October 2016). COFADEPA-HG submitted a third proposal to the Commission of Government on February 24, 2011 under the name "Draft Bill through which 9 June is established as the National Day of the Disappeared and Assassinated during the Military Dictatorship in Panama" (COFADEPA-HG February 24, 2011),

11 Despite the fact that lack of time is invoked, a more likely reason is the fact that, of the 7 members of the Human Rights Commission, 3 were members of the PRD, 3 were members of the *Partido Panameñista*, and the swing vote went to Javier Tejeira, of the *Partido Nacional Liberal*, a party that had, at times, been on both sides of the debate on historic memory.

but it is unclear what progress, if any, has been made (Maestre, Interview, October 2016). Fourth, the Roundtable of Mutual Understanding produced a draft bill on this topic on August 20, 2012 (MIREP 2012), but it was shelved by the civil servants in charge of the Roundtable (La Crítica June 9, 2014). Draft Bill No. 550, which saw its first debate on September 19, 2017 in the Commission for Education, Culture and Sports, is the fifth attempt at a Remembrance Day. The text of the document refers to June 9 as a "civic day of reflection for the victims of the military dictatorship." The demand for a monument is replaced with the inclusion of texts on historic memory in the primary education curriculum and the incorporation of programs and articles that promote human rights and democratic values in state-owned media (La Prensa September 21, 2017). Finally, the friendly settlement also refers these past attempts and commits the Foreign Ministry to resume efforts to work with Congress to approve legislation in this direction (IAComHR 2019). As there is no remembrance day to this date (Panamá América September 13, 2021), this recommendation can only be regarded as unimplemented.

5.9. EXCAVATION OF POSSIBLE BURIAL SITES

9. *To carry out systematic excavations in those sites where remains of victims are presumed to be located.*

According to Maestre, there have only been two stages of excavations since the PTC. In the first phase, excavations were quite extensive, and were carried out by the Follow-up Office. The second phase lasted for a few days in the beginning of 2012, and were carried out by Dimas Guevara, the Auxiliary Prosecutor in charge of the PTC cases at that time, with the help of the *Instituto de Medicina Legal y Ciencias Forenses* (Institute of Legal Medicine and Forensic Sciences, IMELCF) (Panamá América January 4, 2012). In the phase conducted by the Follow-up Office, excavations were carried out in three main areas. The first large area comprised the headquarters of the military regiment where the remains that initially prompted the creation of the PTC were found and next to the landing strip of the *Servicio Aéreo Nacional* (National Air Service, SAN). The second area was the Penal Island of Coiba and the third was made up of three sites in the province of Chiriquí. Where remains surfaced, they were deemed too small for forensic analyses (CIVP 2004, 11–32). The Follow-up Office reported that only 59, or 29 per cent, of the potential clandestine gravesites they investigated were excavated (CIVP 2004, 38). The excavations carried out by Guevara, on the other hand, concentrated on the Penal Island of Coiba, and had the explicit purpose of locating the remains of the student leader, Floyd Britton, in light of new information received the previous year (La Prensa June 14, 2012). A series of remains wrapped in fabric was uncovered, but identification is yet to be carried out (Panamá América May 2, 2015). Since excavations were not systematic, nor did they lead to any new identifications as the recommendation requests, this recommendation is judged as only partially implemented.

5.10. ANALYSIS OF VICTIMS' AND RELATIVES' DNA

10. *To send saliva samples of the relatives of the forcibly disappeared persons and of the remains recovered, for their subsequent analysis using mitochondrial DNA and identification.*

Once the mandate of the Follow-up Office ended, the saliva samples and the remains it had collected were placed in the custody of the Institute of Legal Medicine (Ross and Pachar Lucio 2015, 250). The Follow-up Office report claims that it collected 42 saliva samples of the 54 necessary for the identification of the 40 persons determined to have been forcibly disappeared (CIVP 2004, 38). Besides the identification of Heliodoro Portugal, which preceded the creation of the PTC, the PTC and the Follow-up Office successfully identified seven other sets of remains (La Prensa February 11, 2012). A further two forcibly disappeared persons were identified in 2017 (La Prensa August 30, 2017).

A report put together by the Institute of Legal Medicine and Forensic Sciences for the relatives on October 12, 2015 details the state of the remains in its possession. It refers to the evaluation of the remains made by the *Equipo Argentino de Antropología Forense* (Argentine Forensic Anthropology Team, EAAF) in February 2012 at the invitation of the Panamanian Foreign Ministry. This inventory showed that there were three groups of remains there: first, those resulting from excavations carried out prior to the PTC; second, those transferred by the PTC; and third, "cases exhumed by the Truth Commission in Coiba and Chiriquí", which probably refer to the excavations of the Follow-up Office. About "80% of the cases cannot be DNA tested because the remains are either not human, too old, or too deteriorated" (La Estrella October 15, 2015). Many of the remains found by the PTC have to be reassessed due to the Anderson debacle (CIVP 2004, 39). Referring to the DNA samples provided by the Follow-up Office, the same report claims that the lists of relatives attached to it do not match, some DNA profiles are missing, and they lack samples for new analyses. Further, it is now believed that these samples are contaminated (Panamá América June 29, 2012), forcing the Institute of Legal Medicine to collect new samples from the relatives to create a new master registry (IMELCF October 13, 2015). The friendly settlement commits the Institute of Legal Medicine to carry out the remaining identifications within a year (CIDH 2019), but no further remains have been returned to their relatives (Panamá América September 13, 2021). Despite the lack of progress in the last decade, this recommendation is deemed partly implemented on the basis of previous efforts.

5.11. CREATE A FOLLOW-UP BODY

11. *To create a follow-up body to lend continuity to all the material investigated, the declassified documents, the DNA evidence, as well as the remains recovered, which were produced by the investigations of the Panamanian Truth Commission.*

The PTC reconstituted itself of its own accord into a Follow-up Office immediately after it handed over its report to President Moscoso (CIVP 2004: 7). In an arguably suspect move, the *Comisión Institucional de la Verdad*, or the Institutional Truth Commission (CIVP), arose from this body. Formally acknowledged by Executive Decree 559 of October 20, 2003, the CIVP was to "give continuity to the activities that could not be carried to term by the Truth Commission" by boosting the process of recovery and identification of remains, advising the relatives of the forcibly disappeared and extra-judicially assassinated on their judicial proceedings, and advising state organs on measures dealing with the past. The same document set December 31, 2004 as a time-limit for its work and clarified that this body was expected to function with the personnel and the funds left in the PTC accounts.

The materials the PTC had collected and its archives remained in the custody of the Follow-up Office throughout the duration of the mandate of the latter. COFADEPA-HG became the guardians of the archives of both bodies once the Follow-up Office shut its doors (CIVP 2004, 83). The remains recovered, together with the DNA bank, were handed over to the Institute of Legal Medicine and Forensic Sciences, as outlined above. The Follow-up Office also assisted the relatives of the victims in bringing their case before the IAComHR. The reason why this recommendation is deemed only partially implemented is the incoherent fashion in which it gave continuity to the work of the PTC. It carried out limited investigations into the areas known to be clandestine internment sites, identified a small number of victims, and collected insufficient DNA samples.

Table 2. Typology and Implementation of the Recommendations of the Panamanian Truth Commission

# Rec	Recommendation type	Targeted actor	Status of Implementation	Observations on Implementation
1	**Criminal** Reopen cases where the TC has gathered new evidence	Judicial branch, i.e. Office of the General Prosecutor	Limited implementation	Majority of the cases closed due to lack of evidence, witnesses or statutes of limitations
2	**Reparation** Moral and material reparation for victims	Executive or Legislative branch	Limited implementation	Mainly thanks to IACtHR and IAComHR

(continued)

Table 2 *continued*

# Rec	Recommendation type	Targeted actor	Status of Implementation	Observations on Implementation
3	**Criminal** **Non-repetition** **Follow-up** Create Prosecutor in charge of investigating the crimes of the military regime	Judicial branch, i.e. Office of the General Prosecutor	Limited implementation	General Prosecutor Ana Matilde Gomez in response to IAComHR meeting
4	**Institutional reform** **Legal** **Non-repetition** Reform legislation governing the National Police to ensure civilian control	Legislative branch	Negative implementation	Judicial Investigations Department now answers to both the National Police and the Public Ministry
5	**Legal** **Criminal** **Non-repetition** Comply with international HR obligations to ensure effective guarantees of rights	Panamanian state, i.e. Judicial branch	Difficult to assess	IACtHR influence: Criminalization of enforced disappearance and torture; inclusion in the Penal Code of crimes against humanity
6	**Non-repetition** **Educational reform** Strengthen HR education in schools and law enforcement sector	National government, i.e. Department of Education	Limited implementation	2004: Department of Education – Follow-up Office: History of Panama 2015–16: Department of Education – COFADEPA-HG meetings
7	**Reparation** Publicize the TC report	"National Government"	Limited implementation	Ombudsman Follow-up Office + local newspapers
8	**Reparation** **Legal reform** National day of the Disappeared	"a State organ" i.e. Legislative or Executive branch	Unimplemented	several failed attempts by COFADEPA-HG Project now with Legislative Assembly
9	**Criminal** **Investigations** Excavations where human remains are presumed to be located	Judicial branch, i.e. Office of the General Prosecutor	Limited implementation	Follow-up Office 2002–04 Auxiliary Prosecutor 2012

(continued)

Table 2 *continued*

# Rec	Recommendation type	Targeted actor	Status of Implementation	Observations on Implementation
10	**Follow-up** **Criminal Reparations** Saliva of relatives and remains for their identification	Judicial branch, i.e. Office of the General Prosecutor	Limited implementation	Follow-up Office: 7 identifications Remains collected, DNA samples: IMELCF since 2004 2 identifications 2017
11	**Follow-up** Follow-up body to give continuity to the work of TC	Legislative or Executive branch	Limited implementation	Executive Decree 559 of October 20, 2003

Sources: Comisión de la Verdad de Panamá (CVP) (2002). *Informe final* and sources cited throughout section 5 of this chapter. See Bibliography for details.
Note: Table prepared by author.

6. HOW TO UNDERSTAND THE RECORD OF IMPLEMENTATION?

Despite the best efforts of the commissioners, the Office of the Ombudsman, and the print media, the PTC report is far from widely known in Panama today. The general perception is that the PTC produced an important historic document on a politically divisive and legally sensitive topic (Perez Jaramillo, Interview, October 2016; Tejada Mora, Interview, October 2016). The IACtHR, for instance, praised the report in the *Heliodoro Portugal vs. Panama* 2008 judgment, as did the IAComHR in the 2015 admissibility proceedings of Petition 882-03 "Victims of the Military Dictatorship." Furthermore, according to Maestre (Interview, October 2016) the PTC was also an opportunity for many of the victims to meet for the first time, as the process galvanized previously weak denunciation efforts.

Indeed, just as Hayner broadly claimed about the general record of implementation of truth commissions' recommendations (Hayner 2011, 6), the majority of the PTC recommendations have been found to be only partially implemented, as the steps taken in this direction produced few visible results. Three main points can be made in relation to this outcome.

First, wherever there has been implementation, however partial, the IACtHR and the CIDH functioned as supporting actors. The reparations in the cases of Rita Wald and Heliodoro Portugal are clear examples of this. One ingenious approach has been to use the pressure exerted by these regional bodies to work against the absence of domestic political will. Thus, although General Prosecutor Gomez was acting under an administration openly opposed to the work of the PTC, she sought to salvage the legacy of the PTC where she had been the head of the Legal Department. Gomez called for statutes of limitation not to be imposed on the human rights violations perpetrated by the military regime, created the position of the Special Investigative Prosecutor to look into the abuses of the military regime, and sought the legal domestic codification of torture and enforced disappearance in accordance with the IACtHR mandate in the *Heliodoro Portugal vs. Panama* 2008 judgment.

Second, when implementation depended on legislators and sitting Presidents, the rule has been very little advancement, because what one administration built, the next tore down (Maestre, Interview, April 2011; Perez Jaramillo, Interview, October 2016; Tejada Mora, Interview, October 2016). As was the case with the Endara administration that immediately followed the fall of the military regime, dragging out matters relating to the human rights violations of the military regime now formally established by the PTC was the biggest mistake made by Moscoso. Yet, if the views put forward by Wald, Tejeira, and de Britton are to be considered, the creation of the PTC did not respond to a sincere and sustained commitment by Moscoso to censure the actions of the military regime. The implementation record is less surprising if we take stock of the delicate, yet necessary, political balance between the two largest parties with histories on either side of the military coup and ensuring regime. The news of evidence planting by Anderson further compounded the issue by humiliating the PTC. Finally, once the 2004 presidential elections transferred executive power to the PRD, a party with the majority in Congress throughout the Torrijos administration, all traces of the PTC were obliterated. Thus, the talks between the government representatives and victims recommended by the IAComHR never took place, the history handbook for school children disappeared from the repositories of the Department of Education, and the moral reparations mandated by the IACtHR in the *Heliodoro Portugal vs. Panama* case were delayed until the next administration.

The Martinelli administration somewhat recovered the issue, most likely because it saw it as a powerful tool against the PRD. Martinelli formally established the Roundtable of Mutual Understanding with the victims, but the talks were slow, and stalled over the identification of the remains. The Presidency of Juan Carlos Varela was expected to bode well for victims. Not only was Varela the leader of the *Partido Panameñista*, led by Moscoso when the PTC was created, but he was at the helm of the Foreign Ministry where the Roundtable was launched. However, as Varela began flirting with the PRD in what became an on-again-off-again relationship, the commitment to victims' issues became patchy during his time as president (La Vanguardia July 1, 2014). The act acknowledging state responsibility in the Wald disappearance should be understood in this evolving context (La Estrella October 30, 2016). The friendly settlement reached before the CIDH as the PRD leader Laurentino Cortizo assumed office as President in July 2019 has, unsurprisingly, stalled given the position of his party on dealing with the past.

Third, the weakness of Panamanian civil society, where victims' organizations are no exception, can be linked to both the lack of demand for transitional justice policies during the transition and the lack of progress on implementation since the PTC (Castillo, Interview, April 2011; Leis, Interview, April 2011). Although COFADEPA-HG is formally registered as an NGO representing victims and acknowledged by Executive Decree No. 449 of December 30, 2011 as their only representative, it is the result of the fragmentation of a larger association in late 2000 (Rudling 2019). While COFADEPA-HG still exists today, it is in a debilitated state, with no offices or resources. Its counterpart ceased to exist shortly after the split. If old age and deficient education were serious issues for victims prior to the PTC, they now face the added problem of the near absence of interest in these matters from the younger generation. Maestre claimed that the near total apathy of younger relatives means that there is no possibility for renewal of COFADEPA-HG's organizational structures (Maestre, Interview, October 2016). Thus, unlike Hayner (1994, 609) would have envisioned, the recommendations of the PTC are unlikely to be used as "pressure points around which the civilian society or the international community can lobby for change" in the future.

7. CONCLUSIONS

Tracing the record of implementation of the recommendations of the PTC gives support to the claims made by Hayner (2011) and Correa (2013) that the recommendations are usually neglected by policy-makers and elected officials. This state of affairs is arguably related to two sets of factors, the first of which were directly linked to the very creation of the PTC and the second that came into being once its work was completed. Although the architects of the PTC might have seen its recommendations as contributing to the long-term impact of this body of inquiry, the PTC itself did not stand for a genuine commitment on the part of the Moscoso administration to deal with the past. Rather, it was a one-off measure, forgotten once more pressing concerns captured its attention. As matters relating to the PTC became protracted, the implementation of the recommendations was left to legislators and executives with intermittent interest. While little could be expected of the Torrijos administration who opposed the PTC from the start, Prosecutor Gomez was able to use the pressure exerted by the IACtHR to criminalize forced disappearance. The Martinelli and Varela governments were more instrumental in their approach, calling attention to the human rights abuses of the military regime when they could be used to keep their political opponent, the PRD, in check. Thus, as efforts waxed and waned over the decades, the CIDH push for Petition 882-03 "Victims of the Military Dictatorship" seemed to be the only mechanism to offer victims and their families a glimmer of hope. With the PRD leader Cortizo taking office in 2019, it appears that the issue of the human rights abuses of the military regime will be deferred again.

BIBLIOGRAPHY

Asamblea Nacional Panama (ANP) (2000). "Acta de la sesión ordinaria de la Asamblea Legislativa correspondiente al 26 y 27 de diciembre de 2000".

—— (2000a). "Acta de la sesión ordinaria de la Asamblea Legislativa correspondiente al 31 de diciembre de 2000".

Beluche, Olmedo (1994).*Diez años de luchas políticas y sociales en Panamá. 1980–1990.* Panamá.

Caumartin, Corinne (2007). "'Depoliticisation' in the Reform of the Panamanian Security Apparatus". *Journal of Latin American Studies* no. 39 (1): 107–132.

CIVICUS. World Alliance for Citizen Participation. 2015. "Enabling Environment National Assessment: Panama". Available at: http://www.civicus.org/index.php/eena-country/panama.

Comité de Familiares de Asesinados y Detenidos-Desaparecidos Panamá – Héctor Gallego (COFADEPA-HG) (2002). "Evaluación del Informe de la Comisón de la Verdad y Nuevas Perspectivas de Lucha Contra la Impunidad". Unpublished document dated May 2.

—— (2011). "Señores diputados". Unpublished document dated February 24.

—— (2014). "Comunicado". Unpublished document dated June 23.

—— (2016). "Planes escolares". Unpublished document dated January 14.

Comisión de la Verdad de Panamá (CVP) (2002). *Informe final* [Final report]. Panamá: Impresos Tavial. http://www.defensoriadelpueblo.gob.pa/sub.php?spid=436.

Comisión Institucional de la Verdad de Pamanamá (CIVP) (2004). *Avance de tareas* [Progress Report]. Panama: Panamanian Institutional Truth Commission.

Correa, Cristián (2013). *Reparations in Peru: From Recommendations to Implementation.* New York: International Center for Transitional Justice. Available at: https://www.ictj.org/publication/reparations-peru-recommendations-implementation.

Defensoría del Pueblo Panamá (DDP) (2006). *Instrumentos internacionales sobre Derechos Humanos reconocidos por la República de Panamá.* Panamá: Dirección de Relaciones Publicas e Imagen Institucional.

El País (1978). "Los tratados de la discordia disgustan en Panamá". Published: May, 13. Available at: https://elpais.com/diario/1978/05/13/internacional/263858403_850215.html [Referenced: 9 October 2021].

General Prosecutor (2011). "Señor Vicepresidente de la República" Unpublished document dated 2 February.

González, Alberto (2010). *La prescripción penal. Extincion de la acción penal y de la pena.* Panamá: Cultural Portobello.

Guevara, Carlos (1994). *Ilegitimidad y hegemonía: una interpretación histórica del militarismo panameño.* Panamá: Editorial La Prensa.

Hayner, Priscilla (1994). "Fifteen Truth Commissions -1974 to 1994: A Comparative Study". *Human Rights Quarterly* no. 16 (4): 597–655.

—— (2011). *Unspeakable Truths: Confronting State Terror and Atrocity*, New York: Routledge, 2nd edn.

Instituto de Medicina Legal y Ciencias Forenses (IMELCF) (2015). "Informe sobre estudio de osamentas que reposan en el IMELCF". Unpublished document dated October 13.

Inter-American Court of Human Rights (IACtHR) (2008). Case of *Heliodoro Portugal v. Panama*. Judgment of August 12, 2008. (Preliminary objections, Merits, Reparations and Costs). Available at: www.corteidh.or.cr/docs/casos/articulos/seriec_186_ing.pdf.

—— (2010). *Heliodoro Portugal vs. Panama*. Supervisión de cumplimiento de sentencia. Published: 20 April. Available at: https://www.corteidh.or.cr/docs/supervisiones/portugal_20_04_10.pdf.

—— (2010a). *Heliodoro Portugal vs. Panama*. Supervisión de cumplimiento de sentencia. 28 May. Available at: https://www.corteidh.or.cr/docs/supervisiones/portugal_28_05_10.pdf.

Inter-American Commission on Human Rights (CIDH) (2015). "Informe No 68/2015 de admisibilidad Petition 882/03 'Víctimas de la dictadura militar Panama'". Available at: https://www.oas.org/es/cidh/decisiones/2015/PNAD882-03ES.docx.

Inter-American Commission on Human Rights (CIDH) (2019). Informe No. 102/19. Caso 13.017A. Informe de solución amistosa. Familiares de víctimas de la dictadura militar, octubre de 1968 a diciembre de 1989 Panamá." Available at: https://www.oas.org/es/cidh/decisiones/2019/PNSA13017AES.pdf

La Crítica (2001). "Acusan a Sossa de obstruir investigación". Published: January 10, 2a.

—— (2004). "Cuestionan idulto de Almanza". Published: August 28. Available at: http://portal.critica.com.pa/archivo/08282004/suc03.html.

—— (2014). "Sanjur: Gallego solo vive en el campesinado". Published: June 9. Available at: http://www.critica.com.pa/sucesos/sanjur-gallego-vive-solo-en-el-campesinado-336238.

—— (2014). "Panamá, con más oficiales que un Ejército". Published: June 26. Available at: http://www.critica.com.pa/nacional/panama-con-mas-oficiales-que-un-ejercito-344252.

La Crítica Libre (2001). "Balbina cuestiona Comisión de Verdad". Published: January 18. 2a.

—— (2001). "Piden presupuesto para Comisión de la Verdad". Published: February 6. 2a.

La Estrella (2015). "Revivirán casos de la dictadura militar". Published: September 24. Available at: http://laestrella.com.pa/panama/politica/reviviran-casos-dictadura-militar/23893684.

—— (2015). "Mayoría de restos de víctimas dictadura en Panamá no sirven para prueba ADN". Published: October 15. Available at: http://laestrella.com.pa/panama/nacional/mayoria-restos-victimas-dictadura-sirven-para-prueba/23897952.

—— (2016). "PRD se declara como la única oposición a Varela". Published: October 10. Available at: http://laestrella.com.pa/panama/politica/declara-como-unica-oposicion-varela/23968448.

Loxton, James (2015). "Authoritarian Successor Parties". *Journal of Democracy* no. 26 (3): 157–170.

Ministerio de Educación (MEDUCA) (2004). *Síntesis Informe Final "... la verdad os hará libres"*. Panama: Comisión de la Verdad.

—— (n/a). "Contenidos de las asignaturas por grados relacionados con temas de los derechos humanos". Unpublished document.

Ministerio de Relaciones Exteriores (MIREP) (2005). "Partes Pertinentes". Unpublished document dated 26 January.

Ministerio de Relaciones Exteriores (MIREP) (2012). Comité de Familiares de Asesinados y Desaparecidos de Panama, Héctor Gallego (COFADEPA) se reúnen con autoridades.

Published: August 20. Available at: http://mire.gob.pa/noticias/2012/08/20/comite-de-familiares-de-asesinados-y-desaparecidos-de-panama-hector-gallego-cofa.
La Nación (2001). "Recabarán información sobre crímenes en régimen militar panameño". Published: January 19. Available at: http://wvw.nacion.com/ln_ee/2001 /enero/19/ultima3.html.
Panamá América (2000). "Exhumaciones seguirán 'hasta el final,' Moscoso". Published: December 28, 1a-2a.
—— (2001). "Golpes y contragolpes entre PRD y arnulfismo". Published: January 15. Available at: http://m.panamaamerica.com.pa/content/golpes-y-contragolpes-entre-prd-y-arnulfismo.
—— (2001). "Gobierno no dará recursos a la Comisión de la Verdad". Published: February 5, 1a.
—— (2001). "Renuncia Britton a la Comisión de la Verdad". Published: April 18. Available at: http://www.panamaamerica.com.pa/content/renuncia-britton-la-comisi%C3%B3n-de-la-verdad
—— (2001). "Acusan a gerente de BNP de proteger a torturador". Published: May 26, 1a.
—— (2002). "Moscoso apoya indemnizar a las víctimas de la dictadura". Published: April 18, 1a.
—— (2003). "Comisión pide crear el Día del Desaparecido". Published: September 30. Available at: http://www.panamaamerica.com.pa/content/comisi%C3%B3n-pide-crear-el-d%C3%ADa-del-desaparecido.
—— (2004). "Comisón de la Verdad entrega texto a MEDUCA". Published: March 3, 3a.
—— (2005). "Osvaldo Velasquez, defensor de derechos humanos". Published: January 9. Available at: http://www.panamaamerica.com.pa/content/osvaldo-vel%C3%A1squez-defensor-de-los-derechos-humanos.
—— (2009). "Día del desaparecido". Published: November 30. Available at: http://www.panamaamerica.com.pa/content/d%C3%ADa-del-desaparecido.
—— (2012). "Encuentran restos óseos en Coiba durante exhumación". Published: January 4. Available at: http://www.panamaamerica.com.pa/content/encuentran-restos-%C3%B3seos-en-coiba-durante-exhumaci%C3%B3n.
—— (2012). "Falta de muestras pone en peligro identificación". Published: June 29. Available at: http://www.panamaamerica.com.pa/content/falta-de-muestras-pone-en-peligro-identificaci%C3%B3n.
—— (2015). "Viuda de Floyd Britton: 'Seguiré la lucha por la justicia y la verdad'". Published: May 2. Available at: http://www.panamaamerica.com.pa/tema-del-dia/viuda-de-floyd-britton-seguire-la-lucha-por-la-justicia-y-la-verdad-974690.
—— (2016). "Intento en vano por oficializar día". Published: June 9. Available at: http://www.panamaamerica.com.pa/nacion/intento-en-vano-por-oficializar-dia-1029678.
—— (2021). "Víctimas de la dictadura militar denuncian falta de cumplimiento". Published: September 13. https://www.panamaamerica.com.pa/nacion/victimas-de-la-dictadura-militar-denuncian-falta-de-cumplimiento-1194023.
—— (2021). "¿Y los asesinados por la dictadura?". Published: May 19. Available at: https://www.panamaamerica.com.pa/opinion/y-los-asesinados-por-la-dictadura-1187323.
Pérez, Orlando (2011). *Political Culture in Panama. Democracy after Invasion*. New York: Palgrave Macmillan.

La Prensa (2001). "Comisión es una entidad política". Published: March 2, 2a.

—— (2001). "Solicitan separación de Sossa". Published: November 12, 2a.

—— (2002). "Comisión de la Verdad divulga sus gastos". Published: February, 20, 2a.

—— (2003). "Asegura Alberto Almanza, indemnizarán a familiares de desaparecidos". Published: July 31. Available at: http://impresa.prensa.com/opinion/Asegura-Alberto-Almanza-Indemnizaran-desaparecidos_0_980152202.html.

—— (2003). "Encausan a la dueña de Eagle". Published: August 21. Available at: http://impresa.prensa.com/opinion/Encausan-duena-Eagle_0_995900588.html.

—— (2003). "Labor de Comisión de la Verdad no será empañada". Published: August 23. Available at: http://impresa.prensa.com/mas_de_la_prensa/Labor-Comision-Verdad-empanada_0_996650437.html.

—— (2004). "El PRD, el Perro 'Eagle' y la Comisión de la Verdad". Published: March 28. Available at: http://impresa.prensa.com/opinion/PRD-perro-Eagle-Comision-Verdad_0_1160884047.html.

—— (2012). "Vuelta al cuartel de Los Pumas". Published: February 11. Available at: http://impresa.prensa.com/panorama/Vuelta-cuartel-Pumas_0_3317668266.html.

—— (2012). "Fiscalía no avala más exhumaciones en Coiba" Published: June 14. Available at: http://impresa.prensa.com/panorama/Fiscalia-avala-excavaciones-Coiba_0_3410659141.html.

—— (2012). "Tomarán muestras de ADN a familiares de desaparecidos". Published: August 19. Available at: http://impresa.prensa.com/panorama/Tomaran-muestras-ADN-familiares-desaparecidos_0_3460154038.html.

—— (2013). "La Ley 74 es inconstitucional". Published: December 17. Available at: http://impresa.prensa.com/panorama/Ley-inconstitucional_0_3823867655.html.

—— (2014). "Rechazan plaza en honor a víctimas en casa de Noriega". Published: June 24. Available at: http://impresa.prensa.com/panorama/Rechazan-plaza-honor-victimas-Noriega_2_3965623403.html.

——(2016). "Tribunales rechazan casos de la dictadura militar". Published: April 18. Available at: http://www.prensa.com/judiciales/Casos-dictadura-archivados_0_4462803792.html.

—— (2017). "Panamá pide perdón por la víctima de régimen militar en 1977". Published: March 15. Available at: http://www.laprensa.hn/mundo/1053064-410/panam%C3%A1-pide-perd%C3%B3n-por-v%C3%ADctima-de-r%C3%A9gimen-militar-en-1977.

—— (2017). "Restos pertenecen a Fistonich". Published: August 30. Available at: https://impresa.prensa.com/panorama/Restos-pertenecen-Fistonich_0_4837016389.html.

—— (2017). "Avanza Proyecto sobre víctimas de dictadura". Published: September 21. Available at: https://impresa.prensa.com/panorama/Avanza-proyecto-victimas-dictadura_0_4853514732.html.

—— (2018). "Cancelan licitación de monument a víctimas de la dictadura por falta de presupuesto". Available at: https://www.prensa.com/politica/Cancelan-licitacion-monumento-dictadura-presupuesto_0_4969752985.html.

Red de Derechos Humanos-Panamá (RDH-P) (2008). "Lista de cuestiones que deben abordarse al examinar el Tercer Informe Periódico de Panamá". Available at: http://www2.ohchr.org/english/bodies/hrc/docs/AdvanceDocs/WRPanama92_sp.doc.

—— (2010). "Examen Periodico Universal". Available at: http://lib.ohchr.org/HRBodies/UPR/Documents/session9/PA/RDH_Red%20de%20Derechos%20Humanos%20_JS.pdf.

Ropp, Steve C. (1992). "Explaining the Long-Term Maintenance of the Military Regime: Panama before the US Invasion". *World Politics* no. 44 (2): 210–234.

Ross, Ann and Vicente Pachar Lucio (2015). "Forensic Scientific Practice in Panama". In Groen, Micke W.J., Nicholas Márquez-Grant, and Robert C. Janaway (eds.), *Forensic Archaeology. A Global Perspective*. Chichester: Wiley Blackwell, 247–254.

Rouquié, Alain and Stephen Suffern (1998). "The Military in Latin American Politics since 1930". In Bethell, Leslie (ed.), *Latin America. Politics and Society since 1930*. Cambridge: Cambridge University Press, 145–218.

Rudling, Adriana (2013). "¿Algo más que verdad? Un estudio sobre la implementación de las recomendaciones de la Comisión de la Verdad de Panamá". *Revista Panameña de Ciencia Política* no. 12 (1): 73–93.

Rudling, Adriana (2019). "What's Inside the Box? Mapping Agency and Conflict within Victims' Organizations". *International Journal of Transitional Justice*, no. 13(3): 458–477.

Scranton, Margaret E. (1995). "Panama's First Post-Transition Election". *Journal of Interamerican Studies and World Affairs* no. 37 (1): 69–100.

El Siglo (2017). "Asesinados tendrán monumento". Published: April 4. Available at: http://elsiglo.com.pa/panama/asesinados-tendran-monumento/23994231.

Special Investigative Agent (2010). "Informe de gestión del Agente de Instrucción Especial".

Supreme Court of Justice (CSJ) (2003). "Registro Judicial". Published: July n.d. Available at: https://www.organojudicial.gob.pa/uploads/blogs.dir/1/2019/07/406/registro-judicial-julio-2003.pdf.

Supreme Court of Justice (CSJ) (2008). Judgment, June 30, 2008. Published in Official Gazette No. 26,337-A/ August 3, 2009.

Supreme Court of Justice (CSJ) (2011). Judgment, December 29, 2011. Published in Official Gazette No. 27,485/ February 28, 2014.

UN Doc. S/ 25500/ April 1, 1993 El Salvador: Mexico Peace Agreements – Provisions Creating the Commission on Truth. Available at: https://www.usip.org/publications/1992/07/truth-commission-el-salvador.

La Vanguardia (2014). "Opositor PRD aprueba pacto legislativo que permite 'gobernabilidad' a Varela". Published: July 1. Available at: http://www.lavanguardia.com/politica/20140701/54410593200/opositor-prd-aprueba-pacto-legislativo-que-permite-gobernabilidad-a-varela.html.

LEGISLATION

Decree 187/ 83 Comisión Nacional sobre la Desaparición de Personas of 15 December 1983. Published in the Official Bulletin 19 December 1983

Decreto de Gabinete 42/ 13 November 2013. Published in Official Gazette No. 27164-A / 15 November 2012

Executive Decree 2/ 18 January 2001. Published in Official Gazette No. 24,224/ 22 January 2001
Executive Decree 268/ 19 October 2001. Published in Official Gazette No. 24,416/ 24 October 2001
Executive Decree 559/ 20 October 2003. Published in Official Gazette No. 24, 914/ 22 October 2003
Executive Decree 317/ 25 August 2004. Published in Official Gazette No. 25,124/ 26 August 2004
Executive Decree 449/ 30 December 2011. Published in Official Gazette No. 26945-B/ 5 January 2012
Law 15/ 28 October 1976. Published in Official Gazette 18,373/ 18 July 1977
Law 12/ 18 June 1991. Published in Official Gazette 21,815/ 25 June 1991
Law 18/ 3 June 1997. Published in Official Gazette 23,302/ 4 June 1997
Law 69/ 27 December 2007. Published in Official Gazette No. 25,949/ 28 December 2007
Law 63/ 28 August 2008. Published in Official Gazette 26,114/ 29 August 2008
Law 27/ 21 May 2008. Published in Official Gazette No. 26,045/ 22 May 2008
Law 74/ 29 October 2010. Published Official Gazette No. 26,654-A/ 1 November 2010
Law 1/ 13 January 2011. Published in Official Gazette No. 26,702-A/ 17 January 2011
Penal Code. Published in Official Gazette 26,519/ 26 April 2010
Resolution 2/ 2 March 2005. Published in Official Gazette No. 25,273/ 7 April 2005.
Resolution 51/ 15 November 2006. Published in Official Gazette No. 25,684/ 4 December 2006

ANNEX: LIST OF INTERVIEWEES

Alberto Almanza, President of the Panamanian Truth Commission and the Panamanian Institutional Truth Commission, Panama City, April 19, 2011.

José I. Blandón, MP of the *Partido Panameñista*, Panama City, April 25, 2011.

Rosa María de Britton, former commissioner of the Panamanian Truth Commission (until April 2001), Panama City, April 15, 2011.

Magaly J. Castillo, Executive Director of Allianza Pro Justicia, Panama City, April 28, 2011.

Ana Matilde Gómez, Head of the Legal Department of the Panamanian Truth Commission, former General Prosecutor, Panama City, April 29, 2011; October 10, 2016.

Rafael Perez Jaramillo, Head of the Report Department, Panama City, April 29, 2011; October 9, 2016.

Raul Leis, General Secretary of the Council for Adult Education in Latin America, Panama City, April 18, 2011.

Maritza Maestre, President of COFADEPA-HG, Panama City, April 20, 2011; October 9, 2016.

Juan Antonio Tejada Mora, commissioner of the Panamanian Truth Commission, Panama City, October 8, 2016.

Otilia Tejeira, former commissioner of the Panamanian Truth Commission (until May 2001), Panama City, April 27, 2011.

Edwin Wald, brother of the disappeared Rita Wald, Panama City, May 3, 2011; October 10, 2016.

Civil servants, Department of Education MEDUCA, Panama City, April 13, 2011; October 5, 2016.

CONCLUSION

Onur Bakiner

Few other fact-finding panels have harnessed the energy and imagination of scholars and activists interested in making the world a better place as much as truth commissions. Since Argentina's National Commission on the Disappearance of Persons submitted its final report in 1984, much has been said about what truth commissions can do, should do, and have been able to do. For skeptics, the emphasis on "*truth*" – understood in the context of political transitions from authoritarian rule and/or internal armed conflict as the documentation of past human rights violations, and drafting a list of victims (but not necessarily the victimizers) – amounts to little more than the denial of *justice* for victims and their relatives. At best, truth commissions fail to produce the hoped-for impact (Snyder and Vinjamuri 2003; Mendeloff 2004). Countering truth commission skeptics, however, other observers have pointed out that despite (or perhaps, thanks to) their lack of authority to punish offenders, truth commissions may expand the horizon in terms of how societies understand justice, recognition, and reconciliation. Far from being a tool of injustice, it is hoped, truth commissions can serve as the most appropriate mechanism to promote restorative justice without sacrificing retribution altogether, while also helping affected individuals to narrate their experiences, promoting an honest and reflective engagement with past wrongs, and ultimately fostering a culture of peace and respect for human rights (Minow 1998; Zalaquett 1991). Nuanced analyses assess whether and how truth commissions produce impact by going beyond the justice/injustice dichotomy (Olsen, Payne, and Reiter 2010; Sikkink and Kim 2013; Wiebelhaus-Brahm 2010).

In what ways does a truth commission produce impact? The process matters: victims may feel a sense of closure through narrating their experiences; commissioners may extend recognition of individual pain and suffering by simply listening to, and affirming, victims' narratives; perpetrators may participate in this process by confessing to their crimes (though admittedly, massive confessions are the exception rather than the norm around the world); and ultimately, it is hoped, the existence of a panel tasked to uncover and publicize human rights violations forces the entire society to reflect on past wrongs. Ever since South Africa's Truth and Reconciliation Commission made headlines around the world in the mid-1990s with its public hearings featuring highly emotional testimonies from victims and confessions from perpetrators, a participatory truth commission process aimed at reconciling former adversaries has been praised for its capacity for changing politics and society performatively – though this optimistic view has not gone uncontested, either.[1]

In addition to the process and performance of a truth commission, change is likely to result from a crucial yet under-studied aspect of a commission's work: its recommendations. Almost all truth commissions have published in their final reports recommendations for legal and institutional reform, some kind of relief for victims, and policy measures to cultivate respect for human rights. Some final reports confine their recommendations to a few brief paragraphs, while others submit long to-do lists to the political authorities. A reparations program for victims is found in almost every commission's list of recommendations. Defying skeptics who consider truth commissions a distraction from retributive justice, many commissions have demanded criminal prosecution of presumed perpetrators and shared their findings with prosecutors. Some of the more ambitious commissions seek nothing less than the elimination of socioeconomic inequality, ethnic/racial discrimination, and hegemonic notions of identity and belonging.

Do governments and state institutions heed commissions' recommendations? This is the missing link connecting a truth commission to truth commission impact. Admittedly, research on this question has remained rudimentary, in part because large-N regression analyses that ignore causal mechanisms in favor of causal inference have become increasingly dominant in transitional justice scholarship, and in part because tracking government responses to recommendations many years after a truth commission has stopped working is a daunting task. Truth commissions operate in fast-changing political contexts where policy adoption of their recommendations depends on factors outside their control. Sometimes early sympathy for the human rights cause gives way

1 For critical assessments, see: Hayner (2010); Wilson (2001).

to apathy, or even hostility, when newly elected governments do not share their predecessor's respect for human rights or when a government that once appeared to support human rights initiatives deprioritizes them later. In other cases, documenting truth commission impact is difficult because politicians who are sympathetic to the human rights movement come to power many years after a commission has completed its work, which makes the adoption of rights-oriented policies more likely, but it may not be clear whether the truth commission's recommendations inspired the new policies. In some countries, a truth commission elicits no official response at all; therefore, tracking the impact of recommendations is analogous to what statisticians call a null finding. Given all these twists and turns of political life, and the resulting methodological difficulties for researchers, then, who would dare to document truth commission recommendations and trace the history of their adoption across decades?

The researchers who have contributed to this volume have done precisely this. The meticulous case studies from 13 truth commissions in 11 Latin American countries (Chile and Uruguay have had two truth commissions) represent the most focused effort to document truth commission recommendations and their policy adoption to date. It is the first database that documents *all* truth commission recommendations, rather than a subsection of them, and definitely the first to assess the implementation record of all these recommendations. The project combines the descriptive goals of documenting recommendations and policy responses with the analytical goals of explaining the variation in the policy adoption of recommendations. In methodological terms, it is small-N research with detailed descriptions in each country under study. Thus, the case studies are stand-alone contributions, while the comparative character of the overall project allows broader generalizations.

My goal in this concluding chapter is to discuss the challenges that research on truth commission recommendations face, list the achievements of this research project, and suggest avenues for future research. *Beyond Words* has undertaken an ambitious research project that requires not only the documentation of the recent history of truth commissions, but also attentiveness to present and future developments around human rights in Latin America. This volume should inspire a line of future research that goes beyond the volume's temporal and spatial scope.

1. CHALLENGES

1.1. CONCEPTUALIZING TRUTH COMMISSION RECOMMENDATIONS

Truth commission recommendations appear easy to conceptualize at first sight: they are a set of statements found in each commission's final report. Taking into consideration the varieties of recommendations and the varieties of contexts in which they are written, however, the challenge becomes obvious. Straightforward recommendations demand a specific intervention in a well-defined policy area, e.g. "a specific article of the criminal code should be abolished". At the other extreme, a recommendation may expect nothing less than the total transformation of economic, political, and cultural structures, e.g. "society should reflect on the exclusion and marginalization that is inherent in its foundation". Although both sets of demands are recommendations in the abstract, the differences in terms of their content, political weight, and the likelihood of quick implementation could not be any greater.

Variation in content is aggravated (and perhaps caused to some degree) by contextual differences. Recommendations written at the end of a civil war reflect different priorities from those written at the start of a democratic transition – not to mention the possibility of contexts in which peace and democratization occur simultaneously. Even though truth commissions are typically associated with the broad field of scholarship and practice called "transitional justice", many commissions have been established in the absence of a clear political transformation, as built-in authoritarian enclaves (e.g., Chile after 1990) or ideological continuities between the authoritarian and democratic periods (e.g., Paraguay after 1989) eliminate the possibility of a clean break with the past. Furthermore, commissions that address the challenges of transition are likely to produce radically different recommendations than their non-transitional counterparts, raising the question of cross-context comparability of truth commission recommendations.

1.2. CONCEPTUALIZING THE IMPLEMENTATION RECORD

Codifying the implementation record of transitional justice tools is difficult. For truth commissions in particular, the implementation record tends to be messy: early gains are reversible; any policy leaves behind dissatisfied individuals and groups; and the evolving challenges of social and political life make successful implementation a moving target. Added to these concerns is the intrinsic difficulty of measuring concepts like "prosecution", which involves preliminary investigation, trial, sentencing, and appeals, or "reparations", which have no upper limit in terms of the number of victims covered, amount of resources spent, or symbolic closure offered.

Traditions of quantitative and qualitative data collection and analysis in the social sciences have produced their own responses to the challenges of conceptualizing the implementation record. Quantification strategies tend to codify implementation as either binary (implementation/no implementation) or discrete (there are levels of implementation, including none). Some researchers build composite measures of implementation to check for robustness: for example, they may check if a country's prosecution trend observed in the number of trials initiated follows a similar pattern when it comes to guilty verdicts. Finding correlating patterns is likely to suggest a robust trend (e.g., some trials of human rights violators result in guilty verdicts), while lack of correlation (e.g., if all trials end in acquittals, suggesting a willful policy of impunity) is likely to mean that trials do not signify a striving for justice, and therefore, the mere existence of trials should not be taken as a proxy for the implementation of prosecutions.

Qualitative researchers, who collect information through interviews, ethnographic research, and archival research, have long criticized quantification strategies for using very rough measures that ignore the multi-faceted nature of implementation. One of the fundamental advantages of the qualitative approach is to assess implementation from the relevant actors' perspective. Furthermore, adopting a qualitative data collection and analysis methodology offers much greater detail in terms of whether, how much, and why implementation is observed. A potential drawback of this approach is comparability, in part because reliance on the relevant actors' own assessments may produce incomparable results (i.e., one person's "lack of implementation" may be someone else's "a little bit of implementation"), and in part because the task of producing generalizable explanations requires systematizing contextual details in some way.

1.3. THE TEMPORAL SCOPE

Human affairs are dynamic; therefore, social sciences cannot rest content with time-invariant theories to make sense of them. Theoretical propositions in the transitional justice field face particular difficulties because many of the foundational concepts of the field, such as peace and reconciliation, can be attained, if at all, in the long-run only, while most of the transitional justice tools around the world are quite new – products of the 1990s and 2000s. To give an example, some of the truth commissions in Latin America have completed their work less than a decade before the contributors to this volume began to compile information. Brazil's truth commission was still underway when the *Beyond Words* project was conceived. It will become increasingly more possible for researchers to conduct long-term analysis of transitional justice tools, but meanwhile experts in countries with recent transitions should confine themselves to studying the short-term effects of these tools.

Truth commission impact is a moving target even decades after a commission has completed its work because policy adoption, policy reversal, or both, may happen at any time. What is true today may be false tomorrow. Thus, a researcher's choice of time-frame and definitions may influence what counts as compliance with truth commission findings. To give an example, the

Supreme Court of Peru annulled the presidential pardon for former dictator Alberto Fujimori in October 2018, reversing the pardon that was granted 10 months earlier. Considering that effective and fair prosecutions for human rights violations were one of the recommendations of the country's Truth and Reconciliation Commission back in 2003, one could perhaps code compliance with this recommendation as achieved, at least to some degree, until December 2017, when the presidential pardon was announced. Then one would have to assign a lower level of compliance in the 10 months when Fujimori was free, and then reassign higher compliance after the most recent Supreme Court ruling. However, this raises a conceptual question in addition to the one about the time-frame: at what stage of a judicial process should scholars acknowledge progress in human rights accountability?

Taking the Fujimori case as an example, if one assumed that the existence of a sentence would be sufficient for compliance, then compliance would be coded as constant over time, but if the execution of a punishment is conceptualized as intrinsic to justice, then the ebbs and flows of the case would complicate operationalization efforts. Conceptual and analytical efforts should pay attention to specific details while not losing sight of broader patterns, which may become increasingly more difficult to track over time.

1.4. ESTABLISHING CAUSAL MECHANISMS

An additional challenge is that a country's overall progress may or may not be caused by truth commission recommendations. In fact, the successful implementation of policies that once appeared in a commission's recommendations chapter is not proof that those recommendations were the causal factor. This problem cannot be fully overcome, since "smoking-gun" evidence is hard to find in this line of social-scientific inquiry, but it can be alleviated. Sometimes a few recommendation items are implemented soon after the publication of the final report, which is a strong indicator that the commission was a causal factor. Sometimes implementation takes longer, in which case the researcher should delve deeper into the mechanism for implementation to understand whether the commission had anything to do with it. For example, Argentina's reparations program was legislated more than two decades after the completion of the truth commission's work. Although the commission recommended such a program, there is no evidence to suggest that the commission's text was a motivating factor for the politicians or civil society activists at the time of policy adoption. Even when a government implements policies that are broadly consistent with a truth commission's recommendations, claiming that the recommendations were a causal factor requires attention to the processes that connect the recommendations to actual policy adoption.

1.5. DATA PROBLEMS

Data problems should be mentioned, too. The afterlife of a truth commission influences what can be studied about that commission. For example, a return to authoritarian rule and/or violent conflict may eliminate the possibility of conducting research in the post-commission period. Even when the space for reflection and research is not entirely closed, an inauspicious political climate may stifle societal debate around a commission's findings and message, and limit scholars' access to commission archives and personnel. Thus, the study of post-commission success is endogenous to its own subject matter: the more political and societal support a commission receives, the better researchers can study it. Added to this challenge are differences in how "popular" a country (and its truth commission) is perceived to be among funding agencies, scholarly journals, and international scholars. While the journalistic and scholarly production of knowledge on some of the more famous commissions, such as the South African or Argentine ones, establishes a baseline to conduct more research, very little has been written on, say, the Panamanian Truth Commission. This presents a challenge and an opportunity for comparative researchers: a challenge, because the absence of evidence on truth commission impact should be investigated further to make sure it reflects the empirical reality rather than the absence of work on that commission, and opportunity, because careful research design and meticulous case studies can close the gap between so-called over-studied and under-studied cases in terms of measurement metrics and empirical evidence.

2. ASSESSING *BEYOND WORDS*

Latin America, alongside Sub-Saharan Africa, has led the world in the number and variety of transitional justice measures, including truth commissions. Argentina's 1983 commission may not have been the first of its kind (some transitional justice databases include a 1974 commission established in Uganda as the first truth commission), but it definitely was the first one to receive some degree of official post-commission endorsement. When Chilean human rights lawyers looked for a workable model for discovering and publicizing human rights violations in the late 1980s, Argentina's commission stood out as an example; a few years later, Chile's commissioners shared their insights and the commission's name ("Truth and *Reconciliation* Commission") with South Africans, whose commission became a global trend-setter. Since then, most countries in South and Central America, and a few in the Caribbean have established truth commissions to address legacies of internal armed conflict, authoritarianism, or both.

Beyond Words combines an ambitious descriptive project with an analytical one. It lists all the recommendations contained in the final reports of 13 truth commissions from 11 Latin American countries. Broken down to their components, these recommendations constitute nearly 1,000 potential policy interventions. As expected, the number and content of recommendations vary by country. The analytical side of the endeavor concerns understanding whether, to what extent, how, and why truth commission recommendations are implemented into policy. Is it about the political context in which a commission operates? Or the political context in the post-commission period? Does the type or complexity of a given recommendation influence its likelihood of being implemented? Do non-governmental actors play a role in shaping official responses to a truth commission?

What are the recommendations about? It appears that Latin American truth commissions have asked for material reparations uniformly. Another popular recommendation item is memorialization, or what some commissions label symbolic reparations. All commissions demand institutional reform aimed at fostering a culture of respect for human rights and non-violence; naturally, the content of the list of recommendations depends on the political history of that particular country. While Chile's 1990 commission suggested that the military be trained in human rights in the immediate wake of a military dictatorship, its Brazilian 2014 counterpart asked for prison reform, as riots and massacres in prisons have continued in the democratic period. In addition to recommendations for reparations and institutional reform, a number of commissions call for the prosecution of human rights violators, or their removal from public office.

In what follows, I offer a categorization of truth commission recommendations found in the volume, organized by theme. Truth commissions do not necessarily label their recommendations by these names, but these broad themes are found in most of them.

(i) Investigation into forced disappearances: truth commissions established in countries with a history of forced disappearances, like Argentina, Chile, Paraguay and Uruguay, recommend measures to investigate forced disappearances, either through courts or through special forensic units.

(ii) Reparations: material reparations, to be disbursed in cash or in kind, are another key recommendation agenda. Most commissions demand individual reparations, but some (e.g., the Peruvian one) ask for collective reparations, to be distributed in the form of public works, for communities affected by the conflict.

(iii) Attention to victims: beyond material reparations, some commissions ask the government to provide victims with legal assistance and psychological support structures.

(iv) Memorialization: often labelled "symbolic reparations", this recommendation item concerns the construction of human rights memorials and spaces, and the official recognition of past violations. In addition to requesting official steps to memorialize the past, a few commissions (e.g., the Brazilian one) also ask politicians and the broader society to not praise repressive regimes. Although the national government is the addressee of memorialization recommendations for the most part, local governments are also expected to play a key role in these efforts.

(v) Legislative change: a number of truth commissions recommend the abolition of certain laws (typically amnesty laws and repressive national security/emergency laws), ratification of international human rights treaties, and the codification of certain violent acts (like torture and sexual violence) as grave human rights violations in the criminal code.

(vi) Institutional reform: since the cultivation of a culture of respect for human rights and ensuring the non-recurrence of political violence are among the core goals of all truth commissions, their recommendations often contain a mixture of institutional reform and legislation (see above). The content of reform-driven recommendations varies, but generally, commissions demand the creation of new institutions (like the Ombudsman's office), rule-of-law reform, judicial reform, and security-sector reform.

(vii) Educational incorporation: commissions generally expect the lessons from the past to be incorporated into educational curricula at various levels of learning. Toward that end, a few commissions have asked for the incorporation of their findings into textbooks. Policies of memorialization (see above) are also justified on the basis of their educational value.

(viii) Creation of follow-up institutions: since commissions typically disband once they publish their final report, they ask for the creation of follow-up institutions to oversee compliance with the recommendations.

The case studies in this volume find considerable variation across countries in terms of compliance with truth commission recommendations: on the one hand there are commissions, like Chile's 1990 Rettig Commission, that have seen a relatively high degree of implementation. On the other hand, the work of commissions in Panama and Haiti has been left to oblivion for the most part. The other countries appear to occupy a space somewhere in between.

A common thread found in all of the case studies is that politicians' willingness to implement truth commission recommendations matters. A government that genuinely cares about a commission's findings and recommendations, or at least pays lip service to them in order to boost its domestic or international legitimacy, is likely to pass legislation to implement the recommendations. The book reports a few examples of relatively high implementation records, though no government to date has implemented 100 per cent of a commission's recommendations. Juxtaposed to this relatively uplifting story is the record of non-compliance by some other governments: given that a truth commission's recommendations are not binding (and practically unenforceable even when legally binding, as was the case in El Salvador), politicians can simply choose to ignore them. Politicians with ties to an abusive regime in the past are likely to brush aside a commission's work, as the case study of Paraguay illustrates. Even when such a clear motivation to derail a commission's work is absent, decision-makers who do not consider human rights a top priority do little or nothing to implement truth commission recommendations, as the example of Peru between 2003 and 2006 suggests.

Another common pattern concerns the supportive role of victims' associations and human rights organizations. Almost every case study mentions non-governmental initiatives that demand accountability for past violations, and legislation to implement truth commission recommendations. In countries like Chile, where a narrowly mandated reparations program was legislated soon after a truth commission, victims mobilized for the expansion of the scope of the program. Limits on civil society participation are also notable: in El Salvador, the commission sponsored by the United Nations in 1992 excluded domestic civil society groups. In Panama, the government's decision to exclude human rights groups from the creation of the commission strained these groups' overall participation in the commission process. There does not appear to be an overarching pattern to explain cross-national and temporal variation in terms of when, how, and how much civil society groups get involved with a truth commission, but the fact that so many case studies mention so many non-governmental actors suggests that future studies should analyze the relationship between these actors and truth commissions.

Most case studies in this volume find evidence that truth commissions seek to forge a shared memory of past events through their findings and recommendations. The overall sense one gets from reading about each country's post-commission period is that building a shared culture of respect for fundamental rights based on a shared awareness of past violations is an elusive task, in part because symbolic reparations and gestures recommended by commissions (memorials, apologies, etc.) are either not implemented at all, or implemented in a haphazard way. In addition, change of government can have a profound impact on a country's memory politics, above and beyond the potential of a truth commission to set the tone. To give two examples: the rise of Fujimorismo in Peru since the mid-2000s, and the ongoing influence of the Colorado Party in Paraguayan politics have limited truth commissions' ability to steer the national debate in a victim-centered direction.

Beyond the common patterns, country-specific dynamics should be acknowledged. For example, Haiti's truth commission failed to generate much impact as much because of natural disasters as because of political adversity.

Brazil's truth commission may have been received much more positively had the Rousseff government not been deposed. The fact that Paraguay's commission was established many years after the democratic transition meant that the already-existing reparation and memorialization policies were not initialized by the truth commission. El Salvador's truth commission was unique in the degree of United Nations control over the process, and the failure of international community involvement in the Salvadorian truth commission has forced United Nations officials to take local ownership much more seriously in Guatemala. These country-specific details, found throughout the volume, point to the interplay of structural and contextual factors that influence the adoption of truth commission recommendations.

Striking a balance between case study methodology and comparative design is in part a methodological challenge: case studies are best known for documenting the contextual background and the unique dynamics of the case at hand in rich detail, while comparative methods need common metrics to find patterns of similarities and differences. It is a practical challenge, too: each area expert is likely to collect information on the basis of the political and intellectual priorities of their context, and the knowledge produced in one context may not speak to similar developments in another, unless the area experts make a conscious effort to model their conceptual and theoretical framework as both area-specific and comparable.

Beyond Words achieves the goal of offering stand-alone case studies that speak to one another. Each chapter is structured around the same set of questions: What is the context in which a truth commission is established? What are its recommendations? To what degree have successive governments implemented those recommendations? What explains the relative success or failure of implementation? On the one hand, the questions are generic enough to allow discussion of unique features: each case study contains not only a list of recommendations and their implementation record, but also an assessment of that truth commission's role in societal and political debates around human rights and national history. In addition, the volume offers detailed data for comparative analysis, and the comparative perspective does not come at the expense of detail: each case study narrates a meticulous history of that country's human rights issues, transitional justice efforts, and truth commission process. The project can generate insights that are generalizable enough to enable theory-building and -testing using comparative methodologies, while each case study presents context-specific details that can be used to set scope conditions for the applicability of theories, and to identify outliers and extreme cases.

The case studies in this volume present a rich repository of data for researchers. The qualitative nature of the research project and its potential for quantification allow researchers to use a variety of methodological tools to analyze the content. For the qualitative tradition, data analysis using process-tracing appears to be ideal because the project links an outcome of interest (implementation) to an initial condition (the nature of recommendations), while maintaining that contextual and structural factors may influence the outcome as well. In addition, it features a relatively small number of decision-makers making a small number of decisions in each country, which can be treated as critical junctures. The data are predominantly qualitative. All these features make process-tracing an ideal method to assess the validity of stated hypotheses, and confirm/discount alternative hypotheses in each country, and comparatively.

Other qualitative traditions will also find this volume useful. It contains translated texts of truth commission recommendations, which lend themselves to textual analysis not only of topic headings and content, but also commissions' affective engagement with victims, perpetrators, and broader society. Experts in qualitative comparative analysis may find this work helpful, too: this methodology, typically used for comparing a small number of cases when the research design features a large number of potential independent variables, is a good candidate for analyzing truth commission recommendations. Qualitative comparative analysis requires the codification of variables as binary, which can be achieved for truth commission recommendations and their implementation record.

Taking the quantification strategies one step further, incorporating the volume's findings into discrete variables to conduct quantitative analysis appears plausible, as well. A key variable like the implementation record can be codified as binary (see above), but it is also possible to conceptualize it as ordinal (e.g. no implementation/little progress/high progress/total implementation). The number of countries is admittedly small, but the number of country-years is not: most of the countries in this volume have had 15–20 years of post-commission developments. In addition, the data collection method used in the project is generalizable to other geographies, so building a global database of truth commission recommendations is plausible.

3. FUTURE RESEARCH

One of the outstanding challenges ahead for transitional justice scholars is to reassess conventional notions of truth commission impact in light of new evidence. Are there general patterns, or do we observe nothing more than *ad hoc* policy adoption and reversal as a result of changing political fortunes? If there are general patterns, does the answer lie with the resources, interests and ideas of those who govern? In other words, is it simply a question of political will? Alternatively, does mobilization by human rights groups stand out as a key factor in explaining the variation in truth commission impact? What about structural factors, like a country's wealth and human development, political system, etc.?

A related question concerns the recommendations themselves. Do their form, content, comprehensiveness, and other relevant characteristics explain their likelihood of getting implemented? Are there "easy" and "difficult" recommendations? What can future truth commissions learn from earlier ones in terms of drafting a list of recommendations? From a normative standpoint, how much should the commissioners of the future value the implementability of recommendations? On the one hand, giving more weight to implementable recommendations may be a practical solution to the problem of non-compliance. On the other hand, what if the recommendations that are most necessary for a society coming to terms with its past are those that provoke difficult questions and set aspirational standards?

Most of the time, truth commissions are part of a broader reform movement, yet this insight keeps eluding scholars and practitioners in their analyses. Commissions and their recommendations often build upon reports written by civil society organizations, government agencies and international bodies. In turn, their findings and recommendations are cited by reform-minded individuals and organizations. To give some examples, the influence of prior civil society efforts on the commissions in Brazil and Uruguay is noted. Likewise, the case study of Haiti mentions the *Xaragua* report written in the Ministry of Justice, which followed up on the work of the truth commission in that country. Needless to say, truth commission recommendations do not map onto other reformist texts perfectly; in a way, their textual autonomy needs to be respected. Yet, in assessing compliance with these recommendations, the intertextual connections should be taken into account as well. As the Haiti case study suggests, it is plausible to argue that recommendations that find their way into existing reform agendas have a greater likelihood of getting implemented.

Another area for future research is what can be called "non-recommendations": demands for change that were being circulated at the time of a truth commission's work, which the commission chose not to incorporate into its list of recommendations. To give a famous example, Chile's 1990 Commission did not recommend the abolition of the 1978 Amnesty Law. The case study of Argentina mentions recommendations by human rights groups that were ignored by the truth commission. The divergence between civil society agendas and truth commissions can be instructive in terms of a commission's position within the broader human rights movement.

The members of truth commissions should receive more attention from scholars. Their personal histories and professional backgrounds reveal as much about a commission as its codified mandate. Judging by their professional outlook, it is easy to conclude that the commissioners in Argentina understood their job to conduct forensic investigation; the all-international panel in El Salvador remained a foreign intervention with little domestic input. Ideological makeup matters, too: in my own research, I found that the 1990 Chilean Rettig

Commission reflected an intentional effort to strike a balance between the Left and the Right, while its Peruvian counterpart was predominantly composed of social-democrats.[2] The striking differences in terms of the two commissions' recommendations result in great part from this variation in commissioner profiles.

In addition to who is included in a commission, exclusions on the basis of class, gender, ethnicity, profession, or victim status are likely to shape a commission's overall outlook. The tendency of almost all governments is to disallow victims from participating as commissioners, although Paraguay, where four of the nine commissioners were former victims, is an outlier. Peru's commission had no indigenous members, much to the dismay of viable candidates. Future research should look into these commissioner-level factors to understand cross-national variation in the content of recommendations. Finally, a truth commission is the typical example of a small-group dynamic. Patterns of cooperation and conflict, the formation of alliances on the basis of shared interests and values, and commissioners' quest for respect and recognition within the group may determine the process and outcome of a commission's work.

4. CONCLUDING REMARKS

The achievements of the *Beyond Words* project – as a comprehensive list of truth commission recommendations and their implementation record in Latin America, and as a repository of causal explanations grounded in rich empirical detail – are impressive. Yet, there are many more truth commissions to cover, in Latin America and beyond. At the time of writing, truth commissions investigating massive violations are underway in Bolivia and Colombia, and Mexico's government has recently announced the creation of a truth commission to investigate a massacre. This volume's combination of case studies and comparative analysis can set an example for studying these new commissions.

Scholarship on truth commissions should not only expand to new geographies; it should also deepen our understanding of past and present commissions. Reckoning with past wrongs through truth commissions has remained a popular idea for at least two decades, yet *Beyond Words* reveals that systematic analysis of the post-commission adoption of their recommendations has only recently begun as a serious research agenda. This is not to ignore the vast scholarship that has been produced on truth commissions in the past two decades, but, rather, to admit that what we know about the commission process, the commissioners, and the post-commission dynamics in many countries,

2 Bakiner (2015).

including the so-called "emblematic" ones, is quite limited. Moreover, what we do know about commissions can be put to better use through comparative analysis.

The findings of *Beyond Words* encourage transitional justice specialists to engage in dialogue with scholars and practitioners of post-conflict reform in general. Truth commissions are typically established in the context of a broader agenda of rule-of-law, and security-sector and judicial reform, to name a few. Their recommendations may echo those of other reform-minded proposals coming from civil society organizations, international organizations, and government agencies, though divergence across reformist agendas is a fascinating area of research, too. Needless to say, truth commissions do not *only* produce reform proposals; their fact-finding mission, and their contributions to an honest, reflective reckoning with past wrongs, set them apart from institutions and organizations with otherwise-similar reformist outlooks. What I suggest is conceptualizing truth commissions as a special participant in the broader context of social and political reform, rather than as stand-alone agents of change.

Finally, *Beyond Words* is bound to be a work in progress by virtue of its subject matter. This volume's chapters on Argentina and Chile present rich analyses of human rights policy by tracing 35- and 28-year trajectories, respectively. The varying time-frames complicate comparative analysis, however. Brazil's truth commission, established in 2011 and completed in 2014, only offers short-term insights for the time being. Researchers of truth commissions have to constantly update their findings as time passes. For all these reasons, I hope the ambitious research project presented in *Beyond Words* will be the beginning of even more ambitious research in the future.

BIBLIOGRAPHY

Bakiner, Onur (2015). *Truth Commissions: Memory, Power, and Legitimacy*. Philadelphia, PA: University of Pennsylvania Press.

Hayner, Priscilla B. (2010). *Unspeakable Truths: Transitional Justice and the Challenge of Truth Commissions*. London: Routledge, 2nd edn.

Mendeloff, David (2004). "Truth-Seeking, Truth-Telling, and Postconflict Peacebuilding: Curb the Enthusiasm?" *International Studies Review* no. 6 (3): 355–380.

Minow, Martha (1998). *Between Vengeance and Forgiveness: Facing History after Genocide and Mass Violence*. Boston, MA: Beacon Press.

Olsen, Tricia D., Leigh A. Payne, and Andrew G. Reiter (2010). *Transitional Justice in Balance: Comparing Processes, Weighing Efficacy*. Washington, DC: US Institute of Peace Press.

Sikkink, Kathryn, and Hun Joon Kim (2013). "The Justice Cascade: The Origins and Effectiveness of Prosecutions of Human Rights Violations." *Annual Review of Law and Social Science* no. 9: 269–285.

Snyder, Jack, and Leslie Vinjamuri (2003). "Trials and Errors: Principle and Pragmatism in Strategies of International Justice." *International Security* no. 28 (3): 5–44.

Wiebelhaus-Brahm, Eric (2010). *Truth Commissions and Transitional Societies: The Impact on Human Rights and Democracy*. New York: Routledge.

Wilson, Richard A. (2001). *The Politics of Truth and Reconciliation in South Africa: Legitimizing the Post-Apartheid State*. Cambridge University Press.

Zalaquett, José (1991). "Balancing Ethical Imperatives and Political Constraints: The Dilemma of New Democracies Confronting Past Human Rights Violations." *Hastings Law Journal* no. 43 (6): 1425–1438.

APPENDIX

Latin American Truth Commission Reports

ARGENTINA, 1984
National Commission on the Disappeared
Comisión Nacional sobre la Desaparición de Personas (CONADEP)

TC report: *Informe de la Comisión Nacional Sobre la Desaparición de Personas*

Spanish version available at:
http://www.desaparecidos.org/arg/conadep/nuncamas/

English version available at:
http://web.archive.org/web/20031004074316/nuncamas.org/english/library/nevagain/nevagain_001.htm

English version available at: https://www.amazon.com/Nunca-Mas-Never-Again-Report/dp/0571138497/ref=sr_1_1?ie=UTF8&qid=1489094735&sr=8-1&keywords=nunca+mas+argentina (official English translation, for sale)

URUGUAY, 1985
Investigative Commission on the Situation of Disappeared People and its Causes
Comisión Investigadora Parlamentaria Sobre la Situación de Personas Desaparecidas y Hechos que la Motivaron

TC report: *Informe Final de la Comisión Investigadora Parlamentaria Sobre Situación de Personas Desaparecidas y Hechos que la Motivaron*

Spanish version available at (see only pp. 1–25):
http://archivo.presidencia.gub.uy/_web/noticias/2007/06/tomo4.pdf

Note that the original report is not publicly available. However, there is a modern reproduction made by the Uruguayan government, online available, edited in 4 volumes by Presidency in 2007. This 2007 publication by the Uruguayan government of the TC reports was reproduced as part of implementing a recommendation from the ComiPaz. The five-volume publication is titled *Investigación Histórica sobre Detenidos Desaparecidos*, and the TC reports are re-produced in Vol. IV. See:
http://archivo.presidencia.gub.uy/_web/noticias/2007/06/2007060509.htm

The entire 2007 volume is available in Spanish here:

Volume 1:
http://archivo.presidencia.gub.uy/_web/noticias/2007/06/tomo1.pdf

Volume 2:
http://archivo.presidencia.gub.uy/_web/noticias/2007/06/tomo2.pdf

Volume 3:
http://archivo.presidencia.gub.uy/_web/noticias/2007/06/tomo3.pdf

Volume 4:
http://archivo.presidencia.gub.uy/_web/noticias/2007/06/tomo4.pdf

Volume 5:
http://archivo.presidencia.gub.uy/_web/noticias/2007/06/tomo5.pdf

The re-production is also available through this site:
http://www.desaparecidos.org/uru/

English version not available.

CHILE RETTIG, 1991
National Commission for Truth and Reconciliation "The Rettig Commission"
Comisión Rettig

TC report: *Informe de la Comisión Nacional de Verdad y Reconciliación* ("Informe Rettig"). Vol. 1–3.

Spanish version available at:
http://www.ddhh.gov.cl/wp-content/uploads/2015/12/tomo1.pdf (Volume 1),

http://www.ddhh.gov.cl/wp-content/uploads/2015/12/tomo2.pdf (Volume 2), and

http://www.ddhh.gov.cl/wp-content/uploads/2015/12/tomo3.pdf (Volume 3)

English version (Report of the Chilean National Commission on Truth and Reconciliation) available at:
http://www.usip.org/sites/default/files/resources/collections/truth_commissions/Chile90-Report/Chile90-Report.pdf

EL SALVADOR, 1993
Commission on the Truth for El Salvador
Comisión de la Verdad para El Salvador (CVES)

TC report: *De la locura a la esperanza. La guerra de 12 años en El Salvador.*

Spanish version available at:
http://www.derechoshumanos.net/lesahumanidad/informes/elsalvador/informe-de-la-locura-a-la-esperanza.htm and

https://www.scribd.com/document/137504386/De-la-locura-a-la-esperanza-La-guerra-de-12-anos-en-El-Salvador

English version available at:
http://www.usip.org/sites/default/files/file/ElSalvador-Report.pdf

HAITI, 1996
National Truth and Justice Commission
Commission Nationale de Vérité et de Justice (CNVJ)

TC report: *Si m pa rele: 29 September 1991–14 Octobre 1994.*

French version available at:
http://ufdcweb1.uflib.ufl.edu/UF00085926/00001
Annex I and II available at: http://ufdc.ufl.edu/UF00085926/00002 and Annex III available at: http://ufdc.ufl.edu/UF00085926/00003, or both available at: https://kuscholarworks.ku.edu/handle/1808/10910.

English version not available, but a very rough translation of the recommendations are listed in USAID's report:
http://pdf.usaid.gov/pdf_docs/PNABZ701.pdf, Appendix B, 18 pages.

GUATEMALA, 1999
Commission for Historical Clarification of Guatemala
Comisión para el Esclarecimiento Histórico de Guatemala (CEH)

TC report: *Guatemala: Memoria del Silencio*

Spanish versions available at:
http://www.undp.org/content/dam/guatemala/docs/publications/UNDP_gt_PrevyRecu_MemoriadelSilencio.pdf (short, 96 pages) and http://www.centrodememoriahistorica.gov.co/descargas/guatemala-memoria-silencio/guatemala-memoria-del-silencio.pdf (long, 4383 pages)

English version (short, 82 pages) available at:
https://www.aaas.org/sites/default/files/migrate/uploads/mos_en.pdf

PANAMA, 2002
Panama Truth Commission
Comisión de la Verdad de Panamá

TC report: *Informe Final de la Comisión de la Verdad. "La verdad os hará libres"*

Spanish version available at:
http://www.defensoriadelpueblo.gob.pa/index.php?option=com_flippingbook&view=book&id=6:informe-final-de-la-comision-de-la-verdad&catid=6:informes

English version not available.

URUGUAY, 2003
Commission for Peace
Comisión para la Paz (COMIPAZ/ComiPaz)

TC report: *Informe Final de la Comisión para la Paz*

Spanish version available at:
https://www.usip.org/sites/default/files/file/resources/collections/commissions/Uruguay-Report_Informal.pdf

English version not available.

PERU, 2003
Truth and Reconciliation Commission
Comisión de la Verdad y Reconciliación (CVR)

TC report: *Informe Final de la Comisión de la Verdad y Reconciliación* (Abbreviated version: *Hatun Willakuy*)

Full Spanish 2003 version available, in several separate files, at: http://www.cverdad.org.pe/ifinal/index.php and http://www.usip.org/publications/truth-commission-peru-01

Abbreviated Spanish 2004 version available at:
http://idehpucp.pucp.edu.pe/wp-content/uploads/2012/11/hatun-willakuy-cvr-espanol.pdf

English version of the Conclusions, available at the CVR's webpage: http://www.cverdad.org.pe/ingles/ifinal/conclusiones.php

CHILE VALECH, 2004
National Commission on Political Imprisonment and Torture
Comisión Nacional sobre Prisión Politica y Tortura ("Comisión Valech")

TC report: *Informe de la Comisión Nacional sobre Prisión Politica y Tortura* (Informe Valech)

Spanish version of the first report and the complimentary report available at:
http://www.comisiontortura.cl/
and http://www.archivochile.com/Derechos_humanos/com_valech/

PARAGUAY, 2008
Truth and Justice Commission
Comisión de Verdad y Justicia (CVJ)

TC report: *Informe Final. Anive haguã oiko*

Spanish version, in several separate files, available at: http://www.cipae.org.py/V2/informe-final-anive-agua-oiko/

English version not available.

ECUADOR, 2010
Truth Commission to Impede Impunity
Comisión de la Verdad para Impedir la Impunidad

TC report: *Informe de la Comisión de la Verdad Ecuador 2010: Sin verdad no hay justicia*

Spanish version available at:
https://issuu.com/triguero/docs/ecuador._sin_verdad_no_hay_justicia

English version not available.

BRAZIL, 2014
National Truth Commission
Comissão Nacional da Verdade (CNV)

TC report: *Relatório da Comissão Nacional da Verdade, volume I, II & III*

Portuguese version available at:
http://www.cnv.gov.br/index.php?option=com_content&view=article&id=571

Read the conclusions and recommendations contained in the final report of the National Truth Commission in Portuguese:

http://www.cnv.gov.br/images/pdf/relatorio/Capitulo%2018.pdf (official site)

English version not available.

INDEX*

* Some entries and page references are in bold to indicate that they are core entries.

ABOUT THE EDITORS

ELIN SKAAR (Research Professor, Chr. Michelsen Institute, Bergen, Norway) works in the intersection between law and politics and has published widely on transitional justice, human rights, and courts.

ERIC WIEBELHAUS-BRAHM (Associate Professor, School of Public Affairs, University of Arkansas at Little Rock) is the author of three books and over two dozen articles and book chapters on transitional justice, human rights, and peacebuilding.

JEMIMA GARCÍA-GODOS (Professor, Dept. Sociology and Human Geography, University of Oslo) is a human geographer working and publishing on transitional justice, human rights, victims' rights, and state-society relations.

www.ingramcontent.com/pod-product-compliance
Ingram Content Group UK Ltd.
Pitfield, Milton Keynes, MK11 3LW, UK
UKHW051043120926
8556IPUK00031B/868

9 781839 701795